hand**book**

Mathematics

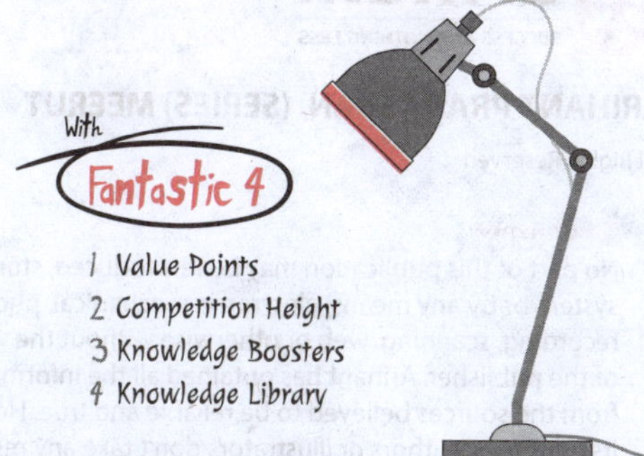

Highly useful for XI-XII, Engg., & Other Competitions

Laxman Prasad

Supported by

Anjali Sharma

Sachin Kumar

ARIHANT PRAKASHAN, (SERIES) MEERUT

卐 **Administrative & Production Offices**

Regd. Office

'Ramchhaya' 4577/15, Agarwal Road, Darya Ganj, New Delhi -110002
Tele: 011- 47630600, 43518550

卐 **Head Office**

Kalindi, TP Nagar, Meerut (UP) - 250002
Tel: 0121-7156203, 7156204

卐 **Sales & Support Offices**

Agra, Ahmedabad, Bengaluru, Bareilly, Chennai, Delhi, Guwahati, Hyderabad, Jaipur, Jhansi, Kolkata, Lucknow, Nagpur & Pune.

PO No. : TXT-59-T071230-5-26

卐 **PRICE** ₹345.00

Published by Arihant Publications (India) Ltd.

For further information about the books published by Arihant, log on to www.arihantbooks.com or e-mail at info@arihantbooks.com

Follow us on 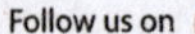  

Preface

This Arihant handbook is unique multipurpose Revision book, developed to facilitate quick and powerpacked revision of various **Key Notes, Terms, Definitions & Formulae.**

The book is equally useful for revisions before board exam and all relevant competitions like **JEE, NDA, CDS, UPSC etc.**

The handful nature of book help in quick revision anytime from anywhere even between the exam shifts or while travelling as well.

This revised edition of Arihant handbook Mathematics is now even more powerful with Fantastic 4.

1. **Value Points** - Assorted pointers with enhanced importance for more impactful revision.
2. **Competition Insight** - Most valuable competition related concepts segregated to create more focus.
3. **Knowledge Booster** - Concept enhancers to elevate knowledge sphere outline.
4. **Knowledge Library** Unique compendium of indispensable facts excluded from Rationalised NCERT.

However, we have put our best efforts in preparing this book, but if any error or what so ever has been skipped out, we will by heart welcome your suggestions. A part from all those who helped in the compilation of this book a special note of thanks goes to Mr. Ashwani of Arihant Publications.

Author

CONTENTS

1. Sets and Relations 1-11
   - Set
   - Subset and Superset
   - Venn Diagram
   - Operations on Sets
   - Ordered Pair
   - Relation
   - Equivalence Relation

2. Functions 12-27
   - Function
   - Real Valued and Real Functions
   - Standard Real Functions and their Graphs
   - Operations on Real Functions
   - Equal Functions
   - Even and Odd Functions

3. Complex Numbers 28-44
   - Equality of Complex Numbers
   - Iota
   - Algebra of Complex Numbers
   - Argand Plane and Argument of a Complex Number
   - Cube Roots of Unity
   - *n*th Roots of Unity
   - Geometry of Complex Numbers

4. Theory of Equations and Inequations 45-60
   - Polynomial
   - Quadratic Equation
   - Quadratic Expression
   - Inequality
   - Linear Inequality
   - Solution Set

5. Sequences and Series 61-73
   - Sequence
   - Series
   - Arithmetic Progression (AP)
   - Geometric Progression (GP)
   - Harmonic Progression (HP)

6. Permutations and Combinations 74-83
   - Fundamental Principles of Counting
   - Factorial
   - Permutation
   - Circular Permutation
   - Combination

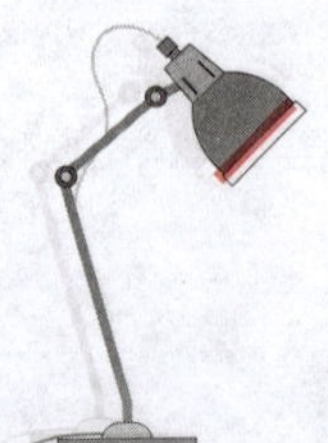

7. Binomial Theorem and Principle of Mathematical Induction 84-90
- Binomial Theorem for Positive Integer
- General Term in a Binomial Expansion
- Middle Term in a Binomial Expansion
- Greatest Term

8. Matrices 91-99
- Matrix
- Algebra of Matrices
- Transpose of Matrix
- Symmetric and Skew-Symmetric Matrices
- Conjugate of a Matrix
- Rank of a Matrix

9. Determinants 100-109
- Minors and Cofactors
- Adjoint of a Matrix
- Inverse of a Matrix
- Homogeneous and Non-homogeneous System of Linear Equations

10. Probability 110-120
- Experiment
- Algebra of Events
- Baye's Theorem
- Random Variable

11. Trigonometric Functions, Identities and Equations 121-133
- Measurement of Angles
- Trigonometric Ratios For Acute Angle
- Trigonometric (or Circular) Functions
- Graph of Trigonometric Functions
- Fundamental Trigonometric Identities
- Trigonometric Functions of Compound Angles
- Transformation Formulae
- Trigonometric Functions of Multiple Angles
- Periodic Functions

12. Triangle 134-139
- Basic Rules of Triangle
- Trigonometrical Ratios of Half of the Angles of Triangle
- Area of a Triangle

13. Inverse Trigonometric Functions 140-148
- Domain and Range of Inverse Trigonometric Functions
- Graphs of Inverse Trigonometric Functions
- Elementary Properties of Inverse Trigonometric Functions

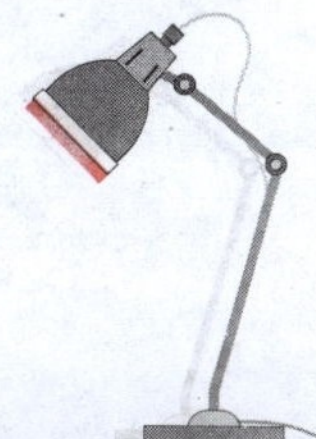

14. Rectangular Axis 149-154
- Rectangular Axis
- Quadrants
- Distance Formulae
- Section Formulae
- Area of Triangle/ Quadrilateral
- Shifting of Origin/Rotation of Axes
- Equation of Locus

15. Straight Line 155-163
- Slope (Gradient) of a Line
- Angle between Two Lines
- Equation of a Straight Line
- Distance of a Point from a Line
- Pair of Lines

16. Circles 164-176
- Standard Equation of a Circle
- Equation of Circle Passing Through Three Points
- Parametric Equation of Circle
- Equation of Tangent
- Equation of Normal
- Pair of Tangents
- Common Tangents of Two Circles
- Family of Circles
- Diameter of Circle

17. Parabola 177-186
- Conic Section
- General Equation of Conic
- Equation of Tangent
- Point of Intersection of Two Tangents
- Equation of Normal
- Length of Tangent and Normal
- Equation of Diameter
- Pair of Tangents
- Chord of Contact

18. Ellipse 187-194
- Parametric Equation
- Equation of Tangent
- Equation of Normal

19. Hyperbola 195-204
- Hyperbola of the Form $\frac{x^2}{a^2} - \frac{y^2}{b^2} = 1$
- Conjugate Hyperbola $-\frac{x^2}{a^2} + \frac{y^2}{b^2} = 1$
- Equation of Hyperbola in Different Forms
- Tangent Equation of Hyperbola
- Normal Equation of Hyperbola
- Asymptote
- Rectangular Hyperbola

20. Limits, Continuity & Differentiability 205-218
- Limit
- Methods of Evaluating Limits
- Sandwich Theorem
- Continuity
- Differentiability
- Fundamental Theorems of Differentiability

21. Derivatives 219-226
- Derivatives of Standard Functions
- Fundamental Rules for Derivatives
- Derivatives of Different Types of Function
- Differentiation of a Determinant
- Successive Differentiations
- Partial Differentiations

22. Application of Derivatives 227-238
- Derivatives as the Rate of Change
- Tangents and Normals
- Rolle's Theorem
- Lagrange's Mean Value Theorem
- Approximations and Errors
- Increasing Function
- Maxima and Minima of Functions

23. Indefinite Integrals 239-253
- Some Standard Integral Formulae
- Properties of Integration
- Integration by Substitution
- Integration by Parts
- Integration by Partial Fractions
- Integration of Irrational Algebraic Function

24. Definite Integrals 254-260
- Fundamental Theorem of Calculus
- Properties of Definite Integral
- Integral Function

25. Applications of Integrals 261-269
- Area of Curves Given by Polar Equations
- Area of Curves Given by Parametric Curves
- Curve Sketching
- Volume and Surface Area

26. Differential Equations 270-276
- Order and Degree of a Differential Equation
- Linear and Non-Linear Differential Equations
- Solution of Differential Equations
- Formation of Differential Equations

27. Vectors 277-287
- Types of Vectors
- Addition of Vectors
- Difference (Subtraction) of Vectors
- Multiplication of a Vector by a Scalar
- Components of a Vector
- Vector Joining Two Points
- Section Formulae
- Scalar or Dot Product of Two Vectors
- Vector or Cross Product of Two Vectors

28. Three Dimensional Geometry 288-299
- Coordinate System
- Direction Cosines
- Line in Space
- Plane
- Angle Between Two Planes
- Parallelism and Perpendicularity of Two Planes

29 Statistics 300-313
- Graphical Representation of Frequency Distributions
- Measures of Central Tendency
- Arithmetic Mean
- Geometric Mean
- Harmonic Mean
- Median
- Mode

Knowledge Library 317-429

Appendix 430-438

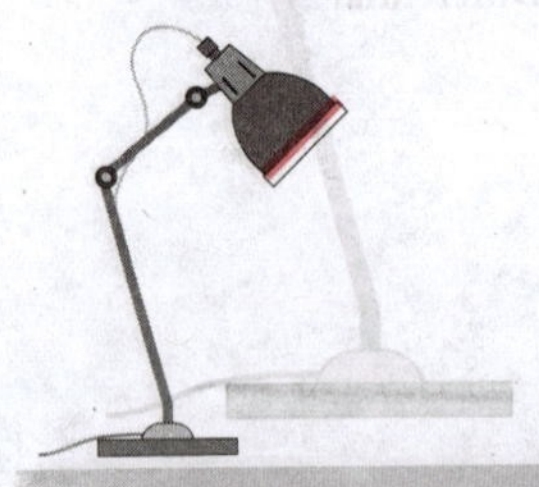

Chapter 01

Sets and Relations

Set

Set is a collection of well defined objects which are distinct from each other. Sets are usually denoted by capital letters $A, B, C, \ldots$ and elements are usually denoted by small letters $a, b, c, \ldots$.

If a is an element of a set A, then we write $a \in A$ and say a belongs to A or a is in A or a is a member of A. If a does not belongs to A, we write $a \notin A$.

Standard Notations

N	:	A set of all natural numbers.
W	:	A set of all whole numbers.
Z	:	A set of all integers.
Z^+ / Z^-	:	A set of all positive/negative integers.
Q	:	A set of all rational numbers.
Q^+ / Q^-	:	A set of all positive/negative rational numbers.
R	:	A set of all real numbers.
R^+ / R^-	:	A set of all positive/negative real numbers.
C	:	A set of all complex numbers.

Methods for Describing a Set

(i) **Roster Form / Listing Method / Tabular Form** In this method, a set is described by listing the elements, separated by commas and enclosed within braces.

e.g. If A is the set of vowels in English alphabet, then $A = \{a, e, i, o, u\}$

(ii) **Set Builder Form / Rule Method** In this method, we write down a property or rule which gives us all the elements of the set.

e.g. $A = \{x : x \text{ is a vowel in English alphabet}\}$

Types of Sets

(i) **Empty/Null/Void Set** A set containing no element, it is denoted by ϕ or $\{\}$.

(ii) **Singleton Set** A set containing a single element.

(iii) **Finite Set** A set containing finite number of elements or no element.

Value Point

Cardinal Number (or Order) of a Finite Set The number of elements in a given finite set is called its cardinal number. If A is a finite set, then its cardinal number is denoted by $n(A)$. e.g. if $A = \{a, b, c\}$, then $n(A) = 3$

(iv) **Infinite Set** A set containing infinite number of elements.

(v) **Equivalent Sets** Two sets are said to be equivalent, if they have same number of elements.

If $n(A) = n(B)$, then A and B are equivalent sets.

(vi) **Equal Sets** Two sets A and B are said to be equal, if every element of A is a member of B and every element of B is a member of A and we write it as $A = B$.

Subset and Superset

Let A and B be two sets. If every element of A is an element of B, then A is called subset of B and B is called superset of A and written as $A \subseteq B$ or $B \supseteq A$.

Power Set

The set formed by all the subsets of a given set A, is called power set of A, denoted by $P(A)$.

Universal Set U

A set consisting of all possible elements which occurs under consideration is called a universal set.

Proper Subset

If A is a subset of B and $A \neq B$, then A is called proper subset of B and we write it as $A \subset B$.

Comparable Sets

Two sets A and B are comparable, if $A \subseteq B$ or $B \subseteq A$.

Non-comparable Sets

For two sets A and B, if neither $A \subseteq B$ nor $B \subseteq A$, then A and B are called non-comparable sets.

Intervals as Subsets of R

(i) The set of real numbers x, such that $a \le x \le b$ is called a **closed interval** and denoted by $[a, b]$ i.e. $[a, b] = \{x : x \in R, a \le x \le b\}$.

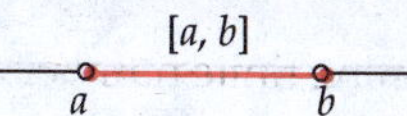

(ii) The set of real number x, such that $a < x < b$ is called an **open interval** and is denoted by (a, b).

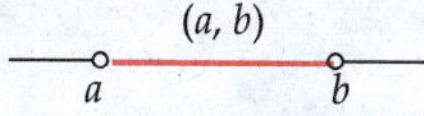

i.e. $(a,b) = \{x : x \in R, a < x < b\}$

(iii) The sets $[a, b) = \{x : x \in R, a \le x < b\}$ and $(a, b] = \{x : x \in R, a < x \le b\}$ are called **semi-open** or **semi-closed** intervals.

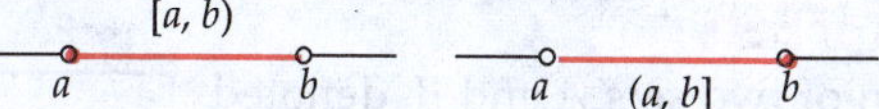

Value Points

- An interval contains infinitely many points.
- The number $(b - a)$ is called the length of any of the interval $[a, b]$, (a, b), $[a, b)$, $(a, b]$.

Venn Diagram

In a Venn diagram, the universal set is represented by a rectangular region and its subset is represented by circle or a closed geometrical figure inside the rectangular region.

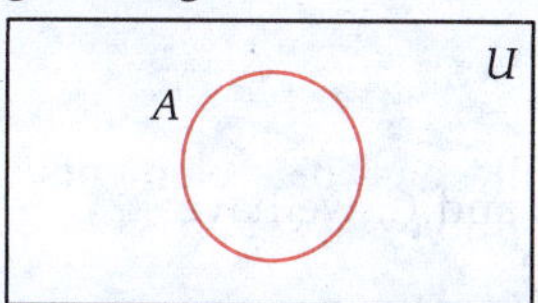

Operations on Sets

1. Union of Sets

The union of two sets A and B, denoted by $A \cup B$, is the set of all those elements which are either in A or in B or both in A and B.

Symbolically, $A \cup B = \{x : x \in A \text{ or } x \in B\}$

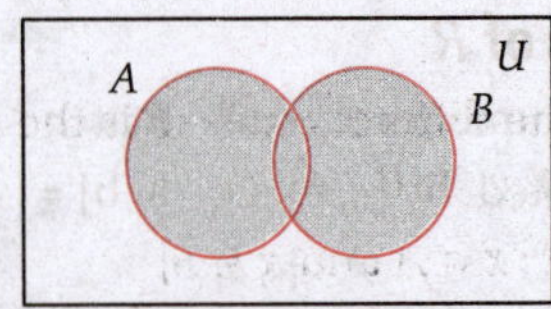

Laws of Union of Sets

For any three sets A, B and C, we have

(i) $A \cup \phi = A$ (Identity law)

(ii) $U \cup A = U$ (Universal law)

(iii) $A \cup A = A$ (Idempotent law)

(iv) $A \cup B = B \cup A$ (Commutative law)

(v) $(A \cup B) \cup C = A \cup (B \cup C)$ (Associative law)

2. Intersection of Sets

The intersection of two sets A and B, denoted by $A \cap B$, is the set of all those elements which are common to both A and B.

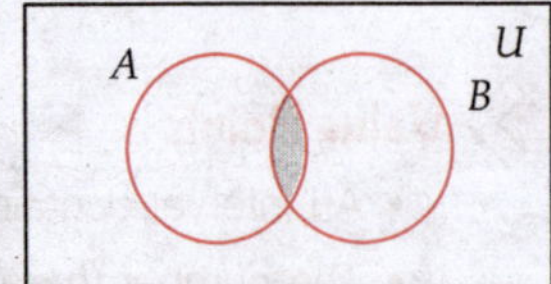

If $A_1, A_2, \ldots, A_n$ is a finite family of sets, then their intersection is denoted by

$$\bigcap_{i=1}^{n} A_i \text{ or } A_1 \cap A_2 \cap \ldots \cap A_n.$$

Symbolically, $A \cap B = \{x : x \in A \text{ and } x \in B\}$

Disjoint Sets

Two sets A and B are called disjoint, if $A \cap B = \phi$ i.e. they do not have any common element.

Laws of Intersection

For any three sets, A, B and C, we have

(i) $A \cap \phi = \phi$ (Identity law)

(ii) $U \cap A = A$ (Universal law)

(iii) $A \cap A = A$ (Idempotent law)

(iv) $A \cap B = B \cap A$ (Commutative law)

(v) $(A \cap B) \cap C = A \cap (B \cap C)$ (Associative law)

(vi) $A \cap (B \cup C) = (A \cap B) \cup (A \cap C)$

(intersection distributes over union)

(vii) $A \cup (B \cap C) = (A \cup B) \cap (A \cup C)$

(union distributes over intersection)

3. Difference of Sets

For two sets A and B, the difference $A-B$ is the set of all those elements of A which do not belong to B.

Symbolically, $A-B=\{x : x \in A \text{ and } x \notin B\}$

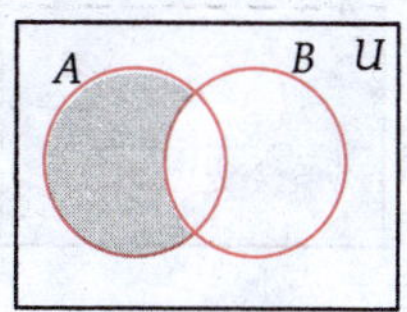

The sets $A-B$, $A\cap B$ and $B-A$ are mutually disjoint sets i.e. the intersection of any of these two sets is the null set.

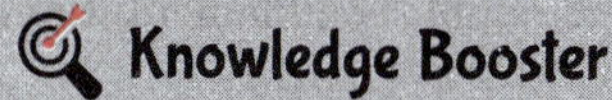

Knowledge Booster

Symmetric Difference

For two sets A and B, symmetric difference is the set $(A-B)\cup(B-A)$ denoted by $A\,\Delta\,B$.

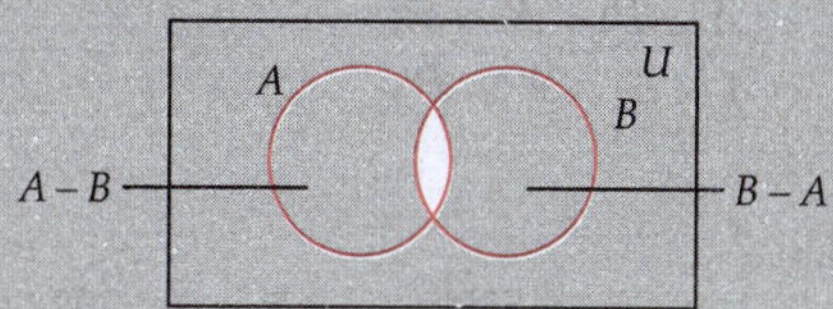

Symbolically, $A\Delta B=(A-B)\cup(B-A)=(A\cap B')\cup(B\cap A')$.

Laws of Difference of Sets

(a) For any two sets A and B, we have

(i) $A-B=A\cap B'$ (ii) $B-A=B\cap A'$

(iii) $A-B\subseteq A$ (iv) $B-A\subseteq B$

(v) $A-B=A \Leftrightarrow A\cap B=\phi$

(vi) $(A-B)\cup B=A\cup B$

(vii) $(A-B)\cap B=\phi$

(viii) $(A-B)\cup(B-A)=(A\cup B)-(A\cap B)$

(b) If A, B and C are any three sets, then

(i) $A-(B\cap C)=(A-B)\cup(A-C)$

(ii) $A-(B\cup C)=(A-B)\cap(A-C)$

(iii) $A\cap(B-C)=(A\cap B)-(A\cap C)$

(iv) $A\cap(B\,\Delta\,C)=(A\cap B)\,\Delta\,(A\cap C)$

4. Complement of a Set

If A is a set with U as universal set, then complement of a set A, denoted by A' or A^c is the set $U - A$.

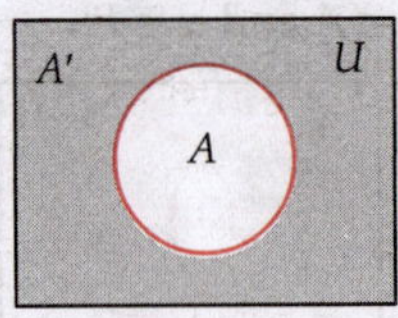

Symbolically, $A' = \{x : x \notin A \text{ but } x \in U\}$

Properties of Complement of Sets are

(i) (a) $A' = U - A$ (b) $(A')' = A = U - A'$

(law of double complementation)

(ii) (a) $A \cup A' = U$

(b) $A \cap A' = \phi$ (complement laws)

(iii) (a) $\phi' = U$

(b) $U' = \phi$ (laws of empty set and universal set)

(iv) $(A \cup B)' = U - (A \cup B) = A' \cap B'$

(v) $(A \cap B)' = U - (A \cap B) = A' \cup B'$

Value Points

(i) Every set is a subset of itself i.e. $A \subseteq A$, for any set A.

(ii) Empty set ϕ is a subset of every set i.e. $\phi \subset A$, for any set A.

(iii) For any set A and its universal set U, $A \subseteq U$

(iv) If $A = \phi$, then power set has only one element, i.e. $n(P(A)) = 1$.

(v) Power set of any set is always a non-empty set.

(vi) Suppose $A = \{1, 2\}$, then $P(A) = \{\{1\}, \{2\}, \{1, 2\}, \phi\}$.

(a) $A \in P(A)$ (b) $\{A\} \notin P(A)$

(vii) If a set A has n elements, then $P(A)$ has 2^n elements.

(viii) Equal sets are always equivalent but equivalent sets may or may not be equal.

(ix) The set $\{\phi\}$ is not a null set. It is a set containing one element ϕ.

Results on Number of Elements in Sets

If A, B and C are finite sets and U is the universal set, then

(i) $n(A \cup B) = n(A) + n(B) - n(A \cap B)$

(ii) $n(A \cup B) = n(A) + n(B)$, if A and B are disjoint sets.

(iii) $n(A - B) = n(A) - n(A \cap B)$

(iv) $n(B - A) = n(B) - n(A \cap B)$

(v) $n(A \Delta B) = n(A) + n(B) - 2n(A \cap B)$

(vi) $n(A \cup B \cup C) = n(A) + n(B) + n(C) - n(A \cap B) - n(B \cap C) - n(A \cap C) + n(A \cap B \cap C)$

(vii) n (number of elements in exactly two of the sets A, B, C) $= n(A \cap B) + n(B \cap C) + n(C \cap A) - 3n(A \cap B \cap C)$

(viii) n (number of elements in exactly one of the sets A, B, C) $= n(A) + n(B) + n(C) - 2n(A \cap B) - 2n(B \cap C) - 2n(A \cap C) + 3n(A \cap B \cap C)$

(ix) $n(A' \cup B') = n(A \cap B)' = n(U) - n(A \cap B)$

(x) $n(A' \cap B') = n(A \cup B)' = n(U) - n(A \cup B)$

(xi) If $A_1, A_2, \ldots\ldots, A_m$ are disjoint sets, then
$n(A_1 \cup A_2 \cup \ldots\ldots \cup A_m) = n(A_1) + n(A_2) + \ldots\ldots + n(A_m)$

Ordered Pair

An ordered pair consists of two objects or elements grouped in a particular order.

Equality of Ordered Pairs

Two ordered pairs (a_1, b_1) and (a_2, b_2) are equal iff $a_1 = a_2$ and $b_1 = b_2$.

Cartesian (or Cross) Product of Sets

For two non-empty sets A and B, the set of all ordered pairs (a, b) such that $a \in A$ and $b \in B$ is called Cartesian product $A \times B$, i.e.

$$A \times B = \{(a, b) : a \in A \text{ and } b \in B\}$$

Ordered Triplet

If there are three sets A, B, C and $a \in A$, $b \in B$ and $c \in C$, then we form an ordered triplet (a, b, c). It is also called 3-triple. The set of all ordered triplets (a, b, c) is called the **cartesian product** of three sets A, B and C.

i.e. $A \times B \times C = \{(a, b, c) : a \in A, b \in B \text{ and } c \in C\}$

Diagramatic Representation of Cartesian Product of Two Sets

We first draw two circles representing sets A and B one opposite to the other as shown in the given figure and write the elements of sets in the corresponding circles.

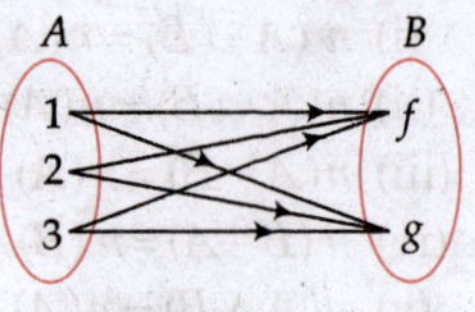

Now, we draw line segments starting from each element of set A and terminating to each element of set B.

Properties of Cartesian Product

For three sets A, B and C,

(i) $n(A \times B) = n(A) \times n(B)$

(ii) $A \times B = \phi$, if either A or B is an empty set.

(iii) $A \times (B \cup C) = (A \times B) \cup (A \times C)$

(iv) $A \times (B \cap C) = (A \times B) \cap (A \times C)$

(v) $A \times (B - C) = (A \times B) - (A \times C)$

(vi) $(A \times B) \cap (C \times D) = (A \cap C) \times (B \cap D)$

(vii) $A \times (B' \cup C')' = (A \times B) \cap (A \times C)$

(viii) $A \times (B' \cap C')' = (A \times B) \cup (A \times C)$

(ix) If $A \subseteq B$ and $C \subseteq D$, then $(A \times C) \subseteq (B \times D)$

(x) If $A \subseteq B$, then $A \times A \subseteq (A \times B) \cap (B \times A)$

(xi) If $A \subseteq B$, then $A \times C \subseteq B \times C$ for any set C.

(xii) $A \times B = B \times A \Leftrightarrow A = B$

(xiii) If $A \neq B$, then $A \times B \neq B \times A$

(xiv) If either A or B is an infinite set, then $A \times B$ is an infinite set.

(xv) If A and B be any two non-empty sets having n elements in common, then $A \times B$ and $B \times A$ have n^2 elements in common.

Relation

If A and B are two non-empty sets, then a relation R from A to B is a subset of $A \times B$.

If $R \subseteq A \times B$ and $(a, b) \in R$, then we say that a is related to b by the relation R, written as aRb.

If $R \subseteq A \times A$, then we simply say R is a relation on A.

Representation of a Relation

(i) **Roster form** In this form, we represent the relation by the set of all ordered pairs belongs to R.

e.g. Let R is a relation from set $A=\{-3,-2,-1,1,2,3\}$ to set $B=\{1,4,9,10\}$, defined by $aRb \Leftrightarrow a^2=b$,

Then, $(-3)^2=9, (-2)^2=4, (-1)^2=1, (2)^2=4, (3)^2=9$.

Then, in roster form, R can be written as

$$R=\{(-1,1),(-2,4),(1,1),(2,4),(-3,9),(3,9)\}$$

(ii) **Set-builder form** In this form, we represent the relation R from set A to set B as

$R=\{(a,b): a\in A, b\in B$ and the rule which relate the elements of A and $B\}$

e.g. Let R is a relation from set $A=\{1,2,4,5\}$ to set

$B=\left\{1,\frac{1}{2},\frac{1}{4},\frac{1}{5}\right\}$ such that

$$R=\left\{(1,1),\left(2,\frac{1}{2}\right)\left(4,\frac{1}{4}\right)\left(5,\frac{1}{5}\right)\right\}$$

Then, in set-builder form, R can be written as

$$R=\left\{(a,b): a\in A, b\in B \text{ and } b=\frac{1}{a}\right\}$$

EXPERT Scale Up

We cannot write every relation from set A to set B in set-builder form.

Domain, Codomain and Range of a Relation

Let R be a relation from a non-empty set A to a non-empty set B. Then, set of all first components or coordinates of the ordered pairs belonging to R is called the **domain** of R, while the set of all second components or coordinates of the ordered pairs belonging to R is called the **range** of R. Also, the set B is called the **codomain** of relation R.

Thus, domain of $R=\{a:(a,b)\in R\}$ and range of $R=\{b:(a,b)\in R\}$

Types of Relations

(i) **Empty or Void Relation** For any set A, $R = \phi \subset A \times A$ is a relation on A, called the empty or void relation.

(ii) **Universal Relation** For any set A, $R = A \times A \subseteq A \times A$ is a relation on A, called the universal relation.

(iii) **Identity Relation** The relation $I_A = \{(a, a) : a \in A\}$ is called the identity relation on A.

(iv) **Reflexive Relation** A relation R on a set A is said to be reflexive relation, if every element of A is related to itself.

Thus, $(a, a) \in R, \forall a \in A \Rightarrow R$ is reflexive.

(v) **Symmetric Relation** A relation R on a set A is said to be symmetric relation iff $(a, b) \in R \Rightarrow (b, a) \in R, \forall a, b \in A$

i.e. $$a R b \Rightarrow bRa, \forall a, b \in A$$

(vi) **Transitive Relation** A relation R on a set A is said to be transitive relation, iff $(a, b) \in R$ and $(b, c) \in R$

$$\Rightarrow \quad (a, c) \in R, \forall a, b, c \in A$$

i.e. aRb and $bRc \Rightarrow aRc, \forall a, b, c \in A$.

Equivalence Relation

A relation R on a set A is said to be an equivalence relation, if it is simultaneously reflexive, symmetric and transitive on A.

Equivalence Classes

Let R be an equivalence relation on A $(\neq \phi)$. Let $a \in A$.

Then, the equivalence class of a denoted by $[a]$ or (a) is defined as the set of all those points of A which are related to a under the relation R.

Inverse Relation If A and B are two non-empty sets and R be a relation from A to B, then the inverse of R, denoted by R^{-1}, is a relation from B to A and is defined by $R^{-1} = \{(b, a) : (a, b) \in R\}$.

Composition of Relation Let R and S be two relations from sets A to B and B to C respectively, then we can define relation SoR from A to C such that $(a, c) \in SoR \Leftrightarrow \exists\, b \in B$ such that $(a, b) \in R$ and $(b, c) \in S$.

This relation SoR is called the composition of R and S.

(i) $RoS \neq SoR$ (ii) $(SoR)^{-1} = R^{-1} o S^{-1}$ known as **reversal rule**.

Value Points

(i) If R and S are two equivalence relations on a set A, then $R \cap S$ is also an equivalence relation on A.

(ii) The union of two equivalence relations on a set is not necessarily an equivalence relation on the set.

(iii) If R is an equivalence relation on a set A, then R^{-1} is also an equivalence relation on A.

(vi) Let A and B be two non-empty finite sets consisting of m and n elements, respectively. Then, $A \times B$ consists of mn ordered pairs. So, the total number of relations from A to B is 2^{nm}.

(v) If a set A has n elements, then number of reflexive relations from A to A is $2^{n^2 - n}$.

Chapter 02

Functions

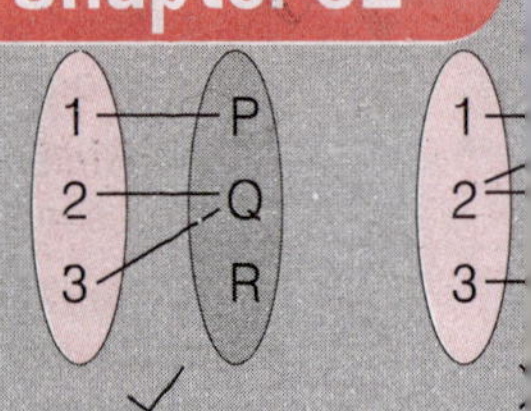

Function

Let A and B be two non-empty sets, then a function f from set A to set B is a rule which associates each element of A to a unique element of B. It is represented as $f : A \rightarrow B$ or $A \xrightarrow{f} B$ and function is also called the **mapping**.

Domain, Codomain and Range of a Function

If $f : A \rightarrow B$ is a function from A to B, then

(i) the set A is called the **domain** of $f(x)$.

(ii) the set B is called the **codomain** of $f(x)$.

(iii) the subset of B containing only the image elements of A is called the **range** of $f(x)$.

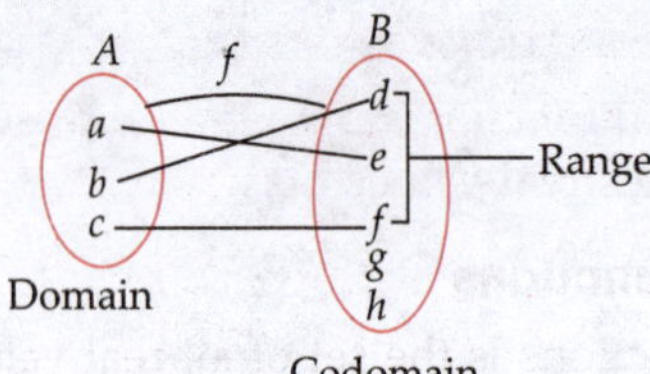

Characteristics of a Function $f : A \rightarrow B$

(i) For each element $x \in A$, there is unique element $y \in B$.

(ii) The element $y \in B$ is called the **image** of x under the function f. Also, y is called the **value of function** f at x i.e. $f(x) = y$.

(iii) $f : A \rightarrow B$ is not a function, if there is an element in A which has more than one image in B. But more than one element of A may be associated to the same element of B.

(iv) $f : A \rightarrow B$ is not a function, if an element in A does not have an image in B.

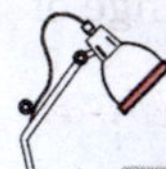

EXPERT Scale Up

Identification of a Function from its Graph

For a vertical line drawn parallel to Y-axis, such that it intersects the graph of the given expression. If it intersects the graph at more than one point, then the **expression is a relation** else, if it intersects at only one point, then the **expression is a function**.

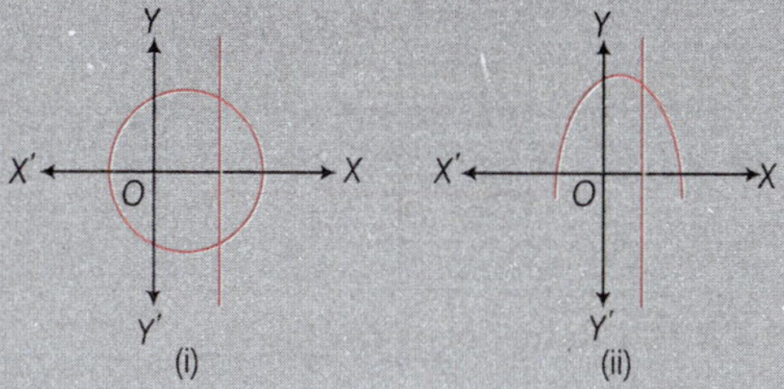

In figure (i), the vertical parallel line intersects the curve at two points, thus the expression is a relation whereas in figure (ii), the vertical parallel line intersects the curve at one point. So, the expression is a function.

Real Valued and Real Functions

A function $f: A \to B$ is called a **real valued function**, if $B \subseteq R$ and it is called a **real function**, if $A \subseteq R$ and $B \subseteq R$.

1. Domain of Real Functions

The domain of the real function $f(x)$ is the set of all those real numbers for which $f(x)$ assumes real values only.

2. Range of Real Functions

The range of real functions is the set of all real values taken by $f(x)$ at points of its domain.

Working Rule for Finding Range of Real Functions

Let $y = f(x)$ be a real function, then for finding the range we may use the following steps.

Step **I** Find the domain of the function $y = f(x)$.

Step **II** Transform the equation $y = f(x)$ as $x = g(y)$. i.e. convert x in terms of y.

Step **III** Find the values of y from $x = g(y)$ such that the values of x are real and lying in the domain of f.

***Step* IV** The set of values of y obtained in step III will be the range of function f.

Standard Real Functions and their Graphs

1. Constant Function

Let c be a fixed real number. The function which associates each real number x to this fixed number c, is called a constant function.
i.e. $y = f(x) = c$ for all $x \in R$.

Domain of $f(x) = R$ and Range of $f(x) = \{c\}$.

2. Identity Function

The function which associates each real number x to the same number x, is called the identity function.
i.e. $y = f(x) = x, \forall x \in R$.

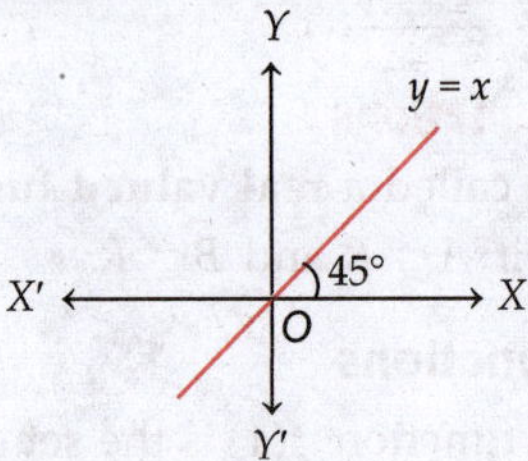

Domain of $f(x) = R$ and Range of $f(x) = R$

3. Linear Function

If a and b are fixed real numbers, then the linear function is defined as $y = f(x) = ax + b$. The graph of a linear function is given in the following diagram, which is a straight line with slope $\tan\alpha$.

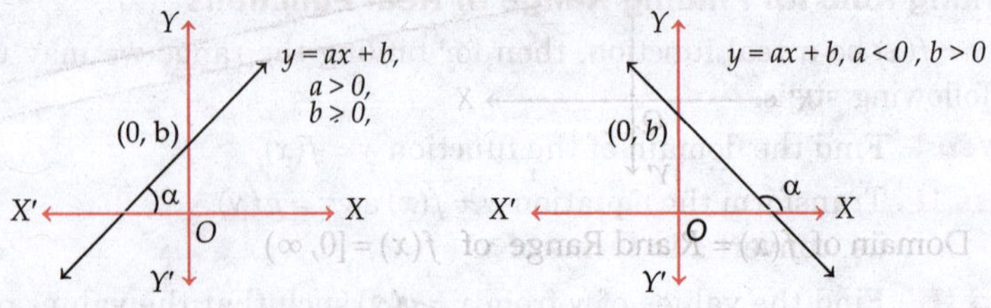

Domain of $f(x) = R$ and Range of $f(x) = R$.

4. Quadratic Function

If a, b and c are fixed real numbers, then the quadratic function is expressed as

$$y = f(x) = ax^2 + bx + c, a \neq 0$$

$$\Rightarrow \quad y = a\left(x + \frac{b}{2a}\right)^2 + \frac{4ac - b^2}{4a}$$

which represents a downward parabola, if $a < 0$ and upward parabola, if $a > 0$ and vertex of this parabola is at $\left(-\frac{b}{2a}, \frac{4ac - b^2}{4a}\right)$.

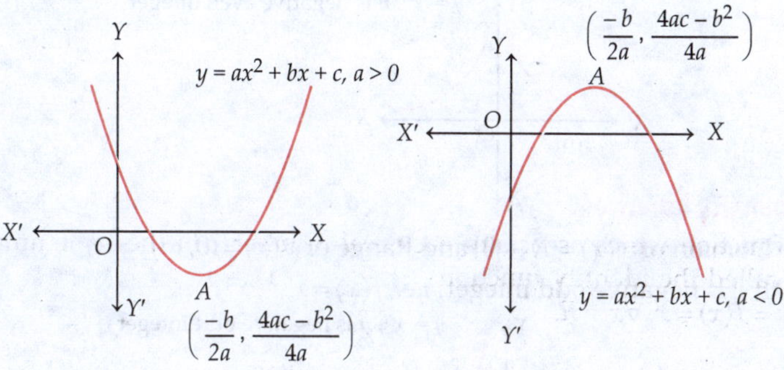

Domain of $f(x) = R$

Range of $f(x)$ is $\left(-\infty, \frac{4ac - b^2}{4a}\right]$, if $a < 0$ and $\left[\frac{4ac - b^2}{4a}, \infty\right)$, if $a > 0$.

5. Power Function

The power function is given by $y = f(x) = x^n$, $n \in I, n \neq 0, 1$.
The domain and range of $y = f(x)$, depend on n.

(a) If n is positive even integer, i.e. $f(x) = x^2, x^4, \ldots$

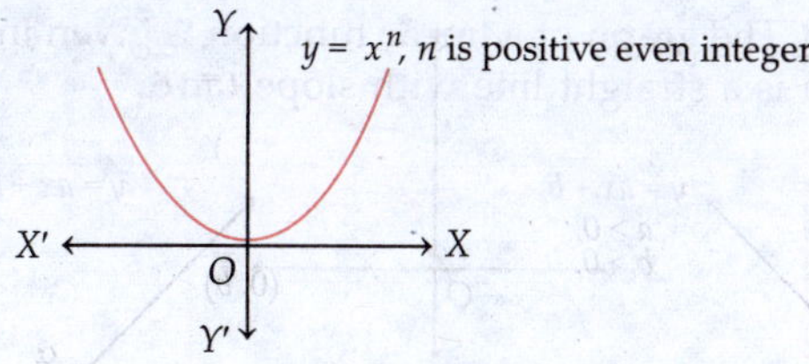

Domain of $f(x) = R$ and Range of $f(x) = [0, \infty)$

(b) If n is positive odd integer, i.e. $f(x) = x^3, x^5, \ldots$

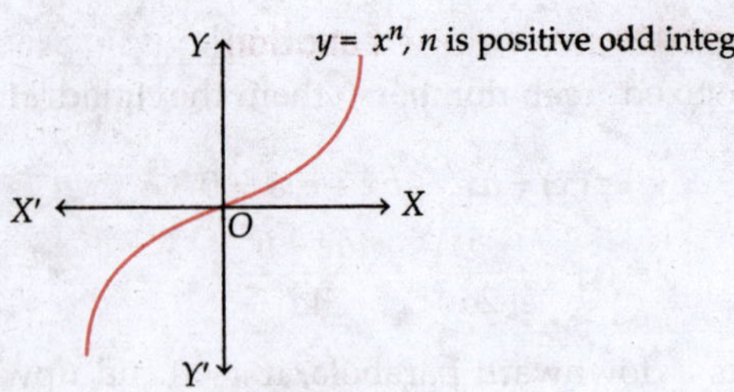

Domain of $f(x) = R$ and Range of $f(x) = R$

(c) If n is negative even integer, i.e. $f(x) = x^{-2}, x^{-4}, \ldots$

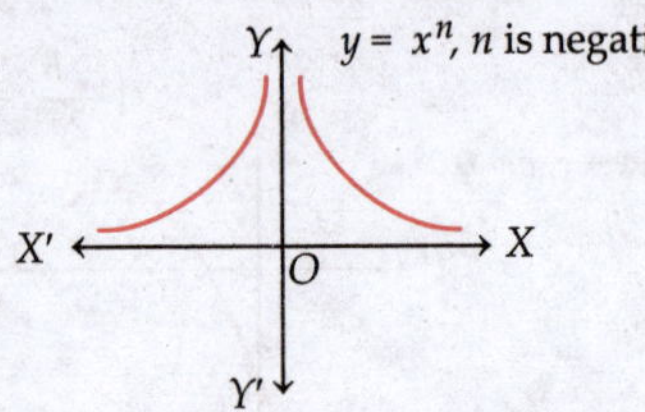

Domain of $f(x) = R - \{0\}$ and Range of $f(x) = (0, \infty)$

(d) If n is negative odd integer, i.e. $f(x) = x^{-1}, x^{-3}, \ldots$

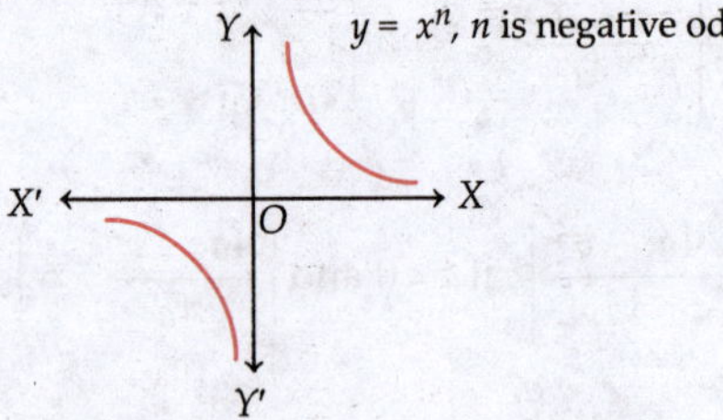

Domain of $f(x) = R - \{0\}$ and Range of $f(x) = R - \{0\}$

6. Square Root Function

Square root function is defined by $y = f(x) = \sqrt{x}, x \geq 0$.

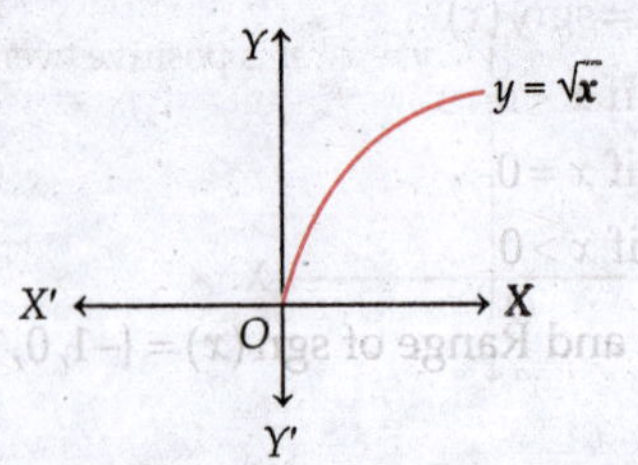

Domain of $f(x) = [0, \infty)$ and Range of $f(x) = [0, \infty)$

7. Modulus (or Absolute Value) Function

Modulus function is given by $y = f(x) = |x|$, where $|x|$ denotes the absolute value of x,

i.e. $$|x| = \begin{cases} x, \text{ if } x \geq 0 \\ -x, \text{ if } x < 0 \end{cases}$$

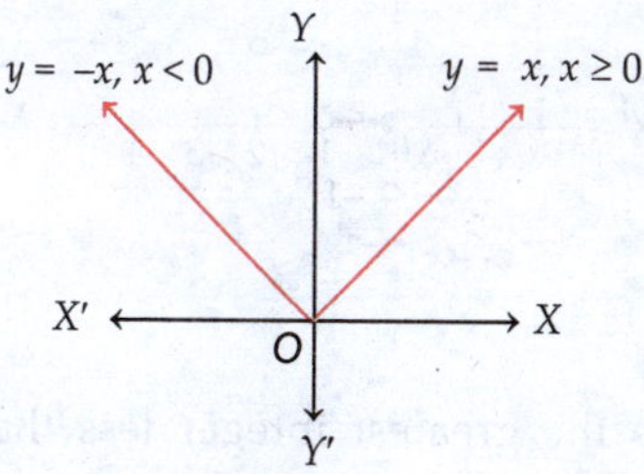

Domain of $f(x) = R$ and Range of $f(x) = [0, \infty)$.

8. Signum Function

Signum function is defined as follows

$$y = f(x) = \begin{cases} \dfrac{|x|}{x}, \text{ if } x \neq 0 \\ 0, \quad \text{if } x = 0 \end{cases} \text{ or } \begin{cases} \dfrac{x}{|x|}, \text{ if } x \neq 0 \\ 0, \quad \text{if } x = 0 \end{cases}$$

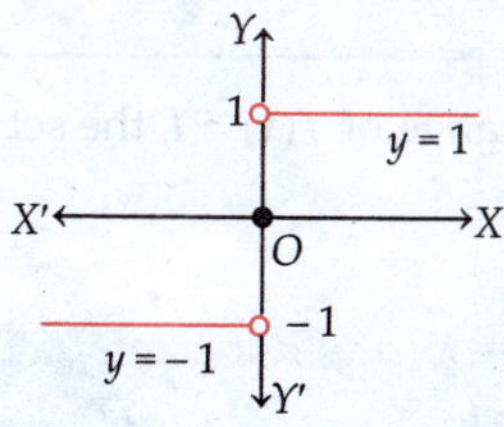

Symbolically, signum function is denoted by sgn (x).

Thus, $$y = f(x) = \text{sgn }(x)$$

where, $$\text{sgn }(x) = \begin{cases} -1, \text{ if } x < 0 \\ 0, \text{ if } x = 0 \\ 1, \text{ if } x > 0 \end{cases}$$

Domain of sgn $(x) = R$ and Range of sgn $(x) = \{-1, 0, 1\}$.

9. Greatest Integer Function/Step Function/Floor Function

The greatest integer function is defined as $y = f(x) = [x],\ x \in R$

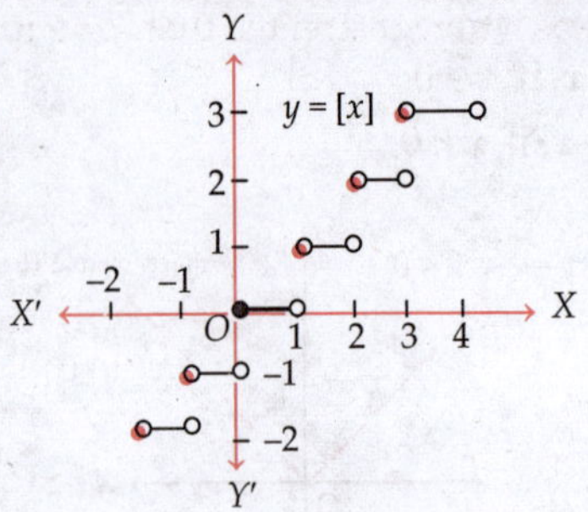

where, $[x]$ represents the greatest integer less than or equal to x. In general, if $n \le x < n+1$ for any integer n, $[x] = n$.

Thus, $[2.304] = 2$, $[4] = 4$ and $[-8.05] = -9$

x	$[x]$
$0 \le x < 1$	0
$1 \le x < 2$	1
$-1 \le x < 0$	-1
$-2 \le x < -1$	-2
⋮	⋮

Domain of $f(x) = R$ and Range of $f(x) = I$, the set of integers.

Value Points

- $[x+n] = n + [x],\ n \in I$
- $[-x] = \begin{cases} -[x], & x \in I \\ -[x]-1, & x \notin I \end{cases}$
- $[x] \ge n \Rightarrow x \ge n,\ n \in I$
- $[x] > n \Rightarrow x \ge n+1,\ n \in I$
- $[x] \le n \Rightarrow x < n+1,\ n \in I$
- $[x] < n \Rightarrow x < n,\ n \in I$
- $[x+y] = [x] + [y + x - [x]]$ for all $x, y \in R$
- $[x+y] \ge [x] + [y]$
- $[x] + \left[x + \frac{1}{n}\right] + \left[x + \frac{2}{n}\right] + \dots + \left[x + \frac{n-1}{n}\right] = [nx],\ n \in N.$

10. Least Integer Function/Ceiling Function/Smallest Function

The least integer function is defined as $y = f(x) = (x)$, $x \in R$, where (x) represents the least integer greater than or equal to x.

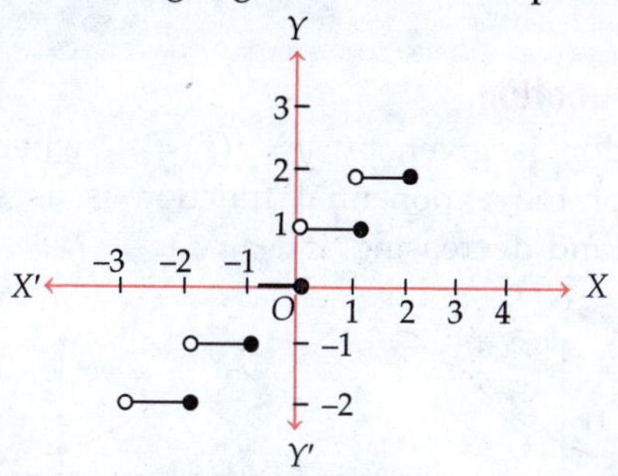

Thus, $(3.578) = 4$, $(0.87) = 1$, $(4) = 4$, $(-8.239) = -8$, $(-0.7) = 0$

In general, if n is an integer and x is any real number such that $n < x \leq n+1$, then $(x) = n+1$

$$\therefore \quad f(x) = (x) = [x] + 1$$

x	(x)
$-1 < x \leq 0$	0
$0 < x \leq 1$	1
$1 < x \leq 2$	2
$2 < x \leq 3$	3
$-2 < x \leq -1$	-1
⋮	⋮

Domain of $f = R$ and Range of $f = I$

11. Fractional Part Function

It is defined as $f(x) = \{x\}$, where $\{x\}$ represents the fractional part of x, i.e., if $x = n + f$, where $n \in I$ and $0 \leq f < 1$, then $\{x\} = f$

e.g. $\{0.7\} = 0.7$, $\{3\} = 0$, $\{-3.6\} = 0.4$

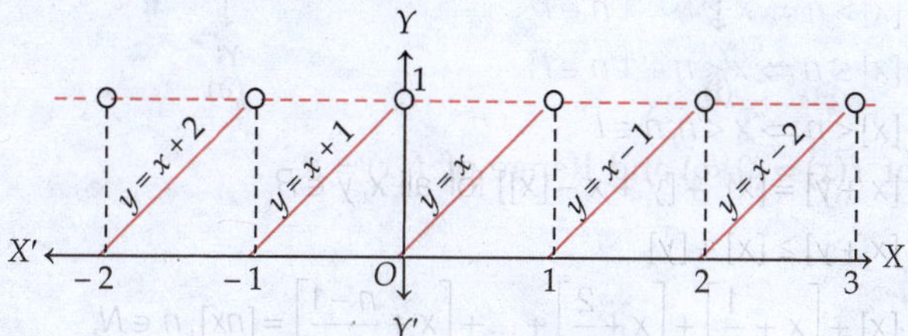

Domain of $f = R$ and Range of $f = [0, 1)$.

Value Points

- $\{x\} = x - [x]$
- $\{x\} = x$, if $0 \le x < 1$
- $\{x\} = 0$, if $x \in I$
- $\{-x\} = 1 - \{x\}$, if $x \notin I$

12. Exponential Function

Exponential function is given by $y = f(x) = a^x$, where $a > 0, a \neq 1$ and $x > 0$. The graph of the exponential function is as shown, which is increasing, if $a > 1$ and decreasing, if $0 < a < 1$.

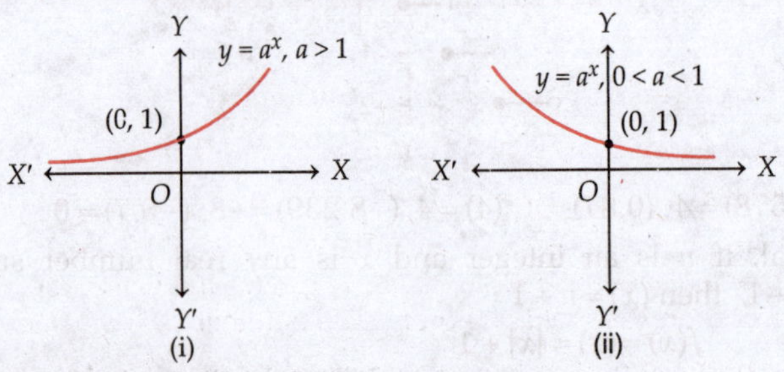

Domain of $f(x) = R$ and Range of $f(x) = (0, \infty)$

13. Logarithmic Function

A logarithmic function is given by $y = f(x) = \log_a x$, where $a > 0, a \neq 1$ and $x > 0$.

The graph of the function is as shown below, which is increasing, if $a > 1$ and decreasing, if $0 < a < 1$.

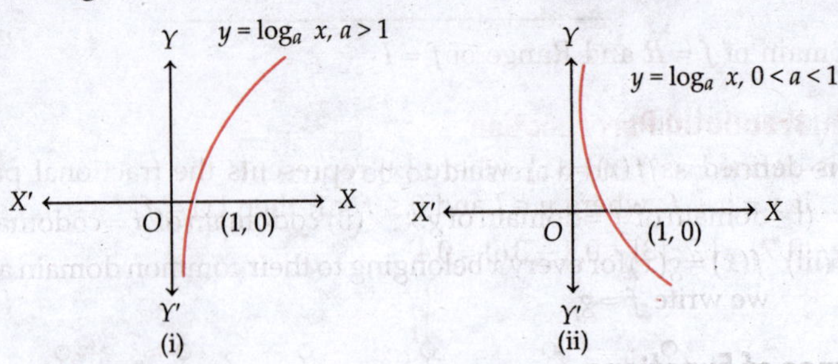

Domain of $f(x) = (0, \infty)$ and Range of $f(x) = R$

Operations on Real Functions

Let $f: A \to B$ and $g: A \longrightarrow B$ be two real functions, then

(i) **Addition** The addition $f + g$ is defined as $f + g: A \longrightarrow B$ such that $(f + g)(x) = f(x) + g(x)$, for all $x \in A$.

(ii) **Difference** The difference $f - g$ is defined as $f - g: A \to B$ such that $(f - g)(x) = f(x) - g(x)$, for all $x \in A$.

(iii) **Product** The product fg is defined as $fg: A \longrightarrow B$ such that $(fg)(x) = f(x)\, g(x)$, for all $x \in A$.

This is also called pointwise multiplication.

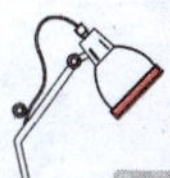

EXPERT Scale Up

$f \pm g$ and fg are defined only, if f and g have the same domain. In case, the domains of f and g are different, then

domain of $f + g$ or fg = domain of $f \cap$ domain of g.

(iv) **Multiplication by a Number** (or a Scalar) The function cf, where c is a real number is defined as $cf: A \longrightarrow B$, such that $(cf)(x) = cf(x)$, $x \in A$.

(v) **Quotient** The quotient $\frac{f}{g}$ is defined as $\frac{f}{g}: A \to B$ such that $\frac{f}{g}(x) = \frac{f(x)}{g(x)}$, provided $g(x) \neq 0$, for all $x \in A$.

Equal Functions

Two functions f and g are said to be equal iff

(i) domain of f = domain of g. (ii) codomain of f = codomain of g.

(iii) $f(x) = g(x)$ for every x belonging to their common domain and then we write $f = g$.

Types of Functions

1. One-One (or Injective) Function

A mapping $f: A \to B$ is called one-one (or injective) function, if different elements in A have different images in B.

Methods to Test One-One

(i) **Analytically** If $f(x_1) = f(x_2) \Rightarrow x_1 = x_2$ or equivalently

$x_1 \neq x_2 \Rightarrow f(x_1) \neq f(x_2), \forall x_1, x_2 \in A,$

then the function is one-one.

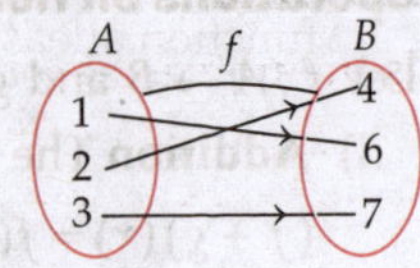

(ii) **Graphically** If every line parallel to X-axis cuts the graph of the function atmost at one point, then the function is one-one.

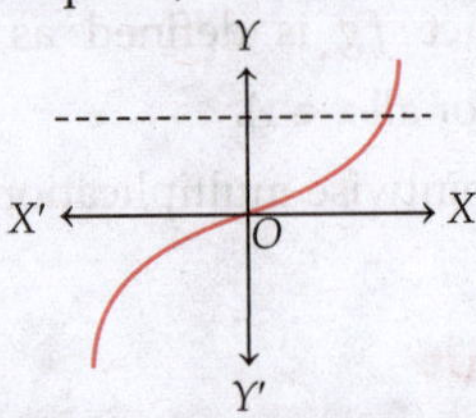

(iii) **Monotonically** If the function is increasing or decreasing in whole domain, then the function is one-one.

Knowledge Booster

Number of One-One Functions

Let A and B be finite sets having m and n elements respectively, then the number of one-one functions from A to B is

$$\begin{cases} {}^nP_m, n \geq m \\ 0, n < m \end{cases} = \begin{cases} n(n-1)(n-2)\dots(n-(m-1)), & n \geq m \\ 0, & n < m \end{cases}$$

2. Many-One Function

A function $f: A \longrightarrow B$ is called many-one function, if two or more than two different elements in A have the same image in B.

Method to Test Many-One

(i) **Analytically** If $x_1 \neq x_2 \Rightarrow f(x_1) = f(x_2)$ for some $x_1, x_2 \in A$, then the function is many-one.

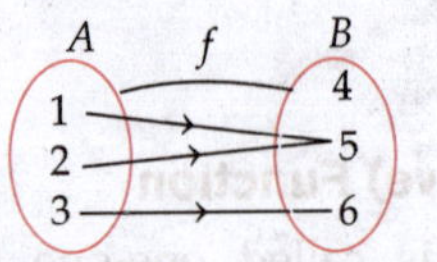

(ii) **Graphically** If any line parallel to X-axis cuts the graph of the function atleast at two points, then the function is many-one.

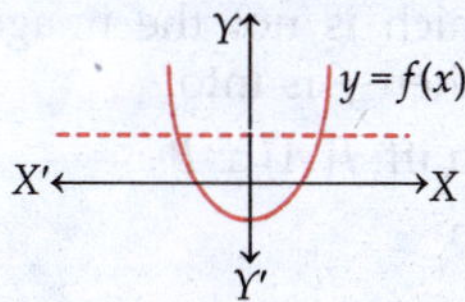

(iii) **Monotonically** If the function is neither strictly increasing nor strictly decreasing, then the function is many-one.

Number of Many-One Function

Let A and B be finite sets having m and n elements respectively, then the number of many-one function from A to B is

$$= \text{Total number of functions} - \text{Number of one-one functions}$$

$$= \begin{cases} n^m - {}^nP_m, \text{ if } n \geq m \\ n^m, \text{ if } n < m \end{cases}$$

3. Onto (or Surjective) Function

If the function $f : A \longrightarrow B$ is such that each element in B (codomain) is the image of atleast one element of A, then we say that f is a function of A onto B. Thus, $f : A \longrightarrow B$ is onto iff $f(A) = B$.

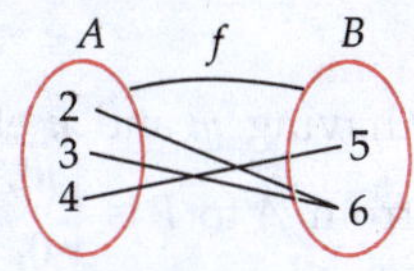

i.e. Range = Codomain

 **Value Point**

Every polynomial function $f : R \longrightarrow R$ of odd degree is onto.

Number of Onto (or Surjective) Functions

Let A and B are finite sets having m and n elements respectively, then number of onto (or surjective) functions from A to B is

$$= \begin{cases} n^m - {}^nC_1(n-1)^m + {}^nC_2(n-2)^m - {}^nC_3(n-3)^m + \ldots, & n < m \\ n!, & n = m \\ 0, & n > m \end{cases}$$

4. Into Function

If $f : A \longrightarrow B$ is such that there exists atleast one element in codomain which is not the image of any element in domain, then f is into.

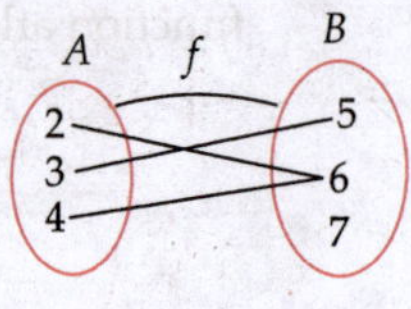

Thus, $f : A \longrightarrow B$, is into iff $f(A) \subset B$

i.e. Range $\subset$ Codomain

Number of Into Function

Let A and B be finite sets having m and n elements respectively, then number of into functions from A to B is

$$= \begin{cases} {}^nC_1(n-1)^m - {}^nC_2(n-2)^m + {}^nC_3(n-3)^m \ldots, & n \leq m \\ n^m, & n > m \end{cases}$$

5. One-One and Onto Function (or Bijective)

A function $f : A \to B$ is said to be one-one and onto (or bijective), if f is both one-one and onto.

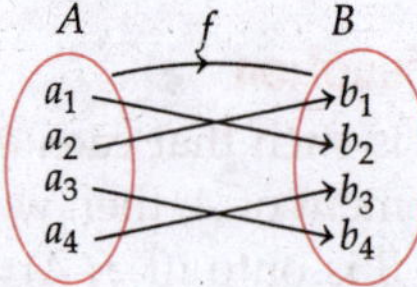

Number of Bijective Functions

Let A and B be finite sets having m and n elements respectively, then number of onto functions from A to B is $\begin{cases} n!, \text{ if } n = m \\ 0, \text{ if } n > m \text{ or } n < m \end{cases}$.

Competition Insight

Composition of Two Functions

Let $f : A \longrightarrow B$ and $g : B \longrightarrow C$ be two functions. Then, we define $gof : A \longrightarrow C$, such that $gof(x) = g(f(x)), \forall x \in A$

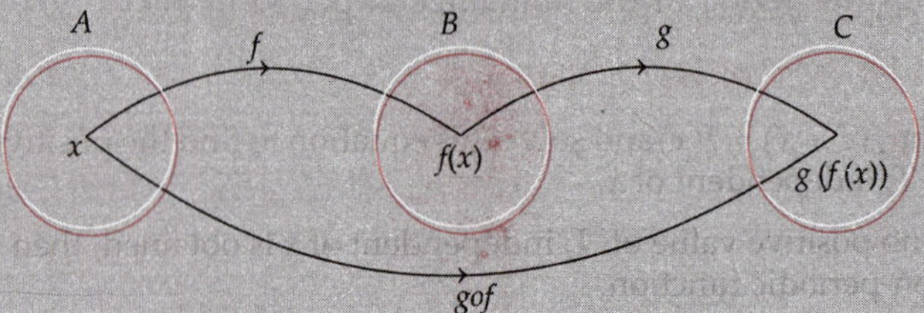

(i) If f and g are injective, then fog and gof are injective.

(ii) If f and g are surjective, then fog and gof are surjective.

(iii) If f and g are bijective, then fog and gof are bijective.

Inverse of a Function

Let $f : A \longrightarrow B$ be a bijective function, i.e. it is one-one and onto function. Then, we can define a function $g : B \longrightarrow A$, such that $f(x) = y \Rightarrow g(y) = x$, which is called inverse of f and *vice-versa*. Symbolically, we write $g = f^{-1}$

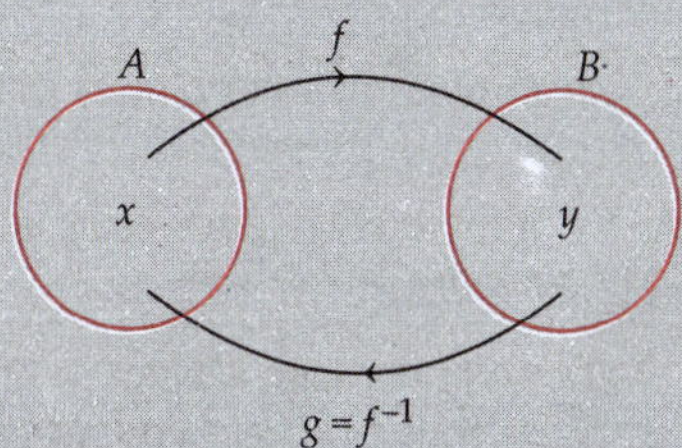

A function whose inverse exists, is called an **invertible function or inversible**.

(i) Domain (f^{-1}) = Range (f)

(ii) Range (f^{-1}) = Domain (f)

(iii) If $f(x) = y$, then $f^{-1}(y) = x$ and *vice-verse*.

(iv) The inverse of a bijection is also a bijection.

(v) If f and g are two bijections $f : A \to B, g : B \to C$ and gof exists, then the inverse of gof also exists and $(gof)^{-1} = f^{-1}og^{-1}$.

Periodic Functions

A function $f(x)$ is said to be a periodic function of x, if there exists a real number $T > 0$, such that

$$f(T + x) = f(x), \forall\ x \in \text{Dom}(f).$$

The smallest positive real number T, satisfying the above condition is known as the period or the fundamental period of $f(x)$.

Testing the Periodicity of a Function

(i) Put $f(T + x) = f(x)$ and solve this equation to find the positive values of T; independent of x.

(ii) If no positive value of T, independent of x is obtained, then $f(x)$ is a non-periodic function.

(iii) If positive values of T which is independent of x are obtained, then $f(x)$ is a periodic function and the least positive value of T is the period of the function $f(x)$.

Value Points

- Constant function is periodic with no fundamental period.
- If $f(x)$ is periodic with period T, then $\frac{1}{f(x)}$ and $\sqrt{f(x)}$ are also periodic with same period T.
- If $f(x)$ is periodic with period T_1 and $g(x)$ is periodic with period T_2, then $f(x) + g(x)$ is periodic with period equal to
  - (a) LCM of $\{T_1, T_2\}$, if there is no positive k, such that $f(k + x) = g(x)$ and $g(k + x) = f(x)$.
  - (b) $\frac{1}{2}$ LCM of $\{T_1, T_2\}$, if there exist a positive number k such that $f(k + x) = g(x)$ and $g(k + x) = f(x)$
- If $f(x)$ is periodic with period T, then $kf(ax + b)$ is periodic with period $\frac{T}{|a|}$, where $a, b, k \in R$ and $a, k \neq 0$.
- If $f(x)$ is a periodic function with period T and $g(x)$ is any function, such that range of $f \subseteq$ domain of g, then gof is also periodic with period T.

Even and Odd Functions

Even Function A real function $f(x)$ is an even function, if $f(-x) = f(x)$.

Odd Function A real function $f(x)$ is an odd function, if $f(-x) = -f(x)$.

Properties of Even and Odd Functions

(i) Even function ± Even function = Even function.

(ii) Odd function ± Odd function = Odd function.

(iii) Even function × Odd function = Odd function.

(iv) Even function × Even function = Even function.

(v) Odd function × Odd function = Even function.

(vi) gof or fog is even, if both f and g are even or if f is odd and g is even or if f is even and g is odd.

(vii) gof or fog is odd, if both of f and g are odd.

(viii) If $f(x)$ is an even function, then $\frac{d}{dx} f(x)$ or $\int f(x)\, dx$ is an odd function and if $f(x)$ is an odd function, then $\frac{d}{dx} f(x)$ or $\int f(x)\, dx$ is an even function.

(ix) The graph of an even function is symmetrical about Y-axis.

(x) The graph of an odd function is symmetrical about origin or symmetrical in opposite quadrants.

(xi) An even function can never be one-one, however an odd function may or may not be one-one.

Chapter 03

Complex Numbers

z = a +

Real Part

Complex Number

A number of the form $z = x + iy$, where $x, y \in R$, is called a complex number. Here, the symbol i is used to denote $\sqrt{-1}$ and it is called iota. The set of complex numbers is denoted by C.

Real and Imaginary Parts of a Complex Number Let $z = x + iy$ be a complex number, then x is called the **real part** and y is called the **imaginary part** of z and it may be denoted as $\text{Re}(z)$ and $\text{Im}(z)$, respectively.

Purely Real and Purely Imaginary Complex Number A complex number z is a purely real, if its imaginary part is 0.

i.e. $\text{Im}(z) = 0$. And purely imaginary, if its real part is 0 i.e. $\text{Re}(z) = 0$.

Zero Complex Number A complex number is said to be zero, if its both real and imaginary parts are zero.

Equality of Complex Numbers

Two complex numbers $z_1 = a_1 + ib_1$ and $z_2 = a_2 + ib_2$ are equal, iff $a_1 = a_2$ and $b_1 = b_2$ i.e. $\text{Re}(z_1) = \text{Re}(z_2)$ and $\text{Im}(z_1) = \text{Im}(z_2)$.

Iota

Mathematician Euler, introduced the symbol i (read as iota) for $\sqrt{-1}$ with property $i^2 + 1 = 0$. i.e. $i^2 = -1$. He also called this symbol as the imaginary unit. Integral power of iota (i) are given below.

$$i = \sqrt{-1}, i^2 = -1, i^3 = -i, i^4 = 1$$

So, $i^{4n+1} = i, i^{4n+2} = -1, i^{4n+3} = -i, i^{4n+4} = 1$

In other words, $i^n = \begin{cases} (-1)^{n/2}, & \text{if } n \text{ is an even integer} \\ (-1)^{\frac{n-1}{2}} \cdot i, & \text{if } n \text{ is an odd integer} \end{cases}$

Algebra of Complex Numbers

1. Addition of Complex Numbers

Let $z_1 = x_1 + iy_1$ and $z_2 = x_2 + iy_2$ be any two complex numbers, then their sum will be defined as

$$z_1 + z_2 = (x_1 + iy_1) + (x_2 + iy_2) = (x_1 + x_2) + i(y_1 + y_2)$$

Properties of Addition of Complex Numbers

(i) **Closure Property** Sum of two complex numbers is also a complex number.

(ii) **Commutative Property** $z_1 + z_2 = z_2 + z_1, \forall z_1, z_2 \in C$

(iii) **Associative Property** $(z_1 + z_2) + z_3 = z_1 + (z_2 + z_3), \forall z_1, z_2, z_3 \in C$

(iv) **Existence of Additive Identity** $z + 0 = z = 0 + z$

Here, 0 is additive identity element.

(v) **Existence of Additive Inverse** $z + (-z) = 0 = (-z + z)$

Here, $(-z)$ is additive inverse or negative of complex number z.

2. Subtraction of Complex Numbers

Let $z_1 = x_1 + iy_1$ and $z_2 = x_2 + iy_2$ be any two complex numbers, then the difference $z_1 - z_2$ is defined as

$$z_1 - z_2 = (x_1 + iy_1) - (x_2 + iy_2)$$
$$= (x_1 - x_2) + i(y_1 - y_2)$$

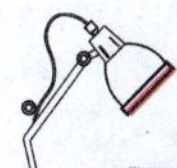

EXPERT Scale Up

The difference of two complex numbers $z_1 - z_2$, follows the closure property, but this operation is neither commutative nor associative, like in real numbers. Also, there does not exist any identity element for this operation and so inverse element also does not exist.

3. Multiplication of Complex Numbers

Let $z_1 = x_1 + iy_1$ and $z_2 = x_2 + iy_2$ be any two complex numbers, then their multiplication is defined as

$$z_1 z_2 = (x_1 + iy_1)(x_2 + iy_2) = (x_1 x_2 - y_1 y_2) + i(x_1 y_2 + x_2 y_1)$$

Properties of Multiplication of Complex Numbers

(i) **Closure Property** Product of two complex numbers is also a complex number.

(ii) **Commutative Property** $z_1 z_2 = z_2 z_1, \forall z_1, z_2 \in C.$

(iii) **Associative Property** $(z_1 z_2) z_3 = z_1(z_2 z_3) \forall z_1, z_2, z_3 \in C$.

(iv) **Existence of Multiplicative Identity** $z \cdot 1 = z = 1 \cdot z$

Here, 1 is multiplicative identity element of z.

(v) **Existence of Multiplicative Inverse** For every non-zero complex number z there exists a complex number z_1 such that $z \cdot z_1 = 1 = z_1 \cdot z$.

Then, complex number z_1 is called multiplicative inverse element of complex number z.

(vi) **Distributive Property** For each $z_1, z_2, z_3 \in C$

(a) $z_1(z_2 + z_3) = z_1 z_2 + z_1 z_3$ [left distribution]

(b) $(z_2 + z_3) z_1 = z_2 z_1 + z_3 z_1$ [right distribution]

4. Division of Complex Numbers

Let $z_1 = x_1 + iy_1$ and $z_2 = x_2 + iy_2$ be two complex numbers, then their division $\frac{z_1}{z_2}$ is defined as

$$\frac{z_1}{z_2} = \frac{(x_1 + iy_1)}{(x_2 + iy_2)} = \frac{(x_1 x_2 + y_1 y_2) + i(x_2 y_1 - x_1 y_2)}{x_2^2 + y_2^2}$$

provided, $z_2 \neq 0$.

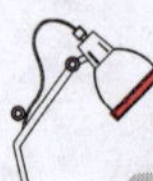

EXPERT Scale Up

The division of two complex numbers $\frac{z_1}{z_2}$, follows the closure property, but this operation is neither commutative nor associative, like in real numbers. Also, there does not exist any identity element for this operation and so inverse element also does not exists.

Identities Related to Complex Numbers

For any complex numbers z_1, z_2, we have

(i) $(z_1 + z_2)^2 = z_1^2 + 2 z_1 z_2 + z_2^2$

(ii) $(z_1 - z_2)^2 = z_1^2 - 2 z_1 z_2 + z_2^2$

(iii) $(z_1 + z_2)^3 = z_1^3 + 3z_1^2 z_2 + 3z_1 z_2^2 + z_2^3$

(iv) $(z_1 - z_2)^3 = z_1^3 - 3z_1^2 z_2 + 3z_1 z_2^2 - z_2^3$

(v) $z_1^2 - z_2^2 = (z_1 + z_2)(z_1 - z_2)$

These identities are similar as the algebraic identities in real numbers.

Conjugate of a Complex Number

If $z = x + iy$ is a complex number, then conjugate of z is denoted by $\bar{z}$,

i.e. $$\bar{z} = x - iy$$

Properties of Conjugate of Complex Numbers

For any complex number z, z_1, z_2, we have

(i) $\overline{(\bar{z})} = z$

(ii) $z + \bar{z} = 2\,\text{Re}(z), z + \bar{z} = 0 \Leftrightarrow z$ is purely imaginary.

(iii) $z - \bar{z} = 2i\,[\text{Im}(z)], z - \bar{z} = 0 \Leftrightarrow z$ is purely real.

(iv) $\overline{z_1 + z_2} = \bar{z}_1 + \bar{z}_2$

(v) $\overline{z_1 - z_2} = \bar{z}_1 - \bar{z}_2$

(vi) $\overline{z_1 \cdot z_2} = \bar{z}_1 \cdot \bar{z}_2$

(vii) $\overline{\left(\dfrac{z_1}{z_2}\right)} = \dfrac{\bar{z}_1}{\bar{z}_2}, z_2 \neq 0$

(viii) $z_1\,\bar{z}_2 \pm \bar{z}_1\,z_2 = 2\,\text{Re}(\bar{z}_1\,z_2) = 2\,\text{Re}(z_1\,\bar{z}_2)$

(ix) $(\bar{z})^n = \overline{(z^n)}$

(x) If $z = f(z_1)$, then $\bar{z} = f(\bar{z}_1)$

(xi) If $z = \begin{vmatrix} a_1 & a_2 & a_3 \\ b_1 & b_2 & b_3 \\ c_1 & c_2 & c_3 \end{vmatrix}$, then $\bar{z} = \begin{vmatrix} \bar{a}_1 & \bar{a}_2 & \bar{a}_3 \\ \bar{b}_1 & \bar{b}_2 & \bar{b}_3 \\ \bar{c}_1 & \bar{c}_2 & \bar{c}_3 \end{vmatrix}$

where, $a_i, b_i, c_i; (i = 1, 2, 3)$ are complex numbers.

(xii) $z\bar{z} = \{\text{Re}(z)\}^2 + \{\text{Im}(z)\}^2$

Reciprocal/Multiplicative Inverse of a Complex Number

Let $z = x + iy$ be a non-zero complex number, then the multiplicative inverse

$$z^{-1} = \frac{1}{z} = \frac{1}{x + iy} = \frac{1}{x + iy} \times \frac{x - iy}{x - iy}$$

[multiply and divide by conjugate of $z = x + iy$]

$$= \frac{x - iy}{x^2 + y^2} = \frac{x}{x^2 + y^2} + \frac{i(-y)}{x^2 + y^2}$$

Modulus (or Absolute value) of a Complex Number

If $z = x + iy$, then modulus or magnitude of z is denoted by $|z|$ and is given by $$|z| = \sqrt{x^2 + y^2}$$

Geometrically it represents a distance of point $z(x, y)$ from origin.

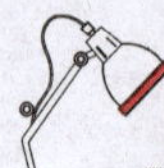

EXPERT Scale Up

In the set of non-real complex number, the order relation is not defined i.e. $z_1 > z_2$ or $z_1 < z_2$ has no meaning but $|z_1| > |z_2|$ or $|z_1| < |z_2|$ has got its meaning, since $|z_1|$ and $|z_2|$ are real numbers.

Properties of Modulus of Complex Numbers

(i) $|z| \ge 0$

(ii) (a) $|z| = 0$, iff $z = 0$ i.e. $\text{Re}(z) = 0 = \text{Im}(z)$ (b) $|z| > 0$, iff $z \ne 0$

(iii) $-|z| \le \text{Re}(z) \le |z|$ and $-|z| \le \text{Im}(z) \le |z|$

(iv) $|z| = |\bar{z}| = |-z| = |-\bar{z}|$

(v) $z\bar{z} = |z|^2$

(vi) $|z_1 z_2| = |z_1||z_2|$

In general, $|z_1 z_2 z_3 \dots z_n| = |z_1||z_2||z_3| \dots |z_n|$

(vii) $\left|\dfrac{z_1}{z_2}\right| = \dfrac{|z_1|}{|z_2|}$, provided $z_2 \ne 0$

(viii) $|z_1 \pm z_2| \le |z_1| + |z_2|$

In general, $|z_1 \pm z_2 \pm z_3 \pm \dots \pm z_n| \le |z_1| + |z_2| + |z_3| + \dots + |z_n|$

(ix) $|z_1 \pm z_2| \ge ||z_1| - |z_2||$

(x) $|z^n| = |z|^n$

(xi) $||z_1| - |z_2|| \le |z_1 + z_2| \le |z_1| + |z_2|$ i.e. greatest and least possible value of $|z_1 + z_2|$ is $|z_1| + |z_2|$ and $||z_1| - |z_2||$ respectively.

(xii) $z_1\bar{z}_2 + \bar{z}_1 z_2 = 2|z_1||z_2|\cos(\theta_1 - \theta_2) = 2\,\text{Re}(z_1\bar{z}_2)$, where $\theta_1 = \arg(z_1)$ and $\theta_2 = \arg(z_2)$

(xiii) $|z_1 \pm z_2|^2 = (z_1 \pm z_2)(\overline{z_1} \pm \overline{z_2})$

$$= |z_1|^2 + |z_2|^2 \pm (z_1\overline{z_2} + z_2\overline{z_1})$$
$$= |z_1|^2 + |z_2|^2 \pm 2\,\text{Re}(z_1\overline{z_2})$$
$$= |z_1|^2 + |z_2|^2 \pm 2|z_1||z_2|\cos(\theta_1 - \theta_2)$$

(xiv) $|z_1 + z_2|^2 + |z_1 - z_2|^2 = 2\{|z_1|^2 + |z_2|^2\}$

(xv) $|z_1 + z_2|^2 = |z_1|^2 + |z_2|^2 \Leftrightarrow \frac{z_1}{z_2}$ is purely imaginary.

(xvi) $|az_1 - bz_2|^2 + |bz_1 + az_2|^2 = (a^2 + b^2)(|z_1|^2 + |z_2|^2)$ where $a, b \in R$.

(xvii) z is **unimodulus** i.e. unit modulus, if $|z| = 1$

Argand Plane and Argument of a Complex Number

Argand Plane

Any complex number $z = x + iy$ can be represented geometrically by a point (x, y) in a plane, called **Argand plane** or **Gaussian plane.**

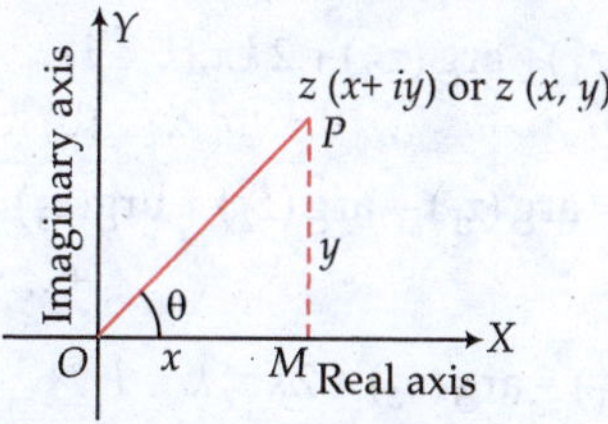

There exists a one-one correspondence between the points of the plane and the members of the set C of all complex numbers.

The length of the line segment OP is the modulus of z,

i.e. $|z|$= length of $OP = \sqrt{x^2 + y^2}$.

Argument

The angle made by the line joining point z to the origin, with the positive direction of real axis is called argument of that complex number. It is denoted by the symbol arg (z) or amp (z).

$$\arg(z) = \theta = \tan^{-1}\left(\frac{y}{x}\right)$$

Argument of z is not unique, general value of the argument of z is $2n\pi + \theta$, where n is an integer. But arg (0) is not defined.

 **Value Points**

- A purely real number is represented by a point on real axis.
- A purely imaginary number is represented by a point on imaginary axis.

Principal Value of Argument

The value of the argument which lies in the interval $(-\pi, \pi]$ is called principal value of argument.

(i) If $x > 0$ and $y > 0$, then $\arg(z) = \theta$

(ii) If $x < 0$ and $y > 0$, then $\arg(z) = \pi - \theta$

(iii) If $x < 0$ and $y < 0$, then $\arg(z) = -(\pi - \theta)$

(iv) If $x > 0$ and $y < 0$, then $\arg(z) = -\theta$

where, $\theta = \tan^{-1}\left|\frac{y}{x}\right|$.

Properties of Argument

(i) $\arg(\bar{z}) = \begin{cases} \pi, & \text{if } z \text{ is purely negative real number} \\ -\arg(z), & \text{otherwise} \end{cases}$

(ii) $\arg(z_1 z_2) = \arg(z_1) + \arg(z_2) + 2k\pi, (k \in I)$

In general,

$\arg(z_1 z_2 z_3 \dots z_n) = \arg(z_1) + \arg(z_2) + \arg(z_3) + \dots + \arg(z_n) + 2k\pi, (k \in I)$

(iii) $\arg\left(\frac{z_1}{z_2}\right) = \arg(z_1) - \arg(z_2) + 2k\pi, k \in I$

(iv) $\arg(z_1 \bar{z}_2) = \arg(z_1) - \arg(z_2) + 2k\pi, k \in I$

(v) $\arg\left(\frac{z}{\bar{z}}\right) = 2\arg(z) + 2k\pi, k \in I$

(vi) $\arg(z^n) = n\arg(z) + 2k\pi, k \in I$

(vii) If $\arg\left(\frac{z_2}{z_1}\right) = \theta$, then $\arg\left(\frac{z_1}{z_2}\right) = 2k\pi - \theta, (k = 0, 1 \text{ or } -1)$

(viii) If $\arg(z) = 0 \Rightarrow z$ is real

(ix) $\arg(z) - \arg(-z) = \begin{cases} \pi, & \text{if } \arg(z) > 0 \\ -\pi, & \text{if } \arg(z) < 0 \end{cases}$

(x) If $|z_1 + z_2| = |z_1 - z_2|$, then

$\arg\left(\frac{z_1}{z_2}\right) \Rightarrow \arg(z_1) - \arg(z_2) = \frac{\pi}{2}$

(xi) If $|z_1 + z_2| = |z_1| + |z_2|$, then $\arg(z_1) = \arg(z_2)$

(xii) If $|z - 1| = |z + 1|$, then $\arg(z) = \pm\frac{\pi}{2}$

(xiii) If $\arg\left(\frac{z-1}{z+1}\right) = \frac{\pi}{2}$, then $|z| = 1$

(xiv) (a) If $z = 1 + \cos\theta + i\sin\theta$, then $\arg(z) = \frac{\theta}{2}$ and $|z| = 2\cos\frac{\theta}{2}$

(b) If $z = 1 + \cos\theta - i\sin\theta$, then $\arg(z) = -\frac{\theta}{2}$ and $|z| = 2\cos\frac{\theta}{2}$

(c) If $z = 1 - \cos\theta + i\sin\theta$, then $\arg(z) = \frac{\pi}{2} - \frac{\theta}{2}$ and $|z| = 2\sin\frac{\theta}{2}$

(d) If $z = 1 - \cos\theta - i\sin\theta$, then $\arg(z) = \frac{\theta}{2} - \frac{\pi}{2}$ and $|z| = 2\sin\frac{\theta}{2}$

(xv) If $|z_1| \le 1, |z_2| \le 1$, then

(a) $|z_1 - z_2|^2 \le (|z_1| - |z_2|)^2 + [\arg(z_1) - \arg(z_2)]^2$

(b) $|z_1 + z_2|^2 \le (|z_1| + |z_2|)^2 - [\arg(z_1) - \arg(z_2)]^2$

Polar Form of a Complex Number

If $z = x + iy$ is a complex number, then z can be written as $z = r(\cos\theta + i\sin\theta)$, where $\theta = \arg(z)$ and $r = \sqrt{x^2 + y^2}$, this is called polar form.

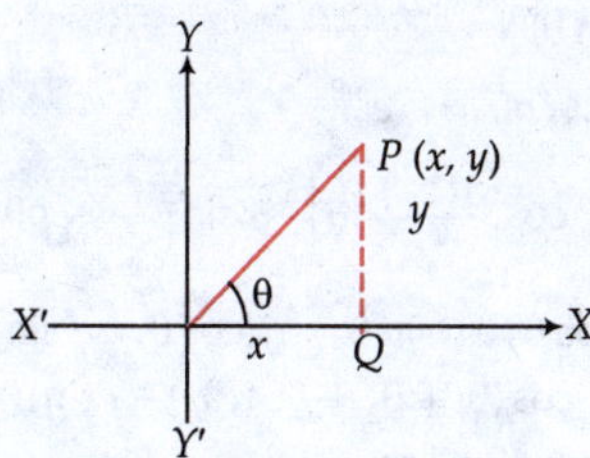

If the general value of the argument is considered, then the polar form of z is $z = r[\cos(2n\pi + \theta) + i\sin(2n\pi + \theta)]$, where n is an integer.

Eulerian Form of a Complex Number

If $z = x + iy$ is a complex number, then it can be written as

$$z = re^{i\theta}$$

where, $r = |z|$ and $\theta = \arg(z)$

This is called Eulerian form and $e^{i\theta} = \cos\theta + i\sin\theta$ and

$$e^{-i\theta} = \cos\theta - i\sin\theta.$$

From this, $\cos\theta = \frac{e^{i\theta} + e^{-i\theta}}{2}$, $\sin\theta = \frac{e^{i\theta} - e^{-i\theta}}{2i}$

Competition Insight

De-Moivre's Theorem

A simplest formula for calculating powers of complex numbers in the standard polar form is known as De-Moivre's theorem.

If $n \in I$ (set of integers), then $(\cos\theta + i\sin\theta)^n = \cos n\theta + i\sin n\theta$ and if $n \in Q$ (set of rational numbers), then $\cos n\theta + i\sin n\theta$ is one of the values of $(\cos\theta + i\sin\theta)^n$.

Properties of De-Moivre's Theorem

(i) If $\frac{p}{q}, q \neq 0$ is a rational number, then

$$(\cos\theta + i\sin\theta)^{p/q} = \left(\cos\frac{p}{q}\theta + i\sin\frac{p}{q}\theta\right)$$

(ii) $\frac{1}{\cos\theta + i\sin\theta} = (\cos\theta + i\sin\theta)^{-1} = \cos\theta - i\sin\theta$

(iii) More generally, for a complex number $z = r(\cos\theta + i\sin\theta) = re^{i\theta}$

$$z^n = r^n(\cos\theta + i\sin\theta)^n$$
$$= r^n(\cos n\theta + i\sin n\theta) = r^n e^{in\theta}$$

(iv) $(\sin\theta + i\cos\theta)^n = \left[\cos\left(\frac{n\pi}{2} - n\theta\right) + i\sin\left(\frac{n\pi}{2} - n\theta\right)\right]$

(v) $(\cos\theta_1 + i\sin\theta_1)(\cos\theta_2 + i\sin\theta_2)\dots(\cos\theta_n + i\sin\theta_n)$
$= \cos(\theta_1 + \theta_2 + \dots + \theta_n) + i\sin(\theta_1 + \theta_2 + \dots + \theta_n)$

(vi) $(\sin\theta \pm i\cos\theta)^n \neq \sin n\theta \pm i\cos n\theta$

(vii) $(\cos\theta + i\sin\phi)^n \neq \cos n\theta + i\sin n\phi$

e.g.

(i) $\cos 0 + i\sin 0 = 1$ (ii) $\cos\pi + i\sin\pi = -1$

(iii) $\cos\frac{\pi}{2} + i\sin\frac{\pi}{2} = i$ (iv) $\cos\frac{\pi}{2} - i\sin\frac{\pi}{2} = -i$

Cube Roots of Unity

Cube roots of unity are $1, \omega, \omega^2$,

where $\omega = \frac{-1}{2} + i\frac{\sqrt{3}}{2} = e^{i2\pi/3}$ and $\omega^2 = \frac{-1}{2} - \frac{i\sqrt{3}}{2}$

$$\arg(\omega) = \frac{2\pi}{3} \text{ and } \arg(\omega^2) = \frac{4\pi}{3}$$

Properties of Cube Roots of Unity

(i) $1+\omega^2+\omega^{2r}=\begin{cases}0, & \text{if } r \text{ is not a multiple of 3.}\\ 3, & \text{if } r \text{ is a multiple of 3.}\end{cases}$

(ii) $\omega^3=1$ and $1+\omega+\omega^2=0$

(iii) $\omega^{3r}=1$, $\omega^{3r+1}=\omega$ and $\omega^{3r+2}=\omega^2$, where $r\in I$.

(iv) Cube roots of unity lie on the unit circle $|z|=1$ and divide its circumference into 3 equal parts. It always forms an equilateral triangle.

(v) Cube roots of -1 are $-1, -\omega, -\omega^2$.

Some Important Identities

(i) $x^2+x+1=(x-\omega)(x-\omega^2)$ (ii) $x^2-x+1=(x+\omega)(x+\omega^2)$

(iii) $x^2+xy+y^2=(x-y\omega)(x-y\omega^2)$ (iv) $x^2-xy+y^2=(x+\omega y)(x+y\omega^2)$

(v) $x^2+y^2=(x+iy)(x-iy)$ (vi) $x^3+y^3=(x+y)(x+y\omega)(x+y\omega^2)$

(vii) $x^3-y^3=(x-y)(x-y\omega)(x-y\omega^2)$

(viii) $x^2+y^2+z^2-xy-yz-zx=(x+y\omega+z\omega^2)(x+y\omega^2+z\omega)$
or $(x\omega+y\omega^2+z)(x\omega^2+y\omega+z)$ or $(x\omega+y+z\omega^2)(x\omega^2+y+z\omega)$

(ix) $x^3+y^3+z^3-3xyz=(x+y+z)(x+\omega y+\omega^2 z)(x+\omega^2 y+\omega z)$

*n*th Roots of Unity

The *n*th roots of unity, it means any complex number z, which satisfies the equation $z^n=1$ or $z=(1)^{1/n}$

or $z=\cos\dfrac{2k\pi}{n}+i\sin\dfrac{2k\pi}{n}$, where $k=0,1,2,\ldots,(n-1)$

Properties of nth Roots of Unity

(i) nth roots of unity form a GP with common ratio $e^{i2\pi/n}$.

(ii) Sum of nth roots of unity is always 0.

(iii) Sum of pth powers of nth roots of unity is n, if p is a multiple of n.

(iv) Sum of pth powers of nth roots of unity is zero, if p is not a multiple of n.

(v) Product of nth roots of unity is $(-1)^{n-1}$.

(vi) The nth roots of unity lie on the unit circle $|z|=1$ and divide its circumference into n equal parts.

Knowledge Booster

Square Root of a Complex Number

If $z = x + iy$, then $\sqrt{z} = \sqrt{x + iy} = \pm\left[\sqrt{\frac{|z| + x}{2}} + i\sqrt{\frac{|z| - x}{2}}\right]$, for $y > 0$

$$= \pm\left[\sqrt{\frac{|z| + x}{2}} - i\sqrt{\frac{|z| - x}{2}}\right], \text{ for } y < 0$$

Logarithm of a Complex Number

Let $z = x + iy$ be a complex number and in polar form z is $re^{i\theta}$, then

$$\log(x + iy) = \log(re^{i\theta}) = \log(r) + i\theta = \log(\sqrt{x^2 + y^2}) + i\tan^{-1}\frac{y}{x}$$

or $\qquad \log(z) = \log(|z|) + i\,\text{amp}(z),$

In general, $\quad z = re^{i(\theta + 2n\pi)}$

$$\log(z) = \log|z| + i\arg(z) + 2n\pi i,\ n \in I$$

Geometry of Complex Numbers

1. **Geometrical Representation of Addition** If two points P and Q represent complex numbers z_1 and z_2, respectively, in the argand plane, then the sum $z_1 + z_2$ is represented by the extremity R of the diagonal OR of parallelogram $OPRQ$ having OP and OQ as two adjacent sides.

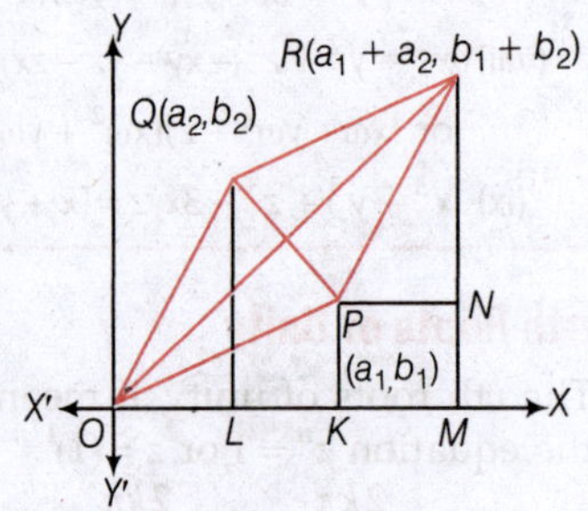

2. **Geometrical Representation of Subtraction** Let $z_1 = a_1 + ib_1$ and $z_2 = a_2 + ib_2$ be two complex numbers represented by points $P(a_1, b_1)$ and $Q(a_2, b_2)$ in the argand plane. Q' represents the complex number $(-z_2)$. Complete the parallelogram $OPRQ'$ by taking OP and OQ' as two adjacent sides.

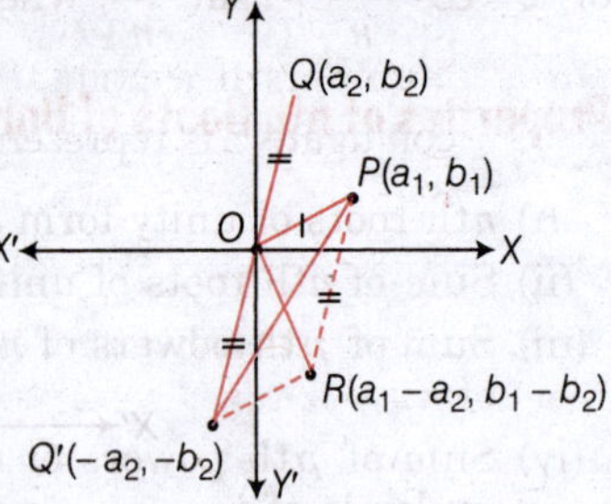

The sum of z_1 and $-z_2$ is represented by the extremity R of the diagonal OR of parallelogram $OPRQ'$. R represents the complex number $z_1 - z_2$.

3. **Geometrical Representation of Multiplication**

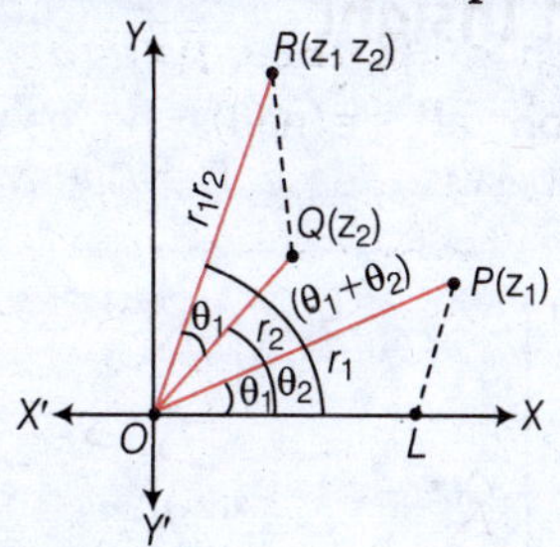

R has the polar coordinates $(r_1r_2, \theta_1 + \theta_2)$ and it represents the complex numbers z_1z_2.

4. **Geometrical Representation of the Division**

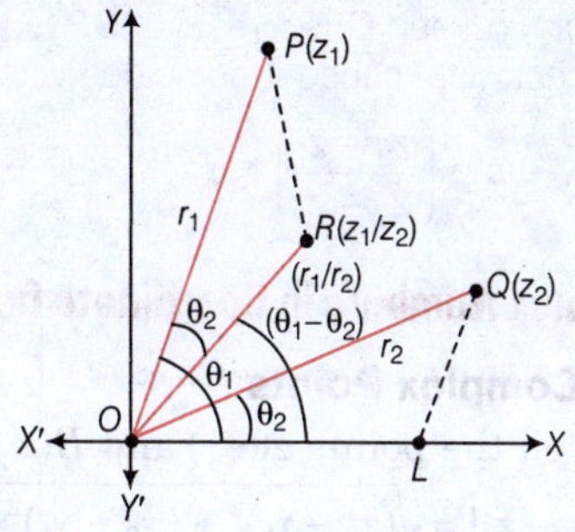

R has the polar coordinates $\left(\dfrac{r_1}{r_2}, \theta_1 - \theta_2\right)$ and it represents the complex number z_1/z_2.

5. **Geometrical Representation of the Conjugate of Complex Numbers** If a point P represents a complex number z, then its conjugate $\bar{z}$ is represented by the image of P in the real axis.

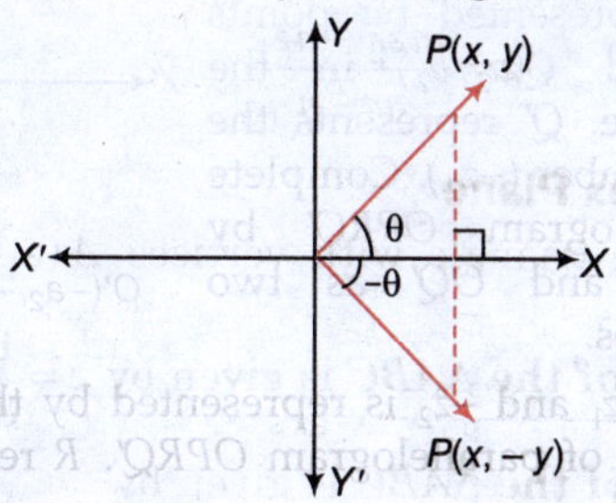

Geometrically, the point $(x, -y)$ is the mirror image of the point (x, y) on the real axis.

Competition Insight

Concept of Rotation Let z_1, z_2 and z_3 be the vertices of a ΔABC described in anti-clockwise sense. Draw OP and OQ parallel and equal to AB and AC, respectively.

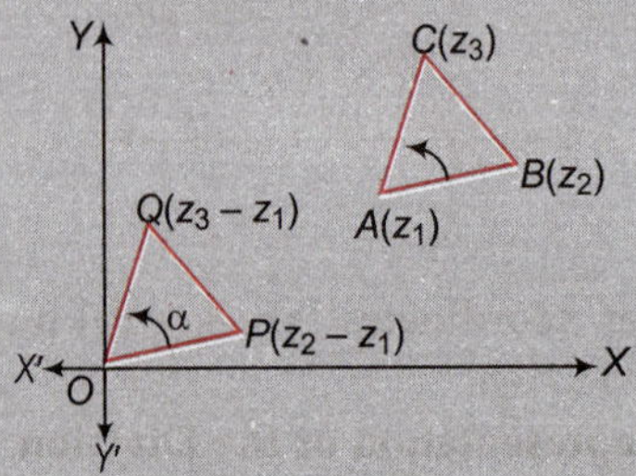

Then, point P is $z_2 - z_1$ and Q is $z_3 - z_1$. If OP is rotated through angle α in anti-clockwise, sense it coincides with OQ.

$$\therefore \quad \text{amp}\left(\frac{z_3 - z_1}{z_2 - z_1}\right) = \alpha$$

Applications of Complex Numbers in Coordinate Geometry

Distance between Complex Points

(i) Distance between the points $A(z_1)$ and $B(z_2)$ is given by

$$AB = |z_2 - z_1| = \sqrt{(x_2 - x_1)^2 + (y_2 - y_1)^2}$$

where, $z_1 = x_1 + iy_1$ and $z_2 = x_2 + iy_2$.

(ii) The point $P(z)$ which divides the join of segment AB internally in the ratio $m:n$ is given by

$$z = \frac{mz_2 + nz_1}{m + n}$$

If P divides the line externally in the ratio $m : n$, then

$$z = \frac{mz_2 - nz_1}{m - n}$$

Triangle in Complex Plane

(i) Let ABC be a triangle with vertices $A(z_1), B(z_2)$ and $C(z_3)$, then

(a) **Centroid of the ΔABC** is given by $z = \frac{1}{3}(z_1 + z_2 + z_3)$

(b) **Incentre of the ΔABC** is given by

$$z = \frac{az_1 + bz_2 + cz_3}{a + b + c}$$

(ii) **Area of the triangle** with vertices $A(z_1), B(z_2)$ and $C(z_3)$ is given by

$$\Delta = \frac{i}{4}\begin{vmatrix} z_1 & \bar{z}_1 & 1 \\ z_2 & \bar{z}_2 & 1 \\ z_3 & \bar{z}_3 & 1 \end{vmatrix}$$

(iii) The triangle whose vertices are the points represented by complex numbers z_1, z_2 and z_3 is equilateral, if

$$\frac{1}{z_2 - z_3} + \frac{1}{z_3 - z_1} + \frac{1}{z_1 - z_2} = 0$$

i.e. $$z_1^2 + z_2^2 + z_3^2 = z_1 z_2 + z_2 z_3 + z_3 z_1$$

Straight Line in Complex Plane

(i) The general equation of a straight line is $\bar{a}z + a\bar{z} + b = 0$, where a is a complex number and b is a real number.

(ii) The complex and real slopes of the line $\bar{a}z + a\bar{z} + b = 0$ are $-\frac{a}{\bar{a}}$ and $-i\left(\frac{a+\bar{a}}{a-\bar{a}}\right)$.

(iii) The equation of straight line through z_1 and z_2 is $z = tz_1 + (1-t)z_2$, where t is real.

(iv) If z_1 and z_2 are two fixed points, then $|z - z_1| = |z - z_2|$ represents perpendicular bisector of the line segment joining z_1 and z_2.

Knowledge Booster

Three points z_1, z_2 and z_3 are collinear, if $\begin{vmatrix} z_1 & \bar{z}_1 & 1 \\ z_2 & \bar{z}_2 & 1 \\ z_3 & \bar{z}_3 & 1 \end{vmatrix} = 0$

This is also, the equation of the line passing through z_1, z_2 and z_3 and slope is defined to be $\frac{z_1 - z_2}{\bar{z}_1 - \bar{z}_2}$.

(v) **Length of Perpendicular** The length of perpendicular from a point z_1 to $\bar{a}z + a\bar{z} + b = 0$ is given by $\frac{|\bar{a}z_1 + a\bar{z}_1 + b|}{2|a|}$

(vi) The equation of a line parallel to the line $a\bar{z} + \bar{a}z + b = 0$ is $\bar{a}z + a\bar{z} + \lambda = 0$, where $\lambda \in R$.

(vii) The equation of a line perpendicular to the line $a\bar{z} + \bar{a}z + b = 0$ is $a\bar{z} - \bar{a}z + i\lambda = 0$, where $\lambda \in R$.

(viii) The equation of the perpendicular bisector of the line segment joining points $A(z_1)$ and $B(z_2)$ is
$z(\bar{z}_1 - \bar{z}_2) + \bar{z}(z_1 - z_2) = |z_1|^2 - |z_2|^2$

(ix) If z is a variable point in the argand plane such that $\arg(z) = \theta$, then locus of z is a straight line through the origin inclined at an angle θ with X-axis.

(x) If z is a variable point and z_1 is fixed point in the argand plane such that $(z - z_1) = \theta$, then locus of z is a straight line passing through the point z_1 and inclined at an angle θ with the X-axis.

(xi) If z is a variable point and z_1, z_2 are two fixed points in the argand plane, such that

(a) $|z - z_1| + |z - z_2| = |z_1 - z_2|$, then locus of z is the line segment joining z_1 and z_2.

(b) $||z - z_1| - |z - z_2|| = |z_1 - z_2|$, then locus of z is a straight line joining z_1 and z_2 but z does not lie between z_1 and z_2.

(c) $\arg\left(\dfrac{z - z_1}{z - z_2}\right) = 0$ or π, then locus z is a straight line passing through z_1 and z_2.

(xii)

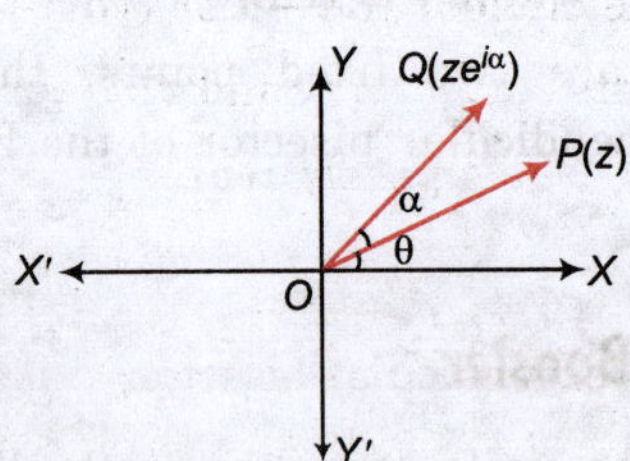

(a) $ze^{i\alpha}$ is the complex number whose modulus is $|z|$ and argument $\theta + \alpha$.

(b) Multiplication by $e^{-i\alpha}$ to z rotates the vector **OP** in clockwise sense through an angle α.

(xiii) If z_1, z_2 and z_3 are the affixes of the points A, B and C in the argand plane, then

(a) $\angle BAC = \arg\left(\dfrac{z_3 - z_1}{z_2 - z_1}\right)$

(b) $\dfrac{z_3 - z_1}{z_2 - z_1} = \left|\dfrac{z_3 - z_1}{z_2 - z_1}\right|(\cos\alpha + i\sin\alpha)$, where $\alpha = \angle BAC$.

(xiv) If z_1, z_2, z_3 and z_4 are the affixes of the points A, B, C and D, respectively in the argand plane.

(a) AB is inclined to CD at the angle $\arg\left(\frac{z_2 - z_1}{z_4 - z_3}\right)$.

(b) If CD is inclined at 90° to AB, then $\arg\left(\frac{z_2 - z_1}{z_4 - z_3}\right) = \pm\frac{\pi}{2}$.

Circle in Complex Plane

(i) An equation of the circle with centre at z_0 and radius r is $|z - z_0| = r$ or $z\bar{z} - z_0\bar{z} - \bar{z}_0 z + z_0\bar{z}_0 - r^2 = 0$

(a) $|z - z_0| < r$, represents interior of the circle.

(b) $|z - z_0| > r$, represents exterior of the circle.

(c) $|z - z_0| \le r$ is the set of points lying inside and on the circle $|z - z_0| = r$. Similarly, $|z - z_0| \ge r$ is the set of points lying outside and on the circle $|z - z_0| = r$.

(d) **General equation of a circle is**

$z\bar{z} + a\bar{z} + \bar{a}z + b = 0$

where, a is a complex number and b is a real number.
Centre of the circle $= -a$

Radius of the circle $= \sqrt{a\bar{a} - b}$ or $\sqrt{|a|^2 - b}$

(e) Four points z_1, z_2, z_3 and z_4 are concyclic, if $\frac{(z_4 - z_1)(z_2 - z_3)}{(z_4 - z_3)(z_2 - z_1)}$ is purely real.

(ii) $\frac{|z - z_1|}{|z - z_2|} = k \Rightarrow \begin{cases} \text{Circle,} & \text{if } k \ne 1 \\ \text{Perpendicular bisector,} & \text{if } k = 1 \end{cases}$

(iii) The equation of a circle described on the line segment joining z_1 and z_2 as diameter is $(z - z_1)(\bar{z} - \bar{z}_2) + (z - z_2)(\bar{z} - \bar{z}_1) = 0$.

(iv) $\arg \frac{z - z_1}{z - z_2} = \beta$, then locus is the arc of a circle for which the segment joining z_1 and z_2 is a chord.

(v) If z_1 and z_2 are the fixed complex numbers, then the locus of a point z satisfying $\arg\left(\frac{z - z_1}{z - z_2}\right) = \pm\pi/2$ is a circle having z_1 and z_2 at the end points of a diameter.

(vi) If $\arg\left(\frac{z + 1}{z - 1}\right) = \frac{\pi}{2}$, then z lies on circle of radius unity and centre as origin.

(vii) If $|z - z_1|^2 + |z - z_2|^2 = |z_1 - z_2|^2$, then locus of z is a circle with z_1 and z_2 as the extremities of diameter.

Conic in Complex Plane

Let z_1 and z_2 be two fixed points, and k be a positive real number.

(i) If $k > |z_1 - z_2|$, then $|z - z_1| + |z - z_2| = k$ represents an ellipse with foci at $A(z_1)$ and $B(z_2)$ and length of the major axis is k.

(ii) If $k < |z_1 - z_2|$, then $||z - z_1| - |z - z_2|| = k$ represents hyperbola with foci at $A(z_1)$ and $B(z_2)$.

Value Points

- $\sqrt{-a} \times \sqrt{-b} \neq \sqrt{ab}$
  $\sqrt{a} \times \sqrt{b} = \sqrt{ab}$ is possible only, iff atleast one of the quantity either a or b is/are non-negative. e.g. $i^2 = \sqrt{-1} \times \sqrt{-1} \neq \sqrt{1}$
- i is neither positive, zero nor negative.
- Argument of 0 is not defined.
- Argument of purely imaginary number is $\frac{\pi}{2}$ or $-\frac{\pi}{2}$.
- Argument of purely real number is 0 or π.
- If $\left|z + \frac{1}{z}\right| = a$, then greatest value of $|z| = \frac{a + \sqrt{a^2 + 4}}{2}$ and least value of $|z| = \frac{-a + \sqrt{a^2 + 4}}{2}$
- The value of $i^i = e^{-\pi/2}$
- The non-real complex numbers do not possess the property of order,
  i.e. $x + iy <$ (or) $> c + id$ is not defined.
- The area of the triangle on the argand plane formed by the complex numbers z, iz and $z + iz$ is $\frac{1}{2}|z|^2$.
- If ω_1 and ω_2 are the complex slope of two lines on the argand plane, then the lines are
  (a) perpendicular, if $\omega_1 + \omega_2 = 0$.
  (b) parallel, if $\omega_1 = \omega_2$.

Chapter 04

Theory of Equations and Inequations

Polynomial

An algebraic expression of the form $a_0 + a_1x + a_2x^2 + ... + a_nx^n$, where $n \in N$, is called a polynomial. It is generally denoted by $p(x), q(x), f(x), g(x)$ etc.

Real Polynomial

Let $a_0, a_1, a_2, \ldots, a_n$ be real numbers and x is a real variable, then $f(x) = a_0 + a_1x + a_2x^2 + \ldots + a_nx^n$ is called a real polynomial of real variable x with real coefficients.

Complex Polynomial

If $a_0, a_1, a_2, \ldots, a_n$ be complex numbers and x is a varying complex number, then $f(x) = a_0 + a_1x + a_2x^2 + \ldots + a_{n-1}x^{n-1} + a_nx^n$ is called a complex polynomial or a polynomial of complex variable x with complex coefficients.

Degree of a Polynomial

A polynomial $f(x) = a_0 + a_1x + a_2x^2 + a_3x^3 + \ldots + a_nx^n$, real or complex is a polynomial of degree n, if $a_n \neq 0$.

Some Important Deduction

(i) **Linear Polynomial** A polynomial of degree one is known as linear polynomial.

(ii) **Quadratic Polynomial** A polynomial of second degree is known as quadratic polynomial.

(iii) **Cubic Polynomial** A polynomial of degree three is known as cubic polynomial.

(iv) **Biquadratic Polynomial** A polynomial of degree four is known as biquadratic polynomial.

Polynomial Equation

If $f(x)$ is a polynomial, real or complex, then $f(x)=0$ is called a polynomial equation.

Quadratic Equation

A quadratic polynomial $f(x)$ when equated to zero is called quadratic equation.

i.e. $ax^2 + bx + c = 0$, where $a, b, c \in R$ and $a \neq 0$.

Roots of a Quadratic Equation

The values of variable x which satisfy the quadratic equation is called roots of quadratic equation.

Solution of Quadratic Equation

1. Factorisation Method

Let $ax^2 + bx + c = a(x - \alpha)(x - \beta) = 0$. Then, $x = \alpha$ and $x = \beta$ will satisfy the given equation.

2. Direct Formula

Quadratic equation $ax^2 + bx + c = 0$ $(a \neq 0)$ has two roots, given by

$$\alpha = \frac{-b + \sqrt{b^2 - 4ac}}{2a}, \beta = \frac{-b - \sqrt{b^2 - 4ac}}{2a}$$

or $$\alpha = \frac{-b + \sqrt{D}}{2a}, \beta = \frac{-b - \sqrt{D}}{2a}$$

where, $D = \Delta = b^2 - 4ac$ is called discriminant of the equation.

Above formulas also known as **Sridharacharya formula.**

Nature of Roots

(i) Let quadratic equation be $ax^2 + bx + c = 0$, whose discriminant is D.

Also, let $a, b, c \in R$ and $a \neq 0$. Then,

(a) $D < 0 \Rightarrow$ Complex roots

(b) $D > 0 \Rightarrow$ Real and distinct roots

(c) $D = 0 \Rightarrow$ Real and equal roots as $\alpha = \beta = -\dfrac{b}{2a}$

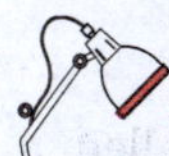

EXPERT Scale Up

If $a, b, c \in Q, a \neq 0$, then

(a) $D > 0$ and D is a perfect square.
$\Rightarrow$ Roots are unequal and rational.

(b) $D > 0$, $a = 1$; $b, c \in I$ and D is a perfect square.
$\Rightarrow$ Roots are integral.

(c) $D > 0$ and D is not a perfect square.
$\Rightarrow$ Roots are irrational and unequal.

(ii) **Conjugate Roots** The irrational (complex) roots of a quadratic equation, whose coefficients are rational (real) always occur in conjugate pairs. Thus,

(a) if one root be $\alpha + i\beta$, then other root will be $\alpha - i\beta$.

(b) if one root be $\alpha + \sqrt{\beta}$, then other root will be $\alpha - \sqrt{\beta}$.

(iii) Let D_1 and D_2 are the discriminants of two quadratic equations.

(a) If $D_1 + D_2 \geq 0$, then atleast one of D_1 and $D_2 \geq 0$
Thus, if $D_1 < 0$, then $D_2 > 0$, if $D_2 < 0$, then $D_1 > 0$ or D_1 and D_2 both can be non-negative (means positive or zero).

(b) If $D_1 + D_2 < 0$, then atleast one of D_1 and $D_2 < 0$
Thus, if $D_1 > 0$, then $D_2 < 0$, if $D_2 > 0$, then $D_1 < 0$ or D_1 and D_2 both can be negative.

Roots Under Particular Conditions

For the quadratic equation $ax^2 + bx + c = 0$.

(i) If $a > 0$ and $b = 0$, roots are real/complex according as $c < 0$ or $c > 0$. These roots are equal in magnitude but of opposite sign.

(ii) If $c = 0$, one root is zero, other is $-b/a$.

(iii) If $b = c = 0$, both roots are zero.

(iv) If $a = c$, roots are reciprocal to each other.

(v) If $\left.\begin{matrix} a > 0, & c < 0 \\ a < 0, & c > 0 \end{matrix}\right\} \Rightarrow$ Roots are of opposite sign.

(vi) If $\left.\begin{matrix} a > 0, & b > 0, & c > 0 \\ a < 0, & b < 0, & c < 0 \end{matrix}\right\} \Rightarrow$ Both roots are negative, provided $D \geq 0$

(vii) If $\left.\begin{matrix} a > 0, & b < 0, & c > 0 \\ a < 0, & b > 0, & c < 0 \end{matrix}\right\} \Rightarrow$ Both roots are positive, provided $D \geq 0$

(viii) If sign of $a =$ sign of $b \neq$ sign of c
$\Rightarrow$ Greater root in magnitude is negative.

(ix) If sign of $b =$ sign of $c \neq$ sign of a
$\Rightarrow$ Greater root in magnitude is positive.

(x) If $a + b + c = 0 \Rightarrow$ One root is 1 and second root is c/a.

Relation between Roots and Coefficients

1. Quadratic Equation

If roots of quadratic equation $ax^2 + bx + c = 0$ $(a \neq 0)$ are α and β, then

$$\text{Sum of roots} = S = \alpha + \beta = \frac{-b}{a} = -\frac{\text{coefficient of } x}{\text{coefficient of } x^2}$$

$$\text{Product of roots} = P = \alpha \cdot \beta = \frac{c}{a} = \frac{\text{constant term}}{\text{coefficient of } x^2}$$

$$\text{Also, } |\alpha - \beta| = \frac{\sqrt{D}}{|a|}$$

2. Cubic Equation

If α, β and γ are the roots of cubic equation $ax^3 + bx^2 + cx + d = 0$.

Then,
$$\sum \alpha = \alpha + \beta + \gamma = -\frac{b}{a}$$

$$\sum \alpha\beta = \alpha\beta + \beta\gamma + \gamma\alpha = \frac{c}{a}$$

$$\alpha\beta\gamma = -\frac{d}{a}$$

Knowledge Booster

Biquadratic Equation

If α, β, γ and δ are the roots of the biquadratic equation $ax^4 + bx^3 + cx^2 + dx + e = 0$, then $S_1 = \alpha + \beta + \gamma + \delta = -\frac{b}{a}$,

$$S_2 = \alpha\beta + \alpha\gamma + \alpha\delta + \beta\gamma + \beta\delta + \gamma\delta = (-1)^2 \frac{c}{a} = \frac{c}{a}$$

or $S_2 = (\alpha + \beta)(\gamma + \delta) + \alpha\beta + \gamma\delta = \frac{c}{a}$

$$S_3 = \alpha\beta\gamma + \beta\gamma\delta + \gamma\delta\alpha + \alpha\beta\delta = (-1)^3 \frac{d}{a} = -\frac{d}{a}$$

or $S_3 = \alpha\beta(\gamma + \delta) + \gamma\delta(\alpha + \beta) = -\frac{d}{a}$ and $S_4 = \alpha \cdot \beta \cdot \gamma \cdot \delta = (-1)^4 \frac{e}{a} = \frac{e}{a}$

Symmetric Roots

If the roots of quadratic equation $ax^2 + bx + c = 0$ $(a \neq 0)$ are α and β, then

(i) $(\alpha - \beta) = \sqrt{(\alpha + \beta)^2 - 4\alpha\beta} = \pm \dfrac{\sqrt{b^2 - 4ac}}{a} = \dfrac{\pm\sqrt{D}}{a}$

(ii) $\alpha^2 + \beta^2 = (\alpha + \beta)^2 - 2\alpha\beta = \dfrac{b^2 - 2ac}{a^2}$

(iii) $\alpha^2 - \beta^2 = (\alpha + \beta)\sqrt{(\alpha + \beta)^2 - 4\alpha\beta} = \pm \dfrac{b\sqrt{b^2 - 4ac}}{a^2} = \dfrac{\pm b\sqrt{D}}{a^2}$

(iv) $\alpha^3 + \beta^3 = (\alpha + \beta)^3 - 3\alpha\beta(\alpha + \beta) = -\dfrac{b(b^2 - 3ac)}{a^3}$

(v) $\alpha^3 - \beta^3 = (\alpha - \beta)^3 + 3\alpha\beta(\alpha - \beta) = \dfrac{\pm(b^2 - ac)\sqrt{b^2 - 4ac}}{a^3}$

(vi) $\alpha^4 + \beta^4 = \{(\alpha + \beta)^2 - 2\alpha\beta\}^2 - 2\alpha^2\beta^2 = \left(\dfrac{b^2 - 2ac}{a^2}\right)^2 - \dfrac{2c^2}{a^2}$

(vii) $\alpha^4 - \beta^4 = (\alpha^2 - \beta^2)(\alpha^2 + \beta^2) = \dfrac{\pm b(b^2 - 2ac)\sqrt{b^2 - 4ac}}{a^4}$

(viii) $\alpha^2 + \alpha\beta + \beta^2 = (\alpha + \beta)^2 - \alpha\beta = \dfrac{b^2 - ac}{a^2}$

(ix) $\dfrac{\alpha}{\beta} + \dfrac{\beta}{\alpha} = \dfrac{\alpha^2 + \beta^2}{\alpha\beta} = \dfrac{(\alpha + \beta)^2 - 2\alpha\beta}{\alpha\beta} = \dfrac{b^2 - 2ac}{ac}$

(x) $\alpha^2\beta + \beta^2\alpha = \alpha\beta(\alpha + \beta) = -\dfrac{bc}{a^2}$

(xi) $\left(\dfrac{\alpha}{\beta}\right)^2 + \left(\dfrac{\beta}{\alpha}\right)^2 = \dfrac{\alpha^4 + \beta^4}{\alpha^2\beta^2} = \dfrac{(\alpha^2 + \beta^2)^2 - 2\alpha^2\beta^2}{\alpha^2\beta^2} = \dfrac{b^2D + 2a^2c^2}{a^2c^2}$

Formation of Polynomial Equation from Given Roots

If $\alpha_1, \alpha_2, \alpha_3, \ldots, \alpha_n$ are the roots of an nth degree equation, then the equation is $x^n - S_1x^{n-1} + S_2x^{n-2} - S_3x^{n-3} + \ldots + (-1)^n S_n = 0$, where S_n denotes the sum of the products of roots taken n at a time.

1. Quadratic Equation

If α and β are the roots of a quadratic equation, then the equation is $x^2 - S_1x + S_2 = 0$, where S_1 = sum of roots and S_2 = multiplication of roots.

i.e. $\quad x^2 - (\alpha + \beta)x + \alpha\beta = 0.$

2. Cubic Equation

If α, β and γ are the roots of cubic equation, then the equation is

$$x^3 - S_1x^2 + S_2x - S_3 = 0$$

i.e. $$x^3 - (\alpha + \beta + \gamma)x^2 + (\alpha\beta + \beta\gamma + \gamma\alpha)x - \alpha\beta\gamma = 0$$

Equation in Terms of the Roots of another Equation

If α, β are roots of the equation $ax^2 + bx + c = 0$, then the equation whose roots are

(i) $-\alpha, -\beta \Rightarrow ax^2 - bx + c = 0$ [replace x by $-x$]

(ii) $\alpha^n, \beta^n; n \in N \Rightarrow a(x^{1/n})^2 + b(x^{1/n}) + c = 0$ [replace x by $x^{1/n}$]

(iii) $k\alpha, k\beta \Rightarrow ax^2 + kbx + k^2c = 0$ [replace x by x/k]

(iv) $k + \alpha, k + \beta \Rightarrow a(x - k)^2 + b(x - k) + c = 0$ [replace x by $(x - k)$]

(v) $\frac{\alpha}{k}, \frac{\beta}{k} \Rightarrow k^2ax^2 + kbx + c = 0$ [replace x by kx]

(vi) $\alpha^{1/n}, \beta^{1/n}; n \in N \Rightarrow a(x^n)^2 + b(x^n) + c = 0$ [replace x by x^n]

The quadratic function $f(x) = ax^2 + 2hxy + by^2 + 2gx + 2fy + c$ is always resolvable into linear factor, iff $abc + 2fgh - af^2 - bg^2 - ch^2 = 0$

or $$\begin{vmatrix} a & h & g \\ h & b & f \\ g & f & c \end{vmatrix} = 0$$

Competition Insight

Condition for Common Roots in Quadratic Equations

1. Only One Root is Common

If α is the common root of quadratic equations $a_1x^2 + b_1x + c_1 = 0$ and $a_2x^2 + b_2x + c_2 = 0$, then $a_1\alpha^2 + b_1\alpha + c_1 = 0$ and $a_2\alpha^2 + b_2\alpha + c_2 = 0$.

By Cramer's Rule

$$\frac{\alpha^2}{\begin{vmatrix} -c_1 & b_1 \\ -c_2 & b_2 \end{vmatrix}} = \frac{\alpha}{\begin{vmatrix} a_1 & -c_1 \\ a_2 & -c_2 \end{vmatrix}} = \frac{1}{\begin{vmatrix} a_1 & b_1 \\ a_2 & b_2 \end{vmatrix}}$$

or $$\frac{\alpha^2}{b_1c_2 - b_2c_1} = \frac{\alpha}{a_2c_1 - a_1c_2} = \frac{1}{a_1b_2 - a_2b_1}$$

$\therefore$ $$\alpha = \frac{a_2c_1 - a_1c_2}{a_1b_2 - a_2b_1} = \frac{b_1c_2 - b_2c_1}{a_2c_1 - a_1c_2}, \alpha \neq 0$$

Hence, the condition for only one root common is

$$(c_1a_2 - c_2a_1)^2 = (b_1c_2 - b_2c_1)(a_1b_2 - a_2b_1)$$

2. Both Roots are Common

The required condition is

$$\frac{a_1}{a_2} = \frac{b_1}{b_2} = \frac{c_1}{c_2}$$

(i) To find the common roots of two equations, make the coefficient of second degree term in the two equations equal and subtract. The value of x obtained is the required common root.

(ii) Two different quadratic equations with rational coefficient can not have single common root which is complex or irrational as imaginary and surd roots always occur in pair.

Properties of Polynomial Equation

1. Let $f(x) = 0$ be a polynomial equation, then we have the following results.

   (i) $f(a) \cdot f(b) < 0$, then atleast one or in general odd number of roots of the equation $f(x) = 0$ lies between a and b.

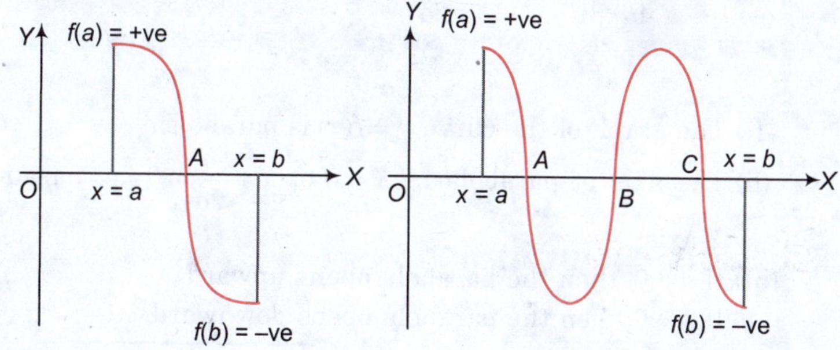

   (ii) $f(a) \cdot f(b) > 0$, then in general even number of roots of the equation $f(x) = 0$ lies between a and b or no root exist.

   (iii) $f(a) = f(b)$, then there exists a point c between a and b such that $f'(c) = 0, a < c < b$.

2. **Repeated roots** A polynomial equation $f(x) = 0$ has exactly n roots equal to α if $f(\alpha) = f'(\alpha) = f''(\alpha) ... = f^{n-1}(\alpha) = 0$ and $f^n(\alpha) \neq 0$.

   (i) If the roots of the quadratic equation $a_1x^2 + b_1x + c_1 = 0$, $a_2x^2 + b_2x + c_2 = 0$ are in the same ratio $\left(\text{i.e. } \frac{\alpha_1}{\beta_1} = \frac{\alpha_2}{\beta_2}\right)$, then

$$\frac{b_1^2}{b_2^2} = \frac{a_1c_1}{a_2c_2}.$$

(ii) If one root is k times the other root of the quadratic equation $ax^2 + bx + c = 0$,then $\frac{(k+1)^2}{k} = \frac{b^2}{ac}$.

Quadratic Expression

An expression of the form $ax^2 + bx + c$, where $a, b, c \in R$ and $a \neq 0$ is called a quadratic expression in x.

1. **Graph of a Quadratic Expression**

We have,

$$y = ax^2 + bx + c = f(x)$$

$$y = a\left[\left(x + \frac{b}{2a}\right)^2 - \frac{D}{4a^2}\right]$$

$$\Rightarrow \quad y + \frac{D}{4a} = a\left(x + \frac{b}{2a}\right)^2$$

Let $y + \frac{D}{4a} = Y$ and $x + \frac{b}{2a} = X$

$$Y = a \cdot X^2 \Rightarrow X^2 = \frac{Y}{a}$$

(i) The graph of the curve $y = f(x)$ is parabolic.

(ii) The axis of parabola is $X = 0$ or $x + \frac{b}{2a} = 0$ i.e. parallel to Y-axis.

(iii) If $a > 0$, then the parabola opens upward.

If $a < 0$, then the parabola opens downward.

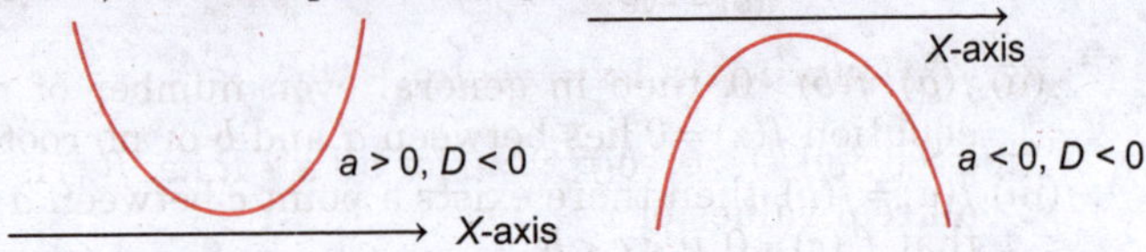

2. **Position of $y = ax^2 + bx + c$ with Respect to Axes**

(i) For $D > 0$, parabola cuts X-axis and has two real and distinct points i.e. $x = \frac{-b \pm \sqrt{D}}{2a}$.

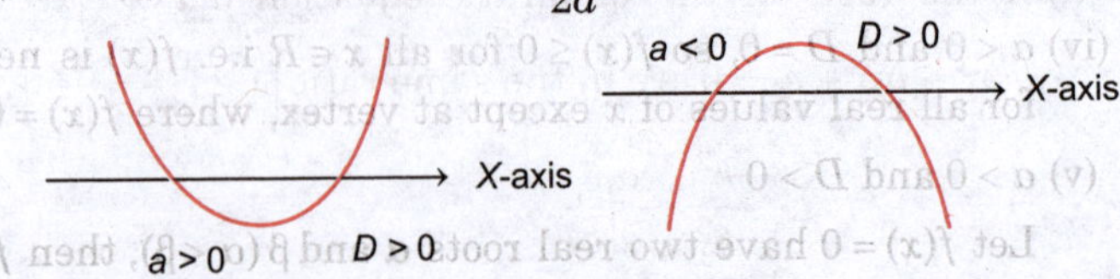

(ii) For $D = 0$, parabola touch X-axis in one point, $x = -\dfrac{b}{2a}$.

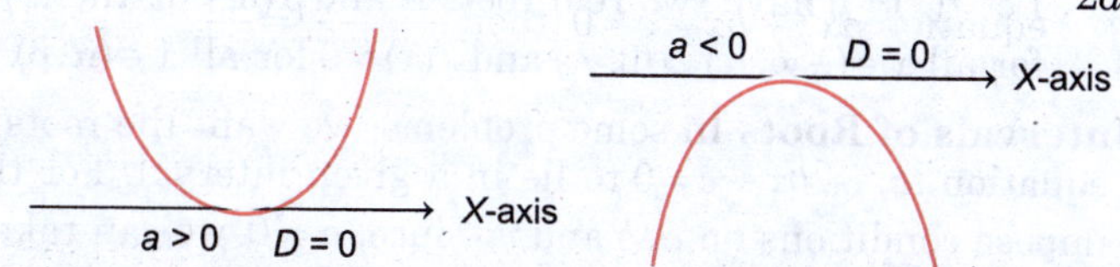

(iii) For $D < 0$, parabola does not cut X-axis (i.e. imaginary value of x).

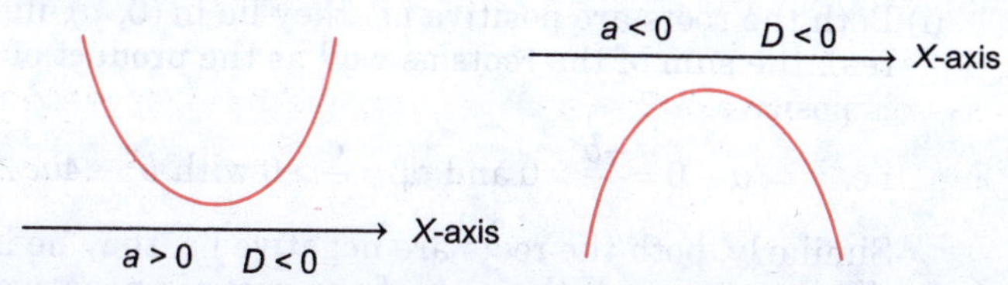

Competition Insight

Maximum and Minimum Values of Quadratic Expression

(i) If $a > 0$, quadratic expression has least value at $x = \dfrac{-b}{2a}$. This least value is given by $\dfrac{4ac - b^2}{4a} = -\dfrac{D}{4a}$. But there is no greatest value.

(ii) If $a < 0$, quadratic expression has greatest value at $x = -\dfrac{b}{2a}$. This greatest value is given by $\dfrac{4ac - b^2}{4a} = -\dfrac{D}{4a}$. But their is no least value.

3. Sign of Quadratic Expression

(i) $a > 0$ and $D < 0$, so $f(x) > 0$ for all $x \in R$ i.e. $f(x)$ is positive for all real values of x.

(ii) $a < 0$ and $D < 0$, so $f(x) < 0$ for all $x \in R$ i.e. $f(x)$ is negative for all real values of x.

(iii) $a > 0$ and $D = 0$, so $f(x) \geq 0$ for all $x \in R$ i.e. $f(x)$ is positive for all real values of x except at vertex, where $f(x) = 0$.

(iv) $a < 0$ and $D = 0$, so $f(x) \leq 0$ for all $x \in R$ i.e. $f(x)$ is negative for all real values of x except at vertex, where $f(x) = 0$.

(v) $a > 0$ and $D > 0$

Let $f(x) = 0$ have two real roots α and β $(\alpha < \beta)$, then $f(x) > 0$ for $x \in (-\infty, \alpha) \cup (\beta, \infty)$ and $f(x) < 0$ for all $x \in (\alpha, \beta)$.

(vi) $a < 0$ and $D > 0$

Let $f(x) = 0$ have two real roots α and β $(\alpha < \beta)$, then, $f(x) < 0$ for all $x \in (-\infty, \alpha) \cup (\beta, \infty)$ and $f(x) > 0$ for all $x \in (\alpha, \beta)$.

4. **Intervals of Roots** In some problems, we want the roots of the equation $ax^2 + bx + c = 0$ to lie in a given interval. For this we impose conditions on a, b and c. Since, $a \neq 0$, we can take $f(x) = x^2 + \frac{b}{a}x + \frac{c}{a}$.

(i) Both the roots are positive i.e. they lie in $(0, \infty)$, iff roots are real, the sum of the roots as well as the product of the roots is positive.

i.e. $\alpha + \beta = \frac{-b}{a} > 0$ and $\alpha\beta = \frac{c}{a} > 0$ with $b^2 - 4ac \geq 0$

Similarly, both the roots are negative i.e. they lie in $(-\infty, 0)$, iff roots are real, the sum of the roots is negative and the product of the roots is positive.

i.e. $\alpha + \beta = \frac{-b}{a} < 0$ and $\alpha\beta = \frac{c}{a} > 0$ with $b^2 - 4ac \geq 0$

(ii) Both the roots are greater than a given number k, iff the following conditions are satisfied $D \geq 0, \frac{-b}{2a} > k$ and $af(k) > 0$

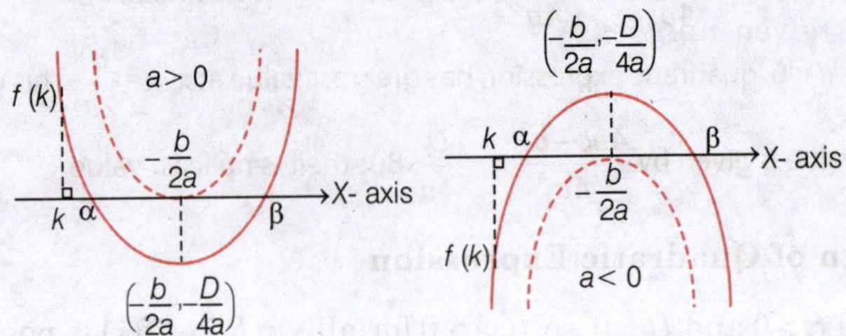

(iii) Both the roots are less than a given number k, iff the following conditions are satisfied

$$D \geq 0, \frac{-b}{2a} < k \text{ and } af(k) > 0$$

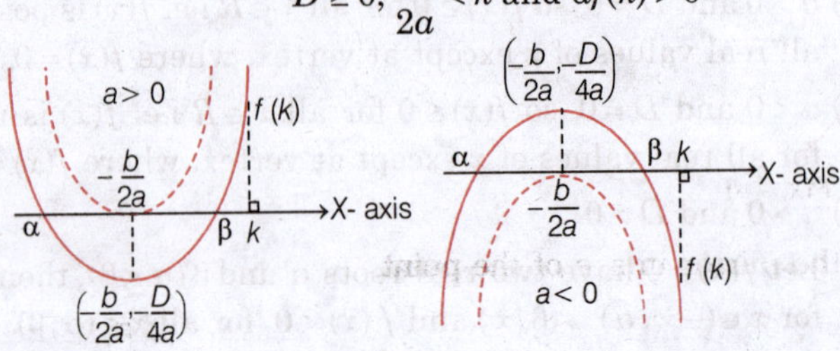

(iv) Both the roots lie in a given interval (k_1, k_2), iff the following conditions are satisfied

$$D \geq 0, k_1 < \frac{-b}{2a} < k_2 \text{ and } af(k_1) > 0, af(k_2) > 0$$

or $$f(k_1) \cdot f(k_2) > 0$$

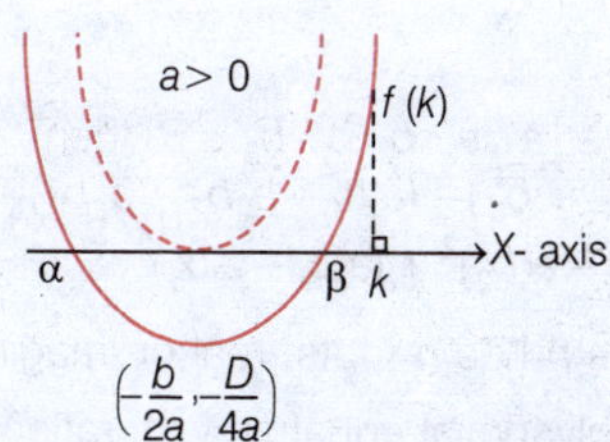

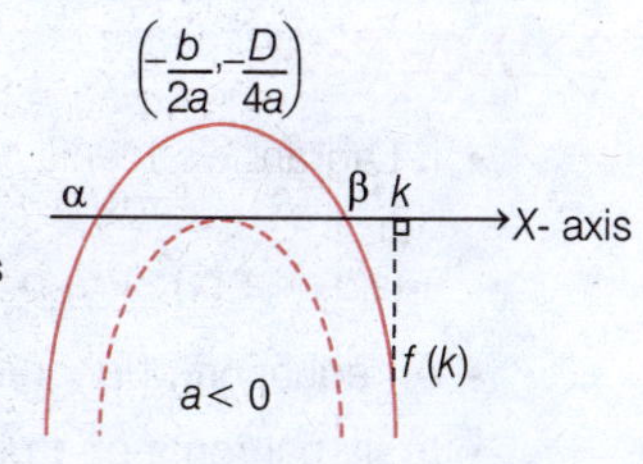

(v) Exactly one of the roots lies in a given interval (k_1, k_2), iff $D > 0$ and $f(k_1)\, f(k_2) < 0$.

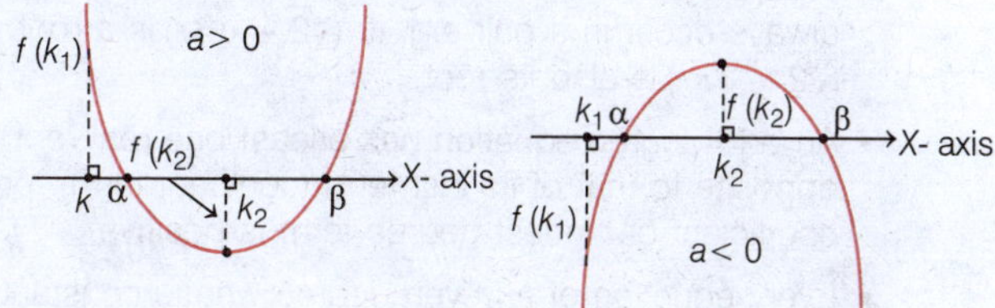

(vi) A given number k lies between the roots, iff $af(k) < 0$ and $D > 0$.

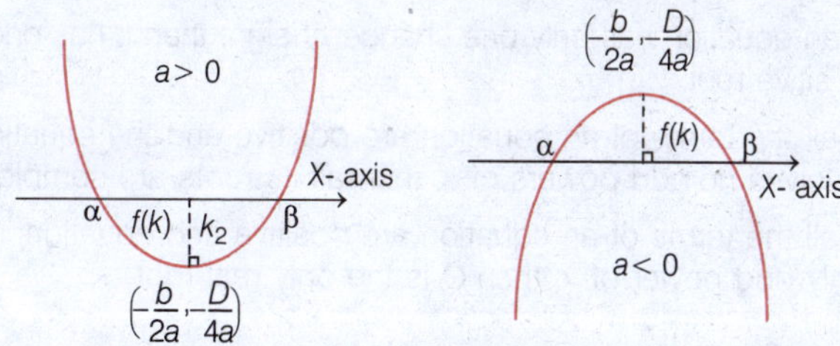

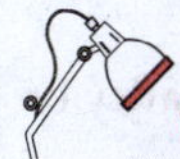

EXPERT Scale Up

The roots of the equation will be of opposite sign, iff 0 lies between the roots.

$\Rightarrow$ $$af(0) < 0, D > 0$$

Descarte's Rule of Signs

The maximum number of positive real roots of a polynomial equation $f(x) = 0$ is the number of changes of sign in $f(x)$.

The maximum number of negative real roots of a polynomial equation $f(x) = 0$ is the number of changes of sign in $f(-x)$.

Value Points

- If Lagrange's Identity $a_1, a_2, a_3, b_1, b_2, b_3 \in R$, then
  $(a_1^2 + a_2^2 + a_3^2)(b_1^2 + b_2^2 + b_3^2) - (a_1b_1 + a_2b_2 + a_3b_3)^2$
  $= (a_1b_2 - a_2b_1)^2 + (a_2b_3 - a_3b_2)^2 + (a_3b_1 - a_1b_3)^2$
- An equation of degree n has n roots, real or imaginary.
- Irrational roots of a polynomial equation with rational coefficients, always occurs in a pair, e.g. if $2 + \sqrt{3}$ is a root, then $2 - \sqrt{3}$ is also its root.
- Imaginary roots of a polynomial equation with real coefficients always occur in a pair e.g. if $(\sqrt{2} + \sqrt{3}i)$ is a root, then $(\sqrt{2} - \sqrt{3}i)$ is also its root.
- An odd degree equation has atleast one real root whose sign is opposite to that of its last term (constant term), provided that the coefficient of highest degree term is positive.
- Every equation of an even degree whose constant term is negative and the coefficient of highest degree term is positive has atleast two real roots, one positive and one negative.
- If an equation has only one change of sign, then it has one positive root.
- If all the terms of an equation are positive and the equation involves no odd powers of x, then all its roots are complex.
- If all the terms of an equation are positive and equation involves only odd power of x, then O is the only real root.

Inequality

A statement involving the symbols $>, <, \leq$ or $\geq$ is called an **inequality** or **inequation.**

Here, the symbols $<$ (less than), $>$ (greater than), $\leq$ (less than or equal to) and $\geq$ (greater than or equal to) are known as symbol of **inequalities.**

e.g. $5 < 7,\ x \leq 2,\ x + y \geq 11$

Types of Inequalities

(i) **Numerical inequality** An inequality which does not involve any variable is called a numerical inequality.

e.g. $4 > 2, 8 < 21$

(ii) **Literal inequality** An inequality which have variables is called literal inequality.

e.g. $x < 7, y \geq 11, x - y \leq 4$

(iii) **Strict inequality** An inequality which have only < or > is called strict inequality.

e.g. $3x + y < 0, x > 7$

(iv) **Slack inequality** An inequality which have only ≥ or ≤ is called slack inequality.

e.g. $3x + 2y \leq 0, y \geq 4$

Linear Inequality

An inequality is said to be linear, if the variable(s) occurs in first degree only and there is no term involving the product of the variables. e.g. $ax + b \leq 0$, $ax + by + c > 0$, $ax \leq 4$.

Linear Inequality in One Variable

A linear inequality which has only one variable, is called linear inequality in one variable.

e.g. $ax + b < 0$, where $a \neq 0$

Linear Inequality in Two Variables

A linear inequality which have only two variables, is called linear inequality in two variables.

e.g. $3x + 11y \leq 0$, $4t + 3y > 0$

Concept of Intervals on a Number Line

On number line or real line, various types of infinite subsets, known as intervals, are defined below

Closed Interval

The set of all real numbers x such that $a \leq x \leq b$, is called a closed interval and is denoted by **[*a*, *b*]**.

On the number line, [*a*, *b*] may be represented as follows

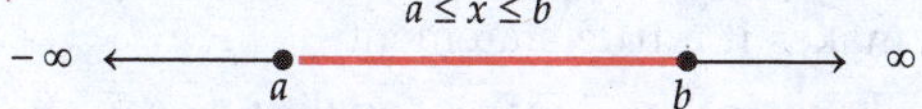

Open Interval

The set of all real numbers x such that $a < x < b$, is called an open interval and is denoted by **(a, b) or $]a, b[$.**

On the number line, (a, b) may be represented as follows

$a < x < b$

$-\infty$ a b ∞

Semi-open or Semi-closed Intervals

Here, $(a, b] = \{x : a < x \leq b, x \in R\}$ and $[a, b) = \{x : a \leq x < b, x \in R\}$ are known as semi-open or semi-closed intervals.

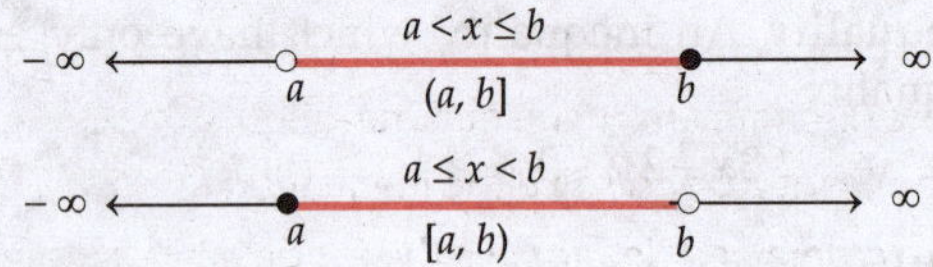

Solution of an Inequality

Any solution of an inequality is the value(s) of variable(s) which makes it a true statement.

1. Addition or Subtraction

Some number may be added (or subtracted) to (from) both sides of an inequality i.e. if $a > b$, then for any number c,

$$a + c > b + c \text{ or } a - c > b - c$$

2. Multiplication or Division

Let a, b and c be three real numbers such that $a > b$ and $c \neq 0$.

(i) If $c > 0$, then $\frac{a}{c} > \frac{b}{c}$ and $ac > bc$.

(ii) If $a > b$ and $c < 0$, then $\frac{a}{c} < \frac{b}{c}$ and $ac < bc$.

Solution Set

The set of all solutions of an inequality is called the solution set of the inequality.

Algebraic Solution of Linear Inequalities in One Variable

Any solution of an linear inequality in one variable is a value of the variable which makes it a true statement.

e.g. $x = 1$ is the solution of the linear inequality $4x + 7 > 0$.

Solution of System of Linear Inequalities in One Variable

The common point which satisfy both the inequations is said to be the solution of system of equation.

Competition Insight

Steps to solve the rational expression

To find the values attained by rational expression of the form $\dfrac{a_1x^2 + b_1x + c_1}{a_2x^2 + b_2x + c_2}$ for real values of x, proceed as follows

(a) Equate the given rational expression to y.

(b) Obtain a quadratic equation in x by simplifying the expression.

(c) Obtain the discriminant of the quadratic equation.

(d) Put discriminant ≥ 0 and solve the inequation for y.

The values of y, so obtained determines the set of values attained by the given rational expression.

Inequation Containing Absolute Value

(i) $|x| < a \Rightarrow -a < x < a \ (a > 0)$

(ii) $|x| \leq a \Rightarrow -a \leq x \leq a \ (a > 0)$

(iii) $|x| > a \Rightarrow x < -a$ or $x > a \ (a > 0)$

(iv) $|x| \geq a \Rightarrow x \leq -a$ or $x \geq a \ (a > 0)$

Important Inequalities

1. Arithmetic, Geometric and Harmonic Mean Inequalities

(i) If $a, b > 0$, then $\dfrac{a+b}{2} \geq \sqrt{ab} \geq \dfrac{2}{(1/a) + (1/b)}$

(ii) If $a_i > 0$, where $i = 1, 2, 3, \ldots, n$, then

$$\frac{a_1 + a_2 + \ldots + a_n}{n} \geq (a_1 \cdot a_2 \cdot \ldots \cdot a_n)^{1/n} \geq \frac{n}{\dfrac{1}{a_1} + \dfrac{1}{a_2} + \ldots + \dfrac{1}{a_n}}$$

2. Relation between Weighted AM and Weighted GM

If $a_1, a_2, \ldots, a_n$ are n positive real numbers and $m_1, m_2, \ldots, m_n$ are n positive rational numbers, then

$$\frac{m_1a_1 + m_2a_2 + \ldots + m_na_n}{m_1 + m_2 + \ldots + m_n} \geq (a_1^{m_1} \cdot a_2^{m_2} \cdot \ldots \cdot a_n^{m_n})^{\frac{1}{m_1 + m_2 + \ldots + m_n}}$$

i.e. Weighted AM $\geq$ Weighted GM

Value Points

(i) If $a > b$ and $b > c$, then $a > c$. Generally, if $a_1 > a_2, a_2 > a_3, \dots, a_{n-1} > a_n$, then $a_1 > a_n$.

(ii) If $a > b$, then $a \pm c > b \pm c, \forall c \in R$

(iii) (a) If $a > b$ and $m > 0$, $am > bm$, $\frac{a}{m} > \frac{b}{m}$

(b) If $a > b$ and $m < 0$, $bm > am$, $\frac{b}{m} > \frac{a}{m}$

(iv) If $a > b > 0$, then

(a) $a^2 > b^2$ (b) $|a| > |b|$ (c) $\frac{1}{a} < \frac{1}{b}$

(v) If $a < b < 0$, then

(a) $a^2 > b^2$ (b) $|a| > |b|$ (c) $\frac{1}{a} > \frac{1}{b}$

(vi) If $a < 0 < b$, then

(a) $a^2 > b^2$, if $|a| > |b|$

(b) $a^2 < b^2$, if $|a| < |b|$

(vii) If $a < x < b$ and a, b are positive real numbers, then $a^2 < x^2 < b^2$

(viii) If $a < x < b$ and a is negative number and b is positive number, then

(a) $0 \le x^2 < b^2$, if $|b| > |a|$

(b) $0 \le x^2 < a^2$, if $|a| > |b|$

(ix) If $\frac{a}{b} > 0$, then

(a) $a > 0$, if $b > 0$

(b) $a < 0$, if $b < 0$

(x) If $a_i > b_i > 0$, where $i = 1, 2, 3, \dots, n$, then

$$a_1 a_2 a_3 \dots a_n > b_1 b_2 b_3 \dots b_n$$

(xi) If $a_i > b_i$, where $i = 1, 2, 3, \dots, n$, then

$$a_1 + a_2 + a_3 + \dots + a_n > b_1 + b_2 + \dots + b_n$$

(xii) If $0 < a < 1$ and n is a positive rational number, then

(a) $0 < a^n < 1$ (b) $a^{-n} > 1$

Chapter 05

Sequences and Series

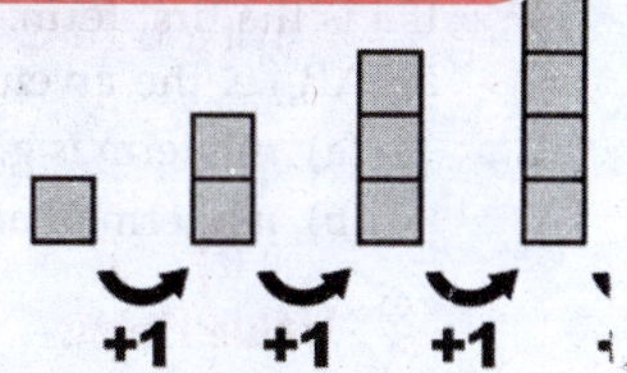

Sequence

Sequence is a function whose domain is the set of natural numbers or some subset of the type $\{1,2,3,...,k\}$. We represents the images of $1,2,3,...,n, ...$ as $f_1, f_2, f_3, ..., f_n ...$, where $f_n = f(n)$.

In other words, a sequence is an arrangement of numbers in definite order according to some rule.

- A sequence containing a finite number of terms is called a **finite sequence.**
- A sequence containing an infinite number of terms is called an **infinite sequence.**
- A sequence whose range is a subset of real number R, is called a **real sequence.**

Progression

A sequence whose terms follow a certain pattern is called a progression.

Series

If $a_1, a_2, a_3, ..., a_n, ...$ is a sequence, then the sum expressed as $a_1 + a_2 + a_3 + ... + a_n + ...$ is called a series and abbreriated as $\sum_{k=1}^{n} a_k$.

- A series having finite number of terms is called **finite series.**
- A series having infinite number of terms is called **infinite series.**

Arithmetic Progression (AP)

A sequence in which terms increase or decrease regularly by a fixed number. This fixed number is called the common difference of AP.

e.g. a, $a + d$, $a + 2d$, ... is an AP, where a = first term and d = common difference.

nth Term (or General Term) of an AP

If a is the first term, d is the common difference and l is the last term of an AP, i.e. the given AP is $a, a+d, a+2d, a+3d, \ldots, l$, then

(a) nth term is given by $a_n = a + (n-1)d$

(b) nth term of an AP from the last term is given by $a'_n = l - (n-1)d$

Value Points

- $a_n + a'_n = a + l$

  i.e. nth term from the begining + nth term from the end = first term + last term

- Common difference of an AP

$$d = a_n - a_{n-1}, \forall n > 1$$

- $a_n = \frac{1}{2}[a_{n-k} + a_{n+k}], k < n$

Properties of Arithmetic Progression

(i) If a constant is added or subtracted from each term of an AP, then the resulting sequence is also an AP with same common difference.

(ii) If each term of an AP is multiplied or divided by a non-zero constant k, then the resulting sequence is also an AP, with common difference kd or $\frac{d}{k}$ respectively, where d = common difference of given AP.

(iii) If a_n, a_{n+1} and a_{n+2} are three consecutive terms of an AP, then $2a_{n+1} = a_n + a_{n+2}$.

(iv) If the terms of an AP are chosen at regular intervals, then they form an AP.

(v) If a sequence is an AP, then its nth term is a linear expression in n, i.e. its nth term is given by $An + B$, where A and B are constants and A = common difference.

Selection of Terms in an AP

(i) Any three terms in AP can be taken as

$$(a-d), a, (a+d)$$

(ii) Any four terms in AP can be taken as

$$(a-3d), (a-d), (a+d), (a+3d)$$

(iii) Any five terms in AP can be taken as

$$(a-2d), (a-d), a, (a+d), (a+2d)$$

Sum of First n Terms of an AP

Sum of first n terms of AP, is given by

$$S_n = \frac{n}{2}[2a + (n-1)d] = \frac{n}{2}[a + l], \text{ where } l = \text{last term}$$

Knowledge Booster

- If the pth term of an AP is c and qth term is d, then its rth term will be
$$\frac{c(r-q) - d(r-p)}{p-q}$$
- A sequence is an AP iff the sum of its first n terms is of the form $An^2 + Bn$, where A and B are constants and common difference in such case will be $2A$.
- $a_n = S_n - S_{n-1}$ i.e.
nth term of AP = Sum of first n terms – Sum of first $(n-1)$ terms

Arithmetic Mean (AM)

(i) If a, A and b are in AP, then A is called the arithmetic mean of a and b and it is given by $A = \frac{a+b}{2}$

(ii) If $a_1, a_2, a_3, \ldots, a_n$ are n numbers, then their AM is given by,
$$A = \frac{a_1 + a_2 + \ldots + a_n}{n}$$

(iii) If $a, A_1, A_2, A_3, \ldots, A_n, b$ are in AP, then

(a) $A_1, A_2, A_3, \ldots, A_n$ are called n arithmetic mean between a and b, where
$$A_1 = a + d = \frac{na + b}{n+1}$$
$$A_2 = a + 2d = \frac{(n-1)a + 2b}{n+1}$$
$$\vdots \qquad \vdots \qquad \vdots$$
$$A_n = a + nd = \frac{a + nb}{n+1} \text{ and } d = \frac{b-a}{n+1}$$

(b) Sum of n AM's between a and b is nA

i.e. $A_1 + A_2 + A_3 + \ldots + A_n = nA$, where $A = \frac{a+b}{2}$

Value Points

- If $a_p = q$ and $a_q = p$, then $a_{p+q} = 0$, $a_r = p + q - r$
- If $pa_p = qa_q$, then $a_{p+q} = 0$
- If $a_p = \frac{1}{q}$ and $a_q = \frac{1}{p}$, then $a_{pq} = 1$
- If $S_p = q$ and $S_q = p$, then $S_{p+q} = -(p+q)$
- If $S_p = S_q$, then $S_{p+q} = 0$
- If a^2, b^2 and c^2 are in AP, then $\frac{1}{b+c}, \frac{1}{c+a}, \frac{1}{a+b}$ and $\frac{a}{b+c}, \frac{b}{c+a}, \frac{c}{a+b}$ both are also in AP.
- If $a_1, a_2, \ldots, a_n$ are the non-zero terms of an AP, then
$$\frac{1}{a_1 a_2} + \frac{1}{a_2 a_3} + \frac{1}{a_3 a_4} + \ldots + \frac{1}{a_{n-1} a_n} = \frac{n-1}{a_1 a_n}$$
- Between any two number $\frac{\text{sum of } m \text{ AM's}}{\text{sum of } n \text{ AM's}} = \frac{m}{n}$

Geometric Progression (GP)

A sequence in which the ratio of any term (except first term) to its just preceding term is constant throughout. The constant ratio is called common ratio (r).

i.e. $$\frac{a_{n+1}}{a_n} = r, \ \forall \ n \ge 1$$

If a is the first term, r is the common ratio and l is the last term of a GP, then the GP can be written as $a, ar, ar^2, \ldots, ar^{n-1}, \ldots l$.

*n*th Term (or General Term) of a GP

If a is the first term, r is the common ratio and l is the last term, then

(i) nth term of a GP from the beginning is given by $a_n = ar^{n-1}$

(ii) nth term of a GP from the end is given by $a'_n = \frac{l}{r^{n-1}}$.

(iii) The nth term from the end of a finite GP consisting of m terms is ar^{m-n}.

(iv) $a_n a'_n = al$

i.e. nth term from the beginning × nth term from the end = first term × last term

Properties of Geometric Progression

(i) If all the terms of GP are multiplied or divided by same non-zero constant, then the resulting sequence is also a GP with the same common ratio.

(ii) The reciprocal of terms of a given GP also form a GP.

(iii) If each term of a GP is raised to same power, then the resulting sequence also forms a GP.

(iv) If the terms of a GP are chosen at regular intervals, then the resulting sequence is also a GP.

(v) If $a_1, a_2, a_3, \ldots, a_n$ are non-zero and non-negative term of a GP, then $\log a_1, \log a_2, \log a_3, \ldots, \log a_n$ are in an AP and *vice-versa*.

(vi) If a, b and c are three consecutive terms of a GP, then $b^2 = ac$.

Knowledge Booster

If the pth term of a GP is P and qth term is Q, then nth term will be $(P^{n-q} \cdot Q^{p-n}) \cdot \frac{1}{p-q}$

Selection of Terms in a GP

(i) Any three terms in a GP can be taken as $\frac{a}{r}$, a and ar.

(ii) Any four terms in a GP can be taken as $\frac{a}{r^3}, \frac{a}{r}, ar$ and ar^3.

(iii) Any five terms in a GP can be taken as $\frac{a}{r^2}, \frac{a}{r}, a, ar$ and ar^2.

Sum of First n Terms of a GP

(i) Sum of first n terms of a GP is given by

$$S_n = \begin{cases} \frac{a(1-r^n)}{1-r}, & \text{if } r < 1 \\ \frac{a(r^n - 1)}{r-1}, & \text{if } r > 1 \\ na, & \text{if } r = 1 \end{cases}$$

(ii) $S_n = \frac{a - lr}{1-r}, r < 1$ or $S_n = \frac{lr - a}{r-1}, r > 1,$

where l = last term of the GP

Sum of Infinite Terms of a GP

(i) If $|r|<1$, then $S_\infty = \dfrac{a}{1-r}$

(ii) If $|r|\geq 1$, then S_∞ does not exist.

Value Points

- If $a_p = x$ and $a_q = y$, then $a_n = \left(\dfrac{x^{n-q}}{y^{n-p}}\right)^{\frac{1}{p-q}}$
- If $a_{m+n} = p$ and $a_{m-n} = q$, then $a_m = \sqrt{pq}$ and $a_n = p\left(\dfrac{q}{p}\right)^{\frac{m}{2n}}$
- If a, b and c are the pth, qth and rth terms of a GP, then
  $$a^{q-r} \times b^{r-p} \times c^{p-q} = 1$$
- Sum of n terms of $b + bb + bbb + \ldots$ is
  $$a_n = \frac{b}{9}\left(\frac{10(10^n - 1)}{9} - n\right); b = 1, 2, \ldots, 9$$
- Sum of n terms of $0 \cdot b + 0 \cdot bb + 0 \cdot bbb + \ldots$ is
  $$a_n = \frac{b}{9}\left(n - \frac{(1 - 10^{-n})}{9}\right); b = 1, 2, \ldots, 9$$
- If $a_1, a_2, a_3, \ldots, a_n$ and $b_1, b_2, b_3, \ldots, b_n$ are in GP, then the sequence $a_1 \pm b_1$, $a_2 \pm b_2$, $a_3 \pm b_3 \ldots$ will not be a GP.
- If pth, qth and rth term of geometric progression are also in geometric progression, then p, q and r are in arithmetic progression.
- If a, b and c are in AP as well as in GP, then $a = b = c$.
- If a, b and c are in AP, then x^a, x^b and x^c are in geometric progression.

Geometric Mean GM

(i) If a, G, b are in GP, then G is called the geometric mean of a and b and is given by $G = \sqrt{ab}$.

(ii) GM of n positive numbers $a_1, a_2, a_3, \ldots, a_n$ are given by $G = (a_1 a_2 \ldots a_n)^{1/n}$

(iii) If $a, G_1, G_2, G_3, \ldots, G_n, b$ are in GP, then

(a) $G_1, G_2, G_3, \ldots, G_n$, are called n GM's between a and b, where

$$G_1 = ar = a\left(\frac{b}{a}\right)^{\frac{1}{n+1}},$$

$$G_2 = ar^2 = a\left(\frac{b}{a}\right)^{\frac{2}{n+1}}$$

$$\vdots \quad \vdots \quad \vdots$$

$$G_n = ar^n = a\left(\frac{b}{a}\right)^{\frac{n}{n+1}} \text{ and } r = \left(\frac{b}{a}\right)^{\frac{1}{n+1}}$$

(b) Product of n GM's,

$$G_1 \times G_2 \times G_3 \times \ldots \times G_n = G^n, \text{ where } G = \sqrt{ab}$$

Harmonic Progression (HP)

A sequence $a_1, a_2, a_3, \ldots, a_n, \ldots$ of non-zero numbers is called a Harmonic Progression (HP), if the sequence $\frac{1}{a_1}, \frac{1}{a_2}, \frac{1}{a_3}, \ldots, \frac{1}{a_n}, \ldots$ is in AP.

*n*th Term (or General Term) of Harmonic Progression

(i) nth term of the HP from the beginning

$$a_n = \frac{1}{\frac{1}{a_1} + (n-1)\left(\frac{1}{a_2} - \frac{1}{a_1}\right)}$$

$$= \frac{a_1 a_2}{a_2 + (n-1)(a_1 - a_2)}$$

(ii) nth term of the HP from the end

$$a'_n = \frac{1}{\frac{1}{l} - (n-1)\left(\frac{1}{a_2} - \frac{1}{a_1}\right)} = \frac{a_1 a_2 l}{a_1 a_2 - l(n-1)(a_1 - a_2)},$$

where l is the last term.

(iii) $\frac{1}{a_n} + \frac{1}{a'_n} = \frac{1}{a} + \frac{1}{l} = \frac{1}{\text{First term of HP}} + \frac{1}{\text{Last term of HP}}$

(iv) $a_n = \frac{1}{a + (n-1)d}$, if a, d are the first term and common difference of the corresponding AP.

Harmonic Mean

(i) If a, H and b are in HP, then H is called the harmonic mean of a and b and is given by $H = \frac{2ab}{a+b}$

(ii) Harmonic Mean (HM) of $a_1, a_2, a_3, \ldots, a_n$ is given by

$$\frac{1}{H} = \frac{1}{n}\left(\frac{1}{a_1} + \frac{1}{a_2} + \frac{1}{a_3} + \ldots.. + \frac{1}{a_n}\right)$$

(iii) If $a, H_1, H_2, H_3, \ldots., H_n, b$ are in HP, then

(a) $H_1, H_2, H_3, \ldots, H_n$

are called n harmonic means between a and b, where

$$H_1 = \frac{(n+1)ab}{a+nb},$$

$$H_2 = \frac{(n+1)ab}{2a+(n-1)b},$$

$$H_3 = \frac{(n+1)ab}{3a+(n-2)b}$$

$$\vdots \qquad \vdots$$

$$H_n = \frac{(n+1)ab}{na+(n-(n-1))b} = \frac{(n+1)ab}{na+b}$$

(b) $\frac{1}{H_1} + \frac{1}{H_2} + \frac{1}{H_3} + \ldots + \frac{1}{H_n} = \frac{n}{H}$, where $H = \frac{2ab}{a+b}$

If in a HP, $a_m = n$ and $a_n = m$, then

$$a_{m+n} = \frac{mn}{m+n}, \quad a_{mn} = 1$$

and $$a_p = \frac{mn}{p}$$

If in a HP, $a_p = qr$ and $a_q = pr$, then $a_r = pq$.

If H is HM between a and b, then

(a) $(H-2a)(H-2b) = H^2$

(b) $\frac{1}{H-a} + \frac{1}{H-b} = \frac{1}{a} + \frac{1}{b}$

(c) $\frac{H+a}{H-a} + \frac{H+b}{H-b} = 2$

Properties of AM, GM and HM between Two Numbers

1. If A, G and H are arithmetic, geometric and harmonic means of two positive numbers a and b, then

   (i) $A = \frac{a+b}{2}, G = \sqrt{ab}, H = \frac{2ab}{a+b}$

   (ii) $A \geq G \geq H$

EXPERT Scale Up

The inequality $A \geq G \geq H$ can be remember by A Great Hope which means that Arithmetic is greater than Harmonic.

   (iii) $G^2 = AH$ and so A, G, H are in GP.

   (iv) $$\frac{a^{n+1} + b^{n+1}}{a^n + b^n} = \begin{cases} A, & \text{if } n = 0 \\ G, & \text{if } n = -\frac{1}{2} \\ H, & \text{if } n = -1 \end{cases}$$

2. If A, G, H are AM, GM and HM of three positive numbers a, b and c, then the equation having a, b and c as its root is

   $$x^3 - 3Ax^2 + \frac{3G^3}{H}x - G^3 = 0,$$

   where $A = \frac{a+b+c}{3}$ and $G = (abc)^{1/3}$

   and $$\frac{1}{H} = \left(\frac{\frac{1}{a} + \frac{1}{b} + \frac{1}{c}}{3}\right)$$

3. If number of terms in AP/GP/HP are odd, then AM/GM/HM of first and last term is middle term of progression.

4. If A_1 and A_2 are two AM's, G_1 and G_2 are two GM's and H_1 and H_2 are two HM's between two numbers a and b, then

   $$\frac{G_1 G_2}{H_1 H_2} = \frac{A_1 + A_2}{H_1 + H_2}$$

Competition Insight

Arithmetic-Geometric Progression

A sequence in which every term is a product of corresponding term of AP and GP is known as arithmetic-geometric progression.

The series may be written as

$$a, (a+d)r, (a+2d)r^2, (a+3d)r^3, \dots, [a+(n-1)d]r^{n-1}$$

Then, $S_n = \dfrac{a}{1-r} + \dfrac{dr(1-r^{n-1})}{(1-r)^2} - \dfrac{\{a+(n-1)d\}r^n}{1-r}$, if $r \neq 1$

$S_n = \dfrac{n}{2}[2a + (n-1)d]$, if $r = 1$

Also, $S_\infty = \dfrac{a}{1-r} + \dfrac{dr}{(1-r)^2}$, if $|r| < 1$

Method of Difference

Let $a_1 + a_2 + a_3 + \dots$ be a given series.

Case I If $a_2 - a_1, a_3 - a_2, \dots$ are in AP or GP, then a_n and S_n can be found by the method of difference.

Clearly, $S_n = a_1 + a_2 + a_3 + a_4 + \dots + a_n$ or $S_n = \quad a_1 + a_2 + a_3 + \dots + a_{n-1} + a_n$

So, $S_n - S_n = a_1 + (a_2 - a_1) + (a_3 - a_2) + (a_4 - a_3) + (a_n - a_{n-1}) - a_n$

$\Rightarrow \quad a_n = a_1 + (a_2 - a_1) + (a_3 - a_2) + \dots + (a_n - a_{n-1})$

$\therefore \quad a_n = a_1 + T_1 + T_2 + T_3 + \dots + T_{n-1}$,

where $T_1, T_2, T_3, \dots$ are terms of new series and $S_n = \Sigma a_n$

Case II It is not always necessary that the sequence of first order of differences i.e. $a_2 - a_1, a_3 - a_2, \dots, a_n - a_{n-1}, \dots$ is always in AP or in GP. In such cases, we proceed as follows.

Let $a_1 = T_1, a_2 - a_1 = T_2, a_3 - a_2 = T_3, \dots, a_n - a_{n-1} = T_n$

So,

$$a_n = T_1 + T_2 + \dots + T_n \quad \dots\text{(i)}$$

$$a_n = T_1 + T_2 + \dots + T_{n-1} + T_n \quad \dots\text{(ii)}$$

On subtracting Eq. (ii) from Eq. (i), we get

$$T_n = T_1 + (T_2 - T_1) + (T_3 - T_2) + \dots + (T_n - T_{n-1})$$

Now, the series $(T_2 - T_1) + (T_3 - T_2) + \dots + (T_n - T_{n-1})$ is series of second order of differences and if it is either in AP or in GP, then $a_n = \Sigma T_r$.

Otherwise, in the similar way, we find series of higher order of differences and the nth term of the series.

Exponential Series

The sum of the series $1+\frac{1}{1!}+\frac{1}{2!}+\frac{1}{3!}+\frac{1}{4!}+\ldots\infty$ is denoted by the number e.

$$\therefore \qquad e=1+\frac{1}{1!}+\frac{1}{2!}+\frac{1}{3!}+\frac{1}{4!}+\ldots$$

(i) e lies between 2 and 3.

(ii) e is an irrational number.

(iii) $e^x=1+\frac{x}{1!}+\frac{x^2}{2!}+\frac{x^3}{3!}+\ldots\infty, x\in R$

(iv) $e^{-x}=1-\frac{x}{1!}+\frac{x^2}{2!}-\frac{x^3}{3!}+\ldots\infty, x\in R$

(v) For any $a>0$, $a^x=e^{x\log_e a}$

$$=1+x(\log_e a)+\frac{x^2}{2!}(\log_e a)^2+\frac{x^3}{3!}(\log_e a)^3+\ldots\infty, x\in R$$

Logarithmic Series

(i) $\log_e(1+x)=x-\frac{x^2}{2}+\frac{x^3}{3}-\frac{x^4}{4}+\ldots\infty, (-1<x\le 1)$

$$=\sum_{n=1}^{\infty}(-1)^{n-1}\frac{x^n}{n}, (-1<x\le 1)$$

(ii) $\log_e(1-x)=-x-\frac{x^2}{2}-\frac{x^3}{3}-\frac{x^4}{4}-\ldots\infty, (-1\le x<1)$

$$\Rightarrow -\log_e(1-x)=x+\frac{x^2}{2}+\frac{x^3}{3}+\frac{x^4}{4}+\ldots\infty, (-1\le x<1)$$

(iii) $\log_e\left(\frac{1+x}{1-x}\right)=2\left(x+\frac{x^3}{3}+\frac{x^5}{5}+\ldots\infty\right), (-1<x<1)$

(iv) $\log_e 2=1-\frac{1}{2}+\frac{1}{3}-\frac{1}{4}+\frac{1}{5}-\ldots\infty$

Summation of Series

(i) $\sum_{n=0}^{\infty}\frac{1}{n!}=e=\sum_{n=1}^{\infty}\frac{1}{(n-1)!}=\sum_{n=k}^{\infty}\frac{1}{(n-k)!}=e$

(ii) $\sum_{n=1}^{\infty}\frac{1}{n!}=\frac{1}{1!}+\frac{1}{2!}+\frac{1}{3!}+\ldots\infty=e-1$

(iii) $\sum_{n=2}^{\infty} \frac{1}{n!} = \frac{1}{2!} + \frac{1}{3!} + \frac{1}{4!} + \dots \infty = e - 2$

(iv) $\sum_{n=0}^{\infty} \frac{1}{(n+1)!} = \frac{1}{1!} + \frac{1}{2!} + \frac{1}{3!} + \dots \infty = e - 1$

(v) $\sum_{n=1}^{\infty} \frac{1}{(n+1)!} = \sum_{n=0}^{\infty} \frac{1}{(n+2)!} = \frac{1}{2!} + \frac{1}{3!} + \frac{1}{4!} + \dots \infty = e - 2$

(vi) $\sum_{n=0}^{\infty} \frac{1}{(2n)!} = 1 + \frac{1}{2!} + \frac{1}{4!} + \frac{1}{6!} + \dots = \frac{e + e^{-1}}{2} = \sum_{n=1}^{\infty} \frac{1}{(2n-2)!}$

(vii) $\sum_{n=1}^{\infty} \frac{1}{(2n-1)!} = \frac{1}{1!} + \frac{1}{3!} + \frac{1}{5!} + \dots = \frac{e - e^{-1}}{2} = \sum_{n=0}^{\infty} \frac{1}{(2n+1)!}$

(viii) $e^{ax} = 1 + \frac{(ax)}{1!} + \frac{(ax)^2}{2!} + \frac{(ax)^3}{3!} + \dots + \frac{(ax)^n}{n!} + \dots \infty$

(ix) $\sum_{n=0}^{\infty} \frac{n}{n!} = e = \sum_{n=1}^{\infty} \frac{n}{n!}$

(x) $\sum_{n=0}^{\infty} \frac{n^2}{n!} = 2e = \sum_{n=1}^{\infty} \frac{n^2}{n!}$

(xi) $\sum_{n=0}^{\infty} \frac{n^3}{n!} = 5e = \sum_{n=1}^{\infty} \frac{n^3}{n!}$

(xii) $\sum_{n=0}^{\infty} \frac{n^4}{n!} = 15e = \sum_{n=1}^{\infty} \frac{n^4}{n!}$

(xiii) $\sum_{r=1}^{n} (a_r \pm b_r) = \sum_{r=1}^{n} a_r \pm \sum_{r=1}^{n} b_r$

(xiv) $\sum_{r=1}^{n} ka_r = k \sum_{r=1}^{n} a_r$

(xv) $\sum_{r=1}^{n} k = k + k + \dots n$ times $= n.k$, where k is a constant.

(xvi) $\sum_{r=1}^{n} r = 1 + 2 + \dots + n = \frac{n(n+1)}{2}$

(xvii) Sum of first n even natural numbers.
i.e. $2 + 4 + 6 + \dots + 2n = n(n+1)$

(xviii) Sum of first n odd natural numbers.
i.e. $1 + 3 + 5 + \dots + (2n-1) = n^2$

(xix) $\sum_{r=1}^{n} r^2 = 1^2 + 2^2 + 3^2 + \ldots + n^2 = \frac{n(n+1)(2n+1)}{6}$

(xx) $\sum_{r=1}^{n} r^3 = 1^3 + 2^3 + 3^3 + \ldots + n^3 = \left[\frac{n(n+1)}{2}\right]^2$

(xxi) $\sum_{r=1}^{n} r^4 = 1^4 + 2^4 + 3^4 + \ldots + n^4 = \frac{n(n+1)(6n^3 + 9n^2 + n - 1)}{30}$

(xxii) Sum of n terms of series

$1^2 - 2^2 + 3^2 - 4^2 + 5^2 - 6^2 + 7^2 - 8^2 + \ldots$

Case I When n is odd $= \frac{n(n+1)}{2}$

Case II When n is even $= \frac{-n(n+1)}{2}$

(xxiii) $2 \sum_{i<j=1}^{n} a_i a_j = (a_1 + a_2 + \ldots + a_n)^2 - (a_1^2 + a_2^2 + \ldots + a_n^2)$

Chapter 06

Permutations and Combinations

Fundamental Principles of Counting

There are two Fundamental Principles of Counting

1. Multiplication Principle

If an operation can be performed in m ways and another operation can be performed in n ways. Then, the two operations taken together can be performed in mn ways. This can be extended to any finite number of operations.

2. Addition Principle

If an operation can be performed in m ways and another operation, which is independent of the first, can be performed in n ways. Then, either of the two operations can be performed in $m+n$ ways. This can be extended to any finite number of mutually exclusive events.

Factorial

For any natural number n, we define factorial as

$$n! \text{ or } \underline{|n} = n(n-1)(n-2)\ldots 3\times 2\times 1.$$

The notation $n!$ represent the product of first n natural numbers.

 Value Points

- $0! = 1! = 1$
- Factorials of negative integers and fractions are not defined.
- $n! = n(n-1)! = n(n-1)(n-2)!$
- $\dfrac{n!}{r!} = n(n-1)(n-2)\cdots(r+1)$
- $n!+1$ is not divisible by any natural number between 2 and n.

Exponent of a Prime p in $n!$

If p is prime and p^r divides $n!$, then maximum exponent of prime p in $n!$ is given by $E_p(n!) = \left[\frac{n}{p}\right] + \left[\frac{n}{p^2}\right] + \left[\frac{n}{p^3}\right] + \dots$

Permutation

Each of the different arrangement which can be made by taking some or all of a number of things is called a permutation.

Mathematically The number of ways of arranging n distinct objects in a row taking $r (0 < r \le n)$ at a time is denoted by $P(n, r)$ or ${}^nP_r$.

i.e. $${}^nP_r = \frac{n!}{(n-r)!}$$

Properties of Permutation

(i) ${}^nP_n = n(n-1)(n-2)\dots 1 = n!$ (ii) ${}^nP_0 = \frac{n!}{n!} = 1$

(iii) ${}^nP_1 = n$ (iv) ${}^nP_{n-1} = n!$

(v) ${}^nP_r = n \cdot {}^{n-1}P_{r-1} = n(n-1) \cdot {}^{n-2}P_{r-2} = n(n-1)(n-2) \cdot {}^{n-3}P_{r-3}$

(vi) ${}^{n-1}P_r + r \cdot {}^{n-1}P_{r-1} = {}^nP_r$

(vii) $\frac{{}^nP_r}{{}^nP_{r-1}} = n - r + 1$

Value Points

- The number of permutations of n different things taken r at a time, when each thing may be repeated any number of times is n^r.
- The number of permutations of n different objects taken r at a time, where $0 < r \le n$ and the objects do not repeat, is $n(n-1)(n-2)\dots(n-r+1)$, which is denoted by ${}^nP_r$ or $P(n, r)$.
- The number of permutations of n different things taken all at a time is ${}^nP_n = n!$.
- The number of permutations of n things taken all at a time, in which p are alike of one kind, q are alike of second kind and r are alike of third kind and rest are different is $\frac{n!}{p!q!r!}$.
- The number of permutations of n things taken all at a time, in which p_1 are alike of one kind p_2 are alike of second kind, p_3 are alike of third kind,...., p_r are alike of rth kind and

  $p_1 + p_2 + p_3 + \dots + p_r = n$ is $\frac{n!}{p_1!p_2!p_3!\dots p_r!}$

Restricted Permutation

(i) Number of permutations of n different things taken r at a time,

(a) when a particular thing is to be included in each arrangement is $r \cdot {}^{n-1}P_{r-1}$.

(b) when a particular thing is always excluded is ${}^{n-1}P_r$.

(ii) Number of permutations of n different objects taken r at a time in which m particular objects are always

(a) excluded $= {}^{n-m}P_r$ (b) included $= {}^{n-m}P_{r-m} \times r!$

(iii) Number of permutations of n different things taken all at a time, when m specified things always come together is $m!\,(n-m+1)!$.

(iv) Number of permutations of n different things taken all at a time, when m specified things never come together is

$$n! - m! \times (n-m+1)!.$$

(v) Number of permutations of n different things, taken r at a time, when $p\,(p<r)$ particular things are to be always included in each arrangement is $p!\{r-(p-1)\} \cdot {}^{n-p}P_{r-p}$.

Circular Permutation

In a circular permutation, firstly we fix the position of one of the objects and then arrange the other objects in all possible ways.

(i) Number of circular permutations of n different things taken all at a time is $(n-1)!$, if clockwise and anti-clockwise orders are taken as different.

(ii) Number of circular permutations of n different things taken all at a time, when clockwise or anti-clockwise orders are not different $= \frac{1}{2}(n-1)!$.

(iii) Number of circular permutations of n different things taken r at a time, when clockwise or anti-clockwise orders are taken as different is $\frac{{}^nP_r}{r}$.

(iv) Number of circular permutations of n different things, taken r at a time, when clockwise or anti-clockwise orders are not different is $\frac{{}^nP_r}{2r}$.

(v) If we mark numbers 1 to n on chairs in a round table, then n persons sitting around table is $n!$.

Combination

Each of the different groups or selections which can be made by some or all of a number of given things without reference to the order of the things in each group is called a combination.

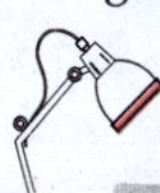

EXPERT Scale Up

'Permutations Prioritise, Combinations Choose'. This can help us to remember that permutations are about ordered arrangements and combinations are simply about choosing items.

Mathematically The number of combinations of n different things taken r at a time is $C(n, r)$ or ${}^nC_r$ or $\binom{n}{r}$ i.e. ${}^nC_r = \dfrac{n!}{r!(n-r)!}$, $0 \le r \le n$

Properties of Combination

(i) ${}^nC_0 = {}^nC_n = 1$ (ii) ${}^nC_1 = n$ (iii) ${}^nC_r = {}^nC_{n-r}$

(iv) If ${}^nC_r = {}^nC_p$, then either $r = p$ or $r + p = n$

(v) ${}^nC_r = \dfrac{{}^nP_r}{r!}$ (vi) ${}^nC_r + {}^nC_{r-1} = {}^{n+1}C_r$

(vii) $n \cdot {}^{n-1}C_{r-1} = (n-r+1)\,{}^nC_{r-1}$

(viii) ${}^nC_r = \dfrac{n}{r}\,{}^{n-1}C_{r-1} = \dfrac{n(n-1)}{r(r-1)}\,{}^{n-2}C_{r-2}$

(ix) ${}^nC_0 + {}^nC_1 + {}^nC_2 + \ldots + {}^nC_n = 2^n$

(x) ${}^nC_0 + {}^nC_2 + {}^nC_4 + \ldots = {}^nC_1 + {}^nC_3 + \ldots = 2^{n-1}$

(xi) ${}^{2n+1}C_0 + {}^{2n+1}C_1 + {}^{2n+1}C_2 + \ldots + {}^{2n+1}C_n = 2^{2n}$

(xii) ${}^nC_n + {}^{n+1}C_n + {}^{n+2}C_n + \ldots + {}^{2n-1}C_n = {}^{2n}C_{n+1}$

(xiii) If n is even, then the greatest value of ${}^nC_r$ is ${}^nC_{n/2}$.

(xiv) If n is odd, then the greatest value of ${}^nC_r$ is ${}^nC_{\frac{(n+1)}{2}}$.

Knowledge Booster

- The number of combinations of n different things taken r at a time allowing repetitions is ${}^{n+r-1}C_r$.
- The total number of combinations of n different objects taken r at a time in which
  - (a) m particular objects are excluded = ${}^{n-m}C_r$.
  - (b) m particular objects are included = ${}^{n-m}C_{r-m}$.

Applications of Permutation and Combination

1. Number of Functions

If a set A has m elements and set B has n elements, then

(i) number of functions from A to B is n^m.

(ii) number of one-one function from A to B is ${}^nP_m, m \le n$.

(iii) number of onto functions from A to B is
$$n^m - {}^nC_1(n-1)^m + {}^nC_2(n-2)^m \dots ; m \le n.$$

(iv) number of increasing (decreasing) functions from A to B is ${}^nC_m, m \le n$.

(v) number of non-increasing (non-decreasing) functions from A to B is ${}^{m+n-1}C_m$.

(vi) number of bijective (one-one, onto) functions from A to B is $n!$, if $m = n$.

2. Use in Geometry

(i) Given, n distinct points in the plane, no three of which are collinear, then the number of line segments formed $= {}^nC_2$.

(ii) Given, n distinct points in the plane, in which m are collinear $(m \ge 3)$, then the number of line segments is $({}^nC_2 - {}^mC_2) + 1$.

(iii) Given, n distinct points in the plane, no three of which are collinear, then the number of triangle formed $= {}^nC_3$

(iv) Given, n distinct points in a plane, in which m are collinear $(m \ge 3)$, then the number of triangle formed $= {}^nC_3 - {}^mC_3$

(v) The number of diagonals in a n-sided closed polygon $= {}^nC_2 - n$

(vi) Given, n points on the circumference of a circle, then
(a) number of straight lines $= {}^nC_2$ (b) number of triangles $= {}^nC_3$
(c) number of quadrilaterals $= {}^nC_4$

(vii) Number of rectangles of any size in a square of $n \times n$ is $\sum_{r=1}^{n} r^3$ and number of square of any size is $\sum_{r=1}^{n} r^2$.

(viii) In a rectangle of $n \times p\,(n < p)$, numbers of rectangles of any size is ${}^{n+1}C_2 \cdot {}^{P+1}C_2$ or $\dfrac{np}{4}(n+1)(p+1)$ and number of squares of any size is $\sum_{r=1}^{n}(n+1-r)(p+1-r)$.

(ix) Suppose n straight lines are drawn in the plane such that no two lines are parallel and no three lines are concurrent, then number of parts which these divides the plane is equal to $1 + \sum n$.

Competition Insight

Prime Factors

Any natural number >1, can be expressed as product of primes.

Let $n = p_1^{\alpha_1} p_2^{\alpha_2} p_3^{\alpha_3} \dots p_r^{\alpha_r}$, where

$p_i, i = 1, 2, 3, \dots, r,$ are prime numbers.

$\alpha_i, i = 1, 2, 3, \dots, r,$ are positive integers.

(i) Number of distinct positive integral divisors of n (including 1 and n) is $(\alpha_1 + 1)(\alpha_2 + 1)(\alpha_3 + 1)\dots(\alpha_r + 1)$.

(ii) Sum of distinct positive integral divisors of n is

$$\frac{(p_1^{\alpha_1+1} - 1)}{p_1 - 1} \cdot \frac{(p_2^{\alpha_2+1} - 1)}{p_2 - 1} \cdot \frac{(p_3^{\alpha_3+1} - 1)}{p_3 - 1} \dots \frac{(p_r^{\alpha_r+1} - 1)}{p_r - 1}$$

(iii) Total number of divisors of n (excluding 1 and n), is $(\alpha_1 + 1)(\alpha_2 + 1)(\alpha_3 + 1)\dots(\alpha_r + 1) - 2$.

(iv) Total number of divisors of n (excluding 1 or n), is $(\alpha_1 + 1)(\alpha_2 + 1)(\alpha_3 + 1)\dots(\alpha_r + 1) - 1$.

(v) The number of ways in which n can be resolved as a product of two factors is

(a) $\frac{1}{2}(\alpha_1 + 1)(\alpha_2 + 1)(\alpha_3 + 1)\dots(\alpha_r + 1)$, if n is not a perfect square.

(b) $\frac{1}{2}[(\alpha_1 + 1)(\alpha_2 + 1)(\alpha_3 + 1)\dots(\alpha_r + 1) + 1]$, if n is a perfect square.

(vi) The number of ways in which n can be resolved into two factors which are prime to each other is 2^{r-1}, where r is the number of different factors in n.

3. Integral Solutions

(i) The number of integral solutions of $x_1 + x_2 + \dots + x_r = n$, where $x_1, x_2, \dots x_r \geq 0$ is ${}^{n+r-1}C_{r-1}$ or ${}^{n+r-1}C_n$.

(ii) Number of integral solutions of $x_1 + x_2 + \dots + x_r = n$, where $x_1, x_2, \dots, x_r \geq 1$, is ${}^{n-1}C_{r-1}$.

4. Sum of Digits

(i) Sum of the numbers formed by taking all the given n digits

$$= (\text{Sum of all the } n \text{ digits}) \times (n-1)! \times \underbrace{(111\dots\dots1)}_{n\text{-times}}.$$

(ii) The sum of all digits in the unit place of all numbers formed with the help of $a_1, a_2, \ldots, a_n$ all at a time (repetition of digits is not allowed) is $(n-1)!(a_1 + a_2 + \ldots + a_n)$.

(iii) The sum of all digits of numbers that can be formed by using the digits $a_1, a_2, \ldots, a_n$ (repetition of digits is not allowed) is
$(n-1)!(a_1 + a_2 + \ldots + a_n)\left(\frac{10^n - 1}{9}\right)$ and if repetition of digits is allowed, then sum of all digits is

$$n^{n-1}(a_1 + a_2 + a_3 + \ldots + a_n)\left(\frac{10^n - 1}{9}\right)$$

5. Arrangements

(i) The number of ways in which m (one type of different things) and n (another type of different things) can be arranged in a row so that all the second type of things come together is $n!(m+1)!$.

(ii) The number of ways in which m (one type of different things) and n (another type of different things) can be arranged in a row so that no two things of the same type come together is

$$2 \times m!n!, \text{ provided } m = n$$

(iii) The number of ways in which m (one type of different things) and n (another type of different things) $(m \geq n)$, can be arranged in a circle so that no two things of second type come together $(m-1)!\,{}^mP_n$ and when things of second type come together $= m!n!$

Knowledge Booster

Number of permutations of n different objects, taken r at a time, when $p(p < r)$ particular objects are to be always included in each arrangements, is $p!(r-(p-1))^{n-p}P_{r-p}$

(iv) The number of ways in which m things of one type and n things of another type (all different) $(m \geq n)$, can be arranged in the form of a garland so that all the second type of things come together, is $\frac{m!n!}{2}$ and if no two things of second type come together, is $\frac{(m-1)!\,{}^mP_n}{2}$

(v) If there are l objects of one kind, m objects of second kind, n objects of third kind and so on. Then, the number of possible arrangements permutations of r objects out of these objects = Coefficient of x^r in the expansion of

$$r!\left(1+\frac{x}{1!}+\frac{x^2}{2!}+\dots+\frac{x^l}{l!}\right)\left(1+\frac{x}{1!}+\frac{x^2}{2!}+\dots+\frac{x^m}{m!}\right)\left(1+\frac{x}{1!}+\frac{x^2}{2!}+\dots+\frac{x^n}{n!}\right).$$

Competition Insight

Dearrangements

If n distinct objects are arranged in a row, then the number of ways in which they can be dearranged so that no one of them occupies the place assigned to it is $n!\left[1-\frac{1}{1!}+\frac{1}{2!}-\frac{1}{3!}+\dots(-1)^n\frac{1}{n!}\right]$ and it is denoted by $D(n)$.

6. Selection

There are two types of selection, which are as follows

1. Selection from Different Items

(i) The number of ways of selecting at least one item from n distinct items is 2^n-1.

(ii) The number of ways of answering one or more of n questions is 2^n-1.

(iii) The number of ways of answering one or more of n questions when each question has an alternative is 3^n-1.

2. Selection from Identical Items

(i) The number of ways of selecting r items out of n identical items is 1.

(ii) The number of ways of selecting zero or more items out of n identical items is $(n+1)$.

(iii) The number of ways of selecting one or more out of $p+q+r$ items, where p are alike of one kind, q are alike of second kind and rest are alike of third kind, is $[(p+1)(q+1)(r+1)]-1$.

(iv) The number of ways of selecting one or more items from p identical items of one kind; q identical items of second kind; r identical items of third kind and other n are distinct, is $(p+1)(q+1)(r+1)2^n-1$.

(v) The number of ways of selecting r items from a group of n items in which p are identical $n \ge p+r$, is

${}^{n-p}C_r+{}^{n-p}C_{r-1}+{}^{n-p}C_{r-2}+\dots+{}^{n-p}C_0$, if $r \le p$

and ${}^{n-p}C_r+{}^{n-p}C_{r-1}+{}^{n-p}C_{r-2}+\dots+{}^{n-p}C_{r-p}$, if $r>p$

(vi) If there are m items of one kind, n items of another kind and so on. Then, the number of ways of choosing r items out of these items = coefficient of x^r in
$(1 + x + x^2 + \ldots + x^m)(1 + x + x^2 + \ldots + x^n)\ldots$

(vii) If there are m items of one kind, n items of another kind and so on. Then, the number of ways of choosing r items out of these items such that atleast one item of each kind is included in every selection = coefficient of x^r in

$$(x + x^2 + \ldots + x^m)(x + x^2 + \ldots + x^n)\ldots$$

7. Division into Groups

There are two types of division into groups, which are as follow

1. Division of Distinct Items into Groups

(i) The number of ways in which $(m + n)$ different things can be divided into two groups which contain m and n things respectively

$$= \frac{(m+n)!}{m!n!}, \text{ where } m \neq n$$

This can be extended to $(m + n + p)$ different things divided into three groups of m, n and p things respectively. In this case, number of ways $\frac{(m+n+p)!}{m!n!p!}$, where $m \neq n \neq p$.

(ii) The number of ways of dividing $2n$ different elements into two groups of n objects each is $\frac{(2n)!}{(n!)^2}$, when the distinction can be made between the groups, i.e. if the order of group is important. This can be extended to $3n$ different elements divided into 3 groups of n objects each. In this case, number of ways $= \frac{(3n)!}{(n!)^3}$.

(iii) The number of ways of dividing $2n$ different elements into two groups of n objects when no distinction can be made between the groups i.e. order of the group is not important is $\frac{(2n)!}{2!(n!)^2}$.

This can be extended to $3n$ different elements divided into 3 groups of n objects each.

In this case, number of ways $= \frac{(3n)!}{3!(n!)^3}$.

(iv) The number of ways in which mn different things can be divided equally into m groups each containing n objects, if order of the group is not important is $\frac{(mn)!}{(n!)^m m!}$.

(v) If the order of the group is important, then number of ways of dividing mn different things equally into m distinct groups each containing n objects is $\frac{(mn)!}{(n!)^m}$.

(vi) The number of ways of dividing n different things into r groups is $\frac{1}{r!}[r^n - {}^rC_1(r-1)^n + {}^rC_2(r-2)^n - {}^rC_3(r-3)^n + \dots]$.

(vii) The number of ways of dividing n different things into r groups taking into account the order of the groups and also the order of things in each group is

$$^{n+r-1}P_n = r(r+1)(r+2)\dots(r+n-1).$$

2. Division of Identical Items into Groups

(i) The number of ways of dividing n identical items among r persons, each of whom, can receive 0, 1, 2 or more items ($\le n$) is $^{n+r-1}C_{r-1}$.

Or The number of ways of dividing n identical items into r groups, if blank groups are allowed is $^{n+r-1}C_{r-1}$.

(ii) The number of ways of dividing n identical items among r persons, each one of whom receives at least one item is $^{n-1}C_{r-1}$.

Or The number of ways of dividing n identical items into r groups such that blank groups are not allowed is $^{n-1}C_{r-1}$.

(iii) The number of ways of dividing n identical things among r persons such that each gets 1, 2, 3, ... or k things is the coefficient of x^{n-r} in the expansion of $(1 + x + x^2 + \dots + x^{k-1})^r$.

(iv) The number of ways in which n identical items can be divided into r groups so that no group contains less than m items and more than $k (m < k)$ is coefficient of x^n in the expansion of $(x^m + x^{m+1} + \dots + x^k)^r$.

Chapter 07

Binomial Theorem and Principle of Mathematical Induction

An algebraic expression consisting of two terms with positive and negative sign between them is called **binomial expression.**

Binomial Theorem for Positive Integer

If n is any positive integer, then

$$(x+a)^n = {}^nC_0 x^n + {}^nC_1 x^{n-1} a + {}^nC_2 x^{n-2} a^2 + \ldots + {}^nC_n a^n.$$

i.e.
$$(x+a)^n = \sum_{r=0}^{n} {}^nC_r \, x^{n-r} a^r \qquad \ldots(\text{i})$$

where, x and a are real numbers and ${}^nC_0, {}^nC_1, {}^nC_2, \ldots, {}^nC_n$ are called **binomial coefficients.**

Also, here Eq. (i) is called **Binomial theorem**, where

$${}^nC_r = \frac{n!}{r!(n-r)!} \text{ for } 0 \le r \le n.$$

Pascal's Triangle

A Pascal's triangle is an arrangement of numbers (binomical coefficients) in a triangular form.

Index	Coefficients
0	${}^0C_0(=1)$
1	${}^1C_0(=1)$ ${}^1C_1(=1)$
2	${}^2C_0(=1)$ ${}^2C_1(=2)$ ${}^2C_2(=1)$
3	${}^3C_0(=1)$ ${}^3C_1(=3)$ ${}^3C_2(=3)$ ${}^3C_3(=1)$

Properties of Binomial Theorem for Positive Integer

(i) Total number of terms in the expansion of $(x + a)^n$ is $(n + 1)$ i.e. finite number of terms.

(ii) The sum of the indices of x and a in each term is n.

(iii) The above expansion is also true when x and a are complex numbers.

(iv) The coefficient of terms equidistant from the beginning and the end are equal. These coefficients are known as the binomial coefficients i.e. ${}^nC_r = {}^nC_{n-r}$, where $r = 0, 1, 2, \ldots, n$.

(v) The values of the binomial coefficients steadily increase to maximum and then steadily decrease.

(vi) In the binomial expansion of $(x + a)^n$, the r th term from the end is $(n - r + 2)$th term from the beginning.

(vii) If n is a positive integer, then number of terms in $(x + y + z)^n$ is $\dfrac{(n+1)(n+2)}{2}$.

Knowledge Booster

The number of terms in the expansion of $(x_1 + x_2 + \ldots + x_r)^n$ is ${}^{n+r-1}C_{r-1}$.

Some Special Cases

(i) $(x - a)^n = {}^nC_0\, x^n - {}^nC_1 x^{n-1} a + {}^nC_2 x^{n-2} a^2 - {}^nC_3 x^{n-3} a^3 + \ldots + (-1)^n\, {}^nC_n\, a^n$

i.e. $(x - a)^n = \sum_{r=0}^{n} (-1)^r\, {}^nC_r \cdot x^{n-r} \cdot a^r$

(ii) $(1 + x)^n = {}^nC_0 + {}^nC_1 x + {}^nC_2 x^2 + \ldots + {}^nC_r\, x^r + \ldots + {}^nC_n\, x^n$

i.e. $(1 + x)^n = \sum_{r=0}^{n} {}^nC_r \cdot x^r$

(iii) $(1 - x)^n = {}^nC_0 - {}^nC_1 x + {}^nC_2 x^2 - {}^nC_3 x^3 + \ldots + (-1)^r\, {}^nC_r x^r + \ldots + (-1)^n\, {}^nC_n x^n$

i.e. $(1 - x)^n = \sum_{r=0}^{n} (-1)^r\, {}^nC_r \cdot x^r$

(iv) The coefficient of x^r in the expansion of $(1 + x)^n$ is ${}^nC_r$ and in the expansion of $(1 - x)^n$ is $(-1)^r\, {}^nC_r$.

(v) (a) $(x+a)^n+(x-a)^n=2\,({}^nC_0x^na^0+{}^nC_2x^{n-2}a^2+\ldots)$

(b) $(x+a)^n-(x-a)^n=2\,({}^nC_1x^{n-1}a+{}^nC_3x^{n-3}a^3+\ldots)$

(vi) (a) If n is odd, then $(x+a)^n+(x-a)^n$ and $(x+a)^n-(x-a)^n$ both have the same number of terms equal to $\left(\frac{n+1}{2}\right)$.

(b) If n is even, then $(x+a)^n+(x-a)^n$ has $\left(\frac{n}{2}+1\right)$ terms and $(x+a)^n-(x-a)^n$ has $\left(\frac{n}{2}\right)$ terms.

General Term in a Binomial Expansion

(i) General term in the expansion of $(x+a)^n$ is

$$T_{r+1}={}^nC_r\,x^{n-r}\,a^r$$

(ii) General term in the expansion of $(x-a)^n$ is

$$T_{r+1}=(-1)^r\,{}^nC_r\,x^{n-r}\,a^r$$

(iii) General term in the expansion of $(1+x)^n$ is $T_{r+1}={}^nC_r\,x^r$

(iv) General term in the expansion of $(1-x)^n$ is

$$T_{r+1}=(-1)^r\,{}^nC_r\,x^r$$

Value Points

- Coefficient of x^m in the expansion of $\left(ax^p+\frac{b}{x^q}\right)^n$ is the coefficient of T_{r+1}, where $r=\frac{np-m}{p+q}$.
- The term independent of x in the expansion of $\left(ax^p+\frac{b}{x^q}\right)^n$ is the coefficient of T_{r+1}, where $r=\frac{np}{p+q}$.
- If the coefficient of rth, $(r+1)$ th and $(r+2)$ th term of $(1+x)^n$ are in AP, then $n^2-(4r+1)n+4r^2=2$
- In the expansion of $(x+a)^n$, $\frac{T_{r+1}}{T_r}=\frac{n-r+1}{r}\times\frac{a}{x}$
- (a) The coefficient of x^{n-1} in the expansion of
  $$(x-1)(x-2)\ldots.(x-n)=-\frac{n(n+1)}{2}$$
- The coefficient of x^{n-1} in the expansion of
  $$(x+1)(x+2)\ldots.(x+n)=\frac{n(n+1)}{2}$$

- If the coefficients of pth and qth terms in the expansion of $(1+x)^n$ are equal, then $p+q=n+2$.
- If the coefficients of x^r and x^{r+1} in the expansion of $\left(a+\frac{x}{b}\right)^n$ are equal, then $n=(r+1)(ab+1)-1$.

Middle Term in a Binomial Expansion

(i) If n is even in the expansion of $(x+a)^n$ or $(x-a)^n$, then the middle term is $\left(\frac{n}{2}+1\right)$th term.

(ii) If n is odd in the expansion of $(x+a)^n$ or $(x-a)^n$, then the middle terms are $\frac{(n+1)}{2}$th term and $\frac{(n+3)}{2}$th term.

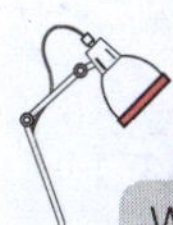

EXPERT Scale Up

When there are two middle terms in the expansion, then their binomial coefficients are equal.

Greatest Coefficient

Binomial coefficient of middle term is the greatest binomial coefficient.

(i) If n is even, then in $(x+a)^n$, the greatest coefficient is ${}^nC_{n/2}$.

(ii) If n is odd, then in $(x+a)^n$, the greatest coefficient is ${}^nC_{\frac{n-1}{2}}$ $\left(\text{or } {}^nC_{\frac{n+1}{2}}\right)$.

Greatest Term

In the expansion of $(x+a)^n$,

(i) If $\dfrac{n+1}{\left|\frac{x}{a}\right|+1}$ is an integer $=p$ (say), then greatest terms are T_p and T_{p+1}.

(ii) If $\dfrac{n+1}{\left|\frac{x}{a}\right|+1}$ is not an integer with m as integral part of $\dfrac{n+1}{\frac{x}{a}+1}$, then T_{m+1} is the greatest term.

Knowledge Booster

Let T_{r+1} be the greatest term in $(x+a)^n$.

Then, $\frac{T_{r+1}}{T_r} \geq 1$ and $\frac{T_{r+2}}{T_{r+1}} \leq 1 \Rightarrow r \leq \frac{n+1}{\left|\frac{x}{a}\right|+1}$

Divisibility Problems

From the expansion, $(1+x)^n = 1 + {}^nC_1 x + {}^nC_2 x^2 + \ldots + {}^nC_n x^n$

We can conclude that

(i) $(1+x)^n - 1 = {}^nC_1 x + {}^nC_2 x^2 + \ldots + {}^nC_n x^n$ is divisible by x i.e. it is a multiple of x.

or $$(1+x)^n - 1 = M(x)$$

(ii) $(1+x)^n - 1 - nx = {}^nC_2 x^2 + {}^nC_3 x^3 + \ldots + {}^nC_n x^n = M(x^2)$

(iii) $(1+x)^n - 1 - nx - \frac{n(n-1)}{2} x^2 = {}^nC_3 x^3 + {}^nC_4 x^4 + \ldots + {}^nC_n x^n = M(x^3)$

Important Formulae on Binomial Coefficients

If $C_0, C_1, C_2, \ldots, C_n$ are the coefficients of $(1+x)^n$, where $C_r = {}^nC_r$, then

(i) ${}^nC_r + {}^nC_{r-1} = {}^{n+1}C_r$ (ii) $\frac{{}^nC_r}{{}^{n-1}C_{r-1}} = \frac{n}{r}$

(iii) $\frac{{}^nC_r}{{}^nC_{r-1}} = \frac{n-r+1}{r}$

(iv) $C_0 + C_1 + C_2 + \ldots + C_n = 2^n$

(v) $C_0 + C_2 + C_4 + \ldots = C_1 + C_3 + C_5 + \ldots = 2^{n-1}$

(vi) $C_0 - C_2 + C_4 - C_6 + \ldots = (\sqrt{2})^n \cos \frac{n\pi}{4}$

(vii) $C_1 - C_3 + C_5 - C_7 + \ldots = (\sqrt{2})^n \sin \frac{n\pi}{4}$

(viii) $C_0 - C_1 + C_2 - C_3 + \ldots + (-1)^n C_n = 0$

(ix) $C_1 - 2 \cdot C_2 + 3 \cdot C_3 - \ldots = 0$

(x) $C_0 + 2 \cdot C_1 + 3 \cdot C_2 + \ldots + (n+1) \cdot C_n = (n+2) 2^{n-1}$

(xi) $C_0 C_r + C_1 C_{r+1} + \ldots + C_{n-r} C_n = {}^{2n}C_{n-r}$

$$= {}^{2n}C_{n+r} = \frac{(2n)!}{(n-r)!(n+r)!}$$

(xii) $C_0^2 + C_1^2 + C_2^2 + \ldots + C_n^2 = {}^{2n}C_n = \dfrac{(2n)!}{(n!)^2}$

(xiii) $C_0^2 - C_1^2 + C_2^2 - C_3^2 + \ldots + (-1)^n \cdot C_n^2 = \begin{cases} 0 & \text{if } n \text{ is odd.} \\ (-1)^{n/2} \cdot {}^nC_{n/2} & \text{if } n \text{ is even.} \end{cases}$

(xiv) $C_1^{\,2} - 2C_2^{\,2} + 3C_3^2 - \ldots + (-1)^n \; n \cdot C_n^2$

$$= (-1)^{\frac{n}{2}-1} \cdot \frac{n}{2} \cdot \frac{n!}{\left(\frac{n}{2}\right)! \left(\frac{n}{2}\right)!}, \text{ when } n \text{ is even.}$$

(xv) $C_0 + \dfrac{C_1}{2} + \dfrac{C_2}{3} + \ldots + \dfrac{C_n}{n+1} = \dfrac{2^{n+1} - 1}{(n+1)}$

(xvi) $C_0 - \dfrac{C_1}{2} + \dfrac{C_2}{3} - \dfrac{C_3}{4} + \ldots + (-1)^n \dfrac{C_n}{n+1} = \dfrac{1}{n+1}$

(xvii) $C_0 + \dfrac{C_1}{2} + \dfrac{C_2}{2^2} + \dfrac{C_3}{2^3} + \ldots + \dfrac{C_n}{2^n} = \left(\dfrac{3}{2}\right)^n$

(xviii) $\displaystyle\sum_{r=0}^{n} (-1)^r \; {}^nC_r \left\{ \frac{1}{2^r} + \frac{3^r}{2^{2r}} + \frac{7^r}{2^{3r}} + \frac{15^r}{2^{4r}} + \ldots \text{ upto } m \text{ terms} \right\}$

$$= \frac{2^{mn} - 1}{2^{mn} \, (2^n - 1)}$$

Competition Insight

Binomial Theorem for Any Index

If n is any rational number, then

$$(1+x)^n = 1 + nx + \frac{n(n-1)}{1 \cdot 2} x^2 + \frac{n(n-1)(n-2)}{1 \cdot 2 \cdot 3} x^3 + \ldots, |x| < 1$$

(i) In the above expansion, if n is any positive integer, then the series in RHS is finite and if n is negative/ rational number, then there are infinite number of terms exist.

(ii) General term in the expansion of $(1+x)^n$ is

$$T_{r+1} = \frac{n(n-1)(n-2)\ldots[n-(r-1)]}{r!} x^r.$$

(iii) Expansion of $(x+a)^n$ for any rational index

Case I When $x > a$ i.e. $\frac{a}{x} < 1$

In this case, $(x+a)^n = \left\{x\left(1+\frac{a}{x}\right)\right\}^n = x^n\left(1+\frac{a}{x}\right)^n$

$$= x^n\left\{1 + n\cdot\frac{a}{x} + \frac{n(n-1)}{2!}\left(\frac{a}{x}\right)^2 + \frac{n(n-1)(n-2)}{3!}\left(\frac{a}{x}\right)^3 + \dots\right\}$$

Case II When $x < a$ i.e. $\frac{x}{a} < 1$

In this case, $(x+a)^n = \left\{a\left(1+\frac{x}{a}\right)\right\}^n = a^n\left(1+\frac{x}{a}\right)^n$

$$= a^n\left\{1 + n\cdot\frac{x}{a} + \frac{n(n-1)}{2!}\left(\frac{x}{a}\right)^2 + \frac{n(n-1)(n-2)}{3!}\left(\frac{x}{a}\right)^3 + \dots\right\}$$

(iv) $(1-x)^{-n} = 1 + nx + \frac{n(n+1)}{2!}x^2 + \frac{n(n+1)(n+2)}{3!}x^3 + \dots + \frac{n(n+1)(n+2)\dots(n+r-1)}{r!}x^r + \dots$

(v) $(1+x)^{-n} = 1 - nx + \frac{n(n+1)}{2!}x^2 - \frac{n(n+1)(n+2)}{3!}x^3 + \dots + (-1)^r\frac{n(n+1)(n+2)\dots(n+r-1)}{r!}x^r + \dots$

(vi) $(1-x)^n = 1 - nx + \frac{n(n-1)}{2!}x^2 - \frac{n(n-1)(n-2)}{3!}x^3 + \dots + (-1)^r\frac{n(n-1)(n-2)\dots(n-r+1)}{r!}x^r + \dots$

(vii) $(1+x)^n = 1 + nx$, if $x^2, x^3, \dots$ are all very small as compared to x.

Chapter 08

Matrices

Matrix

A matrix is a rectangular arrangement of numbers (real or complex) which may be represented as

$$A = \begin{bmatrix} a_{11} & a_{12} & a_{13} & \cdots & a_{1n} \\ a_{21} & a_{22} & a_{23} & \cdots & a_{2n} \\ \cdots & \cdots & \cdots & \cdots & \cdots \\ a_{m1} & a_{m2} & a_{m3} & \cdots & a_{mn} \end{bmatrix}.$$

Matrix is enclosed by [ ] or ( ).

Compact form of the above matrix is represented by $[a_{ij}]_{m\times n}$ or $A=[a_{ij}]$.

Element of a Matrix

The numbers $a_{11}, a_{12}, \ldots$ etc., in the above matrix are known as the elements of the matrix, generally represented as a_{ij}, which denotes element in the ith row and jth column.

Order of a Matrix

The above matrix has m rows and n columns, then matrix A is of order $m\times n$.

EXPERT Scale Up

A matrix has number of elements equal to product of its number of rows and number of columns.

Types of Matrices

(i) **Row Matrix** A matrix having only one row and any number of columns is called a row matrix. i.e. $A=[a_{ij}]_{1\times n}$

(ii) **Column Matrix** A matrix having only one column and any number of rows is called column matrix. i.e. $A=[a_{ij}]_{m\times 1}$

(iii) **Null/Zero Matrix** A matrix of any order, having all its elements as zero, is called a null/zero matrix, i.e. $a_{ij} = 0, \forall\ i, j$.

(iv) **Square Matrix** A matrix of order $m \times n$, such that $m = n$, is called a square matrix.

(v) **Diagonal Matrix** A square matrix $A = [a_{ij}]_{m \times n}$ is called a diagonal matrix, if all the elements except those in the leading diagonals are zero, i.e. $a_{ij} = 0$ for $i \neq j$.

It can be represented as $A = \text{diag}\,[a_{11}\ a_{22} \dots a_{nn}]$.

(vi) **Scalar Matrix** A square matrix in which every non-diagonal element is zero and all diagonal elements are equal, is called scalar matrix, i.e. in scalar matrix, $a_{ij} = 0$, for $i \neq j$ and $a_{ij} = k$, for $i = j$.

(vii) **Unit/Identity Matrix** A square matrix, in which every non-diagonal element is zero and every diagonal element is 1, is called unit matrix or an identity matrix

i.e. $a_{ij} = \begin{cases} 0, \text{ when } i \neq j \\ 1, \text{ when } i = j \end{cases}$

(viii) **Rectangular Matrix** A matrix of order $m \times n$, such that $m \neq n$, is called rectangular matrix.

(ix) **Horizontal Matrix** A matrix in which the number of rows is less than the number of columns, is called a horizontal matrix.

(x) **Vertical Matrix** A matrix in which the number of rows is greater than the number of columns, is called a vertical matrix.

(xi) **Upper Triangular Matrix** A square matrix $A = [a_{ij}]_{n \times n}$ is called a upper triangular matrix, if $a_{ij} = 0, \forall\ i > j$.

(xii) **Lower Triangular Matrix** A square matrix $A = [a_{ij}]_{n \times n}$ is called a lower triangular matrix, if $a_{ij} = 0, \forall\ i < j$.

Knowledge Booster

Number of zeros in a diagonal matrix is given by $n^2 - n$ and minimum number of zeros in a triangular matrix is given by $\frac{n(n-1)}{2}$, where n is a order of matrix.

(xiii) **Submatrix** A matrix which is obtained from a given matrix by deleting any number of rows or columns or both is called a submatrix of the given matrix.

(xiv) **Equal Matrices** Two matrices A and B are said to be equal, if both having same order and corresponding elements of the matrices are equal.

(xv) **Singular Matrix** A square matrix A is said to be singular matrix, if determinant of A denoted by det (A) or $|A|$ is zero i.e. $|A|=0$, otherwise it is a non-singular matrix.

Algebra of Matrices

1. Addition of Matrices

Let A and B be two matrices each of order $m \times n$. Then, the sum of matrices $A+B$ is defined only if matrices A and B are of same order.

If $A=[a_{ij}]_{m \times n}$ and $B=[b_{ij}]_{m \times n}$. Then, $A+B=[a_{ij}+b_{ij}]_{m \times n}$.

Properties of Addition of Matrices

If A, B and C are three matrices of order $m \times n$, then

(i) **Commutative Law** $A+B=B+A$

(ii) **Associative Law** $(A+B)+C=A+(B+C)$

(iii) **Existence of Additive Identity** A zero matrix O of order $m \times n$ (same as of A), is additive identity, if

$$A+O=A=O+A$$

(iv) **Existence of Additive Inverse** If A is a square matrix, then the matrix $(-A)$ is called additive inverse, if

$$A+(-A)=0=(-A)+A$$

(v) **Cancellation Law** $A+B=A+C \Rightarrow B=C$ [left cancellation law]

$B+A=C+A \Rightarrow B=C$ [right cancellation law]

2. Subtraction of Matrices

Let A and B be two matrices of the same order, then subtraction of matrices, $A-B$, is defined as

$$A-B=[a_{ij}-b_{ij}]_{m \times n}$$

where $A=[a_{ij}]_{m \times n}$ and $B=[b_{ij}]_{m \times n}$

3. Multiplication of a Matrix by a Scalar

Let $A=[a_{ij}]_{m \times n}$ be a matrix and k be any scalar. Then, the matrix obtained by multiplying each element of A by k is called the scalar multiple of A by k and is denoted by kA, given as

$$kA=[ka_{ij}]_{m \times n}$$

Properties of Scalar Multiplication

If A and B are two matrices of order $m \times n$, then

(i) $k(A+B) = kA + kB$ (ii) $(k_1 + k_2)A = k_1 A + k_2 A$

(iii) $k_1 k_2 A = k_1(k_2 A) = k_2(k_1 A)$ (iv) $(-k)A = -(kA) = k(-A)$

4. Multiplication of Matrices

Let $A = [a_{ij}]_{m \times n}$ and $B = [b_{ij}]_{n \times p}$ are two matrices such that the number of columns of A is equal to the number of rows of B, then multiplication of A and B is denoted by AB, is given by $c_{ij} = \sum_{k=1}^{n} a_{ik} b_{kj}$,

where c_{ij} is the element of matrix C and $C = AB$ of order $m \times p$.

e.g. If $A = \begin{bmatrix} a_1 & a_2 \\ a_3 & a_4 \end{bmatrix}$ and $B = \begin{bmatrix} b_1 & b_2 \\ b_3 & b_4 \end{bmatrix}$, then $AB = \begin{bmatrix} a_1 b_1 + a_2 b_3 & a_1 b_2 + a_2 b_4 \\ a_3 b_1 + a_4 b_3 & a_3 b_2 + a_4 b_4 \end{bmatrix}$.

Properties of Multiplication of Matrices

(i) **Associative Law** $(AB)C = A(BC)$

(ii) **Existence of Multiplicative Identity** $A \cdot I = A = I \cdot A$,

where I is called multiplicative Identity.

(iii) **Distributive Law** $A(B+C) = AB + AC$

(iv) **Cancellation Law** If A is non-singular matrix, then

$AB = AC \Rightarrow B = C$ [left cancellation law]

$BA = CA \Rightarrow B = C$ [right cancellation law]

(v) **Zero Matrix as the Product of Two Non-zero Matrices** $AB = O$, does not necessarily imply that $A = O$ or $B = O$ or both A and $B = O$.

Value Points

- If A and B are square matrices of the same order, (say n), then both the product AB and BA are defined and each is a square matrix of order n.
- In the matrix product AB, the matrix A is called premultiplier (prefactor) and B is called postmultiplier (postfactor).
- The rule of multiplication of matrices is row columnwise (or $\rightarrow \downarrow$ wise) the first row of AB is obtained by multiplying the first row of A with first, second, third,... columns of B respectively; similarly second row of A with first, second, third, ... columns of B, respectively and so on.
- Multiplication of diagonal matrices of same order will be commutative.

Positive Integral Powers of a Square Matrix

Let A be a square matrix. Then, we can define

(i) $A^{n+1} = A^n \cdot A$, where $n \in N$.

(ii) $A^m \cdot A^n = A^{m+n}$.

(iii) $(A^m)^n = A^{mn}, \forall m, n \in N$

Matrix Polynomial

Let $f(x) = a_0x^n + a_1x^{n-1} + a_2x^{n-2} + \ldots + a_n$.

Then, $f(A) = a_0A^n + a_1A^{n-1} + \ldots + a_n I_n$ is called the matrix polynomial.

Transpose of a Matrix

Let $A = [a_{ij}]_{m \times n}$ be a matrix of order $m \times n$. Then, the $n \times m$ matrix obtained by interchanging the rows and columns of A is called the transpose of A and is denoted by A' or A^T.

$$A' = A^T = [a_{ji}]_{n \times m}$$

Properties of Transpose

For any two matrices A and B of suitable orders, we have

(i) $(A')' = A$

(ii) $(A \pm B)' = A' \pm B'$

(iii) $(kA)' = kA'$

(iv) $(AB)' = B'A'$

(v) $(A^n)' = (A')^n$

(vi) $(ABC)' = C'B'A'$

Symmetric and Skew-Symmetric Matrices

(i) A square matrix $A = [a_{ij}]_{n \times n}$ is said to be **symmetric**, if $A' = A$. i.e. $a_{ij} = a_{ji}$, $\forall i$ and j.

(ii) A square matrix A is said to be **skew-symmetric**, if $A' = -A$, i.e. $a_{ij} = -a_{ji}$, $\forall i$ and j.

Properties of Symmetric and Skew-symmetric Matrices

(i) Elements of principal diagonal of a skew-symmetric matrix are all zero. i.e. $a_{ii} = -a_{ii} \Rightarrow 2a_{ii} = 0$ or $a_{ii} = 0$, for all values of i.

(ii) If A is a square matrix, then

(a) $A + A'$ is symmetric. (b) $A - A'$ is skew-symmetric matrix.

(iii) If A and B are two symmetric (or skew-symmetric) matrices of same order, then $A + B$ is also symmetric (or skew-symmetric).

(iv) If A is symmetric (or skew-symmetric), then kA (k is a scalar) is also symmetric (or skew-symmetric) matrix.

(v) If A and B are symmetric matrices of the same order, then the product AB is symmetric, iff $BA = AB$.

(vi) Every square matrix can be expressed uniquely as the sum of a symmetric and a skew-symmetric matrix.
i.e. Matrix A can be written as $\frac{1}{2}(A + A') + \frac{1}{2}(A - A')$

(vii) The matrix $B'AB$ is symmetric or skew-symmetric according as A is symmetric or skew-symmetric matrix.

(viii) All positive integral powers of a symmetric matrix are symmetric.

(ix) All positive odd integral powers of a skew-symmetric matrix are skew-symmetric and positive even integral powers of a skew-symmetric are symmetric matrix.

(x) If A and B are symmetric matrices of the same order, then
(a) $AB - BA$ is a skew-symmetric and
(b) $AB + BA$ is symmetric.

(xi) For a square matrix A, AA' and $A'A$ are symmetric matrices.

Invertible Matrices

If A is a square matrix of order m and B is another square matrix of order m such that $AB = BA = I$, then B is called the inverse matrix of A i.e. $B = A^{-1}$. Here, A is called invertible matrix.

 **Value Points**

A rectangular matrix is not invertible as $AB \neq BA$

- Every invertible matrix has a unique inverse.
- If A and B are invertible matrices of same order, then $(AB)^{-1} = B^{-1}A^{-1}$.

Trace of a Matrix

The sum of the diagonal elements of a square matrix A is called the trace of A, denoted by trace (A) or tr (A).

Properties of Trace of a Matrix

(i) Trace $(A \pm B) =$ Trace $(A) \pm$ Trace (B)
(ii) Trace $(kA) = k$ Trace (A)
(iii) Trace $(A') =$ Trace (A)
(iv) Trace $(I_n) = n$
(v) Trace $(O) = 0$
(vi) Trace $(AB) \neq$ Trace $(A) \times$ Trace (B)
(vii) Trace $(AA') \geq 0$

Competition Insight

Conjugate of a Matrix

The matrix obtained from a matrix A containing complex number as its elements, on replacing its elements by the corresponding conjugate complex number is called conjugate of A and is denoted by $\bar{A}$.

Properties of Conjugate of a Matrix

Let A and B are two matrices of order $m \times n$ and k be a scalar, then

(i) $(\overline{\bar{A}}) = A$

(ii) $(\overline{A+B}) = \bar{A} + \bar{B}$

(iii) $(\overline{AB}) = \bar{A}\bar{B}$

(iv) $(\overline{kA}) = k\bar{A}$

(v) $(\overline{A^n}) = (\bar{A})^n$

Transpose Conjugate of a Matrix

The transpose of the conjugate of a matrix A is called transpose conjugate of A and is denoted by A^θ or A^*

i.e. $(\overline{A'}) = (\bar{A})' = A^\theta$ or A^*

Properties of Transpose Conjugate of a Matrix

(i) $(A^*)^* = A$

(ii) $(A+B)^* = A^* + B^*$

(iii) $(kA)^* = \bar{k}A^*$

(iv) $(AB)^* = B^* A^*$

(v) $(A^n)^* = (A^*)^n$

Some Special Types of Matrices

1. Orthogonal Matrix

A square matrix of order n is said to be orthogonal, if $AA' = I_n = A'A$

Properties of Orthogonal Matrix

(i) If A is orthogonal matrix, then A' is also orthogonal matrix.

(ii) For any two orthogonal matrices A and B, AB and BA is also an orthogonal matrix.

(iii) If A is an orthogonal matrix, then A^{-1} is also orthogonal matrix, where $A^{-1} = A'$.

2. Idempotent Matrix

A square matrix A is said to be idempotent, if $A^2 = A$.

Properties of Idempotent Matrix

(i) If A and B are two idempotent matrices, then
  (a) AB is idempotent, iff $AB = BA$.
  (b) $A + B$ is an idempotent matrix, iff $AB = BA = O$
  (c) $AB = A$ and $BA = B$, then $A^2 = A$, $B^2 = B$

(ii) (a) If A is an idempotent matrix and $A + B = I$, then B is an idempotent and $AB = BA = O$.
  (b) Diagonal (1, 1, 1, ...,1) is an idempotent matrix.

3. Involutory Matrix

A square matrix A is said to be involutory, if $A^2 = I$

4. Nilpotent Matrix

A square matrix A is said to be nilpotent matrix, if there exists a positive integer m such that $A^m = O$. If m is the least positive integer such that $A^m = O$, then m is called the index of the nilpotent matrix A.

5. Unitary Matrix

A square matrix A is said to be unitary, if $\overline{A'}A = I$

6. Periodic Matrix

If $A^{k+1} = A$, where k is a positive integer, then A is known as periodic matrix and k is known as period of matrix A.

Competition Insight

Rank of a Matrix

A positive integer r is said to be the rank of a non-zero matrix A, if
  (i) there exists at least one minor in A of order r which is not zero.
  (ii) every minor in A of order greater than r, is zero,
  rank of a matrix A is denoted by $\rho(A) = r$.

Properties of Rank of a Matrix

(i) The rank of a null matrix is zero i.e. $\rho(O) = 0$
(ii) If I_n is an identity matrix of order n, then $\rho(I_n) = n$.
(iii) (a) If a matrix A doesn't possess any minor of order r, then $\rho(A) \geq r$.
  (b) If atleast one minor of order r of the matrix is not equal to zero, then $\rho(A) \leq r$.
(iv) If every $(r + 1)$ th order minor of A is zero, then any higher order minor will also be zero.

(v) If A is of order n, then for a non-singular matrix A, $\rho(A) = n$

(vi) $\rho(A') = \rho(A)$

(vii) $\rho(A^*) = \rho(A)$

(viii) $\rho(A + B) \leq \rho(A) + \rho(B)$

(ix) If A and B are two matrices such that the product AB is defined, then rank (AB) cannot exceed the rank of the either matrix.

(x) If A and B are square matrices of same order and $\rho(A) = \rho(B) = n$, then $\rho(AB) = n$

(xi) Every skew-symmetric matrices of odd order has rank less than its order.

(xii) Elementary operations do not change the rank of a matrix.

Chapter 09

Determinants

Every square matrix A is associated with a number, called its **determinant** and it is denoted by Δ (read as delta) or det (A) or $|A|$.

Only square matrices have determinants. The matrices which are not square do not have determinants.

(i) First Order Determinant

If $A=[a]$, then det $(A)=|A|=a.$

(ii) Second Order Determinant

If $A=\begin{bmatrix} a_{11} & a_{12} \\ a_{21} & a_{22} \end{bmatrix}$, then $|A|=a_{11}a_{22}-a_{21}a_{12}$

(iii) Third Order Determinant

If $A=\begin{bmatrix} a_{11} & a_{12} & a_{13} \\ a_{21} & a_{22} & a_{23} \\ a_{31} & a_{32} & a_{33} \end{bmatrix}$, then

$$|A|=a_{11}\begin{vmatrix} a_{22} & a_{23} \\ a_{32} & a_{33} \end{vmatrix}-a_{12}\begin{vmatrix} a_{21} & a_{23} \\ a_{31} & a_{33} \end{vmatrix}+a_{13}\begin{vmatrix} a_{21} & a_{22} \\ a_{31} & a_{32} \end{vmatrix}$$

or $|A|=a_{11}(a_{22}a_{33}-a_{32}a_{23})-a_{12}(a_{21}a_{33}-a_{31}a_{23})+a_{13}(a_{21}a_{32}-a_{22}a_{31})$

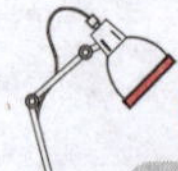

EXPERT Scale Up

We shall expand the determinant along that row or column which contains maximum number of zeros.

e.g. The expansion of the determinant $A = \begin{vmatrix} 1 & 3 & -2 \\ 4 & -2 & 1 \\ 2 & -5 & 4 \end{vmatrix}$ is

$$A = 1\begin{vmatrix} -2 & 1 \\ -5 & 4 \end{vmatrix} - 3\begin{vmatrix} 4 & 1 \\ 2 & 4 \end{vmatrix} - 2\begin{vmatrix} 4 & -2 \\ 2 & -5 \end{vmatrix}$$

$$= 1(-8+5) - 3(16-2) - 2(-20+4)$$
$$= -3 - 42 + 32 = -13$$

Competition Insight

Evaluation of Determinant of Square Matrix of Order 3 by Sarrus Rule

If $A = \begin{bmatrix} a_{11} & a_{12} & a_{13} \\ a_{21} & a_{22} & a_{23} \\ a_{31} & a_{32} & a_{33} \end{bmatrix}$, then determinant can be found by enlarging the matrix by adjoining the first two columns on the right and draw lines as show below parallel and perpendicular to the diagonal.

$$\begin{matrix} a_{11} & a_{12} & a_{13} & a_{11} & a_{12} \\ a_{21} & a_{22} & a_{23} & a_{21} & a_{22} \\ a_{31} & a_{32} & a_{33} & a_{31} & a_{32} \end{matrix}$$

The value of the determinant will be the sum of the product of element in line parallel to the diagonal minus the sum of the product of elements in line perpendicular to the line segment. Thus,

$\Delta = a_{11}a_{22}a_{33} + a_{12}a_{23}a_{31} + a_{13}a_{21}a_{32} - a_{13}a_{22}a_{31} - a_{11}a_{23}a_{32} - a_{12}a_{21}a_{33}$.

This method does not work for determinants of order greater than 3.

Some Important Points

(i) $|AB| = |A||B|$, where A and B are square matrices of the same order.

(ii) $|A^n| = |A|^n$

(iii) If A, B and C are square matrices of the same order such that ith columns (or rows) of A is the sum of i th columns (or rows) of B and C and all other columns (or rows) of A, B and C are identical, then $|A| = |B| + |C|$

(iv) $|I_n| = 1$, where I_n is identity matrix of order n.

(v) $|O_n| = 0$, where O_n is a zero matrix of order n.

(vi) If $\Delta(x)$ be a 3rd order determinant having polynomials as its elements.

(a) If $\Delta(a)$ has 2 rows (or columns) proportional, then $(x-a)$ is a factor of $\Delta(x)$.

(b) If $\Delta(a)$ has 3 rows (or columns) proportional, then $(x-a)^2$ is a factor of $\Delta(x)$.

(vii) A square matrix A is **non-singular**, if $|A| \neq 0$ and **singular**, if $|A| = 0$.

(viii) Determinant of a skew-symmetric matrix of odd order is zero and of even order is a non-zero perfect square.

(ix) In general, $|B+C| \neq |B| + |C|$

(x) Determinant of a diagonal matrix
= Product of its diagonal elements

(xi) Determinant of a triangular matrix
= Product of its diagonal elements

(xii) A square matrix of order n is non-singular, if its rank $r = n$ i.e. if $|A| \neq 0$, then rank $(A) = n$

(xiii) If $\Delta(x) = \begin{vmatrix} f_1(x) & f_2(x) & f_3(x) \\ g_1(x) & g_2(x) & g_3(x) \\ a & b & c \end{vmatrix}$, then

(a) $$\sum_{x=1}^{n} \Delta(x) = \begin{vmatrix} \sum_{x=1}^{n} f_1(x) & \sum_{x=1}^{n} f_2(x) & \sum_{x=1}^{n} f_3(x) \\ \sum_{x=1}^{n} g_1(x) & \sum_{x=1}^{n} g_2(x) & \sum_{x=1}^{n} g_3(x) \\ a & b & c \end{vmatrix}$$

(b) $$\prod_{x=1}^{n} \Delta(x) = \begin{vmatrix} \prod_{x=1}^{n} f_1(x) & \prod_{x=1}^{n} f_2(x) & \prod_{x=1}^{n} f_3(x) \\ \prod_{x=1}^{n} g_1(x) & \prod_{x=1}^{n} g_2(x) & \prod_{x=1}^{n} g_3(x) \\ a & b & c \end{vmatrix}$$

(xiv) If A is a non-singular matrix, then $|A^{-1}| = \dfrac{1}{|A|} = |A|^{-1}$.

(xv) Determinant of a orthogonal matrix $= 1$ or -1.

(xvi) Determinant of a hermitian matrix is purely real.

(xvii) If A and B are non-zero matrices and $AB = O$, then it implies $|A| = O$ and $|B| = O$.

Applications of Determinants in Geometry

Let the three points in a plane be $A(x_1, y_1)$, $B(x_2, y_2)$ and $C(x_3, y_3)$, then

(i) Area of $\Delta ABC = \frac{1}{2}\begin{vmatrix} x_1 & y_1 & 1 \\ x_2 & y_2 & 1 \\ x_3 & y_3 & 1 \end{vmatrix}$

$$= \frac{1}{2}[x_1 (y_2 - y_3) + x_2 (y_3 - y_1) + x_3 (y_1 - y_2)]$$

EXPERT Scale Up

Since, area cannot be negative, therefore we always take the absolute value of the determinant.

(ii) If the given points are collinear, then $\begin{vmatrix} x_1 & y_1 & 1 \\ x_2 & y_2 & 1 \\ x_3 & y_3 & 1 \end{vmatrix} = 0.$

(iii) Let two points be $A(x_1, y_1)$, $B(x_2, y_2)$ and $P(x, y)$ be a point on the line joining points A and B, then the equation of line is given by

$$\frac{1}{2}\begin{vmatrix} x & y & 1 \\ x_1 & y_1 & 1 \\ x_2 & y_2 & 1 \end{vmatrix} = 0$$

Minors and Cofactors

If $\Delta = \begin{vmatrix} a_{11} & a_{12} & a_{13} \\ a_{21} & a_{22} & a_{23} \\ a_{31} & a_{32} & a_{33} \end{vmatrix}$, then the **minor** M_{ij} of the element a_{ij} is the determinant obtained by deleting the ith row and jth column,

i.e. $M_{11} = \text{minor of } a_{11} = \begin{vmatrix} a_{22} & a_{23} \\ a_{32} & a_{33} \end{vmatrix}$

$M_{12} = \text{minor of } a_{12} = \begin{vmatrix} a_{21} & a_{23} \\ a_{31} & a_{33} \end{vmatrix}$

and $M_{13} = \text{minor of } a_{13} = \begin{vmatrix} a_{21} & a_{22} \\ a_{31} & a_{32} \end{vmatrix}$

The **cofactor** of the element a_{ij} is $C_{ij} = (-1)^{i+j} M_{ij}$

Properties of Minors and Cofactors

(i) The sum of the products of elements of any row (or column) of a determinant with the cofactors of the corresponding elements of any other row (or column) is zero

i.e. if $\Delta = \begin{vmatrix} a_{11} & a_{12} & a_{13} \\ a_{21} & a_{22} & a_{23} \\ a_{31} & a_{32} & a_{33} \end{vmatrix}$, then $a_{11}C_{31} + a_{12}C_{32} + a_{13}C_{33} = 0$

and so on.

(ii) The sum of the product of elements of any row (or column) of a determinant with the cofactors of the corresponding elements of the same row (or column) is Δ

i.e. if $A = \begin{vmatrix} a_{11} & a_{12} & a_{13} \\ a_{21} & a_{22} & a_{23} \\ a_{31} & a_{32} & a_{33} \end{vmatrix}$, then $|A| = \Delta = a_{11}C_{11} + a_{12}C_{12} + a_{13}C_{13}$

In general, if $|A| = \Delta$, then $|A| = \sum_{i=1}^{n} a_{ij} C_{ij}$

where A is a matrix of order $n \times n$.

Adjoint of a Matrix

Adjoint of a matrix is the transpose of the matrix of cofactors of the given matrix,

i.e. $$\text{adj}(A) = \begin{bmatrix} C_{11} & C_{12} & C_{13} \\ C_{21} & C_{22} & C_{23} \\ C_{31} & C_{32} & C_{33} \end{bmatrix}^T = \begin{bmatrix} C_{11} & C_{21} & C_{31} \\ C_{12} & C_{22} & C_{32} \\ C_{13} & C_{23} & C_{33} \end{bmatrix}$$

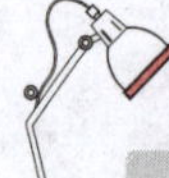

EXPERT Scale Up

If $A = \begin{bmatrix} a_{11} & a_{12} \\ a_{21} & a_{22} \end{bmatrix}$, then adj A obtained by interchanging a_{11} and a_{22} and by changing signs of a_{12} and a_{21} i.e. adj $A = \begin{bmatrix} a_{22} & -a_{12} \\ -a_{21} & a_{11} \end{bmatrix}$.

Properties of Adjoint of a Matrix

If A and B are two non-singular matrices of same order n, then

(i) $A(\text{adj } A) = (\text{adj } A)A = |A|I$, where I is identity matrix of order n.

(ii) $\text{adj}(A') = (\text{adj } A)'$

(iii) $\text{adj}(AB) = (\text{adj } B)(\text{adj } A)$

(iv) $\text{adj}(kA) = k^{n-1}(\text{adj } A), k \in R$

(v) $\text{adj}(A^m) = (\text{adj } A)^m$

(vi) $\text{adj}(\text{adj } A) = |A|^{n-2} A$

(vii) $|\text{adj } A| = |A|^{n-1}$

(viii) $|\text{adj}(\text{adj } A)| = |A|^{(n-1)^2}$

(ix) $\text{adj}(I_n) = I_n$, $\text{adj}(O) = O$

Value Points

- Adjoint of a diagonal matrix is a diagonal matrix.
- Adjoint of a triangular matrix is a triangular matrix.
- Adjoint of a symmetric matrix is a symmetric matrix.

Inverse of a Matrix

Let A be a non-zero square matrix of order n, then a square matrix B, such that $AB = BA = I$, is called inverse of A, denoted by A^{-1}.

i.e. $$A^{-1} = \frac{1}{|A|}(\text{adj } A), \text{ where } |A| \neq 0$$

Value Points

- Square matrix A is invertible iff it is non-singular.
- Every invertible matrix possesses a unique inverse.
- If a non-singular square matrix A is symmetric, then A^{-1} is also symmetric.
- Inverse of a triangular matrix is a triangular matrix.

Properties of Inverse of a Matrix

Let A and B be two square matrices of same order n. Then,

(i) $(A^{-1})^{-1} = A$

(ii) $(AB)^{-1} = B^{-1}A^{-1}$

In general, $(A_1 A_2 A_3 \dots A_n)^{-1} = A_n^{-1} A_{n-1}^{-1} \dots A_3^{-1} A_2^{-1} A_1^{-1}$

(iii) $(A')^{-1} = (A^{-1})'$

(iv) $|A^{-1}| = |A|^{-1}$

(v) $AA^{-1} = A^{-1}A = I$

(vi) $(A^k)^{-1} = (A^{-1})^k, k \in N$

(vii) If $A = \begin{bmatrix} a & 0 & 0 \\ 0 & b & 0 \\ 0 & 0 & c \end{bmatrix}$ and $abc \neq 0$, then $A^{-1} = \begin{bmatrix} 1/a & 0 & 0 \\ 0 & 1/b & 0 \\ 0 & 0 & 1/c \end{bmatrix}$

(viii) If A, B and C are square matrices of the same order and A is a non-singular matrix, then

(a) $AB = AC \Rightarrow B = C$ [left cancellation law]

(b) $BA = CA \Rightarrow B = C$ [right cancellation law]

Competition Insight

Differentiation of Determinant

If $\Delta(x) = \begin{vmatrix} a(x) & b(x) & c(x) \\ p(x) & q(x) & r(x) \\ u(x) & v(x) & w(x) \end{vmatrix}$, then

$$\frac{d\Delta}{dx} = \begin{vmatrix} a'(x) & b'(x) & c'(x) \\ p(x) & q(x) & r(x) \\ u(x) & v(x) & w(x) \end{vmatrix} + \begin{vmatrix} a(x) & b(x) & c(x) \\ p'(x) & q'(x) & r'(x) \\ u(x) & v(x) & w(x) \end{vmatrix} + \begin{vmatrix} a(x) & b(x) & c(x) \\ p(x) & q(x) & r(x) \\ u'(x) & v'(x) & w'(x) \end{vmatrix}$$

Integration of Determinant

If $\Delta(x) = \begin{vmatrix} a_{11}(x) & a_{12}(x) & a_{13}(x) \\ a_{21} & a_{22} & a_{23} \\ a_{31} & a_{32} & a_{33} \end{vmatrix}$, then

$$\int \Delta(x)dx = \begin{vmatrix} \int a_{11}(x)dx & \int a_{12}(x)dx & \int a_{13}(x)dx \\ a_{21} & a_{22} & a_{23} \\ a_{31} & a_{32} & a_{33} \end{vmatrix}$$

If the elements of more than one column or rows are functions of x, then the integration can be done only after evaluation/expansion of the determinant.

Application of Determinants and Matrices

Homogeneous and Non-homogeneous System of Linear Equations

A system of equations $AX = B$, is called a **homogeneous system**, if $B = O$ and if $B \neq O$, then it is called a **non-homogeneous system** of equations.

Solution of System of Linear Equations

The value of the variables satisfying all the linear equations in the system, is called solution of system of linear equations.

Solution of System of Equations by Matrix Method

(i) **Non-homogeneous System of Equations** Let $AX = B$ be a system of n linear equations in n variables.

(a) If $|A| \neq 0$, then the system of equations is consistent and has a unique solution given by $X = A^{-1}B$.

(b) If $|A| = 0$ and $(\text{adj } A)B = O$, then the system of equations is consistent and has infinitely many solutions.

(c) If $|A| = 0$ and $(\text{adj } A)\ B \neq O$, then the system of equations is inconsistent i.e. having no solution.

(ii) **Homogeneous System of Equations** Let $AX = O$ be a system of n linear equations in n variables.

(a) If $|A| \neq 0$, then it has only one solution $X = O$, is called the **trivial solution.**

(b) If $|A| = 0$, then the system has infinitely many solutions and it is called **non-trivial solution.**

Competition Insight

Solution of Linear Equations by Determinant/Cramer's Rule

Case I The solution of the system of simultaneous linear equations

$$a_1x + b_1y = c_1 \quad \text{...(i)}$$

$$a_2x + b_2y = c_2 \quad \text{...(ii)}$$

is given by $x = \dfrac{D_1}{D}, y = \dfrac{D_2}{D}$

where, $D = \begin{vmatrix} a_1 & b_1 \\ a_2 & b_2 \end{vmatrix}$, $D_1 = \begin{vmatrix} c_1 & b_1 \\ c_2 & b_2 \end{vmatrix}$ and $D_2 = \begin{vmatrix} a_1 & c_1 \\ a_2 & c_2 \end{vmatrix}$ provided that $D \neq 0$.

(i) If $D \neq 0$, then the given system of equations is **consistent** and **has a unique solution** given by $x = \dfrac{D_1}{D}, y = \dfrac{D_2}{D}$.

(ii) If $D = 0$ and $D_1 = D_2 = 0$, then the system is **consistent** and has **infinitely many solutions.**

(iii) If $D = 0$ and one of D_1 and D_2 is non-zero, then the system is **inconsistent** and has no solution.

Case II Let the system of equations be $a_1x + b_1y + c_1z = d_1$, $a_2x + b_2y + c_2z = d_2$ and $a_3x + b_3y + c_3z = d_3$. Then, the solution of the system of equation is $x = \frac{D_1}{D}$, $y = \frac{D_2}{D}$, $z = \frac{D_3}{D}$, it is called **Cramer's rule**.

where, $D = \begin{vmatrix} a_1 & b_1 & c_1 \\ a_2 & b_2 & c_2 \\ a_3 & b_3 & c_3 \end{vmatrix}$, $D_1 = \begin{vmatrix} d_1 & b_1 & c_1 \\ d_2 & b_2 & c_2 \\ d_3 & b_3 & c_3 \end{vmatrix}$, $D_2 = \begin{vmatrix} a_1 & d_1 & c_1 \\ a_2 & d_2 & c_2 \\ a_3 & d_3 & c_3 \end{vmatrix}$

and $D_3 = \begin{vmatrix} a_1 & b_1 & d_1 \\ a_2 & b_2 & d_2 \\ a_3 & b_3 & d_3 \end{vmatrix}$.

(i) If $D \neq 0$, then the system of equations is consistent with unique solution.

(ii) If $D = 0$ and atleast one of the determinant D_1, D_2, D_3 is non-zero, then the given system is inconsistent, i.e. having no solution.

(iii) If $D = 0$ and $D_1 = D_2 = D_3 = 0$, then the system is consistent, with infinitely many solutions.

(iv) If $D \neq 0$ and $D_1 = D_2 = D_3 = 0$, then system has only trivial solution, $(x = y = z = 0)$.

Some Important Results

(i) $\begin{vmatrix} 1 & 1 & 1 \\ a & b & c \\ a^2 & b^2 & c^2 \end{vmatrix} = (a-b)(b-c)(c-a)$

(ii) $\begin{vmatrix} 1 & 1 & 1 \\ a & b & c \\ a^3 & b^3 & c^3 \end{vmatrix} = (a-b)(b-c)(c-a)(a+b+c)$

(iii) $\begin{vmatrix} 1 & 1 & 1 \\ a & b & c \\ a^4 & b^4 & c^4 \end{vmatrix} = (a-b)(b-c)(c-a)\,[(a^2+b^2+c^2)+(ab+bc+ca)]$

(iv) $\begin{vmatrix} 1 & 1 & 1 \\ a^2 & b^2 & c^2 \\ a^3 & b^3 & c^3 \end{vmatrix} = (a-b)(b-c)(c-a)(ab+bc+ca)$

(v) $\begin{vmatrix} x^2 & (x+a)^2 & (x-a)^2 \\ y^2 & (y+a)^2 & (y-a)^2 \\ z^2 & (z+a)^2 & (z-a)^2 \end{vmatrix} = -4a^3(x-y)(y-z)(z-x)$

(vi) $\begin{vmatrix} 1 & 1 & 1 \\ a & b & c \\ b & a & c \end{vmatrix} = a^2 + b^2 + c^2 - ab - bc - ca$

$= \frac{1}{2}[(b-c)^2 + (c-a)^2 + (a-b)^2]$

(vii) $\begin{vmatrix} a & b & c \\ b & c & a \\ c & a & b \end{vmatrix} = -(a+b+c)(a^2 + b^2 + c^2 - ab - bc - ca)$

$= -(a^3 + b^3 + c^3 - 3abc)$

(viii) $\begin{vmatrix} x+a & b & c & d \\ a & x+b & c & d \\ a & b & x+c & d \\ a & b & c & x+d \end{vmatrix} = x^3 (x + a + b + c + d)$

Chapter 10

Probability

Experiment

An operation which produce some well-defined results or outcomes is called an experiment.

Types of Experiments

1. Deterministic Experiment

Those experiments, which when repeated under identical conditions produce the same result or outcome are known as deterministic experiment.

2. Probabilistic/Random Experiment

Those experiments, which when repeated under identical conditions, do not produce the same outcome every time but the outcome produced is one of the several possible outcomes, are called random experiment.

Some Basic Definitions

(i) **Trial** Performing an experiment is called a trial. The number of times an experiment is repeated is called the number of trials.

(ii) **Sample Space** The set of all possible outcomes of a random experiment is called the sample space of the experiment and it is denoted by S.

(iii) **Sample Point** The outcome of an experiment is called the sample point, i.e. the elements of set S are called the sample points.

(iv) **Event** Any subset of the sample space associated with a random experiment is called event or case.

(v) **Elementary** (or Simple) **Event** An event containing only one sample point is called elementary event (or indecomposable event).

(vi) **Compound Event** An event containing more than one sample points is called compound event (or decomposable event).

(vii) **Occurrence of an Event** An event associated to a random experiment is said to occur, if any one of the elementary events associated to it is an outcome.

(viii) **Certain Event** An event which must occur, whatever be the outcomes, is called a certain event (or sure event).

(ix) **Impossible Event** An event which cannot occur in a random experiment, is called an impossible event.

(x) **Favourable Outcomes** Let S be the sample space associated with a random experiment and $E \subset S$. Then, the elementary events belonging to E are known as the favourable outcomes to E.

(xi) **Equally likely Outcomes** The outcomes of a random experiment are said to be equally likely, when each outcome is as likely to occur as the other.

Algebra of Events

Let A and B be two events associated with a random experiment, whose sample space is S. Then,

(i) the event 'not A' is the set A' or $S - A$

(ii) the events A or B is the set $A \cup B$

(iii) the events A and B is the set $A \cap B$

(iv) the events A but not B is the set $A - B$ or $A \cap B'$

Probability–

Theoretical (Classical) Approach

If there are n equally likely outcomes associated with a random experiment and m of them are favourable to an event A, then the probability of happening or occurrence of A, denoted by $P(A)$, is given by

$$P(A) = \frac{m}{n} = \frac{\text{Number of favourable outcomes to } A}{\text{Total number of possible outcomes}}$$

Axiomatic Approach

Let $S = \{w_1, w_2, w_3, \ldots w_n\}$ be a sample space, then according to axiomatic approach we have the following

(i) $0 \le P(w_i) \le 1$ for each $w_i \in S$

(ii) $P(w_1) + P(w_2) + \ldots + P(w_n) = 1$

(iii) For any event A, $P(A) = \Sigma P(w_i)$, $w_i \in A$.

Value Points

- Theoretical approach is valid only when the outcomes are equally likely and number of total outcomes is known.
- $P(\text{sure event}) = P(S) = 1$ and $P(\text{impossible event}) = P(\phi) = 0$

Different Types of Events and Their Probabilities

(i) **Equally Likely Events** The given events are said to be equally likely, if none of them is expected to occur in preference to the other.

Thus, if the events E and F are equally likely, then $P(E) = P(F)$

(ii) **Mutually Exclusive Events** A set of events is said to be mutually exclusive, if the happening of one event excludes the happening of the other.

If A and B are mutually exclusive events, then $(A \cap B) = \phi$.
$\therefore$ The probability of mutually exclusive events is $P(A \cap B) = 0$.

(iii) **Probability of Exhaustive Events** A set of events is said to be exhaustive, if atleast one of them necessarily occurs whenever the experiment is performed.

If $E_1, E_2, \ldots, E_n$ are exhaustive events, then

$$E_1 \cup E_2 \cup \ldots \cup E_n = S.$$

and so $$P(E_1 \cup E_2 \cup E_3 \cup \ldots \cup E_n) = 1.$$

EXPERT Scale Up

If $E_i \cap E_j = \phi$ for $i \neq j$ and $\bigcup_{i=1}^{n} E_i = S$, then events $E_1, E_2, \ldots, E_n$ are called **mutually exclusive and exhaustive events.**

(iv) **Independent Events** Two events A and B, associated to a random experiment, are independent if the probability of occurrence or non-occurrence of A is not affected by the occurrence or non-occurrence of B.

Knowledge Booster

If A and B are independent events associated with a random experiment, then

(a) $P(A \cap B) = P(A)\,P(B)$

(b) $\overline{A}$ and B are independent events.

(c) A and $\overline{B}$ are independent events.

(d) $\overline{A}$ and $\overline{B}$ are independent events.

(v) **Complementary Event** Let A be an event of a sample space S, the complementary event to A is the event containing all sample points other than the sample point in A and it is denoted by A' or $\overline{A}$ i.e. A' or $\overline{A} = \{n : n \in S, n \notin A\}$

$\therefore$ The probability of complementary event to A is

$$P(\overline{A}) = 1 - P(A)$$

Value Points

- $P(A) + P(A') = 1$
- $P(A \cup A') = P(S) = 1$
- $P(A \cap A') = P(\phi) = 0$
- $P(A')' = P(A)$

Partition of a Sample Space

The events $A_1, A_2, \ldots, A_n$ represent a partition of the sample space S, if they are pairwise disjoint, exhaustive and have non-zero probabilities. i.e.

(i) $A_i \cap A_j = \phi; i \neq j; i, j = 1, 2, \ldots, n$

(ii) $A_1 \cup A_2 \cup \ldots \cup A_n = S$

(iii) $P(A_i) > 0, \forall\ i = 1, 2, \ldots, n$

Important Results on Probability

(i) **Addition Theorem of Probability**

(a) For two events A and B

$$P(A \cup B) = P(A) + P(B) - P(A \cap B)$$

(b) For three events A, B and C

$$P(A \cup B \cup C) = P(A) + P(B) + P(C) - P(A \cap B) - P(B \cap C) - P(A \cap C) + P(A \cap B \cap C)$$

(c) For n events $A_1, A_2, \ldots, A_n$

$$P\left(\bigcup_{i=1}^{n} A_i\right) = \sum_{i=1}^{n} P(A_i) - \sum_{1 \le i < j \le n} \sum P(A_i \cap A_j) + \sum_{1 \le i} \sum_{< j < k} \sum_{\le n} P(A_i \cap A_j \cap A_k) - \ldots + (-1)^{n-1} P(A_1 \cap A_2 \cap \ldots \cap A_n)$$

(ii) If A and B are two events associated with a random experiment, then

(a) $P(\overline{A} \cap B) = P(B) - P(A \cap B)$

(b) $P(A \cap \overline{B}) = P(A) - P(A \cap B)$

(c) $P[(A \cap \overline{B}) \cup (\overline{A} \cap B)] = P(A) + P(B) - 2P(A \cap B)$

(d) $P(\overline{A} \cap \overline{B}) = P(\overline{A \cup B}) = 1 - P(A \cup B)$

(e) $P(\overline{A} \cup \overline{B}) = P(\overline{A \cap B}) = 1 - P(A \cap B)$

(f) $P(A) = P(A \cap B) + P(A \cap \overline{B})$

(g) $P(B) = P(A \cap B) + P(B \cap \overline{A})$

(iii) (a) P (exactly one of A, B occurs)

$$= P(A) + P(B) - 2P(A \cap B) = P(A \cup B) - P(A \cap B)$$

(b) P(neither A nor B occurs) $= P(A' \cap B') = 1 - P(A \cup B)$

(iv) If $B \subseteq A$, then

(a) $P(A \cap \overline{B}) = P(A) - P(B)$

(b) $P(B) \le P(A)$

(v) If A and B are two events, then

$$P(A \cap B) \le P(A) (\text{or } P(B)) \le P(A \cup B) \le P(A) + P(B)$$

(vi) If A, B and C are three events, then

(a) P(exactly one of A, B, C occurs)

$$= P(A) + P(B) + P(C) - 2P(A \cap B) - 2P(B \cap C) - 2P(A \cap C) + 3P(A \cap B \cap C)$$

(b) P (atleast two of A, B, C occurs)

$$= P(A \cap B) + P(B \cap C) + P(C \cap A) - 2P(A \cap B \cap C)$$

(c) P (exactly two of A, B, C occurs)

$$= P(A \cap B) + P(B \cap C) + P(A \cap C) - 3P(A \cap B \cap C)$$

(vii) (a) $P(A \cup B) = P(A) + P(B)$, if A and B are mutually exclusive events.

(b) $P(A \cup B \cup C) = P(A) + P(B) + P(C)$, if A, B and C are mutually exclusive events.

(viii) If the events $A_1, A_2, \ldots, A_n$ are mutually exclusive, i.e. $A_i \cap A_j = \phi$ for $i \ne j$, then

$$P(A_1 \cup A_2 \cup A_3 \cup \ldots \cup A_n) = P(A_1) + (A_2) + \ldots + P(A_n)$$

and $P(A_1 \cap A_2 \cap A_3 \cap \ldots \cap A_n) = P(\phi) = 0$

(ix) If $A_1, A_2, \ldots, A_n$ are independent events associated with a random experiment, then probability of occurrence of atleast one

$$= P(A_1 \cup A_2 \cup \ldots \cup A_n) = 1 - P(\overline{A_1 \cup A_2 \cup \ldots \cup A_n})$$

$$= 1 - P(\overline{A}_1) P(\overline{A}_2) \ldots P(\overline{A}_n)$$

(x) If $A_1, A_2, \ldots, A_n$ are n events associated with a random experiment, then

(a) $P(A_1 \cap A_2 \cap \ldots \cap A_n) \geq \sum_{i=1}^{n} P(A_i) - (n-1)$

(Bonferroni's Inequality)

Or

$$P(A_1 \cap A_2 \cap \ldots \cap A_n) \geq 1 - P(\overline{A}_1) - P(\overline{A}_2) \ldots - P(\overline{A}_n)$$

(b) $P(\bigcup_{i=1}^{n} A_i) \leq \sum_{i=1}^{n} P(A_i)$ (Booley's Inequality)

Odds in Favour and Against of an Event

(i) Odds in favour of an event E is given by $\dfrac{P(E)}{P(\overline{E})}$

(ii) Odds in against of an event E is given by $\dfrac{P(\overline{E})}{P(E)}$

Value Point

If odds in favour of an event E are $a : b$, then $P(E) = \dfrac{a}{a+b}$ and $P(\overline{E}) = \dfrac{b}{a+b}$.

Conditional Probability

Let A and B be two events associated with a random experiment. Then, the probability of occurrence of event A under the condition that B has already occurred and $P(B) \neq 0$, is called the conditional probability and it is given by

$$P(A/B) = \frac{P(A \cap B)}{P(B)}$$

If A has already occurred and $P(A) \neq 0$, then $P(B/A) = \dfrac{P(A \cap B)}{P(A)}$

EXPERT Scale Up

If A and B are independent events, then $P(B/A) = P(B)$ and $P(A/B) = P(A)$.

Properties of Conditional Probability

(i) $P\left(\frac{A}{B}\right)+P\left(\frac{\overline{A}}{B}\right)=1$

(ii) $P((A \cup B)/F) = P\left(\frac{A}{F}\right) + P\left(\frac{B}{F}\right) - P\left(\frac{(A \cap B)}{F}\right)$, where F is an event of sample space S such that $P(F) \neq 0$.

In particular, $P\left(\frac{(A \cup B)}{F}\right) = P\left(\frac{A}{F}\right) + P\left(\frac{B}{F}\right)$, if A and B are disjointevents.

Multiplication Theorem on Probability

(i) If A and B are two events associated with a random experiment, then

$$P(A \cap B) = P(A)P(B/A), \text{ if } P(A) \neq 0$$

or

$$P(A \cap B) = P(B)P(A/B), \text{ if } P(B) \neq 0$$

(ii) If $A_1, A_2, \ldots, A_n$ are n events associated with a random experiment, then

$$P(A_1 \cap A_2 \cap \ldots \cap A_n) = P(A_1)\, P(A_2 / A_1)\, P(A_3 / (A_1 \cap A_2)) \ldots P(A_n / (A_1 \cap A_2 \cap A_3 \cap \ldots \cap A_{n-1}))$$

Theorem of Total Probability

Let S be the sample space and let $E_1, E_2, \ldots, E_n$ be a partition of the sample space S. If A is any event which occurs with E_1 or E_2 or ... or E_n, then

$$P(A) = P(E_1)P(A/E_1) + P(E_2)P(A/E_2) + \ldots + P(E_n)\, P(A/E_n) = \sum_{r=1}^{n} P(E_r)P(A/E_r)$$

Baye's Theorem

Let S be the sample space and let $E_1, E_2, \ldots, E_n$ be a partition of the sample space S. If A is any event which occurs with E_1 or E_2 or ... or E_n, then probability of occurrence of E_i, when A occurred, is

$$P(E_i / A) = \frac{P(E_i)P(A/E_i)}{\sum_{i=1}^{n} P(E_i)P(A/E_i)}, \; i = 1, 2, \ldots, n$$

where, $P(E_i), i = 1, 2, \ldots, n$ is known as the **priori probability**

and $P\left(\frac{E_i}{A}\right), i = 1, 2, \ldots, n$ is known as **posteriori probability**

Coin

A coin has two sides, head and tail. If an experiment consists of more than one coin, then coins are considered as distinct, if not otherwise stated.

Die

A die has six face marked with 1, 2, 3, 4, 5 and 6. If an experiment consists of more than one die, then all dice are considered as distinct, if not otherwise stated.

Playing Cards

A pack of playing cards has 52 cards, which are divided into 4 suits (spade, heart, diamond and club) each having 13 cards.

The cards in each suit are ace, king, queen, jack, 10, 9, 8, 7, 6, 5, 4, 3 and 2.

King, queen and jack are called face cards, so there are in all 12 face cards. Also, there are 16 honour cards, 4 of each suit namely ace, king, queen and jack. The suits, clubs and spades are of black colour while the suits hearts and diamonds are of red colour. So, there are 26 red cards and 26 black cards.

Random Variable

Let S be a sample space associated with a given random experiment. A real valued function X defined on S, i.e. $X : S \to R$, is called a random variable.

There are two types of random variable

(i) **Discrete Random Variable** If the range of the function $X : S \to R$ is a finite set or countably infinite set of real numbers, then it is called a discrete random variable.

e.g. In tossing of two coins $S = \{HH, HT, TH, TT\}$, let X denotes number of heads in tossing of two coins, then

$$X(HH) = 2, X(TH) = 1, X(HT) = 1, X(TT) = 0$$

(ii) **Continuous Random Variable** If the range of X is an interval (a, b) of R, then X is called a continuous random variable.

Probability Distribution of a Random Variable

If a random variable X takes values $x_1, x_2, \ldots, x_n$ with respective probabilities $p_1, p_2, \ldots, p_n$, then the representation

X	x_1	x_2	x_3 ...	x_n
P(X)	p_1	p_2	p_3 ...	p_n

is known as the probability distribution of X.

or

Probability distribution gives the values of the random variable along with the corresponding probabilities.

Mathematical Expectation/Mean of a Random Variable

If X is a discrete random variable which assume values $x_1, x_2, \ldots, x_n$ with respective probabilities $p_1, p_2, \ldots, p_n$, then the mean μ of X is defined as

$$E(X) = \mu = p_1x_1 + p_2x_2 + \ldots + p_nx_n = \sum_{i=1}^{n} p_ix_i$$

Competition Insight

Variance of a Random Variable

Variance of a random variable is denoted by σ^2 and it is defined as

$$V(X) = \sigma^2 = E(X^2) - [E(X)]^2$$

where, $$E(X^2) = \sum_{i=1}^{n} x_i^2 p_i$$

Standard Deviation

$$\sigma = \sqrt{V(X)} = \sqrt{E(X^2) - (E(X))^2}$$

Important Points

(i) If $Y = aX + b$, then

(a) $E(Y) = E(aX + b) = aE(X) + b$

(b) $\sigma_y^2 = V(Y) = a^2V(X) = a^2\sigma_x^2$

(c) $\sigma_y = \sqrt{V(Y)} = |a|\,\sigma_x$

(ii) If $Y = aX^2 + bX + c$, then

$E(Y) = E(aX^2 + bX + c) = aE(X^2) + bE(X) + c$

Formulae on Mean, Variance and Standard Deviation

(i) If $p = q$, then probability of r successes in n trials is ${}^nC_r p^n$.

(ii) Mean $= E(X) = \mu = np$

(iii) Variance $= \sigma_x^2 = npq$

(iv) Standard deviation $= \sigma_x = \sqrt{npq}$

(v) Mean is always greater than variance.

Geometrical Probability

If the total number of possible outcomes of a random experiment is infinite, in such cases, the definition of probability is modified and the general expression for the probability P of occurrence of an event is given by

$$P = \frac{\text{Measure of region occupied by the event}}{\text{Measure of the whole region}}$$

where, measure means length or area or volume of the region, if we are dealing with one, two or three dimensional space respectively.

Important Points

(i) When two dice are thrown, the number of ways of getting a total r is

(a) $(r-1)$, if $2 \le r \le 7$ and (b) $(13-r)$, if $8 \le r \le 12$

Knowledge Booster

Experiment of insertion of n letters in n addressed envelopes.

(a) Probability of inserting all the n letters in right envelopes $= \frac{1}{n!}$

(b) Probability that atleast one letter is not in right envelope $= 1 - \frac{1}{n!}$

(c) Probability of keeping all the letters in wrong envelopes

$$= \frac{1}{2!} - \frac{1}{3!} + \dots + \frac{(-1)^n}{n!}$$

(d) Probability that exactly r letters are in right envelopes

$$= \frac{1}{r!}\left[\frac{1}{2!} - \frac{1}{3!} + \frac{1}{4!} - \dots + (-1)^{n-r}\frac{1}{(n-r)!}\right]$$

(ii) (a) **Selection of Shoes from a Cupboard** Out of n pair of shoes, if k shoes are selected at random, the probability that there is no pair is $P = \frac{{}^nC_k 2^k}{{}^{2n}C_k}$

(b) The probability that there is atleast one pair is $(1-P)$.

(iii) **Selection of Squares from the Chessboard** If r $(1 \le r \le 7)$ squares are selected at random from a chessboard, then probability that they lie on a diagonal is

$$\frac{4[{}^7C_r + {}^6C_r + \dots + {}^1C_r] + 2({}^8C_r)}{{}^{64}C_r}$$

(iv) If A and B are two finite sets and if a mapping is selected at random from the set of all mapping from A to B, then the probability that the mapping is

(a) a one-one function $= \dfrac{{}^{n(B)}P_{n(A)}}{n(B)^{n(A)}}$, provided $n(B) \geq n(A)$

(b) a many-one function $= 1 - \dfrac{{}^{n(B)}P_{n(A)}}{n(B)^{n(A)}}$, provided $n(B) \geq n(A)$

(c) a constant function $= \dfrac{n(B)}{n(B)^{n(A)}}$

(d) a one-one onto function $= \dfrac{n(A)!}{n(B)^{n(A)}}$, provided $n(A) = n(B)$

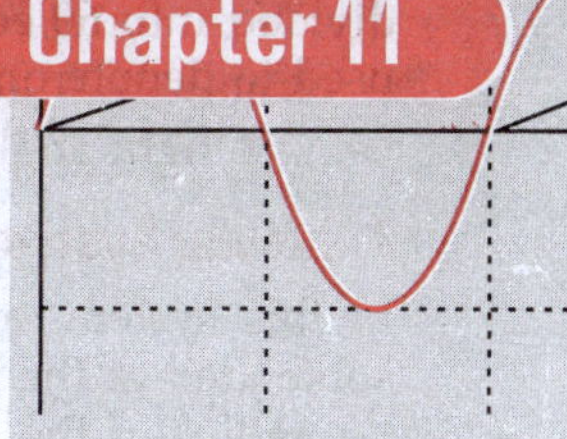

Chapter 11

Trigonometric Functions, Identities and Equations

Angle

When a ray OA starting from its initial position OA rotates about its end point O and takes the final position OB, we say that angle AOB (written as $\angle AOB$) has been formed.

The amount of rotation from the initial side to the terminal side is called the measure of the angle.

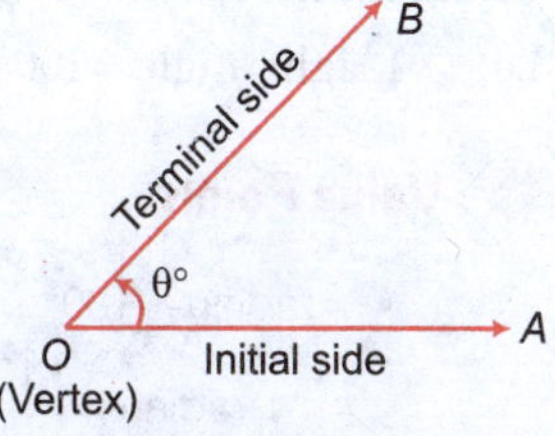

Positive and Negative Angles

An angle formed by a rotating ray is said to be positive or negative depending on whether it moves in an anti-clockwise or a clockwise direction, respectively.

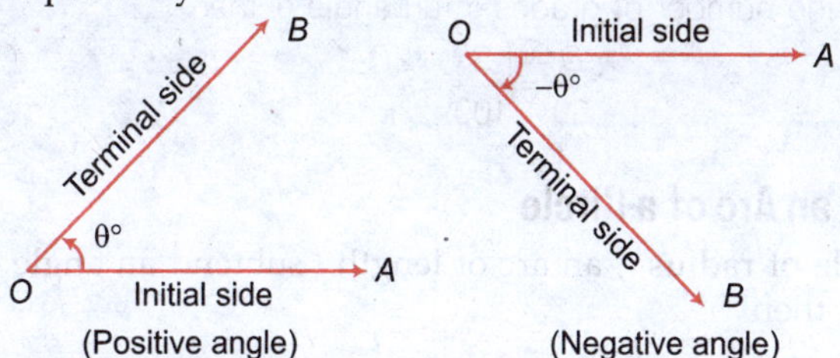

Measurement of Angles

There are three system for measuring the angles, which are given below

1. Sexagesimal System (Degree Measure)

In this system, a right angle is divided into 90 equal parts, called the degrees. The symbol 1° is used to denote one degree. Each degree is divided into 60 equal parts, called the minutes and one minute is divided into 60 equal parts, called the seconds. Symbols 1′ and 1″ are used to denote one minute and one second, respectively.

i.e. 1 right angle $= 90°$, $1° = 60'$, $1' = 60''$

2. Circular System (Radian Measure)

In this system, angle is measured in radian. A radian is the angle subtended at the centre of a circle by an arc, whose length is equal to the radius of the circle. The number of radians in an angle subtended by an arc of circle at the centre is equal to $\dfrac{\text{arc}}{\text{radius}}$.

3. Centesimal System (French System)

In this system, a right angle is divided into 100 equal parts, called the grades. Each grade is subdivided into 100 min and each minute is divided into 100 s.

i.e. 1 right angle $= 100$ grades $= 100^g$, $1^g = 100'$, $1' = 100''$

Value Points

- π radian $= 180°$

  or 1 radian $= \left(\dfrac{180°}{\pi}\right) = 57°16'22''$ where, $\pi = \dfrac{22}{7} = 3.14159$
- $1° = \left(\dfrac{\pi}{180}\right)$ rad $= 0.01746$ rad
- If D is the number of degrees, R is the number of radians and G is the number of grades in an angle θ, then

$$\frac{D}{90} = \frac{G}{100} = \frac{2R}{\pi}$$

Length of an Arc of a Circle

If in a circle of radius r, an arc of length l subtend an angle θ radian at the centre, then

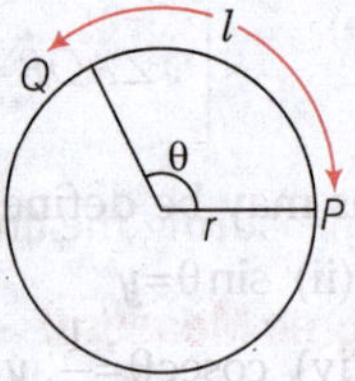

$$\theta = \frac{l}{r} = \frac{\text{Length of arc}}{\text{Radius}} \text{ or } l = r\theta$$

Trigonometric Ratios For acute Angle

Relation between different sides and angles of a right angled triangle are called trigonometric ratios or T-ratios.

Trigonometric ratios can be represented as

$$\sin\theta = \frac{\text{Perpendicular}}{\text{Hypotenuse}} = \frac{BC}{AC}$$

$$\cos\theta = \frac{\text{Base}}{\text{Hypotenuse}} = \frac{AB}{AC}$$

$$\tan\theta = \frac{\text{Perpendicular}}{\text{Base}} = \frac{BC}{AB}$$

$$\text{cosec}\,\theta = \frac{\text{Hypotenuse}}{\text{Perpendicular}} = \frac{AC}{BC}$$

$$\sec\theta = \frac{\text{Hypotenuse}}{\text{Base}} = \frac{AC}{AB}$$

$$\cot\theta = \frac{\text{Base}}{\text{perpendicular}} = \frac{AB}{BC}$$

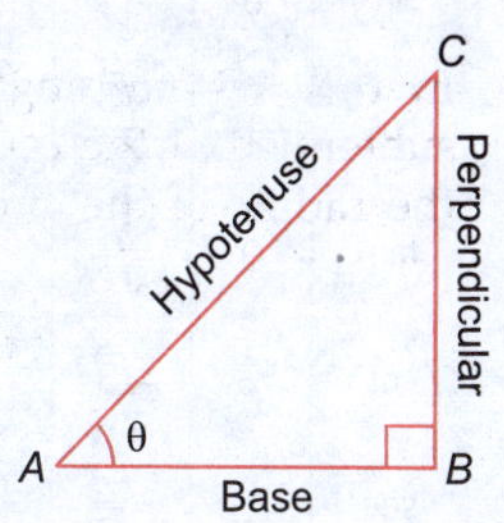

Trigonometric (or Circular) Functions

Let $X'OX$ and YOY' be the coordinate axes. Taking O as the centre and a unit radius, draw a circle, cutting the coordinate axes at A, B, A' and B', as shown in the figure.

$$\left[\because \angle AOP = \frac{\text{arc } AP}{\text{radius } OP} = \frac{l}{1} = \theta^c, \text{ using } \theta = \frac{l}{r}\right]$$

Now, six circular functions may be defined as

(i) $\cos\theta = x$ (ii) $\sin\theta = y$

(iii) $\sec\theta = \frac{1}{x}, x \neq 0$ (iv) $\text{cosec}\,\theta = \frac{1}{y}, y \neq 0$

(v) $\tan\theta = \frac{y}{x}, x \neq 0$ (vi) $\cot\theta = \frac{x}{y}, y \neq 0$

Trigonometric Function of Some Standard Angles

Angle	0°	30°	45°	60°	90°	120°	135°	150°	180°
sin	0	$\frac{1}{2}$	$\frac{1}{\sqrt{2}}$	$\frac{\sqrt{3}}{2}$	1	$\frac{\sqrt{3}}{2}$	$\frac{1}{\sqrt{2}}$	$\frac{1}{2}$	0
cos	1	$\frac{\sqrt{3}}{2}$	$\frac{1}{\sqrt{2}}$	$\frac{1}{2}$	0	$-\frac{1}{2}$	$-\frac{1}{\sqrt{2}}$	$-\frac{\sqrt{3}}{2}$	-1
tan	0	$\frac{1}{\sqrt{3}}$	1	$\sqrt{3}$	∞	$-\sqrt{3}$	-1	$-\frac{1}{\sqrt{3}}$	0
cot	∞	$\sqrt{3}$	1	$\frac{1}{\sqrt{3}}$	0	$-\frac{1}{\sqrt{3}}$	-1	$-\sqrt{3}$	$-\infty$
sec	1	$\frac{2}{\sqrt{3}}$	$\sqrt{2}$	2	∞	-2	$-\sqrt{2}$	$-\frac{2}{\sqrt{3}}$	-1
cosec	∞	2	$\sqrt{2}$	$\frac{2}{\sqrt{3}}$	1	$\frac{2}{\sqrt{3}}$	$\sqrt{2}$	2	∞

Graph of Trigonometric Functions

1. **Graph of sin x**

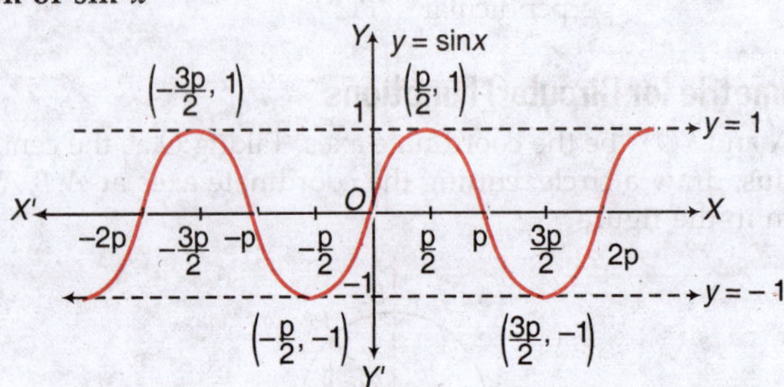

(i) Domain = R (ii) Range $= [-1, 1]$ (iii) Period $= 2\pi$

2. **Graph of cos x**

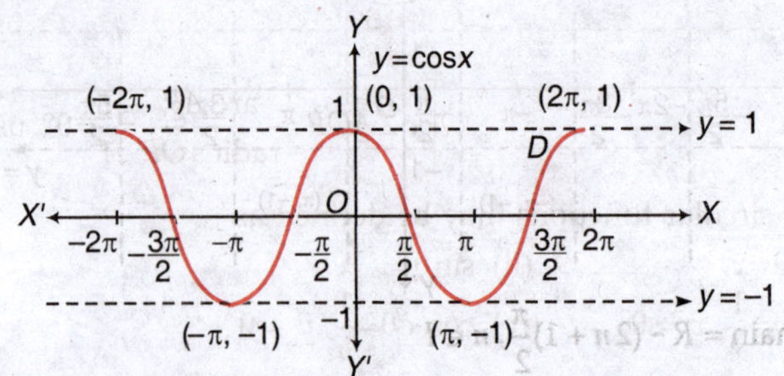

(i) Domain = R (ii) Range $= [-1, 1]$ (iii) Period $= 2\pi$

3. **Graph of tan x**

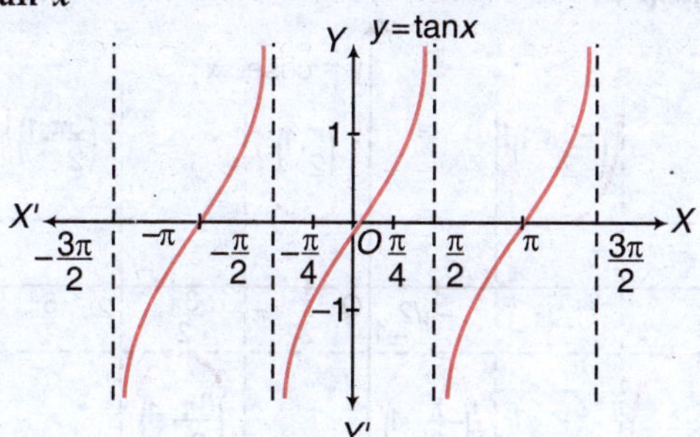

(i) Domain $= R \sim (2n+1)\frac{\pi}{2}, n \in I$

(ii) Range $= (-\infty, \infty)$

(iii) Period $= \pi$

4. **Graph of cot x**

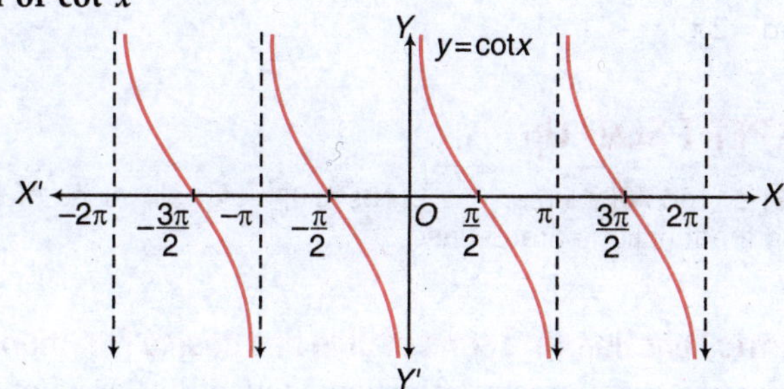

(i) Domain $= R \sim n\pi, n \in I$ (ii) Range $= (-\infty, \infty)$ (iii) Period $= \pi$

5. **Graph of sec x**

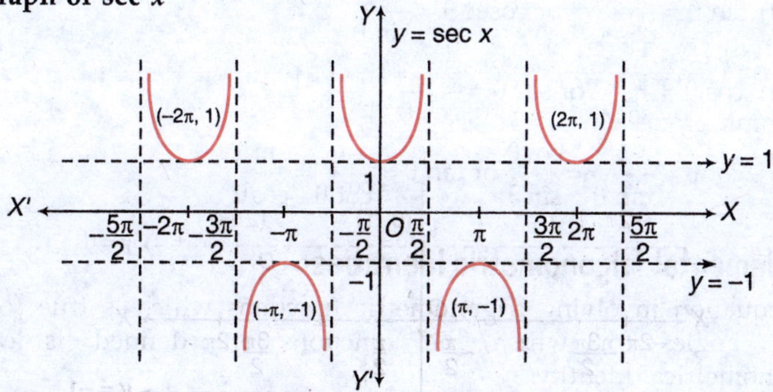

(i) Domain $= R \sim (2n+1)\frac{\pi}{2}, n \in I$

(ii) Range $= (-\infty, -1] \cup [1, \infty)$

(iii) Period $= 2\pi$

6. **Graph of cosec x**

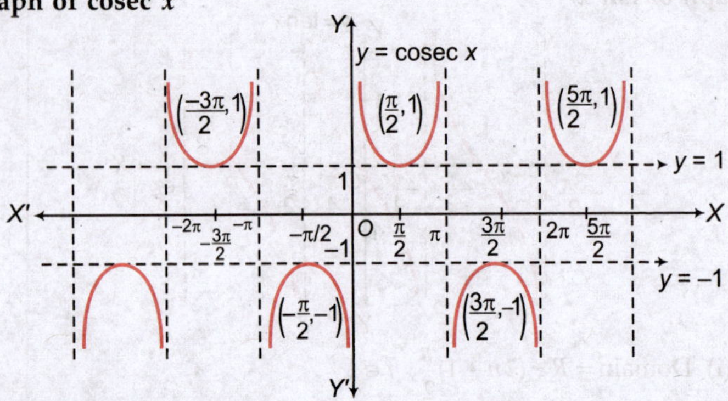

(i) Domain $= R \sim n\pi, n \in I$

(ii) Range $= (-\infty, -1] \cup [1, \infty)$

(iii) Period $= 2\pi$

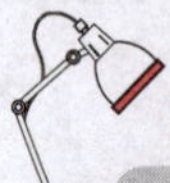

EXPERT Scale Up

$|\sin\theta| \le 1, |\cos\theta| \le 1, |\sec\theta| \ge 1, |\text{cosec}\,\theta| \ge 1$ for all values of θ, for which the functions are defined.

Trigonometric Functions in Terms of sine and cosine Functions

Given below are trigonometric functions defined in terms of sine and cosine functions

(i) $\sin\theta = \dfrac{1}{\text{cosec}\,\theta}$ or $\text{cosec}\,\theta = \dfrac{1}{\sin\theta}$

(ii) $\cos\theta = \dfrac{1}{\sec\theta}$ or $\sec\theta = \dfrac{1}{\cos\theta}$

(iii) $\cot\theta = \dfrac{1}{\tan\theta} = \dfrac{\cos\theta}{\sin\theta}$ or $\tan\theta = \dfrac{1}{\cot\theta} = \dfrac{\sin\theta}{\cos\theta}$

Fundamental Trigonometric Identities

An equation involving trigonometric functions which is true for all those angles for which the functions are defined is called trigonometrical identity.

(i) $\cos^2\theta + \sin^2\theta = 1$ or $1 - \cos^2\theta = \sin^2\theta$ or $1 - \sin^2\theta = \cos^2\theta$

(ii) $1 + \tan^2\theta = \sec^2\theta$ or $\tan^2\theta = \sec^2\theta - 1$ or $\sec^2\theta - \tan^2\theta = 1$

(iii) $1 + \cot^2\theta = \text{cosec}^2\theta$ or $\cot^2\theta = \text{cosec}^2\theta - 1$ or $\text{cosec}^2\theta - \cot^2\theta = 1$

Transformation of One Trigonometric Function to Another Trigonometric Function

Trigonometric function	$\sin\theta$	$\cos\theta$	$\tan\theta$	$\cot\theta$	$\sec\theta$	$\operatorname{cosec}\theta$
$\sin\theta$	$\sin\theta$	$\sqrt{(1-\cos^2\theta)}$	$\frac{\tan\theta}{\sqrt{(1+\tan^2\theta)}}$	$\frac{1}{\sqrt{1+\cot^2\theta}}$	$\frac{\sqrt{(\sec^2\theta-1)}}{\sec\theta}$	$\frac{1}{\operatorname{cosec}\theta}$
$\cos\theta$	$\sqrt{(1-\sin^2\theta)}$	$\cos\theta$	$\frac{1}{\sqrt{(1+\tan^2\theta)}}$	$\frac{\cot\theta}{\sqrt{(1+\cot^2\theta)}}$	$\frac{1}{\sec\theta}$	$\frac{\sqrt{(\operatorname{cosec}^2\theta-1)}}{\operatorname{cosec}\theta}$
$\tan\theta$	$\frac{\sin\theta}{\sqrt{(1-\sin^2\theta)}}$	$\frac{\sqrt{(1-\cos^2\theta)}}{\cos\theta}$	$\tan\theta$	$\frac{1}{\cot\theta}$	$\sqrt{(\sec^2\theta-1)}$	$\frac{1}{\sqrt{(\operatorname{cosec}^2\theta-1)}}$
$\cot\theta$	$\frac{\sqrt{(1-\sin^2\theta)}}{\sin\theta}$	$\frac{\cos\theta}{\sqrt{(1-\cos^2\theta)}}$	$\frac{1}{\tan\theta}$	$\cot\theta$	$\frac{1}{\sqrt{(\sec^2\theta-1)}}$	$\sqrt{(\operatorname{cosec}^2\theta-1)}$
$\sec\theta$	$\frac{1}{\sqrt{(1-\sin^2\theta)}}$	$\frac{1}{\cos\theta}$	$\sqrt{(1+\tan^2\theta)}$	$\frac{\sqrt{1+\cot^2\theta}}{\cot\theta}$	$\sec\theta$	$\frac{\operatorname{cosec}\theta}{\sqrt{(\operatorname{cosec}^2\theta-1)}}$
$\operatorname{cosec}\theta$	$\frac{1}{\sin\theta}$	$\frac{1}{\sqrt{(1-\cos^2\theta)}}$	$\frac{\sqrt{(1+\tan^2\theta)}}{\tan\theta}$	$\sqrt{(1+\cot^2\theta)}$	$\frac{\sec\theta}{\sqrt{(\sec^2\theta-1)}}$	$\operatorname{cosec}\theta$

Value Point Above table is applicable only when $\theta\in(0°, 90°)$.

Sign of Trigonometric Functions in Different Quadrants

If we draw two mutually perpendicular (intersecting) lines in the plane of paper, then these lines divide the plane of paper into four parts, known as quadrants.

In anti-clockwise order, these quadrants are numbered as I, II, III and IV. All angles from 0° to 90° are taken in I quardant, 90° to 180° in II quardant, 180° to 270° in III quadrant and 270° to 360° in IV quadrant.

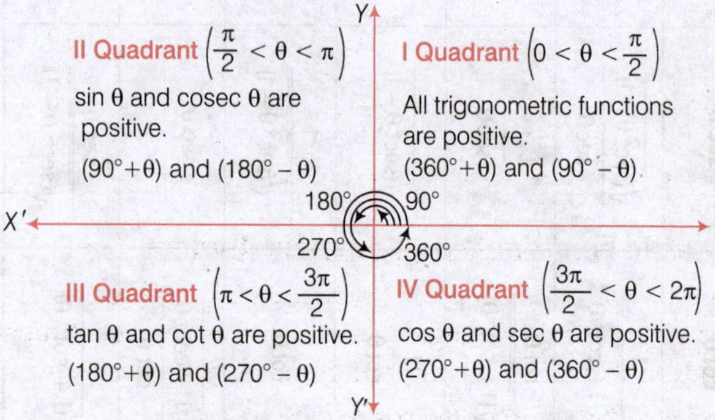

II Quadrant $\left(\frac{\pi}{2} < \theta < \pi\right)$
sin θ and cosec θ are positive.
(90°+θ) and (180° − θ)

I Quadrant $\left(0 < \theta < \frac{\pi}{2}\right)$
All trigonometric functions are positive.
(360°+θ) and (90° − θ)

III Quadrant $\left(\pi < \theta < \frac{3\pi}{2}\right)$
tan θ and cot θ are positive.
(180°+θ) and (270° − θ)

IV Quadrant $\left(\frac{3\pi}{2} < \theta < 2\pi\right)$
cos θ and sec θ are positive.
(270°+θ) and (360° − θ)

Y, Y′, X, X′, 90°, 180°, 270°, 360°

EXPERT Scale Up

There are four quadrants, by using ASTC (Add Sugar To Coffee) we can remember that which trigonometric function is positive quadrantwise.

Add → All
Sugar → Sin
To → Tan
Coffee → Cos

Trigonometric Ratios of Some Special Angles

Angle	$7\frac{1}{2}^\circ$	15°	18°	$22\frac{1}{2}^\circ$	36°
sin θ	$\frac{\sqrt{4-\sqrt{2}-\sqrt{6}}}{2\sqrt{2}}$	$\frac{\sqrt{3}-1}{2\sqrt{2}}$	$\frac{\sqrt{5}-1}{4}$	$\frac{1}{2}\sqrt{2-\sqrt{2}}$	$\frac{1}{4}\sqrt{10-2\sqrt{5}}$
cos θ	$\frac{\sqrt{4+\sqrt{2}+\sqrt{6}}}{2\sqrt{2}}$	$\frac{\sqrt{3}+1}{2\sqrt{2}}$	$\frac{1}{4}\sqrt{10+2\sqrt{5}}$	$\frac{1}{2}\sqrt{2+\sqrt{2}}$	$\frac{\sqrt{5}+1}{4}$
tan θ	$(\sqrt{3}-\sqrt{2})(\sqrt{2}-1)$	$2-\sqrt{3}$	$\frac{\sqrt{5}-1}{\sqrt{10+2\sqrt{5}}}$	$\sqrt{2}-1$	$\frac{\sqrt{10-2\sqrt{5}}}{\sqrt{5}+1}$

Trigonometric Ratios (or Functions) of Allied Angles

Two angles are said to be allied when their sum or difference is either zero or a multiple of 90°. The angles $-\theta, 90° \pm \theta, 180° \pm \theta, 270° \pm \theta$, $360° - \theta$ etc., are angles allied to the angle θ, if θ is measured in degrees.

Allied Angles	$\sin\theta$	$\operatorname{cosec}\theta$	$\cos\theta$	$\sec\theta$	$\tan\theta$	$\cot\theta$
$-\theta$	$-\sin\theta$	$-\operatorname{cosec}\theta$	$\cos\theta$	$\sec\theta$	$-\tan\theta$	$-\cot\theta$
$90°-\theta$	$\cos\theta$	$\sec\theta$	$\sin\theta$	$\operatorname{cosec}\theta$	$\cot\theta$	$\tan\theta$
$90°+\theta$	$\cos\theta$	$\sec\theta$	$-\sin\theta$	$-\operatorname{cosec}\theta$	$-\cot\theta$	$-\tan\theta$
$180°-\theta$	$\sin\theta$	$\operatorname{cosec}\theta$	$-\cos\theta$	$-\sec\theta$	$-\tan\theta$	$-\cot\theta$
$180°+\theta$	$-\sin\theta$	$-\operatorname{cosec}\theta$	$-\cos\theta$	$-\sec\theta$	$\tan\theta$	$\cot\theta$
$270°-\theta$	$-\cos\theta$	$-\sec\theta$	$-\sin\theta$	$-\operatorname{cosec}\theta$	$\cot\theta$	$\tan\theta$
$270°+\theta$	$-\cos\theta$	$-\sec\theta$	$\sin\theta$	$\operatorname{cosec}\theta$	$-\cot\theta$	$-\tan\theta$
$360°-\theta$	$-\sin\theta$	$-\operatorname{cosec}\theta$	$\cos\theta$	$\sec\theta$	$-\tan\theta$	$-\cot\theta$

Trigonometric Functions of Compound Angles

The algebraic sum of two or more angles are generally called compound angles and the angles are known as the constituent angle. Some standard formulae of compound angles have been given below

(i) $\sin(A+B) = \sin A\cos B + \cos A\sin B$

(ii) $\sin(A-B) = \sin A\cos B - \cos A\sin B$

(iii) $\cos(A+B) = \cos A\cos B - \sin A\sin B$

(iv) $\cos(A-B) = \cos A\cos B + \sin A\sin B$

(v) $\tan(A+B) = \dfrac{\tan A + \tan B}{1 - \tan A\tan B}$

(vi) $\tan(A-B) = \dfrac{\tan A - \tan B}{1 + \tan A\tan B}$

(vii) $\cot(A+B) = \dfrac{\cot A\cot B - 1}{\cot B + \cot A}$

(viii) $\cot(A-B) = \dfrac{\cot A\cot B + 1}{\cot B - \cot A}$

(ix) $\sin(A+B)\sin(A-B) = \sin^2 A - \sin^2 B = \cos^2 B - \cos^2 A$

(x) $\cos(A+B)\cos(A-B) = \cos^2 A - \sin^2 B = \cos^2 B - \sin^2 A$

Conditional Identities

(i) $\sin(A+B+C) = \cos A\cos B\sin C + \cos A\sin B\cos C + \sin A\cos B\cos C - \sin A\sin B\sin C$

or $\sin(A+B+C) = \cos A\cos B\cos C(\tan A + \tan B + \tan C - \tan A\tan B\tan C)$

(ii) $\cos(A+B+C)=\cos A\cos B\cos C-\sin A\sin B\cos C$
$-\sin A\cos B\sin C-\cos A\sin B\sin C$

or $\cos(A+B+C)=\cos A\cos B\cos C(1-\tan A\tan B-\tan B\tan C$
$-\tan C\tan A)$

(iii) $\tan(A+B+C)=\dfrac{\tan A+\tan B+\tan C-\tan A\tan B\tan C}{1-\tan A\tan B-\tan B\tan C-\tan C\tan A}$

If $A+B+C=0$, then $\tan A+\tan B+\tan C=\tan A\tan B\tan C$

(iv) (a) $\sin(A_1+A_2+\ldots+A_n)=(\cos A_1\cos A_2\cos A_3\ldots\cos A_n)$
$\times(S_1-S_3+S_5-S_7+\ldots)$

(b) $\cos(A_1+A_2+\ldots+A_n)=(\cos A_1\cos A_2\cos A_3\ldots\cos A_n)$
$\times(1-S_2+S_4-S_6+\ldots)$

(c) $\tan(A_1+A_2+\ldots+A_n)=\dfrac{S_1-S_3+S_5-S_7+\ldots}{1-S_2+S_4-S_6+\ldots}$

where, $S_1=\tan A_1+\tan A_2+\ldots+\tan A_n$
[sum of the tangents of the separate angles]

$S_2=\tan A_1\tan A_2+\tan A_2\tan A_3+\ldots$
[sum of the tangents taken two at a time]

$S_3=\tan A_1\tan A_2\tan A_3+\tan A_2\tan A_3\tan A_4+\ldots$
[sum of the tangents taken three at a time]

Knowledge Booster

If $A_1=A_2=\cdots A_n=A$, then we have
$S_1=n\tan A, S_2={}^nC_2\tan^2 A, S_3={}^nC_3\tan^3 A, \ldots$ so on.

Transformation Formulae

(i) $2\sin A\cos B=\sin(A+B)+\sin(A-B)$

(ii) $2\cos A\sin B=\sin(A+B)-\sin(A-B)$

(iii) $2\cos A\cos B=\cos(A+B)+\cos(A-B)$

(iv) $2\sin A\sin B=\cos(A-B)-\cos(A+B)$

(v) $\sin C+\sin D=2\sin\left(\dfrac{C+D}{2}\right)\cos\left(\dfrac{C-D}{2}\right)$

(vi) $\sin C-\sin D=2\cos\left(\dfrac{C+D}{2}\right)\sin\left(\dfrac{C-D}{2}\right)$

(vii) $\cos C+\cos D=2\cos\left(\dfrac{C+D}{2}\right)\cos\left(\dfrac{C-D}{2}\right)$

(viii) $\cos C - \cos D = -2\sin\left(\frac{C+D}{2}\right)\sin\left(\frac{C-D}{2}\right)$

$$=2\sin\left(\frac{C+D}{2}\right)\sin\left(\frac{D-C}{2}\right)$$

Trigonometric Functions of Multiple Angles

(i) $\sin 2A = 2\sin A\cos A = \frac{2\tan A}{1+\tan^2 A}$

(ii) $\cos 2A = \cos^2 A - \sin^2 A = 2\cos^2 A - 1 = 1 - 2\sin^2 A = \frac{1-\tan^2 A}{1+\tan^2 A}$

(iii) $\tan 2A = \frac{2\tan A}{1-\tan^2 A}$

(iv) $\sin 3A = 3\sin A - 4\sin^3 A$

(v) $\cos 3A = 4\cos^3 A - 3\cos A$

(vi) $\tan 3A = \frac{3\tan A - \tan^3 A}{1-3\tan^2 A}$

Trigonometric Functions of Sub-multiple Angles

(i) $\sin A = 2\sin\frac{A}{2}\cos\frac{A}{2} = \frac{2\tan\frac{A}{2}}{1+\tan^2\frac{A}{2}}$

(ii) $\cos A = \cos^2\frac{A}{2} - \sin^2\frac{A}{2} = 2\cos^2\frac{A}{2} - 1 = 1 - 2\sin^2\frac{A}{2} = \frac{1-\tan^2\frac{A}{2}}{1+\tan^2\frac{A}{2}}$

(iii) $\tan A = \frac{2\tan\frac{A}{2}}{1-\tan^2\frac{A}{2}}$

(iv) $1 - \cos A = 2\sin^2\frac{A}{2}$

(v) $1 + \cos A = 2\cos^2\frac{A}{2}$

(vi) $\frac{1-\cos A}{1+\cos A} = \tan^2\frac{A}{2}$

(vii) $\sin\left(\frac{A}{2}\right) + \cos\left(\frac{A}{2}\right) = \pm\sqrt{1+\sin A}$

(viii) $\sin\left(\frac{A}{2}\right) - \cos\left(\frac{A}{2}\right) = \pm\sqrt{1-\sin A}$

Competition Insight

Some Important Results

Product of Trigonometric Ratio

(i) $\sin\theta \sin(60^\circ - \theta)\sin(60^\circ + \theta) = \frac{1}{4}\sin 3\theta$

(ii) $\cos\theta \cos(60^\circ - \theta)\cos(60^\circ + \theta) = \frac{1}{4}\cos 3\theta$

(iii) $\tan\theta \tan(60^\circ - \theta)\tan(60^\circ + \theta) = \tan 3\theta$

(iv) (a) $\sin^2\theta + \sin^2(60^\circ + \theta) + \sin^2(60^\circ - \theta) = \frac{3}{2}$

(b) $\cos^2\theta + \cos^2(60^\circ + \theta) + \cos^2(60^\circ - \theta) = \frac{3}{2}$

(v) $\cos A \cos 2A \cos 4A \ldots \cos 2^{n-1}A = \frac{1}{2^n \sin A}\sin(2^n A)$

Sum of Trigonometric Ratios

(i) $\sin A + \sin(A+B) + \sin(A+2B) + \ldots + \sin(A+(n-1)B)$

$$= \frac{\sin\left\{A + (n-1)\frac{B}{2}\right\}\sin\frac{nB}{2}}{\sin\frac{B}{2}}$$

(ii) $\cos A + \cos(A+B) + \cos(A+2B) + \ldots + \cos(A+(n-1)B)$

$$= \frac{\sin\frac{nB}{2}}{\sin\frac{B}{2}}\cos\left\{A + \frac{(n-1)B}{2}\right\}$$

Identities for Angles of a Triangle

If A, B and C are angles of a triangle (or $A + B + C = \pi$), then

(i) (a) $\sin(B+C) = \sin A$ (b) $\cos(B+C) = -\cos A$

(c) $\sin\left(\frac{B+C}{2}\right) = \cos\frac{A}{2}$ (d) $\cos\left(\frac{B+C}{2}\right) = \sin\frac{A}{2}$

(ii) $\sin 2A + \sin 2B + \sin 2C = 4\sin A \sin B \sin C$

(iii) $\cos 2A + \cos 2B + \cos 2C = -1 - 4\cos A \cos B \cos C$

(iv) $\sin A + \sin B + \sin C = 4\cos\frac{A}{2}\cos\frac{B}{2}\cos\frac{C}{2}$

(v) $\cos A + \cos B + \cos C = 1 + 4\sin\frac{A}{2}\sin\frac{B}{2}\sin\frac{C}{2}$

(vi) $\tan A + \tan B + \tan C = \tan A \tan B \tan C$

(vii) $\cot B \cot C + \cot C \cot A + \cot A \cot B = 1$

(viii) $\cot\frac{A}{2} + \cot\frac{B}{2} + \cot\frac{C}{2} = \cot\frac{A}{2}\cot\frac{B}{2}\cot\frac{C}{2}$

(ix) $\tan\frac{A}{2}\tan\frac{B}{2} + \tan\frac{B}{2}\tan\frac{C}{2} + \tan\frac{C}{2}\tan\frac{A}{2} = 1$

Periodic Functions

A function $f(x)$ is said to be periodic, if there exists a real number $T > 0$ such that $f(x+T) = f(x)$ for all x. T is called the period of the function, all trigonometric functions are periodic.

Value Points

(i) $\sin\theta$, $\cos\theta$, $\operatorname{cosec}\theta$ and $\sec\theta$ have a period of 2π.

(ii) $\tan\theta$, $\cot\theta$ have a period of π.

(iii) Period of $\sin k\theta$ is $2\pi/k$.

(iv) Period of $\tan k\theta$ is π/k.

(v) Period of $\sin^n\theta$, $\cos^n\theta$, $\sec^n\theta$ and $\operatorname{cosec}^n\theta$ is 2π, if n is odd and, π if n is even.

(vi) Period of $\tan^n\theta$, $\cot^n\theta$ is π, if n is even or odd.

(vii) Period of $|\sin\theta|$, $|\cos\theta|$, $|\tan\theta|$, $|\cot\theta|$, $|\sec\theta|$ and $|\operatorname{cosec}\theta|$ is π.

(viii) Period of $|\sin\theta| + |\cos\theta|$, $|\tan\theta| + |\cot\theta|$ and $|\sec\theta| + |\operatorname{cosec}\theta|$ is $\pi/2$.

Maximum and Minimum Values of a Trigonometric Expression

(i) Maximum value of $a\cos\theta \pm b\sin\theta = \sqrt{a^2+b^2}$

Minimum value of $a\cos\theta \pm b\sin\theta = -\sqrt{a^2+b^2}$

(ii) Maximum value of $a\cos\theta \pm b\sin\theta + c = c + \sqrt{a^2+b^2}$

Minimum value of $a\cos\theta \pm b\sin\theta + c = c - \sqrt{a^2+b^2}$

Chapter 12

Triangle

Basic Rules of Triangle

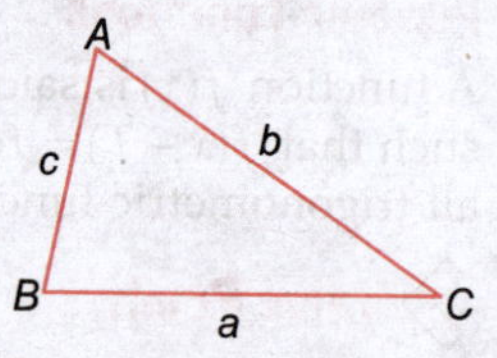

In a ΔABC, the angles are denoted by capital letters A, B and C and the lengths of the sides opposite to these angles are denoted by small letters a, b and c, respectively. Area and perimeter of a triangle are denoted by Δ and 2s respectively, where s = semi-perimeter of ΔABC.

Semi-perimeter of the triangle is written as $s = \dfrac{a+b+c}{2}$.

(i) **Sine Rule** $\dfrac{\sin A}{a} = \dfrac{\sin B}{b} = \dfrac{\sin C}{c} = \dfrac{1}{2R}$, where R is radius of the circumcircle of ΔABC.

(ii) **Cosine Rule** $\cos A = \dfrac{b^2 + c^2 - a^2}{2bc}$, $\cos B = \dfrac{a^2 + c^2 - b^2}{2ac}$

and $\cos C = \dfrac{a^2 + b^2 - c^2}{2ab}$

(iii) **Projection Rule** $a = b\cos C + c\cos B$, $b = c\cos A + a\cos C$ and $c = a\cos B + b\cos A$

Trigonometrical Ratios of Half of the Angles of Triangle

(i) $\sin\dfrac{A}{2} = \sqrt{\dfrac{(s-b)(s-c)}{bc}}$, $\sin\dfrac{B}{2} = \sqrt{\dfrac{(s-c)(s-a)}{ac}}$, $\sin\dfrac{C}{2} = \sqrt{\dfrac{(s-a)(s-b)}{ab}}$

(ii) $\cos\dfrac{A}{2} = \sqrt{\dfrac{s(s-a)}{bc}}$, $\cos\dfrac{B}{2} = \sqrt{\dfrac{s(s-b)}{ac}}$, $\cos\dfrac{C}{2} = \sqrt{\dfrac{s(s-c)}{ab}}$

(iii) $\tan\dfrac{A}{2} = \sqrt{\dfrac{(s-b)(s-c)}{s(s-a)}}$, $\tan\dfrac{B}{2} = \sqrt{\dfrac{(s-a)(s-c)}{s(s-b)}}$, $\tan\dfrac{C}{2} = \sqrt{\dfrac{(s-a)(s-b)}{s(s-c)}}$

Area of a Triangle

Consider a triangle of side a, b and c.

(i) $\Delta = \frac{1}{2} bc \sin A = \frac{1}{2} ca \sin B = \frac{1}{2} ab \sin C$

(ii) $\Delta = \frac{c^2 \sin A \sin B}{2 \sin C} = \frac{a^2 \sin B \sin C}{2 \sin A} = \frac{b^2 \sin C \sin A}{2 \sin B}$

(iii) $\Delta = \sqrt{s(s-a)(s-b)(s-c)}$, is known as **Heron's formula.**

where $s = \frac{a+b+c}{2}$ [semi-perimeter of triangle]

(iv) $\Delta = \frac{abc}{4R} = rs$, where R and r are radii of the circumcircle and the incircle of ΔABC, respectively.

Solutions of a Triangle

Elements of a Triangle

There are six elements of a triangle, in which three are its sides and other three are its angle. If three elements of a triangle are given, atleast one of which is its side, then other elements can be uniquely calculated. This is called **solving the triangle**.

Solutions of a Right Angled Triangle

Let ΔABC be a given triangle with right angle at C, then

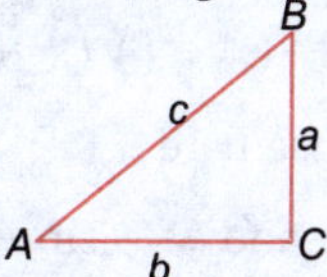

(i) the solution when two sides are given

Given	To be calculated
a, b	$\tan A = \frac{a}{b}; B = 90° - A, c = \frac{a}{\sin A}$
a, c	$\sin A = \frac{a}{c}; B = 90° - A$ $b = c \cos A$ or $b = \sqrt{c^2 - a^2}$

(ii) the solution when one side and one acute angle are given

Given	To be calculated
a, A	$B = 90° - A, b = a \cot A, c = \frac{a}{\sin A}$
c, A	$B = 90° - A, a = c \sin A, b = a \cot A$

Competition Insight

Solutions of a Triangle in General

(i) When three sides a, b and c are given, then

$$\sin A = \frac{2\Delta}{bc}, \sin B = \frac{2\Delta}{ac}, \sin C = \frac{2\Delta}{ab}$$

where, $\Delta = \sqrt{s(s-a)(s-b)(s-c)}$ in which $s = \frac{a+b+c}{2}$

and $A + B + C = 180°$.

(ii) When two sides and the included angle are given, then

(a) $\tan\left(\frac{A-B}{2}\right) = \frac{a-b}{a+b}\cot\frac{C}{2}, \frac{A+B}{2} = 90° - \frac{C}{2}, c = \frac{a\sin C}{\sin A}$

(b) $\tan\left(\frac{B-C}{2}\right) = \frac{b-c}{b+c}\cot\frac{A}{2}, \frac{B+C}{2} = 90° - \frac{A}{2}, a = \frac{b\sin A}{\sin B}$

(c) $\tan\left(\frac{C-A}{2}\right) = \frac{c-a}{c+a}\cot\frac{B}{2}, \frac{C+A}{2} = 90° - \frac{B}{2}, b = \frac{c\sin B}{\sin C}$

This is called as **Napier's analogy.**

(iii) When one side a and two angles A and B are given, then

$$C = 180° - (A+B) \Rightarrow b = \frac{c\sin B}{\sin C} \text{ and } c = \frac{a\sin C}{\sin A}$$

(iv) When two sides a, b and the opposite $\angle A$ is given, then

$$\sin B = \frac{b}{a}\sin A, C = 180° - (A+B), c = \frac{a\sin C}{\sin A}$$

Now, different cases arise here

(a) If A is an acute angle and $a < b\sin A$, then $\sin B = \frac{b}{a}\sin A$ gives $\sin B > 1$, which is not possible, so no such triangle is possible.

(b) When A is an acute angle and $a = b\sin A$. In this case, only one triangle is possible, which is right angled at B.

(c) If A is an acute angle and $a > b\sin A$. In this case, there are two values of B given by $\sin B = \frac{b\sin A}{a}$, say B_1 and B_2 such that $B_1 + B_2 = 180°$, hence two triangles are possible.

Circles Connected with Triangle

1. Circumcircle

The circle passing through the vertices of the ΔABC is called the circumcircle and its radius R is called the circumradius.

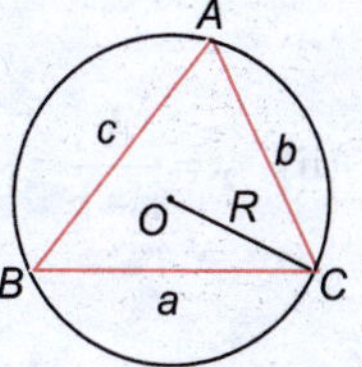

$$\therefore \quad R = \frac{a}{2\sin A} = \frac{b}{2\sin B} = \frac{c}{2\sin C} = \frac{abc}{4\Delta}$$

2. Incircle

The circle touches the three sides of the triangle internally is called the inscribed or the incircle of the triangle and its radius r is called the inradius of circle.

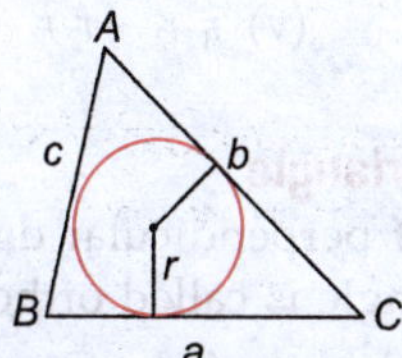

$$\therefore \quad r = \frac{\Delta}{s} = (s-a)\tan\frac{A}{2}$$

$$r = (s-b)\tan\frac{B}{2} = (s-c)\tan\frac{C}{2} = 4R\sin\frac{A}{2}\sin\frac{B}{2}\sin\frac{C}{2}$$

and $$r = \frac{a\sin\frac{B}{2}\sin\frac{C}{2}}{\cos\frac{A}{2}} = \frac{b\sin\frac{C}{2}\sin\frac{A}{2}}{\cos\frac{B}{2}} = \frac{c\sin\frac{A}{2}\sin\frac{B}{2}}{\cos\frac{C}{2}}$$

3. Escribed Circle

The circle touches BC and the two sides AB and AC produced of ΔABC externally is called the escribed circle opposite to A. Its radius is denoted by r_1.

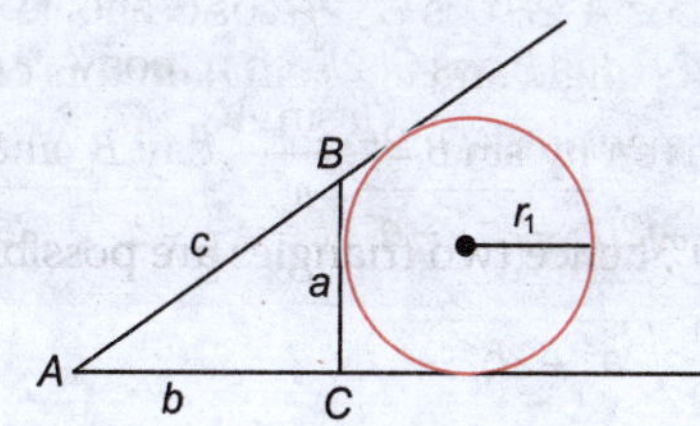

Similarly, r_2 and r_3 denote the radii of the escribed circles opposite to angles B and C, respectively. Hence, r_1, r_2 and r_3 are called the exradius of ΔABC. Here,

(i) $r_1 = \dfrac{\Delta}{s-a} = s\tan\dfrac{A}{2} = 4R\sin\dfrac{A}{2}\cos\dfrac{B}{2}\cos\dfrac{C}{2} = \dfrac{a\cos\dfrac{B}{2}\cos\dfrac{C}{2}}{\cos\dfrac{A}{2}}$

(ii) $r_2 = \dfrac{\Delta}{s-b} = s\tan\dfrac{B}{2} = 4R\sin\dfrac{B}{2}\cos\dfrac{C}{2}\cos\dfrac{A}{2} = \dfrac{b\cos\dfrac{C}{2}\cos\dfrac{A}{2}}{\cos\dfrac{B}{2}}$

(iii) $r_3 = \dfrac{\Delta}{s-c} = s\tan\dfrac{C}{2} = 4R\sin\dfrac{C}{2}\cos\dfrac{A}{2}\cos\dfrac{B}{2} = \dfrac{c\cos\dfrac{A}{2}\cos\dfrac{B}{2}}{\cos\dfrac{C}{2}}$

(iv) $r_1 + r_2 + r_3 = 4R + r$ (v) $r_1 r_2 + r_2 r_3 + r_3 r_1 = \dfrac{r_1 r_2 r_3}{r}$

4. Orthocentre and Pedal Triangle

The point of intersection of perpendicular drawn from the vertices on the opposite sides of a triangle is called orthocentre.

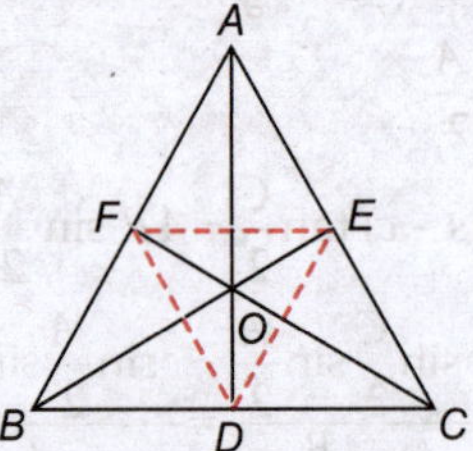

The ΔDEF formed by joining the feet of the altitudes is called the pedal triangle.

Value Points

- Distance of the orthocentre of the triangle from the angular points are $2R\cos A$, $2R\cos B$, $2R\cos C$ and its distances from the sides are $2R\cos B\cos C$, $2R\cos C\cos A$, $2R\cos A\cos B$.
- The length of medians AD, BE and CF of a ΔABC are
$$AD = \frac{1}{2}\sqrt{2b^2 + 2c^2 - a^2},\ BE = \frac{1}{2}\sqrt{2c^2 + 2a^2 - b^2}$$
and $CF = \dfrac{1}{2}\sqrt{2a^2 + 2b^2 - c^2}$
- Distance between circumcentre and orthocentre
$$= R^2[1 - 8\cos A\cos B\cos C]$$

- Distance between circumcentre and incentre

$$= R^2\left[1 - 8\sin\frac{A}{2}\sin\frac{B}{2}\sin\frac{C}{2}\right] = R^2 - 2Rr$$

- Distance between circumcentre and centroid

$$= R^2 - \frac{1}{9}(a^2 + b^2 + c^2)$$

Radii of the Inscribed and Circumscribed Circles of Regular Polygon

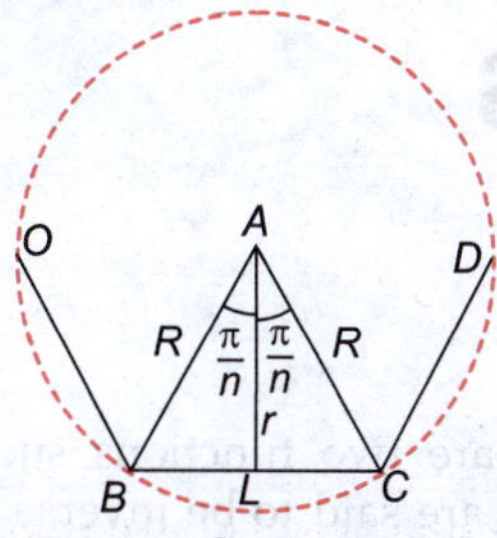

(i) Radius of circumcircle $(R) = \frac{a}{2}\operatorname{cosec}\frac{\pi}{n}$

(ii) Radius of incircle $(r) = \frac{a}{2}\cot\frac{\pi}{n}$, where a is the length of a side of polygon.

(iii) The area of the polygon $= n$ (Area of ΔABC)

$$= \frac{1}{4}na^2\cot\left(\frac{\pi}{n}\right) = nr^2\tan\frac{\pi}{n} = \frac{n}{2}R^2\sin\left(\frac{2\pi}{n}\right)$$

Knowledge Booster

***m-n* Theorem** In a ΔABC, D is a point on the line BC such that $BD : DC = m : n$ and $\angle ADC = \theta$, $\angle BAD = \alpha$, $\angle DAC = \beta$, then

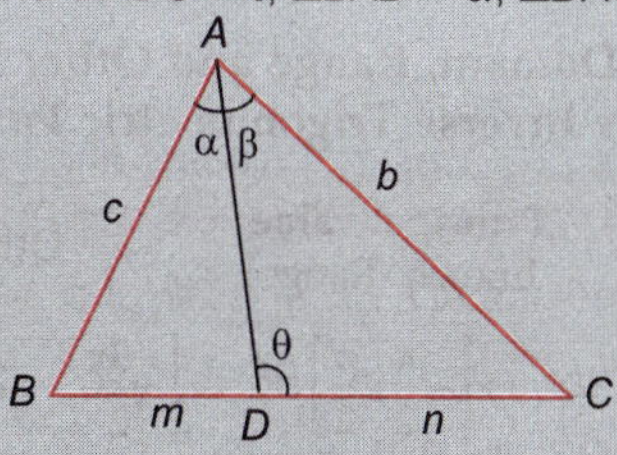

(a) $(m + n)\cot\theta = m\cot\alpha - n\cot\beta$

(b) $(m + n)\cot\theta = n\cot B - m\cot C$

Apollonius Theorem In a ΔABC, $AB^2 + AC^2 = 2(AD^2 + BD^2)$, where D is mid-point of BC. This theorem relates the length of a median of a triangle to the length of its side.

Chapter 13

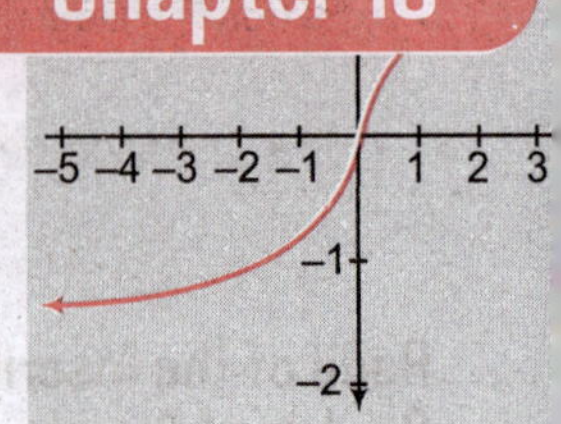

Inverse Trigonometric Functions

Inverse Function

If $y = f(x)$ and $x = g(y)$ are two functions such that $f(g(y)) = y$ and $g(f(y)) = x$, then f and g are said to be inverse of each other, i.e. $g = f^{-1}$. If $y = f(x)$, then $x = f^{-1}(y)$.

Inverse Trigonometric Functions

As we know that trigonometric functions are not one-one and onto in their natural domain and range, so their inverse do not exist but if we restrict their domain and range, then their inverse may exists.

Domain and Range of Inverse Trigonometric Functions

The range of trigonometric functions becomes the domain of inverse trigonometric functions and restricted domain of trigonometric functions becomes range or principal value branch of inverse trigonometric functions.

Table for Domain, Range and Other Possible Range of Inverse Trigonometric Functions

Function	Domain	Principal value branch (Range)	Other possible range
$y = \sin^{-1} x$	$[-1, 1]$	$\left[-\frac{\pi}{2}, \frac{\pi}{2}\right]$	$\left[\frac{-3\pi}{2}, \frac{-\pi}{2}\right], \left[\frac{\pi}{2}, \frac{3\pi}{2}\right]$ etc.
$y = \cos^{-1} x$	$[-1, 1]$	$[0, \pi]$	$[-\pi, 0], [\pi, 2\pi]$ etc.
$y = \tan^{-1} x$	R	$\left(-\frac{\pi}{2}, \frac{\pi}{2}\right)$	$\left(\frac{-3\pi}{2}, \frac{-\pi}{2}\right), \left(\frac{\pi}{2}, \frac{3\pi}{2}\right)$ etc.

Function	Domain	Principal value branch (Range)	Other possible range
$y = \sec^{-1} x$	$R - (-1, 1)$	$[0, \pi] - \left\{\frac{\pi}{2}\right\}$	$[-\pi, 0] - \left\{-\frac{\pi}{2}\right\}, [\pi, 2\pi] - \left\{\frac{3\pi}{2}\right\}$ etc.
$y = \operatorname{cosec}^{-1} x$	$R - (-1, 1)$	$\left[\frac{-\pi}{2}, \frac{\pi}{2}\right] - \{0\}$	$\left[\frac{-3\pi}{2}, \frac{-\pi}{2}\right] - \{-\pi\}, \left[\frac{\pi}{2}, \frac{3\pi}{2}\right] - \{\pi\}$
$y = \cot^{-1} x$	R	$(0, \pi)$	$(-\pi, 0), (\pi, 2\pi)$ etc.

EXPERT Scale Up

$\sin^{-1} x$ should not be confused with $(\sin x)^{-1}$. In fact $(\sin x)^{-1} = \frac{1}{\sin x}$ and similarly for other inverse trigonometric functions.

Graphs of Inverse Trigonometric Functions

The graphs of inverse trigonometric functions with respect to line $y = x$ are given in the following table

Function	Graph (By interchanging axes)	Graph (By mirror image)
$y = \sin^{-1} x$	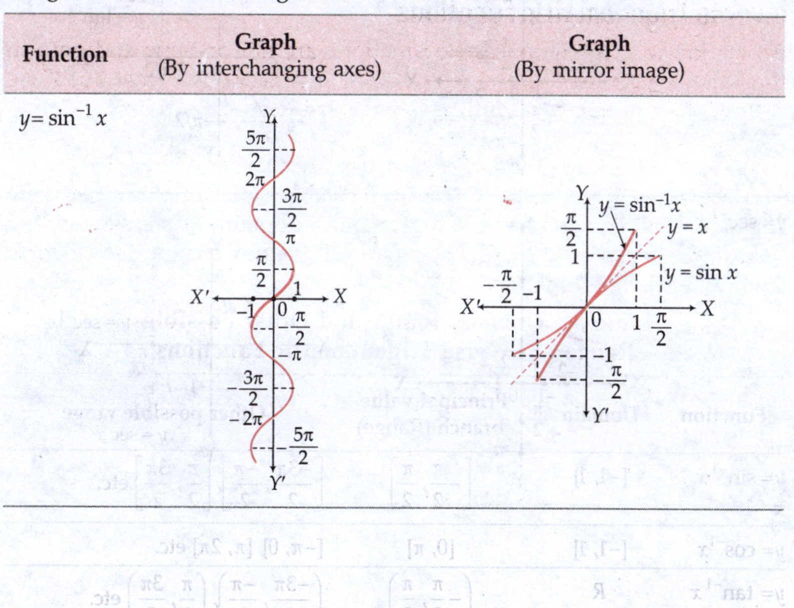	

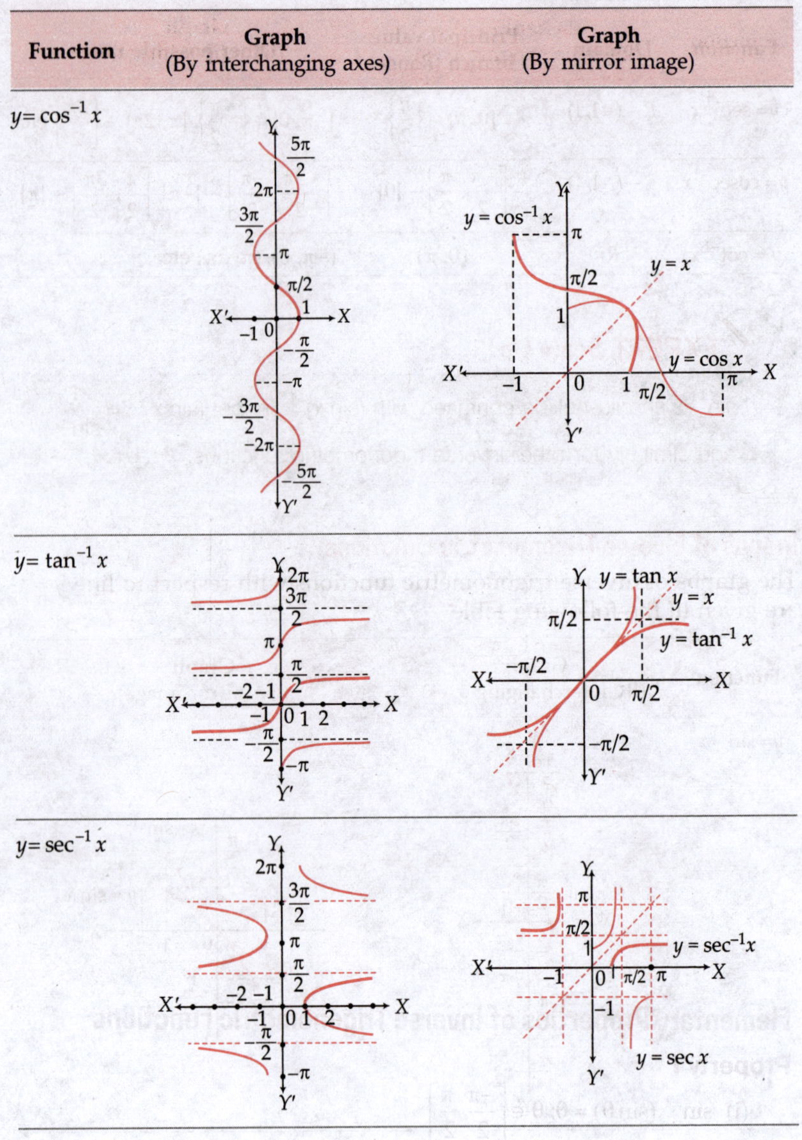
Function
Graph (By interchanging axes)
Graph (By mirror image)
y= cos⁻¹ x
Y
5π/2
2π
3π/2
π
π/2
1
X′
X
−1
0
−π/2
−π
−3π/2
−2π
−5π/2
Y′
y = cos⁻¹ x
π
π/2
y = x
1
y = cos x
X′
−1
0
1
π/2
π
X
Y′
y= tan⁻¹ x
Y
2π
3π/2
π
π/2
−2
−1
X′
X
−1
0
1
2
−π/2
−π
Y′
y = tan x
y = x
π/2
y = tan⁻¹ x
−π/2
X′
0
π/2
X
−π/2
Y′
y= sec⁻¹ x
Y
2π
3π/2
π
π/2
−2
−1
X′
X
−1
0
1
2
−π/2
−π
Y′
Y
π
π/2
1
y = sec⁻¹x
X′
−1
0
π/2
π
X
−1
y = sec x
Y′

Function	Graph (By interchanging axes)	Graph (By mirror image)
$y = \text{cosec}^{-1} x$		
$y = \cot^{-1} x$		

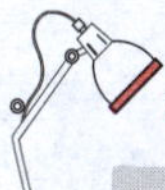

EXPERT Scale Up

If no branch of an inverse trigonometric function is mentioned, then the principal value branch is taken for the inverse trigonometric function.

Elementary Properties of Inverse Trigonometric Functions

Property I

(i) $\sin^{-1}(\sin\theta) = \theta;\ \theta \in \left[\frac{-\pi}{2}, \frac{\pi}{2}\right]$

(ii) $\cos^{-1}(\cos\theta) = \theta;\ \theta \in [0, \pi]$

(iii) $\tan^{-1}(\tan\theta) = \theta;\ \theta \in \left(-\frac{\pi}{2}, \frac{\pi}{2}\right)$

(iv) $\text{cosec}^{-1}(\text{cosec}\,\theta) = \theta; \theta \in \left[-\frac{\pi}{2}, \frac{\pi}{2}\right], \theta \neq 0$

(v) $\sec^{-1}(\sec\theta) = \theta; \theta \in [0, \pi], \theta \neq \frac{\pi}{2}$

(vi) $\cot^{-1}(\cot\theta) = \theta; \theta \in (0, \pi)$

Property II

(i) $\sin(\sin^{-1} x) = x; x \in [-1, 1]$

(ii) $\cos(\cos^{-1} x) = x; x \in [-1, 1]$

(iii) $\tan(\tan^{-1} x) = x; x \in R$

(iv) $\text{cosec}(\text{cosec}^{-1} x) = x; x \in (-\infty, -1) \cup (1, \infty)$

(v) $\sec(\sec^{-1} x) = x; x \in (-\infty, -1) \cup (1, \infty)$

(vi) $\cot(\cot^{-1} x) = x; x \in R$

Property III

(i) $\sin^{-1}(-x) = -\sin^{-1} x; x \in [-1, 1]$

(ii) $\cos^{-1}(-x) = \pi - \cos^{-1} x; x \in [-1, 1]$

(iii) $\tan^{-1}(-x) = -\tan^{-1} x; x \in R$

(iv) $\text{cosec}^{-1}(-x) = -\text{cosec}^{-1} x; x \in (-\infty, -1] \cup [1, \infty)$

(v) $\sec^{-1}(-x) = \pi - \sec^{-1} x; x \in (-\infty, -1] \cup [1, \infty)$

(vi) $\cot^{-1}(-x) = \pi - \cot^{-1} x; x \in R$

Property IV

(i) $\sin^{-1}\left(\frac{1}{x}\right) = \text{cosec}^{-1} x; x \in (-\infty, -1] \cup [1, \infty)$

(ii) $\cos^{-1}\left(\frac{1}{x}\right) = \sec^{-1} x; x \in (-\infty, -1] \cup [1, \infty)$

(iii) $\tan^{-1}\left(\frac{1}{x}\right) = \begin{cases} \cot^{-1} x, & \text{if } x > 0 \\ -\pi + \cot^{-1} x, & \text{if } x < 0 \end{cases}$

Property V

(i) $\sin^{-1} x + \cos^{-1} x = \frac{\pi}{2}; x \in [-1, 1]$

(ii) $\tan^{-1} x + \cot^{-1} x = \frac{\pi}{2}; x \in R$

(iii) $\sec^{-1} x + \text{cosec}^{-1} x = \frac{\pi}{2}; x \in (-\infty, -1] \cup [1, \infty)$

Property VI

(i) $\sin^{-1} x + \sin^{-1} y = \begin{cases} \sin^{-1} \{x\sqrt{1-y^2} + y\sqrt{1-x^2}\}, \\ \quad \text{if } -1 \le x, y \le 1 \text{ and } x^2 + y^2 \le 1 \text{ or} \\ \quad \text{if } xy < 0 \text{ and } x^2 + y^2 > 1 \\ \pi - \sin^{-1} \{x\sqrt{1-y^2} + y\sqrt{1-x^2}\}, \\ \quad \text{if } 0 < x, y \le 1 \text{ and } x^2 + y^2 > 1 \\ -\pi - \sin^{-1} \{x\sqrt{1-y^2} + y\sqrt{1-x^2}\}, \\ \quad \text{if} -1 \le x, y < 0 \text{ and } x^2 + y^2 > 1 \end{cases}$

(ii) $\sin^{-1} x - \sin^{-1} y = \begin{cases} \sin^{-1} \{x\sqrt{1-y^2} - y\sqrt{1-x^2}\}; \\ \quad \text{if } -1 \le x, y \le 1 \text{ and } x^2 + y^2 \le 1 \\ \quad \text{or if } xy > 0 \text{ and } x^2 + y^2 > 1 \\ \pi - \sin^{-1} \{x\sqrt{1-y^2} - y\sqrt{1-x^2}\}, \\ \quad \text{if } 0 < x \le 1, -1 \le y \le 0 \text{ and } x^2 + y^2 > 1 \\ -\pi - \sin^{-1} \{x\sqrt{1-y^2} - y\sqrt{1-x^2}\}, \\ \quad \text{if } -1 \le x < 0, 0 < y \le 1 \text{ and } x^2 + y^2 > 1 \end{cases}$

Property VII

(i) $\cos^{-1} x + \cos^{-1} y$

$$= \begin{cases} \cos^{-1} \{xy - \sqrt{1-x^2}\sqrt{1-y^2}\}; & \text{if} -1 \le x, y \le 1 \text{ and } x + y \ge 0 \\ 2\pi - \cos^{-1} \{xy - \sqrt{1-x^2}\sqrt{1-y^2}\}; & \text{if } -1 \le x, y \le 1 \text{ and } x + y \le 0 \end{cases}$$

(ii) $\cos^{-1} x - \cos^{-1} y$

$$= \begin{cases} \cos^{-1} \{xy + \sqrt{1-x^2}\sqrt{1-y^2}\}; & \text{if } -1 \le x, y \le 1 \text{ and } x \le y \\ -\cos^{-1} \{xy + \sqrt{1-x^2}\sqrt{1-y^2}\}; & \text{if } -1 \le y \le 0, 0 < x \le 1 \text{ and } x \ge y \end{cases}$$

Property VIII

(i) $\tan^{-1} x + \tan^{-1} y$

$$= \begin{cases} \tan^{-1}\left(\dfrac{x+y}{1-xy}\right), & \text{if } xy < 1 \\ \pi + \tan^{-1}\left(\dfrac{x+y}{1-xy}\right), & \text{if } x > 0, y > 0 \text{ and } xy > 1 \\ -\pi + \tan^{-1}\left(\dfrac{x+y}{1-xy}\right), & \text{if } x < 0, y < 0 \text{ and } xy > 1 \end{cases}$$

(ii) $\tan^{-1} x - \tan^{-1} y$

$$= \begin{cases} \tan^{-1}\left(\dfrac{x-y}{1+xy}\right), & \text{if } xy > -1 \\ \pi + \tan^{-1}\left(\dfrac{x-y}{1+xy}\right), & \text{if } x > 0, y < 0 \text{ and } xy < -1 \\ -\pi + \tan^{-1}\left(\dfrac{x-y}{1+xy}\right), & \text{if } x < 0, y > 0 \text{ and } xy < -1 \end{cases}$$

Knowledge Booster

$\tan^{-1} x_1 + \tan^{-1} x_2 + \ldots + \tan^{-1} x_n = \tan^{-1}\left(\dfrac{S_1 - S_3 + S_5 - \ldots}{1 - S_2 + S_4 - S_6 + \ldots}\right)$ where,

S_k denotes the sum of the products of $x_1, x_2, \ldots, x_n$ takes k at a time.

Property IX

(i) $\sin^{-1} x = \cos^{-1} \sqrt{1-x^2} = \tan^{-1} \dfrac{x}{\sqrt{1-x^2}} = \cot^{-1} \dfrac{\sqrt{1-x^2}}{x}$

$$= \sec^{-1}\left(\frac{1}{\sqrt{1-x^2}}\right) = \operatorname{cosec}^{-1}\left(\frac{1}{x}\right), x \in (0, 1)$$

(ii) $\cos^{-1} x = \sin^{-1} \sqrt{1-x^2} = \tan^{-1} \dfrac{\sqrt{1-x^2}}{x}$

$$= \cot^{-1} \frac{x}{\sqrt{1-x^2}} = \sec^{-1}\left(\frac{1}{x}\right) = \operatorname{cosec}^{-1}\left(\frac{1}{\sqrt{1-x^2}}\right), x \in (0, 1)$$

(iii) $\tan^{-1} x = \sin^{-1}\left(\dfrac{x}{\sqrt{1+x^2}}\right) = \cos^{-1}\left(\dfrac{1}{\sqrt{1+x^2}}\right) = \cot^{-1}\left(\dfrac{1}{x}\right)$

$$= \operatorname{cosec}^{-1}\left(\frac{\sqrt{1+x^2}}{x}\right) = \sec^{-1}(\sqrt{1+x^2}), x \in (0, \infty)$$

Competition Insight

(i) $2\sin^{-1}x = \begin{cases} \sin^{-1}(2x\sqrt{1-x^2}), & \text{if } -\frac{1}{\sqrt{2}} \le x \le \frac{1}{\sqrt{2}} \\ \pi - \sin^{-1}(2x\sqrt{1-x^2}), & \text{if } \frac{1}{\sqrt{2}} \le x \le 1 \\ -\pi - \sin^{-1}(2x\sqrt{1-x^2}), & \text{if } -1 \le x \le -\frac{1}{\sqrt{2}} \end{cases}$

(ii) $2\cos^{-1}x = \begin{cases} \cos^{-1}(2x^2-1), & \text{if } 0 \le x \le 1 \\ 2\pi - \cos^{-1}(2x^2-1), & \text{if } -1 \le x \le 0 \end{cases}$

(iii) $2\tan^{-1}x = \begin{cases} \tan^{-1}\left(\frac{2x}{1-x^2}\right), & \text{if } -1 < x < 1 \\ \pi + \tan^{-1}\left(\frac{2x}{1-x^2}\right), & \text{if } x > 1 \\ -\pi + \tan^{-1}\left(\frac{2x}{1-x^2}\right), & \text{if } x < -1 \end{cases}$

Property X

(i) $3\sin^{-1}x = \begin{cases} \sin^{-1}(3x-4x^3), & \text{if } -\frac{1}{2} \le x \le \frac{1}{2} \\ \pi - \sin^{-1}(3x-4x^3), & \text{if } \frac{1}{2} < x \le 1 \\ -\pi - \sin^{-1}(3x-4x^3), & \text{if } -1 \le x < -\frac{1}{2} \end{cases}$

(ii) $3\cos^{-1}x = \begin{cases} \cos^{-1}(4x^3-3x), & \text{if } \frac{1}{2} \le x \le 1 \\ 2\pi - \cos^{-1}(4x^3-3x), & \text{if } -\frac{1}{2} \le x \le \frac{1}{2} \\ 2\pi + \cos^{-1}(4x^3-3x), & \text{if } -1 \le x \le -\frac{1}{2} \end{cases}$

(iii) $3\tan^{-1}x = \begin{cases} \tan^{-1}\left(\frac{3x-x^3}{1-3x^2}\right), & \text{if } -\frac{1}{\sqrt{3}} < x < \frac{1}{\sqrt{3}} \\ \pi + \tan^{-1}\left(\frac{3x-x^3}{1-3x^2}\right), & \text{if } x > \frac{1}{\sqrt{3}} \\ -\pi + \tan^{-1}\left(\frac{3x-x^3}{1-3x^2}\right), & \text{if } x < -\frac{1}{\sqrt{3}} \end{cases}$

Property XI

(i) $$2\tan^{-1}x = \begin{cases} \sin^{-1}\left(\dfrac{2x}{1+x^2}\right), & \text{if } -1 \le x \le 1 \\ \pi - \sin^{-1}\left(\dfrac{2x}{1+x^2}\right), & \text{if } x > 1 \\ -\pi - \sin^{-1}\left(\dfrac{2x}{1+x^2}\right), & \text{if } x < -1 \end{cases}$$

(ii) $$2\tan^{-1}x = \begin{cases} \cos^{-1}\left(\dfrac{1-x^2}{1+x^2}\right), & \text{if } 0 \le x < \infty \\ -\cos^{-1}\left(\dfrac{1-x^2}{1+x^2}\right), & \text{if } -\infty < x < 0 \end{cases}$$

Value Points

(i) $\tan^{-1}x + \tan^{-1}y + \tan^{-1}z = \tan^{-1}\left(\dfrac{x+y+z-xyz}{1-xy-yz-zx}\right)$,

if $x > 0, y > 0, z > 0$ and $(xy + yz + zx) < 1$

(ii) If $\tan^{-1}x + \tan^{-1}y + \tan^{-1}z = \dfrac{\pi}{2}$, then $xy + yz + zx = 1$

(iii) If $\tan^{-1}x + \tan^{-1}y + \tan^{-1}z = \pi$, then $x + y + z = xyz$

(iv) If $\sin^{-1}x + \sin^{-1}y + \sin^{-1}z = \dfrac{\pi}{2}$, then $x^2 + y^2 + z^2 + 2xyz = 1$

(v) If $\sin^{-1}x + \sin^{-1}y + \sin^{-1}z = \pi$, then

$$x\sqrt{1-x^2} + y\sqrt{1-y^2} + z\sqrt{1-z^2} = 2xyz$$

(vi) If $\cos^{-1}x + \cos^{-1}y + \cos^{-1}z = 3\pi$, then $xy + yz + zx = 3$

(vii) If $\cos^{-1}x + \cos^{-1}y + \cos^{-1}z = \pi$, then $x^2 + y^2 + z^2 + 2xyz = 1$

(viii) If $\sin^{-1}x + \sin^{-1}y + \sin^{-1}z = \dfrac{3\pi}{2}$, then $xy + yz + zx = 3$

(ix) If $\sin^{-1}x + \sin^{-1}y = \theta$, then $\cos^{-1}x + \cos^{-1}y = \pi - \theta$

(x) If $\cos^{-1}x + \cos^{-1}y = \theta$, then $\sin^{-1}x + \sin^{-1}y = \pi - \theta$

(xi) If $\tan^{-1}x + \tan^{-1}y = \pi/2$, then $xy = 1$

(xii) If $\cot^{-1}x + \cot^{-1}y = \pi/2$, then $xy = 1$

(xiii) If $\cos^{-1}\dfrac{x}{a} + \cos^{-1}\dfrac{y}{b} = \theta$, then $\dfrac{x^2}{a^2} - \dfrac{2xy}{ab}\cos\theta + \dfrac{y^2}{b^2} = \sin^2\theta$

Chapter 14

Rectangular Axis

Coordinate Geometry

The branch of mathematics in which we study the position of any object lying in a plane with the help of two mutually perpendicular lines in the same plane, is called coordinate geometry.

Rectangular Axis

Let XOX' and YOY' be two fixed straight lines, which meet at right angles at O. Then,

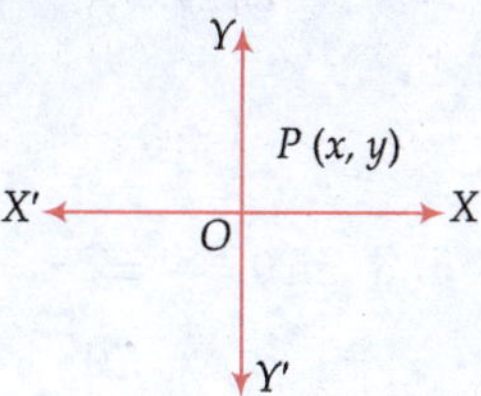

(i) $X'OX$ is called axis of X or abscissa or the **X-axis.**

(ii) $Y'OY$ is called axis of Y or ordinate or the **Y-axis.**

(iii) The ordered pair of real numbers (x, y) is called **cartesian coordinate**.

(iv) Coordinates of the **origin** are $(0, 0)$.

(v) y-coordinate of a point on X-axis is zero.

(vi) x-coordinate of a point on Y-axis is zero.

Quadrants

The X and Y-axes divide the coordinate plane into four parts, each part is called a quadrant which is given below

(–, +) II Quadrant $x < 0, y > 0$	(+, +) I Quadrant $x > 0, y > 0$
(–, –) III Quadrant $x < 0, y < 0$	(+, –) IV Quadrant $x > 0, y < 0$

(Axes: $X'OX$ and YOY')

Polar Coordinates

In ΔOPQ,

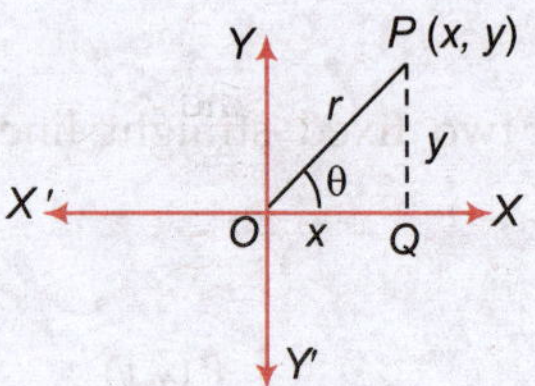

$$\cos\theta = \frac{x}{r} \text{ and } \sin\theta = \frac{y}{r} \Rightarrow x = r\cos\theta \text{ and } y = r\sin\theta$$

where, $r = \sqrt{x^2 + y^2}$ and $\theta = \tan^{-1}\left(\frac{y}{x}\right)$

The polar coordinate is represented by the symbol $P(r, \theta)$.

Distance Formulae

(i) Distance between two points $P(x_1, y_1)$ and $Q(x_2, y_2)$, is

$$PQ = \sqrt{(x_2 - x_1)^2 + (y_2 - y_1)^2}.$$

$P(x_1, y_1)$ $\qquad$ $Q(x_2, y_2)$

(ii) If points are (r_1, θ_1) and (r_2, θ_2), then distance between them is

$$\sqrt{r_1^2 + r_2^2 - 2r_1r_2\cos(\theta_1 - \theta_2)}.$$

(iii) Distance of a point (x_1, y_1) from the origin is $\sqrt{x_1^2 + y_1^2}$.

(iv) If the coordinate axes are inclined at an angle ω, then distance between (x_1, y_1) and (x_2, y_2) is

$$= \sqrt{(x_1 - x_2)^2 + (y_1 - y_2)^2 + 2(x_1 - x_2)(y_1 - y_2)\cos\omega}$$

Section Formulae

(i) The coordinate of the point which divides the joint of (x_1, y_1) and (x_2, y_2) in the ratio $m_1 : m_2$ **internally**, is

$$\left(\frac{m_1x_2 + m_2x_1}{m_1 + m_2}, \frac{m_1y_2 + m_2y_1}{m_1 + m_2}\right)$$

A (x_1, y_1) —— m_1 —— R —— m_2 —— C (x_2, y_2)

and **externally** is $\left(\frac{m_1x_2 - m_2x_1}{m_1 - m_2}, \frac{m_1y_2 - m_2y_1}{m_1 - m_2}\right)$.

(ii) X-axis divides the line segment joining (x_1, y_1) and (x_2, y_2) in the ratio $-y_1 : y_2$.

Similarly, Y-axis divides the same line segment in the ratio $-x_1 : x_2$.

Value Points

- Mid-point of the joint of (x_1, y_1) and (x_2, y_2) is $\left(\frac{x_1 + x_2}{2}, \frac{y_1 + y_2}{2}\right)$.
- Centroid of ΔABC with vertices (x_1, y_1), (x_2, y_2) and (x_3, y_3), is $\left(\frac{x_1 + x_2 + x_3}{3}, \frac{y_1 + y_2 + y_3}{3}\right)$.
- Circumcentre of ΔABC with vertices $A(x_1, y_1)$, $B(x_2, y_2)$ and $C(x_3, y_3)$, is
$$\left(\frac{x_1 \sin 2A + x_2 \sin 2B + x_3 \sin 2C}{\sin 2A + \sin 2B + \sin 2C}, \frac{y_1 \sin 2A + y_2 \sin 2B + y_3 \sin 2C}{\sin 2A + \sin 2B + \sin 2C}\right)$$
- Incentre of ΔABC with vertices $A(x_1, y_1)$, $B(x_2, y_2)$ and $C(x_3, y_3)$ and whose sides are a, b and c, is
$$\left(\frac{ax_1 + bx_2 + cx_3}{a + b + c}, \frac{ay_1 + by_2 + cy_3}{a + b + c}\right)$$

- Excentre of ΔABC with vertices $A(x_1, y_1)$, $B(x_2, y_2)$, $C(x_3, y_3)$ and whose sides are a, b and c, is given by

$$I_1 = \left(\frac{-ax_1 + bx_2 + cx_3}{-a+b+c}, \frac{-ay_1 + by_2 + cy_3}{-a+b+c}\right),$$

$$I_2 = \left(\frac{ax_1 - bx_2 + cx_3}{a-b+c}, \frac{ay_1 - by_2 + cy_3}{a-b+c}\right)$$

and $$I_3 = \left(\frac{ax_1 + bx_2 - cx_3}{a+b-c}, \frac{ay_1 + by_2 - cy_3}{a+b-c}\right)$$

- Orthocentre of ΔABC with vertices $A(x_1, y_1)$, $B(x_2, y_2)$ and $C(x_3, y_3)$, is $\left(\frac{x_1 \tan A + x_2 \tan B + x_3 \tan C}{\tan A + \tan B + \tan C}, \frac{y_1 \tan A + y_2 \tan B + y_3 \tan C}{\tan A + \tan B + \tan C}\right)$.

- Orthocentre, centroid and circumcentre are collinear and centroid divides line joining the circumcentre and orthocentre in the ratio of 2 : 1.

Area of Triangle/Quadrilateral

(i) Area of ΔABC with vertices $A(x_1, y_1)$, $B(x_2, y_2)$ and $C(x_3, y_3)$, is

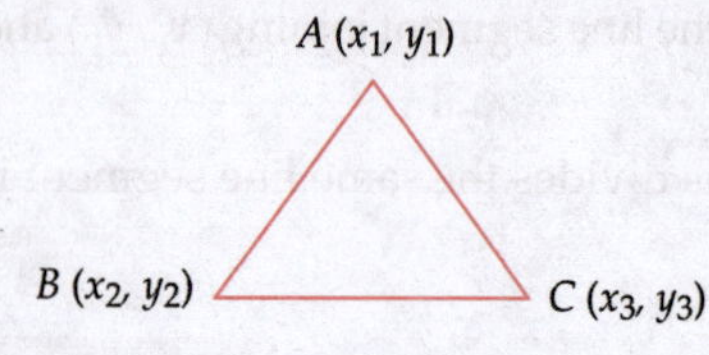

$$\Delta = \frac{1}{2}\left\|\begin{matrix} x_1 & y_1 & 1 \\ x_2 & y_2 & 1 \\ x_3 & y_3 & 1 \end{matrix}\right\| = \frac{1}{2}\left\|\begin{matrix} x_1 - x_3 & x_2 - x_3 \\ y_1 - y_3 & y_2 - y_3 \end{matrix}\right\|$$

These points A, B and C will be collinear, if $\Delta = 0$.

EXPERT Scale Up

Solution of system of equations, $a_1x + b_1y + c_1 = 0$, $a_2x + b_2y + c_2 = 0$ and $a_3x + b_3y + c_3 = 0$.

$\therefore$ Area of triangle, $\Delta = \frac{1}{2}\begin{vmatrix} x_1 & y_1 & 1 \\ x_2 & y_2 & 1 \\ x_3 & y_3 & 1 \end{vmatrix}$

(ii) Area of the quadrilateral formed by joining the vertices (x_1, y_1), (x_2, y_2), (x_3, y_3) and (x_4, y_4) is $\frac{1}{2}\left\|\begin{matrix} x_1 - x_3 & x_2 - x_4 \\ y_1 - y_3 & y_2 - y_4 \end{matrix}\right\|$.

(iii) Area of trapezium formed by joining the vertices $(x_1, y_1), (x_2, y_2), (x_3, y_3)$ and (x_4, y_4) is

$$\frac{1}{2}|[(y_1 + y_2)(x_1 - x_2) + (y_2 + y_3)(x_2 - x_3) + (y_3 + y_4)(x_3 - x_4) + (y_4 + y_1)(x_4 - x_1)]|$$

Competition Insight

Shifting of Origin/Rotation of Axes

Shifting of Origin

Let the origin is shifted to a point $O'(h, k)$. If $P(x, y)$ are coordinates of a point referred to old axes and $P'(X, Y)$ are the coordinates of the same points referred to new axes, then $x = X + h, y = Y + k$

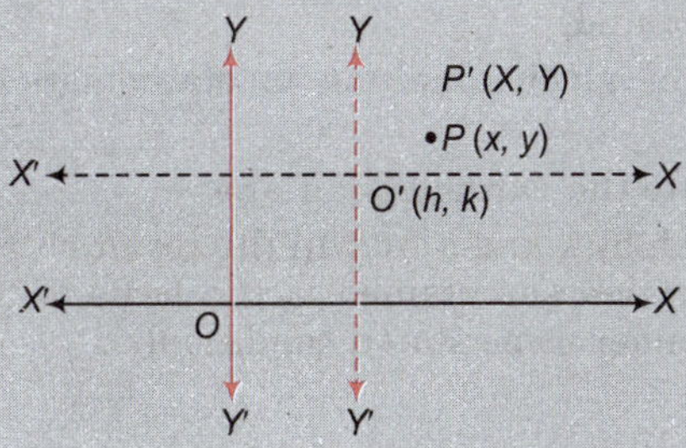

Rotation of Axes

Let (x, y) be the coordinates of any point P referred to the old axes and (X, Y) be its coordinates referred to the new axes (after rotating the old axes by angle θ). Then, $X = x\cos\theta + y\sin\theta$ and $Y = y\cos\theta - x\sin\theta$

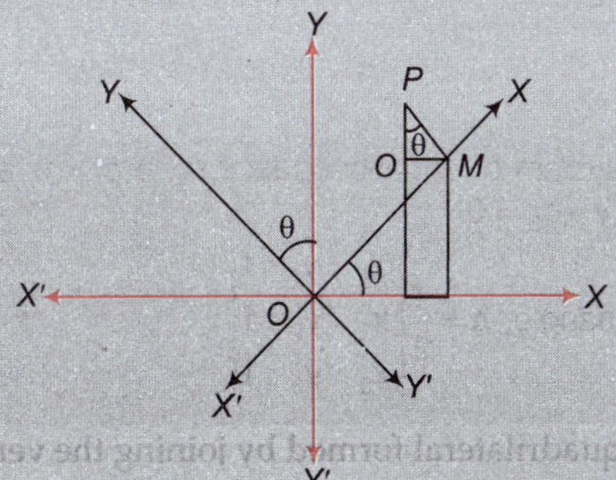

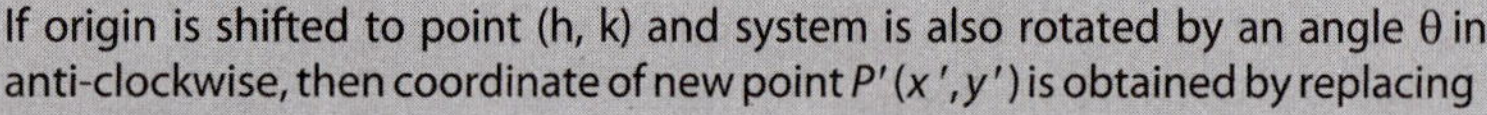

If origin is shifted to point (h, k) and system is also rotated by an angle θ in anti-clockwise, then coordinate of new point $P'(x', y')$ is obtained by replacing

$$x' = h + x\cos\theta + y\sin\theta$$

and

$$y' = k - x\sin\theta + y\cos\theta$$

Locus

The curve described by a point which moves under given condition(s) is called its locus.

Equation of Locus

The equation of curve described by a point, which moves under given conditions(s), is called the equation of locus.

Step Taken to Find the Equation of Locus of a Point

Step I Assume the coordinates of the point say (h, k) whose locus is to be found.

Step II Write the given condition in mathematical form involving h, k.

Step III Eliminate the variable(s), if any.

Step IV Replace h by x and k by y in the result obtained in step III. The equation so obtained is the locus of the point, which moves under some stated condition(s).

Chapter 15

Straight Line

A straight line is the locus of all those points which are collinear with two given points.

General equation of a line is $ax + by + c = 0$

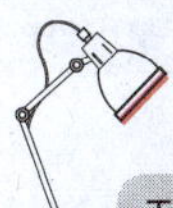

EXPERT Scale Up

The equation of a straight line is the relation between x and y which is satisfied by the coordinates of each and every point on the line.

- We can have one and only one line through a fixed point in a given direction.
- We can have infinitely many lines through a given point.

Slope (Gradient) of a Line

The trigonometrical tangent of the angle that a line makes with the positive direction of the X-axis in anti-clockwise sense is called the slope or gradient of the line.

So, slope of a line, $m = \tan\theta$

where, θ is the angle made by the line with positive direction of X-axis.

Value Points

- Slope of a line parallel to X-axis, $m = 0$.
- Slope of a line parallel to Y-axis, $m = \infty$.
- Slope of a line equally inclined with axes is 1 or –1 as it makes an angle of 45° or 135°, with X-axis.
- Slope of a line passing through (x_1, y_1) and (x_2, y_2) is given by

$$m = \tan\theta = \frac{y_2 - y_1}{x_2 - x_1}.$$

Angle between Two Lines

The angle θ between two lines having slopes m_1 and m_2, is

$$\tan\theta = \left|\frac{m_2 - m_1}{1 + m_1 m_2}\right|.$$

(i) Two lines are parallel, iff $m_1 = m_2$.

(ii) Two lines are perpendicular to each other, iff $m_1 m_2 = -1$.

Equation of a Straight Line

General equation of a straight line is $Ax + By + C = 0$.

(i) The equation of a line parallel to X-axis at a distance b from it, is given by $y = b$

(ii) The equation of a line parallel to Y-axis at a distance a from it, is given by $x = a$

(iii) Equation of X-axis is $y = 0$

(iv) Equation of Y-axis is $x = 0$

Different Forms of the Equation of a Straight Line

(i) **Slope Intercept Form** The equation of a line with slope m and making an intercept c on Y-axis, is

$$y = mx + c$$

If the line passes through the origin, then its equation will be

$$y = mx$$

(ii) **One Point Slope Form** The equation of a line which passes through the point (x_1, y_1) and has the slope m is given by

$$(y - y_1) = m(x - x_1)$$

(iii) **Two Points Form** The equation of a line passing through the points (x_1, y_1) and (x_2, y_2) is given by

$$(y - y_1) = \left(\frac{y_2 - y_1}{x_2 - x_1}\right)(x - x_1)$$

This equation can also be determined by the determinant method, i.e.

$$\begin{vmatrix} x & y & 1 \\ x_1 & y_1 & 1 \\ x_2 & y_2 & 1 \end{vmatrix} = 0$$

(iv) **Intercept Form** The equation of a line which cuts off intercept a and b respectively on the X and Y-axes is given by

$$\frac{x}{a}+\frac{y}{b}=1$$

The general equation $Ax + By + C = 0$ can be converted into the intercept form, as

$$\frac{x}{-(C/A)}+\frac{y}{-(C/B)}=1$$

(v) **Normal Form** The equation of a straight line upon which the length of the perpendicular from the origin is p and angle made by this perpendicular to the X-axis is α, is given by

$$x\cos\alpha + y\sin\alpha = p$$

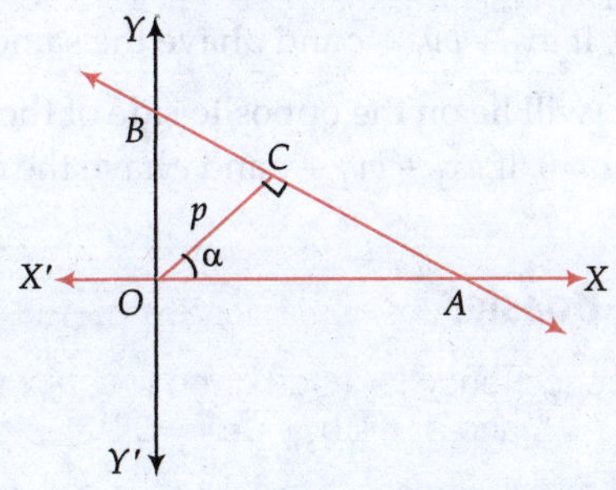

(vi) **Distance** (Parametric) **Form** The equation of a straight line passing through (x_1, y_1) and making an angle θ with the positive direction of X-axis, is

$$\frac{x-x_1}{\cos\theta}=\frac{y-y_1}{\sin\theta}=r$$

where, r is the distance between two points $P(x, y)$ and $Q(x_1, y_1)$.

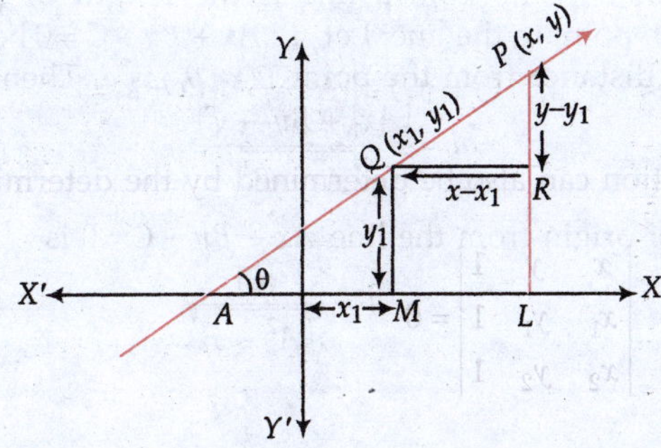

Thus, the coordinates of any point on the line at a distance r from the given point (x_1, y_1) are $(x_1 + r\cos\theta, y_1 + r\sin\theta)$. If P is on the right side of (x_1, y_1), then r is positive and if P is on the left side of (x_1, y_1), then r is negative.

Position of Point(s) Relative to a Given Line

Let the equation of the given line be $ax + by + c = 0$ and let the coordinates of the two given points be $P(x_1, y_1)$ and $Q(x_2, y_2)$.

(i) The two points are on the same side of the straight line $ax + by + c = 0$, if $ax_1 + by_1 + c$ and $ax_2 + by_2 + c$ have the same sign.

(ii) The two points are on the opposite side of the straight line $ax + by + c = 0$, if $ax_1 + by_1 + c$ and $ax_2 + by_2 + c$ have opposite sign.

(iii) A point (x_1, y_1) will lie on the side of the origin relative to a line $ax + by + c = 0$, if $ax_1 + by_1 + c$ and c have the same sign.

(iv) A point (x_1, y_1) will lie on the opposite side of the origin relative to a line $ax + by + c = 0$, if $ax_1 + by_1 + c$ and c have the opposite sign.

Knowledge Booster

Condition of concurrency for three given lines $a_1x + b_1y + c_1 = 0$, $a_2x + b_2y + c_2 = 0$ and $a_3x + b_3y + c_3 = 0$ is

$$a_3(b_1c_2 - b_2c_1) + b_3(c_1a_2 - a_1c_2) + c_3(a_1b_2 - a_2b_1) = 0$$

or

$$\begin{vmatrix} a_1 & b_1 & c_1 \\ a_2 & b_2 & c_2 \\ a_3 & b_3 & c_3 \end{vmatrix} = 0$$

Distance of a Point from a Line

The distance of a point from a line is the **length of perpendicular** drawn from the point to the line. Let $L: Ax + By + C = 0$ be a line, whose perpendicular distance from the point $P(x_1, y_1)$ is d. Then,

$$d = \frac{|Ax_1 + By_1 + C|}{\sqrt{A^2 + B^2}}$$

The distance of origin from the line $Ax + By + C = 0$ is

$$d = \frac{|C|}{\sqrt{A^2 + B^2}}$$

Distance between Two parallel Lines

The distance between two parallel lines

$$y = m\,x + c_1 \quad \text{...(i)}$$

$$y = m\,x + c_2 \quad \text{...(ii)}$$

is given by $d = \dfrac{|c_1 - c_2|}{\sqrt{1+m^2}}$

Point of Intersection of Two Lines

Let equation of lines be $a_1x + b_1y + c_1 = 0$ and $a_2x + b_2y + c_2 = 0$, then their point of intersection is $\left(\dfrac{b_1c_2 - b_2c_1}{a_1b_2 - a_2b_1}, \dfrac{c_1a_2 - c_2a_1}{a_1b_2 - a_2b_1}\right)$.

Line Parallel and Perpendicular to a Given Line

(i) The equation of a line parallel to a given line $ax + by + c = 0$ is $ax + by + \lambda = 0$, where λ is a constant.

(ii) The equation of a line perpendicular to a given line $ax + by + c = 0$ is $bx - ay + \lambda = 0$, where λ is a constant.

Knowledge Booster

The equation of bisectors of the angles between the lines $a_1x + b_1y = c_1$ and $a_2x + b_2y = c_2$ is given by

$$\frac{a_1x + b_1y + c_1}{\sqrt{a_1^2 + b_1^2}} = \pm \frac{a_2x + b_2y + c_2}{\sqrt{a_2^2 + b_2^2}}$$

- If $a_1a_2 + b_1b_2 > 0$, then positive sign will be for obtuse angle and negative sign for acute angle.
- If $a_1a_2 + b_1b_2 < 0$, then positive sign will be for acute angle and negative sign for obtuse angle.

Image of a Point with Respect to a Line

Let the image of a point (x_1, y_1) with respect to $ax + by + c = 0$ be (x_2, y_2), then

$$\frac{x_2 - x_1}{a} = \frac{y_2 - y_1}{b} = \frac{-2\,(ax_1 + by_1 + c)}{a^2 + b^2}$$

(i) The image of the point $P(x_1, y_1)$ with respect to X-axis is $Q(x_1, -y_1)$.

(ii) The image of the point $P(x_1, y_1)$ with respect to Y-axis is $Q(-x_1, y_1)$.

(iii) The image of the point $P(x_1, y_1)$ with respect to mirror $y = x$ is $Q(y_1, x_1)$.

(iv) The image of the point $P(x_1, y_1)$ with respect to the line mirror $y = x \tan\theta$ is

$$x = x_1 \cos 2\theta + y_1 \sin 2\theta \Rightarrow y = x_1 \sin 2\theta - y_1 \cos 2\theta$$

(v) The image of the point $P(x_1, y_1)$ with respect to the origin is the point $Q(-x_1, -y_1)$.

Pair of Lines

General equation of second degree

$$ax^2 + 2hxy + by^2 + 2gx + 2fy + c = 0.$$

It will represent a pair of straight line iff

$$abc + 2fgh - af^2 - bg^2 - ch^2 = 0 \text{ or } \begin{vmatrix} a & h & g \\ h & b & f \\ g & f & c \end{vmatrix} = 0$$

Homogeneous Equation of Second Degree

An equation in two variables x and y (whose RHS is zero) is said to be a homogeneous equation of the second degree, if the sum of the indices of x and y in each term is equal to 2. The general form of homogeneous equation of the second degree in x and y is $ax^2 + 2hxy + by^2 = 0$.

Any homogeneous equation of second degree in x and y represents two straight lines through the origin.

Important Properties of Pair of Lines

(i) Let $ax^2 + 2hxy + by^2 = 0$ or $ax^2 + 2hxy + by^2 + 2gx + 2fy + c = 0$ be an equation of pair of straight lines. Then,

(a) Slope of first line, $m_1 = \dfrac{-h + \sqrt{h^2 - ab}}{b}$

and slope of the second line, $m_2 = \dfrac{-h - \sqrt{h^2 - ab}}{b}$

$$\therefore \quad m_1 + m_2 = -\frac{2h}{b} = -\frac{\text{Coefficient of } xy}{\text{Coefficient of } y^2}$$

$$\text{and} \quad m_1 m_2 = \frac{a}{b} = \frac{\text{Coefficient of } x^2}{\text{Coefficient of } y^2}$$

Here, m_1 and m_2 are

(1) real and distinct, if $h^2 > ab$.

(2) coincident, if $h^2 = ab$.

(3) imaginary, if $h^2 < ab$.

(b) Angle between the pair of lines is given by $\tan\theta = \dfrac{2\sqrt{h^2 - ab}}{|a + b|}$

(1) If lines are coincident, then $h^2 = ab$.

(2) If lines are perpendicular, then $a + b = 0$.

(c) The angle between the lines represented by $ax^2 + 2hxy + by^2 + 2gx + 2fy + c = 0$ is equal to angle between the lines represented by

$$ax^2 + 2hxy + by^2 = 0$$

(d) The joint equation of bisector of the angles between the lines represented by the equation $ax^2 + 2hxy + by^2 = 0$ is

$$\frac{x^2 - y^2}{a - b} = \frac{xy}{h} \Rightarrow hx^2 - (a - b)xy - hy^2 = 0.$$

(e) The equation of the pair of lines through the origin and perpendicular to the pair of lines given by $ax^2 + 2hxy + by^2 = 0$ is $bx^2 - 2hxy + ay^2 = 0$.

Competition Insight

(i) If the equation of a pair of straight lines is $ax^2 + 2hxy + by^2 + 2gx + 2fy + c = 0$, then the point of intersection is given by $\left(\dfrac{hf - bg}{ab - h^2}, \dfrac{gh - af}{ab - h^2}\right)$.

(ii) The general equation $ax^2 + 2hxy + by^2 + 2gx + 2fy + c = 0$ will represent two parallel lines, if $g^2 - ac > 0$ and $\dfrac{a}{h} = \dfrac{h}{b} = \dfrac{g}{f}$ and the distance between them is $2\sqrt{\dfrac{g^2 - ac}{a(a + b)}}$ or $2\sqrt{\dfrac{f^2 - bc}{b(a + b)}}$.

(iii) The equation of the bisectors of the angles between the lines represented by $ax^2 + 2hxy + by^2 + 2gx + 2fy + c = 0$ are given by

$$\frac{(x - x_1)^2 - (y - y_1)^2}{a - b} = \frac{(x - x_1)(y - y_1)}{h},$$

where (x_1, y_1) is the point of intersection of the lines represented by the given equation.

(iv) Equation of the straight lines joining the origin to the points of intersection of a second degree curve $ax^2 + 2hxy + by^2 + 2gx + 2fy + c = 0$ and a straight line $lx + my + n = 0$ is

$$ax^2 + 2hxy + by^2 + 2gx\left(\frac{lx + my}{-n}\right) + 2fy\left(\frac{lx + my}{-n}\right) + c\left(\frac{lx + my}{-n}\right)^2 = 0.$$

Important Points

(i) In an equilateral triangle, orthocentre, centroid, circumcentre, incentre coincide.

(ii) The circumcentre of a right angled triangle is the mid-point of the hypotenuse.

(iii) Orthocentre, centroid, circumcentre of a triangle are collinear. Centroid divides the line joining orthocentre and circumcentre in the ratio 2 : 1.

(iv) If D, E and F are the mid-point of the sides BC, CA and AB of ΔABC, then the centroid of $\Delta\, ABC =$ centroid of ΔDEF.

(v) Orthocentre of the right angled ΔABC, right angled at A is A.

(vi) Distance between two parallel lines $ax + by + c_1 = 0$ and $ax + by + c_2 = 0$ is given by $d = \left|\dfrac{c_2 - c_1}{\sqrt{a^2 + b^2}}\right|$.

(vii) The area of the triangle formed by the lines $y = m_1x + c_1$, $y = m_2x + c_2$ and $y = m_3x + c_3$ is $\Delta = \dfrac{1}{2}\left|\Sigma \dfrac{(c_1 - c_2)^2}{m_1 - m_2}\right|$.

(viii) Three given points A, B, C are collinear i.e. lie on the same straight line, if any of the three points (say B) lie on the straight line joining the other two points.

$$\Rightarrow \qquad AB + BC = AC$$

(ix) Area of the triangle formed by the line $ax + by + c = 0$ with the coordinate axes is $\Delta = \dfrac{c^2}{2|ab|}$.

(x) The foot of the perpendicular (h, k) from (x_1, y_1) to the line $ax + by + c = 0$ is given by $\dfrac{h - x_1}{a} = \dfrac{k - y_1}{b} = -\dfrac{(ax_1 + by_1 + c)}{a^2 + b^2}$.

(xi) Area of rhombus formed by $ax \pm by \pm c = 0$ is $\left|\dfrac{2c^2}{ab}\right|$.

(xii) Area of the parallelogram formed by the lines

$$a_1x + b_1y + c_1 = 0, a_2x + b_2y + c_2 = 0, a_1x + b_1y + d_1 = 0$$

and $a_2x + b_2y + d_2 = 0$ is $\left|\dfrac{(d_1 - c_1)(d_2 - c_2)}{a_1b_2 - a_2b_1}\right|$.

(xiii) (a) Foot of the perpendicular from (a, b) on $x - y = 0$ is $\left(\dfrac{a + b}{2}, \dfrac{a + b}{2}\right)$.

(b) Foot of the perpendicular from (a, b) on $x + y = 0$ is $\left(\frac{a-b}{2}, \frac{a-b}{2}\right)$.

(xiv) The image of the line $a_1x + b_1y + c_1 = 0$ about the line $ax + by + c = 0$ is

$$2(aa_1 + bb_1)(ax + by + c) = (a^2 + b^2)(a_1x + b_1y + c_1).$$

Value Point

Given two vertices (x_1, y_1) and (x_2, y_2) of an equilateral ΔABC, then its third vertex is given by

$$\left[\frac{x_1 + x_2 \pm \sqrt{3}(y_1 - y_2)}{2}, \frac{y_1 + y_2 \mp \sqrt{3}(x_1 - x_2)}{2}\right]$$

(xv) The equation of the straight line which passes through a given point (x_1, y_1) and makes an angle α with the given straight line $y = mx + c$ are $(y - y_1) = \frac{m \pm \tan\alpha}{1 \mp m\tan\alpha}(x - x_1)$

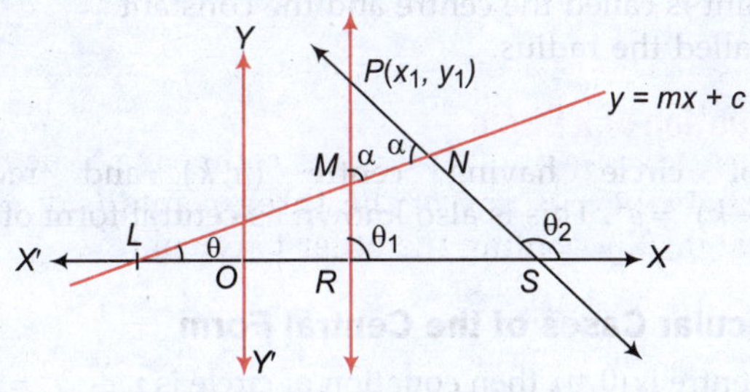

(xvi) The equation of the family of lines passing through the intersection of the lines $a_1x + b_1y + c_1 = 0$ and $a_2x + b_2y + c_2 = 0$ is $(a_1x + b_1y + c_1) + \lambda(a_2x + b_2y + c_2) = 0$ where, λ is any real number.

(xvii) Line $ax + by + c = 0$ divides the line joining the points (x_1, y_1) and (x_2, y_2) in the ratio $\lambda : 1$, then $\lambda = -\left(\frac{ax_1 + by_1 + c}{ax_2 + by_2 + c}\right)$.

If λ is positive it divides internally and if λ is negative, then it divides externally.

(xviii) Area of a polygon of n-sides with vertices $A_1(x_1, y_1)$, $A_2(x_2, y_2), \ldots, A_n(x_n, y_n)$

$$= \frac{1}{2}\left[\begin{vmatrix} x_1 & y_1 \\ x_2 & y_2 \end{vmatrix} + \begin{vmatrix} x_2 & y_2 \\ x_3 & y_3 \end{vmatrix} + \ldots + \begin{vmatrix} x_n & y_n \\ x_1 & y_1 \end{vmatrix}\right]$$

(xix) Equation of the pair of lines through (α, β) and perpendicular to the pair of lines $ax^2 + 2hxy + by^2 = 0$ is $b(x - \alpha)^2 - 2h(x - \alpha)(y - \beta) + a(y - \beta)^2 = 0$.

Chapter 16

Circles

Circle

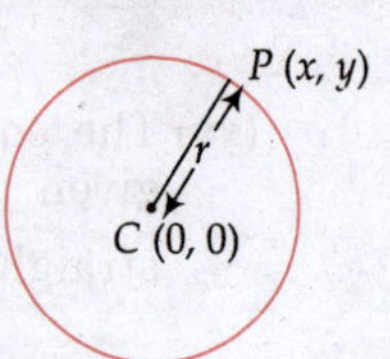

Circle is defined as the locus of a point which moves in a plane such that its distance from a fixed point in that plane is constant.

The fixed point is called the centre and the constant distance is called the radius.

Standard Equation of a Circle

Equation of circle having centre (h, k) and radius a is $(x-h)^2+(y-k)^2=a^2$. This is also known as central form of equation of a circle.

Some Particular Cases of the Central Form

(i) When centre is $(0, 0)$, then equation of circle is $x^2+y^2=a^2$.

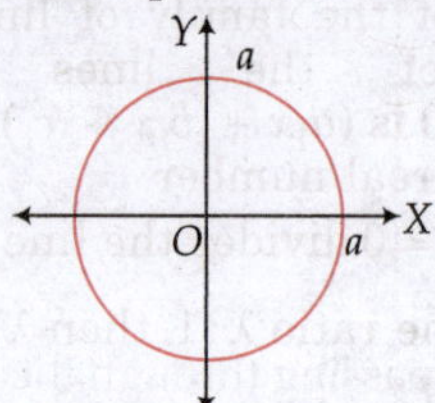

(ii) When the circle passes through the origin, then equation of the circle is $x^2+y^2-2hx-2ky=0$.

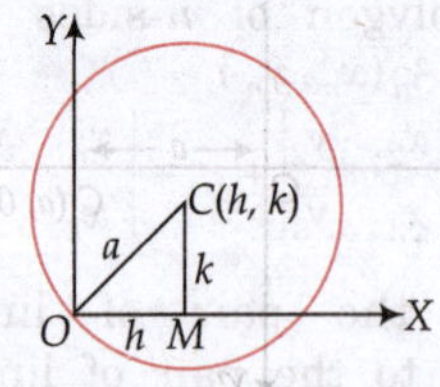

(iii) When the circle touches the X-axis, the equation is $x^2 + y^2 - 2hx - 2ay + h^2 = 0$.

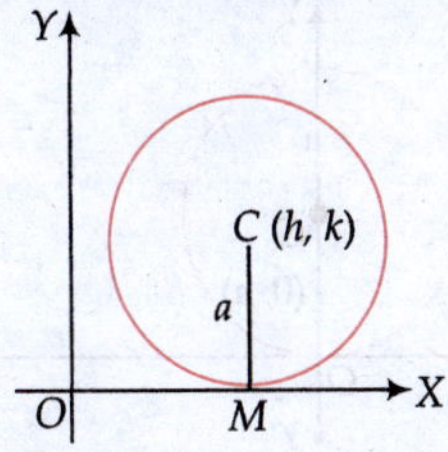

(iv) Equation of the circle, touches the Y-axis is
$$x^2 + y^2 - 2ax - 2ky + k^2 = 0.$$

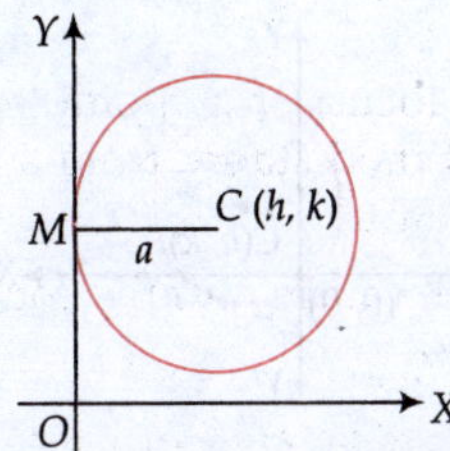

(v) Equation of the circle, touching both axes is
$$x^2 + y^2 - 2ax - 2ay + a^2 = 0.$$

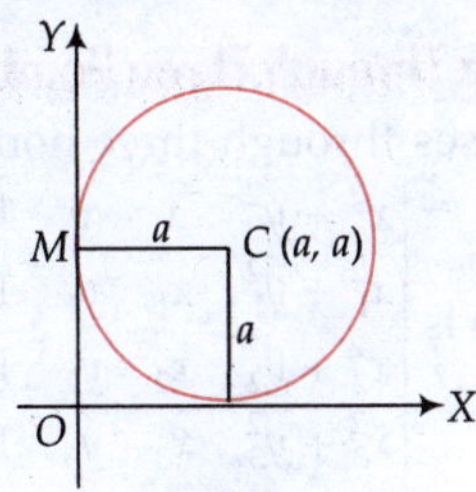

(vi) Equation of the circle passing through the origin and centre lying on the X-axis is $x^2 + y^2 - 2ax = 0$.

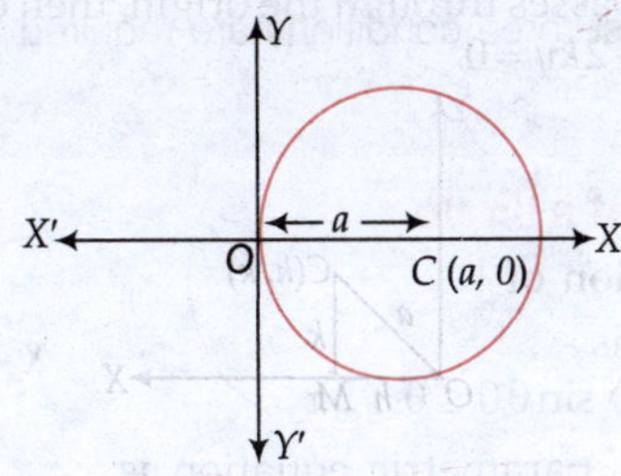

(vii) Equation of the circle passing through the origin and centre lying on the Y-axis is $x^2 + y^2 - 2ay = 0$.

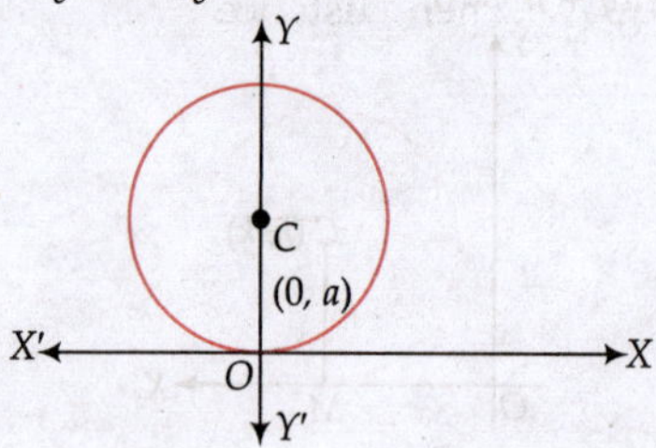

(viii) Equation of the circle through the origin and cutting intercepts a and b on the coordinate axes is $x^2 + y^2 - ax - by = 0$.

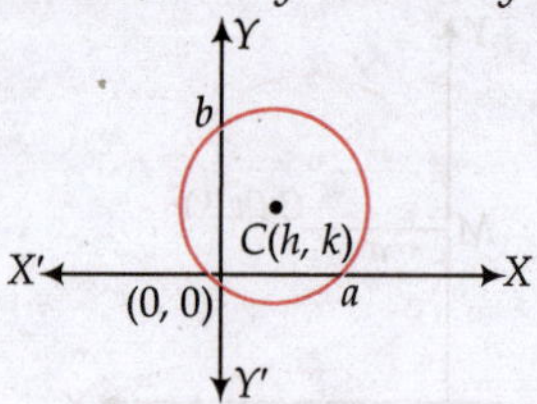

Equation of Circle When Ends Points of Diameter are Given

Equation of the circle, when the coordinates of end points of a diameter are (x_1, y_1) and (x_2, y_2) is $(x - x_1)(x - x_2) + (y - y_1)(y - y_2) = 0$.

Equation of Circle Passing Through Three Points

Equation of the circle passes through three non-collinear points

$(x_1, y_1), (x_2, y_2)$ and (x_3, y_3) is $\begin{vmatrix} x^2 + y^2 & x & y & 1 \\ x_1^2 + y_1^2 & x_1 & y_1 & 1 \\ x_2^2 + y_2^2 & x_2 & y_2 & 1 \\ x_3^2 + y_3^2 & x_3 & y_3 & 1 \end{vmatrix} = 0.$

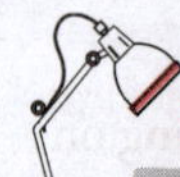

EXPERT Scale Up

The general equation of the circle involves three constants which implies that atleast three conditions are required to determine circle uniquely.

Parametric Equation of a Circle

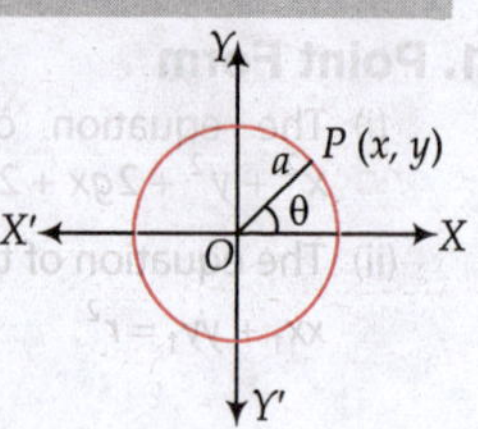

The parametric equation of $(x - h)^2 + (y - k)^2 = a^2$ is $x = h + a\cos\theta, y = k + a\sin\theta, 0 \le \theta \le 2\pi$

For circle $x^2 + y^2 = a^2$, parametric equation is $x = a\cos\theta, y = a\sin\theta$

General Equation of a Circle

The general equation of a circle is given by $x^2 + y^2 + 2gx + 2fy + c = 0$, whose centre $= (-g, -f)$ and radius $= \sqrt{g^2 + f^2 - c}$

(i) If $g^2 + f^2 - c > 0$, then the radius of the circle is real and hence the circle is also real.

(ii) If $g^2 + f^2 - c = 0$, then the radius of the circle is 0 and the circle is known as point circle.

(iii) If $g^2 + f^2 - c < 0$, then the radius of the circle is imaginary. Such a circle is imaginary, which is not possible to draw.

Value Point

A point (x_1, y_1) lies outside, on or inside a circle
$S \equiv x^2 + y^2 + 2gx + 2fy + c = 0$, according as $S_1 >, =$ or < 0
where, $S_1 = x_1^2 + y_1^2 + 2gx_1 + 2fy_1 + c$

Intercepts on the Axes

The length of the intercepts made by the circle $x^2 + y^2 + 2gx + 2fy + c = 0$ with X and Y-axes are $2\sqrt{g^2 - c}$ and $2\sqrt{f^2 - c}$ respectively.

(i) If $g^2 > c$, then the roots of the equation $x^2 + 2gx + c = 0$ are real and distinct, so the circle $x^2 + y^2 + 2gx + 2fy + c = 0$ meets the X-axis in two real and distinct points.

(ii) If $g^2 = c$, then the roots of the equation $x^2 + 2gx + c = 0$ are real and equal, so the circle touches X-axis, then intercept on X-axis is 0.

(iii) If $g^2 < c$, then the roots of the equation $x^2 + 2gx + c = 0$ are imaginary, so the given circle does not meet X-axis in real point.
Similarly, the circle $x^2 + y^2 + 2gx + 2fy + c = 0$ cuts the Y-axis in real and distinct points, touches or does not meet in real point according to $f^2 >, =$ or $< c$.

Equation of Tangent

A line which touch only one point of a circle.

1. Point Form

(i) The equation of the tangent at the point $P(x_1, y_1)$ to a circle $x^2 + y^2 + 2gx + 2fy + c = 0$ is $xx_1 + yy_1 + g(x + x_1) + f(y + y_1) + c = 0$

(ii) The equation of the tangent at the point $P(x_1, y_1)$ to a circle $x^2 + y^2 = r^2$ is $xx_1 + yy_1 = r^2$.

2. Slope Form

(i) The equation of the tangent of slope m to the circle $x^2 + y^2 + 2gx + 2fy + c = 0$ are

$$y + f = m(x + g) \pm \sqrt{(g^2 + f^2 - c)(1 + m^2)}$$

(ii) The equation of the tangents of slope m to the circle $(x - a)^2 + (y - b)^2 = r^2$ are $y - b = m(x - a) \pm r\sqrt{1 + m^2}$ and the coordinates of the points of contact are $\left(a \pm \frac{mr}{\sqrt{1 + m^2}}, b \mp \frac{r}{\sqrt{1 + m^2}}\right)$.

(iii) The equation of tangents of slope m to the circle $x^2 + y^2 = r^2$ are $y = mx \pm r\sqrt{1 + m^2}$ and the coordinates of the point of contact are $\left(\pm \frac{rm}{\sqrt{1 + m^2}}, \mp \frac{r}{\sqrt{1 + m^2}}\right)$.

3. Parametric Form

The equation of the tangent to the circle $(x - a)^2 + (y - b)^2 = r^2$ at the point $(a + r\cos\theta, b + r\sin\theta)$ is $(x - a)\cos\theta + (y - b)\sin\theta = r$.

Equation of Normal

A line which is perpendicular to the tangent is known as a normal.

1. Point Form

(i) The equation of normal at the point (x_1, y_1) to the circle $x^2 + y^2 + 2gx + 2fy + c = 0$ is

$$y - y_1 = \frac{y_1 + f}{x_1 + g}(x - x_1) \text{ or } (y_1 + f)x - (x_1 + g)y + (gy_1 - fx_1) = 0.$$

(ii) The equation of normal at the point (x_1, y_1) to the circle $x^2 + y^2 = r^2$ is $\frac{x}{x_1} = \frac{y}{y_1}$.

2. Slope Form

The equation of a normal of slope m to the circle $x^2 + y^2 = r^2$ is $my = -x \pm r\sqrt{1 + m^2}$.

3. Parametric Form

The equation of normal to the circle $x^2 + y^2 = r^2$ at the point $(r\cos\theta, r\sin\theta)$ is $\frac{x}{r\cos\theta} = \frac{y}{r\sin\theta}$ or $y = x\tan\theta$.

Important Points

(i) If (x_1, y_1) is one end of a diameter of the circle $x^2 + y^2 + 2gx + 2fy + c = 0$, then the other end will be $(-2g - x_1, -2f - y_1)$.

(ii) If a line is perpendicular to the radius of a circle at its end points on the circle, then the line is a tangent to the circle and *vice-versa*.

(iii) Normal at any point on the circle is a straight line which is perpendicular to the tangent to the curve at the point and it passes through the centre of circle.

(iv) The line $y = mx + c$ meets the circle in unique real point or touch the circle $x^2 + y^2 = r^2$, if $r = \left|\frac{c}{\sqrt{1+m^2}}\right|$ and the point of contacts are $\left(\frac{\pm mr}{\sqrt{1+m^2}}, \frac{\mp r}{\sqrt{1+m^2}}\right)$.

(v) The line $lx + my + n = 0$ touches the circle $x^2 + y^2 = r^2$, if $r^2(l^2 + m^2) = n^2$.

(vi) Tangent at the point $P(r\cos\theta, r\sin\theta)$ to the circle $x^2 + y^2 = r^2$ is $x\cos\theta + y\sin\theta = r$.

(vii) The point of intersection of the tangent at the points $P(\theta_1)$ and $Q(\theta_2)$ on the circle $x^2 + y^2 = r^2$ is given by

$$x = \frac{r\cos\left(\frac{\theta_1+\theta_2}{2}\right)}{\cos\left(\frac{\theta_1-\theta_2}{2}\right)} \text{ and } y = \frac{r\sin\left(\frac{\theta_1+\theta_2}{2}\right)}{\cos\left(\frac{\theta_1-\theta_2}{2}\right)}.$$

(viii) A line intersect a given circle at two distinct real points, if the length of the perpendicular from the centre is less than the radius of the circle.

(ix) Length of the intercept cut off from the line $y = mx + c$ by the circle $x^2 + y^2 = a^2$ is $2\sqrt{\frac{a^2(1+m^2) - c^2}{1+m^2}}$

(x) If P is a point and C is the centre of a circle of radius r, then the maximum and minimum distances of P from the circle are $CP + r$ and $|CP - r|$, respectively.

(xi) Power of a point (x_1, y_1) with respect to the circle $x^2 + y^2 + 2gx + 2fy + c = 0$ is $x_1^2 + y_1^2 + 2gx_1 + 2fy_1 + c$.

Pair of Tangents

(i) The combined equation of the pair of tangents drawn from a point $P(x_1, y_1)$ to the circle $x^2 + y^2 = r^2$ is

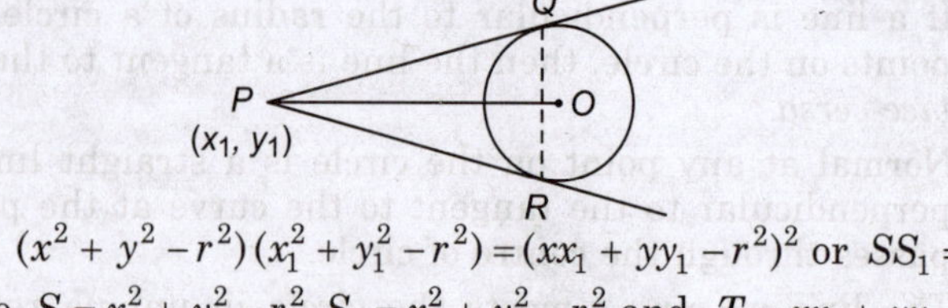

$$(x^2 + y^2 - r^2)(x_1^2 + y_1^2 - r^2) = (xx_1 + yy_1 - r^2)^2 \text{ or } SS_1 = T^2$$

where, $S = x^2 + y^2 - r^2, S_1 = x_1^2 + y_1^2 - r^2$ and $T = xx_1 + yy_1 - r^2$

(ii) The length of the tangents from the point $P(x_1, y_1)$ to the circle $x^2 + y^2 + 2gx + 2fy + c = 0$ is equal to
$\sqrt{x_1^2 + y_1^2 + 2gx_1 + 2fy_1 + c} = \sqrt{S_1}$

Competition Insight

Chord of contact QR of two tangents, drawn from $P(x_1, y_1)$ to the circle $x^2 + y^2 = r^2$ is $xx_1 + yy_1 = r^2$ or $T = 0$.

Similarly, for the circle

$x^2 + y^2 + 2gx + 2fy + c = 0$ is $xx_1 + yy_1 + g(x + x_1) + f(y + y_1) + c = 0$

(iii) Let AB is a chord of contact of tangents from C to the circle $x^2 + y^2 = r^2$. M is the mid-point of AB.

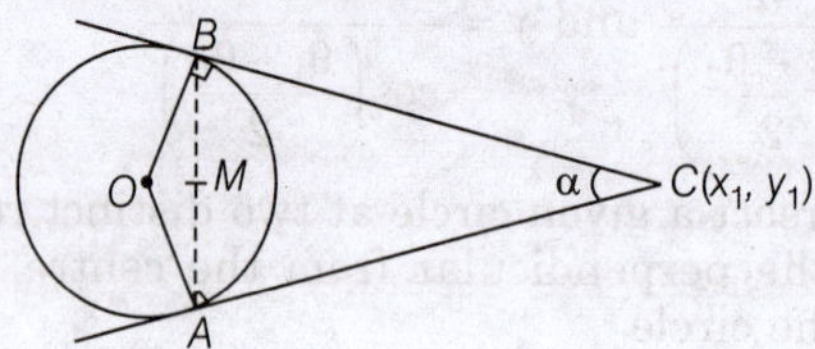

(a) Coordinates of $M\left(\dfrac{r^2x_1}{x_1^2 + y_1^2}, \dfrac{r^2y_1}{x_1^2 + y_1^2}\right)$

(b) $AB = 2r\dfrac{\sqrt{x_1^2 + y_1^2 - r^2}}{\sqrt{x_1^2 + y_1^2}}$

(c) $BC = \sqrt{x_1^2 + y_1^2 - r^2}$

(d) Area of quadrilateral $OACB = r\sqrt{x_1^2 + y_1^2 - r^2}$

(e) Area of $\Delta ABC = \dfrac{r}{x_1^2 + y_1^2}(x_1^2 + y_1^2 - r^2)^{3/2}$

(f) Area of $\Delta OAB = \dfrac{r^3}{x_1^2 + y_1^2}\sqrt{x_1^2 + y_1^2 - r^2}$

(g) Angle between two tangents $\angle ACB$ is $2\tan^{-1}\dfrac{r}{\sqrt{S_1}}$.

(iv) In general, two tangents can be drawn to a circle from a given point in its plane. If m_1 and m_2 are slope of the tangents drawn from the point $P(x_1, y_1)$ to the circle $x^2 + y^2 = a^2$, then

$$m_1 + m_2 = \frac{2x_1y_1}{x_1^2 - a^2} \quad \text{and} \quad m_1 \times m_2 = \frac{y_1^2 - a^2}{x_1^2 - a^2}$$

(v) The pair of tangents from $(0, 0)$ to the circle $x^2 + y^2 + 2gx + 2fy + c = 0$ are at right angle, if $g^2 + f^2 = 2c$.

 **Competition Insight**

Equation of Chord Bisected at a Given Point

The equation of chord of the circle $S \equiv x^2 + y^2 + 2gx + 2fy + c = 0$ bisected at the point (x_1, y_1) is given by $T = S_1$.

i.e. $xx_1 + yy_1 + g(x + x_1) + f(y + y_1) + c = x_1^2 + y_1^2 + 2gx_1 + 2fy_1 + c$

Director Circle

The locus of the point of intersection of two perpendicular tangents to a given circle is called a director circle. For circle $x^2 + y^2 = r^2$, the equation of director circle is $x^2 + y^2 = 2r^2$.

Common Tangents of Two Circles

Let the centres and radii of two circles are C_1, C_2 and r_1, r_2 respectively. Then, the following cases of intersection of these two circles may arise.

(i) When two circles are separate, four common tangents are possible.

Condition, $C_1C_2 > r_1 + r_2$

Clearly, $\frac{C_1D}{C_2D} = \frac{r_1}{r_2}$ [externally]

and $\frac{C_1T}{C_2T} = \frac{r_1}{r_2}$ [internally]

Length of direct common tangent

$$AB = A'B' = \sqrt{(C_1C_2)^2 - (r_1 - r_2)^2}$$

Length of transverse common tangent

$$PQ = P'Q' = \sqrt{(C_1C_2)^2 - (r_1 + r_2)^2}$$

(ii) When two circles touch externally, three common tangents are possible.

Condition, $C_1C_2 = r_1 + r_2$

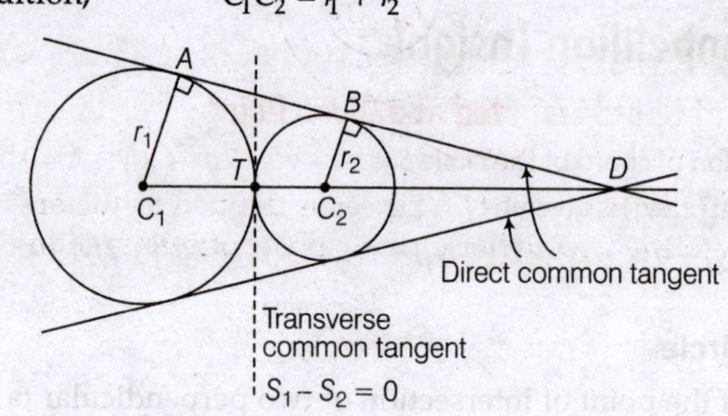

Clearly, $\frac{C_1D}{C_2D} = \frac{r_1}{r_2}$ [externally]

and $\frac{C_1T}{C_2T} = \frac{r_1}{r_2}$ [internally]

(iii) When two circles intersect, two common tangents are possible.

Condition, $|r_1 - r_2| < C_1C_2 < (r_1 + r_2)$

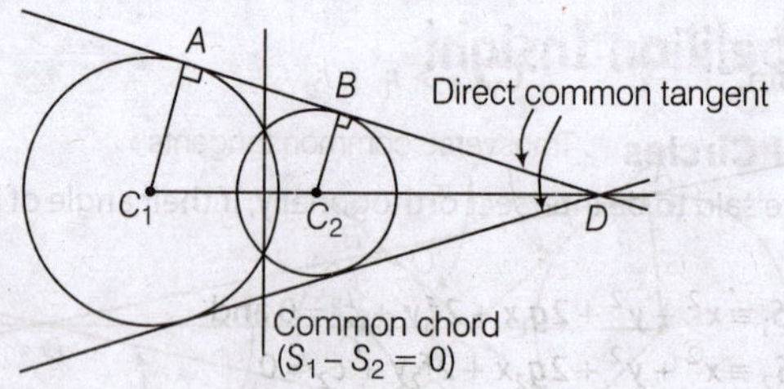

(iv) When two circles touch internally, one common tangent is possible.

Condition, $C_1C_2 = |r_1 - r_2|$

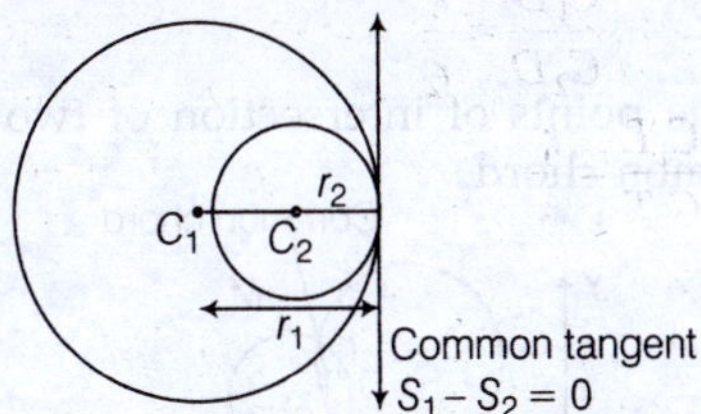

(v) When one circle contains another circle, no common tangent is possible.

Condition, $C_1C_2 < |r_1 - r_2|$

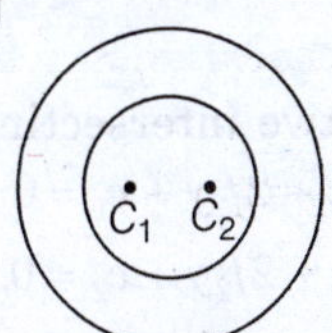

Angle of Intersection of Two Circles

The angle of intersection of two circles is defined as the angle between the tangents to the two circles at their point of intersection is given by

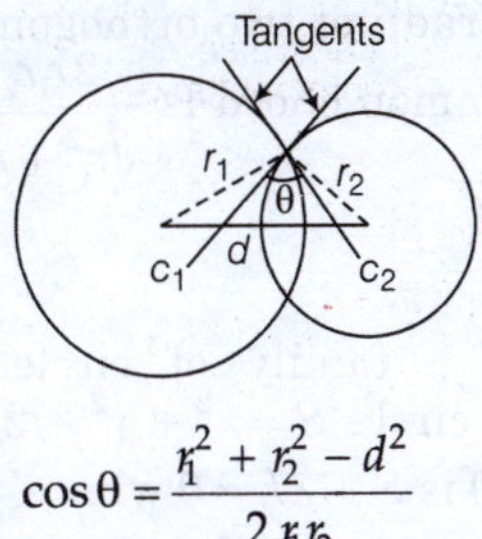

$$\cos\theta = \frac{r_1^2 + r_2^2 - d^2}{2 r_1 r_2}$$

Competition Insight

Orthogonal Circles

Two circles are said to be intersect orthogonally, if their angle of intersection is a right angle.

If two circles $S_1 \equiv x^2 + y^2 + 2g_1x + 2f_1y + c_1 = 0$ and

$$S_2 \equiv x^2 + y^2 + 2g_2x + 2f_2y + c_2 = 0$$

are orthogonal, then $2g_1g_2 + 2f_1f_2 = c_1 + c_2$

Common Chord

The chord joining the points of intersection of two given intersecting circles is called common chord.

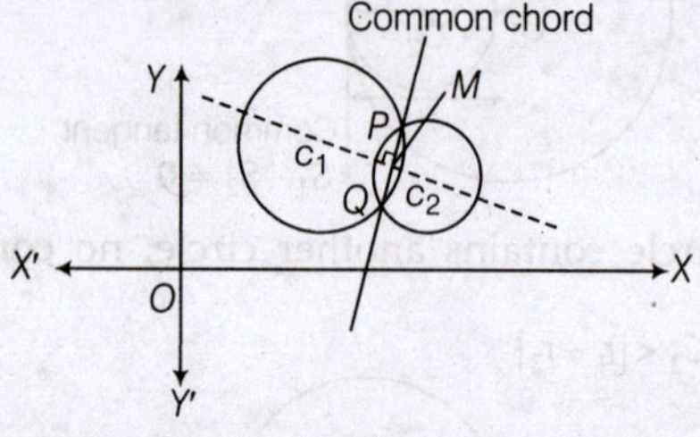

(i) If $S_1 = 0$ and $S_2 = 0$ be two intersecting circles, such that
$$S_1 \equiv x^2 + y^2 + 2g_1x + 2f_1y + c_1 = 0$$
and $S_2 \equiv x^2 + y^2 + 2g_2x + 2f_2y + c_2 = 0$,
then their common chord is given by $S_1 - S_2 = 0$

(ii) If C_1, C_2 denote the centre of the given intersecting circles, then their common chord
$PQ = 2\,PM = 2\sqrt{(C_1P)^2 - (C_1M)^2}$

(iii) If r_1 and r_2 be the radii of two orthogonally intersecting circles, then length of common chord is $\dfrac{2r_1r_2}{\sqrt{r_1^2 + r_2^2}}$.

Family of Circles

(i) The equation of a family of circles passing through the intersection of a circle $S = x^2 + y^2 + 2gx + 2fy + c = 0$ and line $L = lx + my + n = 0$ is $S + \lambda L = 0$ where, λ is any real number.

(ii) The equation of the family of circles passing through the point $A(x_1, y_1)$ and $B(x_2, y_2)$ is
$$(x - x_1)(x - x_2) + (y - y_1)(y - y_2) + \lambda \begin{vmatrix} x & y & 1 \\ x_1 & y_1 & 1 \\ x_2 & y_2 & 1 \end{vmatrix} = 0.$$

(iii) The equation of the family of circles touching the circle $S \equiv x^2 + y^2 + 2gx + 2fy + c = 0$ at point $P(x_1, y_1)$ is
$$x^2 + y^2 + 2gx + 2fy + c + \lambda\,[xx_1 + yy_1 + g(x + x_1) + f(y + y_1) + c] = 0$$
or $S + \lambda L = 0$, where $L = 0$ is the equation of the tangent to $S = 0$ at (x_1, y_1) and $\lambda \in R$.

(iv) Any circle passing through the point of intersection of two circles S_1 and S_2 is $S_1 + \lambda S_2 = 0$, (where $\lambda \neq -1$).

(v) Pole of $lx + my + n = 0$ with respect to $x^2 + y^2 = a^2$ is $\left(-\frac{a^2 l}{n}, -\frac{a^2 m}{n}\right)$.

(vi) Let $S_1 = 0, S_2 = 0$ be two circles with radii r_1, r_2, then $\frac{S_1}{r_1} \pm \frac{S_2}{r_2} = 0$ will meet at right angle.

(vii) Family of circles touching a line $L = 0$ at a point (x_1, y_1) on it is $(x - x_1)^2 + (y - y_1)^2 + \lambda L = 0$.

(viii) Circumcircle of a Δ with vertices $(x_1, y_1), (x_2, y_2), (x_3, y_3)$ is

$$\frac{(x - x_1)(x - x_2) + (y - y_1)(y - y_2)}{(x_3 - x_1)(x_3 - x_2) + (y_3 - y_1)(y_3 - y_2)} = \frac{\begin{vmatrix} x & y & 1 \\ x_1 & y_1 & 1 \\ x_2 & y_2 & 1 \end{vmatrix}}{\begin{vmatrix} x_3 & y_3 & 1 \\ x_1 & y_1 & 1 \\ x_2 & y_2 & 1 \end{vmatrix}}$$

Knowledge Booster

If the equation of two circles are $S_1 \equiv x^2 + y^2 + 2g_1x + 2f_1y + c_1 = 0$ and $S_2 \equiv x^2 + y^2 + 2g_2x + 2f_2y + c_2 = 0$, then equation of common chord is $S_1 - S_2 = 0$

$\Rightarrow \quad 2x(g_1 - g_2) + 2y(f_1 - f_2) + c_1 - c_2 = 0$

Image of the Circle by the Line Minor

Let the circle be $x^2 + y^2 + 2gx + 2fy + c = 0$

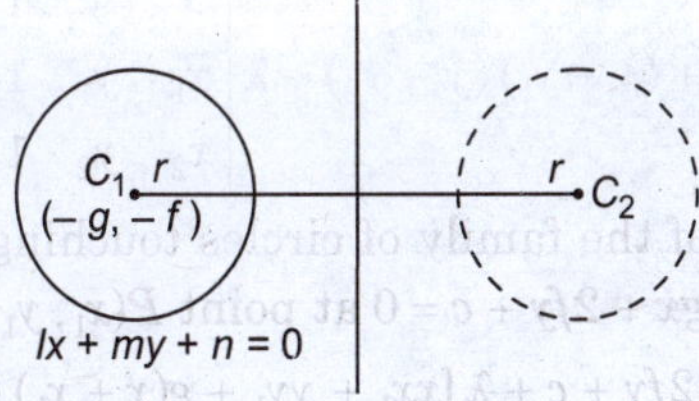

and line minor is $lx + my + n = 0$.

Then, the image of the circle is

$$(x - x_1)^2 + (y - y_1)^2 = r^2$$

where, (x_1, y_1) is mirror image of centre $(-g, -f)$ with respect to mirror line $lx + my + n = 0$ and $r = \sqrt{g^2 + f^2 - c}$.

Diameter of a Circle

The locus of the middle points of a system of parallel chords of a circle is called a diameter of the circle.

(i) The equation of the diameter bisecting parallel chords $y = mx + c$ of the circle $x^2 + y^2 = a^2$ is $x + my = 0$.

(ii) The diameter corresponding to a system of parallel chords of a circle always passes through the centre of the circle and is perpendicular to the parallel chords.

Chapter 17

Parabola

Conic Section

A conic is the locus of a point whose distance from a fixed point bears a constant ratio to its distance from a fixed line. The fixed point is the focus S and the fixed line is directrix l.

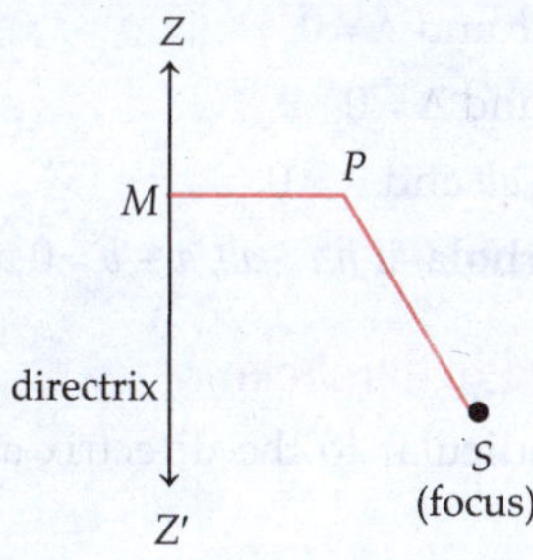

The constant ratio is called the eccentricity denoted by e.

(i) If $0 < e < 1$, conic is an ellipse.

(ii) $e = 1$, conic is a parabola.

(iii) $e > 1$, conic is a hyperbola.

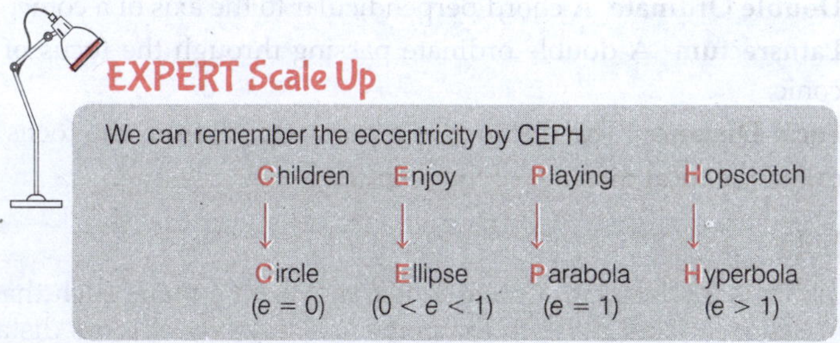

General Equation of Conic

If fixed point of curve is (x_1, y_1) and fixed line is $ax + by + c = 0$, then equation of the conic is

$$(a^2 + b^2)[(x - x_1)^2 + (y - y_1)^2] = e^2(ax + by + c)^2$$

which on simplification takes the form

$$ax^2 + 2hxy + by^2 + 2gx + 2fy + c = 0,$$

where a, b, c, f, g and h are constants.

A second degree equation $ax^2 + 2hxy + by^2 + 2gx + 2fy + c = 0$ represents

(i) **a pair of straight lines,** if $\Delta = \begin{vmatrix} a & h & g \\ h & b & f \\ g & f & c \end{vmatrix} = 0$

(ii) **a pair of parallel** (or coincident) **straight lines,** if $\Delta = 0$ and $h^2 = ab$.

(iii) **a pair of perpendicular straight lines,** if $\Delta = 0$ and $a + b = 0$

(iv) **a point,** if $\Delta = 0$ and $h^2 < ab$

(v) **a circle,** if $a = b \neq 0, h = 0$ and $\Delta \neq 0$

(vi) **a parabola,** if $h^2 = ab$ and $\Delta \neq 0$

(vii) **a ellipse,** if $h^2 < ab$ and $\Delta \neq 0$

(viii) **a hyperbola,** if $h^2 > ab$ and $\Delta \neq 0$

(ix) **a rectangular hyperbola,** if $h^2 > ab$, $a + b = 0$ and $\Delta \neq 0$

Important Terms Related to Parabola

(i) **Axis** A line perpendicular to the directrix and passes through the focus.

(ii) **Vertex** The intersection point of the conic and axis.

(iii) **Centre** The point which bisects every chord of the conic passing through it.

(iv) **Focal Chord** Any chord passing through the focus.

(v) **Double Ordinate** A chord perpendicular to the axis of a conic.

(vi) **Latusrectum** A double ordinate passing through the focus of the conic.

(vii) **Focal Distance** The distance of a point $P(x, y)$ from the focus S is called the focal distance of the point P.

Parabola

A parabola is the locus of a point which moves in a plane such that its distance from a fixed point in the plane is always equal to its distance from a fixed straight line in the same plane.

If focus of a parabola is $S(x_1, y_1)$ and equation of the directrix is $ax + by + c = 0$, then the equation of the parabola is

$$(a^2+b^2)[(x-x_1)^2+(y-y_1)^2]=(ax+by+c)^2$$

The point (x_1, y_1) lies inside, on or outside the parabola $y^2 = 4ax$ according to $y_1^2 - 4ax_1 >, = \text{or} < 0$.

Standard Forms of a Parabola and Related Terms

Terms	$y^2 = 4ax$	$y^2 = -4ax$	$x^2 = 4ay$	$x^2 = -4ay$
Vertex	$A(0, 0)$	$A(0, 0)$	$A(0, 0)$	$A(0, 0)$
Focus	$S(a, 0)$	$S(-a, 0)$	$S(0, a)$	$S(0, -a)$
Equation of axis	$y = 0$	$y = 0$	$x = 0$	$x = 0$
Equation of directrix	$x + a = 0$	$x - a = 0$	$y + a = 0$	$y - a = 0$
Eccentricity	$e = 1$	$e = 1$	$e = 1$	$e = 1$
Extremities of latusrectum	$(a, \pm 2a)$	$(-a, \pm 2a)$	$(\pm 2a, a)$	$(\pm 2a, -a)$
Length of latusrectum	$4a$	$4a$	$4a$	$4a$
Equation of tangent at vertex	$x = 0$	$x = 0$	$y = 0$	$y = 0$
Parametric equation	$\begin{cases} x = at^2 \\ y = 2at \end{cases}$	$\begin{cases} x = -at^2 \\ y = 2at \end{cases}$	$\begin{cases} x = 2at \\ y = at^2 \end{cases}$	$\begin{cases} x = 2at \\ y = -at^2 \end{cases}$

Terms	$y^2 = 4ax$	$y^2 = -4ax$	$x^2 = 4ay$	$x^2 = -4ay$
Focal distance of any point $P(h, k)$ on the parabola	$h + a$	$a - h$	$k + a$	$a - k$
Equation of latusrectum	$x - a = 0$	$x + a = 0$	$y - a = 0$	$y + a = 0$

Knowledge Booster

The length of the side of an equilateral triangle inscribed in parabola $y^2 = 4ax$ is $8a\sqrt{3}$ (one angular point is of the vertex)

Other Forms of a Parabola

If the vertex of the parabola is at a point $A(h, k)$ and its latusrectum is of length $4a$, then its equation is

(i) $(y - k)^2 = 4a(x - h)$, if its axis is parallel to OX i.e. parabola opens rightward.

(ii) $(y - k)^2 = -4a(x - h)$, if its axis is parallel to OX' i.e. parabola opens leftward.

(iii) $(x - h)^2 = 4a(y - k)$, if its axis is parallel to OY i.e. parabola opens upward.

(iv) $(x - h)^2 = -4a(y - k)$, if its axis is parallel to OY' i.e. parabola opens downward.

(v) The general equation of a parabola whose axis is parallel to X-axis, is $x = ay^2 + by + c$ and the general equation of a parabola whose axis is parallel to Y-axis, is $y = ax^2 + bx + c$.

Position of a Point

The point (x_1, y_1) lies outside, on or inside the parabola $y^2 = 4ax$ according as $y_1^2 - 4ax_1 >, =, < 0$.

Chord of Parabola

Joining any two points on a curve is called chord.

(i) **Parametric Equation of a Chord** Let $P(at_1^2, 2at_1)$ and $Q(at_2^2, 2at_2)$ be any two points on the parabola $y^2 = 4ax$, then the equation of the chord is

$$(y - 2at_1) = \frac{2at_2 - 2at_1}{at_2^2 - at_1^2}(x - at_1^2) \quad \text{or} \quad y(t_1 + t_2) = 2x + 2at_1t_2$$

(ii) Let $P(at^2, 2at)$ be the one end of a focal chord PQ of the parabola $y^2 = 4ax$, then the coordinates of the other end Q are $\left(\frac{a}{t^2}, \frac{-2a}{t}\right)$

(iii) If l_1 and l_2 are the length of the focal segments, then length of the latusrectum = 2 (harmonic mean of focal segment)

i.e. $$4a = \frac{4l_1l_2}{l_1 + l_2}$$

(iv) For a chord joining points $P(at_1^2, 2at_1)$ and $Q(at_2^2, 2at_2)$ and passing through focus, then $t_1t_2 = -1$.

(v) Length of the focal chord having t_1 and t_2 as end points is $a(t_2 - t_1)^2$.

Equation of Tangent

A line which touch only one point of a parabola.

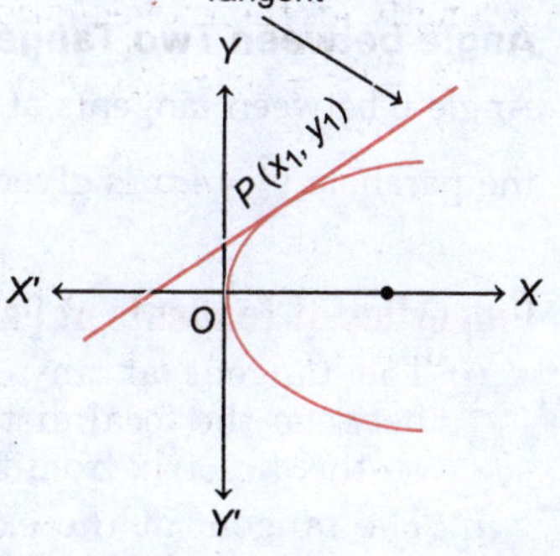

Point Form

The equation of the tangent to the parabola $y^2 = 4ax$ at a point (x_1, y_1) is given by $yy_1 = 2a(x + x_1)$.

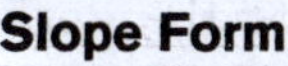

Slope Form

(a) The equation of the tangent of slope m to the parabola $y^2 = 4ax$ is $y = mx + \frac{a}{m}$

(b) The equation of the tangent of slope m to the parabola $(y - k)^2 = 4a(x - h)$ is given by $(y - k) = m(x - h) + \frac{a}{m}$.

The coordinates of the point of contact are $\left(h + \frac{a}{m^2}, k + \frac{2a}{m}\right)$.

Parametric Form

The equation of the tangent to the parabola $y^2 = 4ax$ at a point $(at^2, 2at)$ is $yt = x + at^2$.

Competition Insight

Condition of Tangency

(i) The line $y = mx + c$ touches a parabola, iff $c = \frac{a}{m}$ and the point of contact is $\left(\frac{a}{m^2}, \frac{2a}{m}\right)$.

(ii) The straight line $lx + my + n = 0$ touches $y^2 = 4ax$, if $nl = am^2$ and $x \cos\alpha + y \sin\alpha = p$ touches $y^2 = 4ax$, if $p \cos\alpha + a \sin^2\alpha = 0$.

Point of Intersection of Two Tangents

Let two tangents at $P(at_1^2, 2at_1)$ and $Q(at_2^2, 2at_2)$ intersect at R. Then, their point of intersection is $R(at_1t_2, a(t_1 + t_2))$ i.e. (GM of abscissa, AM of ordinate).

Angle between Two Tangents

Angle θ between tangents at two points $P(at_1^2, 2at_1)$ and $Q(at_2^2, 2at_2)$ on the parabola $y^2 = 4ax$ is given by $\tan\theta = \left|\frac{t_2 - t_1}{1 + t_1t_2}\right|$

Properties of Tangents of Parabola

(i) The tangent at any point on a parabola bisects the angle between the focal distance of the point and the perpendicular on the directrix from the point.

(ii) The tangent at the extremities of a focal chord of a parabola intersect at right angle on the directrix.

(iii) The portion of the tangent to a parabola cut off between the directrix and the curve subtends a right angle at the focus.

(iv) The perpendicular drawn from the focus on any tangent to a parabola intersect it at the point where it cuts the tangent at the vertex.

(v) The orthocentre of any triangle formed by three tangents to a parabola lies on the directrix.

(vi) The circumcircle formed by the intersection points of tangents at any three points on a parabola passes through the focus of the parabola.

(vii) The tangent at any point of a parabola is equally inclined to the focal distance of the point and the axis of the parabola.

(viii) The length of the subtangent at any point on a parabola is equal to twice the abscissa of the point.

(ix) Two tangents can be drawn from a point to a parabola. Two tangents are real and distinct or coincident or imaginary according as given point lies outside, on or inside the parabola.

(x) The straight line $y = mx + c$ meets the parabola $y^2 = 4ax$ in two points. These two points are real and distinct, if $c > \frac{a}{m}$, points are real and coincident, if $c = \frac{a}{m}$, points are imaginary, if $c < \frac{a}{m}$.

(xi) Area of the triangle formed by three points on a parabola is twice the area of the triangle formed by the tangents at these points.

Equation of Normal

A line which is perpendicular to the tangent at the point of contact with parabola.

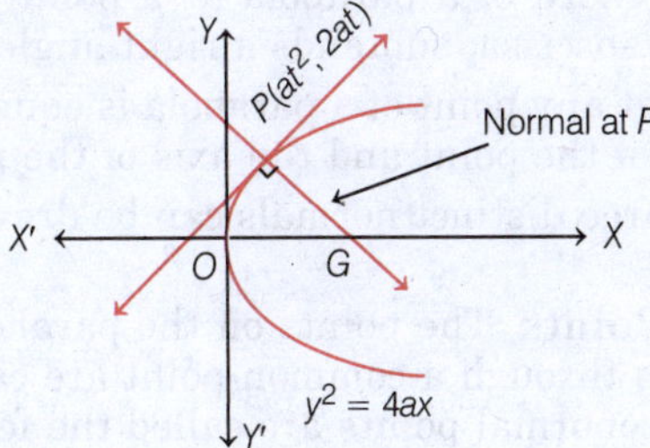

Point Form

The equation of the normal to the parabola $y^2 = 4ax$ at a point (x_1, y_1) is given by $y - y_1 = -\frac{y_1}{2a}(x - x_1)$.

Parametric Form

The equation of the normal to the parabola $y^2 = 4ax$ at point $(at^2, 2at)$ is given by $y + tx = 2at + at^3$.

Slope Form

The equation of the normal to the parabola $y^2 = 4ax$ in terms of its slope m is given by $y = mx - 2am - am^3$ at point $(am^2, -2am)$.

Properties of Normal to Parabola

(i) If the normal at the point $P(at_1^2, 2at_1)$ meets the parabola $y^2 = 4ax$ at $(at_2^2, 2at_2)$, then $t_2 = -t_1 - \frac{2}{t_1}$.

(ii) The tangent at one extremity of the focal chord of a parabola is parallel to the normal at other extremity.

(iii) The normal at points $P(at_1^2, 2at_1)$ and $Q(at_2^2, 2at_2)$ to the parabola $y^2 = 4ax$ intersect at the point

$$[2a + a(t_1^2 + t_2^2 + t_1t_2), -at_1t_2(t_1 + t_2)].$$

(iv) If the normal at points $P(at_1^2, 2at_1)$ and $Q(at_2^2, 2at_2)$ on the parabola $y^2 = 4ax$ meet on the parabola, then $t_1t_2 = 2$.

(v) If the normal at two points P and Q of a parabola $y^2 = 4ax$ intersect at a third point R on the curve, then the product of the ordinates of P and Q is $8a^2$.

(vi) If the normal chord at a point $P(at^2, 2at)$ to the parabola $y^2 = 4ax$ subtends a right angle at the vertex of the parabola, then $t^2 = 2$.

(vii) The normal chord of a parabola at a point whose ordinate is equal to the abscissa, subtends a right angle at the focus.

(viii) The normal at any point of a parabola is equally inclined to the focal radius of the point and the axis of the parabola.

(ix) Maximum three distinct normals can be drawn from a point to a parabola.

(x) **Conormal Points** The points on the parabola at which the normals pass through a common point are called conormal points. The conormal points are called the feet of the normals.

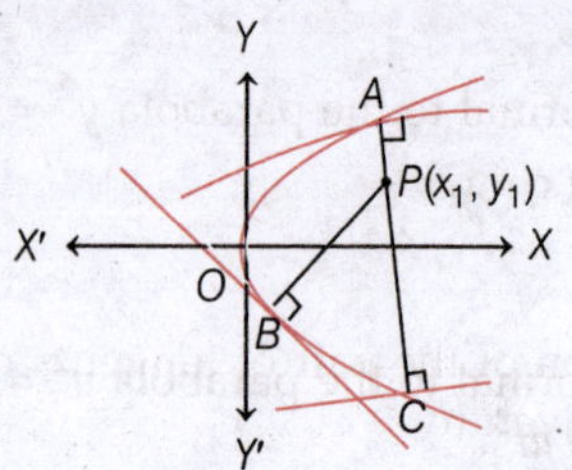

Points A, B and C are called conormal points.

(a) The algebraic sum of the slopes of the normals at conormals point is 0.

(b) The sum of the ordinates of the conormal points is 0.

(c) The centroid of the triangle formed by the conormal points on a parabola lies on its axis.

Length of Tangent and Normal

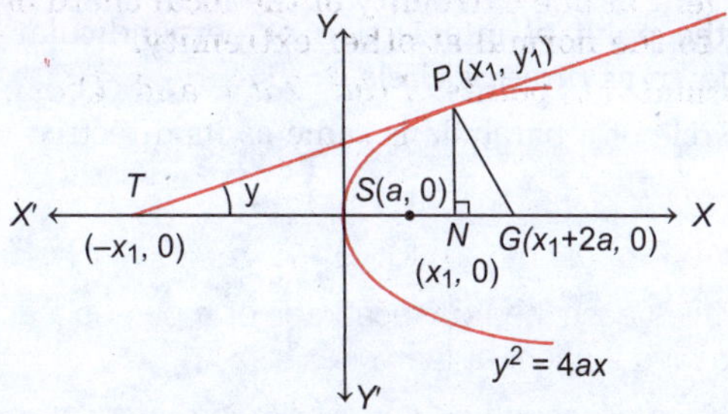

(i) The length of the tangent $= PT = PN$ cosec $\psi = y_1$ cosec ψ

(ii) The length of subtangent $= NT = PN \cot \psi = y_1 \cot \psi$

(iii) The length of normal $= PG = PN \sec \psi = y_1 \sec \psi$

(iv) The length of subnormal $= NG = PN \tan \psi = y_1 \tan \psi$

Competition Insight

Equation of the Chord Bisected at a Given Point

The equation of the chord of the parabola $y^2 = 4ax$ which is bisected at (x_1, y_1) is $yy_1 - 2a(x + x_1) = y_1^2 - 4ax_1$, or $T = S_1$

where, $S_1 = y_1^2 - 4ax_1$ and $T = yy_1 - 2a(x + x_1)$.

Equation of Diameter

The locus of mid-point of a system of parallel chords of a conic is known its diameter.

The diameter bisecting chords of slope m to the parabola $y^2 = 4ax$ is $y = \frac{2a}{m}$.

Pair of Tangents

The combined equation of the pair of tangents drawn from a point to a parabola $y^2 = 4ax$ is given by

$$SS_1 = T^2$$

where, $S = y^2 - 4ax$, $S_1 = y_1^2 - 4ax_1$

and $T = [yy_1 - 2a(x + x_1)]$

Chord of Contact

The chord of contact of tangents drawn from a point (x_1, y_1) to the parabola $y^2 = 4ax$ is $yy_1 = 2a(x + x_1)$.

Director Circle

The locus of the point of intersection of perpendicular tangents to a parabola is known as director circle.

The director circle of a parabola is same as its directrix.

Value Points

- The circles described on focal radii of a parabola as diameter touches the tangent at the vertex.
- The circles described on any focal chord of a parabola as diameter touches the directrix.
- If y_1, y_2, y_3 are the ordinates of the vertices of a triangle inscribed in the parabola $y^2 = 4ax$, then its area is $\frac{1}{8a}|(y_1 - y_2)(y_2 - y_3)(y_3 - y_1)|$.

Chapter 18

Ellipse

Ellipse is the locus of a point in a plane which moves in such a way that the ratio of the distance from a fixed point (focus) in the same plane to its distance from a fixed straight line (directrix) is always constant, which is always less than unity.

Major and Minor Axes

The line segment through the foci of the ellipse with its end points on the ellipse, is called its maj

or axis.

The line segment through the centre and perpendicular to the major axis with its end points on the ellipse, is called its minor axis.

Horizontal Ellipse i.e. $\frac{x^2}{a^2}+\frac{y^2}{b^2}=1, (0 < b < a)$

If the coefficient of x^2 has the larger denominator, then its major axis lies along the X-axis, then it is said to be horizontal ellipse.

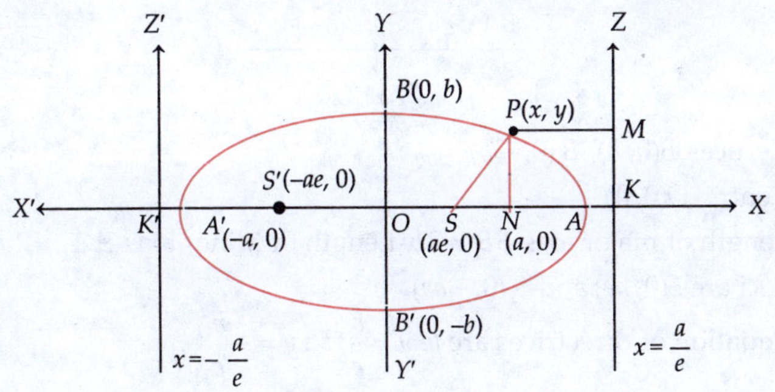

(i) Vertices $A(a,0)$, $A_1(-a,0)$

(ii) Centre $O(0,0)$

(iii) Length of major axis, $AA_1=2a$; Length of minor axis, $BB_1=2b$

(iv) Foci are $S(ae, 0)$ and $S_1(-ae, 0)$

(v) Equation of directrices are $l: x = \frac{a}{e}, l': x = -\frac{a}{e}$

(vi) Length of latusrectum, $LL_1 = L'L_1' = \frac{2b^2}{a}$

(vii) Eccentricity, $e = \sqrt{1 - \frac{b^2}{a^2}} < 1$

(viii) Focal distances of point $P(x, y)$ are SP and S_1P i.e. $|a - ex|$ and $|a + ex|$. Also, $SP + S_1P = 2a =$ major axis.

(ix) Distance between foci $= 2ae$

(x) Distance between directrices $= \frac{2a}{e}$

Vertical Ellipse i.e. $\frac{x^2}{a^2} + \frac{y^2}{b^2} = 1, (0 < a < b)$

If the coefficient of x^2 has the smaller denominator, then its major axis lies along the Y-axis, then it is said to be vertical ellipse.

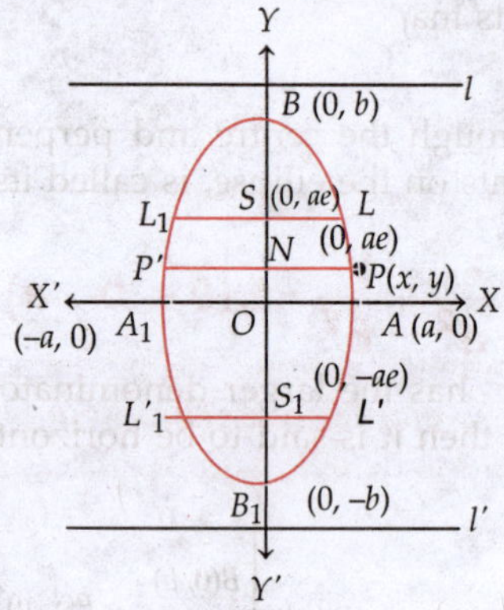

(i) Vertices $B(0, b), B_1(0, -b)$

(ii) Centre $O(0, 0)$

(iii) Length of major axis $BB_1 = 2b$, Length of Minor axis $AA_1 = 2a$

(iv) Foci are $S(0, ae)$ and $S_1(0, -ae)$

(v) Equation of directrices are $l: y = \frac{b}{e}; l': y = -\frac{b}{e}$

(vi) Length of latusrectum $LL_1 = L'L_1' = \frac{2a^2}{b}$

(vii) Eccentricity $e = \sqrt{1 - \frac{a^2}{b^2}} < 1$

(viii) Focal distances of point $P(x, y)$ are SP and S_1P,
i.e. $|b - ex|$ and $|b + ex|$. Also, $SP + S_1P = 2b =$ major axis.

(ix) Distance between foci $= 2be$

(x) Distance between directrices $= \frac{2b}{e}$

Value Point

If focus is zero, then foci merge together with the centre of ellipse and $a^2 = b^2$ i.e. $a = b$ and so ellipse becomes circle. Thus, circle is a special case of an ellipse.

Parametric Equation

The equation $x = a\cos\phi, y = b\sin\phi$, taken together are called the parametric equation of the ellipse $\frac{x^2}{a^2} + \frac{y^2}{b^2} = 1$, where ϕ is any parameter.

Special Form of Ellipse

If centre of the ellipse is (h, k) and the direction of the axes are parallel to the coordinate axes, then its equation is $\frac{(x-h)^2}{a^2} + \frac{(y-k)^2}{b^2} = 1$.

Ordinate and Double Ordinate

Let P be any point on the ellipse and PN be perpendicular to the major axis AA', such that PN produced meets the ellipse at P'. Then, PN is called the ordinate of P and PNP' is the double ordinate of P.

Value Point

The point (x_1, y_1) lies outside, on or inside the ellipse

$$\frac{x^2}{a^2} + \frac{y^2}{b^2} = 1 \text{ according as } \frac{x_1^2}{a^2} + \frac{y_1^2}{b^2} - 1 > 0, = \text{ or } < 0.$$

Auxiliary Circle

The ellipse $\frac{x^2}{a^2} + \frac{y^2}{b^2} = 1$ becomes $x^2 + y^2 = a^2$, if $b = a$.

This is called auxiliary circle of the ellipse. i.e. the circle described on the major axis of an ellipse as diameter is called auxiliary circle.

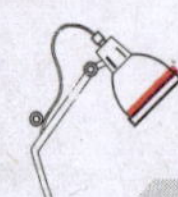

EXPERT Scale Up

If from each point of a circle perpendiculars are drawn upon a fixed diameter, then the locus of the points dividing these perpendiculars in a given ratio is an ellipse of which the given circle is the auxiliary circle.

Eccentric Angle of a Point

Let P be any point on the ellipse $\frac{x^2}{a^2}+\frac{y^2}{b^2}=1$. Draw PM perpendicular from P on the major axis of the ellipse and produce MP to the auxiliary circle in Q. Join CQ.

The $\angle ACQ = \phi$ is called the eccentric angle of the point P on the ellipse.

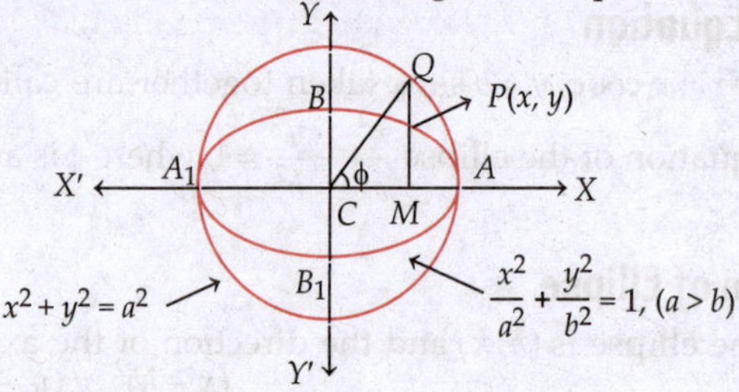

Equation of Tangent

(i) **Point Form** The equation of the tangent to the ellipse $\frac{x^2}{a^2}+\frac{y^2}{b^2}=1$ at the point (x_1, y_1) is $\frac{xx_1}{a^2}+\frac{yy_1}{b^2}=1$ or $T=0$.

(ii) **Parametric Form** The equation of the tangent to the ellipse at the point $(a\cos\theta, b\sin\theta)$ is $\frac{x}{a}\cos\theta+\frac{y}{b}\sin\theta=1$.

(iii) **Slope Form** The equation of the tangent of slope m to the ellipse $\frac{x^2}{a^2}+\frac{y^2}{b^2}=1$ are $y=mx\pm\sqrt{a^2m^2+b^2}$ and the coordinates of the point of contact are $\left(\pm\frac{a^2m}{\sqrt{a^2m^2+b^2}}, \mp\frac{b^2}{\sqrt{a^2m^2+b^2}}\right)$.

(iv) **Point of Intersection of Two Tangents** The equation of the tangents to the ellipse at points $P(a\cos\theta_1, b\sin\theta_1)$ and $Q(a\cos\theta_2, b\sin\theta_2)$ are $\frac{x}{a}\cos\theta_1+\frac{y}{b}\sin\theta_1=1$ and $\frac{x}{a}\cos\theta_2+\frac{y}{b}\sin\theta_2=1$ and these two intersect at the point

$$\left(\frac{a\cos\left(\frac{\theta_1+\theta_2}{2}\right)}{\cos\left(\frac{\theta_1-\theta_2}{2}\right)}, \frac{b\sin\left(\frac{\theta_1+\theta_2}{2}\right)}{\cos\left(\frac{\theta_1-\theta_2}{2}\right)}\right)$$

(v) **Pair of Tangents** The combined equation of the pair of tangents drawn from a point (x_1, y_1) to the ellipse $\frac{x^2}{a^2}+\frac{y^2}{b^2}=1$ is

$$\left(\frac{x^2}{a^2}+\frac{y^2}{b^2}-1\right)\left(\frac{x_1^2}{a^2}+\frac{y_1^2}{b^2}-1\right)=\left(\frac{xx_1}{a^2}+\frac{yy_1}{b^2}-1\right)^2 \text{ i.e. } SS_1=T^2$$

Director Circle

The locus of the point of intersection of perpendicular tangents to an ellipse is a director circle. If equation of an ellipse is $\frac{x^2}{a^2}+\frac{y^2}{b^2}=1$, then equation of director circle is $x^2+y^2=a^2+b^2$.

Competition Insight

Equation of Chord

Let $P(a\cos\theta, b\sin\theta)$ and $Q(a\cos\phi, b\sin\phi)$ be any two points of the ellipse $\frac{x^2}{a^2}+\frac{y^2}{b^2}=1$.

(i) The equation of the chord joining these points will be

$$(y-b\sin\theta)=\frac{b\sin\phi-b\sin\theta}{a\cos\phi-a\cos\theta}(x-a\cos\theta)$$

or $\frac{x}{a}\cos\left(\frac{\theta+\phi}{2}\right)+\frac{y}{b}\sin\left(\frac{\theta+\phi}{2}\right)=\cos\left(\frac{\theta-\phi}{2}\right)$

(ii) The equation of the chord of contact of tangents drawn from a point (x_1, y_1) to the ellipse

$$\frac{x^2}{a^2}+\frac{y^2}{b^2}=1 \text{ is } \frac{xx_1}{a^2}+\frac{yy_1}{b^2}=1 \text{ or } T=0.$$

(iii) The equation of the chord of the ellipse $\frac{x^2}{a^2}+\frac{y^2}{b^2}=1$ bisected at the point (x_1, y_1) is given by

$$\frac{xx_1}{a^2}+\frac{yy_1}{b^2}-1=\frac{x_1^2}{a^2}+\frac{y_1^2}{b^2}-1 \text{ or } T=S_1$$

Equation of Normal

(i) **Point Form** The equation of the normal at (x_1, y_1) to the ellipse $\frac{x^2}{a^2}+\frac{y^2}{b^2}=1$ is $\frac{a^2x}{x_1}-\frac{b^2y}{y_1}=a^2-b^2$

(ii) **Parametric Form** The equation of the normal to the ellipse $\frac{x^2}{a^2}+\frac{y^2}{b^2}=1$ at $(a\cos\theta, b\sin\theta)$ is $ax\sec\theta - by\operatorname{cosec}\theta = a^2-b^2$

(iii) **Slope Form** The equation of the normal of slope m to the ellipse $\frac{x^2}{a^2}+\frac{y^2}{b^2}=1$ are given by $y = mx \pm \frac{m(a^2-b^2)}{\sqrt{a^2+b^2m^2}}$

and the coordinates of the point of contact are

$$\left(\pm\frac{a^2}{\sqrt{a^2+b^2m^2}}, \pm\frac{b^2m}{\sqrt{a^2+b^2m^2}}\right)$$

Knowledge Booster

(i) **Point of Intersection of Two Normals** Point of intersection of the normal at points $(a\cos\theta_1, b\sin\theta_1)$ and $(a\cos\theta_2, b\sin\theta_2)$ are given by

$$\left(\frac{a^2-b^2}{a}\cos\theta_1\cos\theta_2\frac{\cos\left(\frac{\theta_1+\theta_2}{2}\right)}{\cos\left(\frac{\theta_1-\theta_2}{2}\right)}, \frac{-(a^2-b^2)}{b}\sin\theta_1\sin\theta_2\frac{\sin\left(\frac{\theta_1+\theta_2}{2}\right)}{\cos\left(\frac{\theta_1-\theta_2}{2}\right)}\right)$$

(ii) If the line $y = mx + c$ is a normal to the ellipse $\frac{x^2}{a^2}+\frac{y^2}{b^2}=1$, then $c^2=\frac{m^2(a^2-b^2)^2}{a^2+b^2m^2}$

Conormal Points

The points on the ellipse, the normals at which the ellipse passes through a given point are called conormal points.

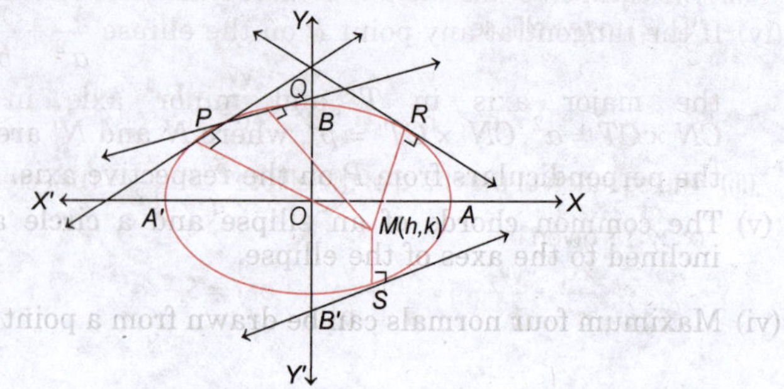

Here, P, Q, R and S are the conormal points.

(i) The sum of the eccentric angles of the conormal points on the ellipse, $\frac{x^2}{a^2}+\frac{y^2}{b^2}=1$ is an odd multiple of π.

(ii) If $\theta_1, \theta_2, \theta_3$ and θ_4 are eccentric angles of four points on the ellipse, the normals at which are concurrent, then

(a) $\Sigma \cos(\theta_1+\theta_2)=0$

(b) $\Sigma \sin(\theta_1+\theta_2)=0$

(iii) If θ_1, θ_2 and θ_3 are the eccentric angles of three points on the ellipse $\frac{x^2}{a^2}+\frac{y^2}{b^2}=1$, such that

$\sin(\theta_1+\theta_2)+\sin(\theta_2+\theta_3)+\sin(\theta_3+\theta_1)=0$,

then the normals at these points are concurrent.

(iv) If the normal at four points $P(x_1, y_1), Q(x_2, y_2), R(x_3, y_3)$ and $S(x_4, y_4)$ on the ellipse $\frac{x^2}{a^2}+\frac{y^2}{b^2}=1$ are concurrent, then

$$(x_1+x_2+x_3+x_4)\left(\frac{1}{x_1}+\frac{1}{x_2}+\frac{1}{x_3}+\frac{1}{x_4}\right)=4$$

Properties of Tangents and Normal to Ellipse

(i) The line $y=mx+c$ touches the ellipse

$\frac{x^2}{a^2}+\frac{y^2}{b^2}=1$, if $c^2=a^2m^2+b^2$

(ii) The tangent and normal at any point of an ellipse bisect the external and internal angles between the focal radii to the point.

(iii) If SM and $S'M'$ are perpendiculars from the foci upon the tangent at any point of the ellipse $\frac{x^2}{a^2}+\frac{y^2}{b^2}=1$, then $SM \times S'M'=b^2$ and M, M' lie on the auxiliary circle.

(iv) If the tangent at any point P on the ellipse $\frac{x^2}{a^2}+\frac{y^2}{b^2}=1$ meets the major axis in T and minor axis in T', then $CN \times CT=a^2, CN' \times CT'=p^2$, where N and N' are the foot of the perpendiculars from P on the respective axis.

(v) The common chords of an ellipse and a circle are equally inclined to the axes of the ellipse.

(vi) Maximum four normals can be drawn from a point to ellipse.

(vii) Polar of the point (x_1, y_1) with respect to the ellipse $\frac{x^2}{a^2}+\frac{y^2}{b^2}=1$ is $\frac{xx_1}{a^2}+\frac{yy_1}{b^2}=1$.

Here, point (x_1, y_1) is the pole of $\frac{xx_1}{a^2}+\frac{yy_1}{b^2}=1$ with respect to ellipse $\frac{x^2}{a^2}+\frac{y^2}{b^2}=1$.

(viii) The pole of the line $lx+my+n=0$ with respect to ellipse $\frac{x^2}{a^2}+\frac{y^2}{b^2}=1$ is $P\left(\frac{-a^2l}{n}, \frac{-b^2m}{n}\right)$.

(ix) Two tangents can be drawn from a point P to an ellipse. These tangents are real and distinct or coincident or imaginary according as the given point lies outside, on or inside the ellipse.

(x) Tangents at the extremities of latusrectum of an ellipse intersect on the corresponding directrix.

(xi) Locus of mid-point of focal chords of an ellipse $\frac{x^2}{a^2}+\frac{y^2}{b^2}=1$ is $\frac{x^2}{a^2}+\frac{y^2}{b^2}=\frac{ex}{a}$.

(xii) Point of intersection of the tangents at two points on the ellipse $\frac{x^2}{a^2}+\frac{y^2}{b^2}=1$, whose eccentric angles differ by a right angle lies on the ellipse $\frac{x^2}{a^2}+\frac{y^2}{b^2}=2$.

(xiii) Locus of mid-point of normal chords of an ellipse $\frac{x^2}{a^2}+\frac{y^2}{b^2}=1$ is

$$\left(\frac{x^2}{a^2}+\frac{y^2}{b^2}\right)^2\left(\frac{a^6}{x^2}+\frac{b^6}{y^2}\right)=(a^2-b^2)^2$$

(xiv) Eccentric angles of the extremities of latusrectum of an ellipse $\frac{x^2}{a^2}+\frac{y^2}{b^2}=1$ are $\tan^{-1}\left(\pm\frac{b}{ae}\right)$.

(xv) The straight lines $y=m_1x$ and $y=m_2x$ are conjugate diameters of an ellipse $\frac{x^2}{a^2}+\frac{y^2}{b^2}=1$, if $m_1 m_2=-\frac{b^2}{a^2}$.

(xvi) The normal at point P on an ellipse with foci S, S_1 is the internal bisector of $\angle SPS_1$.

Chapter 19

Hyperbola

A hyperbola is the locus of a point in a plane which moves in the plane in such a way that the ratio of its distance from a fixed point in the same plane to its distance from a fixed line is always constant, which is always greater than unity.

The fixed point is called the focus and the fixed line is directrix and the ratio is the eccentricity.

Transverse and Conjugate Axes

(i) The line through the foci of the hyperbola is called its transverse axis.

(ii) The line through the centre and perpendicular to the transverse axis of the hyperbola is called its conjugate axis.

Hyperbola of the Form $\frac{x^2}{a^2}-\frac{y^2}{b^2}=1$

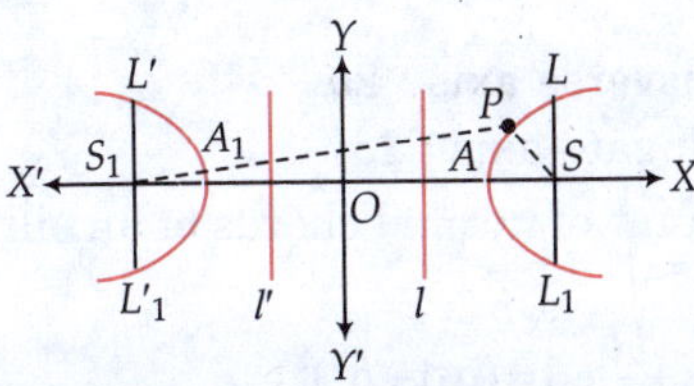

(i) Centre : $O(0,0)$

(ii) Foci : $S(ae,0), S_1(-ae,0)$

(iii) Vertices : $A(a,0)$, $A_1(-a,0)$

(iv) Equation of directrices $l : x=\frac{a}{e}, l' : x=-\frac{a}{e}$

(v) Length of latusrectum : $LL_1 = L'L'_1 = \frac{2b^2}{a}$

(vi) Length of transverse axis : $2a$

(vii) Length of conjugate axis : $2b$

(viii) Eccentricity $e = \sqrt{1 + \left(\frac{b}{a}\right)^2}$

or $b^2 = a^2(e^2 - 1)$

(ix) Distance between foci $= 2ae$

(x) Distance between directrices $= \frac{2a}{e}$

(xi) Coordinates of ends of latusrectum $= \left(\pm ae, \pm \frac{b^2}{a}\right)$

(xii) Focal radii $|SP| = |ex_1 - a|$ and $|S_1 P| = |ex_1 + a|$

Conjugate Hyperbola $-\frac{x^2}{a^2} + \frac{y^2}{b^2} = 1$

(i) Centre : $O(0, 0)$

(ii) Foci : $S(0, be), S_1(0, -be)$

(iii) Vertices : $A(0, b), A_1(0, -b)$

(iv) Equation of directrices

$l : y = \frac{b}{e}, l' : y = -\frac{b}{e}$

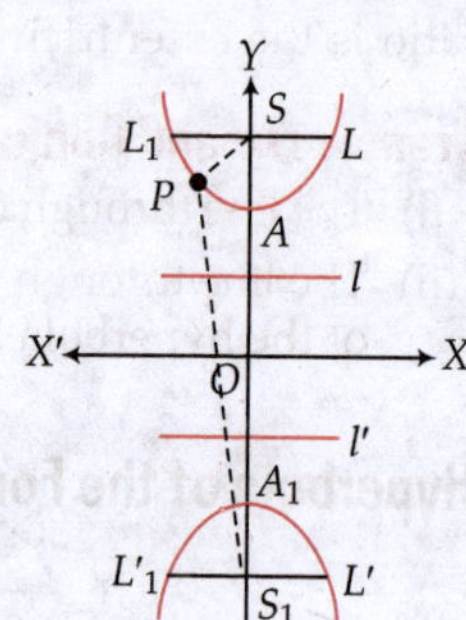

(v) Length of latusrectum :

$LL_1 = L' L_1' = \frac{2a^2}{b}$

(vi) Length of transverse axis : $2b$.

(vii) Length of conjugate axis : $2a$.

(viii) Eccentricity $e = \sqrt{1 + \left(\frac{a}{b}\right)^2}$

(ix) Distance between foci $= 2be$

(x) Distance between directrices $= \frac{2b}{e}$

(xi) Coordinates of ends of latusrectum $= \left(\pm \frac{a^2}{b}, \pm be\right)$

(xii) Focal radii $|SP| = |ey_1 - b|$ and $|S_1P| = |ey_1 + b|$

Value Points

- Two hyperbolas are said to be similar if they have same eccentricity.
- If e_1 and e_2 are the eccentricities of the hyperbola and its conjugate, then $e_1^{-2} + e_2^{-2} = 1$.
- A hyperbola in which $a = b$ is called an equilateral hyperbola.
- The point (x_1, y_1) lies outside, on or inside the hyperbola $\frac{x^2}{a^2} - \frac{y^2}{b^2} = 1$ according as $\frac{x_1^2}{a^2} - \frac{y_1^2}{b^2} - 1 <, =, > 0$.

Focal Distance of a Point

The distance of a point on the hyperbola from the focus is called its focal distance.

The difference of the focal distances of any point on a hyperbola is constant and is equal to the length of transverse axis of the hyperbola i.e.

$$|S_1 P - SP| = 2a$$

where, S and S_1 are the foci and P is any point on the hyperbola $\frac{x^2}{a^2} - \frac{y^2}{b^2} = 1$.

Parametric Equations

(i) Parametric equations of the hyperbola $\frac{x^2}{a^2} - \frac{y^2}{b^2} = 1$ are

$$x = a \sec \theta, y = b \tan \theta \text{ or } x = a \cosh \theta, y = b \sinh \theta$$

(ii) The equations $x = a\left(\frac{e^{\theta} + e^{-\theta}}{2}\right)$, $y = b\left(\frac{e^{\theta} - e^{-\theta}}{2}\right)$ are also the parametric equations of the hyperbola.

Equation of Hyperbola in Different Forms

(i) If the centre of the hyperbola is (h, k) and the directions of the axes are parallel to the coordinate axes, then the equation of the hyperbola, whose transverse and conjugate axes are $2a$ and $2b$ is $\frac{(x-h)^2}{a^2} - \frac{(y-k)^2}{b^2} = 1$.

(ii) If a point $P(x, y)$ moves in the plane of two perpendicular straight lines $a_1 x + b_1 y + c_1 = 0$ and $b_1 x - a_1 y + c_2 = 0$ in such a way that

$$\frac{\left(\frac{a_1x+b_1y+c_1}{\sqrt{a_1^2+b_1^2}}\right)^2}{a^2}-\frac{\left(\frac{b_1x-a_1y+c_2}{\sqrt{a_1^2+b_1^2}}\right)^2}{b^2}=1$$

Then, the locus of P is hyperbola whose transverse axis lies along $b_1x-a_1y+c_2=0$ and conjugate axis along the line $a_1x+b_1y+c_1=0$. The length of transverse and conjugate axes are $2a$ and $2b$, respectively.

Tangent Equation of Hyperbola

(i) **Point Form** The equation of the tangent to the hyperbola $\frac{x^2}{a^2}-\frac{y^2}{b^2}=1$ at (x_1, y_1) is $\frac{xx_1}{a^2}-\frac{yy_1}{b^2}=1$ or $T=0$.

(ii) **Parametric Form** The equation of the tangent to the hyperbola $\frac{x^2}{a^2}-\frac{y^2}{b^2}=1$ at $(a\sec\theta, b\tan\theta)$ is $\frac{x}{a}\sec\theta-\frac{y}{b}\tan\theta=1$.

(iii) **Slope Form** The equation of the tangents of slope m to the hyperbola $\frac{x^2}{a^2}-\frac{y^2}{b^2}=1$ are given by $y=mx\pm\sqrt{a^2m^2-b^2}$.

The coordinates of the point of contact are $\left(\pm\frac{a^2m}{\sqrt{a^2m^2-b^2}}, \pm\frac{b^2}{\sqrt{a^2m^2-b^2}}\right)$.

Important Points

(i) The tangent at the points $P(a\sec\theta_1, b\tan\theta_1)$ and intersect at the point

$$\left(\frac{a\cos\left(\frac{\theta_1-\theta_2}{2}\right)}{\cos\left(\frac{\theta_1+\theta_2}{2}\right)}, \frac{b\sin\left(\frac{\theta_1-\theta_2}{2}\right)}{\cos\left(\frac{\theta_1+\theta_2}{2}\right)}\right)$$

(ii) Two tangents drawn from P are real and distinct, coincident or imaginary according as the roots of the equation $m^2(h^2-a^2)-2khm+k^2+b^2=0$ are real and distinct, coincident or imaginary.

(iii) The line $y=mx+c$ touches the hyperbola, if $c^2=a^2m^2-b^2$ and the point of contacts are $\left(\pm\frac{a^2m}{c}, \pm\frac{b^2}{c}\right)$ where $c=\sqrt{a^2m^2-b^2}$.

(iv) Maximum two tangents can be drawn from a point to a hyperbola.

(v) The combined equation of the pairs of tangent drawn from a point $P(x_1, y_1)$ lying outside the hyperbola $S \equiv \frac{x^2}{a^2} - \frac{y^2}{b^2} = 1$ is $SS_1 = T^2$

i.e. $\left(\frac{x^2}{a^2} - \frac{y^2}{b^2} - 1\right)\left(\frac{x_1^2}{a^2} - \frac{y_1^2}{b^2} - 1\right) = \left(\frac{xx_1}{a^2} - \frac{yy_1}{b^2} - 1\right)^2$

Competition Insight

Equation of Chord

(i) Equations of chord joining two points $P(a \sec \theta_1, b \tan \theta_1)$ and $Q(a \sec \theta_2, b \tan \theta_2)$ on the hyperbola $\frac{x^2}{a^2} - \frac{y^2}{b^2} = 1$ is

$$y - b \tan \theta_1 = \frac{b \tan \theta_2 - b \tan \theta_1}{a \sec \theta_2 - a \sec \theta_1} \cdot (x - a \sec \theta_1)$$

or $$\frac{x}{a} \cos\left(\frac{\theta_1 - \theta_2}{2}\right) - \frac{y}{b} \sin\left(\frac{\theta_1 + \theta_2}{2}\right) = \cos\left(\frac{\theta_1 + \theta_2}{2}\right)$$

(ii) Equations of chord of contact of tangents drawn from a point (x_1, y_1) to the hyperbola $\frac{x^2}{a^2} - \frac{y^2}{b^2} = 1$ is $\frac{xx_1}{a^2} - \frac{yy_1}{b^2} = 1$ or $T = 0$.

(iii) The equation of the chord of the hyperbola $\frac{x^2}{a^2} - \frac{y^2}{b^2} = 1$ bisected at point (x_1, y_1) is given by

$$\frac{xx_1}{a^2} - \frac{yy_1}{b^2} - 1 = \frac{x_1^2}{a^2} - \frac{y_1^2}{b^2} - 1$$

or $$T = S_1$$

Director Circle

The locus of the point of intersection of perpendicular tangents to the hyperbola $\frac{x^2}{a^2} - \frac{y^2}{b^2} = 1$, is called a director circle. The equation of director circle is $x^2 + y^2 = a^2 - b^2$.

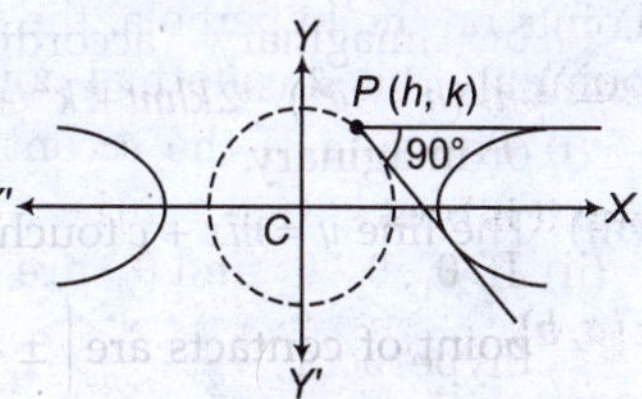

EXPERT Scale Up

Director circle of hyperbola i.e. $\frac{x^2}{a^2} - \frac{y^2}{b^2} = 1$ exist only when $a^2 > b^2$.

Normal Equation of Hyperbola

(i) **Point Form** The equation of the normal to the hyperbola $\frac{x^2}{a^2} - \frac{y^2}{b^2} = 1$ at (x_1, y_1) is $\frac{a^2 x}{x_1} + \frac{b^2 y}{y_1} = a^2 + b^2$.

(ii) **Parametric Form** The equation of the normal at $(a \sec\theta, b \tan\theta)$ to the hyperbola $\frac{x^2}{a^2} - \frac{y^2}{b^2} = 1$ is $ax \cos\theta + by \cot\theta = a^2 + b^2$.

(iii) **Slope Form** The equation of the normal of slope m to the hyperbola $\frac{x^2}{a^2} - \frac{y^2}{b^2} = 1$ are given by $y = mx \mp \frac{m(a^2 + b^2)}{\sqrt{a^2 - b^2 m^2}}$

The coordinates of the point of contact are

$$\left(\pm \frac{a^2}{\sqrt{a^2 - b^2 m^2}}, \mp \frac{b^2 m}{\sqrt{a^2 - b^2 m^2}} \right).$$

Value Points

- The line $y = mx + c$ will be normal to the hyperbola $\frac{x^2}{a^2} - \frac{y^2}{b^2} = 1$, if

$$c^2 = \frac{m^2 (a^2 + b^2)^2}{a^2 - b^2 m^2}$$

- Maximum four normals can be drawn from a point (x_1, y_1) to the hyperbola $\frac{x^2}{a^2} - \frac{y^2}{b^2} = 1$.

Conormal Points

Points on the hyperbola, the normals at which passes through a given point are called conormal points.

(i) The sum of the eccentric angles of conormal points is an odd multiple of π.

(ii) If $\theta_1, \theta_2, \theta_3$ and θ_4 are eccentric angles of four points on the hyperbola $\frac{x^2}{a^2} - \frac{y^2}{b^2} = 1$, then the normal at which they are concurrent, then

(a) $\sum \cos(\theta_1 + \theta_2) = 0$ (b) $\sum \sin(\theta_1 + \theta_2) = 0$

(iii) If θ_1, θ_2 and θ_3 are the eccentric angles of three points on the hyperbola $\frac{x^2}{a^2} - \frac{y^2}{b^2} = 1$, such that
$\sin(\theta_1 + \theta_2) + \sin(\theta_2 + \theta_3) + \sin(\theta_3 + \theta_1) = 0.$
Then, the normals at these points are concurrent.

(iv) If the normals at four points $P(x_1, y_1)$, $Q(x_2, y_2)$, $R(x_3, y_3)$ and $S(x_4, y_4)$ on the hyperbola $\frac{x^2}{a^2} - \frac{y^2}{b^2} = 1$ are concurrent, then

$$(x_1 + x_2 + x_3 + x_4)\left(\frac{1}{x_1} + \frac{1}{x_2} + \frac{1}{x_3} + \frac{1}{x_4}\right) = 4$$

and $$(y_1 + y_2 + y_3 + y_4)\left(\frac{1}{y_1} + \frac{1}{y_2} + \frac{1}{y_3} + \frac{1}{y_4}\right) = 4.$$

Asymptote

An asymptote to a curve is a straight line, at a finite distance from the origin, to which the tangent to a curve tends as the point of contact goes to infinity.

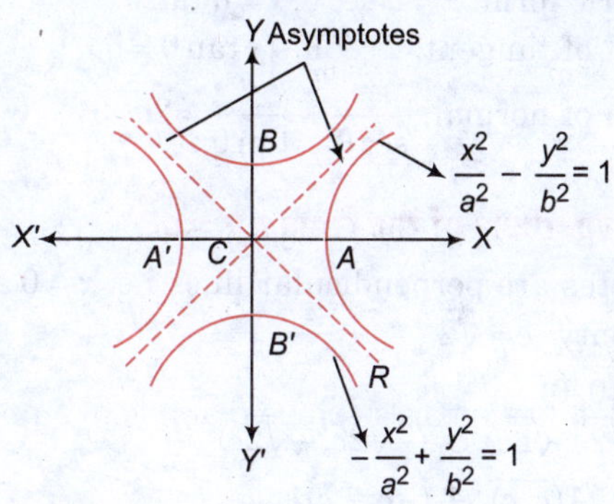

Rectangular Hyperbola

A hyperbola whose asymptotes include a right angle is said to be rectangular hyperbola or we can say that, if the lengths of transverse and conjugate axes of any hyperbola be equal, then it is said to be a rectangular hyperbola.

i.e. In a hyperbola $\frac{x^2}{a^2} - \frac{y^2}{b^2} = 1$, if $b = a$, then it said to be rectangular hyperbola. The eccentricity of a rectangular hyperbola is always $\sqrt{2}$.

Rectangular Hyperbola of the Form $x^2 - y^2 = a^2$

(i) Asymptotes are perpendicular lines i.e. $x \pm y = 0$

(ii) Eccentricity $e = \sqrt{2}$

(iii) Centre $(0, 0)$

(iv) Foci $(\pm \sqrt{2}\, a, 0)$

(v) Vetices $A(a, 0)$ and $A_1\,(-a, 0)$

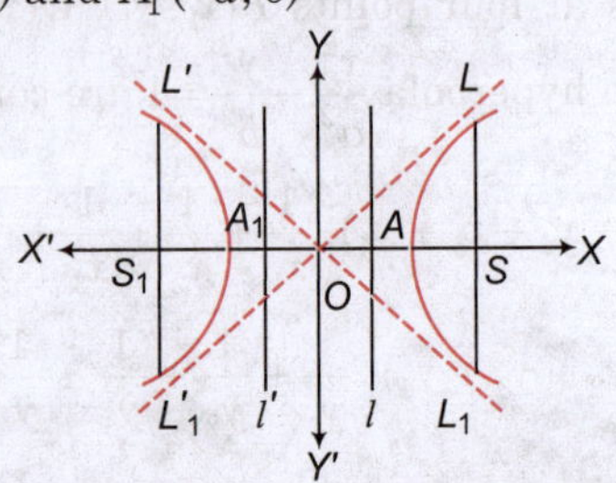

(vi) Equation of directrices $x = \pm \dfrac{a}{\sqrt{2}}$

(vii) Length of latusrectum $= 2a$

(viii) Parametric form $x = a \sec\theta, y = a \tan\theta$

(ix) Equation of tangent, $x \sec\theta - y \tan\theta = a$

(x) Equation of normal, $\dfrac{x}{\sec\theta} + \dfrac{y}{\tan\theta} = 2a$

Rectangular Hyperbola of the Form $xy = c^2$

(i) Asymptotes are perpendicular lines i.e. $x = 0$ and $y = 0$

(ii) Eccentricity $e = \sqrt{2}$

(iii) Centre $(0, 0)$

(iv) Foci $S\,(\sqrt{2}c, \sqrt{2}c), S_1\,(-\sqrt{2}c, -\sqrt{2}c)$

(v) Vertices $A(c, c), A_1(-c, -c)$

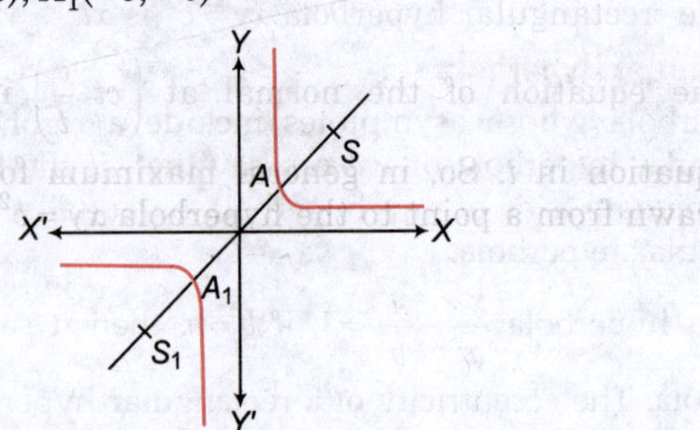

(vi) Equations of directrices $x + y = \pm \sqrt{2}\, c$

(vii) Length of latusrectum $= 2\sqrt{2}\, c$

(viii) Parametric form $x = ct, y = \frac{c}{t}$

Equation of Tangent of Rectangular Hyperbola $xy = c^2$

(i) **Point Form** The equation of tangent at (x_1, y_1) to the rectangular hyperbola is $xy_1 + yx_1 = 2c^2$ or $\frac{x}{x_1} + \frac{y}{y_1} = 2.$

(ii) **Parametric Form** The equation of tangent at $\left(ct, \frac{c}{t}\right)$ to the hyperbola is $\frac{x}{t} + yt = 2c.$

Competition Insight

(i) Tangent at $P\left(ct_1, \frac{c}{t_1}\right)$ and $Q\left(ct_2, \frac{c}{t_2}\right)$ to the rectangular hyperbola intersect at $\left(\frac{2ct_1t_2}{t_1 + t_2}, \frac{2c}{t_1 + t_2}\right)$.

(ii) The equation of the chord of contact of tangents drawn from a point (x_1, y_1) to the rectangular hyperbola is $xy_1 + yx_1 = 2c^2$.

Normal Equation of Rectangular Hyperbola $xy = c^2$

(i) **Point Form** The equation of the normal at (x_1, y_1) to the rectangular hyperbola is $xx_1 - yy_1 = x_1^2 - y_1^2$.

(ii) **Parametric Form** The equation of the normal at $\left(ct, \frac{c}{t}\right)$ to the rectangular hyperbola $xy = c^2$ is $xt^3 - yt - ct^4 + c = 0.$

(iii) The equation of the normal at $\left(ct, \frac{c}{t}\right)$ is a fourth degree equation in t. So, in general maximum four normals can be drawn from a point to the hyperbola $xy = c^2$.

Chord of Rectangular Hyperbola

(i) The equation of the chord of the hyperbola $xy = c^2$ whose mid-point is (x_1, y_1) is $xy_1 + yx_1 = 2x_1y_1$ or $T = S_1$

(ii) Equation of the chord joining t_1, t_2 on $xy = t^2$ is

$$x + yt_1t_2 = c(t_1 + t_2)$$

(iii) If a triangle is inscribed in a rectangular hyperbola, then its orthocentre lies on the hyperbola.

(iv) Any straight line parallel to an asymptotes of a hyperbola intersects the hyperbola at only one point.

Knowledge Booster

A rectangular hyperbola circumscribing a triangle passes through the orthocentre of this triangle.

Chapter 20

Limits, Continuity & Differentiability

Limit

Let $y = f(x)$ be a function of x. If at $x = a, f(x)$ takes indeterminate form $\left(\frac{0}{0}, \frac{\infty}{\infty}, \infty - \infty, 0 \times \infty, 1^{\infty}, 0^0 \text{ and } \infty^0\right)$, then we consider the values of the function at the points which are very near to a. If these values tend to a definite unique number as x tends to a, then the unique number, so obtained is called the limit of $f(x)$ at $x = a$ and we write it as $\lim_{x \to a} f(x)$.

Left Hand and Right Hand Limits

If values of the function, at the points which are very near to the left of a, tends to a definite unique number, then the unique number so obtained is called the left hand limit of $f(x)$ at $x = a$. We write it as

$$f(a-0) = \lim_{x \to a^-} f(x) = \lim_{h \to 0^+} f(a-h)$$

Similarly, right hand limit is written as

$$f(a+0) = \lim_{x \to a^+} f(x) = \lim_{h \to 0^+} f(a+h)$$

Existence of Limit

$\lim_{x \to a} f(x)$ exists, if

(i) $\lim_{x \to a^-} f(x)$ and $\lim_{x \to a^+} f(x)$ both exist

(ii) $\lim_{x \to a^-} f(x) = \lim_{x \to a^+} f(x)$

Uniqueness of Limit

If $\lim_{x \to a} f(x)$ exists, then it is unique, i.e. there cannot be two distinct numbers l_1 and l_2 such that when x tends to a, the function $f(x)$ tends to both l_1 and l_2.

Fundamental Theorems on Limits

If $f(x)$ and $g(x)$ are two functions of x such that $\lim_{x \to a} f(x)$ and $\lim_{x \to a} g(x)$ both exist, then

(i) $\lim_{x \to a} [f(x) \pm g(x)] = \lim_{x \to a} f(x) \pm \lim_{x \to a} g(x)$

(ii) $\lim_{x \to a} [kf(x)] = k \lim_{x \to a} f(x)$, where k is a fixed real number.

(iii) $\lim_{x \to a} [f(x)\, g(x)] = \lim_{x \to a} f(x) \lim_{x \to a} g(x)$

(iv) $\lim_{x \to a} \dfrac{f(x)}{g(x)} = \dfrac{\lim_{x \to a} f(x)}{\lim_{x \to a} g(x)}$, provided $\lim_{x \to a} g(x) \neq 0$

(v) $\lim_{x \to a} [f(x)]^{g(x)} = \left[\lim_{x \to a} f(x)\right]^{\lim_{x \to a} g(x)}$

(vi) $\lim_{x \to a} (gof)(x) = \lim_{x \to a} g[f(x)] = g\left[\lim_{x \to a} f(x)\right]$

(vii) $\lim_{x \to a} \log f(x) = \log\left[\lim_{x \to a} f(x)\right]$, provided $\lim_{x \to a} f(x) > 0$.

(viii) $\lim_{x \to a} e^{f(x)} = e^{\lim_{x \to a} f(x)}$

(ix) If $f(x) \leq g(x)$ for every x excluding a, then $\lim_{x \to a} f(x) \leq \lim_{x \to a} g(x)$.

(x) $\lim_{x \to a} |f(x)| = \left|\lim_{x \to a} f(x)\right|$

(xi) If $\lim_{x \to a} f(x) \to +\infty$ or $-\infty$, then $\lim_{x \to a} \dfrac{1}{f(x)} = 0$

Important Results on Limits

1. Algebraic Limits

(i) $\lim_{x \to a} \dfrac{x^n - a^n}{x - a} = na^{n-1}, n \in Q$ (ii) $\lim_{x \to 0} \dfrac{(1+x)^n - 1}{x} = n, n \in Q$

2. Trigonometric Limits

(i) $\lim_{x \to 0} \dfrac{\sin x}{x} = 1 = \lim_{x \to 0} \dfrac{x}{\sin x}$ (ii) $\lim_{x \to 0} \dfrac{\tan x}{x} = 1 = \lim_{x \to 0} \dfrac{x}{\tan x}$

(iii) $\lim_{x \to 0} \dfrac{\sin^{-1} x}{x} = 1 = \lim_{x \to 0} \dfrac{x}{\sin^{-1} x}$ (iv) $\lim_{x \to 0} \dfrac{\tan^{-1} x}{x} = 1 = \lim_{x \to 0} \dfrac{x}{\tan^{-1} x}$

(v) $\lim_{x\to 0} \frac{\sin x^\circ}{x} = \frac{\pi}{180}$ (vi) $\lim_{x\to 0} \cos x = 1$

(vii) $\lim_{x\to a} \frac{\sin(x-a)}{x-a} = 1$ (viii) $\lim_{x\to a} \frac{\tan(x-a)}{x-a} = 1$

(ix) $\lim_{x\to a} \sin^{-1} x = \sin^{-1} a, |a| \le 1$ (x) $\lim_{x\to a} \cos^{-1} x = \cos^{-1} a, |a| \le 1$

(xi) $\lim_{x\to a} \tan^{-1} x = \tan^{-1} a, -\infty < a < \infty$

(xii) $\lim_{x\to\infty} \frac{\sin x}{x} = \lim_{x\to\infty} \frac{\cos x}{x} = 0$

(xiii) $\lim_{x\to\infty} \frac{\sin\frac{1}{x}}{\frac{1}{x}} = 1$

(xiv) $\lim_{x\to 0} \frac{1-\cos x}{x} = 0$, (where x is measured in radian)

3. **Exponential Limits**

(i) $\lim_{x\to 0} \frac{e^x - 1}{x} = 1$

(ii) $\lim_{x\to 0} \frac{a^x - 1}{x} = \log_e a, \ a > 0$

(iii) $\lim_{x\to 0} \frac{e^{\lambda x} - 1}{x} = \lambda$, where $(\lambda \ne 0)$.

(iv) $\lim_{x\to\infty} a^x = \begin{cases} 0, & 0 \le a < 1 \\ 1, & a = 1 \\ \infty, & a > 1 \\ \text{does not exist}, & a < 0 \end{cases}$

4. **Logarithmic Limits**

(i) $\lim_{x\to 0} \frac{\log_e(1+x)}{x} = 1$ (ii) $\lim_{x\to e} \log_e x = 1$

(iii) $\lim_{x\to 0} \frac{\log_e(1-x)}{x} = -1$ (iv) $\lim_{x\to 0} \frac{\log_a(1+x)}{x} = \log_a e, a > 0, \ne 1$

5. **Limits of the Form $\lim_{x\to a} (f(x))^{g(x)}$**

If $\lim_{x\to a} f(x)$ exists and positive, then $\lim_{x\to a} [f(x)]^{\phi(x)} = e^{\lim_{x\to a} \phi(x)\log f(x)}$

6. **Limits of the Form 1^∞**

To evaluate the exponential form 1^∞, we use following results.

If $\lim_{x\to a} f(x) = \lim_{x\to a} g(x) = 0$, then, $\lim_{x\to a} \{1 + f(x)\}^{1/g(x)} = e^{\lim_{x\to a}\frac{f(x)}{g(x)}}$

Or If $\lim_{x\to a} f(x) = 1$ and $\lim_{x\to a} g(x) = \infty$,

Then, $\lim_{x\to a} \{f(x)\}^{g(x)} = \lim_{x\to a} \{1 + f(x) - 1\}^{g(x)} = e^{\lim_{x\to a}\{f(x)-1\}g(x)}$

Value Points

- $\lim_{x\to 0} (1+x)^{\frac{1}{x}} = e$
- $\lim_{x\to\infty} \left(1+\frac{1}{x}\right)^x = e$
- $\lim_{x\to 0} (1+\lambda x)^{\frac{1}{x}} = e^\lambda$
- $\lim_{x\to\infty} \left(1+\frac{\lambda}{x}\right)^x = e^\lambda$

Methods of Evaluating Limits

1. **Determinate Forms** (Limits by Direct Substitution)

To find $\lim_{x\to a} f(x)$, we substitute $x = a$ in the function. If the value comes out to be a definite value, then it is the limit.

Thus, $\lim_{x\to a} f(x) = f(a)$ provided it exists.

2. **Indeterminate Forms**

While evaluating $\lim_{x\to a} f(x)$, if direct substitution of $x = a$ leads to one of the following form $\frac{0}{0}; \frac{\infty}{\infty}; \infty - \infty; 0\times\infty; 1^\infty, 0^0$ and ∞^0, then these limits can be determined by using L' Hospital's rule or by some other method given below.

(i) **Limits by Factorisation**

If $\lim_{x\to a} \frac{f(x)}{g(x)}$ attains $\frac{0}{0}$ form, then $x - a$ must be a factor of numerator and denominator which can be cancelled out.

(ii) **Limits by Rationalisation**

If $\lim\limits_{x \to a} \dfrac{f(x)}{g(x)}$ attains $\dfrac{0}{0}$ form or $\dfrac{\infty}{\infty}$ form and either $f(x)$ or $g(x)$ or both involve expression consisting of square root, then this can be evaluated by rationalising.

(iii) **Limits by Substitution**

In order to evaluate $\lim\limits_{x \to a} f(x)$, we may substitute $x = a + h$ (or $x = a - h$), so that $x \to a$ changes to $h \to 0$.

Thus, $\lim\limits_{x \to a} f(x) = \lim\limits_{h \to 0} f(a \pm h)$

(iv) **Limits when $x \to \infty$**

If $\lim\limits_{x \to \infty} \dfrac{f(x)}{g(x)}$ is of the form $\dfrac{\infty}{\infty}$ and both $f(x)$ and $g(x)$ are polynomial of x.

Then, we divide numerator and denominator by the highest power of x and put 0 for $\dfrac{1}{x}, \dfrac{1}{x^2}, \dfrac{1}{x^3}$, etc.

Knowledge Booster

If m and n are positive integers and a_0, $b_0 \neq 0$ are real numbers, then

$$\lim_{x \to \infty} \frac{a_0x^m + a_1x^{m-1} + \ldots + a_{m-1}x + a_m}{b_0x^n + b_1x^{n-1} + \ldots + b_{n-1}x + b_n} = \begin{cases} \dfrac{a_0}{b_0}, & \text{if } m = n \\ 0, & \text{if } m < n \\ \infty, & \text{if } m > n, a_0b_0 > 0 \\ -\infty, & \text{if } m > n, a_0b_0 < 0. \end{cases}$$

(v) **L'Hospital's Rule**

If $f(x)$ and $g(x)$ be two functions of x such that

(a) $\lim\limits_{x \to a} f(x) = \lim\limits_{x \to a} g(x) = 0$

(b) both are continuous at $x = a$.

(c) both are differentiable at $x = a$.

(d) $f'(x)$ and $g'(x)$ are continuous at the point $x = a$, then $\lim\limits_{x \to a} \dfrac{f(x)}{g(x)} = \lim\limits_{x \to a} \dfrac{f'(x)}{g'(x)}$.

Above rule is also applicable, if $\lim\limits_{x \to a} f(x) = \infty$ and $\lim\limits_{x \to a} g(x) = \infty$.

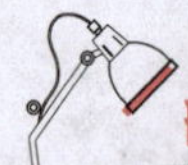

EXPERT Scale Up

If $\lim_{x\to a} \frac{f'(x)}{g'(x)}$ assumes the indeterminate form $\frac{0}{0}$ or $\frac{\infty}{\infty}$ and $f'(x), g'(x)$ satisfy all the condition embeded in L'Hospital's rule, then we can repeat the application of this rule on $\frac{f'(x)}{g'(x)}$ to get $\lim_{x\to a} \frac{f'(x)}{g'(x)}$ i.e. $\lim_{x\to a} \frac{f''(x)}{g''(x)}$.

Limit Using Expansions

Many limits can be evaluated very easily by applying expansion of expressions involving in it. Some of the standard expansions are

(i) $(1+x)^n = 1 + {}^nC_1 x + {}^nC_2 x^2 + \dots + {}^nC_n x^n, n \in N, x \in R$

(ii) $(1+x)^n = 1 + nx + \frac{n(n-1)}{2!} x^2 + \dots \infty, -1 < x < 1, n \in Q$

(iii) $e^x = 1 + \frac{x}{1!} + \frac{x^2}{2!} + \frac{x^3}{3!} + \dots \infty, x \in R$

(iv) $a^x = e^{x \log a} = 1 + x \log_e a + \frac{(x \log_e a)^2}{2!} + \dots \infty, x \in R, a > 0, a \neq 1$

(v) $\log_e (1+x) = x - \frac{x^2}{2} + \frac{x^3}{3} - \frac{x^4}{4} + \dots \infty, -1 < x \le 1$

(vi) $\log_e (1-x) = -x - \frac{x^2}{2} - \frac{x^3}{3} - \dots \infty, -1 \le x < 1$

(vii) $\sin x = x - \frac{x^3}{3!} + \frac{x^5}{5!} - \dots \infty, x \in R$

(viii) $\cos x = 1 - \frac{x^2}{2!} + \frac{x^4}{4!} - \dots \infty, x \in R$

(ix) $\tan x = x + \frac{x^3}{3} + \frac{2}{15} x^5 + \dots, |x| < \frac{\pi}{2}$

(x) $\sin^{-1} x = x + \frac{x^3}{3!} + \frac{9x^5}{5!} + \dots, x \in [-1, 1]$

(xi) $\tan^{-1} x = x - \frac{x^3}{3} + \frac{x^5}{5} - \frac{x^7}{7} + \dots, x \in R$

Some Limit Formulae using Trigonometric Functions

(i) $\lim\limits_{x \to 0} \dfrac{1 - \cos m x}{1 - \cos n x} = \dfrac{m^2}{n^2}$

(ii) $\lim\limits_{x \to 0} \dfrac{\cos ax - \cos bx}{\cos cx - \cos dx} = \dfrac{a^2 - b^2}{c^2 - d^2}$

(iii) $\lim\limits_{x \to 0} \dfrac{\cos mx - \cos nx}{x^2} = \dfrac{n^2 - m^2}{2}$

(iv) $\lim\limits_{x \to 0} \dfrac{\sin^p mx}{(nx)^p} = \left(\dfrac{m}{n}\right)^p$

(v) $\lim\limits_{x \to 0} \dfrac{\tan^p mx}{\tan^p nx} = \left(\dfrac{m}{n}\right)^p$

(vi) $\lim\limits_{x \to a} \dfrac{x^a - a^x}{x^x - a^a} = \dfrac{1 - \log a}{1 + \log a}$

(vii) $\lim\limits_{x \to 0} \dfrac{(1 + x)^m - 1}{(1 + x)^n - 1} = \dfrac{m}{n}$

(viii) $\lim\limits_{x \to 0} \dfrac{(1 + bx)^m - 1}{(1 + ax)^n - 1} = \dfrac{mb}{na}$

(ix) $\lim\limits_{x \to 0} (1 + ax)^{b/x} = \lim\limits_{x \to \infty} \left(1 + \dfrac{a}{x}\right)^{bx} = e^{ab}$

(x) $\lim\limits_{n \to \infty} (x^n + y^n)^{1/n} = y, \ (0 < x < y)$

(xi) $\lim\limits_{x \to 0} (\cos x + a \sin bx)^{1/x} = e^{ab}$

(xii) $\lim\limits_{x \to \infty} \dfrac{x^n}{e^x} = 0, \forall\, n$

(xiii) $\lim\limits_{m \to \infty} \left(\cos \dfrac{x}{m}\right)^m = 1$

(xiv) $\lim\limits_{n \to \infty} \cos \dfrac{x}{2} \cos \dfrac{x}{4} \cos \dfrac{x}{8} \ldots \cos \dfrac{x}{2^n} = \dfrac{\sin x}{x}$

Competition Insight

Sandwich Theorem

Let $f(x)$, $g(x)$ and $h(x)$ be real functions such that

$$f(x) \le g(x) \le h(x), \ \forall \ x \in (\alpha, \beta) - \{a\}$$

If $$\lim_{x \to a} f(x) = l = \lim_{x \to a} h(x),$$

then $$\lim_{x \to a} g(x) = l$$

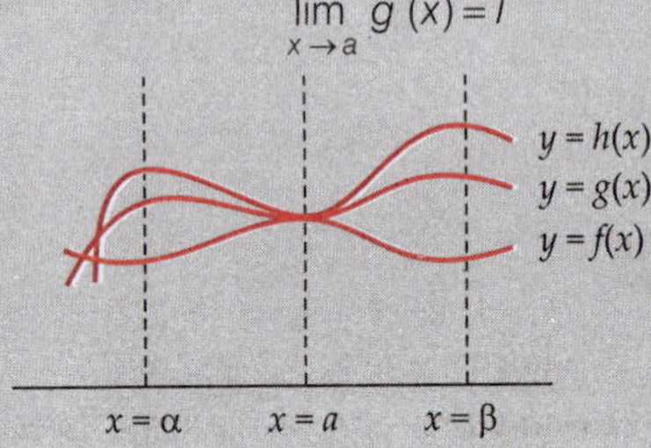

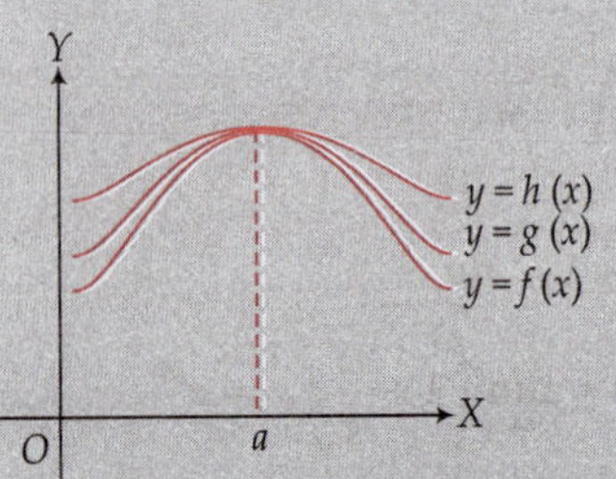

Continuity

If the graph of a function has no break or gap, then it is continuous. A function which is not continuous is called a **discontinuous** function. e.g. $f(x) = \sin x$ is continuous, as its graph has no break or gap.

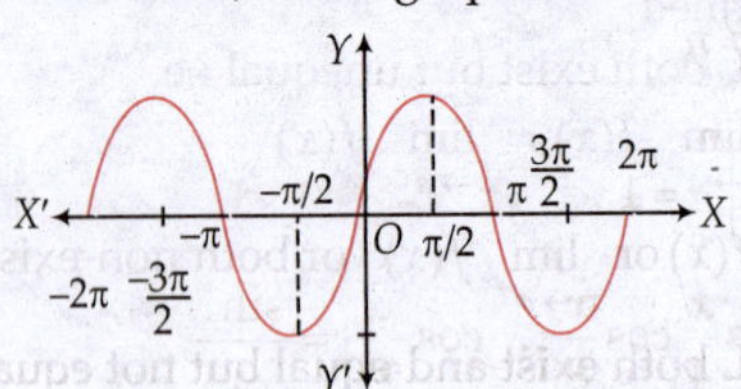

While $f(x) = \dfrac{1}{x}$ is discontinuous at $x = 0$.

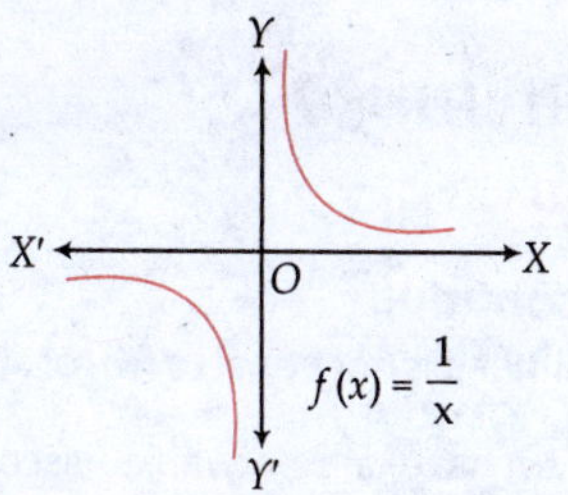

Continuity of a Function at a Point

Let f be a real function and a be a point in the domain of f. We say f is continuous at a, if $\lim_{x \to a} f(x) = f(a)$.

i.e. $$\lim_{x \to a^-} f(x) = \lim_{x \to a^+} f(x) = f(a)$$

Thus, $f(x)$ is continuous at $x = a$, if $\lim_{x \to a} f(x)$ exists and equals to $f(a)$.

If a function is not continuous at $x = a$, then it is said to be discontinuous at $x = a$.

Continuity of a Function in an Interval

(i) A function $f(x)$ is said to be continuous in an open interval (a, b), if $f(x)$ is continuous at every point of the interval.

(ii) A function $f(x)$ is said to be continuous in a closed interval $[a, b]$, if $f(x)$ is continuous in (a, b). In addition, $f(x)$ is continuous at $x = a$ from right and $f(x)$ is continuous at $x = b$ from left.

(iii) A real function f is said to be continuous in its domain, if it is continuous at every point of its domain.

Discontinuity of a Function

A function $f(x)$ can be discontinuous at a point $x = a$ in any one of the following ways.

(i) $f(a)$ is not defined.

(ii) LHL and RHL both exist but unequal i.e.

$$\lim_{x \to a^-} f(x) \neq \lim_{x \to a^+} f(x)$$

(iii) Either $\lim_{x \to a^-} f(x)$ or $\lim_{x \to a^+} f(x)$ or both non-existing or infinite.

(iv) LHL and RHL both exist and equal but not equal to $f(a)$,
i.e. $\lim_{x \to a^-} f(x) = \lim_{x \to a^+} f(x) \neq f(a)$

Competition Insight

Types of Discontinuity

1. Removable Discontinuity

If $\lim_{x \to a} f(x)$ exists and either it is not equal to $f(a)$ or $f(a)$ is not defined, then the function $f(x)$ is said to have a removable discontinuity (**missing point discontinuity**) of $x = a$.

This discontinuity can be removed by suitably defining the function at $x = a$.

2. Non-removable discontinuity

Non-removable discontinuity is of following two types

(i) Discontinuity of first kind

If $\lim_{x \to a^-} f(x)$ and $\lim_{x \to a^+} f(x)$ both exist but are not equal, then the function $f(x)$ is said to have a non-removable discontinuity of first kind at $x = a$.

In this case, we also say that $f(x)$ has jump discontinuity at $x = a$ and we defined

$$\left| \lim_{x \to a^-} f(x) - \lim_{x \to a^+} f(x) \right| = \text{jump of the function at } x = a.$$

(ii) Discontinuity of second kind

If at least one of the limits $\lim_{x \to a^-} f(x)$ or $\lim_{x \to a^+} f(x)$ does not exist or at least one of these is ∞ or $-\infty$, then the function $f(x)$ is said to have a non-removable discontinuity of second kind at $x = a$.

Fundamental Theorems of Continuity

(i) If f and g are continuous functions, then
   (a) $f \pm g$ and fg are continuous.
   (b) cf is continuous, where c is a constant.
   (c) $\dfrac{f}{g}$ is continuous at those points, where $g(x) \neq 0$.

(ii) If g is continuous at a point a and f is continuous at $g(a)$, then fog is continuous at a.

(iii) If f is continuous in $[a, b]$, then it is bounded in $[a, b]$ i.e. there exist m and M such that

$$m \leq f(x) \leq M, \forall\, x \in [a, b],$$

where m and M are called minimum and maximum values of $f(x)$ respectively in the interval $[a, b]$.

(iv) If f is continuous in its domain, then $|f|$ is also continuous in its domain.

(v) If f is continuous at a and $f(a) \neq 0$, then there exists an open interval $(a-\delta, a+\delta)$ such that for all $x \in (a-\delta, a+\delta)$, $f(x)$ has the same sign as $f(a)$.

(vi) If f is a continuous function defined on $[a,b]$ such that $f(a)$ and $f(b)$ are of opposite sign, then there exists atleast one solution of the equation $f(x)=0$ in the open interval (a,b).

(vii) If f is continuous on $[a,b]$ and maps $[a,b]$ into $[a,b]$, then for some $x \in [a,b]$, we have $f(x)=x$.

(viii) If f is continuous in domain D, then $\frac{1}{f}$ is also continuous in $D-\{x : f(x)=0\}$.

Value Points

- If $f(x)$ is continuous and $g(x)$ is discontinuous at $x=a$, then the product function $\phi(x)=f(x)\cdot g(x)$ is not necessarily be discontinuous at $x=a$.
- If $f(x)$ and $g(x)$ both are discontinuous at $x=a$, then the product function $\phi(x)=f(x)\cdot g(x)$ is not necessarily be discontinuous at $x=a$.
- There are some functions which are continuous only at one point.

  e.g. $f(x) = \begin{cases} +x, & \text{if } x \in Q \\ -x, & \text{if } x \notin Q \end{cases}$ and $g(x) = \begin{cases} x, & \text{if } x \in Q \\ 0, & \text{if } x \notin Q \end{cases}$ are both continuous only at $x=0$.

Differentiability

If the curve has no break point and no sharp edge, then it is differentiable.

Differentiability (or Derivability) of a Function at a Point

The function $f(x)$ is differentiable at a point P iff there exists a unique tangent at point P.

In other words, $f(x)$ is differentiable at a point P iff the curve does not have P as a corner point i.e. the function is not differentiable at those points on which function has holes or sharp edges.

If the shape of curve is any of the following forms,

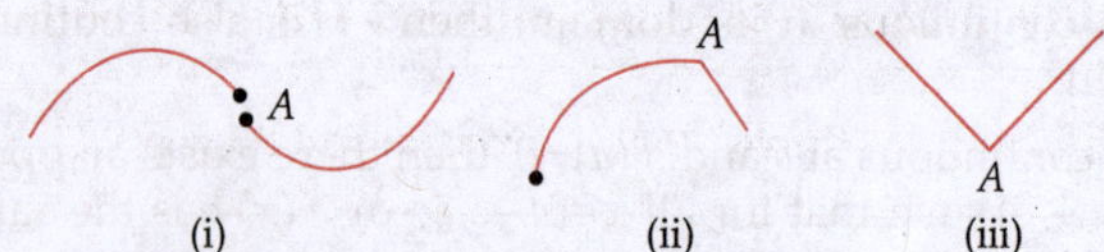

then the function is not differentiable at point A.

Mathematically A function $f(x)$ is said to be differentiable at a point a in its domain, if $\lim_{x \to a} \frac{f(x) - f(a)}{x - a}$ exist finitely

or if $\lim_{x \to a^-} \frac{f(x) - f(a)}{x - a} = \lim_{x \to a^+} \frac{f(x) - f(a)}{x - a}$

i.e. Left Hand Derivative (LHD) = Right Hand Derivative (RHD)

or $$Lf'(a) = Rf'(a)$$

Differentiability of a Function in an Interval

(i) A function $f(x)$ is said to be differentiable in an interval (a, b), if $f(x)$ is differentiable at every point of this interval (a, b).

(ii) A function $f(x)$ is said to be differentiable in a closed interval $[a, b]$, if $f(x)$ is differentiable in (a, b), in addition $f(x)$ is differentiable at $x = a$ from right and at $x = b$ from left.

(iii) A real function f is said to be differentiable if it is differentiable at every point of its domain.

Fundamental Theorems of Differentiability

(i) The sum, difference, product and quotient of two differentiable function, provided it is defined, is differential.

(ii) The composition of differential function is a differential function.

(iii) If $f(x)$ and $g(x)$ both are not differential function, then the sum function $f(x) + g(x)$ and the product function $f(x) \cdot g(x)$ can be differential function.

Relation between Continuity and Differentiability

(i) If a function $f(x)$ is differentiable at $x = a$, then $f(x)$ is necessarily continuous at $x = a$ but the converse is not necessary true, i.e. if a function is continuous at $x = a$, then it is not necessary that f is differentiable at $x = a$

(ii) If f is not continuous at $x = a$, then f is not differential at $x = a$.

Continuity and Differentiability of Different Functions

Function	Curve	Domain and Range	Continuity and Differentiability
Identity	$f(x) = x$	Domain = R, Range = $]-\infty, \infty[= R$	Continuous and Differentiable everywhere
Constant	$f(x) = c$	Domain = R, Range = $\{c\}$, where $c \to$ constant	
Polynomial	$f(x) = a_0 + a_1x + a_2x^2 + \ldots + a_nx^n$, where $a_0, a_1, \ldots, a_n$ are real numbers and $n \in N$.	Domain = R	
Square Root	$f(x) = \sqrt{x}$	Domain = $[0, \infty)$, Range = $[0, \infty)$	Continuous and differentiable in $(0, \infty)$
Greatest integer	$f(x) = [x]$	Domain = R, Range = I	Other than integral values it is continuous and differentiable
Least integer	$f(x) = (x)$	Domain = R, Range = I	
Fractional part	$f(x) = \{x\} = x - [x]$	Domain = R, Range = $[0, 1)$	
Signum	$f(x) = \frac{\lvert x \rvert}{x} = \begin{cases} -1, & x < 0 \\ 0, & x = 0 \\ 1, & x > 0 \end{cases}$	Domain = R, Range = $\{-1, 0, 1\}$	Continuous and differentiable everywhere except at $x = 0$
Exponential	$f(x) = a^x, a > 0, a \neq 1$	Domain = R, Range = $]0, \infty[$	Continuous and differentiable in their domain
Logarithmic	$f(x) = \log_a x; x, a > 0$ and $a \neq 1$	Domain = $(0, \infty)$, Range = R	

Functions	Curve	Domain and Range	Continuity and Differentiability
sine	$y = \sin x$	Domain $= R$, Range $= [-1, 1]$	Continuous and differentiable in their domain
cosine	$y = \cos x$	Domain $= R$, Range $= [-1, 1]$	
tangent	$y = \tan x$	Domain $= R - \left\{(2n+1)\frac{\pi}{2} \mid n \in Z\right\}$, Range $= R$	
cosecant	$y = \text{cosec } x$	Domain $= R - \{n\pi \mid n \in Z\}$ Range $= \{-\infty, -1] \cup [1, \infty)$	
secant	$y = \sec x$	Domain $= R - \left\{(2n+1)\frac{\pi}{2} \mid n \in Z\right\}$, Range $= (-\infty, -1] \cup [1, \infty)$	
cotangent	$y = \cot x$	Domain $= R - \{n\pi \mid n \in Z\}$, Range $= R$	
Arc sine	$y = \sin^{-1} x$	Domain $= [-1, 1]$, Range $= \left[-\frac{\pi}{2}, \frac{\pi}{2}\right]$	Continuous and differentiable in their domain
Arc cosine	$y = \cos^{-1} x$	Domain $= [-1, 1]$, Range $= [0, \pi]$	
Arc tangent	$y = \tan^{-1} x$	Domain $= R$, Range $= \left(-\frac{\pi}{2}, \frac{\pi}{2}\right)$	
Arc cosecant	$y = \text{cosec}^{-1} x$	Domain $= (-\infty, 1] \cup [1, \infty)$, Range $= \left(\frac{\pi}{2}, \frac{\pi}{2}\right) - \{0\}$	
Arc secant	$y = \sec^{-1} x$	Domain $= (-\infty, -1] \cup [1, \infty)$, Range $= [0, \pi] - \left\{\frac{\pi}{2}\right\}$	
Arc cotangent	$y = \cot^{-1} x$	Domain $= R$, Range $= (0, \pi)$	

Chapter 21

Derivatives

Derivative or Differential Coefficient

The rate of change of a quantity y with respect to another quantity x is called the **derivative** or differential coefficient of y with respect to x.

Differentiation

The process of finding derivative of a function is called differentiation.

Differentiation using First Principle

Let $f(x)$ is a function, differentiable at every point on the real number line, then its derivative is given by

$$f'(x) = \frac{d}{dx} f(x) = \lim_{\delta x \to 0} \frac{f(x + \delta x) - f(x)}{\delta x}$$

Derivatives of Standard Functions

(i) $\frac{d}{dx}(x^n) = nx^{n-1}$, where $n \in R$

(ii) $\frac{d}{dx}(k) = 0$, where k is constant.

(iii) $\frac{d}{dx}(e^x) = e^x$

(iv) $\frac{d}{dx}(a^x) = a^x \log_e a$, where $a > 0$ and $a \neq 1$

(v) $\frac{d}{dx}(\log_e x) = \frac{1}{x}$, where $x > 0$

(vi) $\frac{d}{dx}(\log_a x) = \frac{1}{x}(\log_a e) = \frac{1}{x \log_e a}$, where $x > 0$

(vii) $\frac{d}{dx}(\sin x) = \cos x$ (viii) $\frac{d}{dx}(\cos x) = -\sin x$

(ix) $\frac{d}{dx}(\tan x) = \sec^2 x, x \neq (2n+1)\frac{\pi}{2}$, where $n \in I$

(x) $\frac{d}{dx}(\cot x) = -\operatorname{cosec}^2 x, x \neq n\pi$, where $n \in I$

(xi) $\frac{d}{dx}(\sec x) = \sec x \tan x, x \neq (2n+1)\frac{\pi}{2}$, where $n \in I$

(xii) $\frac{d}{dx}(\operatorname{cosec} x) = -\operatorname{cosec} x \cot x, x \neq n\pi$, where $n \in I$

(xiii) $\frac{d}{dx}(\sin^{-1} x) = \frac{1}{\sqrt{1-x^2}}$, where $-1 < x < 1$

(xiv) $\frac{d}{dx}(\cos^{-1} x) = -\frac{1}{\sqrt{1-x^2}}$, where $-1 < x < 1$

(xv) $\frac{d}{dx}(\tan^{-1} x) = \frac{1}{1+x^2}$, where $x \in R$

(xvi) $\frac{d}{dx}(\cot^{-1} x) = -\frac{1}{1+x^2}$, where $x \in R$

(xvii) $\frac{d}{dx}(\sec^{-1} x) = \frac{1}{|x|\sqrt{x^2-1}}$, where $|x| > 1$

(xviii) $\frac{d}{dx}(\operatorname{cosec}^{-1} x) = -\frac{1}{|x|\sqrt{x^2-1}}$, where $|x| > 1$

(xix) $\frac{d}{dx}(\sinh x) = \cos h\, x$

(xx) $\frac{d}{dx}(\cosh x) = \sin h\, x$

(xxi) $\frac{d}{dx}(\tanh x) = \operatorname{sec} h^2 x$

(xxii) $\frac{d}{dx}(\coth x) = -\operatorname{cosec} h^2 x$

(xxiii) $\frac{d}{dx}(\operatorname{sech} x) = -\sec h\, x \tan h\, x$

(xxiv) $\frac{d}{dx}(\operatorname{cosech} x) = -\operatorname{cosec} h\, x \cot h\, x$

(xxv) $\frac{d}{dx}(\sinh^{-1} x) = 1/\sqrt{(x^2+1)}$

(xxvi) $\frac{d}{dx}(\cosh^{-1} x) = 1/\sqrt{(x^2-1)}$, where $x > 1$

(xxvii) $\frac{d}{dx}(\tanh^{-1} x) = 1/(1-x^2)$, where $|x| < 1$

(xxviii) $\frac{d}{dx}(\coth^{-1} x) = 1/(1-x^2)$, where $|x| > 1$

(xxix) $\frac{d}{dx}(\text{sech}^{-1}x) = -1/x\sqrt{(1-x^2)}$, where $x \in (0, 1)$

(xxx) $\frac{d}{dx}(\text{cosech}^{-1}x) = -1/|x|\sqrt{(1+x^2)}$, where $x \neq 0$

Fundamental Rules for Derivatives

(i) $\frac{d}{dx}\{cf(x)\} = c\frac{d}{dx}f(x)$, where c is a constant.

(ii) $\frac{d}{dx}\{f(x) \pm g(x)\} = \frac{d}{dx}f(x) \pm \frac{d}{dx}g(x)$ [sum and difference rule]

(iii) $\frac{d}{dx}\{f(x)\,g(x)\} = f(x)\frac{d}{dx}g(x) + g(x)\frac{d}{dx}f(x)$

[leibnitz product rule or product rule]

Value Point

If $u_1, u_2, u_3, \ldots, u_n$ are functions of x, then

$$\frac{d}{dx}(u_1 u_2 u_3 \ldots u_n) = \left(\frac{du_1}{dx}\right)[u_2 u_3 \ldots u_n] + u_1\left(\frac{du_2}{dx}\right)[u_3 \ldots u_n] + u_1 u_2\left(\frac{du_3}{dx}\right)[u_4 u_5 \ldots u_n] + \ldots + [u_1 u_2 \ldots u_{n-1}]\left(\frac{du_n}{dx}\right)$$

(iv) $\frac{d}{dx}\left\{\frac{f(x)}{g(x)}\right\} = \frac{g(x)\frac{d}{dx}f(x) - f(x)\frac{d}{dx}g(x)}{\{g(x)\}^2}$ [quotient rule]

(v) If $\frac{d}{dx}f(x) = \phi(x)$, then $\frac{d}{dx}f(ax+b) = a\phi(ax+b)$

Derivatives of Different Types of Function

1. Derivatives of Composite Functions (Chain Rule)

If f and g are differentiable functions in their domain, then fog is also differentiable.

Also, $(fog)'(x) = f'\{g(x)\}\,g'(x)$

More easily, if $y = f(u)$ and $u = g(x)$, then $\frac{dy}{dx} = \frac{dy}{du} \times \frac{du}{dx}$.

Extension of Chain Rule

If y is a function of u, u is a function of v and v is a function of x. Then,

$$\frac{dy}{dx}=\frac{dy}{du}\times\frac{du}{dv}\times\frac{dv}{dx}.$$

2. Derivative of Polynomial Functions

If $f(x)=a_nx^n+a_{n-1}x^{n-1}+\ldots+a_1x+a_0$, where a_i's are all real numbers and $a_n\neq 0$. Then, $\frac{df(x)}{dx}=na_nx^{n-1}+(n-1)a_{n-1}x^{n-2}+\ldots+2a_2x+a_1$.

3. Derivatives Functions Using Standard Substitution

Sometimes, it becomes very tedious to differentiate function. It can be made easy by using trigonometrical transformations and standard substitution.

Some Standard Substitution

S. No.	Expression	Substitution
(i)	a^2-x^2	$x=a\sin\theta$ or $a\cos\theta$
(ii)	a^2+x^2	$x=a\tan\theta$ or $a\cot\theta$
(iii)	x^2-a^2	$x=a\sec\theta$ or $a\operatorname{cosec}\theta$
(iv)	$\sqrt{\frac{a-x}{a+x}}$ or $\sqrt{\frac{a+x}{a-x}}$	$x=a\cos 2\theta$
(v)	$\sqrt{\frac{a^2-x^2}{a^2+x^2}}$ or $\sqrt{\frac{a^2+x^2}{a^2-x^2}}$	$x^2=a^2\cos 2\theta$
(vi)	$\sqrt{\frac{x-\alpha}{\beta-x}}$ or $\sqrt{(x-\alpha)(x-\beta)}$	$x=\alpha\cos^2\theta+\beta\sin^2\theta$
(vii)	$a\sin x+b\cos x$	$a=r\cos\alpha,\ b=r\sin\alpha$

4. Derivatives of Implicit Functions

To find $\frac{dy}{dx}$ of a function $f(x,y)=0$, which can not be expressed in the form $y=\phi(x)$, we differentiate both sides of the given relation with respect to x and collect the terms containing $\frac{dy}{dx}$ at one side and find $\frac{dy}{dx}$.

5. Logarithmic Differentiation

(i) If a function is the product or quotient of functions such as $y = f_1(x)\, f_2(x) \ldots f_n(x)$ or $\dfrac{f_1(x)\, f_2(x)\, f_3(x) \ldots}{g_1(x)\, g_2(x)\, g_3(x) \ldots}$, we first take logarithm and then differentiate it.

(ii) If a function is in the form of $[f(x)]^{g(x)}$, we first take logarithm and then differentiate it.

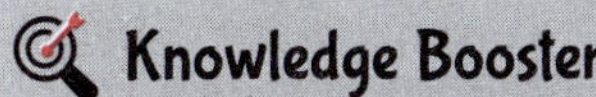

If $\{f(x)\}^{g(y)} = \{g(y)\}^{f(x)}$, then $\dfrac{dy}{dx} = \dfrac{g(y)}{f(x)} \cdot \dfrac{f'(x)}{g'(y)} \left[\dfrac{f(x) \log g(y) - g(y)}{g(y) \log f(x) - f(x)} \right]$

6. Derivatives of Parametric Functions

If the given function is of the form $x = f(t), y = g(t)$, where t is parameter, then

$$\frac{dy}{dx} = \frac{\left(\frac{dy}{dt}\right)}{\left(\frac{dx}{dt}\right)} = \frac{\frac{d}{dt} g(t)}{\frac{d}{dt} f(t)} = \frac{g'(t)}{f'(t)}$$

Derivative of a Function with Respect to Another Function

If $y = f(x)$ and $z = g(x)$, then the differentiation of y with respect to z is

$$\frac{dy}{dz} = \frac{\frac{dy}{dx}}{\frac{dz}{dx}} = \frac{f'(x)}{g'(x)}$$

Competition Insight

Differentiation of Infinite Series

Sometimes, the function is given in the form of an infinite series, e.g. $y = \sqrt{f(x) + \sqrt{f(x) + \ldots \infty}}$, then the process to find the derivative of such infinite series is called differentiation of infinite series.

e.g. Suppose $y = \sqrt{\log x + \sqrt{\log x + \sqrt{\log x + \ldots \infty}}}$

Then, $y = \sqrt{\log x + y} \Rightarrow y^2 = \log x + y$

Now, differentiate it by usual method.

e.g.

(i) If $y = f(x)^{\{f(x)\}^{\cdots\infty}}$, then $\frac{dy}{dx} = \frac{y^2 f'(x)}{f(x)\{1 - y\log f(x)\}}$

(ii) If $y = \sqrt{f(x) + \sqrt{f(x) + \sqrt{f(x) + \ldots \infty}}}$, then $\frac{dy}{dx} = \frac{f'(x)}{2y - 1}$

Differentiation of a Determinant

If $y = \begin{vmatrix} p & q & r \\ u & v & w \\ l & m & n \end{vmatrix}$, where all elements of determinant are differentiable functions of x, then

$$\frac{dy}{dx} = \begin{vmatrix} \frac{dp}{dx} & \frac{dq}{dx} & \frac{dr}{dx} \\ u & v & w \\ l & m & n \end{vmatrix} + \begin{vmatrix} p & q & r \\ \frac{du}{dx} & \frac{dv}{dx} & \frac{dw}{dx} \\ l & m & n \end{vmatrix} + \begin{vmatrix} p & q & r \\ u & v & w \\ \frac{dl}{dx} & \frac{dm}{dx} & \frac{dn}{dx} \end{vmatrix}$$

Successive Differentiations

If the function $y = f(x)$ is differentiated with respect to x, then the result $\frac{dy}{dx}$ or $f'(x)$, so obtained, is a function of x (may be a constant).

Hence, $\frac{dy}{dx}$ can again be differentiated with respect to x.

The differential coefficient of $\frac{dy}{dx}$ with respect to x is written as $\frac{d}{dx}\left(\frac{dy}{dx}\right) = \frac{d^2y}{dx^2}$ or $f''(x)$.

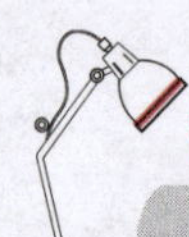

EXPERT Scale Up

Always remember $\frac{dy}{dx} = \frac{\frac{dy}{d\theta}}{\frac{dx}{d\theta}}$ but $\frac{d^2y}{dx^2} \neq \frac{\frac{d^2y}{d\theta^2}}{\frac{d^2x}{d\theta^2}}$

Again, the differential coefficient of $\frac{d^2y}{dx^2}$ with respect to x is written as

$$\frac{d}{dx}\left(\frac{d^2y}{dx^2}\right)=\frac{d^3y}{dx^3} \text{ or } f'''(x) \ldots$$

Here, $\frac{dy}{dx}, \frac{d^2y}{dx^2}, \frac{d^3y}{dx^3}, \ldots$ are respectively known as first, second, third, ... order differential coefficients of y with respect to x. These are alternatively denoted by $f'(x), f''(x), f'''(x), \ldots$ or $y_1, y_2, y_3, \ldots,$ respectively.

Competition Insight

nth Derivative of Some Functions

(i) $\frac{d^n}{dx^n}[\sin(ax+b)]=a^n\sin\left(\frac{n\pi}{2}+ax+b\right)$

(ii) $\frac{d^n}{dx^n}[\cos(ax+b)]=a^n\cos\left(\frac{n\pi}{2}+ax+b\right)$

(iii) $\frac{d^n}{dx^n}(ax+b)^m=\frac{m!}{(m-n)!}a^n(ax+b)^{m-n}$

(iv) $\frac{d^n}{dx^n}[\log(ax+b)]=\frac{(-1)^{n-1}(n-1)!a^n}{(ax+b)^n}$

(v) $\frac{d^n}{dx^n}(e^{ax})=a^ne^{ax}$

(vi) $\frac{d^n}{dx^n}(a^x)=a^x(\log a)^n$

(vii) (a) $\frac{d^n}{dx^n}[e^{ax}\sin(bx+c)]=r^ne^{ax}\sin(bx+c+n\phi)$

(b) $\frac{d^n}{dx^n}[e^{ax}\cos(bx+c)]=r^ne^{ax}\cos(bx+c+n\phi)$,

where $r=\sqrt{a^2+b^2}$ and $\phi=\tan^{-1}\left(\frac{b}{a}\right)$

Partial Differentiation

The partial differential coefficient of $f(x, y)$ with respect to x is the ordinary differential coefficient of $f(x, y)$ when y is regarded as a constant. It is written as $\frac{\partial f}{\partial x}$ or f_x.

Thus, $\frac{\partial f}{\partial x} = \lim_{h \to 0} \frac{f(x+h, y) - f(x, y)}{h}$

Similarly, the differential coefficient of $f(x,y)$ with respect to y is $\frac{\partial f}{\partial y}$ or f_y, where $\frac{\partial f}{\partial y} = \lim_{k \to 0} \frac{f(x, y+k) - f(x, y)}{k}$

e.g. If $z = f(x, y) = x^4 + y^4 + 3xy^2 + x^2y + x + 2y$,

then $\frac{\partial z}{\partial x}$ or $\frac{\partial f}{\partial x}$ or $f_x = 4x^3 + 3y^2 + 2xy + 1$

[here, y is consider as constant]

and $\frac{\partial z}{\partial y}$ or $\frac{\partial f}{\partial y}$ or $f_y = 4y^3 + 6xy + x^2 + 2$ [here, x is consider as constant]

Higher Partial Derivatives

Let $f(x, y)$ be a function of two variables such that $\frac{\partial f}{\partial x}, \frac{\partial f}{\partial y}$ both exist.

(i) The partial derivative of $\frac{\partial f}{\partial x}$ w.r.t. x is denoted by $\frac{\partial^2 f}{\partial x^2}$ or f_{xx}.

(ii) The partial derivative of $\frac{\partial f}{\partial y}$ w.r.t. y is denoted by $\frac{\partial^2 f}{\partial y^2}$ or f_{yy}.

(iii) The partial derivative of $\frac{\partial f}{\partial x}$ w.r.t. y is denoted by $\frac{\partial^2 f}{\partial y \, \partial x}$ or f_{xy}.

(iv) The partial derivative of $\frac{\partial f}{\partial y}$ w.r.t. x is denoted by $\frac{\partial^2 f}{\partial x \, \partial y}$ or f_{yx}.

Euler's Theorem on Homogeneous Function

If $f(x, y)$ is a homogeneous function of x, y of degree n, then

$$x \frac{\partial f}{\partial x} + y \frac{\partial f}{\partial y} = nf$$

Chapter 22

Application of Derivatives

Derivatives as the Rate of Change

If a variable quantity y is some function of time t i.e. $y = f(t)$, then small change in time Δt have a corresponding change Δy in y.

Thus, the average rate of change $= \frac{\Delta y}{\Delta t}$. When limit $\Delta t \to 0$ is applied, the rate of change becomes instantaneous and we get the rate of change with respect to t at any instant y, i.e. $\lim_{\Delta t \to 0} \frac{\Delta y}{\Delta t} = \frac{dy}{dt}$.

Similarly, the differential coefficient of y with respect to x i.e. $\frac{dy}{dx}$ is nothing but the rate of change of y relative to x.

Derivative as the Rate of Change of Two Variables

Let two variables are varying with respect to another variable t, i.e. $y = f(t)$ and $x = g(t)$.

Then, rate of change of y with respect to x is given by

$$\frac{dy}{dx} = \frac{dy/dt}{dx/dt} \quad \text{or} \quad \frac{dy}{dx} = \frac{dy}{dt} \times \frac{dt}{dx}$$

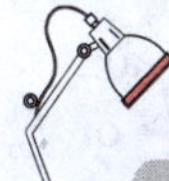

EXPERT Scale Up

$\frac{dy}{dx}$ is positive, if y increases as x increases and is negative, if y decreases as x increases.

Marginal Cost

Marginal cost represents the instantaneous rate of change of the total cost with respect to the number of items produced at an instant. If $C(x)$ represents the cost function for x units produced, then marginal cost, denoted by MC, is given by $MC = \frac{d}{dx}\{C(x)\}$.

Knowledge Booster

Total cost = Fixed cost + Variable cost i.e. $C(x) = f(c) + v(x)$.

Marginal Revenue

Marginal revenue represents the rate of change of total revenue with respect to the number of items sold at an instant. If $R(x)$ represents the revenue function for x units sold, then marginal revenue, denoted by MR, is given by $\text{MR} = \frac{d}{dx}\{R(x)\}$.

Tangents and Normals

A tangent is a straight line, which touches the curve $y = f(x)$ at a point. A normal is a straight line perpendicular to a tangent to the curve $y = f(x)$ intersecting at the point of contact.

Slope of Tangent and Normal

(i) If the tangent at P is perpendicular to X-axis or parallel to Y-axis, then $\theta = \frac{\pi}{2} \Rightarrow \tan\theta = \infty \Rightarrow \left(\frac{dy}{dx}\right)_P = \infty$.

(ii) If the tangent at P is perpendicular to Y-axis or parallel to X-axis, then $\theta = 0 \Rightarrow \tan\theta = 0 \Rightarrow \left(\frac{dy}{dx}\right)_P = 0$.

(iii) Slope of the normal at $P = \frac{-1}{\text{Slope of the tangent at } P}$

$$= \frac{-1}{\left(\frac{dy}{dx}\right)_P} = -\left(\frac{dx}{dy}\right)_P$$

(iv) If $\left(\frac{dy}{dx}\right)_P = 0$, then normal at (x, y) is parallel to Y-axis and perpendicular to X-axis.

(v) If $\left(\frac{dy}{dx}\right)_P = \infty$, then normal at (x, y) is parallel to X-axis and perpendicular to Y-axis.

Equation of Tangents and Normals

The derivative of the curve $y = f(x)$ is $f'(x)$ which represents the slope of tangent and equation of the tangent to the curve at P is $Y - y = \frac{dy}{dx}(X - x)$, where (x, y) is an arbitrary point on the tangent.

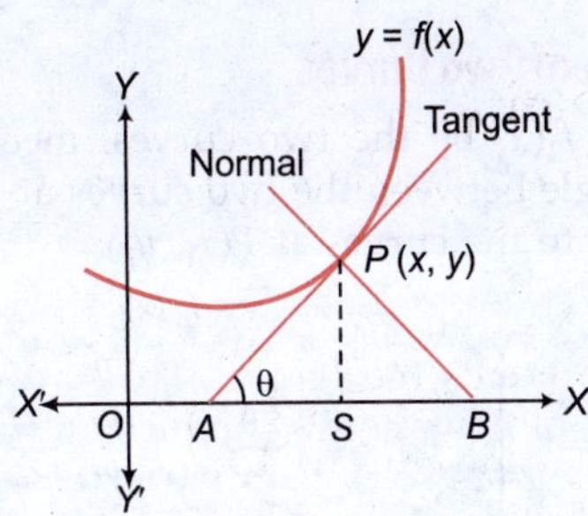

The equation of normal at (x, y) to the curve is $Y - y = -\frac{dx}{dy}(X - x)$

(i) If $\left(\frac{dy}{dx}\right)_{(x,\,y)} = 0$, then the equations of the tangent and normal at (x, y) are $(Y - y) = 0$ and $(X - x) = 0$, respectively.

(ii) If $\left(\frac{dy}{dx}\right)_{(x,\,y)} = \pm\infty$, then the equation of the tangent and normal at (x, y) are $(X - x) = 0$ and $(Y - y) = 0$, respectively.

Knowledge Booster

Length of Tangent and Normal

(i) Length of tangent, $PA = y \operatorname{cosec} \theta = \dfrac{y\sqrt{1+\left(\frac{dy}{dx}\right)^2}}{\left(\frac{dy}{dx}\right)}$

(ii) Length of normal,

$PB = y \sec \theta = y\sqrt{1+\left(\frac{dy}{dx}\right)^2}$

(iii) Length of subtangent,

$AS = y \cot \theta = \dfrac{y}{(dy/dx)}$

(iv) Length of subnormal,

$BS = y \tan \theta = y\left(\frac{dy}{dx}\right)$

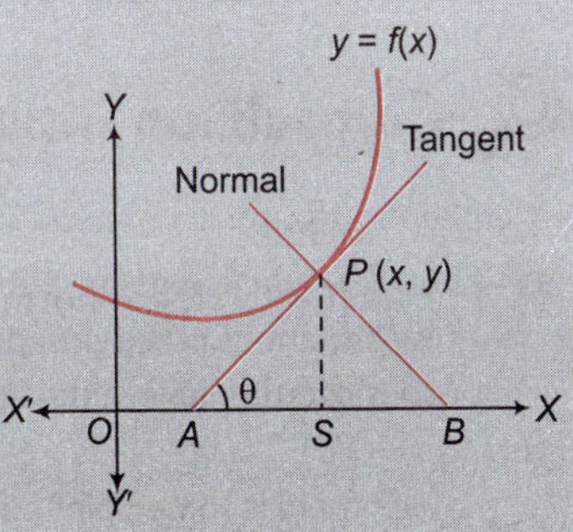

Angle of Intersection of Two Curves

Let $y = f_1(x)$ and $y = f_2(x)$ be the two curves, meeting at some point $P(x_1, y_1)$, then the angle between the two curves at $P(x_1, y_1)$ = the angle between the tangents to the curves at $P(x_1, y_1)$.

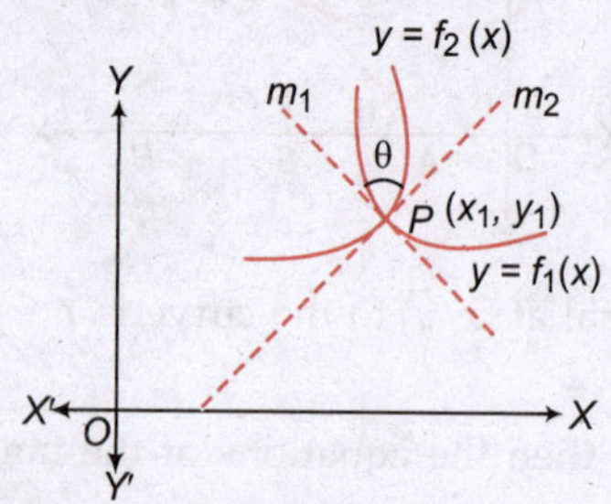

The other angle between the tangents is $(180° - \theta)$. Generally, the smaller of these two angles is taken to be the angle of intersection.

$\therefore$ The angle of intersection of two curves is given by $\tan\theta = \left|\dfrac{m_1 - m_2}{1 + m_1 m_2}\right|$

where, $m_1 = \left(\dfrac{df_1}{dx}\right)_{(x_1, y_1)}$ and $m_2 = \left(\dfrac{df_2}{dx}\right)_{(x_1, y_1)}$

(i) If $\theta = \dfrac{\pi}{2}$, $m_1 m_2 = -1 \Rightarrow \left(\dfrac{df_1}{dx}\right)_{(x_1, y_1)} \left(\dfrac{df_2}{dx}\right)_{(x_1, y_1)} = -1$

such curves are called **orthogonal curves.**

(ii) If $\theta = 0$, $m_1 = m_2 \Rightarrow \left(\dfrac{df_1}{dx}\right)_{(x_1, y_1)} = \left(\dfrac{df_2}{dx}\right)_{(x_1, y_1)}$

such curves are tangential at (x_1, y_1).

Competition Insight

Rolle's Theorem

Let f be a real function defined in the closed interval $[a, b]$, such that

(i) f is continuous in the closed interval $[a, b]$.

(ii) $f(x)$ is differentiable in the open interval (a, b).

(iii) $f(a) = f(b)$

Then, there is some point c in the open interval (a, b), such that $f'(c) = 0$.

Geometrically

Under the assumptions of Rolle's theorem, the graph of $f(x)$ starts at point $(a, f(a))$ and ends at point $(b, f(b))$ as shown in figures.

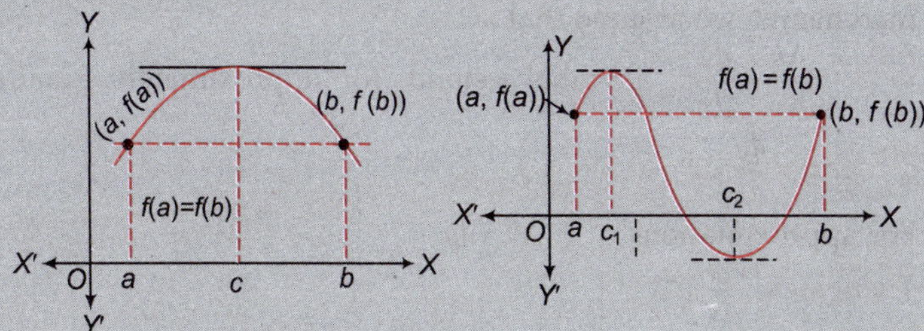

The conclusion is that there is atleast one point c between a and b, such that the tangent to the graph at $(c, f(c))$ is parallel to the X-axis.

Algebraic Interpretation of Rolle's Theorem

Between any two roots of a polynomial $f(x)$, there is always a root of its derivative $f'(x)$.

Lagrange's Mean Value Theorem

Let f be a real function, continuous on the closed interval $[a, b]$ and differentiable in the open interval (a, b). Then, there is atleast one point c in the open interval (a, b) such that $f'(c) = \dfrac{f(b) - f(a)}{b - a}$

Geometrically

For any chord of the curve $y = f(x)$, there is a point on the graph, where the tangent is parallel to this chord.

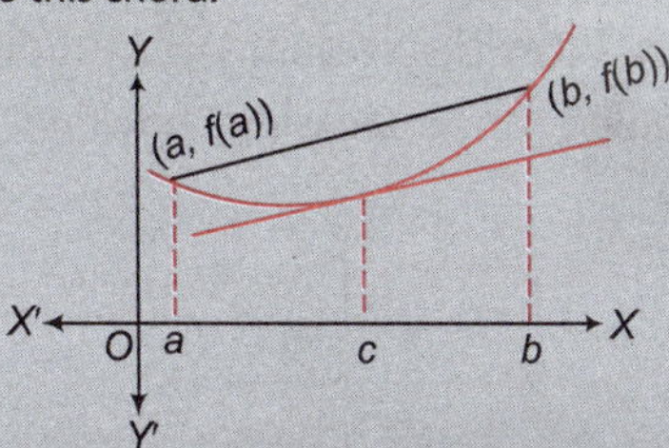

In the particular case, when $f(a) = f(b)$, the expression $\dfrac{f(b) - f(a)}{b - a}$ becomes zero

i.e. when $f(a) = f(b)$, $f'(c) = 0$ for some c in (a, b).

Thus, the Rolle's theorem becomes a particular case of the Lagrange's mean value theorem.

Approximations and Errors

1. Let $y = f(x)$ be a given function and Δx denotes a small increment in x, corresponding which y increases by Δy. Then, for small increments, we assume that

$$\frac{\Delta y}{\Delta x} \approx \frac{dy}{dx} \quad \text{[symbol} \approx \text{stands for 'approximately equal to']}$$

$$\therefore \quad \Delta y = \frac{dy}{dx} \Delta x$$

For approximations of y, $\Delta y \approx dy$

Then, $dy = \left(\frac{dy}{dx}\right) \Delta x$

Thus, $y + \Delta y = f(x + \Delta x) = f(x) + \left(\frac{dy}{dx}\right) \Delta x$

2. Let Δx be the error in the measurement of independent variable x and Δy is corresponding error in the measurement of dependent variable y.

Then, $\quad \Delta y = \left(\frac{dy}{dx}\right) \Delta x$

Δy = Absolute error in measurement of y

$\frac{\Delta y}{y}$ = Relative error in measurement of y

$\frac{\Delta y}{y} \times 100$ = Percentage error in measurement of y

Increasing Function (Non-decreasing Function)

A function f is called an increasing function in domain D, if $x_1 < x_2 \Rightarrow f(x_1) \le f(x_2)$, $\forall\ x_1, x_2 \in D$.

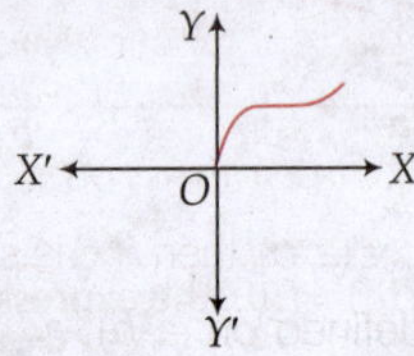

Strictly Increasing Function

$f(x)$ is said to be strictly increasing in D, if for every $x_1, x_2 \in D$; $x_1 < x_2 \Rightarrow f(x_1) < f(x_2)$.

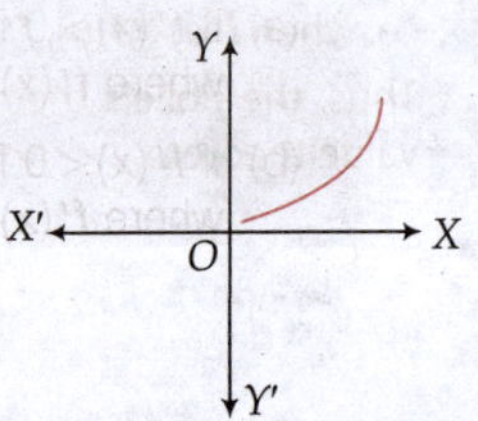

Decreasing Function (Non-increasing Function)

A function f is called a decreasing function in domain D, if $x_1 < x_2 \Rightarrow f(x_1) \geq f(x_2), \forall\, x_1, x_2 \in D$.

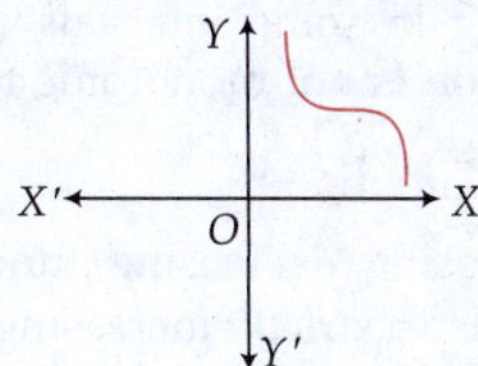

Strictly Decreasing Function

$f(x)$ is said to be strictly decreasing in D, if for every $x_1, x_2 \in D, x_1 < x_2 \Rightarrow f(x_1) > f(x_2)$.

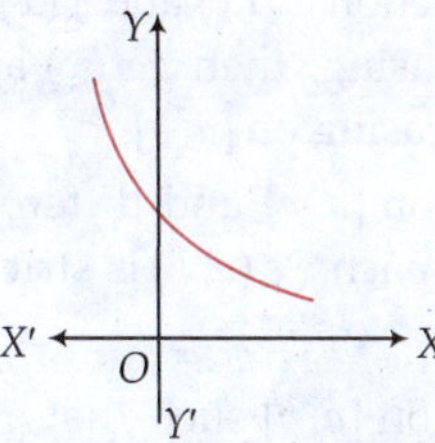

Value Points

- A function $f(x)$ is said to be increasing (decreasing) at point x_0, if there is an interval $(x_0 - h, x_0 + h)$ containing x_0, such that $f(x)$ is increasing (decreasing) on $(x_0 - h, x_0 + h)$.
- A function $f(x)$ is said to be increasing on $[a, b]$, if it is increasing on (a, b) and it is also increasing at $x = a$ and $x = b$.
- Let f be a differentiable real function defined on an open interval (a, b).
  (a) If $f'(x) > 0$ for all $x \in (a, b)$, then $f(x)$ is strictly increasing on (a, b).
  (b) If $f'(x) < 0$ for all $x \in (a, b)$, then $f(x)$ is strictly decreasing on (a, b).
- Let f be a function defined on (a, b).
  (a) If $f'(x) > 0$ for all $x \in (a, b)$ except for a finite number of points, where $f'(x) = 0$, then $f(x)$ is increasing on (a, b).
  (b) If $f'(x) < 0$ for all $x \in (a, b)$ except for a finite number of points, where $f'(x) = 0$, then $f(x)$ is decreasing on (a, b).

Monotonic Function

If a function is either increasing or decreasing on an interval (a,b), then it is said to be a monotonic function.

If a function is increasing in some intervals and decreasing in some intervals, then that function is not monotonic function.

Properties of Monotonic Functions

(i) If $f(x)$ is strictly increasing (decreasing) function on an interval $[a, b]$, then f^{-1} exists and also a strictly increasing (decreasing) function.

(ii) If $f(x)$ and $g(x)$ are strictly increasing (or decreasing) function on $[a, b]$, then $gof(x)$ and $fog(x)$ (provided they exists) is strictly increasing function on $[a, b]$.

(iii) If one of the two functions $f(x)$ and $g(x)$ is strictly increasing and other a strictly decreasing, then $gof(x)$ and $fog(x)$ (provided they exists) is strictly decreasing on $[a, b]$.

(iv) If $f(x)$ is continuous on $[a, b]$ and differentiable on (a, b) such that $f'(c) \geq 0$ $(f'(c) > 0)$ for each $c \in (a, b)$ is strictly increasing function on $[a, b]$.

(v) If $f(x)$ is continuous on $[a, b]$ such that $f'(c) \leq 0$ $(f'(c) < 0)$ for each $c \in (a, b)$, then $f(x)$ is strictly decreasing function on $[a, b]$.

Maxima and Minima of Functions

Local Maximum (Maxima) A function $y = f(x)$ is said to have a **local maximum** at a point $x = a$. If $f(x) \leq f(a)$ for all $x \in (a-h, a+h)$, where h is very small positive quantity.

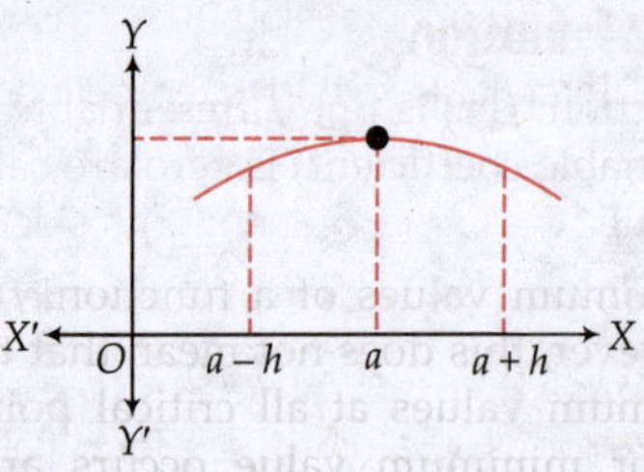

The point $x = a$ is called **a point of local maximum** of the function $f(x)$ and $f(a)$ is known **as the local maximum value** of $f(x)$ at $x = a$.

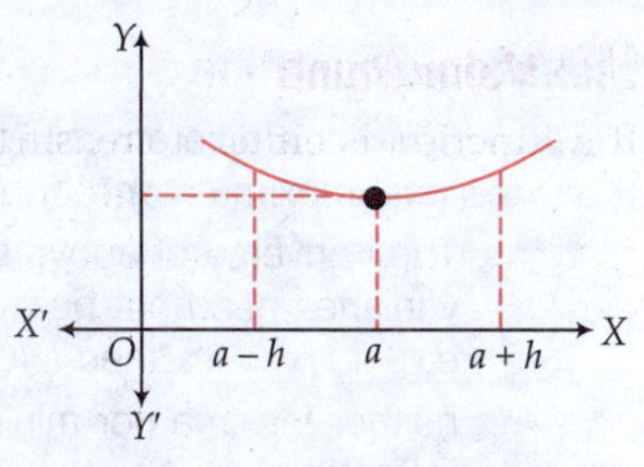

Local Minimum (Minima) A function $y = f(x)$ is said to have a **local minimum** at a point $x = a$, if $f(x) \geq f(a)$ for all $x \in (a - h, a + h)$, where h is very small positive quantity.

The point $x = a$ is called a **point of local minimum** of the function $f(x)$ and $f(a)$ is known as the **local minimum value** of $f(x)$ at $x = a$.

Knowledge Booster

Extreme value A function $f(x)$ have an extreme value in its domain, if there exists a point c in interval I such that $f(c)$ is either a local maximum value or local minimum value in the interval.

Properties of Maxima and Minima

(i) If $f(x)$ is continuous function in its domain, then atleast one maxima and one minima should lie between two different and two equal values of x.

(ii) Maxima and minima occur alternately i.e. between two maxima there is one minima and *vice-versa*.

(iii) If $f(x) \to \infty$ as $x \to a$ or b and $f'(x) = 0$ only for one value of x (say c) between a and b, then $f(c)$ is necessarily the minimum and the least value.

(iv) If $f(x) \to -\infty$ as $x \to a$ or b and $f'(x) = 0$ only for one value of x (say c) between a and b, then $f(c)$ is necessarily the maximum and the greatest value.

Critical Points of a Function

Points where a function $f(x)$ is not differentiable and points where its derivative (differentiable coefficient) is zero are called the critical points of the function $f(x)$.

Maximum and minimum values of a function $f(x)$ can occur only at critical points. However, this does not mean that the function will have maximum or minimum values at all critical points. Thus, the points where maximum or minimum value occurs are necessarily critical points but a function may or may not have maximum or minimum value at a critical point.

Value Points

- If $f(x)$ is a differentiable function, then $f'(x)$ vanishes at every local maximum and at every local minimum.
- The converse of above is not true, i.e. every point at which $f'(x)$ vanishes need not be a local maximum or minimum. e.g. if $f(x) = x^3$, then $f'(0) = 0$, but at $x = 0$ the function has neither maxima nor minima. In general these points are **point of inflection**.
- A function may attain an extreme value at a point without being derivable at that point. e.g. $f(x) = |x|$ has a minima at $x = 0$ but $f'(0)$ does not exist.
- A function $f(x)$ can have several local maximum and local minimum values in an interval. Thus, the maximum and minimum values of $f(x)$ are not necessarily the greatest and the least values of $f(x)$ in a given interval.
- A local minimum value at some point may even be greater than a local maximum value at some other point.

Methods to Find a Local Maxima and Local Minima

1. First Derivative Test

Let $f(x)$ be a differentiable function on an interval I and $a \in I$. Then,

(i) Point a is a local maxima of $f(x)$, if

(a) $f'(a) = 0$

(b) $f'(x) > 0$, if $x \in (a - h, a)$ and $f'(x) < 0$, if $x \in (a, a + h)$, where h is a small positive quantity.

(ii) Point a is a local minima of $f(x)$, if

(a) $f'(a) = 0$

(b) $f'(a) < 0$, if $x \in (a - h, a)$ and $f'(x) > 0$, if $x \in (a, a + h)$, where h is a small positive quantity.

(iii) If $f'(a) = 0$ but $f'(x)$ does not changes sign in $(a - h, a + h)$, for any positive quantity h, then $x = a$ is neither a point of local minima nor a point of local maxima.

2. Second Derivative Test

Let $f(x)$ be a differentiable function on an interval I. Let $a \in I$ is such that $f''(x)$ is continuous at $x = a$. Then,

(i) $x = a$ is a point of local maxima, if $f'(a) = 0$ and $f''(a) < 0$.

(ii) $x = a$ is a point of local minima, if $f'(a) = 0$ and $f''(a) > 0$.

(iii) If $f'(a) = f''(a) = 0$, but $f'''(a) \neq 0$, if exists, then $x = a$ is neither a point of local maxima nor a point of local minima and is called **point of inflection**.

(iv) If $f'(a) = f''(a) = f'''(a) = 0$ and $f^{iv}(a) < 0$, then it is a local maxima. And if $f^{iv}(a) > 0$, then it is a local minima.

3. nth Derivative Test

Let f be a differentiable function on an interval I and let a be an interior point of I such that

$f'(a) = f''(a) = f'''(a) = \dots = f^{n-1}(a) = 0$ and $f^n(a)$ exists and is non-zero.

(i) If n is even and $f^n(a) < 0 \Rightarrow x = a$ is a point of local maxima.

(ii) If n is even and $f^n(a) > 0 \Rightarrow x = a$ is a point of local minima.

(iii) If n is odd, then $x = a$ is neither a point of local maxima nor a point of local minima.

Concept of Global Maxima/Minima

Let $y = f(x)$ be a given function with domain D.

Let $[a, b] \subseteq D$, then global maxima/minima of $f(x)$ in $[a, b]$ is basically the greatest/least value of $f(x)$ in $[a, b]$.

Global maxima/minima in $[a, b]$ would always occur at critical points of $f(x)$ in $[a, b]$ or at end points of the interval.

Global Maxima/Minima in [a,b]

In order to find the global maxima and minima of $f(x)$ in $[a, b]$, find out all critical points $c_1, c_2, \dots, c_n$ of $f(x)$ in $[a, b]$ (i.e. all points at which $f'(x) = 0$) or $f'(x)$ not exists and let $f(c_1), f(c_2), \dots, f(c_n)$ be the values of the function at these points.

Then, $M_1 \rightarrow$ Global maxima or greatest value.

and $M_2 \rightarrow$ Global minima or least value,

where $M_1 = \max\{f(a), f(c_1), f(c_2), \dots, f(c_n), f(b)\}$

and $M_2 = \min\{f(a), f(c_1), f(c_2), \dots, f(c_n), f(b)\}$

Then, M_1 is the greatest value or global maxima in $[a, b]$ and M_2 is the least value or global minima in $[a, b]$.

Value Points

- **To Find Range of a Continuous Function** Let $f(x)$ be a continuous function on $[a, b]$, such that its least value in $[a, b]$ is m and the greatest value in $[a, b]$ is M. Then, range of value of $f(x)$ for $x \in [a, b]$ is $[m, M]$.
- **To Check for the Injectivity of a Function** A strictly monotonic function is always one-one (injective).
  Hence, a function $f(x)$ is one-one in the interval $[a, b]$, if $f'(x) > 0, \forall x \in [a, b]$ or $f'(x) < 0, \forall x \in [a, b]$.
- The points at which a function attains either the local maximum value or local minimum value are known as the **extreme points** or **turning points** and both local maximum and local minimum values are called the extreme values of $f(x)$.

  Thus, a function attains an extreme value at $x = a$, if $f(a)$ is either a local maximum value or a local minimum value. Consequently at an extreme point 'a', $f(x) - f(a)$ keeps the same sign for all values of x in a deleted nbd of a.
- A necessary condition for $f(a)$ to be an extreme value of a function $f(x)$ is that $f'(a) = 0$, if it exists. It is not sufficient, i.e. $f'(a) = 0$ does not necessarily imply that $x = a$ is an extreme point. There are functions for which the derivatives vanish at a point but do not have an extreme value. e.g. the function $f(x) = x^3$, $f'(0) = 0$ but at $x = 0$ the function does not attain an extreme value.
- Geometrically the above condition means that the tangent to the curve $y = f(x)$ at a point, where the ordinate is maximum or minimum, is parallel to the X-axis.
- All x, for which $f'(x) = 0$, do not give us the extreme values. The values of x for which $f'(x) = 0$ are called **stationary values** or **critical values** of x and the corresponding values of $f(x)$ are called stationary or turning values of $f(x)$.

Chapter 23

Indefinite Integrals $\int \frac{e^x}{x} dx$

Let $f(x)$ be a function. Then, the collection of all its primitives is called the **indefinite integral** (or anti-derivative) of $f(x)$ and is denoted by $\int f(x)dx$. Integration is an inverse process of differentiation.

If $\frac{d}{dx}\{\phi(x)\} = f(x)$, then $\int f(x)\,dx = \phi(x) + C$, where C is called the **constant of integration** or **arbitrary constant**.

Symbols $f(x) \to$ Integrand

$f(x)dx \to$ Element of integration

$\int \to$ Sign of integral

$\phi(x) \to$ Anti-derivative or primitive or integral of function $f(x)$

The process of finding functions whose derivative is given, is called anti-differentiation or integration.

Value Point

The derivative of function is unique but integral of a function is not unique.

Some Standard Integral Formulae

	Derivatives	Indefinite Integrals
(i)	$\frac{d}{dx}\left(\frac{x^{n+1}}{n+1}\right) = x^n, n \neq -1$	$\int x^n dx = \frac{x^{n+1}}{n+1} + C, n \neq -1$
(ii)	$\frac{d}{dx}(\log_e x) = \frac{1}{x}$	$\int \frac{1}{x}\,dx = \log_e \lvert x \rvert + C$
(iii)	$\frac{d}{dx}(e^x) = e^x$	$\int e^x dx = e^x + C$
(iv)	$\frac{d}{dx}\left(\frac{a^x}{\log_e a}\right) = a^x, a > 0, a \neq 1$	$\int a^x dx = \frac{a^x}{\log_e a} + C$

	Derivatives	Indefinite Integrals
(v)	$\frac{d}{dx}(-\cos x) = \sin x$	$\int \sin x\, dx = -\cos x + C$
(vi)	$\frac{d}{dx}(\sin x) = \cos x$	$\int \cos x\, dx = \sin x + C$
(vii)	$\frac{d}{dx}(\tan x) = \sec^2 x$	$\int \sec^2 x\, dx = \tan x + C$
(viii)	$\frac{d}{dx}(-\cot x) = \operatorname{cosec}^2 x$	$\int \operatorname{cosec}^2 x\, dx = -\cot x + C$
(ix)	$\frac{d}{dx}(\sec x) = \sec x \tan x$	$\int \sec x \tan x\, dx = \sec x + C$
(x)	$\frac{d}{dx}(-\operatorname{cosec} x) = \operatorname{cosec} x \cot x$	$\int \operatorname{cosec} x \cot x\, dx = -\operatorname{cosec} x + C$
(xi)	$\frac{d}{dx}(\log \sin x) = \cot x$	$\int \cot x\, dx = \log\lvert\sin x\rvert + C$ $= -\log\lvert\operatorname{cosec} x\rvert + C$
(xii)	$\frac{d}{dx}(-\log \cos x) = \tan x$	$\int \tan x\, dx = -\log\lvert\cos x\rvert + C$ $= \log\lvert\sec x\rvert + C$
(xiii)	$\frac{d}{dx}[\log(\sec x + \tan x)] = \sec x$	$\int \sec x\, dx = \log\lvert\sec x + \tan x\rvert + C$ $= \log\left\lvert\tan\left(\frac{\pi}{4} + \frac{x}{2}\right)\right\rvert + C$
(xiv)	$\frac{d}{dx}[\log(\operatorname{cosec} x - \cot x)] = \operatorname{cosec} x$	$\int \operatorname{cosec} x\, dx = \log\lvert\operatorname{cosec} x - \cot x\rvert + C$ $= \log\left\lvert\tan\frac{x}{2}\right\rvert + C$
(xv)	$\frac{d}{dx}\sin^{-1}\left(\frac{x}{a}\right) = \frac{1}{\sqrt{a^2 - x^2}}$	$\int \frac{1}{\sqrt{a^2 - x^2}}\, dx = \sin^{-1}\left(\frac{x}{a}\right) + C$
(xvi)	$\frac{d}{dx}\cos^{-1}\left(\frac{x}{a}\right) = \int \frac{-1}{\sqrt{a^2 - x^2}}$	$\int \frac{-1}{\sqrt{a^2 - x^2}}\, dx = \cos^{-1}\left(\frac{x}{a}\right) + C$
(xvii)	$\frac{d}{dx}\left(\frac{1}{a}\tan^{-1}\frac{x}{a}\right) = \frac{1}{a^2 + x^2}$	$\int \frac{1}{a^2 + x^2}\, dx = \frac{1}{a}\tan^{-1}\left(\frac{x}{a}\right) + C$
(xviii)	$\frac{d}{dx}\left(\frac{1}{a}\cot^{-1}\frac{x}{a}\right) = \frac{-1}{a^2 + x^2}$	$\int \frac{-1}{a^2 + x^2}\, dx = \frac{1}{a}\cot^{-1}\left(\frac{x}{a}\right) + C$
(xix)	$\frac{d}{dx}\left(\frac{1}{a}\sec^{-1}\frac{x}{a}\right) = \frac{1}{x\sqrt{x^2 - a^2}}$	$\int \frac{1}{x\sqrt{x^2 - a^2}}\, dx = \frac{1}{a}\sec^{-1}\left(\frac{x}{a}\right) + C$
(xx)	$\frac{d}{dx}\left(\frac{1}{a}\operatorname{cosec}^{-1}\frac{x}{a}\right) = \frac{-1}{x\sqrt{x^2 - a^2}}$	$\int \frac{-1}{x\sqrt{x^2 - a^2}}\, dx = \frac{1}{a}\operatorname{cosec}^{-1}\left(\frac{x}{a}\right) + C$

Geometrical Interpretation of Indefinite Integral

If $\frac{d}{dx}\{\phi(x)\} = f(x)$, then

$\int f(x)\,dx = \phi(x) + C$. For different values of C, we get different functions, differing only by a constant. The graphs of these functions give us an infinite family of curves such that at the points on these curves with the same x-coordinate, the tangents are parallel as they have the same slope $\phi'(x) = f(x)$.

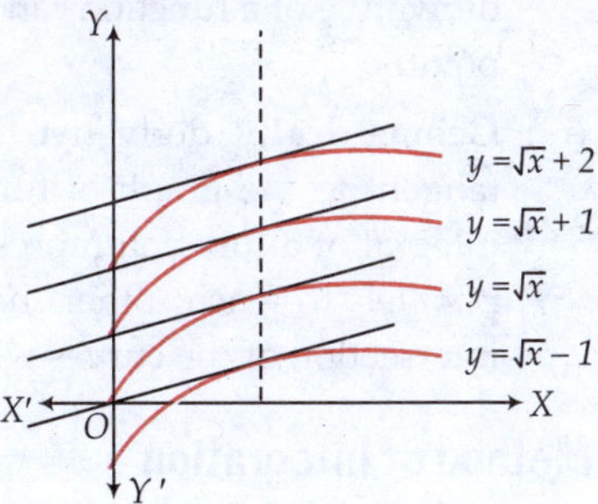

Consider the integral of $\frac{1}{2\sqrt{x}}$

i.e. $$\int \frac{1}{2\sqrt{x}}\,dx = \sqrt{x} + C, C \in R$$

Above figure shows some members of the family of curves given by $y = \sqrt{x} + C$ for different $C \in R$.

Properties of Integration

(i) $\frac{d}{dx}\{\int f(x)dx\} = f(x)$

(ii) $\int k \cdot f(x)dx = k\int f(x)dx$

(iii) $\int \{f_1(x) \pm f_2(x) \pm f_3(x) \pm \ldots \pm f_n(x)\}dx$

$$= \int f_1(x)\,dx \pm \int f_2(x)\,dx \pm \int f_3(x)\,dx \pm \ldots \pm \int f_n(x)\,dx$$

Comparison between Differentiation and Integration

(i) Both differentiation and integration are linear operator on functions as $\frac{d}{dx}\{af(x) \pm bg(x)\} = a\frac{d}{dx}\{f(x)\} \pm b\frac{d}{dx}\{g(x)\}$

and $\int [a \cdot f(x) \pm b \cdot g(x)]dx = a\int f(x)dx \pm b\int g(x)dx.$

(ii) All functions are not differentiable, similarly there are some function which are not integrable.

e.g. Let $f(x) = \frac{1}{x-1}$ and $g(x) = \frac{1}{x-4}$.

Then, $f(x)$ is not differentiable at $x = 1$ and $g(x)$ is not integrable at $x = 4$.

(iii) Integral of a function is always discussed in an interval but derivative of a function can be discussed in a interval as well as at a point.

(iv) **Geometrically** derivative of a function represents slope of the tangent to the graph of function at the point. On the other hand, integral of a function represents an infinite family of curves placed parallel to each other having parallel tangents at points of intersection of the curves with a line parallel to Y-axis.

Method of Integration

Some integrals are not in standard form, to reduce them into standard forms, we use the following methods

1. Integration by Substitution

For integral $\int f'\{g(x)\}g'(x)dx$, we create a new variable $t = g(x)$, so that $g'(x) = \dfrac{dt}{dx}$ or $g'(x)dx = dt$.

Hence, $\int f'\{g(x)\}g'(x)dx = \int f'(t)dt = f(t) + C = f\{g(x)\} + C$

 **Value Points**

- $\int \{f(x)\}^n \cdot f'(x)dx = \dfrac{\{f(x)\}^{n+1}}{n+1} + C, n \neq -1$
- $\int \dfrac{f'(x)}{f(x)} dx = \log|f(x)| + C, f(x) \neq 0$

Basic Formulae Using Method of Substitution

(i) If $\int f(x)\,dx = \phi(x) + C$, then $\int f(ax+b)dx = \dfrac{1}{a}\phi(ax+b) + C.$

(ii) $\int (ax+b)^n dx = \dfrac{1}{a} \cdot \dfrac{(ax+b)^{n+1}}{n+1} + C, n \neq -1$

(iii) $\int \dfrac{1}{ax+b} dx = \dfrac{1}{a} \log|ax+b| + C$

(iv) $\int e^{ax+b} dx = \dfrac{1}{a} e^{ax+b} + C$

(v) $\int a^{bx+c}\, dx = \dfrac{1}{b} \cdot \dfrac{a^{bx+c}}{\log a} + C, a > 0$ and $a \neq 1$

(vi) $\int \sin(ax+b)\, dx = -\dfrac{1}{a} \cos(ax+b) + C$

(vii) $\int \cos(ax+b)dx = \frac{1}{a}\sin(ax+b) + C$

(viii) $\int \sec^2(ax+b)dx = \frac{1}{a}\tan(ax+b) + C$

(ix) $\int \text{cosec}^2(ax+b)dx = -\frac{1}{a}\cot(ax+b) + C$

(x) $\int \sec(ax+b)\tan(ax+b)dx = \frac{1}{a}\sec(ax+b) + C$

(xi) $\int \text{cosec}(ax+b)\cot(ax+b)dx = -\frac{1}{a}\text{cosec}(ax+b) + C$

(xii) $\int \tan(ax+b)dx = -\frac{1}{a}\log|\cos(ax+b)| + C$

(xiii) $\int \cot(ax+b)dx = \frac{1}{a}\log|\sin(ax+b)| + C$

(xiv) $\int \sec(ax+b)\,dx = \frac{1}{a}\log|\sec(ax+b) + \tan(ax+b)| + C$

(xv) $\int \text{cosec}(ax+b)\,dx = \frac{1}{a}\log|\text{cosec}(ax+b) - \cot(ax+b)| + C$

Trigonometric Identities, Used for Conversion of Integrals into the Standard Integrable Forms

(i) $\sin^2 nx = \frac{1-\cos 2nx}{2}$

(ii) $\cos^2 nx = \frac{1+\cos 2nx}{2}$

(iii) $\sin nx = 2\sin\frac{nx}{2}\cos\frac{nx}{2}$

(iv) $\sin^3 nx = \frac{3}{4}\sin nx - \frac{1}{4}\sin 3nx$

(v) $\cos^3 nx = \frac{3}{4}\cos nx + \frac{1}{4}\cos 3nx$

(vi) $\tan^2 nx = \sec^2 nx - 1$

(vii) $\cot^2 nx = \text{cosec}^2 nx - 1$

(viii) $2\sin A\cos B = \sin(A+B) + \sin(A-B)$

(ix) $2\cos A\sin B = \sin(A+B) - \sin(A-B)$

(x) $2\cos A\cos B = \cos(A+B) + \cos(A-B)$

(xi) $2\sin A\sin B = \cos(A-B) - \cos(A+B)$

Standard Substitutions

S.No.	Functions	Substitution
(i)	$(a^2 + x^2), \sqrt{x^2 + a^2}, \frac{1}{\sqrt{x^2 + a^2}}$	$x = a \tan \theta$ or $a \cot \theta$ or $a \sinh \theta$
(ii)	$(a^2 - x^2), \sqrt{a^2 - x^2}, \frac{1}{\sqrt{a^2 - x^2}}$	$x = a \sin \theta$ or $a \cos \theta$
(iii)	$(x \pm \sqrt{x^2 \pm a^2})^n$	expression inside the bracket $= t$
(iv)	$\frac{2x}{a^2 - x^2}, \frac{2x}{a^2 + x^2}, \frac{a^2 - x^2}{a^2 + x^2}$	$x = a \tan \theta$
(v)	$\frac{1}{(x+a)^{1-\frac{1}{n}}(x+b)^{1+\frac{1}{n}}}$ $(n \in N, n > 1)$	$\frac{x+a}{x+b} = t$
(vi)	$(x^2 - a^2), \sqrt{x^2 - a^2}, \frac{1}{\sqrt{x^2 - a^2}}$	$x = a \sec \theta$ or a cosec θ or $a \cosh \theta$
(vii)	$\sqrt{\frac{a - x}{a + x}}$ or $\sqrt{\frac{a + x}{a - x}}$	$x = a \cos 2\theta$
(viii)	$\sqrt{\frac{x - \alpha}{\beta - x}}$ or $\sqrt{(x - \alpha)(\beta - x)}$	$x = \alpha \cos^2 \theta + \beta \sin^2 \theta$
(ix)	$\sqrt{2ax - x^2}$	$x = a(1 - \cos \theta)$
(x)	$\sqrt{\frac{x}{a + x}}, \sqrt{\frac{a + x}{x}}, \sqrt{x(a + x)},$	$x = a \tan^2 \theta$ or $a \cot^2 \theta$
(xi)	$\sqrt{\frac{x}{a - x}}; \sqrt{\frac{a - x}{x}}, \sqrt{x(a - x)}, \frac{1}{\sqrt{x(a - x)}}$	$x = a \sin^2 \theta$ or $a \cos^2 \theta$
(xii)	$\sqrt{\frac{x}{x - a}}; \sqrt{\frac{x - a}{x}}, \sqrt{x(x - a)}, \frac{1}{\sqrt{x(x - a)}}$	$x = a \sec^2 \theta$ or $a \operatorname{cosec}^2 \theta$

Special Integrals

(i) $\int \frac{1}{x^2 + a^2} dx = \frac{1}{a} \tan^{-1} \frac{x}{a} + C$

(ii) $\int \frac{1}{a^2 - x^2} dx = \frac{1}{2a} \log \left| \frac{a + x}{a - x} \right| + C = \frac{1}{a} \tanh^{-1} \left(\frac{x}{a} \right) + C$

(iii) $\int \frac{dx}{x^2 - a^2} dx = \frac{1}{2a} \log \left| \frac{x-a}{x+a} \right| + C = -\frac{1}{a} \coth^{-1}\left(\frac{x}{a}\right) + C$

(iv) $\int \frac{dx}{\sqrt{a^2 - x^2}} = \sin^{-1} \frac{x}{a} + C = -\cos^{-1} \frac{x}{a} + c$

(v) $\int \frac{dx}{\sqrt{x^2 - a^2}} = \log|x + \sqrt{x^2 - a^2}| + C = \cosh^{-1}\left(\frac{x}{a}\right) + C$

(vi) $\int \frac{dx}{\sqrt{x^2 + a^2}} = \log|x + \sqrt{x^2 + a^2}| + C = \sinh^{-1}\left(\frac{x}{a}\right) + C$

Important Forms to be Converted into Special Integrals

Form I $\int \frac{1}{ax^2 + bx + c} dx$ or $\int \frac{1}{\sqrt{ax^2 + bx + c}} dx$

Express $ax^2 + bx + c$ as sum or difference of two squares.

For this write $ax^2 + bx + c = a\left[\left(x + \frac{b}{2a}\right)^2 + \frac{4ac - b^2}{4a^2}\right]$

Form II $\int \frac{px + q}{ax^2 + bx + c} dx$ or $\int \frac{px + q}{\sqrt{ax^2 + bx + c}} dx$

Put $px + q = \lambda \cdot \frac{d}{dx}(ax^2 + bx + c) + \mu$.

Now, find values of λ and μ and then integrate it.

Form III $\int \frac{P(x)}{ax^2 + bx + c} dx$, when $P(x)$ is a polynomial of degree 2 or more carry out the division and express in the form $\frac{P(x)}{ax^2 + bx + c} = Q(x) + \frac{R(x)}{ax^2 + bx + c}$, where $R(x)$ is a linear expression or constant, then integral reduces to the forms discussed earlier.

EXPERT Scale Up

If degree of the numerator of the integrand is equal to or greater than that of denominator divide the numerator by the denominator until the degree of the remainder is less than that of denominator i.e.

$$\frac{\text{Numerator}}{\text{Denominator}} = \text{Quotient} + \frac{\text{Remainder}}{\text{Denominator}}$$

Form IV $\int \frac{dx}{a + b\sin^2 x}, \int \frac{dx}{a + b\cos^2 x}, \int \frac{dx}{a\sin^2 x + b\cos^2 x},$

$\int \frac{dx}{a\sin^2 x + b\cos^2 x + c}, \int \frac{dx}{(a\sin x + b\cos x)^2}$

To evaluate the above type of integrals, we proceed as follows :

(a) Divide numerator and denominator by $\cos^2 x$.

(b) Replace $\sec^2 x$, if any in denominator by $1 + \tan^2 x$.

(c) Put $\tan x = t \Rightarrow \sec^2 x\, dx = dt$

Form V $\int \frac{dx}{a + b\sin x}, \int \frac{dx}{a + b\cos x}, \int \frac{dx}{a\sin x + b\cos x},$

$\int \frac{dx}{a\sin x + b\cos x + c}$

To evaluate the above type of integrals, we proceed as follows:

(a) Put $\sin x = \frac{2\tan\frac{x}{2}}{1 + \tan^2\frac{x}{2}}$ and $\cos x = \frac{1 - \tan^2\frac{x}{2}}{1 + \tan^2\frac{x}{2}}$

(b) Replace $1 + \tan^2\frac{x}{2}$ by $\sec^2\frac{x}{2}$.

(c) Put $\tan\frac{x}{2} = t \Rightarrow \frac{1}{2}\sec^2\frac{x}{2}\,dx = dt$

Form VI $\int \frac{a\sin x + b\cos x}{c\sin x + d\cos x}\,dx,$

Write numerator

= λ (differentiation of denominator)+ μ (denominator)

i.e. $a\sin x + b\cos x = \lambda(c\cos x - d\sin x) + \mu(c\sin x + d\cos x)$

$$\int \frac{a\sin x + b\cos x}{c\sin x + d\cos x}\,dx = \lambda\int \frac{c\cos x - d\sin x}{c\sin x + d\cos x}\,dx + \mu\int \frac{c\sin x + d\cos x}{c\sin x + d\cos x}\,dx$$

$$= \lambda\log|c\sin x + d\cos x| + \mu x + C$$

Form VII $\int \frac{a\sin x + b\cos x + c}{p\sin x + q\cos x + r}\,dx$

Write numerator = λ (differentiation of denominator) + μ(denominator) + γ

i.e. $a\sin x + b\cos x + c = \lambda(p\cos x - q\sin x) + \mu(p\sin x + q\cos x + r) + \gamma$

$$\therefore \int \frac{a \sin x + b \cos x + c}{p \sin x + q \cos x + r} dx = \lambda \int \frac{p \cos x - q \sin x}{p \sin x + q \cos x + r} dx$$

$$+ \mu \int \frac{p \sin x + q \cos x + r}{p \sin x + q \cos x + r} dx + \gamma \int \frac{1}{p \sin x + q \cos x + r} dx$$

$$= \lambda \log | p \sin x + q \cos x + r |$$

$$+ \mu x + \gamma \int \frac{1}{p \sin x + q \cos x + r} dx$$

Form VIII $\int \frac{x^2 + 1}{x^4 + \lambda x^2 + 1} dx$, $\int \frac{x^2 - 1}{x^4 + \lambda x^2 + 1} dx$, $\int \frac{1}{x^4 + \lambda x^2 + 1} dx$, $\int \frac{x^2}{x^4 + \lambda x^2 + 1} dx$

To evaluate this type of integrals we proceed as follows:

(a) Divide numerator and denominator by x^2.

(b) Express the denominator of integrand in the form of $\left(x + \frac{1}{x}\right)^2 \pm k^2$.

(c) Introduce $d\left(x + \frac{1}{x}\right)$ or $d\left(x - \frac{1}{x}\right)$ or both in numerator.

(d) Put $x + \frac{1}{x} = t$ or $x - \frac{1}{x} = t$ as the case may be.

(e) Integral reduced to the form of $\int \frac{1}{x^2 + a^2} dx$ or $\int \frac{1}{x^2 - a^2} dx$.

Form IX $\int \sqrt{\tan x}\, dx, \int \sqrt{\cot x}\, dx, \int \frac{dx}{\sin^4 x + \cos^4 x}$

To evaluate this type of integrals

Put $\tan x = t^2 \Rightarrow \sec^2 x\, dx = 2t\, dt$.

Then, do same as in Form VIII.

2. Integration by Parts

This method is used to integrate the product of two functions.

If $f(x)$ and $g(x)$ are two integrable functions, then

$$\int \underset{\text{I}}{f(x)} \cdot \underset{\text{II}}{g(x)}\, dx = f(x) \int g(x)\, dx - \int \left\{ \frac{d}{dx} f(x) \int g(x)\, dx \right\} dx$$

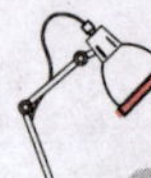

EXPERT Scale Up

We use the following preferential order for taking the first function.

Inverse → **L**ogarithm → **A**lgebraic → **T**rigonometric → **E**xponential. In short, we write it **ILATE**.

(i) If one of the function is not directly integrable, then we take it as the first function.

(ii) If only one function is there, e.g. $\int \log x\, dx$ or $\int \sin^{-1} x\, dx$ etc, then 1 (unity) can be taken as second function.

(iii) If both the functions are directly integrable, then the first function is chosen in such a way that its derivative vanishes easily or the function obtained in integral sign is easily integrable.

(iv) Integration by parts is not applicable to product of functions in all cases e.g. $\int \sqrt{x} \sin x\, dx$

(v) Normally, if any function is a polynomial in x, then we take it as the first function.

Integral of the Form $\int e^x\{f(x)+f'(x)\}dx$

$$\begin{aligned}\int e^x\{f(x)+f'(x)\}dx &= \int \underset{\text{II}}{e^x}\, \underset{\text{I}}{f(x)}dx + \int e^x f'(x)dx \\ &= f(x)\int e^x dx - \int \{f'(x)\int e^x dx\}dx + \int e^x f'(x)dx \\ &= f(x)e^x - \int f'(x)e^x dx + \int e^x f'(x)dx \\ &= e^x \cdot f(x) + C\end{aligned}$$

Knowledge Booster

$\int \{xf'(x)+f(x)\}\,dx = xf(x)+C.$

Integral of the Form $\int e^{ax}\sin(bx+c)dx$ or $\int e^{ax}\cos(bx+c)dx$

(i) $\int e^{ax}\sin(bx+c)\,dx = \dfrac{e^{ax}}{a^2+b^2}\{a\sin(bx+c)-b\cos(bx+c)\}+C$

(ii) $\int e^{ax}\cos(bx+c)dx = \dfrac{e^{ax}}{a^2+b^2}\{a\cos(bx+c)+b\sin(bx+c)\}+C$

Some More Special Integral based on Integration by Parts

(i) $\int \sqrt{x^2 + a^2}\, dx = \frac{1}{2}[x\sqrt{x^2 + a^2} + a^2 \log|x + \sqrt{x^2 + a^2}|] + C$

(ii) $\int \sqrt{a^2 - x^2}\, dx = \frac{1}{2}\left[x\sqrt{a^2 - x^2} + a^2 \sin^{-1}\left(\frac{x}{a}\right)\right] + C$

(iii) $\int \sqrt{x^2 - a^2}\, dx = \frac{1}{2}[x\sqrt{x^2 - a^2} - a^2 \log|x + \sqrt{x^2 - a^2}|] + C$

Important Forms to be converted into special Integrals

Form I $\int \sqrt{ax^2 + bx + c}\, dx$

Express $ax^2 + bx + c$ as sum or difference of two squares. For this write

$$ax^2 + bx + c = a\left[\left(x + \frac{b}{2a}\right)^2 + \frac{4ac - b^2}{4a^2}\right] \text{ or } a\left[\left(x + \frac{b}{2a}\right)^2 \pm k^2\right],$$

where $k^2 = \frac{4ac - b^2}{4a^2}$

Form II $\int (px + q)\sqrt{ax^2 + bx + c}\, dx$

Put $px + q = A\left[\frac{d}{dx}(ax^2 + bx + c)\right] + B = A(2ax + b) + B$

Now, find the values of A and B and then integrate it.

3. Integration by Partial Fractions

Sometimes, an integral of the form $\int \frac{P(x)}{Q(x)} dx$, where $P(x)$ and $Q(x)$ are polynomials in x and $Q(x) \neq 0$, also $Q(x)$ has only linear and quadratic factors. For solving such types of integrals, we use the partial fractions.

Partial Fraction Decomposition

(i) If $f(x)$ and $g(x)$ are two polynomials, then $\frac{f(x)}{g(x)}$ defines a rational algebraic function of x. If degree of $f(x) <$ degree of $g(x)$, then $\frac{f(x)}{g(x)}$ is called a proper rational function.

(ii) If degree of $f(x) \geq$ degree of $g(x)$, then $\frac{f(x)}{g(x)}$ is called an improper rational function.

(iii) If $\dfrac{f(x)}{g(x)}$ is an improper rational function, then we divide $f(x)$ by $g(x)$ and convert it into a proper rational function as $\dfrac{f(x)}{g(x)} = \phi(x) + \dfrac{h(x)}{g(x)}$.

(iv) Any proper rational function $\dfrac{f(x)}{g(x)}$ can be expressed as the sum of rational functions each having a simple factor of $g(x)$. Each such fraction is called a partial fraction and the process of obtaining them, is called the resolution or decomposition of $\dfrac{f(x)}{g(x)}$ into partial fraction.

S.No.	Types of proper rational function	Partial fraction
(i)	$\dfrac{px+q}{(x-a)(x-b)}, a \neq b$	$\dfrac{A}{x-a} + \dfrac{B}{x-b}$
(ii)	$\dfrac{px^2+qx+r}{(x-a)(x-b)(x-c)}, a \neq b \neq c$	$\dfrac{A}{x-a} + \dfrac{B}{x-b} + \dfrac{C}{x-c}$
(iii)	$\dfrac{px+q}{(x-a)^3}$	$\dfrac{A}{x-a} + \dfrac{B}{(x-a)^2} + \dfrac{C}{(x-a)^3}$
(iv)	$\dfrac{px^2+qx+r}{(x-a)^2(x-b)}$	$\dfrac{A}{x-a} + \dfrac{B}{(x-a)^2} + \dfrac{C}{(x-b)}$
(v)	$\dfrac{px^2+qx+r}{(x-a)(x^2+bx+c)}$, where x^2+bx+c cannot be factorised.	$\dfrac{A}{x-a} + \dfrac{Bx+C}{x^2+bx+c}$
(vi)	$\dfrac{px^3+qx^2+rx+s}{(x^2+ax+b)(x^2+cx+d)}$, where (x^2+ax+b) and (x^2+cx+d) can not be factorised.	$\dfrac{Ax+B}{x^2+ax+b} + \dfrac{Cx+D}{x^2+cx+d}$

Shortcut for Finding Values of *A*, *B* and *C* etc.

Suppose rational function in the form of $\dfrac{f(x)}{g(x)}$.

Case I When $g(x)$ is expressible as the product of non-repeated linear factors.

Let $g(x) = (x-a_1)(x-a_2)(x-a_3)\dots(x-a_n)$,

then $\dfrac{f(x)}{g(x)} = \dfrac{A_1}{x-a_1} + \dfrac{A_2}{x-a_2} + \dfrac{A_3}{x-a_3} + \dots + \dfrac{A_n}{x-a_n}$

Now, $A_1 = \dfrac{f(a_1)}{(a_1 - a_2)(a_1 - a_3)(a_1 - a_4)\ldots(a_1 - a_n)}$

$$A_2 = \frac{f(a_2)}{(a_2 - a_1)(a_2 - a_3)(a_2 - a_4)\ldots(a_2 - a_n)} \ldots$$

$$A_n = \frac{f(a_n)}{(a_n - a_1)(a_n - a_2)(a_n - a_3)\ldots(a_n - a_{n-1})}$$

Value Point

To find A_p, put $x = a_p$ in numerator and denominator after deleting the factor $(x - a_p)$.

Case **II** When $g(x)$ is expressible as product of repeated linear factors.

Let $g(x) = (x-a)^k (x - a_1)(x - a_2)\ldots (x - a_n)$,

then $\dfrac{f(x)}{g(x)} = \dfrac{A_1}{x-a} + \dfrac{A_2}{(x-a)^2} + \ldots + \dfrac{A_k}{(x-a)^k} + \dfrac{B_1}{(x-a_1)} + \dfrac{B_2}{(x-a_2)} + \ldots + \dfrac{B_n}{(x-a)^n}$.

Here, all the constant cannot be calculated by using the method in Case I. However, $B_1, B_2, B_3, \ldots, B_n$ can be found using the same method i.e. shortcut can be applied only in the case of non-repeated linear factors.

Integration of Irrational Algebraic Function

Irrational function of the form of $(ax+b)^{1/n}$ and x can be evaluated by substitution $(ax + b) = t^n$, thus

$$\int f\{x, (ax+b)^{1/n}\}dx = \int f\left(\frac{t^n - b}{a}, t\right)\frac{nt^{n-1}}{a}dt.$$

(i) $\displaystyle\int \frac{dx}{(Ax+B)\sqrt{Cx+D}}$, substitute $Cx+D=t^2$, then the given integral reduces into $\displaystyle\int \frac{2\,dt}{At^2 - AD + BC}$.

(ii) $\displaystyle\int \frac{dx}{(Ax^2+B)\sqrt{Cx+D}}$, substitute $Cx+D=t^2$, then the given integral reduces into $\displaystyle\int \frac{2C\,dt}{At^4 - 2DAt^2 + (AD^2 + BC^2)}$.

(iii) $\displaystyle\int \frac{dx}{(x-k)^r\sqrt{Ax^2+Bx+C}}$, substitute $x - k = \dfrac{1}{t}$, then the given integral reduces into $\displaystyle\int \frac{t^{r-1}}{At^2 + Bt + C}dt$.

(iv) $\int \frac{1}{(Ax^2+B)\sqrt{Cx^2+D}}\,dx$, substitute $x=\frac{1}{t}$, then the given integral reduces into $\int \frac{-t}{(A+Bt^2)\sqrt{C+Dt^2}}\,dt$.

Again, substitute $C+Dt^2=u^2$, then it reduces into the form $\int \frac{1}{u^2 \pm a^2}\,du$.

(v) $\int \frac{ax^2+bx+c}{(dx+e)\sqrt{fx^2+gx+h}}\,dx$

Here, we write

$$ax^2+bx+c = A_1(dx+e)\frac{d}{dx}(fx^2+gx+h)+B_1(dx+e)+C_1,$$

where A_1, B_1 and C_1 are constants.

Integrals of the Type $x^m(a+bx^n)^p,\ p\neq 0$

Case **I** If $p \in N$ (natural number) we expand the integral using binomial theorem and integrate it.

Case **II** If $p \in$ negative integer and m and n are rational numbers put $x=t^k$, where k is the LCM of denominator of m and n.

Case **III** If $\frac{m+1}{n}$ is an integer and p is rational number, we put $(a+bx^n)=t^k$, where k is the denominator of the fraction p.

Case **IV** If $\frac{m+p}{n}$ is an integer and p is a rational number, we put $\frac{a+bx^n}{x^n}=t^k$, where k is the denominator of the fraction p.

Competition Insight

Integration of Hyperbolic Functions

(i) $\int \sinh x\,dx = \cosh x + C$

(ii) $\int \cosh x\,dx = \sinh x + C$

(iii) $\int \text{sech}^2 x\,dx = \tanh x + C$

(iv) $\int \text{cosech}^2 x\,dx = -\coth x + C$

(v) $\int \text{sech}\,x \tanh x\,dx = -\text{sech}\,x + C$

(vi) $\int \text{cosech}\,x \coth x\,dx = -\text{cosech}\,x + C$

Important Points

(i) (a) Anti-derivative of signum exists in that interval in which $x = 0$ is not included.

(b) Anti-derivative of odd function is always even and of even function is always odd.

(ii) If $I_n = \int x^n e^{ax} dx$, then $I_n = \frac{x^n e^{ax}}{a} - \frac{n}{a} I_{n-1}$

(iii) (a) $\int (\log x) dx = x \log x - x + C$

(b) $\int \frac{1}{\log x} dx = \log(\log x) + \log x + \frac{(\log x)^2}{2(2!)} + \frac{(\log x)^3}{3(3!)} + \ldots$

(iv) $\int \frac{a \cos x + b \sin x}{c \cos x + d \sin x} dx = \frac{ac + bd}{c^2 + d^2} x + \frac{ad - bc}{c^2 + d^2} \log |c \cos x + d \sin x| + C$

(v) $\int \frac{\sin^n x}{\cos^m x} dx = \frac{1}{m-1} \cdot \frac{\sin^{n-1} x}{\cos^{m-1} x} - \frac{n-1}{m-1} \int \frac{\sin^{n-2} x}{\cos^{m-2} x} dx$

(vi) (a) $\int a^x \cos(bx + c)\, dx = \frac{a^x}{(\log a)^2 + b^2} [(\log a) \cos(bx + c) + b \sin(bx + c)] + C$

(b) $\int a^x \sin(bx + c)\, dx = \frac{a^x}{(\log a)^2 + b^2} [(\log a) \sin(bx + c) - b \cos(bx + c)] + C$

(vii) (a) $\int x e^{ax} \cos(bx + c) dx = \frac{x e^{ax}}{a^2 + b^2} [a \cos(bx + c) + b \sin(bx + c)] - \frac{e^{ax}}{(a^2 + b^2)^2} [(a^2 - b^2) \cos(bx + c) + 2ab \sin(bx + c)] + C$

(b) $\int x e^{ax} \sin(bx + c) dx = \frac{x e^{ax}}{a^2 + b^2} [a \sin(bx + c) - b \cos(bx + c)] - \frac{e^{ax}}{(a^2 + b^2)^2} [(a^2 - b^2) \sin(bx + c) - 2ab \cos(bx + c)] + C$

(viii) (a) $\int \sin^n x\, dx = \frac{-\cos x \cdot \sin^{n-1} x}{n} + \frac{n-1}{n} \int \sin^{n-2} x\, dx$

(b) $\int \cos^n x\, dx = \frac{\sin x \cdot \cos^{n-1} x}{n} + \frac{n-1}{n} \int \cos^{n-2} x\, dx$

(c) $\int \tan^n x\, dx = \frac{\tan^{n-1} x}{n-1} - \int \tan^{n-2} x\, dx$

(d) $\int \sin^n x \cos^m x\, dx = \frac{\sin^{n+1} x \cos^{m-1} x}{n+m} + \frac{m-1}{n+m} \int \sin^n x \cos^{m-2} x\, dx$

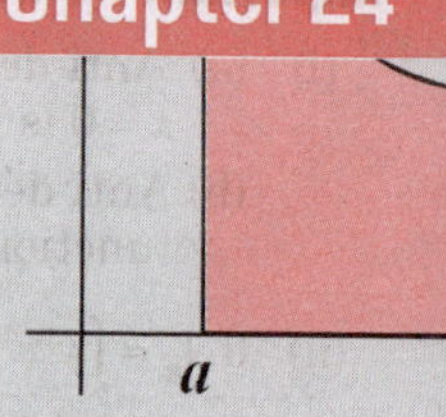

Chapter 24

Definite Integrals

Let $f(x)$ be a function defined on the interval $[a, b]$ and $F(x)$ be its anti-derivative. Then, $\int_a^b f(x)\,dx = F(b) - F(a)$ is defined as the **definite integral** of $f(x)$ from $x = a$ to $x = b$.

The numbers a and b are called lower and upper limits of integration, respectively.

Fundamental Theorem of Calculus

There is a connection between indefinite integral and definite integral is known as fundamental theorem of calculus.

First Fundamental Theorem

Let f be a continuous function defined on the closed interval $[a, b]$ and let $A(x)$ be the area of function i.e. $A(x) = \int_a^b f(x)dx$. Then, $A'(x) = f(x)$ for all $x \in [a, b]$.

Second Fundamental Theorem

Let f be a continuous function defined on the closed integral $[a, b]$ and F be an anti-derivative of f. Then,

$$\int_a^b f(x)dx = [F(x)]_a^b = F(b) - F(a).$$

Value Point

In $\int_a^b f(x)dx$, the function f needs to be well-defined and continuous in $[a, b]$.

For definite integral, there is no need to keep integration constant C.

Evaluation of Definite Integrals by Substitution

Consider a definite integral of the following form

$$\int_a^b f[g(x)] \cdot g'(x)\, dx$$

Step **I** Substitute $g(x) = t \Rightarrow g'(x)\, dx = dt$

Step **II** Find the limits of integration in new system of variable *i.e.*, the lower limit is $g(a)$ and the upper limit is $g(b)$ and the new integral will be $\int_{g(a)}^{g(b)} f(t)\, dt$.

Step **III** Evaluate the integral, so obtained by usual method.

Properties of Definite Integral

1. $\int_a^b f(x)\, dx = \int_a^b f(t)\, dt$

2. $\int_a^b f(x)\, dx = -\int_b^a f(x)\, dx$

3. $\int_a^a f(x)\, dx = 0$

4. $\int_a^b f(x)\, dx = \int_a^c f(x)\, dx + \int_c^b f(x)\, dx$, where $a < c < b$

   Generalisation

   If $a < c_1 < c_2 < \ldots < c_{n-1} < c_n < b$, then

   $$\int_a^b f(x)\, dx = \int_a^{c_1} f(x)\, dx + \int_{c_1}^{c_2} f(x)\, dx + \int_{c_2}^{c_3} f(x)\, dx + \ldots + \int_{c_{n-1}}^{c_n} f(x)\, dx + \int_{c_n}^{b} f(x)\, dx$$

5. $\int_0^a f(x)\, dx = \int_0^a f(a-x)\, dx$

   Deduction $\int_0^a \frac{f(x)}{f(x) + f(a-x)}\, dx = \frac{a}{2}$

6. $\int_a^b f(x)\, dx = \int_a^b f(a+b-x)\, dx$

   Deduction $\int_a^b \frac{f(x)}{f(x) + f(a+b-x)}\, dx = \frac{b-a}{2}$

7. $\int_0^{2a} f(x)\, dx = \int_0^a f(x)\, dx + \int_0^a f(2a-x)\, dx$

If $f(x) = [x] =$ greatest integer function such that $f(x) \le x$, then

$I = \int_0^n [x] dx = \int_0^1 0\, dx + \int_1^2 1\, dx + \ldots + \int_{[n]}^n [n] dx$

8. $\int_{-a}^{a} f(x)\,dx = \int_0^a f(x)\,dx + \int_0^a f(-x)\,dx$

9. $\int_0^{2a} f(x)\,dx = \begin{cases} 2\int_0^a f(x)\,dx \text{ if, } f(2a-x) = f(x) \\ 0, \quad \text{if } f(2a-x) = -f(x) \end{cases}$

10. $\int_a^b f(x)\,dx = \begin{cases} 0, \quad \text{if } f(a+x) = -f(b-x) \\ 2\int_a^{\frac{a+b}{2}} f(x)dx, \text{ if } f(a+x) = f(b-x) \end{cases}$

11. $\int_{-a}^{a} f(x)\,dx = \begin{cases} 2\int_0^a f(x)\,dx, \text{ if } f(x) \text{ is even i.e. } f(-x) = f(x) \\ 0, \quad \text{if } f(x) \text{ is odd i.e. } f(-x) = -f(x) \end{cases}$

12. If $\int_a^b f(x)\,dx = (b-a)\int_0^1 f[(b-a)x+a]dx$

13. If $f(x)$ is periodic function with period T [i.e. $f(x+T) = f(x)$].
Then, $\int_a^{a+T} f(x)dx$ is independent of a.

(a) $\int_0^{nT} f(x)dx = n\int_0^T f(x)dx, n \in I$

(b) $\int_a^{a+nT} f(x)\,dx = n\int_0^T f(x)\,dx, n \in I$

(c) $\int_{a+mT}^{a+nT} f(x)dx = \int_{mT}^{nT} f(x)\,dx = (n-m)\int_0^T f(x)\,dx, m, n \in I$

(d) $\int_{a+mT}^{b+mT} f(x)\,dx = \int_a^b f(x)\,dx, n \in I$

(e) $\int_{nT}^{a+nT} f(x)\,dx = \int_0^a f(x)\,dx$

Competition Insight

- **Leibnitz Rule for Differentiation under Integral Sign**
If $\phi(x)$ and $\psi(x)$ are defined on $[a, b]$ and differentiable at point $x \in (a, b)$ and $f(t)$ is continuous, then
$$\frac{d}{dx}\left[\int_{\phi(x)}^{\psi(x)} f(t)\,dt\right] = f[\psi(x)]\cdot\frac{d}{dx}\psi(x) - f[\phi(x)]\cdot\frac{d}{dx}\phi(x).$$
- If $f(x) \geq 0$ on the interval $[a, b]$, then $\int_a^b f(x) \geq 0$.
- If $f(x) \leq \phi(x)$ for $x \in [a, b]$, then $\int_a^b f(x)dx \leq \int_a^b \phi(x)\,dx$.

Important Points

(i) If at every point x of an interval $[a, b]$ the inequalities $g(x) \le f(x) \le h(x)$ are fulfilled, then $\int_a^b g(x)\,dx \le \int_a^b f(x)\,dx \le \int_a^b h(x)\,dx$.

(ii) $\left|\int_a^b f(x)\,dx\right| \le \int_a^b |f(x)|\,dx$

(iii) If m is the least value and M is the greatest value of the function $f(x)$ on the interval $[a, b]$ (estimation of an integral), then $m(b-a) \le \int_a^b f(x)\,dx \le M(b-a)$.

(iv) If f is continuous on $[a, b]$, then there exists a number c in $[a, b]$ at which $f(c) = \frac{1}{(b-a)} \int_a^b f(x)\,dx$ is called the mean value of the function $f(x)$ on the interval $[a, b]$.

(v) If $f^2(x)$ and $g^2(x)$ are integrable on $[a, b]$, then
$$\left|\int_a^b f(x)\,g(x)\,dx\right| \le \left(\int_a^b f^2(x)dx\right)^{1/2} \left(\int_a^b g^2(x)dx\right)^{1/2}$$

(vi) If $f(t)$ is an odd function, then $\phi(x) = \int_a^x f(t)\,dt$ is an even function.

(vii) If $f(t)$ is an even function, then $\phi(x) = \int_0^x f(t)dt$ is an odd function.

(viii) If $f(t)$ is an even function, then for non-zero a, $\int_a^x f(t)\,dt$ is not necessarily an odd function. It will be an odd function, if $\int_0^a f(t)\,dt = 0$.

(ix) If $f(x)$ is continuous on $[a, \infty)$, then $\int_a^\infty f(x)\,dx$ is called an improper integral and is defined as $\int_a^\infty f(x)\,dx = \lim_{b\to\infty} \int_a^b f(x)\,dx$.

(x) $\int_{-\infty}^b f(x)\,dx = \lim_{a\to-\infty} \int_a^b f(x)\,dx$ and $\int_{-\infty}^\infty f(x)\,dx = \int_{-\infty}^b f(x)\,dx + \int_b^\infty f(x)\,dx$

(xi) **Geometrically** for $f(x) > 0$, the improper integral $\int_a^\infty f(x)\,dx$ gives area of the figure bounded by the curve $y = f(x)$, the axis and the straight line $x = a$.

Integral Function

Let $f(x)$ be a continuous function defined on $[a,b]$, then a function $\phi(x)$ defined by $\phi(x)=\int_a^b f(t)dt, x \in [a,b]$ is called the integral function of the function f.

Properties of Integral Function

(i) The integral function of an integrable function is continuous.

(ii) If $\phi(x)$ is the integral function of continuous function, then $\phi(x)$ is derivable and $\phi'(x)=f(x), \forall\ x \in [a,b]$.

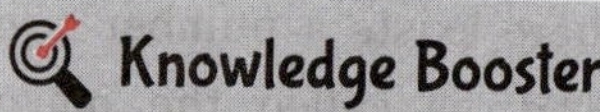

Knowledge Booster

Walli's Formula

$$\int_0^{\pi/2} \sin^n x\, dx = \int_0^{\pi/2} \cos^n x\, dx$$

$$= \begin{cases} \dfrac{n-1}{n} \cdot \dfrac{n-3}{n-2} \cdot \dfrac{n-5}{n-4} \cdots \dfrac{2}{3}, \text{ when } n \text{ is odd.} \\ \dfrac{n-1}{n} \cdot \dfrac{n-3}{n-2} \cdot \dfrac{n-5}{n-4} \cdots \dfrac{3}{4} \cdot \dfrac{1}{2} \cdot \dfrac{\pi}{2}, \text{ when } n \text{ is even.} \end{cases}$$

Some Important Deduction

(i) $\int_0^{\pi/2} \sin^m x \cos^n x\, dx = \dfrac{[(m-1)(m-3)\ldots 2 \text{ or } 1][(n-1)(n-3)\ldots 2 \text{ or } 1]}{[(m+n)(m+n-2)\ldots 2 \text{ or } 1]}$

On multiplying the above by $\dfrac{\pi}{2}$, when both m and n are even.

(a) $\int_0^{\pi/2} \sin^6 x \cos^3 x\, dx = \dfrac{(5\cdot 3\cdot 1)(2)}{9\cdot 7\cdot 5\cdot 3\cdot 1} = \dfrac{2}{63}$

(b) $\int_0^{\pi/2} \sin^8 x \cos^2 x\, dx = \dfrac{(7\cdot 5\cdot 3\cdot 1)}{10\cdot 8\cdot 6\cdot 4\cdot 2} \cdot \dfrac{\pi}{2} = \dfrac{7\pi}{512}$

(ii) Particular case when m or $n=1$

(a) $\int_0^{\pi/2} \sin^m x \cos x\, dx = \left[\dfrac{\sin^{m+1} x}{m+1}\right]_0^{\pi/2} = \dfrac{1}{m+1}$

(b) $\int_0^{\pi/2} \cos^m x \sin x\, dx = \left[\dfrac{-\cos^{m+1} x}{m+1}\right]_0^{\pi/2} = \dfrac{1}{m+1}$

Value Points

(i) (a) $\int_0^{\pi/2} \frac{\sin^n x}{\sin^n x + \cos^n x} dx = \frac{\pi}{4} = \int_0^{\pi/2} \frac{\cos^n x}{\sin^n x + \cos^n x} dx$

(b) $\int_0^{\pi/2} \frac{\tan^n x}{1 + \tan^n x} dx = \frac{\pi}{4} = \int_0^{\pi/2} \frac{dx}{1 + \tan^n x}$

(c) $\int_0^{\pi/2} \frac{dx}{1 + \cot^n x} = \frac{\pi}{4} = \int_0^{\pi/2} \frac{\cot^n x}{1 + \cot^n x} dx$

(d) $\int_0^{\pi/2} \frac{\tan^n x}{\tan^n x + \cot^n x} dx = \frac{\pi}{4} = \int_0^{\pi/2} \frac{\cot^n x}{\tan^n x + \cot^n x} dx$

(e) $\int_0^{\pi/2} \frac{\sec^n x}{\sec^n x + \operatorname{cosec}^n x} dx = \frac{\pi}{4}$

$= \int_0^{\pi/2} \frac{\operatorname{cosec}^n x}{\sec^n x + \operatorname{cosec}^n x} dx$ where, $n \in R$

(ii) $\int_0^{\pi/2} \frac{a^{\sin^n x}}{a^{\sin^n x} + a^{\cos^n x}} dx = \int_0^{\pi/2} \frac{a^{\cos^n x}}{a^{\sin^n x} + a^{\cos^n x}} dx = \frac{\pi}{4}$

(iii) (a) $\int_0^{\pi/2} \log \sin x \, dx = \int_0^{\pi/2} \log \cos x \, dx = -\frac{\pi}{2} \log 2$

(b) $\int_0^{\pi/2} \log \tan x \, dx = \int_0^{\pi/2} \log \cot x \, dx = 0$

(c) $\int_0^{\pi/2} \log \sec x \, dx = \int_0^{\pi/2} \log \operatorname{cosec} x \, dx = \frac{\pi}{2} \log 2$

(iv) (a) $\int_0^{\infty} e^{-ax} \sin bx \, dx = \frac{b}{a^2 + b^2}$

(b) $\int_0^{\infty} e^{-ax} \cos bx \, dx = \frac{a}{a^2 + b^2}$

(c) $\int_0^{\infty} e^{-ax} x^n \, dx = \frac{n!}{a^n + 1}$

Summation of Series by Definite Integral

Let $f(x)$ be a continuous function in $[a, b]$ and h be the length of n equal subintervals, then

$$\int_a^b f(x)\,dx = \lim_{n \to \infty} h \sum_{r=0}^{n} f(a + rh),$$

where $\quad nh = b - a$

Now, $\quad$ put $a = 0, b = 1$

$\therefore \quad nh = 1 - 0 = 1$ or $h = \frac{1}{n}$

$$\therefore \quad \int_0^1 f(x)\,dx = \lim_{n \to \infty} \frac{1}{n} \sum_{r=0}^{n-1} f\left(\frac{r}{n}\right)$$

Method Express the given series in the form of

$$\lim_{n \to \infty} \sum \frac{1}{n} f\left(\frac{r}{n}\right)$$

Replace $\frac{r}{n}$ by x and $\frac{1}{n}$ by dx and the limit of the sum is $\int_0^1 f(x)\,dx$.

Knowledge Booster

$$\lim_{n \to \infty} \sum_{r=1}^{n} \frac{1}{n} f\left(\frac{r}{n}\right) = \int_\alpha^\beta f(x)dx,$$

where $\quad \alpha = \lim_{n \to \infty} \frac{r}{n} = 0 \quad (\text{as } r = 1)$

and $\quad \beta = \lim_{n \to \infty} \frac{r}{n} = p \quad (\text{as } r = pn)$

The method to evaluate the integral, as limit of the sum of an infinite series is known as integration by first principle.

Chapter 25

Applications of Integrals

The space occupied by the curve along with the axis, under the given condition is called **area of bounded region**.

(i) The area bounded by the curve $y = F(x)$ above the X-axis and between the lines $x = a$, $x = b$ is given by

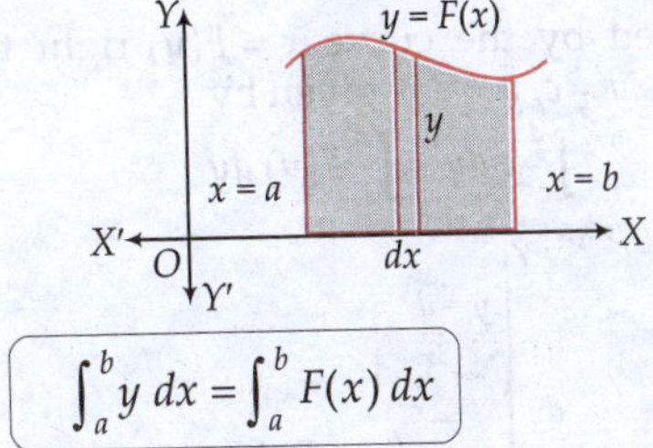

$$\int_a^b y\, dx = \int_a^b F(x)\, dx$$

(ii) If the curve between the lines $x = a$, $x = b$ lies below the X-axis, then the required area is given by

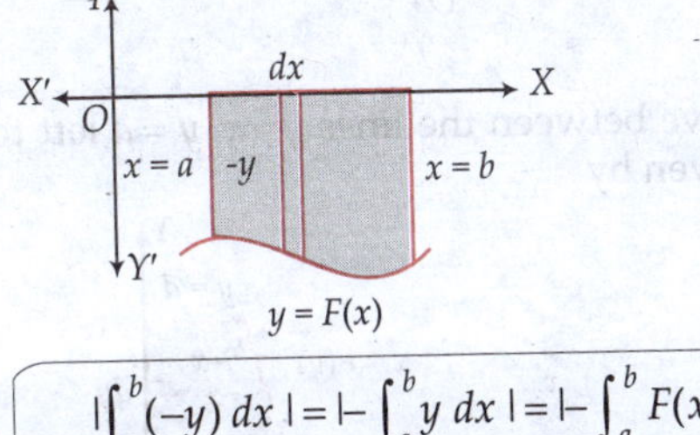

$$\left|\int_a^b (-y)\, dx\right| = \left|-\int_a^b y\, dx\right| = \left|-\int_a^b F(x)\, dx\right|$$

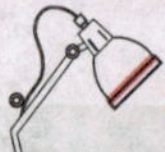

EXPERT Scale Up

If some part of curve lies below X-axis, then its area comes as negative but area cannot be negative, then take modulus.

Here, $a < \alpha < \beta < \gamma < \delta < b$, then

Required area

$$= \int_a^\alpha f(x)dx + \left|\int_\alpha^\beta f(x)dx\right| + \int_\beta^\gamma f(x)dx + \left|\int_\gamma^\delta f(x)dx\right| + \int_\delta^b f(x)dx$$

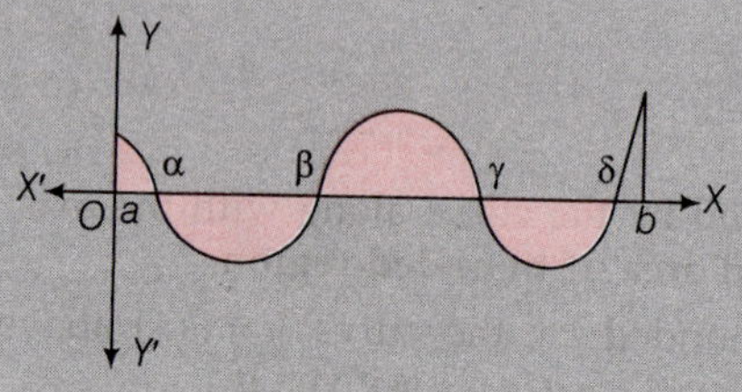

(iii) The area bounded by the curve $x = F(y)$ right to the Y-axis and between the lines $y = c$, $y = d$ is given by

$$\int_c^d x\,dy = \int_c^d F(y)\,dy$$

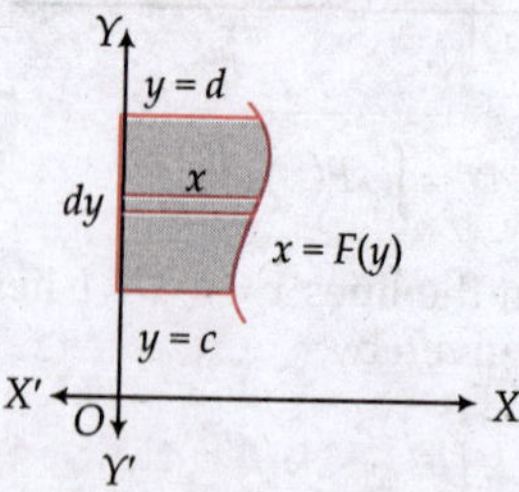

(iv) If the curve between the lines $y = c$, $y = d$ left to the Y-axis, then the area is given by

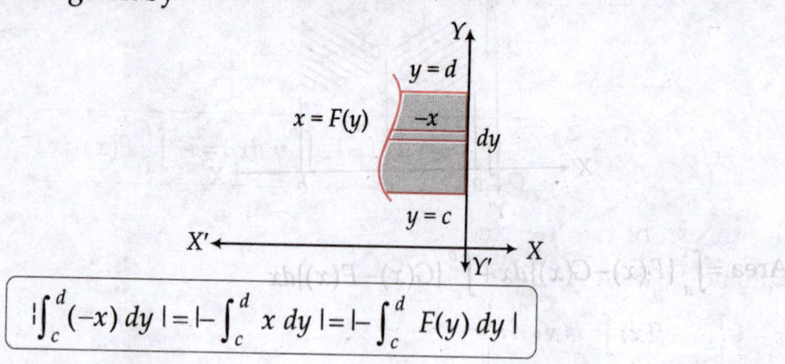

$$\left|\int_c^d (-x)\,dy\right| = \left|-\int_c^d x\,dy\right| = \left|-\int_c^d F(y)\,dy\right|$$

(v) Area bounded by two curves $y = F(x)$ and $y = G(x)$ between $x = a$ and $x = b$ is given by

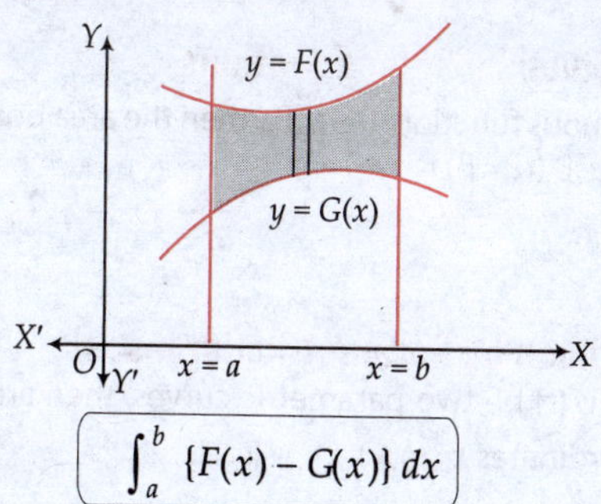

$$\int_a^b \{F(x) - G(x)\}\, dx$$

(vi) Area bounded by two curves $x = F(y)$ and $x = G(y)$ between $y = c$ and $y = d$ is given by

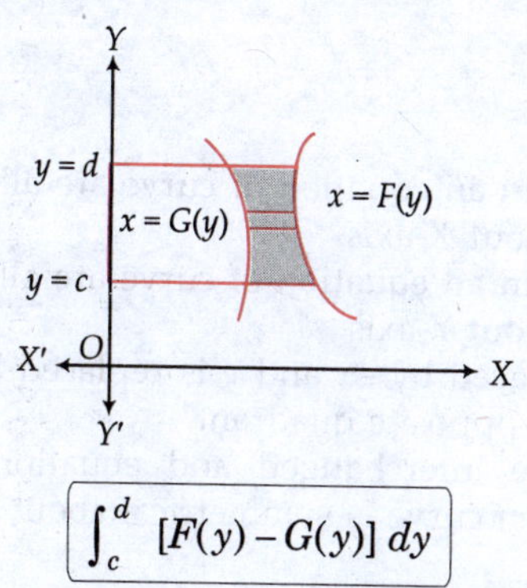

$$\int_c^d [F(y) - G(y)]\, dy$$

(vii) If $F(x) \geq G(x)$ in $[a, c]$ and $F(x) \leq G(x)$ in $[c, d]$, where $a < c < b$, then area of the region bounded by the curves is given as

$$\text{Area} = \int_a^c \{F(x) - G(x)\}dx + \int_c^b \{G(x) - F(x)\}dx$$

Competition Insight

Area of Curves Given by Polar Equations

Let $f(\theta)$ be a continuous function, $\theta \in (\alpha, \beta)$, then the area bounded by the curve $r = f(\theta)$ and radius α, β $(\alpha < \beta)$ is

$$A = \frac{1}{2}\int_{\alpha}^{\beta} r^2 \, d\theta$$

Area of Curves Given by Parametric Curves

Let $x = \phi(t)$ and $y = \psi(t)$ be two parametric curves, then area bounded by the curve, X-axis and ordinates $x = \phi(t_1)$, $x = \psi(t_2)$ is

$$A = \left| \int_{t=t_1}^{t=t_2} y \times \left(\frac{dx}{dt}\right) dt \right|$$

Curve Sketching

1. Symmetry

(i) If powers of y in an equation of curve are all even, then curve is symmetrical about X-axis.

(ii) If powers of x in an equation of curve are all even, then curve is symmetrical about Y-axis.

(iii) When x is replaced by $-x$ and y is replaced by $-y$, then curve is symmetrical in opposite quadrant.

(iv) If x and y are interchanged and equation of curve remains unchanged, then curve is symmetrical about line $y = x$.

2. Nature of Origin

(i) If point (0, 0) satisfies the equation, then curve passes through origin.

(ii) If curve passes through origin, then equate lowest degree term to zero and get equation of tangent. If there are two tangents, then origin is a double point.

3. Point of Intersection with Axes

(i) Put $y = 0$ and get intersection with X-axis, put $x = 0$ and get intersection with Y-axis.

(ii) Now, find equation of tangent at this point i.e. shift origin to the point of intersection and equate the lowest degree term to zero.

(iii) Find regions where curve does not exists i.e. curve will not exit for those values of variable when makes the other imaginary or not defined.

4. Asymptotes

(i) Equate coefficient of highest power of x to get asymptote parallel to X-axis.

(ii) Similarly equate coefficient of highest power of y to get asymptote parallel to Y-axis.

5. The Sign of $\frac{dy}{dx}$

Find points at which $\frac{dy}{dx}$ vanishes or becomes infinite. It gives us the points where tangent is parallel or perpendicular to the X-axis.

6. Points of Inflexion

Put $\frac{d^2y}{dx^2}=0$ or $\frac{d^2x}{dy^2}=0$ and solve the resulting equation. If some point of inflexion is there, then locate it exactly.

Taking in consideration of all above information, we draw an approximate shape of the curve.

Shapes of Some Curves

S.No.	Equations	Curves
(i)	$ay^2 = x^3$ (Semi-cubical parabola)	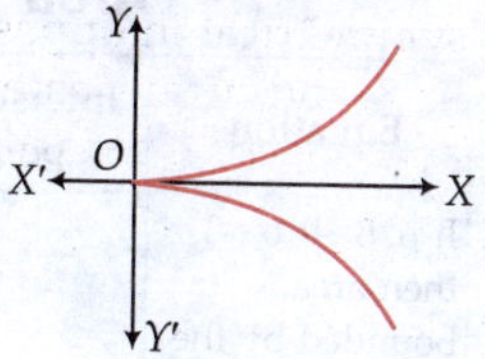 Y, O, X′, X, Y′
(ii)	$y = x^3$ (Cubical parabola)	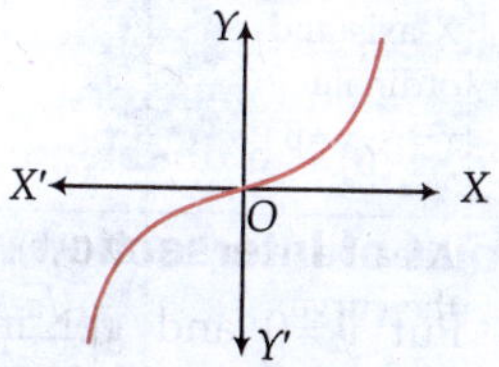 Y, X′, X, O, Y′
(iii)	$(x^2 + 4a^2)y = 8a^3$	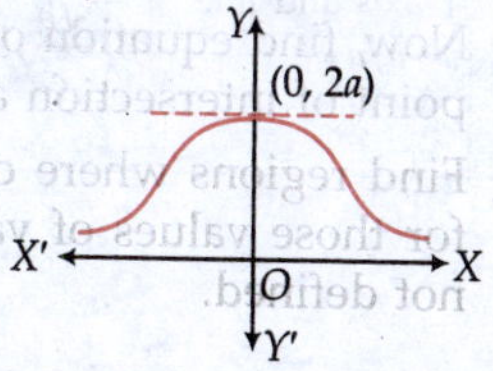 Y, (0, 2a), X′, X, O, Y′

S.No.	Equations	Curves
(iv)	$ay^2 = x^2(a - x)$	Y, $y = x$, $y = -x$, X′, O, X, $(a, 0)$, Y′
(v)	$a^2y^2 = x^2(a^2 - x^2)$	Y, $y = x$, X′, X, O, $y = -x$, Y′

Value Point

If the curve is symmetrical and suppose it has n symmetrical portions, then total area = area of one symmetrical portion $\times n$.

Area bounded by Curves

S.No.	Equations	Intersection points	Area of shaded region	Graphs
(i)	If $\alpha, \beta > 0, \alpha > \beta$, then area bounded by the curve $xy = p^2$, X-axis and ordinate $x = \alpha, x = \beta$	–	$p^2 \log\left(\frac{\alpha}{\beta}\right)$ sq units	Y, X′, X, $x=\beta$, $x=\alpha$, Y′
(ii)	Area between the curve $y = c^2x^2$, Y-axis and line $y = a, y = b$	$O(0,0)$, $A\left(\frac{\sqrt{a}}{c}, a\right)$, $B\left(\frac{\sqrt{b}}{c}, b\right)$	$\frac{2(b^{3/2} - a^{3/2})}{3c}$ sq units	Y, $y = c^2x^2$, $y = b$, $B\left(\frac{\sqrt{b}}{c}, b\right)$, $y = a$, $A\left(\frac{\sqrt{a}}{c}, a\right)$, X′, X, $(0, 0)$ O, Y′

S.No.	Equations	Intersection points	Area of shaded region	Graphs
(iii)	$y = k\cos 3x$, $\forall\, 0 \le x \le \frac{\pi}{6}$,	when $0 \le x \le \frac{\pi}{6}$, then $0 \le 3x \le \frac{\pi}{2}$	$\frac{k}{3}$ sq units	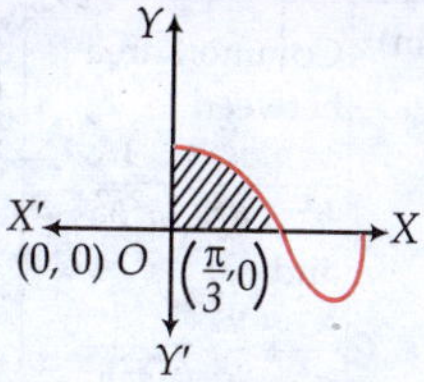
(iv)	$f(x, y); x^2 = 4ay$, $y^2 = 4bx$	$O(0,0)$, $A(4a^{2/3}b^{1/3}, 4a^{1/3}b^{2/3})$	$\frac{16}{3}(ab)$ sq units	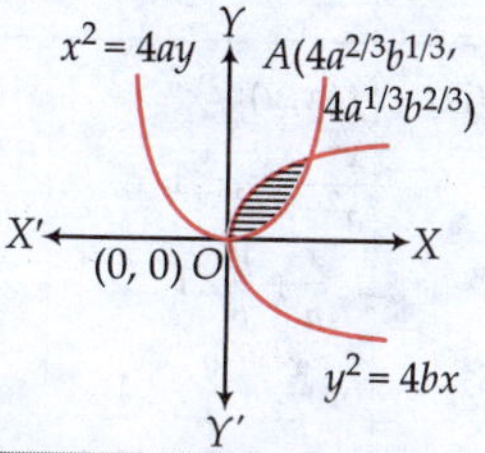
(v)	$f(x, y)$; $x^2 + y^2 \le 2ax$ and $y^2 \ge ax$	$O(0,0)$, $A(a, a)$, $B(a, -a)$	(i) For $x \ge 0, y \ge 0$ Area $= a^2\left(\frac{\pi}{4} - \frac{2}{3}\right)$ sq units (ii) For $x \ge 0$, Area $= 2a^2\left(\frac{\pi}{4} - \frac{2}{3}\right)$ sq units	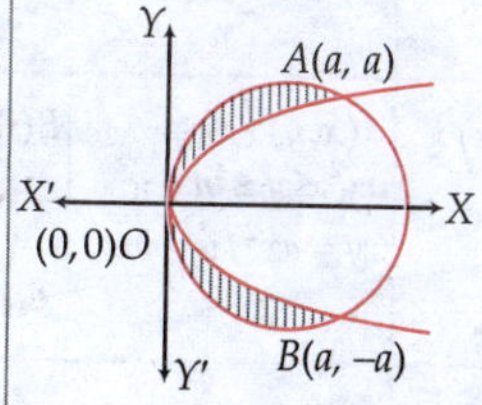
(vi)	Area bounded by the parabola $y^2 = 4ax$ and its latus rectum $x = a$	$A(a, 2a)$, $B(a, -2a)$	$\frac{8}{3}a^2$ sq units	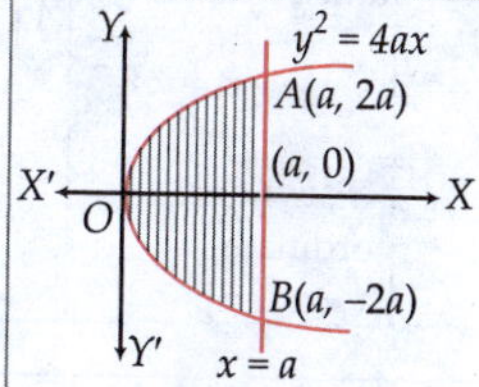
(vii)	Area bounded by the curves $y^2 = 4a(x+a)$ and $y^2 = 4b(b-x)$	$A(b-a, 2\sqrt{ab})$, $B(b-a, -2\sqrt{ab})$	$\frac{8}{3}\sqrt{ab}\,(a+b)$ sq units	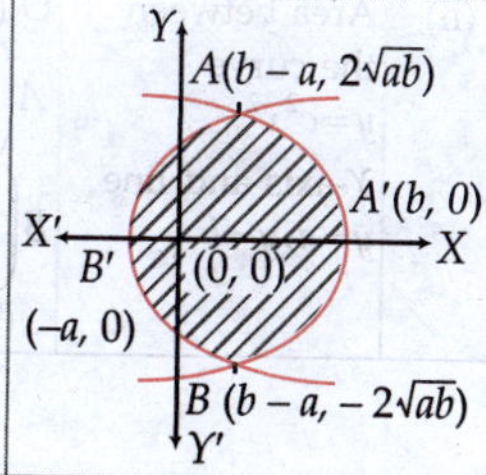

S.No.	Equations	Intersection points	Area of shaded region	Graphs
(viii)	Common area between $\frac{x^2}{b^2}+\frac{y^2}{a^2}=\frac{1}{a^2b^2}$ and $\frac{x^2}{a^2}+\frac{y^2}{b^2}=\frac{1}{a^2b^2}$	$\left(\pm\frac{1}{\sqrt{a^2+b^2}}, \pm\frac{1}{\sqrt{a^2+b^2}}\right)$	Area of region $PQRS$ $=4\times$ Area of $OLQM=\frac{4}{ab}\tan^{-1}\left(\frac{a}{b}\right)$ sq units	Y, M, P, Q, X', X, L, O, R, S, (0, 0), Y'
(ix)	$f(x,y)$: $\frac{x^2}{a^2}+\frac{y^2}{b^2}\le 1$, $\frac{x}{a}+\frac{y}{b}\ge 1$ or $\frac{x^2}{a^2}+\frac{y^2}{b^2}\le 1\le\frac{x}{a}+\frac{y}{b}$	$A(a,0)$, $B(0,b)$	$ab\cdot\frac{(\pi-2)}{4}$ sq units	Y, B(0, b), (−a, 0), A′, A (a, 0), X′, X, (0, 0), Y′
(x)	$f(x,y)$: $ax^2\le y\le mx$ $\therefore y=ax^2, y=mx$	$B(0,0)$, $A\left(\frac{m}{a},\frac{m^2}{a}\right)$	$\frac{1}{6}\cdot\frac{m^3}{a^2}$ sq units	Y, $A\left(\frac{m}{a},\frac{m^2}{a}\right)$, X′, X, B (0, 0), Y′
(xi)	$f(x,y): y^2=4ax$ and $y=\lvert mx\rvert$	$O(0,0)$, $A\left(\frac{4a}{m^2},\frac{4a}{m}\right)$	$\frac{8a^2}{3m^3}$ sq units	Y, $A\left(\frac{4a}{m^2},\frac{4a}{m}\right)$, X′, O, X, (0, 0), Y′

Competition Insight

Volume and Surface Area

If we revolve any plane curve along any line, then solid so generated is called solid of revolution.

1. Volume of Solid Revolution

(i) The volume of the solid generated by revolution of the area bounded by the curve $y = f(x)$, X-axis and the ordinates $x = a, x = b$ is $\int_a^b \pi y^2 dx$, it is being given that $f(x)$ is a continuous function in the interval (a, b).

(ii) The volume of the solid generated by revolution of the area bounded by the curve $x = g(y)$, the axis of Y and two abscissae $y = c$ and $y = d$ is $\int_c^d \pi x^2 dy$, it is being given that $g(y)$ is a continuous function in the interval (c, d).

2. Surface Area of Solid Revolution

(i) The surface area of the solid generated by revolution of the area bounded by the curve $y = f(x)$, X-axis and the ordinates $x = a, x = b$ is $2\pi \int_a^b y \sqrt{\left\{1 + \left(\frac{dy}{dx}\right)^2\right\}} dx$, it is being given that $f(x)$ is a continuous function in the interval (a, b).

(ii) The surface area of the solid generated by revolution of the area bounded by the curve $x = f(y)$, Y-axis and two abscissae $y = c, y = d$ is $2\pi \int_c^d x \sqrt{\left\{1 + \left(\frac{dx}{dy}\right)^2\right\}} dy$, it is being given that $f(y)$ is a continuous function in the interval (c, d).

Chapter 26

Differential Equations

Differential Equation

An equation that involves an independent variable, dependent variable and differential coefficients of dependent variable with respect to the independent variable is called a **differential equation**.

e.g. (i) $x^2\left(\dfrac{d^2y}{dx^2}\right)+x^3\left(\dfrac{dy}{dx}\right)^3=7x^2y^2$

(ii) $(x^2+y^2)\,dx=(x^2-y^2)\,dy$

Order and Degree of a Differential Equation

The **order** of a differential equation is the order of the highest derivative occuring in the equation. The order of a differential equation is always a positive integer.

The **degree** of a differential equation is the exponent of the derivative of the highest order in the equation, when the equation is a polynomial in derivatives.

e.g. The order and degree of a differential equation

$\left(\dfrac{d^3y}{dx^3}\right)^2+2\left(\dfrac{d^2y}{dx^2}\right)^3+3y=0$ are 3 and 2 respectively.

EXPERT Scale Up

If the differential equation is not a polynomial equation in derivatives, then its degree is not defined.

e.g. Degree of $\dfrac{dy}{dx}+\cos\left(\dfrac{dy}{dx}\right)=0$ is not defined,

as $\dfrac{dy}{dx}+\cos\left(\dfrac{dy}{dx}\right)=0$ is not a polynomial in derivatives.

Linear and Non-Linear Differential Equations

A differential equation is said to be linear, if the dependent variable and all of its derivatives occuring in the first power and there are no product of these.

A linear equation of nth order can be written in the form

$$P_0 \frac{d^n y}{dx^n} + P_1 \frac{d^{n-1} y}{dx^{n-1}} + P_2 \frac{d^{n-2} y}{dx^{n-2}} + \ldots + P_{n-1} \frac{dy}{dx} + P_n y = Q$$

where, $P_0, P_1, P_2, \ldots, P_{n-1}, P_n$ and Q must be either constants or functions of x only.

EXPERT Scale Up

A linear differential equation is always of the first degree but every differential equation of the first degree need not be linear.

e.g. The equations $\frac{d^2y}{dx^2} + \left(\frac{dy}{dx}\right)^2 + xy = 0$, $x\frac{d^2y}{dx^2} + y\frac{dy}{dx} + y = x^3$ and $\left(\frac{dy}{dx}\right)\frac{d^2y}{dx^2} + y = 0$ are not linear.

Solutions of Differential Equations

A solution of a differential equation is a relation between the variables, of the equation not involving the differential coefficients, such that it satisfy the given differential equation (i.e., from which the given differential equation can be derived).

e.g. $y = A\cos x + B\sin x$ is a solution of $\frac{d^2y}{dx^2} + y = 0$, because it satisfy this equation.

1. General Solution

If the solution of the differential equation contains as many independent arbitrary constants as the order of the differential equation, then it is called the general solution or the complete integral of the differential equation.

e.g. The general solution of $\frac{d^2y}{dx^2} + y = 0$ is $y = A\cos x + B\sin x$ because it contains two arbitrary constants A and B, which is equal to the order of the equation.

2. Particular Solution

Solution obtained by giving particular values to the arbitrary constants in the general solution is called a particular solution.

e.g. In the previous example, if $A = B = 1$, then $y = \cos x + \sin x$ is a particular solution of the differential equation $\frac{d^2y}{dx^2} + y = 0.$

Solution of a differential equation is also called its **primitive**.

 **Knowledge Booster**

Formation of Differential Equation

Suppose we have an equation $f(x, y, c_1, c_2, \ldots, c_n) = 0$, where $c_1, c_2, \ldots c_n$ are n arbitrary constants.

Then, to form a differential equation differentiate the equation successively n times to get n equations.

Eliminate the arbitrary constants from the $(n + 1)$ equations (the given equation and the n equations obtained above), which leads to the required differential equations.

Solutions of Differential Equations of the First Order and First Degree

A differential equation of first degree and first order can be solved if they belong to any of the following standard forms.

1. Equation of the form

$$f(f_1(x,y))d(f_1(x,y)) + \phi(f_2(x,y))d(f_2(x,y)) + \ldots = 0$$

If the differential equation can be written as $f[f_1(x,y)]d\{f_1(x,y)\} + \phi[f_2(x,y)]d\{f_2(x,y)\} + \ldots = 0$, then each term can be integrated separately.

For this, remember the following results

(i) $x\,dy + y\,dx = d(xy)$

(ii) $dx + dy = d(x + y)$

(iii) $\frac{x\,dy - y\,dx}{x^2} = d\left(\frac{y}{x}\right)$

(iv) $\frac{y\,dx - x\,dy}{y^2} = d\left(\frac{x}{y}\right)$

(v) $\frac{2xy\,dx - x^2\,dy}{y^2} = d\left(\frac{x^2}{y}\right)$

(vi) $\frac{2xy\,dy - y^2\,dx}{x^2} = d\left(\frac{y^2}{x}\right)$

(vii) $\frac{2xy^2\,dx - 2x^2y\,dy}{y^4} = d\left(\frac{x^2}{y^2}\right)$

(viii) $\frac{2x^2y\,dy - 2xy^2\,dx}{x^4} = d\left(\frac{y^2}{x^2}\right)$

(ix) $\frac{x\,dy + y\,dx}{xy} = d(\log xy)$

(x) $\frac{y\,dx - x\,dy}{xy} = d\left(\log \frac{x}{y}\right)$

(xi) $\dfrac{x\,dy - y\,dx}{xy} = d\left(\log\dfrac{y}{x}\right)$ (xii) $\dfrac{dx + dy}{x + y} = d\,(\log(x + y))$

(xiii) $\dfrac{x\,dx + y\,dy}{x^2 + y^2} = d\left(\log\sqrt{x^2 + y^2}\right)$ (xiv) $\dfrac{xdy - ydx}{x^2 + y^2} = d\left(\tan^{-1}\dfrac{y}{x}\right)$

(xv) $\dfrac{y\,dx - x\,dy}{x^2 + y^2} = d\left(\tan^{-1}\dfrac{x}{y}\right)$ (xvi) $\dfrac{xdy + ydx}{x^2y^2} = d\left(\dfrac{-1}{xy}\right)$

(xvii) $\dfrac{ye^x\,dx - e^x\,dy}{y^2} = d\left(\dfrac{e^x}{y}\right)$ (xviii) $\dfrac{xe^y\,dy - e^y\,dx}{x^2} = d\left(\dfrac{e^y}{x}\right)$

(xix) $\dfrac{xdx + ydy}{\sqrt{x^2 + y^2}} = d(\sqrt{x^2 + y^2})$

(xx) $x^{m-1} \cdot y^{n-1}(mydx + nx\,dy) = d(x^m\; y^n)$

(xxi) $\dfrac{xdy - ydx}{x^2 - y^2} = d\left(\dfrac{1}{2}\log\dfrac{x + y}{x - y}\right)$

(xxii) $\dfrac{f'(x, y)}{[f(x, y)]^n} = \dfrac{d\,[f(x, y)]^{1-n}}{1 - n}$ (xxiii) $\dfrac{dx}{x^2} - \dfrac{dy}{y^2} = d\left(\dfrac{1}{y} - \dfrac{1}{x}\right)$

2. **Equations in which the Variables are Separable**

If the equation can be expressed in the form $f(x)\,dx = g(y)\,dy$, we say that the variables have been separated, then $\int f(x)\,dx = \int g(y)\,dy + C$ will be the solution of such differential equation, where C is an arbitrary constant.

3. **Differential Equation Reducible to Variables Separable Form**

A differential equation of the form $\dfrac{dy}{dx} = f(ax + by + c)$

can be reduced to variables separable form by substituting

$$ax + by + c = z \Rightarrow a + b\frac{dy}{dx} = \frac{dz}{dx}$$

The given equation becomes

$$\frac{1}{b}\left(\frac{dz}{dx} - a\right) = f(z) \Rightarrow \frac{dz}{dx} = a + b\,f(z) \Rightarrow \frac{dz}{a + bf(z)} = dx$$

Hence, the variables are separated in terms of z and x.

4. **Homogeneous Differential Equation**

A differential equation of the form

$$\frac{dy}{dx} = \frac{f(x, y)}{g(x, y)}$$

where, $f(x, y)$ and $g(x, y)$ are homogeneous function of same degree is called a homogeneous differential equation.

This equation can be reduced to the form $\frac{dy}{dx} = F\left(\frac{y}{x}\right)$ or $\frac{dx}{dy} = G\left(\frac{x}{y}\right)$.

To solve $\frac{dy}{dx} = F\left(\frac{y}{x}\right)$, we put $y = vx$

$$\Rightarrow \qquad \frac{dy}{dx} = v + x\frac{dv}{dx}.$$

Then, the given equation reduces to

$$v + x\frac{dv}{dx} = F(v) \Rightarrow \quad x\frac{dv}{dx} = F(v) - v$$

which is invariable separable form and so it can be solved in the usual manner.

Similarly, to solve $\frac{dx}{dy} = G\left(\frac{x}{y}\right)$, we put $x = vy$.

Knowledge Booster

A function $f(x, y)$ is said to be homogeneous function of degree n, if $f(\lambda x, \lambda y) = \lambda^n f(x, y)$.

5. Differential Equations Reducible to Homogeneous Form

The differential equation of the form

$$\frac{dy}{dx} = \frac{a_1x + b_1y + c_1}{a_2x + b_2y + c_2}, \text{ where } a_1b_2 - a_2b_1 \neq 0 \text{ i.e. } \frac{a_1}{a_2} \neq \frac{b_1}{b_2} \qquad \text{...(i)}$$

can be reduced to homogeneous form by substituting

$$x = X + h \text{ and } y = Y + k$$

$$\therefore \qquad \frac{dY}{dX} = \frac{a_1X + b_1Y + (a_1h + b_1k + c_1)}{a_2X + b_2Y + (a_2h + b_2k + c_2)} \qquad \text{...(ii)}$$

For finding h and k, put $a_1h + b_1k + c_1 = 0$ and $a_2h + b_2k + c_2 = 0$.

On solving, we get

$$\frac{h}{b_1c_2 - b_2c_1} = \frac{k}{c_1a_2 - c_2a_1} = \frac{1}{a_1b_2 - a_2b_1}$$

$$\Rightarrow \qquad h = \frac{b_1c_2 - b_2c_1}{a_1b_2 - a_2b_1} \text{ and } k = \frac{c_1a_2 - c_2a_1}{a_1b_2 - a_2b_1}$$

Then, Eq. (ii) reduces to $\frac{dY}{dX} = \frac{a_1X + b_1Y}{a_2X + b_2Y}$, which is a homogeneous form and can be solved easily.

6. Linear Differential Equation

A linear differential equation of the first order can be either of the following forms

(i) $\frac{dy}{dx} + Py = Q$, where P and Q are the functions of x or constants.

(ii) $\frac{dx}{dy} + Rx = S$, where R and S are the functions of y or constants.

Consider the differential Eq. (i) i.e. $\frac{dy}{dx} + Py = Q$,

The integrating factor is (IF) $= e^{\int P\,dx}$

and solution is $y \cdot e^{\int P\,dx} = \int Q \cdot e^{\int P\,dx}\,dx + C$

i.e. $$y\,(\text{IF}) = \int Q\,(\text{IF})\,dx + C$$

Similarly, for the second differential equation $\frac{dx}{dy} + Rx = S$, the integrating factor, IF $= e^{\int R\,dy}$ and the general solution is

$$x \cdot e^{\int R dy} = \int S \cdot e^{\int R dy}\,dy + C$$

i.e. $$x\,(\text{IF}) = \int S\,(\text{IF})\,dy + C$$

Value Points

- A differential equation involving derivative of the dependent variable with respect to only one independent variable is called Ordinary Differential Equation, otherwise called Partial Differential Equation.
- Order and degree of Differential Equation are always positive integers.

7. Differential Equation Reducible to the Linear Form

Equation of the form $f'(y)\frac{dy}{dx} + f(y)P = Q$, where P and Q are functions of x only or constants, can be reduced to linear form by substituting

i.e. $$f(y) = u \Rightarrow f'(y)\frac{dy}{dx} = \frac{du}{dx}$$

This will reduce the given equation to $\frac{du}{dx} + uP = Q$,

which is in linear differential equation form and can be solved in the usual manner.

Competition Insight

Bernoulli's Equation

An equation of the form $\frac{dy}{dx} + Py = Qy^n\ (n \neq 0, 1)$, where P and Q are functions of x only or constants, is called **Bernoulli's equation**.

It is easy to reduce the above equation into linear form as below

Dividing both the sides by y^n, we get

$$y^{-n}\frac{dy}{dx} + Py^{-n+1} = Q$$

Put $$y^{-n+1} = z$$

$$\Rightarrow \quad (-n+1)\,y^{-n}\frac{dy}{dx} = \frac{dz}{dx}$$

Then, the equation reduces to

$$\frac{1}{1-n}\frac{dz}{dx} + Pz = Q \Rightarrow \frac{dz}{dx} + (1-n)\,Pz = Q(1-n),$$

which is linear differential equation in z and can be solved in the usual manner.

Orthogonal Trajectory

Any curve, which cuts every member of a given family of curves at right angle, is called an orthogonal trajectory of the family.

Procedure for Finding the Orthogonal Trajectory

(i) Let $f(x, y, c) = 0$ be the equation of the given family of curves, where 'c' is a parameter.

(ii) Differentiate $f = 0$, with respect to 'x' and eliminate c to form a differential equation.

(iii) Substitute $\left(\frac{-dx}{dy}\right)$ in place of $\left(\frac{dy}{dx}\right)$ in the above differential equation. This will give the differential equation of the orthogonal trajectories.

(iv) By solving this differential equation, we get the required orthogonal trajectories.

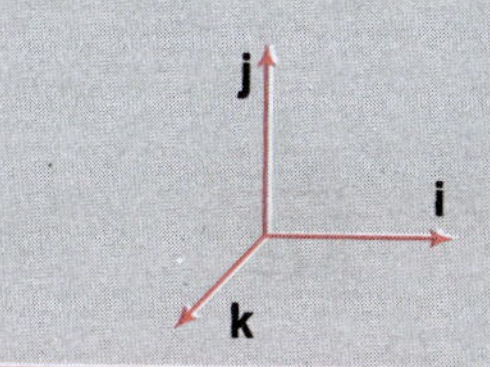

Chapter 27

Vectors

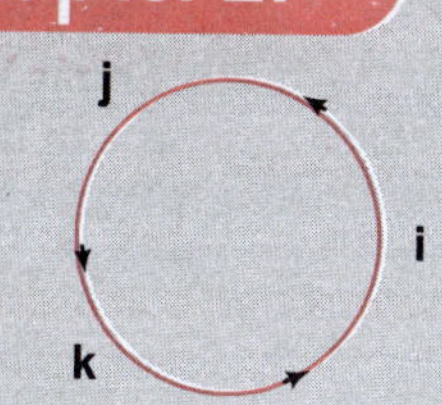

A **vector** has direction and magnitude both but **scalar** has only magnitude. e.g. Vector quantities are displacement, velocity, acceleration, etc. and scalar quantities are length, mass, time, etc.

Characteristics of a Vector

(i) **Magnitude** The length of the vector **AB** or **a** is called the magnitude of **AB** or **a** and it is represented as $|\mathbf{AB}|$ or $|\mathbf{a}|$.

(ii) **Sense** The direction of a line segment from its initial point to its terminal point is called its sense.

e.g. The sense of **AB** is from A to B and that of **BA** is from B to A.

Initial point • A —— B • Terminal point

(iii) **Support** The line of infinite length of which the line segment AB is a part, is called the support of the vector **AB**.

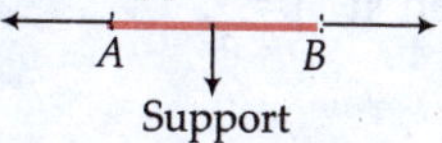

Types of Vectors

(i) **Zero or Null Vector** A vector whose initial and terminal points are coincident is called zero or null vector. It is denoted by **0**.

(ii) **Unit Vector** A vector whose magnitude is unity i.e. 1 is called a unit vector. The unit vector in the direction of **n** is given by $\frac{\mathbf{n}}{|\mathbf{n}|}$ and it is denoted by $\hat{\mathbf{n}}$.

(iii) **Free Vector** If the initial point of a vector is not specified, then it is said to be a free vector.

(iv) **Like and Unlike Vectors** Vectors are said to be like vectors when they have the same direction and unlike when they have opposite direction.

(v) **Collinear or Parallel Vectors** Vectors having the same or parallel supports are called collinear vectors.

(vi) **Equal Vectors** Two vectors **a** and **b** are said to be equal, written as **a** = **b**, if they have same length and same direction.

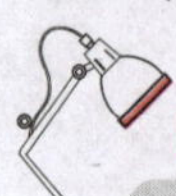

EXPERT Scale Up

Equal vectors may start at different positions.

(vii) **Negative Vector** A vector having the same magnitude as that of a given vector **a** and the direction opposite to that of **a** is called the negative vector **a** and it is denoted by $-\mathbf{a}$.

(viii) **Coinitial Vectors** Vectors having same initial point are called coinitial vectors.

(ix) **Coterminus Vectors** Vectors having the same terminal point are called coterminus vectors.

(x) **Localised Vectors** A vector which is drawn parallel to a given vector through a specified point in space is called localised vector.

(xi) **Coplanar Vectors** A system of vectors is said to be coplanar, if their supports are parallel in the same plane. Otherwise they are called non-coplanar vectors.

(xii) **Reciprocal of a Vector** A vector having the same direction as that of a given vector but magnitude equal to the reciprocal of the given vector is known as the reciprocal of **a** and it is denoted by $\mathbf{a}^{-1}$ i.e. if $|\mathbf{a}| = a$, then $|\mathbf{a}^{-1}| = \frac{1}{a}$.

Addition of Vectors

Triangle Law of Vector Addition

Let **a** and **b** be any two vectors. From the terminal point of **a**, vector **b** is drawn. Then, the vector from the initial point O of **a** to the terminal point B of **b** is called the sum of vectors **a** and **b** and is denoted by **a** + **b**. This is called the triangle law of addition of vectors.

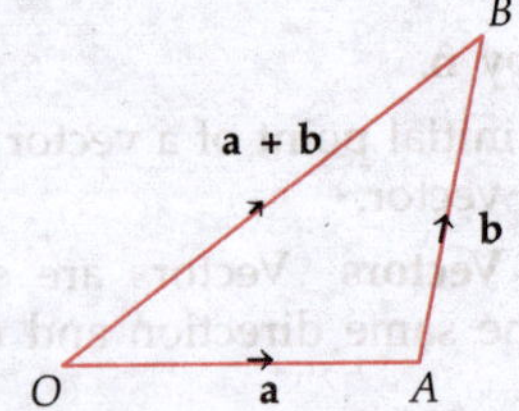

Knowledge Booster

When the sides of a triangle are taken in order, then the resultant will be $AB + BC + CA = 0$.

Parallelogram Law of Vector Addition

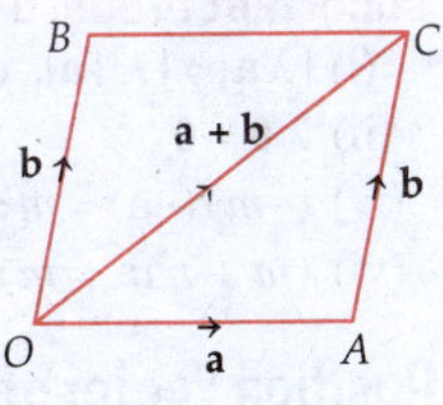

Let **a** and **b** be any two vectors. From the initial point of **a**, vector **b** is drawn and parallelogram *OACB* is completed with *OA* and *OB* as adjacent sides. The diagonal of the parallelogram through the common vertex represents the vector **OC** and it is defined as the sum of **a** and **b**. This is called the parallelogram law of vector addition.

The sum of two vectors is also called their resultant and the process of addition as **composition**.

Properties of Vector Addition

Let **a, b** and **c** be three vectors.

(i) $\mathbf{a} + \mathbf{b} = \mathbf{b} + \mathbf{a}$ (commutative)

(ii) $\mathbf{a} + (\mathbf{b} + \mathbf{c}) = (\mathbf{a} + \mathbf{b}) + \mathbf{c}$ (associative)

(iii) $\mathbf{a} + \mathbf{0} = \mathbf{a}$ (additive identity)

(iv) $\mathbf{a} + (-\mathbf{a}) = \mathbf{0}$ (additive inverse)

Knowledge Booster

The bisector of the angle between two non-collinear vectors **a** and **b** is given by

$$\lambda(\hat{\mathbf{a}} \pm \hat{\mathbf{b}}) \text{ or } \lambda\left(\frac{\mathbf{a}}{|\mathbf{a}|} \pm \frac{\mathbf{b}}{|\mathbf{b}|}\right).$$

Difference (Subtraction) of Vectors

Let **a** and **b** be any two vectors, then their difference $\mathbf{a} - \mathbf{b}$ is defined as $\mathbf{a} + (-\mathbf{b})$. In the given figure the vector **OB′** is said to represent the difference of **a** and **b**.

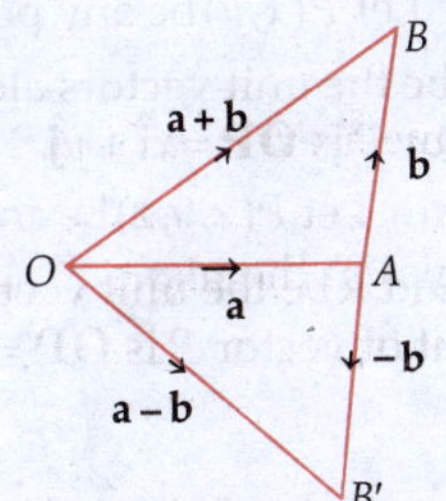

Multiplication of a Vector by a Scalar

Let **a** be a given vector and λ be a scalar. Then, the product of the vector **a** by the scalar λ is $\lambda\,\mathbf{a}$ and is called the multiplication of vector by the scalar.

Important Properties

(i) $|\lambda\mathbf{a}| = |\lambda||\mathbf{a}|$, where λ be a scalar.

(ii) $\lambda\mathbf{0} = \mathbf{0}$

(iii) $m(-\mathbf{a}) = -m\mathbf{a} = -(m\mathbf{a})$

(iv) $(-m)(-\mathbf{a}) = m\mathbf{a}$

(v) $m(n\mathbf{a}) = mn\mathbf{a} = n(m\mathbf{a})$

(vi) $(m+n)\mathbf{a} = m\mathbf{a} + n\mathbf{a}$

(vii) $m(\mathbf{a}+\mathbf{b}) = m\mathbf{a} + m\mathbf{b}$

Position Vector of a Point

The position vector of a point P with respect to a fixed point say O, is the vector **OP**. The fixed point is called the **origin**.

Let **PQ** be any vector. We have,

$$\mathbf{PQ} = \mathbf{PO} + \mathbf{OQ} = -\mathbf{OP} + \mathbf{OQ} = \mathbf{OQ} - \mathbf{OP}$$

$$= \text{Position vector of } Q - \text{Position vector of } P.$$

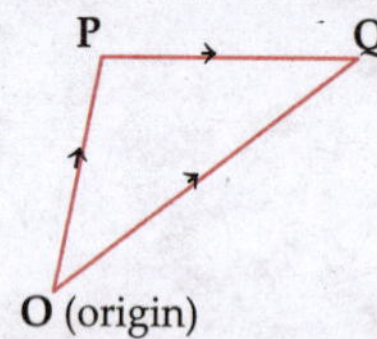

i.e. $\mathbf{PQ} = \text{PV of } \mathbf{Q} - \text{PV of } \mathbf{P}$

Collinear Points

Let A, B and C be any three points.

Points A, B and C are collinear $\Leftrightarrow$ **AB, BC** are collinear vectors $\Leftrightarrow$ $\mathbf{AB} = \lambda\mathbf{BC}$ for some non-zero scalar λ.

Components of a Vector

1. **In two-dimension** Let $P(x,y)$ be any point in a plane and O be the origin. Let $\hat{\mathbf{i}}$ and $\hat{\mathbf{j}}$ be the unit vectors along X and Y-axes, then the component of vector P is $\mathbf{OP} = x\hat{\mathbf{i}} + y\hat{\mathbf{j}}$.
2. **In three-dimension** Let $P(x,y,z)$ be any point in a space and O be the origin. Let $\hat{\mathbf{i}}$, $\hat{\mathbf{j}}$ and $\hat{\mathbf{k}}$ be the unit vectors along X, Y and Z-axes, then the component of vector P is $\mathbf{OP} = x\hat{\mathbf{i}} + y\hat{\mathbf{j}} + z\hat{\mathbf{k}}$.

Vector Joining Two Points

Let $P_1(x_1, y_1, z_1)$ and $P_2(x_2, y_2, z_2)$ be any two points, then the vector joining P_1 and P_2 is the vector $\mathbf{P_1P_2}$.

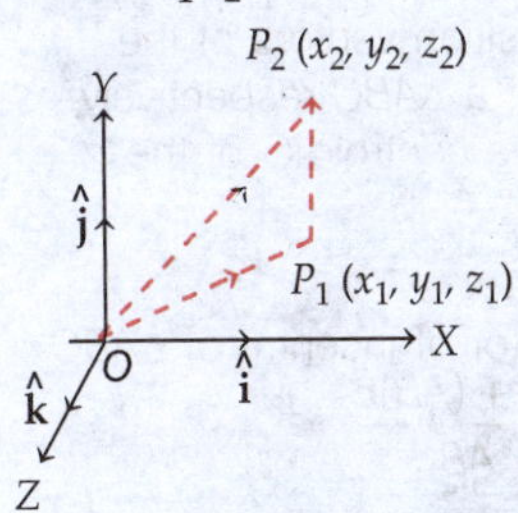

The position vectors of P_1 and P_2 with respect to the origin O are

$$\mathbf{OP_1} = x_1\hat{\mathbf{i}} + y_1\hat{\mathbf{j}} + z_1\hat{\mathbf{k}} \text{ and } \mathbf{OP_2} = x_2\hat{\mathbf{i}} + y_2\hat{\mathbf{j}} + z_2\hat{\mathbf{k}}$$

Then, the component form of $\mathbf{P_1P_2}$ is

$$\mathbf{P_1P_2} = (x_2\hat{\mathbf{i}} + y_2\hat{\mathbf{j}} + z_2\hat{\mathbf{k}}) - (x_1\hat{\mathbf{i}} + y_1\hat{\mathbf{j}} + z_1\hat{\mathbf{k}})$$
$$= (x_2 - x_1)\hat{\mathbf{i}} + (y_2 - y_1)\hat{\mathbf{j}} + (z_2 - z_1)\hat{\mathbf{k}}$$

Here, vector component of $\mathbf{P_1P_2}$ are $(x_2 - x_1)\hat{\mathbf{i}}$, $(y_2 - y_1)\hat{\mathbf{j}}$ and $(z_2 - z_1)\hat{\mathbf{k}}$ along X-axis, Y-axis and Z-axis, respectively.

Its magnitude is $|\mathbf{P_1P_2}| = \sqrt{(x_2 - x_1)^2 + (y_2 - y_1)^2 + (z_2 - z_1)^2}$

Section Formulae

Let A and B be two points with position vectors $\mathbf{a}$ and $\mathbf{b}$, respectively and $\mathbf{OP} = \mathbf{r}$.

(i) **Internal division** Let P be a point dividing AB internally in the ratio $m:n$. Then, position vector of P is

$$\mathbf{OP} = \frac{m\,\mathbf{OB} + n\,\mathbf{OA}}{(m+n)}$$

i.e. $$\mathbf{r} = \frac{m\mathbf{b} + n\mathbf{a}}{m+n}$$

(ii) **External division** Let P be a point dividing AB externally in the ratio $m:n$. Then, position vector of P is

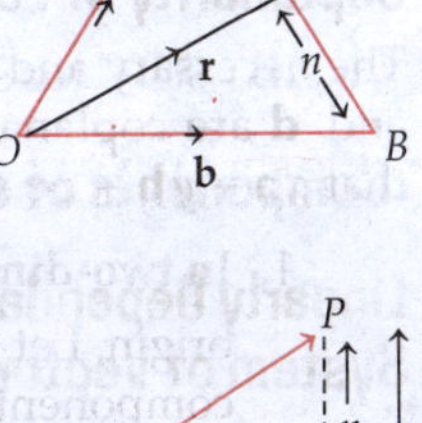

$$\mathbf{OP} = \frac{m\mathbf{OB} - n\mathbf{OA}}{m-n}$$

i.e. $$\mathbf{r} = \frac{m\mathbf{b} - n\mathbf{a}}{m-n}.$$

Value Points

- The position vector of the mid-point of $\mathbf{a}$ and $\mathbf{b}$ is $\dfrac{\mathbf{a}+\mathbf{b}}{2}$.
- Let $\mathbf{a}, \mathbf{b}, \mathbf{c}$ be position vectors of the vertices A, B, C of a ΔABC respectively, then the PV of the centroid G of the triangle is $\dfrac{\mathbf{a}+\mathbf{b}+\mathbf{c}}{3}$.
- The position vector of incentre of ΔABC is $\dfrac{(BC)\,\mathbf{a}+(CA)\mathbf{b}+(AB)\mathbf{c}}{BC+CA+AB}$

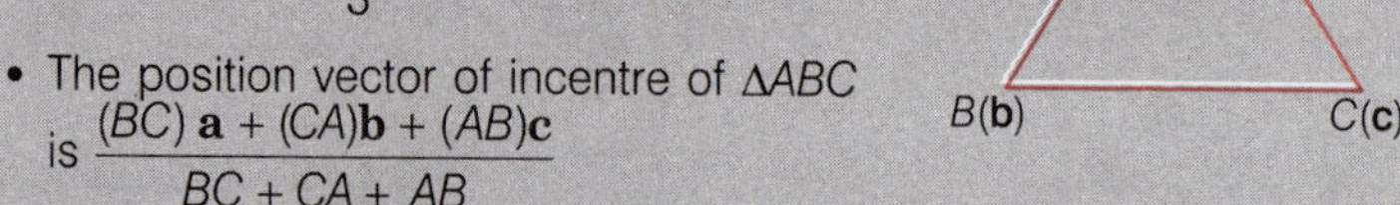

- The position vector of orthocentre of ΔABC is
$$\frac{\mathbf{a}(\tan A)+\mathbf{b}(\tan B)+\mathbf{c}(\tan C)}{\tan A+\tan B+\tan C}$$
- The position vector of circumcentre of ΔABC is
$$\frac{\mathbf{a}(\sin 2A)+\mathbf{b}(\sin 2B)+\mathbf{c}(\sin 2C)}{\sin 2A+\sin 2B+\sin 2C}$$

Linear Combination of Vectors

Let $\mathbf{a}, \mathbf{b}, \mathbf{c}, \ldots$ be vectors and $x, y, z, \ldots$ be scalars, then the expression $x\mathbf{a}+y\mathbf{b}+z\mathbf{c}+\ldots$ is called a linear combination of vectors $\mathbf{a}, \mathbf{b}, \mathbf{c}, \ldots$.

Collinearity of Three Points

The necessary and sufficient condition that three points with PV's $\mathbf{a}, \mathbf{b}, \mathbf{c}$ are collinear, if there exist three scalars x, y, z not all zero such that $x\mathbf{a}+y\mathbf{b}+z\mathbf{c}=\mathbf{0} \Rightarrow x+y+z=0$.

Coplanarity of Four Points

The necessary and sufficient condition that four points with PV's $\mathbf{a}, \mathbf{b}, \mathbf{c}$ and $\mathbf{d}$ are coplanar, if there exist scalar x, y, z and t not all zero, such that $x\mathbf{a}+y\mathbf{b}+z\mathbf{c}+t\mathbf{d}=0 \Leftrightarrow x+y+z+t=0$.

Linearly Dependent and Independent System of Vectors

(i) The system of vectors $\mathbf{a}, \mathbf{b}, \mathbf{c}, \ldots$ is said to be **linearly dependent**, if there exists some scalars x, y, z, ... not all zero, such that $x\mathbf{a}+y\mathbf{b}+z\mathbf{c}+\ldots=\mathbf{0}$.

(ii) The system of vectors $\mathbf{a}, \mathbf{b}, \mathbf{c}, \ldots$ is said to be **linearly independent**, if $x\mathbf{a}+y\mathbf{b}+z\mathbf{c}+t\mathbf{d}=\mathbf{0} \Rightarrow x=y=z=t\ldots=0$.

Value Points

- Two non-zero, non-collinear vectors **a** and **b** are linearly independent.
- Three non-zero, non-coplanar vectors **a**, **b** and **c** are linearly independent.
- More than three vectors are always linearly dependent.

Scalar or Dot Product of Two Vectors

If **a** and **b** are two non-zero vectors, then the scalar or dot product of **a** and **b** is denoted by $\mathbf{a}\cdot\mathbf{b}$ and is defined as

$$\mathbf{a}\cdot\mathbf{b} = |\mathbf{a}||\mathbf{b}|\cos\theta,$$

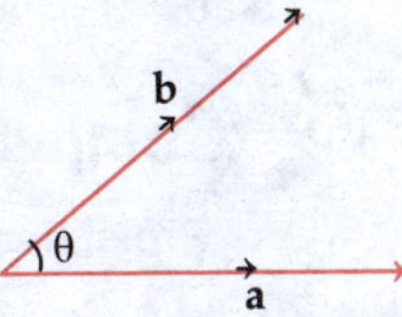

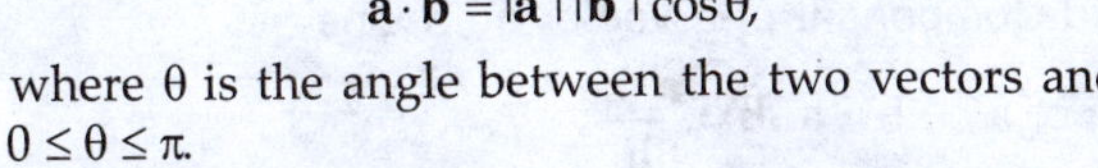

where θ is the angle between the two vectors and $0 \le \theta \le \pi$.

Important Points

(i) Angle between two like vectors is 0 and angle between two unlike vectors is π.

EXPERT Scale Up

The angle between **a** and **b** is acute if $a\cdot b > 0$ and if $a\cdot b < 0$, then the angle between **a** and **b** is obtuse.

(ii) If either **a** or **b** is the null vector, then scalar product of the vector is zero.

(iii) If **a** and **b** are two unit vectors, then $\mathbf{a}\cdot\mathbf{b} = \cos\theta$.

(iv) The scalar product is commutative i.e. $\mathbf{a}\cdot\mathbf{b} = \mathbf{b}\cdot\mathbf{a}$

(v) If $\hat{\mathbf{i}}$, $\hat{\mathbf{j}}$ and $\hat{\mathbf{k}}$ are mutually perpendicular unit vectors then

$$\hat{\mathbf{i}}\cdot\hat{\mathbf{i}} = \hat{\mathbf{j}}\cdot\hat{\mathbf{j}} = \hat{\mathbf{k}}\cdot\hat{\mathbf{k}} = 1 \text{ and } \hat{\mathbf{i}}\cdot\hat{\mathbf{j}} = \hat{\mathbf{j}}\cdot\hat{\mathbf{k}} = \hat{\mathbf{k}}\cdot\hat{\mathbf{i}} = 0$$

(vi) The scalar product of vectors is distributive over vector addition.

(a) $\mathbf{a}\cdot(\mathbf{b}+\mathbf{c}) = \mathbf{a}\cdot\mathbf{b} + \mathbf{a}\cdot\mathbf{c}$ (left distributive)

(b) $(\mathbf{b}+\mathbf{c})\cdot\mathbf{a} = \mathbf{b}\cdot\mathbf{a} + \mathbf{c}\cdot\mathbf{a}$ (right distributive)

(vii) $(m\mathbf{a})\cdot(\mathbf{b}) = m(\mathbf{a}\cdot\mathbf{b}) = \mathbf{a}\cdot(m\mathbf{b})$, where m is any scalar.

(viii) If $\mathbf{a} = a_1\hat{\mathbf{i}} + a_2\hat{\mathbf{j}} + a_3\hat{\mathbf{k}}$, then $|\mathbf{a}|^2 = \mathbf{a}\cdot\mathbf{a} = a_1^2 + a_2^2 + a_3^2$ or $|\mathbf{a}| = \sqrt{a_1^2 + a_2^2 + a_3^2}$

(ix) **Angle between Two Vectors** If θ is angle between two non-zero vectors, **a** and **b**, then we have

$$\mathbf{a} \cdot \mathbf{b} = |\mathbf{a}||\mathbf{b}| \cos\theta \text{ or } \cos\theta = \frac{\mathbf{a}\cdot\mathbf{b}}{|\mathbf{a}||\mathbf{b}|}$$

If $\mathbf{a} = a_1\hat{\mathbf{i}} + a_2\hat{\mathbf{j}} + a_3\hat{\mathbf{k}}$ and $\mathbf{b} = b_1\hat{\mathbf{i}} + b_2\hat{\mathbf{j}} + b_3\hat{\mathbf{k}}$

Then, the angle θ between $\mathbf{a}$ and $\mathbf{b}$ is given by

$$\cos\theta = \frac{\mathbf{a}\cdot\mathbf{b}}{|\mathbf{a}||\mathbf{b}|} = \frac{a_1b_1 + a_2b_2 + a_3b_3}{\sqrt{a_1^2 + a_2^2 + a_3^2}\sqrt{b_1^2 + b_2^2 + b_3^2}}$$

(x) **Condition of perpendicularity**
$\mathbf{a} \cdot \mathbf{b} = 0 \Leftrightarrow \mathbf{a} \perp \mathbf{b}$, $\mathbf{a}$ and $\mathbf{b}$ being non-zero vectors.

Competition Insight

(i) **Projection and Component of a Vector on a Line**

The projection of $\mathbf{a}$ on $\mathbf{b} = \mathbf{a}\cdot\hat{\mathbf{b}} = \dfrac{\mathbf{a}\cdot\mathbf{b}}{|\mathbf{b}|}$

The projection of $\mathbf{b}$ on $\mathbf{a} = \mathbf{b}\cdot\hat{\mathbf{a}} = \dfrac{\mathbf{a}\cdot\mathbf{b}}{|\mathbf{a}|}$

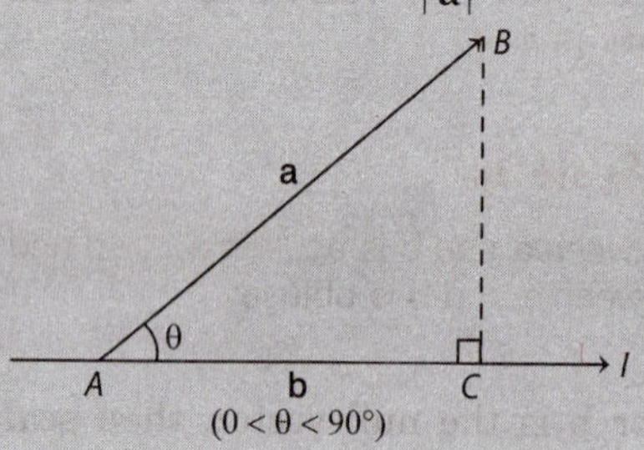

Components of $\mathbf{a}$ along and perpendicular to $\mathbf{b}$ are

$$\frac{\mathbf{a}\cdot\mathbf{b}}{|\mathbf{b}|}\cdot\mathbf{b} \text{ and } \mathbf{a} - \frac{\mathbf{a}\cdot\mathbf{b}}{|\mathbf{b}|^2}\cdot\mathbf{b}, \text{ respectively.}$$

(ii) **Work done by Force** The work done by force is a scalar quantity equal to the product of the magnitude of the force and the resolved part of the displacement.

$\therefore$ $\mathbf{F}\cdot\mathbf{S}$ = dot products of force and displacement.

Suppose $\mathbf{F}_1, \mathbf{F}_2, \ldots, \mathbf{F}_n$ are n forces acted on a particle, then during the displacement $\mathbf{S}$ of the particle, the separate forces to quantities of work $\mathbf{F}_1\cdot\mathbf{S}, \mathbf{F}_2\cdot\mathbf{S}, \ldots, \mathbf{F}_n\cdot\mathbf{S}$.

The total work done is $\displaystyle\sum_{i=1}^{n} \mathbf{F}_i\cdot\mathbf{S} = \sum_{i=1}^{n} \mathbf{S}\cdot\mathbf{F}_i = \mathbf{S}\cdot\mathbf{R}$

Here, system of forces were replaced by its resultant $\mathbf{R}$.

Important Points

(i) $(\mathbf{a}+\mathbf{b})\cdot(\mathbf{a}-\mathbf{b}) = |\mathbf{a}|^2 - |\mathbf{b}|^2$

(ii) $|\mathbf{a}+\mathbf{b}|^2 = |\mathbf{a}|^2 + |\mathbf{b}|^2 + 2(\mathbf{a}\cdot\mathbf{b})$

(iii) $|\mathbf{a}-\mathbf{b}|^2 = |\mathbf{a}|^2 + |\mathbf{b}|^2 - 2(\mathbf{a}\cdot\mathbf{b})$

(iv) $|\mathbf{a}+\mathbf{b}|^2 + |\mathbf{a}-\mathbf{b}|^2 = 2(|\mathbf{a}|^2 + |\mathbf{b}|^2)$

and $|\mathbf{a}+\mathbf{b}|^2 - |\mathbf{a}-\mathbf{b}|^2 = 4(\mathbf{a}\cdot\mathbf{b})$

or $\mathbf{a}\cdot\mathbf{b} = \frac{1}{4}[|\mathbf{a}+\mathbf{b}|^2 - |\mathbf{a}-\mathbf{b}|^2]$

(v) If $|\mathbf{a}+\mathbf{b}| = |\mathbf{a}| + |\mathbf{b}|$, then **a** is parallel to **b**.

(vi) If $|\mathbf{a}+\mathbf{b}| = |\mathbf{a}-\mathbf{b}|$, then **a** is perpendicular to **b**.

(vii) $(\mathbf{a}\cdot\mathbf{b})^2 \le |\mathbf{a}|^2\,|\mathbf{b}|^2$

Vector or Cross Product of Two Vectors

The vector product of the vectors **a** and **b** is denoted by $\mathbf{a}\times\mathbf{b}$ and it is defined as

$$\mathbf{a}\times\mathbf{b} = (|\mathbf{a}||\mathbf{b}|\sin\theta)\,\hat{\mathbf{n}} = ab\sin\theta\,\hat{\mathbf{n}} \quad \text{...(i)}$$

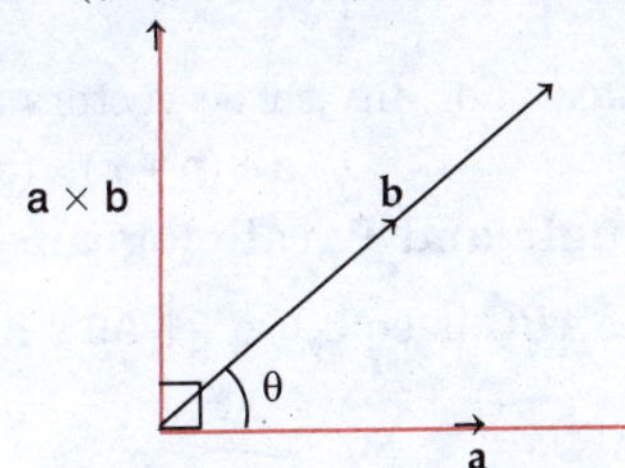

where $a = |\mathbf{a}|$, $b = |\mathbf{b}|$ and θ is the angle between the vectors **a** and **b** and $\hat{\mathbf{n}}$ is a unit vector which is perpendicular to both **a** and **b**.

Important Points

(i) Let $\mathbf{a} = a_1\hat{\mathbf{i}} + a_2\hat{\mathbf{j}} + a_3\hat{\mathbf{k}}$ and $\mathbf{b} = b_1\hat{\mathbf{i}} + b_2\hat{\mathbf{j}} + b_3\hat{\mathbf{k}}$

Then, $$\mathbf{a}\times\mathbf{b} = \begin{vmatrix} \hat{\mathbf{i}} & \hat{\mathbf{j}} & \hat{\mathbf{k}} \\ a_1 & a_2 & a_3 \\ b_1 & b_2 & b_3 \end{vmatrix}$$

(ii) If $\mathbf{a} = \mathbf{b}$ or if **a** is parallel to **b**, then $\sin\theta = 0$ and so $\mathbf{a}\times\mathbf{b} = \mathbf{0}$.

(iii) The direction of $\mathbf{a}\times\mathbf{b}$ is regarded positive, if the rotation from **a** to **b** appears to be anti-clockwise.

(iv) $\mathbf{a} \times \mathbf{b}$ is perpendicular to the plane, which contains both $\mathbf{a}$ and $\mathbf{b}$. Thus, the unit vector perpendicular to both $\mathbf{a}$ and $\mathbf{b}$ or to the plane is given by $\hat{\mathbf{n}} = \dfrac{\mathbf{a} \times \mathbf{b}}{|\mathbf{a} \times \mathbf{b}|} = \dfrac{\mathbf{a} \times \mathbf{b}}{ab \sin \theta}$.

(v) Vector product of two parallel or collinear vectors is zero.

(vi) If $\mathbf{a} \times \mathbf{b} = \mathbf{0}$, then $\mathbf{a} = \mathbf{0}$ or $\mathbf{b} = \mathbf{0}$ or $\mathbf{a}$ and $\mathbf{b}$ are parallel or collinear.

(vii) **Vector Product of Two Perpendicular Vectors**
If $\theta = 90°$, then $\sin \theta = 1$, i.e. $\mathbf{a} \times \mathbf{b} = (ab)\hat{\mathbf{n}}$ or $|\mathbf{a} \times \mathbf{b}| = |ab\hat{\mathbf{n}}| = ab$
$[\because |\mathbf{a}| = a \text{ and } |\mathbf{b}| = b]$

(viii) **Vector Product of Two Unit Vectors** If $\mathbf{a}$ and $\mathbf{b}$ are unit vectors, then

$$a = |\mathbf{a}| = 1, b = |\mathbf{b}| = 1$$

$$\therefore \mathbf{a} \times \mathbf{b} = ab \sin \theta \cdot \hat{\mathbf{n}} = (\sin \theta) \cdot \hat{\mathbf{n}}$$

(ix) **Vector Product is not Commutative** The two vector products $\mathbf{a} \times \mathbf{b}$ and $\mathbf{b} \times \mathbf{a}$ are equal in magnitude but opposite in direction.

i.e. $$\mathbf{b} \times \mathbf{a} = -\mathbf{a} \times \mathbf{b} \quad \text{...(i)}$$

(x) **Distributive Law** For any three vectors $\mathbf{a}, \mathbf{b}, \mathbf{c}$

$$\mathbf{a} \times (\mathbf{b} + \mathbf{c}) = (\mathbf{a} \times \mathbf{b}) + (\mathbf{a} \times \mathbf{c})$$

(xi) **Area of a Triangle and Parallelogram**

(a) The area of ΔABC is equal to $\frac{1}{2}|\mathbf{AB} \times \mathbf{AC}|$ or $\frac{1}{2}|\mathbf{BC} \times \mathbf{BA}|$ or $\frac{1}{2}|\mathbf{CB} \times \mathbf{CA}|$.

(b) The area of ΔABC with vertices having PV's $\mathbf{a}, \mathbf{b}, \mathbf{c}$ respectively, is $1/2|\mathbf{a} \times \mathbf{b} + \mathbf{b} \times \mathbf{c} + \mathbf{c} \times \mathbf{a}|$.

(c) The points whose PV's $\mathbf{a}, \mathbf{b}$ and $\mathbf{c}$ are collinear, if and only if $\mathbf{a} \times \mathbf{b} + \mathbf{b} \times \mathbf{c} + \mathbf{c} \times \mathbf{a} = \mathbf{0}$.

(d) The area of a parallelogram with adjacent sides $\mathbf{a}$ and $\mathbf{b}$ is $|\mathbf{a} \times \mathbf{b}|$.

(e) The area of a parallelogram with diagonals $\mathbf{a}$ and $\mathbf{b}$ is $\frac{1}{2}|\mathbf{a} \times \mathbf{b}|$.

(f) The area of a quadrilateral $ABCD$ is equal to $\frac{1}{2}|\mathbf{AC} \times \mathbf{BD}|$.

Competition Insight

Vector Moment of a Force about a Point The vector moment of torque **M** of a force **F** about the point O is the vector whose magnitude is equal to the product of **F** and the perpendicular distance of the point O from the line of action of **F**.

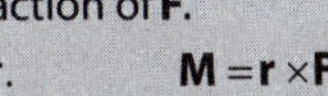

$$\therefore \quad \mathbf{M} = \mathbf{r} \times \mathbf{F}$$

where **r** is the position vector of A referred to O.

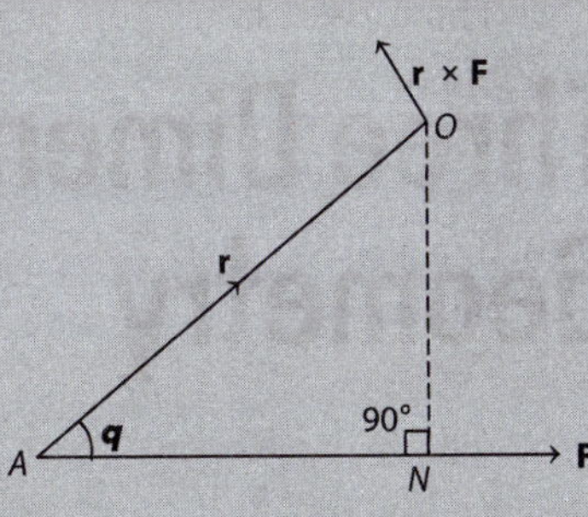

(a) The moment of force **F** about O is independent of the choice of point A on the line of action of **F**.

(b) If several forces are acting through the same point A, then the vector sum of the moments of the separate forces about a point O is equal to the moment of their resultant force about O.

The Moment of a Force about a Line Let **F** be a force acting at a point A, O be any point on the given line l and **a** be the unit vector along the line, then moment of **F** about the line l is a scalar given by $(\mathbf{OA} \times \mathbf{F}) \cdot \mathbf{a}$.

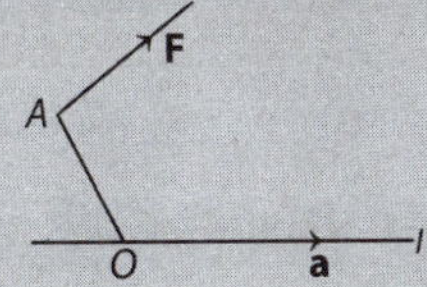

Moment of a Couple

(a) Two equal and unlike parallel forces whose lines of action are different is said to constitute a couple.

(b) Let P and Q be any two points on the lines of action of the forces $-\mathbf{F}$ and $\mathbf{F}$, respectively.

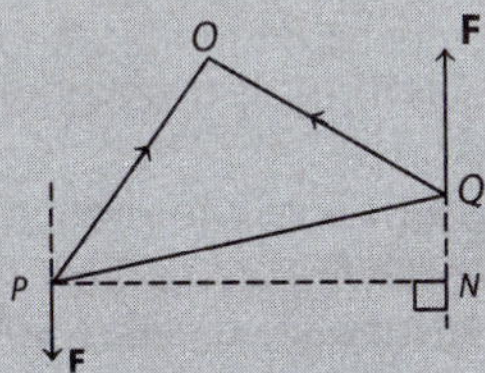

The moment of the couple $= \mathbf{PQ} \times \mathbf{F}$

Chapter 28

Three Dimensional Geometry

Coordinate System

The three mutually perpendicular lines in a space which divides the space into eight parts and if these perpendicular lines are the coordinate axes, then it is said to be a coordinate system.

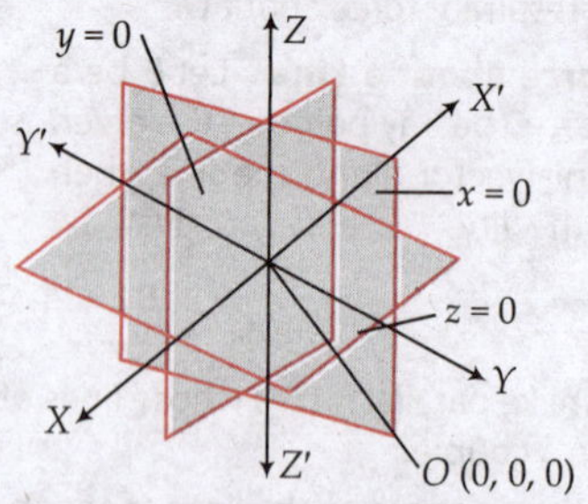

Value Point

The coordinates of any point on the X, Y and Z-axes will be of the form $(x, 0, 0)$, $(0, y, 0)$ and $(0, 0, z)$, respectively.

Octant Coordinate	x	y	z
$OXYZ$	+	+	+
$OX'YZ$	−	+	+
$OXY'Z$	+	−	+
$OXYZ'$	+	+	−
$OX'Y'Z$	−	−	+
$OX'YZ'$	−	+	−
$OXY'Z'$	+	−	−
$OX'Y'Z'$	−	−	−

Distance between Two Points

Let $P(x_1, y_1, z_1)$ and $Q(x_2, y_2, z_2)$ be two given points. Then, distance between these points is given by

$$PQ = \sqrt{(x_2 - x_1)^2 + (y_2 - y_1)^2 + (z_2 - z_1)^2}$$

The distance of a point $P(x, y, z)$ from origin O is

$$OP = \sqrt{x^2 + y^2 + z^2}$$

Section Formulae

(i) The coordinates of any point, which divides the join of points $P(x_1, y_1, z_1)$ and $Q(x_2, y_2, z_2)$ in the ratio $m : n$ internally are

$$\left(\frac{mx_2 + nx_1}{m+n}, \frac{my_2 + ny_1}{m+n}, \frac{mz_2 + nz_1}{m+n}\right)$$

(ii) The coordinates of any point, which divides the join of points $P(x_1, y_1, z_1)$ and $Q(x_2, y_2, z_2)$ in the ratio $m : n$ externally are

$$\left(\frac{mx_2 - nx_1}{m-n}, \frac{my_2 - ny_1}{m-n}, \frac{mz_2 - mz_1}{m-n}\right)$$

(iii) The coordinates of mid-point of P and Q are

$$\left(\frac{x_1 + x_2}{2}, \frac{y_1 + y_2}{2}, \frac{z_1 + z_2}{2}\right)$$

(iv) Coordinates of the centroid of a triangle formed with vertices $P(x_1, y_1, z_1)$, $Q(x_2, y_2, z_2)$ and $R(x_3, y_3, z_3)$ are

$$\left(\frac{x_1 + x_2 + x_3}{3}, \frac{y_1 + y_2 + y_3}{3}, \frac{z_1 + z_2 + z_3}{3}\right)$$

(v) **Centroid of a Tetrahedron**

If (x_1, y_1, z_1), (x_2, y_2, z_2), (x_3, y_3, z_3) and (x_4, y_4, z_4) are the vertices of a tetrahedron, then its centroid G is given by

$$\left(\frac{x_1 + x_2 + x_3 + x_4}{4}, \frac{y_1 + y_2 + y_3 + y_4}{4}, \frac{z_1 + z_2 + z_3 + z_4}{4}\right).$$

Area of Triangle

If the vertices of a triangle are $A(x_1, y_1, z_1)$, $B(x_2, y_2, z_2)$ and $C(x_3, y_3, z_3)$, then

Area of $\Delta ABC = \sqrt{\Delta_{xy}^2 + \Delta_{yz}^2 + \Delta_{zx}^2}$,

where $\Delta_{yz} = \frac{1}{2}\begin{vmatrix} y_1 & z_1 & 1 \\ y_2 & z_2 & 1 \\ y_3 & z_3 & 1 \end{vmatrix}$, $\Delta_{xz} = \frac{1}{2}\begin{vmatrix} x_1 & z_1 & 1 \\ x_2 & z_2 & 1 \\ x_3 & z_3 & 1 \end{vmatrix}$ and $\Delta_{xy} = \frac{1}{2}\begin{vmatrix} x_1 & y_1 & 1 \\ x_2 & y_2 & 1 \\ x_3 & y_3 & 1 \end{vmatrix}$

Direction Cosines

If a directed line segment OP makes angle α, β and γ with OX, OY and OZ respectively, then $\cos\alpha$, $\cos\beta$ and $\cos\gamma$ are called direction cosines of OP and it is represented by l, m, n.

i.e. $l = \cos\alpha$, $m = \cos\beta$ and $n = \cos\gamma$

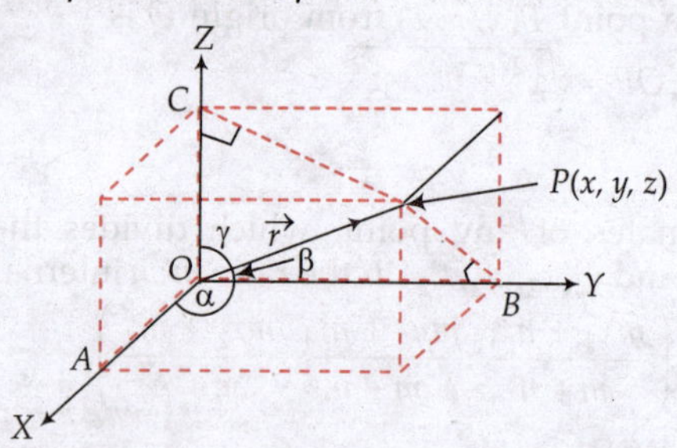

If $OP = r$, then coordinates of OP are (lr, mr, nr)

Angle between Two Intersecting Lines

If l_1, m_1, n_1 and l_2, m_2, n_2 are the direction cosines of two given lines, then the angle θ between them is given by

$$\cos\theta = l_1 l_2 + m_1 m_2 + n_1 n_2$$

(i) The angle between any two diagonals of a cube is $\cos^{-1}\left(\frac{1}{3}\right)$.

(ii) The angle between a diagonal of a cube and the diagonal of a face of the cube is $\cos^{-1}\left(\sqrt{\frac{2}{3}}\right)$.

Value Points

- If l, m, n are direction cosines of a vector $\mathbf{r}$, then
  (a) $\mathbf{r} = |\mathbf{r}|(l\hat{\mathbf{i}} + m\hat{\mathbf{j}} + n\hat{\mathbf{k}}) \Rightarrow \hat{\mathbf{r}} = l\hat{\mathbf{i}} + m\hat{\mathbf{j}} + n\hat{\mathbf{k}}$
  (b) $l^2 + m^2 + n^2 = 1$
  (c) Projections of $\mathbf{r}$ on the coordinate axes are
  $$l|\mathbf{r}|, m|\mathbf{r}|, n|\mathbf{r}|$$
  (d) $|\mathbf{r}| = \sqrt{\text{sum of the squares of projections of } \mathbf{r} \text{ on the coordinate axes}}$
- If $P(x_1, y_1, z_1)$ and $Q(x_2, y_2, z_2)$ are two points such that the direction cosines of **PQ** are l, m, n. Then,
  $$x_2 - x_1 = l|\mathbf{PQ}|, \ y_2 - y_1 = m|\mathbf{PQ}|, \ z_2 - z_1 = n|\mathbf{PQ}|$$
  These are projections of **PQ** on X, Y and Z-axes, respectively.

- If l, m, n are direction cosines of a vector $\mathbf{r}$ and a, b, c are three numbers, such that $\frac{l}{a} = \frac{m}{b} = \frac{n}{c}$. Then, we say that a, b and c are the direction ratios of $\mathbf{r}$ which are proportional to l, m, n.
  Also, we have $l = \pm \frac{a}{\sqrt{a^2 + b^2 + c^2}}$, $m = \pm \frac{b}{\sqrt{a^2 + b^2 + c^2}}$ and
  $$n = \pm \frac{c}{\sqrt{a^2 + b^2 + c^2}}$$
- If θ is the angle between two lines having direction cosines l_1, m_1, n_1 and l_2, m_2, n_2, then $\cos \theta = l_1 l_2 + m_1 m_2 + n_1 n_2$
  (a) Lines are parallel, if $\frac{l_1}{l_2} = \frac{m_1}{m_2} = \frac{n_1}{n_2}$.
  (b) Lines are perpendicular, if $l_1 l_2 + m_1 m_2 + n_1 n_2 = 0$.
- If θ is the angle between two lines whose direction ratios are proportional to a_1, b_1, c_1 and a_2, b_2, c_2 respectively, then the angle θ between them is given by
  $$\cos \theta = \frac{a_1 a_2 + b_1 b_2 + c_1 c_2}{\sqrt{a_1^2 + b_1^2 + c_1^2} \sqrt{a_2^2 + b_2^2 + c_2^2}}.$$
  (a) Lines are parallel, if $\frac{a_1}{a_2} = \frac{b_1}{b_2} = \frac{c_1}{c_2}$.
  (b) Lines are perpendicular, if $a_1 a_2 + b_1 b_2 + c_1 c_2 = 0$.
- The projection of the line segment joining points $P(x_1, y_1, z_1)$ and $Q(x_2, y_2, z_2)$ to the line having direction cosines l, m, n is $|(x_2 - x_1) l + (y_2 - y_1) m + (z_2 - z_1) n|$.
- The direction ratio of the line passing through points $P(x_1, y_1, z_1)$ and $Q(x_2, y_2, z_2)$ are proportional to $x_2 - x_1, y_2 - y_1, z_2 - z_1$. Then, direction cosines of $\mathbf{PQ}$ are $\frac{x_2 - x_1}{|\mathbf{PQ}|}, \frac{y_2 - y_1}{|\mathbf{PQ}|}, \frac{z_2 - z_1}{|\mathbf{PQ}|}$

Line in Space

A line (or straight line) is a curve such that all the points on the line segment joining any two points of it lies on it.

A line can be determined uniquely, if

(i) its direction and the coordinates of a point on it are known.

(ii) it passes through two given points.

1. **Equation of a Line Passing through a given Point and Parallel to a given Vector**

   Vector Equation Equation of a line passing through a point with position vector **a** and parallel to vector **b** is
   $\mathbf{r} = \mathbf{a} + \lambda\, \mathbf{b}$, where λ is a parameter.

   Cartesian Equation Equation of a line passing through a fixed point $A(x_1, y_1, z_1)$ and having direction ratios a, b, c is given by
   $\frac{x - x_1}{a} = \frac{y - y_1}{b} = \frac{z - z_1}{c}$, it is also called the **symmetrically** form of a line.

2. **Equation of Line Passing through Two given Points**

   Vector Equation A line passing through two given points having position vectors **a** and **b** is
   $\mathbf{r} = \mathbf{a} + \lambda(\mathbf{b} - \mathbf{a})$, where λ is a parameter.

   Cartesian Equation Equation of a straight line joining two fixed points $A(x_1, y_1, z_1)$ and $B(x_2, y_2, z_2)$ is given by

   $$\frac{x - x_1}{x_2 - x_1} = \frac{y - y_1}{y_2 - y_1} = \frac{z - z_1}{z_2 - z_1}$$

3. **Perpendicular Distance of a Point from a Line**

   Vector form The length of the perpendicular from a point $P(\vec{\alpha})$ on the line $\mathbf{r} = \mathbf{a} + \lambda\mathbf{b}$ is given by $\sqrt{|\vec{\alpha} - \mathbf{a}|^2 - \left\{\frac{(\vec{\alpha} - \mathbf{a}) \cdot \mathbf{b}}{|\mathbf{b}|}\right\}^2}$

   Cartesian Form The length of the perpendicular from a point $P(x_1, y_1, z_1)$ on the line $\frac{x - a}{l} = \frac{y - b}{m} = \frac{z - c}{n}$ is given by

   $$\sqrt{\{(a - x_1)^2 + (b - y_1)^2 + (c - z_1)^2\} - \{(a - x_1)\,l + (b - y_1)\,m + (c - z_1)\,n\}^2},$$

   where l, m and n are direction cosines of the line.

Skew Lines

Two straight lines in space are said to be skew lines, if they are neither parallel nor intersecting. Thus, skew-lines are such pair of lines which are non-coplanar.

Shortest Distance between two Lines

If l_1 and l_2 are two skew lines, then a line perpendicular to each of lines l_1 and l_2 is known as the line of shortest distance.

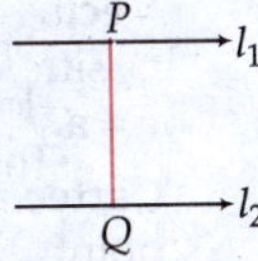

If the line of shortest distance intersects the lines l_1 and l_2 at P and Q respectively, then the distance PQ between points P and Q is known as the shortest distance between l_1 and l_2.

Vector Form

(i) The shortest distance between lines $\mathbf{r} = \mathbf{a}_1 + \lambda\mathbf{b}_1$ and $\mathbf{r} = \mathbf{a}_2 + \mu\mathbf{b}_2$ is given by

$$d = \left| \frac{(\mathbf{b}_1 \times \mathbf{b}_2)\cdot(\mathbf{a}_2 - \mathbf{a}_1)}{|\mathbf{b}_1 \times \mathbf{b}_2|} \right|$$

(ii) The shortest distance between parallel lines $\mathbf{r} = \mathbf{a}_1 + \lambda\mathbf{b}$ and $\mathbf{r} = \mathbf{a}_2 + \mu\mathbf{b}$ is given by

$$d = \left| \frac{(\mathbf{a}_2 - \mathbf{a}_1) \times \mathbf{b}}{|\mathbf{b}|} \right|$$

(iii) Two lines $\mathbf{r} = \mathbf{a}_1 + \lambda\mathbf{b}_1$ and $\mathbf{r} = \mathbf{a}_2 + \mu\mathbf{b}_2$ are intersecting, when $(\mathbf{b}_1 \times \mathbf{b}_2)\cdot(\mathbf{a}_2 - \mathbf{a}_1) = 0$.

Cartesian Form

(i) The shortest distance between the lines

$$\frac{x - x_1}{a_1} = \frac{y - y_1}{b_1} = \frac{z - z_1}{c_1}$$

and $$\frac{x - x_2}{a_2} = \frac{y - y_2}{b_2} = \frac{z - z_2}{c_2}$$ is given by

$$d = \frac{\begin{vmatrix} x_2 - x_1 & y_2 - y_1 & z_2 - z_1 \\ a_1 & b_1 & c_1 \\ a_2 & b_2 & c_2 \end{vmatrix}}{\sqrt{(a_1b_2 - a_2b_1)^2 + (b_1c_2 - b_2c_1)^2 + (c_1a_2 - c_2a_1)^2}}$$

(ii) Two lines $\frac{x - x_1}{a_1} = \frac{y - y_1}{b_1} = \frac{z - z_1}{c_1}$ and $\frac{x - x_2}{a_2} = \frac{y - y_2}{b_2} = \frac{z - z_2}{c_2}$ are intersecting, when

$$\begin{vmatrix} x_2 - x_1 & y_2 - y_1 & z_2 - z_1 \\ a_1 & b_1 & c_1 \\ a_2 & b_2 & c_2 \end{vmatrix} = 0$$

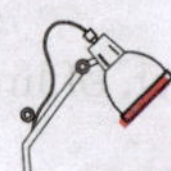

EXPERT Scale Up

Since, *X*, *Y* and *Z*-axes pass through the origin and have direction cosines (1, 0, 0), (0, 1, 0) and (0, 0, 1), respectively. Therefore, their equations are

$$X\text{-axis} \quad \frac{x-0}{1} = \frac{y-0}{0} = \frac{z-0}{0} \text{ or } y=0, z=0$$

$$Y\text{-axis} \quad \frac{x-0}{0} = \frac{y-0}{1} = \frac{z-0}{0} \text{ or } x=0, z=0$$

$$Z\text{-axis} \quad \frac{x-0}{0} = \frac{y-0}{0} = \frac{z-0}{1} \text{ or } x=0, y=0$$

Plane

A plane is a surface such that, if two points are taken on it, a straight line joining them lies completely on the surface. A straight line, which is perpendicular to every line lying on a plane is called a normal to the plane.

General Equation of the Plane

The general equation of the first degree in x, y, z always represents a plane. Hence, the general equation of the plane is $ax + by + cz + d = 0$. The coefficient of x, y and z in the cartesian equation of a plane are the direction ratios of normal to the plane.

Equation of Plane in Normal Form

Vector Form

The equation of plane having normal unit vector $\hat{\mathbf{n}}$ to the plane is $\mathbf{r} \cdot \hat{\mathbf{n}} = d$, where d is the perpendicular distance of the plane from origin and $\mathbf{r}$ is the position vector of any point P on the plane and $\hat{\mathbf{n}}$ is the unit normal vector.

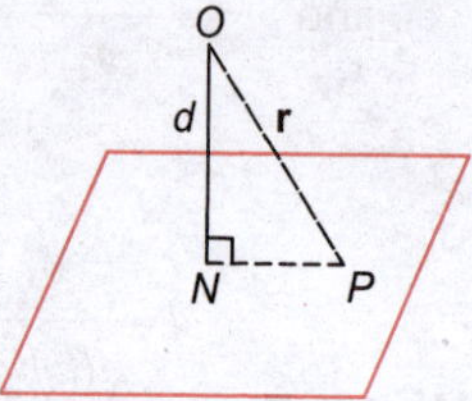

Cartesian Form

The equation of a plane, which is at a distance p from origin and the direction cosines of the normal from the origin to the plane are l, m, n, is given by $lx + my + nz = p$.

The coordinates of foot of perpendicular N from the origin on the plane are (lp, mp, np).

Equation of the Plane Passing Through a Fixed Point

Vector Form

The vector equation of a plane passing through a given point A with position vector $\mathbf{a}$ and perpendicular to a given vector $\mathbf{n}$ is $(\mathbf{r}-\mathbf{a})\mathbf{n}=0$.

Cartesian Form

The equation of a plane passing through a given point (x_1, y_1, z_1) is given by $a(x-x_1)+b(y-y_1)+c(z-z_1)=0$

where, a,b,c are direction ratios of normal to the plane.

Intercept Form

The intercept form of equation of plane represented in the form of

$$\frac{x}{a}+\frac{y}{b}+\frac{z}{c}=1$$

where, a, b and c are intercepts on X, Y and Z-axes, respectively.

For x intercept Put $y=0$, $z=0$ in the equation of the plane and obtain the value of x. Similarly, we can determine other intercepts.

There is no vector form of plane in intercept form.

Competition Insight

The image or reflection (x, y, z) of a point (x_1, y_1, z_1) in a plane $ax+by+cz+d=0$ is given by $\frac{x-x_1}{a}=\frac{y-y_1}{b}=\frac{z-z_1}{c}=\frac{-2(ax_1+by_1+cz_1+d)}{a^2+b^2+c^2}$

The foot (x, y, z) of a point (x_1, y_1, z_1) in a plane $ax+by+cz+d=0$ is given by

$$\frac{x-x_1}{a}=\frac{y-y_1}{b}=\frac{z-z_1}{c}=\frac{-(ax_1+by_1+cz_1+d)}{a^2+b^2+c^2}$$

Equation of Plane Passing Through Three Non-collinear Points

Vector Form

The equation of plane passing through three non-collinear points A, B and C with position vectors $\mathbf{a}$, $\mathbf{b}$ and $\mathbf{c}$ is

$$(\mathbf{r}-\mathbf{a})[(\mathbf{b}-\mathbf{a})\times(\mathbf{c}-\mathbf{a})]=0$$

where, $\mathbf{r}$ is the position vector of any point P on the plane.

Cartesian Form

The cartesian equation of a plane passing through three non-collinear points $A(x_1, y_1, z_1)$, $B(x_2, y_2, z_2)$ and $C(x_3, y_3, z_3)$ is

$$\begin{bmatrix} x-x_1 & y-y_1 & z-z_1 \\ x_2-x_1 & y_2-y_1 & z_2-z_1 \\ x_3-x_1 & y_3-y_1 & z_3-z_1 \end{bmatrix} = 0.$$

where, $P(x,y,z)$ is any point on the plane.

Equation of Plane Passing Through the Intersection of Two given Planes

Vector Form

The equation of plane passing through the intersection of the planes $\mathbf{r}\cdot\mathbf{n}_1 = d_1$ and $\mathbf{r}\cdot\mathbf{n}_2 = d_2$ is $\mathbf{r}\cdot(\mathbf{n}_1 + \lambda\mathbf{n}_2) = d_1 + \lambda d_2$, where λ is a scalar.

Cartesian Form

The carteian equation of plane passing through the intersection of two planes $a_1x + b_1 y + c_1 z - d_1$ and $a_2 x + b_2 y + c_2 z - d_2 = 0$ is
$(a_1 x + b_1 y + c_1 z - d_1) + \lambda(a_2 x + b_2 y + c_2 z - d_2) = 0$
or $x(a_1 + \lambda a_2) + y(b_1 + \lambda b_2) + z(c_1 + \lambda c_2) = d_1 + \lambda d_2$, where $\lambda \in R$.

Equation of a Plane Parallel to a Given Plane

Vector Form

The vector equation of a plane parallel to the given plane $\mathbf{r}.\mathbf{n} = d_1$ is $\mathbf{r}\cdot\mathbf{n} = d_2$.

Cartesian Form

The cartesian equation of a plane parallel to the given plane $ax + by + cz + d_1 = 0$ is $ax + by + cz + d_2 = 0$.

Value Points

- Equation of a plane passing through the point $A(x_1, y_1, z_1)$ and parallel to two given lines with direction ratios a_1, b_1, c_1 and a_2, b_2, c_2 is $\begin{vmatrix} x-x_1 & y-y_1 & z-z_1 \\ a_1 & b_1 & c_1 \\ a_2 & b_2 & c_2 \end{vmatrix} = 0.$
- Equation of a plane passing through two points $A(x_1, y_1, z_1)$ and $B(x_2, y_2, z_2)$ and parallel to a line with direction ratios a, b, c is
$$\begin{vmatrix} x-x_1 & y-y_1 & z-z_1 \\ x_2-x_1 & y_2-y_1 & z_2-z_1 \\ a & b & c \end{vmatrix} = 0.$$

- Four points $A(x_1, y_1, z_1)$, $B(x_2, y_2, z_2)$, $C(x_3, y_3, z_3)$ and $D(x_4, y_4, z_4)$ are coplanar if and only if

$$\begin{vmatrix} x_2 - x_1 & y_2 - y_1 & z_2 - z_1 \\ x_3 - x_1 & y_3 - y_1 & z_3 - z_1 \\ x_4 - x_1 & y_4 - y_1 & z_4 - z_1 \end{vmatrix} = 0.$$

Condition for Coplanarity of Two Lines

Vector Form

Two lines $\vec{\mathbf{r}} = \mathbf{a}_1 + \lambda \mathbf{b}_1$ and $\vec{\mathbf{r}} = \mathbf{a}_2 + \mu \mathbf{b}_2$ are coplanar or intersecting if $(\mathbf{a}_2 - \mathbf{a}_1) \cdot (\mathbf{b}_1 \times \mathbf{b}_2) = 0$ i.e $(\mathbf{a}_2 - \mathbf{a}_1)$ is perpendicular to $(\mathbf{b}_1 \times \mathbf{b}_2)$.

Cartesian Form

The lines $\frac{x - x_1}{a_1} = \frac{y - y_1}{b_1} = \frac{z - z_1}{c_1}$ and $\frac{x - x_2}{a_2} = \frac{y - y_2}{b_2} = \frac{z - z_2}{c_2}$ are coplanar if

$$\begin{vmatrix} x_2 - x_1 & y_2 - y_1 & z_2 - z_1 \\ a_1 & b_1 & c_1 \\ a_2 & b_2 & c_2 \end{vmatrix} = 0.$$

Angle between Two Planes

The angle between two planes is defined as the angle between their normals.

Vector Form

If $\mathbf{n}_1$ and $\mathbf{n}_2$ are normals to the planes and let θ be the angle between the planes $\mathbf{r} \cdot \mathbf{n}_1 = d_1$ and $\mathbf{r} . \mathbf{n}_2 = d_2$.

Then, $\cos\theta = \left| \frac{\mathbf{n}_1 \cdot \mathbf{n}_2}{|\mathbf{n}_1||\mathbf{n}_2|} \right|$

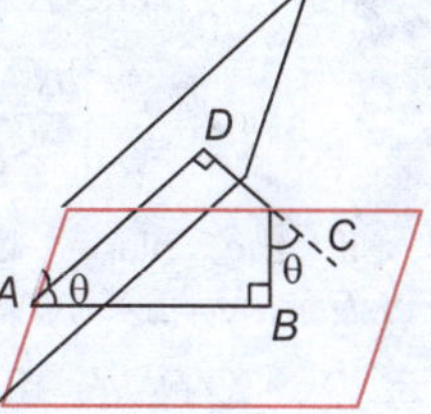

Cartesian Form

The angle between the two planes $a_1 x + b_1 y + c_1 z + d_1 = 0$ and $a_2 x + b_2 y + c_2 z + d_2 = 0$ is $\cos\theta = \left| \frac{a_1 a_2 + b_1 b_2 + c_1 c_2}{\sqrt{a_1^2 + b_1^2 + c_1^2}\sqrt{a_2^2 + b_2^2 + c_2^2}} \right|$

Parallelism and Perpendicularity of Two Planes

Two planes are parallel or perpendicular according as their normals are parallel or perpendicular.

Vector Form

Two planes $\mathbf{r}\cdot\mathbf{n}_1 = d_1$ and $\mathbf{r}\cdot\mathbf{n}_2 = d_2$ are parallel, if $\mathbf{n}_1 = \lambda\mathbf{n}_2$ for some scalar λ and perpendicular, if $\mathbf{n}_1\cdot\mathbf{n}_2 = 0$.

Cartesian Form

The planes $a_1x + b_1y + c_1z + d_1 = 0$ and $a_2x + b_2y + c_2z + d_2 = 0$ are parallel, if $\frac{a_1}{a_2} = \frac{b_1}{b_2} = \frac{c_1}{c_2}$ and perpendicular, if $a_1a_2 + b_1b_2 + c_1c_2 = 0$.

Competition Insight

Distance of a Point From a Plane

Vector Form

Let the equation of plane be $\mathbf{r}\cdot\mathbf{n} = d$. The perpendicular distance from a point P whose position vector is $\mathbf{a}$, to the plane is

$$\frac{|\mathbf{a}\cdot\mathbf{n} - d|}{|\mathbf{n}|}$$

The length of perpendicular from origin to the plane $\mathbf{r}\cdot\mathbf{n} = d$ is $\frac{|d|}{|\mathbf{n}|}$. (in vector form)

Cartesian Form

The perpendicular distance of a point $P(x_1, y_1, z_1)$ from the plane $ax + by + cz + d = 0$ is

$$\left|\frac{ax_1 + by_1 + cz_1 + d}{\sqrt{a^2 + b^2 + c^2}}\right|.$$

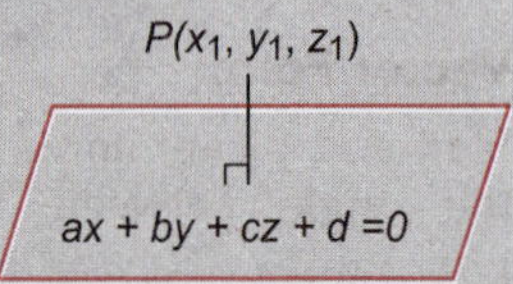

If the plane is given in normal form $lx + my + nz = p$. Then, the distance of the point $P(x_1, y_1, z_1)$ from the plane is $|lx_1 + my_1 + nz_1 - p|$.

The length of perpendicular from origin to the plane

$$ax + by + cz + d = 0 \text{ is } \frac{|d|}{\sqrt{a^2 + b^2 + c^2}}. \text{ (in cartesian form)}$$

Distance between Two Parallel Planes

If $ax + by + cz + d_1 = 0$ and $ax + by + cz + d_2 = 0$ be equation of two parallel planes. Then, the distance between them is

$$\left|\frac{d_2 - d_1}{\sqrt{a^2 + b^2 + c^2}}\right|$$

Angle between a Line and a Plane

The angle between a line and plane is the complement of the angle between the line and normal to the plane.

Vector Form

If the equation of a line is $\mathbf{r} = \mathbf{a} + \lambda \mathbf{b}$ and plane is $\mathbf{r} \cdot \mathbf{n} = d$, then the angle between the line and normal is $\cos \theta = \frac{|\mathbf{n} \cdot \mathbf{b}|}{|\mathbf{n}||\mathbf{b}|}$

and the angle between the line and plane is $\sin \phi = \frac{\mathbf{n} \cdot \mathbf{b}}{|\mathbf{n}||\mathbf{b}|}$ $[\because \phi = 90° - \theta]$

Cartesian Form

The angle between a line $\frac{x - x_1}{a_1} = \frac{y - y_1}{b_1} = \frac{z - z_1}{c_1}$ and normal to the plane $a_2 x + b_2 y + c_2 z + d_2 = 0$ is $\cos \theta = \frac{a_1 a_2 + b_1 b_2 + c_1 c_2}{\sqrt{a_1^2 + b_1^2 + c_1^2}\sqrt{a_2^2 + b_2^2 + c_2^2}}$

and the angle between a line and the plane is

$$\sin \phi = \frac{a_1 a_2 + b_1 b_2 + c_1 c_2}{\sqrt{a_1^2 + b_1^2 + c_1^2}\sqrt{a_2^2 + b_2^2 + c_2^2}} \qquad [\because \phi = 90° - \theta]$$

Knowledge Booster

Bisectors of Angles between Two Planes

The bisector planes of the angles between the planes

$a_1 x + b_1 y + c_1 z + d_1 = 0$ and $a_2 x + b_2 y + c_2 z + d_2 = 0$ is

$$\frac{a_1 x + b_1 y + c_1 z + d_1}{\sqrt{\Sigma a_1^2}} = \pm \frac{a_2 x + b_2 y + c_2 z + d_2}{\sqrt{\Sigma a_2^2}}$$

One of these planes will bisect the acute angle and the other bisect the obtuse angle between the given plane.

(i) If $a_1 a_2 + b_1 b_2 + c_1 c_2 < 0$, then origin lies in acute angle and the acute angle bisector is obtained by taking positive sign in the above equation. The obtuse angle bisector is obtained by taking negative sign in the above equation.

(ii) If $a_1 a_2 + b_1 b_2 + c_1 c_2 > 0$, then origin lies in obtuse angle and the obtuse angle bisector is obtained by taking positive sign in above equation. Acute angle bisector is obtained by taking negative sign.

Chapter 29

Statistics

Statistics is the Science of collection, organisation, presentation, analysis and interpretation of the numerical data.

Useful Terms

1. **Primary and Secondary Data** The data collected by the investigator himself is known as the **primary data**, while the data which are not originally collected but rather obtained from some sources is known as **secondary data**.
2. **Variable or Variate** A characteristics that varies in magnitude from observation to observation. e.g. weight, height, income, age, etc are variables.
3. **Grouped and Ungrouped Data** The data which is organised into several groups is called **grouped data** where as ungrouped data is present in original form, i.e. it is just a list of numbers.
4. **Class-Intervals** The groups which used to condense the data are called classes or class-intervals.
5. **Limit of the Class** The starting and ending values of each class are called **Lower** and **Upper limits**, respectively.
6. **Class Size or Class Width** The difference between upper and lower boundary of a class is called size of the class.
7. **Class Marks** The class marks of a class is given by $\dfrac{\text{Lower limit} + \text{Upper limit}}{2}$.
8. **Frequency** The number of times an observation occurs in the given data, is called the frequency of the observation.
9. **Frequency Distribution** It is a tabular summary of data showing the frequency of observations.

10. **Discrete Frequency Distribution** A frequency distribution is called a discrete frequency distribution, if data are presented in such a way that exact value of the data are clearly shown.
11. **Continuous Frequency Distribution** A frequency distribution in which data are arranged in classes (or groups) which are not exactly measurable.
12. **Cumulative Frequency Distribution** In this type of distribution, the frequencies of each class intervals are added successively from top to bottom or from bottom to top.

    A cumulative frequency distribution is of two types

    (i) **Less than cummulative frequency distribution** In this frequencies are added successively from top to bottom and we represent the cumulative number of observation less than or equal to the class frequency to which it relates.

    (ii) **More than cummulative frequency distribution** In this frequencies are added successively from bottom to top and we represent the cummulative number of observation greater than or equal to the class frequency to which it relates.

Graphical Representation of Frequency Distributions

(i) **Bar Diagrams** In bar diagrams, only the length of the bars are taken into consideration. To draw a bar diagram, we first mark equal lengths for the different classes on the horizontal axis, i.e. on X-axis.

On each of these lengths on the horizontal axis, we erect (vertical) a rectangle whose heights are proportional to **the frequency** of the class.

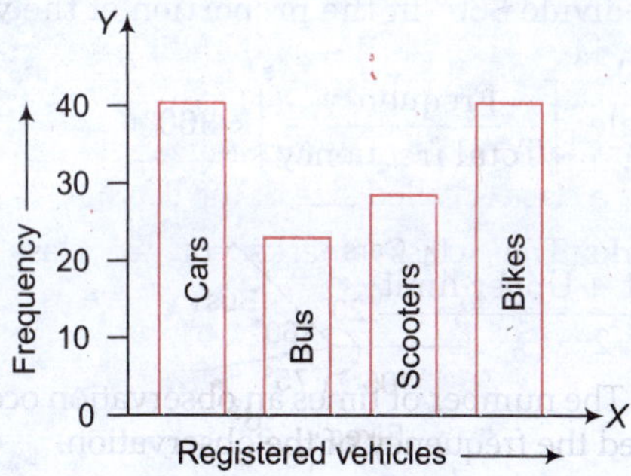

(ii) **Histogram** To draw the histogram of a given continuous frequency distribution, we first mark off all the class intervals along X-axis on a suitable scale.

On each of these class intervals on the horizontal axis, we erect (vertical) a rectangle whose height is proportional to the frequency of that particular class, so that the area of the rectangle is proportional to the frequency of the class.

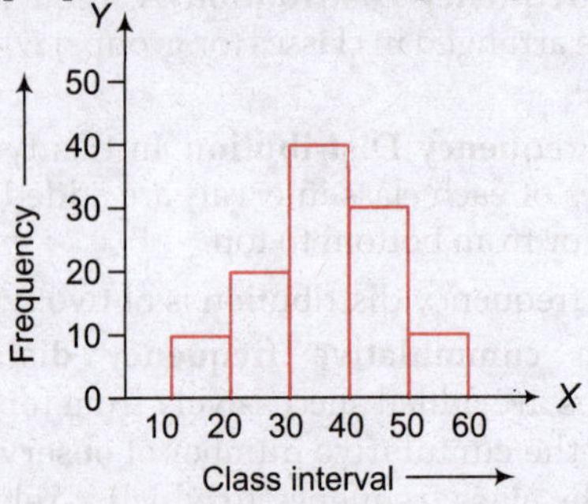

EXPERT Scale Up

If the classes are of unequal width, then the height of the rectangles will be proportional to the ratio of the frequencies to the width of the classes.

(iii) **Pie Diagrams** Pie diagrams are used to represent a relative frequency distribution. A pie diagram consists of a circle divided into as many sectors as there are classes in a frequency distribution. The area of each sector is proportional to the relative frequency of the class.

Now, we make angles at the centre proportional to the relative frequencies. And in order to get the angles of the desired sectors, we divide 360° in the proportion of the various relative frequencies, i.e.

$$\text{Central angle} = \left[\frac{\text{Frequency}}{\text{Total frequency}}\right] \times 360°$$

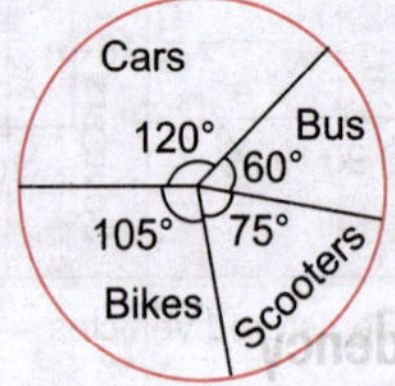

The above pie diagram represent an illustration of types of vehicles and their share in the total number of vehicles of a city.

Competition Insight

Frequency Polygon To draw the frequency polygon of an ungrouped frequency distribution, we plot the points with abscissae as the variate values and the ordinate as the corresponding frequencies. These plotted points are joined by straight lines to obtain the frequency polygon.

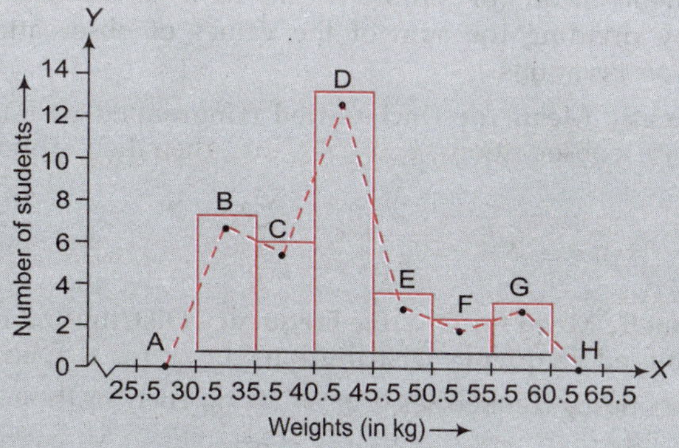

Cumulative Frequency Curve (Ogive) The curve given by the graphical representation of cummulative frequency distribution is called on ogive or commulative frequency curve.

There are two methods of constructing an ogive, (i) 'less than' type ogive (ii) 'more than' type ogive.

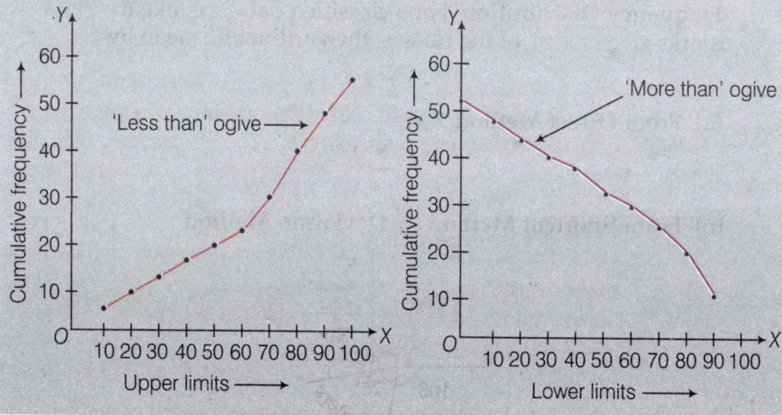

Measures of Central Tendency

A single value which describes the characteristic of the entire data is known as the average. Generally, average value of a distribution lies in the middle part of the distribution, such type of values are known as measures of central tendency.

The following are the five measures of central tendency

1. Arithmetic Mean 2. Geometric Mean 3. Harmonic Mean
4. Median 5. Mode

1. Arithmetic Mean

The arithmetic mean (or simple mean) of a set of observations is obtained by dividing the sum of the values of observations by the number of observations.

(i) **Arithmetic Mean for Unclassified** (Ungrouped or Raw) **Data** If there are n observations, $x_1, x_2, x_3, \ldots, x_n$, then their arithmetic mean

$$A \text{ or } \bar{x} = \frac{x_1 + x_2 + \ldots + x_n}{n} = \frac{\sum_{i=1}^{n} x_i}{n}$$

(ii) **Arithmetic Mean for Discrete Frequency Distribution or Ungrouped Frequency Distribution** Let $f_1, f_2, \ldots, f_n$ be corresponding frequencies of $x_1, x_2, \ldots, x_n$. Then, arithmetic mean

$$A = \frac{x_1 f_1 + x_2 f_2 + \ldots + x_n f_n}{f_1 + f_2 + \ldots + f_n} = \frac{\sum_{i=1}^{n} x_i f_i}{\sum_{i=1}^{n} f_i}$$

(iii) **Arithmetic Mean for Classified** (Grouped) **Data or Grouped Frequency Distribution** For a classified data, we take the class marks $x_1, x_2, \ldots, x_n$ of the classes, then arithmetic mean by

(a) **From Direct Method** $A = \dfrac{\sum_{i=1}^{n} x_i f_i}{\sum_{i=1}^{n} f_i}$

(b) **From Shortcut Method** *Or* **Deviation Method**

$$A = A_1 + \left(\frac{\sum_{i=1}^{n} f_i d_i}{\sum_{i=1}^{n} f_i} \right) h,$$

where A_1 = assumed mean, d_i = deviation = $x_i - A_1$

h = width of interval

(c) **Step Deviation Method** is $\bar{x} = A_1 + \frac{\sum_{i=1}^{n} f_i u_i}{\sum_{i=1}^{n} f_i} \times h,$

where A_1 = assumed mean

u_i = step deviation = $\frac{x_i - A_1}{h}$ and h = width of interval.

(iv) **Combined Mean** If $A_1, A_2, \ldots, A_r$ are means of $n_1, n_2, \ldots, n_r$ observations respectively, then arithmetic mean of the combined group is called the combined mean of the observation

$$A = \frac{n_1 A_1 + n_2 A_2 + \ldots + n_r A_r}{n_1 + n_2 + \ldots + n_r} = \frac{\sum_{i=1}^{r} n_i A_i}{\sum_{i=1}^{r} n_i}$$

(v) **Weighted Arithmetic Mean** If $w_1, w_2, \ldots, w_n$ are the weights assigned to the values $x_1, x_2, \ldots, x_n$ respectively, then the weighted arithmetic mean is

$$A_w = \frac{\sum_{i=1}^{n} w_i x_i}{\sum_{i=1}^{n} w_i}$$

Value Points

- Mean is dependent of change of origin and change of scale.
- Algebraic sum of the deviations of a set of values from their arithmetic mean is zero.
- The sum of the squares of the deviations of a set of values is minimum when taken from mean.
- Change origin means either subtract or add in observations.
- Change of scale means either multiply or divide in observations.

2. Geometric Mean

(i) If $x_1, x_2, \ldots, x_n$ be n positive observations, then their geometric mean is defined as $G = \sqrt[n]{x_1 \, x_2 \ldots x_n}$

or $G = \text{antilog}\left[\frac{\log x_1 + \log x_2 + \ldots + \log x_n}{n}\right]$

(ii) Let $f_1, f_2, \ldots, f_n$ be the corresponding frequencies of positive observations $x_1, x_2, \ldots, x_n$, then geometric mean is defined as

$$G = (x_1^{f_1} x_2^{f_2} \ldots x_n^{f_n})^{\frac{1}{N}}$$

$$\text{or } G = \text{antilog}\left[\frac{1}{N}(f_1 \log x_1 + f_2 \log x_2 + \ldots + f_n \log x_n)\right],$$

$$\text{where } N = \sum_{i=1}^{n} f_i$$

3. Harmonic Mean (HM)

The harmonic mean of n non-zero observations $x_1, x_2, \ldots, x_n$ is defined as

$$\text{HM} = \frac{n}{\frac{1}{x_1} + \frac{1}{x_2} + \ldots + \frac{1}{x_n}} = \frac{n}{\sum_{i=1}^{n} \frac{1}{x_i}}$$

If their corresponding frequencies are $f_1, f_2, \ldots, f_n$ respectively, then

$$\text{HM} = \frac{f_1 + f_2 + \ldots + f_n}{\left(\frac{f_1}{x_1} + \frac{f_2}{x_2} + \ldots + \frac{f_n}{x_n}\right)} = \frac{\sum_{i=1}^{n} f_i}{\sum_{i=1}^{n} \frac{f_i}{x_i}}$$

4. Median

The median of a distribution is the value of the middle observation, when the observations are arranged in ascending or descending order.

(i) Median for Simple Distribution or Raw Data

Firstly, arrange the data in ascending or descending order and then find the number of observations is n.

(a) If n is odd, then $\left(\frac{n+1}{2}\right)$th term is the median.

(b) If n is even, then there are two middle terms namely $\left(\frac{n}{2}\right)$th and $\left(\frac{n}{2}+1\right)$th terms.

Hence, Median = Mean of $\left(\frac{n}{2}\right)$th and $\left(\frac{n}{2}+1\right)$th observations

$$= \frac{1}{2}\left[\left(\frac{n}{2}\right)\text{th} + \left(\frac{n}{2}+1\right)\text{th}\right] \text{ of observations}$$

Value Point

The intersection point of less than ogive and more than ogive is the median of corresponding frequency distribution.

(ii) Median for Unclassified (Ungrouped) Frequency Distribution

(a) Firstly, find $\frac{N}{2}$, where $N = \sum_{i=1}^{n} f_i$.

(b) Find the cumulative frequency which is equal to or just greater than $\frac{N}{2}$.

(c) Take the value of variable corresponding to cummulative frequency obtained in step (ii).

(d) This value of the variable is the required median.

(iii) Median for Classified (Grouped) Data or Grouped Frequency Distribution

If in a continuous distribution, the total frequency be N, then the class whose cumulative frequency is either equal to $N/2$ or is just greater than $N/2$ is called **median class**.

For a continuous distribution, median

$$M_d = l + \frac{\frac{N}{2} - C}{f} \times h,$$

where l = lower limit of the median class

f = frequency of the median class

N = total frequency $= \sum_{i=1}^{n} f_i$

C = cumulative frequency of the class just before the median class

h = length of the median class

Knowledge Booster

The median divides the distribution in two equal parts. Similarly, quartiles divide the distribution in four equal parts.

Q_1 $Q_2 = M_d$ Q_3

Quartiles for a continuous distribution is given by

$$Q_1 \text{ (first quartile)} = l + \frac{\frac{N}{4} - C}{f} \times h$$

Similarly, $$Q_2 \text{ (second quartile)} = l + \frac{\frac{N}{2} - C}{f} \times h = \text{median},$$

$$Q_3 \text{ (third quartile)} = l + \frac{\frac{3N}{4} - C}{f} \times h$$

where, N = total frequency

l = lower limit of the quartile class

f = frequency of the quartile class

C = the cumulative frequency corresponding to the class just before the quartile class

h = the length of the quartile class.

5. Mode

The mode (M_o) of a distribution is the value at the point about which the observations tend to be most heavily concentrated. It is generally the value of the variable which appears to occur most frequently in the distribution.

(i) Mode for a Simple Data or Raw Data

The value which is repeated maximum number of times, is the required mode. e.g. Mode of the data 70, 80, 90, 96, 70, 96, 96, 90 is 96 as 96 occurs maximum number of times.

(ii) Mode for Unclassified (Ungrouped) Frequency Distribution

Mode is the value of the variate corresponding to the maximum frequency.

(iii) Mode for Classified (Grouped) Distribution or Grouped Frequency Distribution

The class having the maximum frequency is called the **modal class** and the middle point of the modal class is called the **crude mode**.

The class just before the modal class is called pre-modal class and the class after the modal class is called the post-modal class.

Mode for classified data (Continuous Distribution) is given by

$$M_o = l + \frac{f_0 - f_1}{2f_0 - f_1 - f_2} \times h$$

where, l = lower limit of the modal class

f_0 = frequency of the modal class

f_1 = frequency of the pre-modal class
f_2 = frequency of the post-modal class
h = length of the class interval

Relation between Mean, Median and Mode

(i) Mean − Mode = 3 (Mean − Median)
(ii) Mode = 3 Median − 2 Mean (iii) 3 Median = 2 Mean + Mode

Competition Insight

Symmetric and Anti-symmetric Distribution

A distribution is symmetric, if the frequencies are symmetrically distributed on both sides of the centre point of the frequency curve. In this, frequency curve is bell shaped.

In symmetrical distribution,

Mean = Median = Mode i.e. $A = M_d = M_o$

A distribution which is not symmetric is called anti-symmetric (or skew-symmetric).

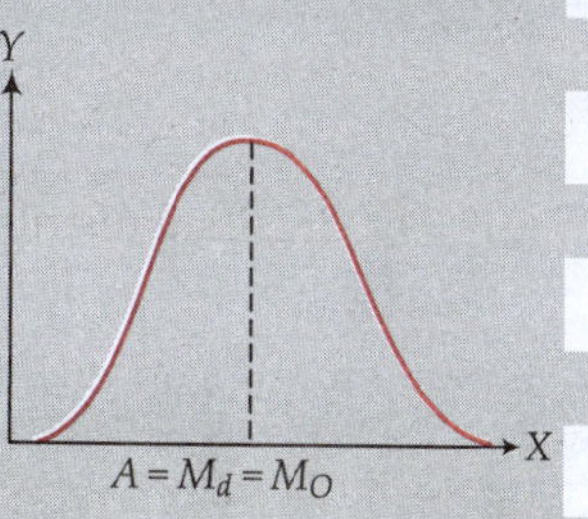

Measure of Dispersion

The degree to which numerical data tend to spread about an average value is called the dispersion of the data. The four measure of dispersion are

1. Range
2. Mean deviation
3. Standard deviation
4. Root mean square deviation

1. Range

The difference between the highest and the lowest observation of a data is called its range.

i.e. $$\text{Range} = X_{max} - X_{min}$$

$\therefore$ The coefficient of range $= \dfrac{X_{max} - X_{min}}{X_{max} + X_{min}}$

Value Points

Quartile is widely used in statistical series relating to quality control in production.

- Inter quartile range $= Q_3 - Q_1$
- Semi-inter quartile range (Quartile deviation) $= \dfrac{Q_3 - Q_1}{2}$

  and coefficient of quartile deviation $= \dfrac{Q_3 - Q_1}{Q_3 + Q_1}$

2. Mean Deviation (MD)

The arithmetic mean of the absolute deviations of the values of the variable from a measure of their average (mean, median, mode) is called Mean Deviation (MD). It is denoted by δ.

(i) For simple (raw) distribution $\delta = \dfrac{\sum_{i=1}^{n} |x_i - \overline{x}|}{n}$

where, n = number of terms, $\overline{x} = A$ or M_d or M_O

(ii) For unclassified frequency distribution $\delta = \dfrac{\sum_{i=1}^{n} f_i |x_i - \overline{x}|}{\sum_{i=1}^{n} f_i}$

(iii) For classified distribution $\delta = \dfrac{\sum_{i=1}^{n} f_i |x_i - \overline{x}|}{\sum_{i=1}^{n} f_i}$

where, x_i is the class mark of the interval.

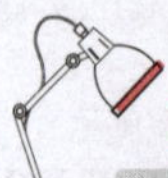

EXPERT Scale Up

The mean deviation will be the least when measured from the median.

Coefficient of Mean Deviation

It is the ratio of MD and the average from which the deviation is measured.

Thus, the coefficient of MD $= \dfrac{\delta_A}{A}$ or $\dfrac{\delta_{M_d}}{M_d}$ or $\dfrac{\delta_{M_O}}{M_O}$

Limitations of Mean Deviation

(i) If the data is more scattered or the degree of variability is very high, then the median is not a valid representative.

(ii) The sum of the deviations from the mean is more than the sum of the deviations from the median.

(iii) The mean deviation is calculated on the basis of absolute values of the deviations and so cannot be subjected to further algebraic treatment.

3. Standard Deviation and Variance

Standard deviation is the square root of the arithmetic mean of the squares of deviations of the terms from their AM and it is denoted by σ.

The square of standard deviation is called the **variance** and it is denoted by the symbol σ^2.

(i) For simple distribution

$$\sigma = \sqrt{\frac{\sum_{i=1}^{n}(x_i - \bar{x})^2}{n}} = \frac{1}{n}\sqrt{n\sum_{i=1}^{n} x_i^2 - \left(\sum_{i=1}^{n} x_i\right)^2}$$

where, n is a number of observations and $\bar{x}$ is mean.

(ii) For discrete frequency distribution

$$\sigma = \sqrt{\frac{\sum_{i=1}^{n} f(x_i - \bar{x})^2}{N}} = \frac{1}{N}\sqrt{N\sum_{i=1}^{n} f_i x_i^2 - \left(\sum_{i=1}^{n} f_i x_i\right)^2}$$

Shortcut Method $\sigma = \frac{1}{N}\sqrt{N\sum_{i=1}^{n} f_i d_i^2 - \left(\sum_{i=1}^{n} f_i d_i\right)^2}$

where, d_i = deviation from assumed mean $= x_i - A$ and A = assumed mean

(iii) For continuous frequency distribution

$$\sigma = \sqrt{\frac{\sum_{i=1}^{n} f_i(x_i - \bar{x})^2}{N}}$$

where, x_i is class mark of the interval.

Shortcut Method $\sigma = \frac{h}{N}\sqrt{N\sum_{i=1}^{n} f_i u_i^2 - \left(\sum_{i=1}^{n} f_i u_i\right)^2}$

where, $u_i = \frac{x_i - A}{h}$, A = assumed mean and h = width of the class

Standard Deviation of the Combined Series

If n_1, n_2 are the sizes, $\overline{X}_1, \overline{X}_2$ are the means and σ_1, σ_2 are the standard deviation of the series, then the standard deviation of the combined series is

$$\sigma = \sqrt{\frac{n_1(\sigma_1^2 + d_1^2) + n_2(\sigma_2^2 + d_2^2)}{n_1 + n_2}}$$

where, $d_1 = \overline{X}_1 - \overline{X}, d_2 = \overline{X}_2 - \overline{X}$

and $\overline{X} = \frac{n_1\overline{X} + n_2\overline{X}_2}{n_1 + n_2}$.

Effects of Average and Dispersion on Change of origin and Scale

	Change of origin	Change of scale
Mean	Dependent	Dependent
Median	Dependent	Dependent
Mode	Dependent	Dependent
Standard Deviation	Not dependent	Dependent
Variance	Not dependent	Dependent

Value Points

- The ratio of SD (σ) and the AM ($\bar{x}$) is called the coefficient of standard deviation $\left(\frac{\sigma}{\bar{x}}\right)$.
- The percentage form of coefficient of SD i.e. $\left(\frac{\sigma}{\bar{x}}\right) \times 100$ is called coefficient of variation.
- Standard deviation of first n natural numbers is $\sqrt{\frac{n^2 - 1}{12}}$.
- Quartile deviation $= \frac{2}{3}$ Standard deviation
- Mean deviation $= \frac{4}{5}$ Standard deviation

4. Root Mean Square Deviation (RMS)

The square root of the AM of squares of the deviations from an assumed mean is called the root mean square deviation.

Thus,

(i) For simple (discrete) distribution

$$S = \sqrt{\frac{\sum (x - A')^2}{n}}, \text{ where } A' = \text{assumed mean}$$

(ii) For frequency distribution

$$S = \sqrt{\frac{\sum f(x - A')^2}{\sum f}}$$

Value Points

- The RMS deviation is the least when measured from AM.
- If $A' = A$ (mean), then $S = \sigma$
- $\sigma^2 + A^2 = \dfrac{\sum fx^2}{\sum f}$.
- For discrete distribution, if $f = 1$, then $\sigma^2 + A^2 = \dfrac{\sum x^2}{n}$.
- The mean deviation about the mean is less than or equal to the SD i.e. $\text{MD} \le \sigma$.

Handbook of Mathematics

Knowledge LIBRARY

Linear Programming Problem (LPP)

Linear programming problem is one that is concerned with finding the maximum or minimum value of a linear function of several variables, subject to conditions that the variables are non-negative and satisfy a set of linear inequalities.

Objective Function

The linear function which is to be optimised (maximised/minimised) is called an objective function.

Constraints

The system of linear inequations under which the objective function is to be optimised is called constraints.

Non-negative Restrictions

All the variables considered for making decisions assume non-negative values.

Optimal Value

The maximum or minimum value of an objective function is known as the optimal value of LPP.

Mathematical Description of a General Linear Programming Problem

A general LPP can be stated as (Max/Min)

$Z = c_1x_1 + c_2x_2 + \ldots + c_nx_n$ (Objective function) subject to constraints

$$\left\{\begin{array}{l} a_{11}\, x_1 + a_{12}\, x_2 + \ldots + a_{1n}\, x_n\, (\le = \ge) b_1 \\ a_{21}\, x_1 + a_{22}\, x_2 + \ldots + a_{2n}\, x_n (\le = \ge) b_2 \\ \ldots\ldots\ldots\ldots\ldots \quad \ldots\ldots\ldots\ldots\ldots \\ \ldots\ldots\ldots\ldots\ldots \quad \ldots\ldots\ldots\ldots\ldots \end{array}\right\}$$

$a_{m_1} x_1 + a_{m_2}\, x_2 + \ldots + a_{m_n}\, x_n\, (\le = \ge)\, b_m$ and the non-negative restrictions $x_1, x_2, \ldots, x_n \ge 0$ where all $a_{11}, a_{12}, \ldots, a_{mn}; b_1, b_2, \ldots, b_m; c_1, c_2, \ldots, c_n$ are constants and $x_1, x_2, \ldots, x_n$ are variables.

Some Basic Definitions

(i) **Feasible Region** The common region determined by all the constraints including non-negative constraints is called the feasible region (or solution region)

(ii) **Feasible Solution of a LPP** A set of values of the variables $x_1, x_2, \ldots, x_n$ satisfying the constraints and non-negative restrictions of a LPP is called a feasible solution of the LPP.

or Points within and on the boundary of the feasible region represent feasible solutions of the constraints.

(iii) **Optimal Solution of a LPP** A feasible solution of a LPP is said to be optimal (or optimum), if it also optimises the objective function of the problem.

(iv) **Extreme Point Theorem** An optimum solution of a LPP, if it exists, occurs at one of the extreme points (*i.e.* corner points) of the feasible region.

Value Points

(i) A corner point of a feasible region is the point of intersection of two boundary lines, which form the region.

(ii) The feasible region is always a convex region.

(iii) If two corner points of the feasible region are optimal solutions of same type, then any point on the line segment joining these two points is also an optimal solution of the same type.

Solution of Simultaneous Linear Inequations

The solution set of a system of simultaneous linear inequations is the region containing the points (x, y) which satisfy all the inequations of the given system simultaneously. To draw the graph of the simultaneous linear inequations, we find the region of the XY-plane, common to all the portions comprising the solution sets of the given inequations. If there is no region common to all the solutions of the given inequations, we say that the solution set of the system of inequations is empty.

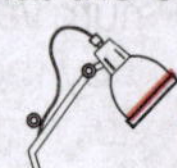

EXPERT Scale Up

The solution set of simultaneous linear inequations may be an empty set or it may be the region bounded by the straight lines corresponding to given linear inequations or it may be an unbounded region with straight line boundaries.

Working Rule to Draw the Graph of an Inequation

(i) Consider the constraint $ax + by \le c$, where $a^2 + b^2 \ne 0$ and $c > 0$.
Firstly, draw the straight line $ax + by = c$. For this find two convenient points satisyfying this equation and then join them. This straight line divides the xy-plane in two parts. The inequation $ax + by \le c$ will represent that part of the xy-plane in which the origin lies.

(ii) Again, consider the constraint $ax + by \ge c$, where $a^2 + b^2 \ne 0$ and $c > 0$. Draw the straight line $ax + by = c$ by joining any two points on it. This straight line divides the xy-plane in two parts. The inequation $ax + by \ge c$ will represent that part of the xy-plane, in which the origin does not lie.

Graphical Method of Solving a Linear Programming Problem

This method of solving a LPP is based on the principle of extreme point theorem, referred as **corner point method.**

The method comprises of the following steps

(i) Consider each constraints as an equation.

(ii) Plot the graph of each equation each of these will geometrically represent a straight line.

(iii) Find the feasible region.

(iv) Determine the vertices (corner points) of the feasible region.

(v) Find the values of the objective function at each of the extreme points.

(vi) (a) If region is bounded, then maximum (say M) or minimum (say m) value out of these values obtained in point (v), is the required maximum or minimum value of the objective function.

(b) If region is unbounded, then maximum (say M) or minimum (say m) value out of these values obtained in point (v) may or may not be required maximum or minimum value of the objective function. In this case, we go to next point.

(vii) Suppose the given objective function is $ax + by$, then for maximum value draw the graph of inequality $ax + by > M$ and for minimum value draw the graph of $ax + by < m$. If open half plane obtained by these inequalities has no point in common with the feasible region obtained in point (iv), then M or m is the required maximum or minimum value. Otherwise, objective function has no maximum or no minimum value.

Different Types of Linear Programming Problems

(i) **Diet Problems** In these types of problem, we have to find the amount of different kinds of constituents/ nutrients which should be included in a diet, so as to minimise the cost of the desired diet.

(ii) **Manufacturing Problems** In these types of problem, we have to find the number of units of different product which should be produced and sold by a firm when each product requires a fixed manpower, machine hours, etc in order to make maximum profit.

(iii) **Transportation Problems** In these types of problem, we have to determine a transportation schedule in order to find the minimum cost of transporting a product from plants/factories situated at different locations to different markets.

Binary Operations

Let S be a non-empty set. A function $*$ from $S \times S$ to S is called a binary operation on S i.e. $* : S \times S \to S$ is a binary operation on set S.

Generally binary operations are represented by the symbols $*$, $\oplus$, ... etc.

Closure Property

An operation $*$ on a non-empty set S is said to satisfy the closure property, if $a \in S, b \in S \Rightarrow a * b \in S, \forall\ a, b \in S$

Also, in this case we say that S is closed under $*$.

An operation $*$ on a non-empty set S, satisfying the closure property is known as a binary operation.

Some Particular Cases

(i) Addition is a binary operation on each one of the sets N, Z, Q, R and C. While addition on the set S of all irrationals is not a binary operation.

(ii) Multiplication is a binary operation on each one of the sets N, Z, Q, R and C. While multiplication on the set S of all irrationals is not a binary operation.

(iii) Subtraction is a binary operation on each one of the sets Z, Q, R and C. While subtraction on the set of natural numbers and irrational number is not a binary operation.

(iv) Let S be a non-empty set and $P(S)$ be its power set. Then, the union, intersection and difference of sets, on $P(S)$ is a binary operation.

(v) Division is not a binary operation on any of the sets N, Z, Q, R and C. However, it is a binary operation on the sets of all non-zero rational (real or complex) numbers.

(vi) Exponential operation $(a, b) \to a^b$ is a binary operation on set N of natural numbers while it is not a binary operation on set Z of integers.

Here, N, Z, Q, R and C represent the set of natural numbers, integers, rationals, real and complex numbers, respectively.

Properties of Binary Operations

(i) **Commutative Property** A binary operation $*$ on a non-empty set S is said to be commutative or abelian, if

$$a * b = b * a,\ \forall\ a, b \in S.$$

Addition and multiplication are commutative binary operations on Z but subtraction is not a commutative binary operation, since $2-3 \neq 3-2$.

Union and intersection are commutative binary operations on the power set $P(S)$ of S. But difference of sets is not a commutative binary operation on $P(S)$.

(ii) **Associative Property** A binary operation $*$ on a non-empty set S is said to be associative, if $(a * b) * c = a * (b * c), \forall\ a, b, c \in S$.

Let R be the set of real numbers, then addition and multiplication on R satisfies the associative property.

(iii) **Distributive Property** Let $*$ and o be two binary operations on a non-empty sets. We say that $*$ is distributed over o, if

$a * (b\, o\, c) = (a * b)\, o\, (a * c), \forall\ a, b, c \in S$ also (called left distributive law) and $(b\ o\ c) * a = (b * a)\ o\ (c * a), \forall\ a, b, c \in S$ also (called right distributive law).

Let R be the set of all real numbers, then multiplication distributes over addition on R.

Since, $a \cdot (b+c) = a \cdot b + a \cdot c, \forall\ a, b, c \in R$.

Identity Element

Let $*$ be a binary operation on a non-empty set S. An element $e \in S$, if it exist, such that $a * e = e * a = a, \forall\ a \in S$, is called an identity element of S, with respect to $*$.

For addition on R, zero is the identity element in R.

Since, $a + 0 = 0 + a = a, \forall\ a \in R$

For multiplication on R, 1 is the identity element in R.

Since, $a \times 1 = 1 \times a = a, \forall\ a \in R$

Let $P(S)$ be the power set of a non-empty set S. Then, ϕ is the identity element for union on $P(S)$, as $A \cup \phi = \phi \cup A = A, \forall\ A \in P(S)$

Also, S is the identity element for intersection on $P(S)$.

Since, $A \cap S = S \cap A = A, \forall\ A \in P(S)$.

For addition on N the identity element does not exist. But for multiplication on N the identity element is 1.

Inverse of an Element

Let $*$ be a binary operation on a non-empty set S and let e be the identity element.

Suppose $a \in S$, we say that a is invertible, if there exists an element $b \in S$ such that $a * b = b * a = e$

Also, in this case, b is called the inverse of a and we write, $a^{-1} = b$

Addition on N has no identity element and accordingly N has no invertible element.

Multiplication on N has 1 as the identity element and no element other than 1 is invertible.

Value Points

If S be a finite set containing n elements, then

(i) the total number of binary operations on S is n^{n^2}.

(ii) the total number of commutative binary operations' on S is $n^{n(n+1)/2}$.

Binomial Theorem and Principle of Mathematical Induction

Principle of Mathematical Induction

In an algebra, there are certain results that are formulated in terms of n, where n is a positive integer. Such results can be proved by specific technique, which is known as the principle of Mathematical Induction.

Statement

A sentence or description which can be judged either true or false, is called the statement.

e.g. (i) 3 divides 9. (ii) Lucknow is the capital of Uttar Pradesh.

1. First Principle of Mathematical Induction

Let $P(n)$ be a statement involving natural number n. To prove statement $P(n)$ is true for all natural number, the following steps are used :

(i) Prove that $P(1)$ is true.

(ii) Assume $P(k)$ is true.

(iii) Using (i) and (ii) prove that statement is true for $n = k + 1$ i.e. $P(k + 1)$ is true.

This is first principle of Mathematical Induction.

2. Second Principle of Mathematical Induction

In second principle of Mathematical Induction following steps are used:

(i) Prove that $P(1)$ is true.

(ii) Assume $P(n)$ is true for all natural numbers such that $2 \le n < k$.

(iii) Using (i) and (ii), prove that $P(k + 1)$ is true.

Matrices

Elementary Operations (Transformations of a Matrix)

Any one of the following operations on a matrix is called an elementary transformation.

(i) Interchanging any two rows (or columns), denoted by

$$R_i \longleftrightarrow R_j \text{ or } C_i \longleftrightarrow C_j.$$

(ii) Multiplication of the element of any row (or column) by a non-zero scalar quantity, denoted by

$$R_i \to kR_i \text{ or } C_i \to kC_i.$$

(iii) Addition of constant multiple of the elements of any row to the corresponding element of any other row, denoted by

$$R_i \to R_i + kR_j \text{ or } C_i \to C_i + kC_j.$$

Elementary Matrix

A matrix obtained from an identity matrix by a single elementary operation is called an elementary matrix.

Equivalent Matrix

Two matrices A and B are said to be equivalent, if one can be obtained from the other by a sequence of elementary transformation.

The symbol $\approx$ is used for equivalence.

Determinant

Properties of Determinants

(i) The value of the determinant remains unchanged, if rows are changed into columns and columns are changed into rows.
e.g. $$|A'| = |A|$$

(ii) If $A = [a_{ij}]_{n \times n}$, $n > 1$ and B be the matrix obtained from A by interchanging two of its rows or columns, then

$$\det(B) = -\det(A)$$

(iii) If two rows (or columns) of a square matrix A are proportional, then $|A| = 0$.

(iv) $|B| = k\,|A|$, where B is the matrix obtained from A, by multiplying one row (or column) of A by k.

(v) $|kA| = k^n |A|$, where A is a matrix of order $n \times n$.

(vi) If each element of a row (or column) of a determinant is the sum of two or more terms, then the determinant can be expressed as the sum of two or more determinants.

e.g. $\begin{vmatrix} a_1+a_2 & b & c \\ p_1+p_2 & q & r \\ u_1+u_2 & v & w \end{vmatrix} = \begin{vmatrix} a_1 & b & c \\ p_1 & q & r \\ u_1 & v & w \end{vmatrix} + \begin{vmatrix} a_2 & b & c \\ p_2 & q & r \\ u_2 & v & w \end{vmatrix}$

(vii) If the same multiple of the elements of any row (or column) of a determinant are added to the corresponding elements of any other row (or column), then the value of the new determinant remains unchanged,

e.g. $\begin{vmatrix} a_{11} & a_{12} & a_{13} \\ a_{21} & a_{22} & a_{23} \\ a_{31} & a_{32} & a_{33} \end{vmatrix} = \begin{vmatrix} a_{11}+ka_{31} & a_{12}+ka_{32} & a_{13}+ka_{33} \\ a_{21} & a_{22} & a_{23} \\ a_{31} & a_{32} & a_{33} \end{vmatrix}$

(viii) If each element of a row (or column) of a determinant is zero, then its value is zero.

(ix) If any two rows (or columns) of a determinant are identical, then its value is zero.

(x) If each element of row (or column) of a determinant is expressed as a sum of two or more terms, then the determinant can be expressed as the sum of two or more determinants.

(xi) If r rows (or r columns) become identical, when a is substituted for x, then $(x-a)^{r-1}$ is a factor of given determinant.

Solution of System of Equations by Rank Method

(i) **Non-homogeneous System of Equations** Let $AX = B$ be a system of n linear equations in n variables, then

Step I Write the augmented matrix $[A:B]$.

Step II Reduce the augmented matrix to Echelon form using elementary row-transformation.

Step III Determine the rank of coefficient matrix A and augmented matrix $[A:B]$ by counting the number of non-zero rows in A and $[A:B]$.

Step IV

(a) If $\rho(A) \neq \rho(A:B)$, then the system of equations is inconsistent.

(b) If $\rho(A) = \rho(A:B) =$ the number of unknowns, then the system of equations is consistent and has a unique solution.

(c) If $\rho(A) = \rho(A:B) <$ the number of unknowns, then the system of equations is consistent and has infinitely many solutions.

(ii) **Homogeneous System of Equations**

(a) If $AX = 0$, is a homogeneous system of linear equations and $\rho(A)$ = number of unknown, then $AX = 0$, have a non-trivial solution i.e. $X = 0$.

(b) If $\rho(A) <$ number of unknowns, then $AX = 0$, have a non-trivial solution, with infinitely many solutions.

Height and Distance

Height and distance is the important application of Trigonometry, in which we measure the height and distance between different objects e.g. towers, building etc.

Angle of Elevation and Angle of Depression

If O be the observer's eye and OX be the horizontal line through O.

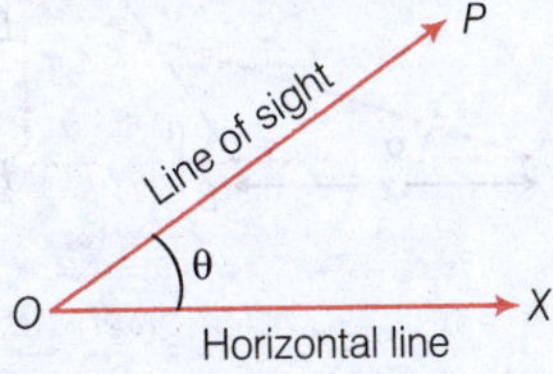

If the object P is at higher level than observer's eye, then $\angle POX$ is called the **angle of elevation**.

If the object P is at lower level than observer's eye, then $\angle POX$ is called the **angle of depression**.

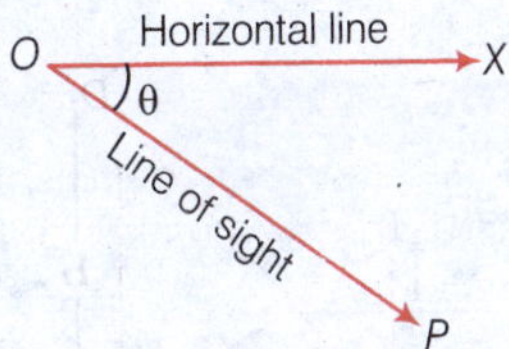

Important Points

(i) Angle of elevation and depression are always an acute angle.

(ii) Angle of elevation of an object from an observer is same as angle of depression of an observer from the object.

Important Results on Height and Distance

(i) $a = h(\cot\alpha - \cot\beta)$

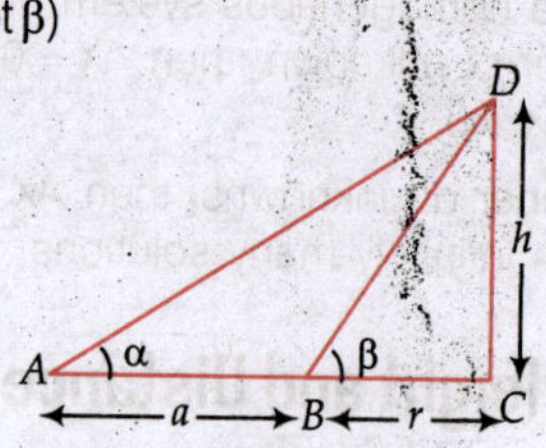

(ii) If $AB = CD$, then $x = y\tan\left(\frac{\alpha+\beta}{2}\right)$

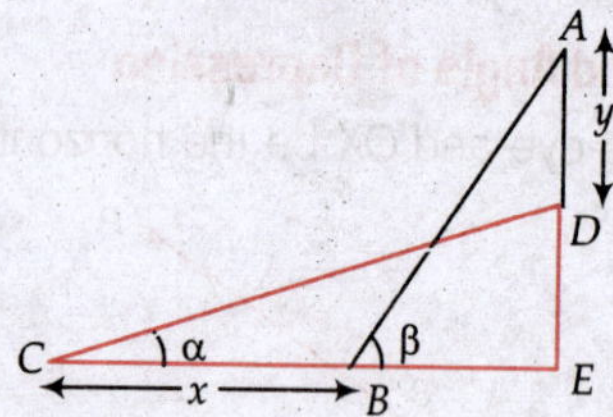

(iii) $h = \frac{H\sin(\beta - \alpha)}{\cos\alpha\sin\beta}$

and $H = \frac{h\cot\alpha}{\cot\alpha - \cot\beta}$

$\Rightarrow \quad H = x\cot\alpha\tan(\alpha + \beta)$

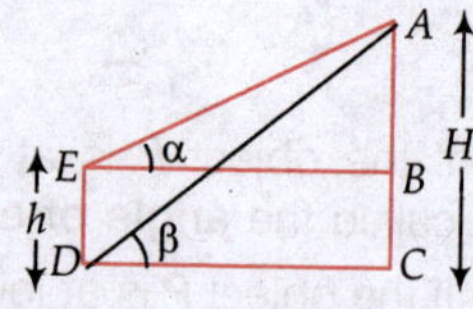

(iv) $H = \frac{h\cot\beta}{\cot\alpha}$

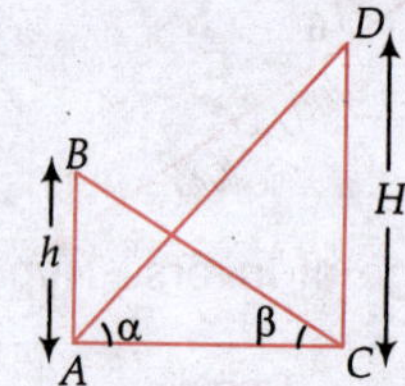

(v) $H = x\cot\alpha\tan(\alpha + \beta)$

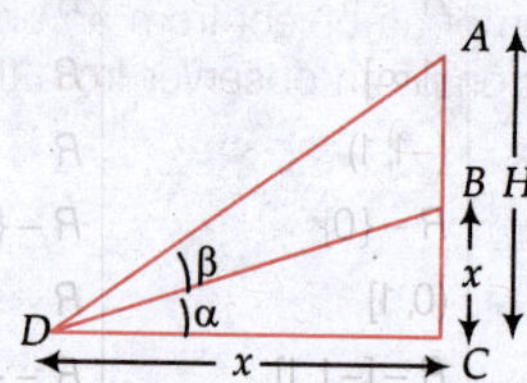

(vi) $H = \dfrac{\alpha \sin(\alpha + \beta)}{\sin(\beta - \alpha)}$

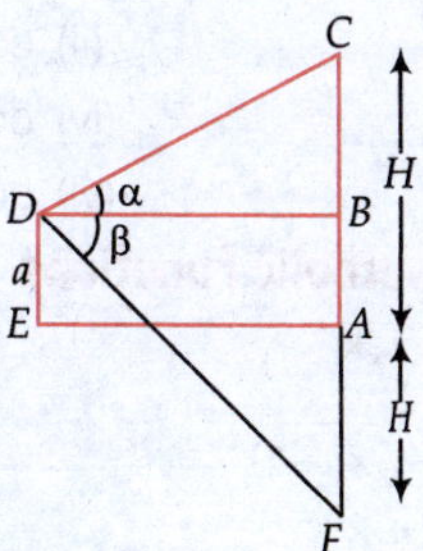

(vii) $a = h(\cot\alpha + \cot\beta)$

$h = a\sin\alpha \sin\beta \ \text{cosec}(\alpha + \beta)$

and $d = h\cot\beta = a\sin\alpha \cos\beta \ \text{cosec}(\alpha + \beta)$

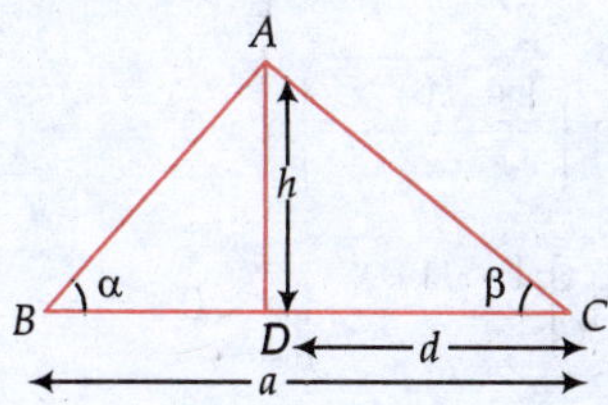

Inverse Trigonometric Functions

(Inverse Hyperbolic Functions)

If $\sinh y = x$, then y is called the inverse hyperbolic sine of x and it is written as $y = \sinh^{-1} x$.

Similarly, $\cosh^{-1} x$, $\tanh^{-1} x$ etc., can be defined.

Domain and Range of Inverse Hyperbolic Functions

Function	Domain	Range
$\sinh^{-1}x$	R	R
$\cosh^{-1}x$	$[1, \infty]$	R
$\tanh^{-1}x$	$(-1, 1)$	R
$\text{cosech}^{-1}x$	$R - \{0\}$	$R - \{0\}$
$\text{sech}^{-1}x$	$(0, 1]$	R
$\coth^{-1}x$	$R - [-1, 1]$	$R - \{0\}$

Relation between Inverse Circular Functions and Inverse Hyperbolic Functions

(i) $\sinh^{-1} x = -i \sin^{-1}(ix)$

(ii) $\cosh^{-1} x = -i \cos^{-1} x$

(iii) $\tanh^{-1} x = -i \tan^{-1}(ix)$

(iv) $\coth^{-1} x = i \cot^{-1}(ix)$

(v) $\sec h^{-1} x = -i \sec^{-1} x$

(vi) $\text{cosech}^{-1} x = i \,\text{cosec}^{-1}(ix)$

Formulae On Inverse Hyperbolic Functions

(i) $\sinh^{-1} x = \log_e (x + \sqrt{x^2 + 1})$

(ii) $\cosh^{-1} x = \log_e (x + \sqrt{x^2 - 1})$

(iii) $\tanh^{-1} x = \dfrac{1}{2} \log_e \left(\dfrac{1+x}{1-x}\right)$

(iv) $\coth^{-1} x = \dfrac{1}{2} \log_e \left(\dfrac{x+1}{x-1}\right), |x| > 1$

(v) $\sec h^{-1} x = \log_e \left(\dfrac{1 + \sqrt{1 - x^2}}{x}\right), x \in (0, 1]$

(vi) $\text{cosech}^{-1} x = \begin{cases} \log_e \left(\dfrac{1 + \sqrt{1 + x^2}}{x}\right), x > 0 \\ \log_e \left(\dfrac{1 - \sqrt{1 + x^2}}{x}\right), x < 0 \end{cases}$

Circles

Pole and Polar

If through a point $P(x_1, y_1)$ (within or outside a circle) there be drawn any straight line to meet the given circle at Q and R, the locus of the point of intersection of tangents at Q and R is called the polar of P and point P is called the pole of polar.

(i) Equation of polar to the circle $x^2 + y^2 = r^2$ is $xx_1 + yy_1 = r^2$.

(ii) Equation of polar to the circle $x^2 + y^2 + 2gx + 2fy + c = 0$ is
$xx_1 + yy_1 + g(x + x_1) + f(y + y_1) + c = 0$

(iii) **Conjugate Points** Two points A and B are conjugate points with respect to a given circle, if each lies on the polar of the other with respect to the circle.

(iv) **Conjugate Lines** If two lines be such that the pole of one lies on the other, then they are called conjugate lines with respect to the given circle.

Radical Axis

The radical axis of two circles is the locus of a point which moves in such a way that the length of the tangents drawn from it to the two circles are equal. A system of circles in which every pair has the same radical axis is called a coaxial system of circles. The equation of radical axis of two circles $S_1 = 0$ and $S_2 = 0$ is given by $S_1 - S_2 = 0$.

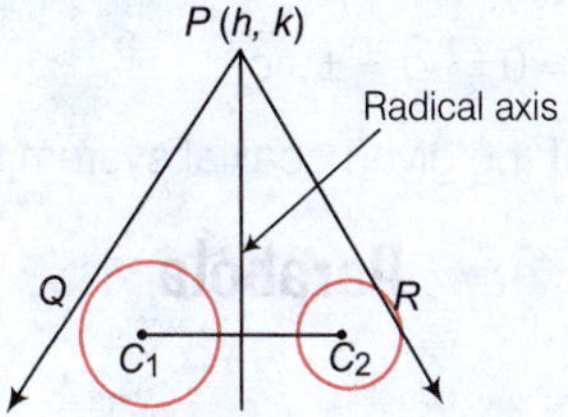

Value Points

(i) The radical axis of two circles is always perpendicular to the line joining the centres of the circles.

(ii) The radical axes of three circles, whose centres are non-collinear taken in pairs are concurrent.

(iii) The centre of the circle cutting two given circles orthogonally, lies on their radical axis.

(iv) **Radical Centre** The point of intersection of radical axis of three circles whose centre are non-collinear, taken in pairs, is called their radical centre.

Coaxial System of Circles

A system of circle is said to be coaxial system of circles, if every pair of the circles in the system has same radical axis.

(i) The equation of a system of coaxial circles, when the equation of the radical axis $P \equiv lx + my + n = 0$ and one of the circle of the system $S \equiv x^2 + y^2 + 2gx + 2fy + c = 0$, is $S + \lambda P = 0$, where λ is an arbitrary constant.

(ii) Since, the lines joining the centres of two circles is perpendicular to their radical axis. Therefore, the centres of all circles of a coaxial system lie on a straight line, which is perpendicular to the common radical axis.

Limiting Points

Limiting points of a system of coaxial circles are the centres of the point circles belonging to the family.

Let equation of circle be $x^2 + y^2 + 2gx + c = 0$

$\therefore$ Radius of circle $= \sqrt{g^2 - c}$

For limiting point, $r = 0$

$$\therefore \quad \sqrt{g^2 - c} = 0 \Rightarrow g = \pm\sqrt{c}$$

Thus, limiting points of the given coaxial system as $(\sqrt{c}, 0)$ and $(-\sqrt{c}, 0)$.

Parabola

Pole and Polar

Let P be a point lying within or outside a given parabola. Suppose any straight line drawn through P intersects the parabola at Q and R. Then, the locus of the point of intersection of the tangents to the parabola at Q and R is called the polar of the given point P with respect to the parabola and the point P is called the pole of the polar.

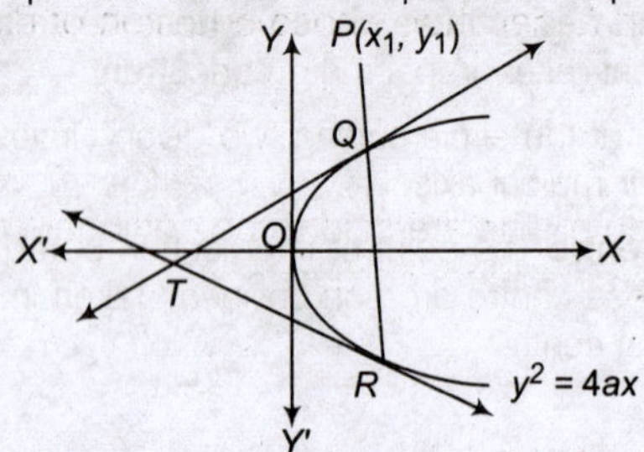

Important Points

(i) The polar of a point $P(x_1, y_1)$ with respect to the parabola $y^2 = 4ax$ is $yy_1 = 2a(x + x_1)$ or $T = 0$.

(ii) Any tangent is the polar of its point of contact.

(iii) Pole of $lx + my + n = 0$ with respect to $y^2 = 4ax$ is $\left(\frac{n}{l}, -\frac{2am}{l}\right)$.

(iv) Pole of the chord joining (x_1, y_1) and (x_2, y_2) is $\left(\frac{y_1 y_2}{4a}, \frac{y_1 + y_2}{2}\right)$.

(v) If the polar of $P(x_1, y_1)$ passes through $Q(x_2, y_2)$, then the polar of Q will passes through P. Here, P and Q are called **conjugate points**.

(vi) If the pole of a line $a_1x + b_1y + c_1 = 0$ lies on another line $a_2x + b_2y + c_2 = 0$, then the pole of the second line will lies on the first line. Such lines are called **conjugate lines**.

(vii) The point of intersection of the polar of two points Q and R is the pole of QR.

(viii) The tangents at the ends of any chord of the parabola meet on the diameter which bisect the chord.

Ellipse

Conjugate Points and Conjugate Lines

Two points are said to be conjugate points with respect to an ellipes, if each lies on the polar of the other. Two lines are said to be conjugate lines with respect to an ellipse, if each passes through the pole of the other.

Diameter and Conjugate Diameter

The locus of the mid-point of a system of parallel chords of an ellipse $\frac{x^2}{a^2} + \frac{y^2}{b^2} = 1$ is called a diameter, whose equation of diameter is

$$y = -\frac{b^2}{a^2 m}x.$$

Two diameters of an ellipse are said to be conjugate diameters, if each bisects the chords parallel to the other.

Properties of Conjugate Diameters

(i) The eccentric angles of the ends of a pair of conjugate diameters of an ellipse differ by a right angle.

(ii) The sum of the squares of any two conjugate semi-diameters of an ellipse is constant and equal to the sum of the squares of the semi-axis of the ellipse i.e. $CP^2 + CD^2 = a^2 + b^2$.

(iii) If PCP' and QCQ' are two conjugate semi-diameters of an ellipse $\frac{x^2}{a^2} + \frac{y^2}{b^2} = 1$ and S, S_1 be two foci of an ellipse, then

$SP \times S_1P = CQ^2$

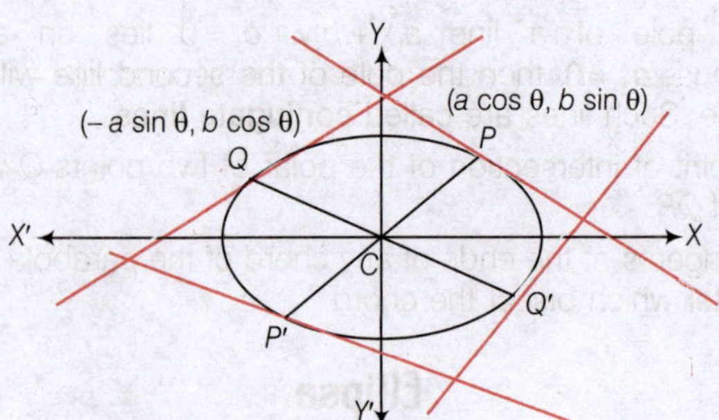

(iv) The tangent at the ends of a pair of conjugate diameters of an ellipse form a parallelogram.

(v) The area of the parallelogram formed by the tangents at the ends of conjugate diameters of an ellipse is constant and is equal to the product of the axes.

Hyperbola

Conjugate Points and Conjugate Lines

(i) Two points are said to be conjugate points with respect to a hyperbola, if each lies on the polar of the other.

(ii) Two lines are said to be conjugate lines with respect to a hyperbola $\frac{x^2}{a^2} - \frac{y^2}{b^2} = 1$, if each passes through the pole of the other.

Diameter and Conjugate Diameter

(i) **Diameter** The locus of the mid-points of a system of parallel chords of a hyperbola is called a diameter.

The equation of the diameter bisecting a system of parallel chords of slope m to the hyperbola $\frac{x^2}{a^2} - \frac{y^2}{b^2} = 1$ is $y = \frac{b^2}{a^2 m} x$

(ii) **Conjugate Diameter** The diameters of a hyperbola are said to be conjugate diameter, if each bisect the chords parallel to the other.

The diameters $y = m_1 x$ and $y = m_2 x$ are conjugate, if $m_1 m_2 = \frac{b^2}{a^2}$.

Important Points

If a pair of diameters is conjugate with respect to a hyperbola, they are conjugate with respect to its conjugate hyperbola also.

(i) The equation of two asymptotes of the hyperbola $\frac{x^2}{a^2}-\frac{y^2}{b^2}=1$ are $y=\pm\frac{b}{a}x$ or $\frac{x}{a}\pm\frac{y}{b}=0$

(ii) The combined equation of the asymptotes of the hyperbola

$$\frac{x^2}{a^2}-\frac{y^2}{b^2}=1 \text{ is } \frac{x^2}{a^2}-\frac{y^2}{b^2}=0.$$

(iii) When $b=a$, i.e. the asymptotes of rectangular hyperbola $x^2-y^2=a^2$ are $y=\pm x$ which are at right angle.

(iv) A hyperbola and its conjugate hyperbola have the same asymptotes.

(v) The equation of the pair of asymptotes differ the hyperbola and the conjugate hyperbola by the same constant only i.e.
Hyperbola – Asymptotes = Asymptotes – Conjugate hyperbola

(vi) The asymptotes pass through the centre of the hyperbola.

(vii) The bisectors of angle between the asymptotes of hyperbola $\frac{x^2}{a^2}-\frac{y^2}{b^2}=1$ are the coordinate axes.

(viii) The angle between the asymptotes of $\frac{x^2}{a^2}-\frac{y^2}{b^2}=1$ is $2\tan^{-1}\left(\frac{b}{a}\right)$ or $2\sec^{-1}(e)$.

Vectors

Scalar Triple Product

If $\mathbf{a}, \mathbf{b}$ and $\mathbf{c}$ are three vectors, then $(\mathbf{a}\times\mathbf{b})\cdot\mathbf{c}$ is called scalar triple product and is denoted by $[\mathbf{a}\ \mathbf{b}\ \mathbf{c}]$.

$\therefore$ $$[\mathbf{a}\ \mathbf{b}\ \mathbf{c}]=(\mathbf{a}\times\mathbf{b})\cdot\mathbf{c}$$

Geometrical Interpretation of Scalar Triple Product

The scalar triple product $(\mathbf{a}\times\mathbf{b})\cdot\mathbf{c}$ represents the volume of a parallelopiped whose coterminus edges are represented by $\mathbf{a}$, $\mathbf{b}$ and $\mathbf{c}$ which form a right handed system of vectors.

Expression of the scalar triple product $(\mathbf{a}\times\mathbf{b})\cdot\mathbf{c}$ in terms of components

$$\mathbf{a}=a_1\hat{\mathbf{i}}+b_1\hat{\mathbf{j}}+c_1\hat{\mathbf{k}},\ \mathbf{b}=a_2\hat{\mathbf{i}}+b_2\hat{\mathbf{j}}+c_2\hat{\mathbf{k}}$$

and $\mathbf{c}=a_3\hat{\mathbf{i}}+b_3\hat{\mathbf{j}}+c_3\hat{\mathbf{k}}$ is

$$[\mathbf{a}\ \mathbf{b}\ \mathbf{c}]=\begin{vmatrix} a_1 & b_1 & c_1 \\ a_2 & b_2 & c_2 \\ a_3 & b_3 & b_3 \end{vmatrix}$$

Properties of Scalar Triple Product

(i) The scalar triple product is independent of the positions of dot and cross i.e. $(\mathbf{a}\times\mathbf{b})\cdot\mathbf{c}=\mathbf{a}\cdot(\mathbf{b}\times\mathbf{c})$.

(ii) The scalar triple product of three vectors is unaltered so long as the cyclic order of the vectors remains unchanged.

i.e. $(\mathbf{a}\times\mathbf{b})\cdot\mathbf{c}=(\mathbf{b}\times\mathbf{c})\cdot\mathbf{a}=(\mathbf{c}\times\mathbf{a})\cdot\mathbf{b}$

or $[\mathbf{a}\ \mathbf{b}\ \mathbf{c}]=[\mathbf{b}\ \mathbf{c}\ \mathbf{a}]=[\mathbf{c}\ \mathbf{a}\ \mathbf{b}]$.

(iii) The scalar triple product changes in sign but not in magnitude, when the cyclic order is changed.

i.e. $[\mathbf{a}\ \mathbf{b}\ \mathbf{c}]=-[\mathbf{a}\ \mathbf{c}\ \mathbf{b}]$

(iv) The scalar triple product vanishes, if any two of its vectors are equal.

i.e. $[\mathbf{a}\ \mathbf{a}\ \mathbf{b}]=0, [\mathbf{a}\ \mathbf{b}\ \mathbf{a}]=0$ and $[\mathbf{b}\ \mathbf{a}\ \mathbf{a}]=0$.

(v) The scalar triple product vanishes, if any two of its vectors are parallel or collinear.

(vi) For any scalar $x, [x\mathbf{a}\ \mathbf{b}\ \mathbf{c}]=x[\mathbf{a}\ \mathbf{b}\ \mathbf{c}]$.

Also, $[x\mathbf{a}\ y\mathbf{b}\ z\mathbf{c}]=xyz[\mathbf{a}\ \mathbf{b}\ \mathbf{c}]$.

(vii) For any vectors $\mathbf{a}, \mathbf{b}, \mathbf{c}, \mathbf{d}$; $[\mathbf{a}+\mathbf{b}\ \mathbf{c}\ \mathbf{d}]=[\mathbf{a}\ \mathbf{c}\ \mathbf{d}]+[\mathbf{b}\ \mathbf{c}\ \mathbf{d}]$

(viii) The scalar triple product of cyclic components $\hat{\mathbf{i}}, \hat{\mathbf{j}}$ and $\hat{\mathbf{k}}$ is 1, i.e. $[\mathbf{i}\ \mathbf{j}\ \mathbf{k}]=1$.

(ix) $(\mathbf{a}\times\mathbf{b})\cdot(\mathbf{c}\times\mathbf{d})=\begin{vmatrix} \mathbf{a}\cdot\mathbf{c} & \mathbf{b}\cdot\mathbf{c} \\ \mathbf{a}\cdot\mathbf{d} & \mathbf{b}\cdot\mathbf{d} \end{vmatrix}$

(x) $[\mathbf{a}\ \mathbf{b}\ \mathbf{c}][\mathbf{u}\ \mathbf{v}\ \mathbf{w}]=\begin{vmatrix} \mathbf{a}\cdot\mathbf{u} & \mathbf{b}\cdot\mathbf{u} & \mathbf{c}\cdot\mathbf{u} \\ \mathbf{a}\cdot\mathbf{v} & \mathbf{b}\cdot\mathbf{v} & \mathbf{c}\cdot\mathbf{v} \\ \mathbf{a}\cdot\mathbf{w} & \mathbf{b}\cdot\mathbf{w} & \mathbf{c}\cdot\mathbf{w} \end{vmatrix}$

(xi) Three non-zero vectors $\mathbf{a}, \mathbf{b}$ and $\mathbf{c}$ are coplanar, if and only if $[\mathbf{a}\ \mathbf{b}\ \mathbf{c}]=0$.

(xii) Four points A, B, C, D with position vectors $\mathbf{a}, \mathbf{b}, \mathbf{c}, \mathbf{d}$ respectively are coplanar, if and only if $[\mathbf{AB}\ \mathbf{AC}\ \mathbf{AD}]=0$.

i.e. if and only if $[\mathbf{b}-\mathbf{a}\ \ \mathbf{c}-\mathbf{a}\ \ \mathbf{d}-\mathbf{a}]=0$.

(xiii) Volume of parallelopiped with three coterminus edges $\mathbf{a}, \mathbf{b}$ and $\mathbf{c}$ is $|[\mathbf{a}\ \mathbf{b}\ \mathbf{c}]|$.

(xiv) Volume of prism on a triangular base with three coterminus edges $\mathbf{a}, \mathbf{b}$ and $\mathbf{c}$ is $\frac{1}{2}|[\mathbf{a}\ \mathbf{b}\ \mathbf{c}]|$.

(xv) Volume of a tetrahedron with three coterminus edges $\mathbf{a}, \mathbf{b}$ and $\mathbf{c}$ is $\frac{1}{6}|[\mathbf{a}\ \mathbf{b}\ \mathbf{c}]|$.

(xvi) If $\mathbf{a}$, $\mathbf{b}$, $\mathbf{c}$ and $\mathbf{d}$ are position vectors of vertices of a tetrahedron, then Volume $= \frac{1}{6}|[\mathbf{b}-\mathbf{a}\ \ \mathbf{c}-\mathbf{a}\ \ \mathbf{d}-\mathbf{a}]|$.

Vector Triple Product

If $\mathbf{a}, \mathbf{b}, \mathbf{c}$ be any three vectors, then $(\mathbf{a}\times \mathbf{b})\times\mathbf{c}$ and $\mathbf{a}\times(\mathbf{b}\times \mathbf{c})$ are known as vector triple product.

$\therefore \qquad \mathbf{a}\times(\mathbf{b}\times \mathbf{c})=(\mathbf{a}\cdot\mathbf{c})\mathbf{b}-(\mathbf{a}\cdot \mathbf{b})\ \mathbf{c}$

and $\qquad (\mathbf{a}\times \mathbf{b})\times \mathbf{c}=(\mathbf{a}\cdot\mathbf{c})\mathbf{b}-(\mathbf{b}\cdot \mathbf{c})\ \mathbf{a}$

Important Properties

(i) The vector $\mathbf{r}=\mathbf{a}\times(\mathbf{b}\times \mathbf{c})$ is perpendicular to $\mathbf{a}$ and lies in the plane $\mathbf{b}$ and $\mathbf{c}$.

(ii) $\mathbf{a}\times(\mathbf{b}\times \mathbf{c})\neq(\mathbf{a}\times \mathbf{b})\times \mathbf{c}$, the cross product of vectors is not associative.

(iii) $\mathbf{a}\times(\mathbf{b}\times \mathbf{c})=(\mathbf{a}\times \mathbf{b})\times \mathbf{c}$, if and only if

$$(\mathbf{a}\cdot \mathbf{c})\mathbf{b}-(\mathbf{a}\cdot \mathbf{b})\mathbf{c}=(\mathbf{a}\cdot \mathbf{c})\mathbf{b}-(\mathbf{b}\cdot \mathbf{c})\ \mathbf{a}, \text{ i.e. } \mathbf{c}=\frac{\mathbf{b}\cdot \mathbf{c}}{\mathbf{a}\cdot \mathbf{b}}\mathbf{a}$$

or vectors $\mathbf{a}$ and $\mathbf{c}$ are collinear.

Reciprocal System of Vectors

Let $\mathbf{a}$, $\mathbf{b}$ and $\mathbf{c}$ be three non-coplanar vectors and let

$$\mathbf{a}'=\frac{\mathbf{b}\times \mathbf{c}}{[\mathbf{a}\ \mathbf{b}\ \mathbf{c}]}$$

$$\mathbf{b}'=\frac{\mathbf{c}\times \mathbf{a}}{[\mathbf{a}\ \mathbf{b}\ \mathbf{c}]}$$

$$\mathbf{c}'=\frac{\mathbf{a}\times \mathbf{b}}{[\mathbf{a}\ \mathbf{b}\ \mathbf{c}]}$$

Then, $\mathbf{a}'$, $\mathbf{b}'$ and $\mathbf{c}'$ are said to form a reciprocal system of a, b and c.

Properties of Reciprocal System

(i) $\mathbf{a}\cdot\mathbf{a}' = \mathbf{b}\cdot\mathbf{b}' = \mathbf{c}\cdot\mathbf{c}' = 1$

(ii) $\mathbf{a}\cdot\mathbf{b}' = \mathbf{a}\cdot\mathbf{c}' = 0, \mathbf{b}\cdot\mathbf{a}' = \mathbf{b}\cdot\mathbf{c}' = 0, \mathbf{c}\cdot\mathbf{a}' = \mathbf{c}\cdot\mathbf{b}' = 0$

(iii) $[\mathbf{a}'\ \mathbf{b}'\ \mathbf{c}'][\mathbf{a}\ \mathbf{b}\ \mathbf{c}] = 1 \Rightarrow [\mathbf{a}'\ \mathbf{b}'\ \mathbf{c}'] = \dfrac{1}{[\mathbf{a}\ \mathbf{b}\ \mathbf{c}]}$

(iv) $\mathbf{a} = \dfrac{\mathbf{b}'\times\mathbf{c}'}{[\mathbf{a}'\ \mathbf{b}'\ \mathbf{c}']}, \mathbf{b} = \dfrac{\mathbf{c}'\times\mathbf{a}'}{[\mathbf{a}'\ \mathbf{b}'\ \mathbf{c}']}, \mathbf{c} = \dfrac{\mathbf{a}'\times\mathbf{b}'}{[\mathbf{a}'\ \mathbf{b}'\ \mathbf{c}']}$

Thus, $\mathbf{a}, \mathbf{b}, \mathbf{c}$ is reciprocal to the system $\mathbf{a}', \mathbf{b}', \mathbf{c}'$.

(v) The orthonormal vector triad $\mathbf{i}, \mathbf{j}, \mathbf{k}$ form self reciprocal system.

(vi) If $\mathbf{a}, \mathbf{b}, \mathbf{c}$ are a system of non-coplanar vectors and $\mathbf{a}', \mathbf{b}', \mathbf{c}'$ are the reciprocal system of vectors, then any vector $\mathbf{r}$ can be expressed as $\mathbf{r} = (\mathbf{r}\cdot\mathbf{a}')\mathbf{a} + (\mathbf{r}\cdot\mathbf{b}')\mathbf{b} + (\mathbf{r}\cdot\mathbf{c}')\mathbf{c}$.

Three Dimensional Geometry

Condition for Tangent Plane to a Sphere

We know that plane touch the sphere, if the perpendicular distance from centre to the sphere is equal to the radius.

Vector Form

The plane $\mathbf{r}\cdot\mathbf{n} = d$ touches the sphere the $|\mathbf{r} - \mathbf{c}| = a$, if $\dfrac{|\mathbf{c}\,\mathbf{n} - d|}{|\mathbf{n}|} = a$.

Cartesian Form

The plane $lx + my + nz = p$ will touch the sphere $x^2 + y^2 + z^2 + 2ux + 2vy + 2wz + d = 0$, if

$$\frac{|lu + mv + nw + p|}{\sqrt{l^2 + m^2 + n^2}} = \sqrt{u^2 + v^2 + w^2 - d}$$

or $$(lu + mv + nw + p)^2 = (u^2 + v^2 + w^2 - d)(l^2 + m^2 + n^2)$$

Plane Section of a Sphere

Consider a sphere intersected by a plane. The set of points common to both sphere and plane is called a plane section of a sphere.

In ΔCNP, $NP^2 = CP^2 - CN^2 = r^2 - p^2$ $\quad [\because NP = \sqrt{r^2 - p^2}]$

Hence, the locus of P is a circle whose centre is at the point N, the foot of the perpendicular from the centre of the sphere to the plane.

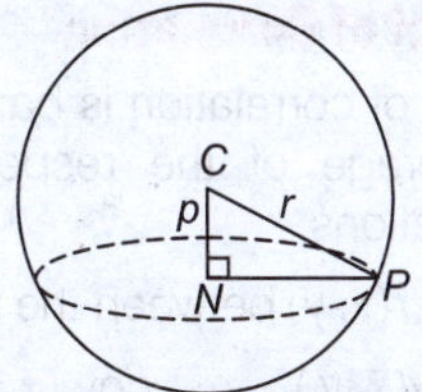

The section of sphere by a plane through its centre is called a great circle. The centre and radius of a great circle are the same as those of the sphere.

Statistics

Correlation

The tendency of simultaneous variation between two variables is called correlation (or covariation). It denotes the degree of inter-dependence between variables.

Types of Correlation

1. Perfect Correlation

If the two variables vary in such a manner that their ratio is always constant, then the correlation is said to be perfect.

2. Positive or Direct Correlation

If an increase or decrease in one variable corresponds to an increase or decrease in the other, then the correlation is said to be positive.

3. Negative or Indirect Correlation

If an increase or decrease in one variable corresponds to a decrease or increase in the other, then correlation is said to be negative.

Covariance

Let $(x_i, y_i), i = 1, 2, 3, \ldots, n$ be a bivariate distribution, where $x_1, x_2, \ldots, x_n$ are the values of variable x and $y_1, y_2, \ldots, y_n$ those of y, then the cov (x, y) is given by

(i) $$\text{cov}(x, y) = \frac{1}{n}\sum_{i=1}^{n}(x_i - \bar{x})(y_i - \bar{y})$$

where, $\bar{x}$ and $\bar{y}$ are mean of variables x and y.

(ii) $$\text{cov}(x, y) = \frac{1}{n}\sum_{i=1}^{n}x_i y_i - \left(\frac{1}{n}\sum_{i=1}^{n}x_i\right)\left(\frac{1}{n}\sum_{i=1}^{n}y_i\right)$$

Karl Pearson's Coefficient of Correlation

Karl Pearson's coefficient of correlation is based on the products of the deviations from the average of the respective variables and their respective standard deviations.

The correlation coefficient $r(x, y)$ between the variables x and y is given

$$r(x, y)=\frac{\operatorname{cov}(x, y)}{\sqrt{\operatorname{var}(x) \operatorname{var}(y)}} \text{ or } \frac{\operatorname{cov}(x, y)}{\sigma_x \sigma_y}$$

$$=\frac{\sum_{i=1}^{n}(x_i-\bar{x})(y_i-\bar{y})}{\sqrt{\sum_{i=1}^{n}(x_i-\bar{x})^2} \sqrt{\sum_{i=1}^{n}(y_i-\bar{y})^2}}$$

$$=\frac{\sum_{i=1}^{n} x_i y_i-\frac{\sum_{i=1}^{n} x_i \sum_{i=1}^{n} y_i}{n}}{\sqrt{\sum_{i=1}^{n} x_i^2-\frac{\left(\sum_{i=1}^{n} x_i\right)^2}{n}} \sqrt{\sum_{i=1}^{n} y_i^2-\frac{\left(\sum_{i=1}^{n} y_i\right)^2}{n}}}$$

$$=\frac{n \sum_{i=1}^{n} x_i y_i-\sum_{i=1}^{n} x_i \sum_{i=1}^{n} y_i}{\sqrt{n \sum_{i=1}^{n} x_i^2-\left(\sum_{i=1}^{n} x_i\right)^2} \sqrt{n \sum_{i=1}^{n} y_i^2-\left(\sum_{i=1}^{n} y_i\right)^2}}$$

Properties of Correlation

(i) Coefficient of correlation lies between −1 and 1 i.e. $-1 \leq r \leq 1$

(ii) If $r=1$, then coefficient of correlation is perfectly positive.

(iii) If $r=-1$, then correlation is perfectly negative.

(iv) The coefficient of correlation is independent of the change of origin and scale.

(v) Correlation coefficient has no unit and it is a pure number.

(vi) If $-1<r<1$, it indicates the degree of linear relationship between x and y, whereas its sign tells about the direction of relationship.

(vii) If x and y are two independent variables, then $r=0$

(viii) If $r=0$, x and y are said to be uncorrelated. It does not imply that the two variates are independent.

(ix) If x and y are random variables and a, b, c and d are any numbers such that $a \neq 0$, $c \neq 0$, then

$$r(ax+b, cy+d) = \frac{|ac|}{ac} r(x, y).$$

(x) **Probable Error and Standard Error** If r is the correlation coefficient in a sample of n pairs of observations, then it standard error is given by $\frac{1-r^2}{\sqrt{n}}$.

And the probable error of correlation coefficient is given by $(0.6745)\left(\frac{1-r^2}{\sqrt{n}}\right)$.

Rank Correlation (Spearman's)

Let d be the difference between paired ranks and n be the number of items ranked. The coefficient of rank correlation is given by

(i) **When ranks are not repeated**

$$r = 1 - \frac{6\sum_{i=1}^{n} d^2}{n(n^2-1)}$$

(ii) **When ranks are repeated** If n ranks are repeated $m_1, m_2, \ldots, m_r$ times, then rank correlation is given by

$$r = 1 - \frac{6\left[\sum_{i=1}^{n} d^2 + \frac{1}{12}\sum_{i=1}^{r}(m_i^3 - m_i)\right]}{n(n^2-1)}$$

Value Points

(i) The rank correlation coefficient lies between -1 and 1.

(ii) If two variables are correlated, then points in the scatter diagram generally cluster around a curve which we call the curve of regression.

Regression

Regression helps to estimate or predict the unknown value of one variable from the known values of the other related variables.

Lines of Regression

A line of regression is the straight line which gives the best fit in the least square sense to the given sets of data.

Regression coefficient of y on x and x on y

The regression coefficient shows that with a unit change in the value of x (or y) variable, what will be the average change in the value of y (or x) variable.

It is denoted by b_{yx} (or b_{xy}).

$$b_{yx} = r\frac{\sigma_y}{\sigma_x} = \frac{\text{cov}(x, y)}{\sigma_x^2} \quad \text{and} \quad b_{xy} = r\frac{\sigma_x}{\sigma_y} = \frac{\text{cov}(x, y)}{\sigma_y^2}$$

Regression Equation Regression equations are the algebraic formulation of regression lines.

(i) Line of regression of y on x is $y - \bar{y} = r\frac{\sigma_y}{\sigma_x}(x - \bar{x})$

(ii) Line of regression of x on y is $x - \bar{x} = r\frac{\sigma_x}{\sigma_y}(y - \bar{y})$

(iii) Angle between two regression lines is given by

$$\theta = \tan^{-1}\left[\left(\frac{1-r^2}{r}\right)\left(\frac{\sigma_x\sigma_y}{\sigma_x^2 + \sigma_y^2}\right)\right] = \tan^{-1}\left[\frac{1-r^2}{b_{xy} + b_{yx}}\right]$$

(a) If $r = 0$, i.e. $\theta = \frac{\pi}{2}$, then two regression lines are perpendicular to each other.

(b) If $r = 1$ or -1, i.e. $\theta = 0$, then two regression lines coincide.

Value Points

(i) Both regression coefficients and r have the same sign.

(ii) Coefficient of correlation is the geometric mean between the regression coefficients.

(iii) $0 < |b_{xy}\, b_{yx}| \le 1$, if $r \ne 0$ i.e. if $|b_{xy}| > 1$, then $|b_{yx}| < 1$

(iv) Regression coefficients are independent of the change of origin but not of scale.

(v) If two regression coefficient have different sign, then $r = 0$.

(vi) Arithmetic mean of the regression coefficients is greater than the correlation coefficient.

i.e. $\frac{b_{yx} + b_{xy}}{2} \ge r$.

Mathematical Reasoning

In mathematical language, there are two kinds of reasoning—inductive and deductive. Here, we will discuss some fundamentals of deductive reasoning.

Statement (Proposition)

A statement is an assertive sentence which is either true or false but not both. Statements are denoted by the small letters i.e. p, q, r ... etc.
e.g. p : A triangle has four sides.

Important Points

(i) A true statement is known as a valid statement and a false statement is known as an invalid statement.

(ii) Imperative, exclamatory, interrogative, optative sentences are not statements.

1. Simple Statement

A statement which cannot be broken into two or more statements is called a simple statement. e.g. p: $\sqrt{2}$ is a real number.

2. Open Statement

A sentence which contains one or more variable such that when certain values are given to the variable it becomes a statement, is called an open statement. e.g. p: 'He is a great man' is an open statement because in this statement, he can be replaced by any person.

3. Compound Statement

If two or more simple statements are combined by the use of words such as 'and', 'or', 'if... then', 'if and only if ', then the resulting statement is called a compound statement.
e.g. Roses are red and sky is blue.

Individual statements of a compound statement are called **component statements.**

Elementary Logical Connectives or Logical Operators

(i) **Negation** A statement which is formed by changing the truth value of a given statement by using the word like 'no', 'not' is called negation of given statement. If p is a statement, then negation of p is denoted by $\sim p$.

(ii) **Conjunction** A compound statement formed by two simple statements p and q using connective 'and' is called the conjunction of p and q and it is represented by $p \wedge q$.

(iii) **Disjunction** A compound statement formed by two simple statements p and q using connective 'or' is called the disjunction of p and q and it is represented by $p \vee q$.

(iv) **Conditional Statement** (Implication) Two simple statements p and q connected by the phrase, 'if ⋯ then', is called conditional statement of $p \cdots q$ and it is denoted by $p \Rightarrow q$.

(v) **Biconditional Statement** (Bi-implication) The two simple statements p and q connected by the phrase, 'if and only if' is called biconditional statement. It is denoted by $p \Leftrightarrow q$.

Truth Value and Truth Table

A statement can be either 'true' or 'false' which is called **truth** value of a statement and it is represented by the symbols T and F, respectively.

A **truth table** is a summary of truth values of the compound statement for all possible truth values of its component statements.

Logical Equivalent Statements

Two compound statements say, $S_1(p,q,r)$ and $S_2(p,q,r,\ldots)$, are said to be logically equivalent if they have the same truth values for all logically possibilities. If statements S_1 and S_2 are logically equivalent, then we write $S_1(p,q,r\ldots) = S_2(p,q,r,\ldots)$

Table for Basic Logical Connections

Number of rows = =

p	q	$\sim p$	$\sim q$	$p \wedge q$	$p \vee q$	$p \Rightarrow q$	$p \Leftrightarrow q$	$\sim(p \wedge q) \equiv \sim p \vee \sim q$	$\sim(p \Rightarrow q) \equiv p \wedge \sim q$	$\sim(p \Leftrightarrow q) \equiv (p \wedge \sim q) \vee (\sim p \wedge q)$
T	T	F	F	T	T	T	T	F	F	F
T	F	F	T	F	T	F	F	T	T	T
F	T	T	F	F	T	T	F	T	F	T
F	F	T	T	F	F	T	T	T	F	F

Tautology and Contradiction

The compound statement which are true for every value of their components are called **tautology**.

The compound statements which are false for every value of their components are called **contradiction** (or fallacy).

Truth Table

p	q	$p \Rightarrow q$	$q \Rightarrow p$	Tautology $(p \Rightarrow q) \vee (q \Rightarrow p)$	Contradiction $\sim\{(p \Rightarrow q) \vee (q \Rightarrow p)\}$
T	T	T	T	T	F
T	F	F	T	T	F
F	T	T	F	T	F
F	F	T	T	T	F

Laws of Algebra of Statements

(i) **Idempotent Laws**

(a) $p \vee p \equiv p$ (b) $p \wedge p \equiv p$

(ii) **Associative Laws**

(a) $(p \vee q) \vee r \equiv p \vee (q \vee r)$ (b) $(p \wedge q) \wedge r \equiv p \wedge (q \wedge r)$

(iii) **Commutative Laws**

(a) $p \vee q \equiv q \vee p$ (b) $p \wedge q \equiv q \wedge p$

(iv) **Distributive Laws**

(a) $p \vee (q \wedge r) \equiv (p \vee q) \wedge (p \vee r)$

(b) $p \wedge (q \vee r) \equiv (p \wedge q) \vee (p \wedge r)$

(v) **De-Morgan's Laws**

(a) $\sim(p \vee q) \equiv (\sim p) \wedge (\sim q)$ (b) $\sim(p \wedge q) \equiv (\sim p) \vee (\sim q)$

(vi) **Identity Laws**

(a) $p \wedge F \equiv F$ (b) $p \wedge T \equiv p$

(c) $p \vee T \equiv T$ (d) $p \vee F \equiv p$

(vii) **Complement Laws**

(a) $p \vee (\sim p) = T$ (b) $p \wedge (\sim p) \equiv F$

(viii) **Involution Laws**

(a) $\sim(\sim p) \equiv p \sim T \equiv F$ (b) $\sim(\sim p) \equiv p$

Value Points

(i) (a) If p is false, then $\sim p$ is true.

(b) If p is true, then $\sim p$ is false.

(ii) (a) The number of rows in truth table is depend on the number of statements.

(b) If the compound statement is made up of n sub-statements, then its truth table will contain 2^n rows.

(iii) (a) The converse of $p \Rightarrow q$ is $q \Rightarrow p$.

(b) The inverse of $p \Rightarrow q$ is $\sim p \Rightarrow \sim q$.

(iv) The contrapositive of $p \Rightarrow q$ is $\sim q \Rightarrow \sim p$.

(v) A statement which is neither a tautology nor a contradiction is a contingency.

Quantifiers

Quantifiers are phrases like, 'There exists' and 'For all'

(i) The symbol '$\forall$' stands 'for all values of '.

This is known as universal quantifier.

(ii) The symbol '$\exists$' stands for 'there exists'.

This is known as existential quantifier.

Quantified Statement

An open statement with a quantifier becomes a quantified statement. e.g. $x^4 > 0, \forall x \in R$ is a quantified statement. Its truth value is T.

Negation of a Quantified Statement

(i) $\sim\{p(x) \text{ is true}, \forall\, x \in A\} = \{\exists\, x \in A \text{ such that (s.t.)} \sim p(x) \text{ is true}\}$

(ii) $\sim\{\exists\, x \in A : p(x) \text{ is true}\} = \{\sim p(x) \text{ is true}, \forall\, x \in A\}$

Validity of Statements

Validity of a statement means checking whether the statement is valid (true) or not. This depends upon which of the connectives and quantifiers used in the statement.

1. Validity of Statement with 'AND'

If p and q are two mathematical statements, then in order to show that the statement '$p \wedge q$' is true, the steps are as follow:

Step I Show that the statement p is true.

Step II Show that the statement q is true.

2. Validity of Statements with 'OR'

If p and q are two mathematical statements, then in order to show that the compound statement 'p or q' is true, one must consider the following.

Case I Assume that p is false, show that q must be true.

Or

Case II Assume that q is false, show that p must be true.

3. Validity of Statements with 'If-then'

If p and q are two mathematical statements, then in order to show that the compound statement, 'if p then q' is true, one must consider the following.

Case I Assume that p is true, show that q must be true (direct method).

CaseII Assume that q is false, show that p must be false (contrapositive method).

4. Validity of the Statement with 'If and only if'

In order to prove that of the statement 'p if and only if q' is true, the steps are as follow:

Step I Show that, if p is true, then q is true.

Step II Show that, if q is true, then p is true.

Elementary Arithmetic-I

Number A number tells us how many times a unit is contained in a given quantity.

Numeral A group of figures (digits), representing a number, is called a numeral.

Face Value and Place Value of the Digits

In a numeral, the face value of a digit is the actual value.

In a numeral, the place value of a digit changes according to the change of its place.

e.g. In the numeral 576432, the face value of 6 is 6 and the place value of 6 is 6000.

Types of Number System

(i) **Binary Number System** (Base-2) It represents numerical values using two digits usually '0' and '1'. This system is used internally for computers and electronics.

For binary system, as we move left to the decimal point, number gets 2 times bigger and as we move right to the decimal, every number gets 2 times smaller.

e.g. $1011.101 = 1\times 2^3 + 0\times 2^2 + 1\times 2^1 + 1\times 2^0 + 1\times 2^{-1} + 0\times 2^{-2} + 1\times 2^{-3}$

Decimal	0	1	2	3	4	5
Binary number	0	1	10	11	100	101

(ii) **Octal Number System** (Base-8) It represents numerical values using 8 digits from '0' to '7'.

As we move left to the decimal point, number gets 8 times bigger and as we move right to the decimal point, number gets 8 times smaller.

Decimal	0	1	2	3	4	5	6	7	8	9	10
Octal	0	1	2	3	4	5	6	7	10	11	12

(iii) **Hexadecimal Number System** (Base-16) Every numerical value in this system is represented by decimal numbers 0 to 9 and letters (A, B, C, D, E, F) in place of number 10 to 15. As we move left to decimal, number gets 16 times bigger and as we move right to the decimal, numbers gets smaller by 16.

Decimal	0	1	2	3	4	5	6	7	8	9	10	11	12	13	14	15
Hexadecimal number	0	1	2	3	4	5	6	7	8	9	A	B	C	D	E	F

(iv) **Roman Number System** Roman Numerals and their corresponding Indo-Arabic numerals

Roman numerals	I	V	X	L	C	D	M
Indo-Arabic numerals	1	5	10	50	100	500	1000

(v) **Decimal Number System** Numeric values are represented by using digits from '0' to '9'.

Classification of Numbers in Decimal Number System

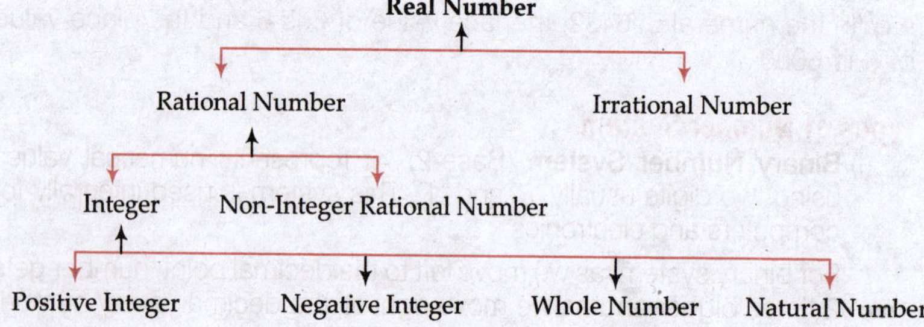

Natural Numbers All the positive integers starting from 1 till infinity and are also used for counting purpose, denoted by N.

$$N = \{1, 2, 3, \dots\}$$

Whole Numbers The system of Natural numbers along with number 0, is called whole number (W).

$$W = \{0, 1, 2, 3, \dots\}$$

Different Types of Natural Number

(i) **Even Number** A number, which is multiple of 2 is called an even number.

(ii) **Odd Number** A number, which is not a multiple of 2 is called an odd number.

(iii) **Prime Number** The number which can be divided only by itself and 1 is called prime number.

e.g. 2, 3, 5, 7, 11, ...

(iv) **Composite Number** The number which can be divided by a number other than 1 and the number itself is called composite number.

(v) **Consecutive Number** A series of numbers in which each number is greater by 1 than the number which precedes it.

Method to Determine a Given Number is Prime or Not

Step I Find a new number larger than the approximate square root of given number.

Step II Test whether the new number is divisible by any prime number.

Step III If the new number is not divisible by any of the prime number, then given number is a prime number otherwise it is a composite number.

Division on Numbers (Division Algorithm)

Let a and b be two integers such that $b \neq 0$, on dividing a by b, let q be the quotient and r the remainder, then the relationship between a, b, q and r is $a = bq + r$.

or in general, we have

$$\text{Dividend} = \text{Divisor} \times \text{Quotient} + \text{Remainder}$$

Test of Divisibility on a Natural Number

(i) **Divisibility by 2** A number is divisible by 2, if digit on unit place is 0, 2, 4, 6, 8.

(ii) **Divisibility by 3** If the sum of the digits of a number is divisible by 3, then the number is divisible by 3.

(iii) **Divisibility by 4** If the last two digits of a number is divisible by 4 or the last two digits are '00', then the number is divisible by 4.

(iv) **Divisibility by 5** A given number is divisible by 5, if 0 or 5 comes at unit place.

(v) **Divisibility by 6** If a given number is divisible by 2 and 3, then it is divisible by 6.

(vi) **Divisibility by 7**

(a) If a number is formed by repeating a digit six times, the number is divisible by 7, 11 and 13. e.g. 666666.

(b) If a number is formed by repeating a two-digit number three times, the number is divisible by 7. e.g. 676767.

(c) If a number is formed by repeating a three-digit number two times, the number is divisible by 7, 11 and 13. e.g. 453453.

(vii) **Divisibility by 8** If the last 3 digits of a number is divisible by 8 or the numbers ends with '000', then it is divisible by 8.

(viii) **Divisibility by 9** If the sum of the digits of a number is divisible by 9, then the number is divisible by 9.

(ix) **Divisibility by 10** If '0' comes at unit place of a number, then it is divisible by 10.

(x) **Divisibility by 11** A given number is divisible by 11, if the difference between the sum of the digits in odd places and the sum of the digits in the even places is either 0 or a multiple by 11.

(xi) **Divisibility by 12** If a given number is divisible by 4 and 3, then it is divisible by 12.

(xii) **Divisibility by 25** When the number formed by last two digits is divisible by 25.

(xiii) **Divisibility by 27** When the sum of the digit of the number is divisible by 27.

(xiv) **Divisibility by 125** When the number formed by last three digits is divisible by 125.

Value Points

(i) If N is a composite number of the form $a^p \cdot b^q \cdot c^r \ldots$, where a, b and c are primes, then the number of divisors of N is given by $(p+1)(q+1)(r+1)\ldots$.

(ii) The sum of the divisors of N is given by

$$S = \frac{(a^{p+1}-1)}{a-1} \cdot \frac{(b^{q+1}-1)}{b-1} \cdot \frac{(c^{r+1}-1)}{c-1}$$

Important Results of Natural Numbers

(i) The sum of first n natural numbers $= \frac{n(n+1)}{2}$

i.e. $$\sum_{r=1}^{n} r = \frac{n(n+1)}{2}$$

(ii) The sum of the squares of first n natural numbers

$$\sum_{r=1}^{n} r^2 = \frac{n(n+1)(2n+1)}{6}$$

(iii) The sum of the cubes of first n natural numbers

$$\sum_{r=1}^{n} r^3 = \left[\frac{n(n+1)}{2}\right]^2 = \left(\sum_{r=1}^{n} r\right)^2$$

(iv) The sum of first n odd numbers

$$(1 + 3 + 5 + 7 + \ldots + \text{upto } n \text{ terms}) = n^2$$

(v) The sum of first n even numbers

$$(2+4+6+\ldots+\text{upto } n \text{ terms}) = n(n+1)$$

(vi) The sum of the square of first n odd numbers

$$(1^2+3^2+5^2+\ldots+\text{upto } n \text{ terms}) = \frac{n}{3}(4n^2-1)$$

(vii) The sum of the square of first n even numbers

$$(2^2+4^2+6^2+\ldots+\text{upto } n \text{ terms}) = \frac{2n(n+1)(2n+1)}{3}$$

(viii) The sum of n terms of the series

$$1+(1+2)+(1+2+3)+\ldots+(1+2+3+\ldots+n)$$
$$=\frac{1}{6}n(n+1)(n+2)$$

Value Points

(i) The product of any n consecutive numbers is divisible by $n!$.

(ii) The product of any two consecutive odd or even numbers increased by 1 is a perfect square.

e.g. (i) $11\times 13+1=144=12^2$ (ii) $12\times 14+1=169=(13)^2$

(iii) The difference between the squares of two consecutive numbers is equal to the sum of those consecutive numbers.

e.g. $15^2-14^2=15+14=29$

Rule to Determine the Digit at Unit Place

Rule 1. For odd numbers When there is an odd digit at the unit place of the base (except 5), multiplying the number itself until you get 1 in the unit place.

$$(\ldots 1)^n=(\ldots 1) \qquad (\ldots 3)^{4n}=(\ldots 1)$$
$$(\ldots 7)^{4n}=(\ldots 1) \qquad (\ldots 9)^{2n}=(\ldots 1)$$

Rule 2. For even numbers When there is an even digit at unit place of the base, multiplying the number by itself until you get 6 in the unit place.

$$(\ldots 2)^{4n}=(\ldots 6) \qquad (\ldots 6)^n=(\ldots 6)$$
$$(\ldots 4)^{2n}=(\ldots 6) \qquad (\ldots 8)^{4n}=(\ldots 6)$$

Rule 3. 1, 5, 6 at unit's place. If there is 1, 5 or 6 at the unit place of base, then any times of its multiplication, it will get the same digit in unit place.

$$(\ldots 1)^n=(\ldots 1) \qquad (\ldots 5)^n=(\ldots 5)$$
$$(\ldots 6)^n=(\ldots 6)$$

Integers

Any number having sign '+' ve or '–' ve without having any fractional part is called integer (including zero).

$$I \text{ or } Z = \{\ldots, -3, -2, -1, 0, 1, 2, 3, \ldots\}$$

Important Points

(i) If n is a natural number, then the number of integers between $-n$ and n is $2n-1$.

(ii) If n and m are natural numbers such that $n < m$, then numbers of integers between n and m is $m-n-1$.

(iii) If n and m are natural number, then number of integers between $-n$ and m is $m+n-1$.

Rational Numbers

A number which can be written in the form of $\dfrac{p}{q}$, where $p, q \in Z$ and $q \neq 0$, is called rational number. A rational number can be expressed as decimal based, on which rational number are of two types :

(i) **Terminating** If the prime factors of denominator contains no factor other than 2 and 5, it is terminating.

(ii) **Non-terminating Recurring** If the prime factors of denominator contains factor other than 2 and 5, is non-terminating recurring rational number.

Rational Number between Two Rational Numbers

If a and b are two distinct rational numbers such that $a < b$, then n rational numbers between a and b, may be

$$a_i = a + \frac{b-a}{n+1} \times i, \text{ where } i = 1, 2, 3, \ldots, n.$$

Irrational Number

An irrational number is a non-terminating, non-recurring decimal, which cannot be written in the form of p/q, is called irrational number.

Value Points

(i) The number $\sqrt{x}$, x is not a perfect square, is an irrational number and $\sqrt{x} + y$ is also irrational.

(ii) π is an irrational number.

(iii) 0 is not an irrational number.

(iv) Sum, difference, product and quotient of two irrational numbers may be rational or irrational.

(v) Sum, difference, product and quotient of one rational and other irrational number is always irrational.

(vi) If a and b are two distinct rational numbers, then for $a < b$, n irrational numbers between a and b can be

$$a_i = a + \frac{b-a}{2(n+1)}\sqrt{2} \times i, \text{ where } i = 1, 2, 3, \dots, n.$$

Real Number

Any number, which is either rational or irrational is called real number and it is denoted by the symbol R.

i.e. R = {Set of all rational and irrational numbers}

Properties of Real Numbers

(i) **Commutative property of addition**

$$a + b = b + a$$

(ii) **Commutative property of multiplication**

$$a \cdot b = b \cdot a$$

(iii) **Associative property of addition**

$$a + (b + c) = (a + b) + c$$

(iv) **Associative property of multiplication**

$$a \cdot (b \cdot c) = (a \cdot b) \cdot c$$

(v) **Left distributive property**

$$a \cdot (b + c) = a \cdot b + a \cdot c$$

(vi) **Right distributive property**

$$(b + c) \cdot a = b \cdot a + c \cdot a$$

(vii) **Additive identity property**

$$a + 0 = a$$

(viii) **Multiplicative identity property**

$$a \cdot 1 = a$$

(ix) **Additive inverse property**

$$a + (-a) = 0$$

(x) **Multiplicative inverse property**

$$a \cdot \left(\frac{1}{a}\right) = 1, a \neq 0$$

(xi) **Zero property** $a \cdot 0 = 0$

Complex Numbers

If a and b are two real numbers, then the number $(a + ib)$ is called the complex number and it is denoted by the symbol C.

i.e. $C = \{a + ib, a, b \in R\}$

Here, a is called real part and b is called imaginary part.

Fraction

A fraction is a number representing ratio or division of two natural numbers.

Types of Fractions

(i) **Proper Fraction** A fraction, having numerator smaller than the denominator. e.g. $\frac{2}{3}, \frac{5}{8}, \frac{3}{7}$.

(ii) **Improper Fraction** A fraction, having numerator greater than or equal to denominator. e.g. $\frac{2}{2}, \frac{2}{1}, \frac{5}{3}, \frac{9}{6}$.

(iii) **Like Fractions** Fractions having same value in denominator. e.g. $\frac{2}{5}, \frac{6}{5}, \frac{11}{5}, \frac{7}{5}$.

(iv) **Unlike Fractions** Fractions having different values in denominator. e.g. $\frac{2}{3}, \frac{2}{5}, \frac{2}{11}, \frac{2}{13}$.

(v) **Equivalent Fraction** Fractions representing the same ratio or numbers are called equivalent fraction. e.g. $\frac{3}{5} = \frac{6}{10} = \frac{9}{15} = \frac{12}{20}$.

(vi) **Mixed Fraction** It consists of two parts, an integer and a fraction. e.g. $2\frac{1}{3}, 5\frac{1}{4}$.

(vii) **Decimal Fraction** A fraction having 10 or power of 10 in the denominator. e.g. $\frac{5}{100}, \frac{2}{10}, \frac{61}{1000}$.

(viii) **Vulgar/Common Fraction** Fraction having denominator other than 10 (or power of 10). e.g. $\frac{7}{3}, \frac{5}{6}$.

(ix) **Complex Fraction** A fraction, in which numerator and denominator, both are fractions. e.g. $\frac{7/3}{2/5}, \frac{2/7}{5/6}$.

Comparison of Fractions

Fraction can be compared by any of the given method.

(i) **LCM Method** By taking LCM of all the denominators in the given fraction, then comparing their numerators by making their denominators equal.

(ii) **Decimal Method** By converting fractional numbers into their corresponding decimal numbers, which can be easily compared.

(iii) **Cross-multiplication Method** If we have two fractions $\frac{a}{b}$ and $\frac{c}{d}$, then cross-multiply the fraction. i.e. we get ad and bc. The fraction, whose numerator after cross-multiplication gives the greater value is greater. *i.e.* If $ad > bc$, then $\frac{a}{b} > \frac{c}{d}$.

Ascending/Descending Orders in Fraction

Rule 1. When numerator and denominator of the fractions increase by a constant value, then the last fraction is the greatest fraction.

i.e. $\frac{x}{y}, \frac{x+a}{y+b}, \frac{x+2a}{y+2b}, \ldots, \frac{x+na}{y+nb}$.

Then, $\frac{x+na}{y+nb}$ is greatest, if $a \geq b$.

Rule 2. In above case, consider $a < b$

(i) If $\frac{a}{b} > \frac{x}{y}$, then $\frac{x+na}{y+nb}$ is greatest. (ii) If $\frac{a}{b} < \frac{x}{y}$, then $\frac{x+na}{y+nb}$ is smallest.

(iii) If $\frac{a}{b} = \frac{x}{y}$, all values are equal.

Rule 3. For arranging fractions in ascending/descending order

***Step* I** Compare first two numbers.

***Step* II** Compare the third number with the one obtained in Step I (larger/smaller depending upon ascending/descending order).

***Step* III** Repeat Step II until the last term.

Power and Index

If a number a is multiplied by itself n times, then product is called ***n*th power** of a and is written as a^n. In a^n, a is called the base and n is the **index**.

Value Points

(i) If a is a rational number and m is a positive integer, then

$a^m = a \times a \times \ldots \times a (m \text{ times})$ or $a^m = a \times a \times a \times \ldots \times a$

(ii) If a is a non-zero rational number and m is a positive integer, then

$a^{-m} = a^{-1} \times a^{-1} \times a^{-1} \times \ldots \times a^{-1} (m \text{ times})$

$$= \frac{1}{a} \times \frac{1}{a} \times \ldots \times \frac{1}{a} \text{ (}m\text{ times)} = \left(\frac{1}{a}\right)^m$$

(iii) If a and b are non-zero rational numbers and m is a positive integer such that $a^m = b$, then we may write $b^{1/m} = a$.

$b^{1/m}$ may also be written as $\sqrt[m]{b}$ (mth root of b).

(iv) Let a be a non-zero rational number and p/q be a positive rational number, then $a^{p/q}$ may be defined as

$a^{p/q} = (a^p)^{1/q}$ read as 'qth root of the pth power of a'.

or $a^{p/q} = (a^{1/q})^p = (\sqrt[q]{a})^p$ read as 'pth power of qth root of a'.

(v) If a is a non-zero rational number, then for positive rational exponent p/q, then number $a^{-p/q}$ may be defined as

$a^{-p/q} = \frac{1}{a^{p/q}} = \left(\frac{1}{a}\right)^{p/q}$. We say $a^{-p/q}$ is reciprocal of $a^{p/q}$ on (p/q)th power of the reciprocal of a.

Laws of Exponents If a and b are positive rational numbers and m and n are rational exponents (positive or negative), then

Rule 1. $a^m \times a^n = a^{m+n}$ **Rule 2.** $a^m \div a^n = a^{m-n}$

Rule 3. $(a^m)^n = a^{m \times n}$ **Rule 4.** $a^m b^m = (a \cdot b)^m$

Rule 5. $a^0 = 1$ **Rule 6.** $(a/b)^m = a^m / b^m$

Rule 7. $a^{-m} = 1/a^m$ **Rule 8.** $(a/b)^{-m} = (b/a)^m$

Exponential Radical Forms If y is a positive rational number and q is a positive integer, then $y^{1/q} = x$, or $x = \sqrt[q]{y}$ denotes the positive real qth root of y.

(a) The form $y^{1/q}$ is called exponential form. The number y is called the base and $1/q$ is called its exponent.

(b) The form $\sqrt[q]{y}$ is called the radical form. The number q is called the index of the radical and y is called the radicand. The index of the radical is always taken positive.

(c) A number written in exponential form can also be expressed in radical form and *vice-versa*.

(d) If a number expressed in exponential form has a negative exponent, then first the exponent must be changed to positive by taking the reciprocal of the base.

Surds

Irrational root of a rational number is called a **surd**. If n is a positive integer and a is a positive rational number, which cannot be expressed as the nth power of some rational number, then the irrational number, $\sqrt[n]{a}$ or $a^{1/n}$ that is the positive nth root of a, is called **surd** or a **radical**. The symbol $\sqrt[n]{\ }$ is called the **radical sign**, n is called the **order of the surd** (or radical) and a is called the **radicand**. Hence, $\sqrt[3]{\sqrt{2}}$ is not a surd as $\sqrt{2}$ is not a rational number. However, $\sqrt{7}$ is a surd as 7 is a rational number and square root of 7 is not a rational number.

$\sqrt{64}$ is not a surd as though 64 is a rational number but $\sqrt{64} = 8$, which is not an irrational number.

$\therefore$ $\sqrt[6]{12}$ is a surd of order 6.

Properties of Surds

- Every surd is a real number. However, every real number is not a surd.
- A surd of order 2 is called a quadratic surd or square root. Hence, $\sqrt{7}, \sqrt{25}, \sqrt{\dfrac{4}{7}}$ are quadratic surds.
- A surd of order 3 is called a cubic surd or cubic root. Hence, $\sqrt[3]{2}, 3\sqrt[3]{5}, \sqrt[3]{2/5}$ are cubic surds.
- A surd of order 4 is called a biquadratic surd.

  H5ence, $\sqrt[4]{5}, 2\sqrt[4]{7}, 4\sqrt[4]{\dfrac{7}{5}}$ are biquadratic surds.
- A surd containing only one term is called a monomial surd.

  Hence, $-2\sqrt[3]{5}, 3\sqrt[4]{7}$ are monomial surds.
- If $\sqrt[n]{a}$ is surd, then $(\sqrt[n]{a})^n = a$.
- If $\sqrt[n]{a}$ and $\sqrt[n]{b}$ are surds, then $\sqrt[n]{a} \times \sqrt[n]{b} = \sqrt[n]{ab}$
- If $\sqrt[n]{a}$ and $\sqrt[n]{b}$ are surds, then $\dfrac{\sqrt[n]{a}}{\sqrt[n]{b}} = \sqrt[n]{\dfrac{a}{b}}$
- If $\sqrt[n]{a}$ is a surd and m is a positive integer, then $\sqrt[m]{\sqrt[n]{a}} = \sqrt[n]{\sqrt[m]{a}} = \sqrt[mn]{a}$.
- If $\sqrt[n]{a^p}$ is a surd and m is a positive integer, then $\sqrt[n]{a^p} = \sqrt[mn]{a^{pm}}$ (index of the radical and the exponent of the radical are multiplied by same positive integer m).
- A surd which has a rational factor other than unity, the other factor being irrational is called a **mixed surd**.

  Thus, $2\sqrt{3}, 7\sqrt[3]{2}, \dfrac{2}{3}\sqrt[4]{7}$ are mixed surds.

- A surd which has unity as its rational factor, the other factor being rational, is called a pure surd. Thus, $\sqrt{10}, \sqrt[3]{4}, \sqrt[5]{7}$ are pure surds.
- Two surds of same order can be compared by just comparing their radicands. If $\sqrt[n]{a}$ and $\sqrt[n]{b}$ are surds, then $\sqrt[n]{a} > \sqrt[n]{b}$, if $a > b$ and $\sqrt[n]{a} < \sqrt[n]{b}$, if $a < b$.
- If two surds are not of same order, then to compare them they must first be reduced to same order.
  Let $\sqrt[n]{a}$ and $\sqrt[m]{b}$ are surds such that $m \neq n$.
  Let LCM of m and n be p. Then, to compare them both must be reduced to pth order.
- Surds having same irrational factor are called **similar** or **like surds**.
  Thus, $3\sqrt{2}, \frac{4}{3}\sqrt{2}, -2\sqrt{2}, -\frac{1}{3}\sqrt{2}$ are similar surds (each has same irrational factor of $\sqrt{2}$).
- Only like surds can be added or subtracted. If $x\sqrt[n]{a}$ and $y\sqrt[n]{a}$ are surds, then $$x\sqrt[n]{a} + y\sqrt[n]{a} = (x+y)\sqrt[n]{a}$$
  and $$x\sqrt[n]{a} - y\sqrt[n]{a} = (x-y)\sqrt[n]{a}.$$
- Product of a surd with a rational number is again a surd.
- If p and q are rational numbers and $\sqrt[n]{a}$ is a surd, then $p \times (q\sqrt[n]{a}) = pq\sqrt[n]{a}$.
- Surds of same order can be multiplied as follows $\sqrt[n]{a} \times \sqrt[n]{b} = \sqrt[n]{a \times b}$ (radicands get multiplied and order remains same).
  Also, $p\sqrt[n]{a} \times q\sqrt[n]{b} = p \times q\sqrt[n]{a \times b}$ (rational factor of first gets multiplied by rational factor of second. Radicand of first gets multiplied by radicand of second. Order remains same).
- If $\sqrt[n]{a}$ is a surd in simplest form, then its simplest rationalising factor is $\sqrt[n]{a^{n-1}}$.
- If $\sqrt[n]{a^p}$ is a surd in simplest form, then its simplest rationalising factor is $\sqrt[n]{a^{n-p}}$.
- If $\sqrt[n]{a^p b^q}$ is a surd in simplest form, then its simplest rationalising factor is $\sqrt[n]{a^{n-p} b^{n-q}}$.
- A surd containing only two distinct terms is called a **binomial surd**. Hence, $\sqrt{2} + \sqrt{3}, 2\sqrt{3} + 3\sqrt{2}, 7 + \sqrt{3}$ are binomial surds.
- Two binomial surds are said to be conjugates of each other, if they differ only in sign (+ or –) connecting them.

Thus, $2\sqrt{2}+3\sqrt{3}$ and $2\sqrt{2}-3\sqrt{3}$ are conjugates of each other.

- Rationalising factor of a binomial surd is its conjugate. e.g. Rationalising factor of $a\sqrt{b}+c\sqrt{d}$ is $a\sqrt{b}-c\sqrt{d}$.
- Surds containing three distinct terms is called a **trinomial surd**. Hence, $\sqrt{7}+\sqrt{2}+3\sqrt{3}, \sqrt{7}-\sqrt{2}+\sqrt{3}$ are trinomial surds.

Some Useful Results

(i) $(\sqrt{a})^2 = a$

(ii) $(a\sqrt{b})^2 = a \times a \times b$

(iii) $\dfrac{1}{\sqrt{a}} = \dfrac{\sqrt{a}}{a}$

(iv) $\dfrac{1}{\sqrt{a}+\sqrt{b}} = \dfrac{\sqrt{a}-\sqrt{b}}{a-b}$

(v) $\dfrac{1}{\sqrt{a}-\sqrt{b}} = \dfrac{\sqrt{a}+\sqrt{b}}{a-b}$

(vi) $\dfrac{\sqrt{a}+\sqrt{b}}{\sqrt{a}-\sqrt{b}} = \dfrac{a+b+2\sqrt{ab}}{a-b}$

(vii) $\dfrac{\sqrt{a}-\sqrt{b}}{\sqrt{a}+\sqrt{b}} = \dfrac{a+b-2\sqrt{ab}}{a-b}$

(viii) $\dfrac{\sqrt{a}+\sqrt{b}}{\sqrt{a}-\sqrt{b}} + \dfrac{\sqrt{a}-\sqrt{b}}{\sqrt{a}+\sqrt{b}} = \dfrac{2(a+b)}{a-b}$

General Formulae Used for Solving Product

(i) $(x \pm y)^2 = x^2 \pm 2xy + y^2$

(ii) $(x+y)(x-y) = x^2 - y^2$

(iii) $(x+y)^3 = x^3 + 3x^2y + 3xy^2 + y^3$

(iv) $(x-y)^3 = x^3 - y^3 - 3xy\,(x-y) = x^3 - y^3 + 3xy^2 - 3x^2y$

(v) $(x+y+z)^2 = x^2 + y^2 + z^2 + 2xy + 2yz + 2xz$

(vi) $x^3 + y^3 = (x+y)(x^2 + y^2 - xy)$

(vii) $x^3 - y^3 = (x-y)^3 + 3xy\,(x-y) = (x-y)(x^2 + y^2 + xy)$

(viii) $(x+a)(x+b) = x^2 + (a+b)x + ab$

(ix) $(x^3 + y^3 + z^3 - 3xyz) = (x+y+z)(x^2 + y^2 + z^2 - xy - yz - zx)$

If $x + y + z = 0 \Leftrightarrow x^3 + y^3 + z^3 = 3xyz$

(x) $x^4 + x^2y^2 + y^4 = (x^2 + xy + y^2)(x^2 - xy + y^2)$

(xi) $x^3 + y^3 + z^3 = (x+y+z)^3 - 3(x+y)(y+z)(x+z)$

(xii) $(x+y)(y+z)(z+x) = (x+y+z)(xy+yz+zx) - xyz$

(xiii) $(x-y)^2 + (y-z)^2 + (z-x)^2 = 2(x^2 + y^2 + z^2 - xy - yz - zx)$

(xiv) $a + b = \sqrt{(a-b)^2 + 4ab}$

(xv) $a - b = \sqrt{(a+b)^2 - 4ab}$

HCF and LCM

Factor A number which can divide a given number exactly, is called a factor of that number.

Multiple A number which is divisible by a given number, is called multiple of that number.

HCF (Highest Common Factor)

HCF of two or more numbers is the greatest number, which divides all the given numbers exactly.

1. Prime Factorization Method

Break the given numbers into their prime factor, the product of the prime factors, common to all numbers gives the HCF.

2. Division Method

Step I Divide the larger number by smaller number.

Step II Take remainder (as obtained in Step I) as divisor and the last divisor as the dividend.

Step III Repeat Step II until 0 is obtained as remainder. The last divisor will be the required HCF.

1. HCF of More than Two Numbers

First, find the HCF of first two numbers by any of the two methods. Next, find HCF of the third number and previously found HCF. Similarly, it can be done for any number of numbers.

2. HCF of Decimals

Step **I** First make the same number of decimal places in all the given numbers.

Step **II** Remove the decimals as if they are integers, thus obtain the HCF of obtained integers.

Step **III** Place as many decimal places in the obtained HCF as there are decimal places in each of the numbers.

3. HCF of Fractions

HCF of fractions, after expressing them in their lowest form

$$= \frac{\text{HCF of numerator}}{\text{LCM of denominator}}$$

LCM (Least Common Multiple)

The least number which is exactly divisible by two or more given numbers is called LCM of those numbers.

Factorisation Method to Find LCM

Step I Find prime factors of each of the given number.

Step II Find the product of all the prime factors which appears greatest number of times in the prime factorization of any given numbers. The product is the required LCM.

1. LCM of Decimals

Step I Make the same number of decimal places in all the given numbers.

Step II Remove the decimal and consider the numbers as integer.

Step III Find LCM of obtained integers.

Step IV Mark as many decimal places as there are decimal places in each of the number.

2. LCM of Fractions

LCM of the fraction numbers, after expressing them in their lowest form

$$= \frac{\text{LCM of numerator}}{\text{HCF of denominator}}.$$

Value Points

(i) For two numbers a and b, HCF × LCM = $a \times b$.

(ii) For three numbers a, b, c; LCM $= \dfrac{a \times b \times c}{(\text{HCF})^2}$.

(iii) For n numbers $a_1, a_2, a_3, a_4, \ldots, a_n$

$$\text{LCM} = \frac{a_1 \times a_2 \times a_3 \times \ldots \times a_n}{(\text{HCF})^{n-1}}.$$

(iv) If x is a factor of y, then HCF = x and LCM = y

(v) To obtain the greatest number that divide x, y and z leaving remainders p, q and r, we will find the HCF of $(x - p)$, $(y - q)$ and $(z - r)$.

(vi) To obtain the lowest number, which when divided by x, y and z leaving remainder p, q and r respectively, then

$$(x - p) = (y - q) = (z - r) = k \text{ (say)}.$$

Required number = (LCM of x, y and z) − k

Simplification

In mathematical expression, which consists of several operations. Then, operations should be performed in the order of each of the letter of 'BODMAS'.

B → Brackets	( ), { }, [ ]
O → Of	of
D → Division	÷
M → Multiplication	×
A → Addition	+
S → Subtraction	–

Brackets must be removed in the order of ( ) , { } and [ ].

Quicker Methods

(i) For addition/subtraction of mixed fraction.

***Step* I** Add/subtract integer part only.

***Step* II** Add/subtract fraction part only.

***Step* III** Add both the results.

(ii) For subtraction of a whole number and fraction.

***Step* I** Subtract 1 from the whole number.

***Step* II** In the fraction number, subtract numerator from the denominator and write in numerator.

***Step* III** Add both the results.

e.g. Consider mixed fraction $6 - \frac{23}{25}$

Step I $6 - 1 = 5$

Step II $\frac{25 - 23}{25} = \frac{2}{25}$

Step III $5 + \frac{2}{25} = 5\frac{2}{25}$

Average

Average is the ratio of the sum of the distributed data among different objects divided by number of data.

i.e. $$\text{Average} = \frac{\text{Sum of data}}{\text{Number of data}}$$

and $$\text{Sum of data} = \text{Average} \times \text{Number of data}$$

Combined Average

(i) If x and y is the average of objects m and n respectively, then the combined average of the data $= \dfrac{mx + ny}{m + n}$

(ii) If x, y and z are the average of objects m, n and p respectively, then combined average of the data $= \dfrac{mx + ny + pz}{m + n + p}$

Some Important Points on Average

(i) When the same value x is added to each element of the data, then new average = original average + x

(ii) When the same value x is subtracted from each element of the data, then new average = original average − x

(iii) When the same value x is multiplied to each element of data, then new average = original average × x

(iv) When one element, x is removed from the data, then

$$\text{New average} = \frac{\text{Sum of data} - x}{\text{Number of elements} - 1}$$

(v) When one element x is added to the data, then

$$\text{New average} = \frac{\text{Sum of data} + x}{\text{Number of elements} + 1}$$

(vi) When one of the data is wrongly taken, then

New average

$$= \frac{\left[\begin{array}{r}\text{Number of data} \times \text{Incorrect average} - \text{Incorrect value} \\ + \text{Correct value}\end{array}\right]}{\text{Number of data}}$$

(vii) When more than one value is wrongly taken,

Correct average

$$= \frac{\left[\begin{array}{r}\text{Number of data} \times \text{Incorrect average} - \text{Sum of incorrect data} \\ + \text{Sum of correct data}\end{array}\right]}{\text{Number of data}}$$

(viii) The average of first n natural numbers $= \dfrac{n + 1}{2}$

(ix) If a person travels half of the distance at x km/h and rest of the distance at y km/h, then average speed during whole journey

$$= \frac{2xy}{x + y}$$

(x) If the average age of m boys is x and the average age of n boys out of them is y, then the average age of the rest of the boys is $\frac{mx - ny}{m - n}$.

Ratio and Proportion

Ratio

Ratio is the relation between one quantity and another quantity, given that both quantity must be of the same kind and same unit, denoted by $x : y$, read as 'x' is to 'y' where, x is called antecedent and y is called consequent.

If antecedent and consequent of a ratio is multiplied/divided by the same number, then ratio remains same.

Compositions of Ratios

(i) **Compound Ratio** Ratio obtained by multiplying together the antecedents of different ratios to get a new antecedent and consequents to get a new consequents is called compound ratio.
i.e., for $a : b, c : d, e : f$, compound ratio $= ace : bdf$

(ii) **Duplicate Ratio** For $x : y$, duplicate ratio $= x^2 : y^2$

(iii) **Triplicate Ratio** For $x : y$, triplicate ratio $= x^3 : y^3$

(iv) **Subduplicate Ratio** For $x : y$, subduplicate ratio $= \sqrt{x} : \sqrt{y}$

(v) **Subtriplicate Ratio** For $x : y$, subtriplicate ratio $= x^{1/3} : y^{1/3}$

(vi) **Inverse Ratio/Reciprocal Ratio** For $x : y$, inverse ratio $= y : x$

Types of Ratios

For a ratio $x : y$,

(i) if $x = y$, then ratio is of equality.

(ii) if $x > y$, then ratio is of greater inequality.

(iii) if $x < y$, then ratio is of lesser inequality.

Value Points

(i) If ratio between first and second quantity is $a : b$ and the ratio between second and third quantity is $c : d$, then ratio among first, second and third quantity is $ac : bc : bd$

(ii) If the ratio between first and second quantity is $a : b$, ratio between second and third quantity is $c : d$ and the ratio between third and fourth quantity is $e : f$, then ratio among first, second, third and fourth quantity is $ace : bce : bde : bdf$

(iii) To divide n things between two objects in the ratio $x : y$, then

First object share $= \frac{x}{x + y} \times n$; Second object share $= \frac{y}{x + y} \times n$

Proportion

When the ratio of two quantities is same as the ratio of two other quantities, then these quantities are said to be in proportion. i.e.
If $a:b=c:d$, then a, b, c and d are in proportions, where a and d are called extremes and b and c are called means. And $a:b=c:d$ is denoted by $a:b::c:d$ or $ad=bc \Rightarrow$ Product of means = Product of extremes

1. Continued Proportion

(i) Quantities a, b and c are called continued proportion, if $a:b=b:c$ i.e. $\frac{a}{b}=\frac{b}{c}$.

b is called mean proportional of a and c and $b=\sqrt{ac}$

and c is called third proportional of a and b and $c=\frac{b^2}{a}$

(ii) Quantities a, b, c, d and e are called in continued proportion, if $a:b=b:c=c:d=d:e$ i.e. $\frac{a}{b}=\frac{b}{c}=\frac{c}{d}=\frac{d}{e}$.

2. Direct Proportion

Two quantities are said to be in direct proportion, if by increasing or decreasing one of the quantities, the other increases or decreases, respectively to the same extent.

3. Indirect Proportion

Two quantities are said to be in indirect proportion, if by increasing or decreasing one of the quantities, the other decreases or increases, respectively to the same extent.

Types of Indirect Proportion

(i) **Invertendo** If $a:b::c:d$, then $b:a::d:c$

(ii) **Alternendo** If $a:b::c:d$, then $a:c::b:d$

(iii) **Componendo** If $a:b::c:d$, then $(a+b):b::(c+d):d$

(iv) **Dividendo** If $a:b::c:d$, then $(a-b):b::(c-d):d$

(v) Componendo and Dividendo If $a:b::c:d$, then

$(a+b):(a-b)::(c+d):(c-d)$

(vi) If $\frac{a}{b}=\frac{c}{d}=\frac{e}{f}=\ldots$, then each ratio is equal to

(a) $\frac{a+c+e+\ldots}{b+d+f+\ldots}$ (b) $\frac{pa+qc+re+\ldots}{pb+qd+rf+\ldots}$

(c) $\left(\frac{pa^n+qc^n+re^n+\ldots}{pb^n+qd^n+rf^n+\ldots}\right)^{1/n}$

Time and Work

Each person has different capabilities to do any work. If a person has lot of capability to do a work, then he takes less time to do that work and if a person has less capability to do a work, then he takes more time to do that work.

∴ A person take a time to do any work

$$\propto \frac{1}{\text{Capability of person to do that work}}$$

Important Points

(i) Work is considered as whole or 1.

(ii) Time and work are always inversely proportional.

(iii) Men and work are directly proportional to each other.

(iv) Men and time are inversely proportional to each other.

(v) Ratio between the wages is equally divided between the work done in a day by men.

(vi) It is assumed that the person works at uniform rate until and unless specified.

(vii) Unit of time is either days or hours.

Fundamental Formula

If M_1 person can do W_1 works in D_1 days and M_2 persons can do W_2 work in D_2 days, when M_1 works T_1 hour with efficiency of E_1 and M_2 works T_2 hour with efficiency of E_2, then

$$M_1D_1T_1E_1W_2 = M_2D_2T_2E_2W_1$$

Formulae Related to Time and Work

- Let X, Y and Z are persons who are assigned a particular job. Working alone 'X' completes the job in 'x' days / hours, 'Y' completes the job in 'y' days/hours and 'Z' completes the job in 'z' days / hours, then

  (i) One day's/hour's work done by $X = \frac{1}{x}$. Similarly, one day's/hour's work done by 'Y' and 'Z' be $\frac{1}{y}$ and $\frac{1}{z}$, respectively.

  (ii) In n days/hours, work completed by x, y and z are $\frac{n}{x}$, $\frac{n}{y}$ and $\frac{n}{z}$.

(iii) If X and Y are working together, then work completed in one day/hour by them $= \frac{1}{x} + \frac{1}{y} = \frac{x+y}{xy}$

or Number of days to complete the work by X and Y together

$$= \frac{xy}{x+y}$$

(iv) Similarly, if X, Y and Z are working together, then work completed in one day/hour $= \frac{xy+yz+zx}{xyz}$

or Number of days to complete the work $= \frac{xyz}{xy+yz+zx}$

(v) If X and Y are working together and complete the work in m days, X can complete the work in x days working alone, then number of days to complete the work by $Y = \frac{xm}{x-m}$

(vi) If X and Y are working together and complete the job in m days. If X takes a days more than m and Y takes b days more than m, completing the job alone, then $m^2 = ab$

(vii) If A completes p/q part of the work in a days, then time taken by him to complete the remaining part of the work $= \frac{a}{p/q}\left(1-\frac{p}{q}\right)$.

(viii) If m men can do $1/n$ of a work in a days, then the number of men p required to complete the work in b days, is $p = \frac{nma}{b}$.

(ix) If X men or Y women can do a piece of work in a days, then m men or n women can do the same work in $\frac{1}{\frac{m}{X \times a} + \frac{n}{Y \times a}}$.

Speed, Time and Distance

Distance Length of the path covered by an object.

Speed Distance travelled by an object in unit time,

i.e. $$\text{Speed} = \frac{\text{Distance}}{\text{Time}}$$

or $$\text{Distance} = \text{Time} \times \text{Speed}$$

Average Speed Ratio of the total distance and the total time taken by an object to cover that distance,

i.e. $$\text{Average speed} = \frac{\text{Total distance covered}}{\text{Total time taken}}$$

Formulae Related to Speed and Distance

(i) If an object covers a distance of x km/h and another object covers the same distance at y km/h, then average speed during whole of the journey $= \dfrac{2xy}{x+y}$ and if the total time taken for the complete journey is t, then distance covered by an object $= \dfrac{2 \times t \times x \times y}{x+y}$

(ii) If an object starts from point P and goes to Q at a speed of x km/h in time t_1 and returns to P from Q in time t_2 at the speed y km/h, then distance between P and $Q = (t_1 + t_2)\dfrac{xy}{x+y}$

(iii) If an object starts at a point (say P) with speed x km/h at particular time (say p a.m.) and another object starts at the same point with speed y km/h at time (say q a.m.), then

Meeting point's distance from starting point

$$= \frac{x \times y \times \text{Difference in starting time}}{\text{Difference of speed}} = \frac{x \times y \times |q-p|}{|x-y|}$$

Now, suppose first object reaches its destiny (say Q) at time p_1 am/pm and second object reaches Q at q_1 am/pm, then first and second object will meet at

$$= \text{First's starting time} + \frac{(\text{Time taken by I})(\text{II reaching time} - \text{I reaching time})}{\text{Sum of time taken by I and II}}$$

$$= p + \frac{(p_1 - p)(q_1 - p_1)}{(p_1 - p) + (q_1 - q)}$$

(iv) If two objects X and Y, starts from point P at speed x and y respectively $(y > x)$, Y reaches at point Q and returns and meet X at point say R, then

distance travelled by $X = 2 \times d \times \left(\dfrac{x}{x+y}\right)$

and distance travelled by $Y = 2 \times d \times \left(\dfrac{y}{x+y}\right)$,

where d = Distance between P and Q.

(v) If P and Q are two points on a straight line, an object A starts from P and reaches at Q in time t_1 and object B starts from Q and reaches at P in time t_2, then

Speed of A : Speed of $B = \sqrt{t_2} : \sqrt{t_1}$

Problems Based on Trains

(i) When two trains are moving with velocities x and y km/h respectively, then relative speed will be

(a) $(x - y)$ km/h, if they are moving in same direction.

(b) $(x + y)$ km/h, if they are moving in opposite direction.

(ii) When a train passes a platform, then to calculate time to pass the platform, we should consider distance as the sum of length of train and the length of the platform.

Formulae Related to Speed and Time of Trains

(i) Suppose a train A of length l_1 and train B of length l_2, are moving at speed of x km/h and y km/h respectively, then

(a) If lengths l_1 and l_2 are negligible, then time taken to cross each other is negligible.

(b) If B is stationary, then time taken by A to cross $B = \frac{l_1 + l_2}{x}$

(c) If A and B are moving in same direction, then time taken to cross each other is given by

$$\frac{l_1 + l_2}{|x - y|}$$

(d) If A and B are moving in opposite direction, then time taken to cross each other is given by

$$\frac{l_1 + l_2}{x + y}$$

(e) Time taken by train A to cross a telegraph post or a stationary man is given by

$$\frac{l_1}{x}$$

(f) Time taken by train A to cross a bridge/railway station of length l is given by

$$\frac{l_1 + l}{x}$$

(g) Time taken by train A to cross a walking man (walking at speed z km/h), is given by

$\frac{l_1}{x - z}$, if man is walking in same direction

and $\frac{l_1}{x + z}$, if man is walking in opposite direction

(ii) Suppose two trains A and B starting from P and Q, with speed x and y respectively, meet at a point R. Between P and Q, difference of the distances travelled by A and B be d km, then distance between P and $Q = d \times \dfrac{x+y}{|x-y|}$.

(iii) If a train passes a man/pole, standing on the platform in t_1 time and passes the platform in t_2 time, then

Length of train $= \dfrac{d}{|t_1 - t_2|} \times t_1$

where, d = Length of the platform

(iv) Suppose there are two trains A and B are of length l_1 and l_2 respectively, if time taken by them to cross each other be t_1, when moving in same direction and t_2 when moving in opposite direction, then

Speed of faster train $= \left(\dfrac{l_1 + l_2}{2}\right)\left(\dfrac{1}{t_1} + \dfrac{1}{t_2}\right)$

and speed of slower train $= \left(\dfrac{l_1 + l_2}{2}\right)\left(\dfrac{1}{t_1} - \dfrac{1}{t_2}\right)$

(v) If a train overtakes two objects a and b moving with speed x and y km/h, respectively and time taken by train to cross a and b be t_1 and t_2 respectively, then

Length of the train $= \left|\dfrac{(x-y) \times t_1 \times t_2}{t_1 - t_2}\right|$

(vi) If two trains A and B are moving from P to Q and Q to P respectively and after meeting at point R, time taken by them to complete the journey be t_1 and t_2 respectively, then

Speed of train B = Speed of train $A \times \sqrt{\dfrac{t_1}{t_2}}$

and speed of train A = speed of train $B \times \sqrt{\dfrac{t_2}{t_1}}$.

Boats and Streams

Still Water When the speed of the water in the stream or river is '0', it is called still water. It has no impact on boat or swimmer.

Moving Water If the water in the river or stream is flowing, it is called moving water. It affects the speed of the boat/swimmer.

Downstream When the boat/swimmer moves in the direction of stream/river, it is called downstream.

Upstream When the boat /swimmer moves against stream/river, it is called upstream.

Formulae Related to Boats and Streams

Let the speed of the boat/river in still water is x km/h and speed of water in stream is y km/h, then

(i) (a) Speed in downstream $= (x + y)$ km/h

Speed in upstream $= (x - y)$ km/h

(b) Speed in downstream > speed in still water

and speed in upstream < speed in still water.

(ii) $x = \frac{1}{2}$ (Speed in upstream + Speed in downstream)

and $y = \frac{1}{2}$ (Speed in downstream − Speed in upstream)

(iii) When the downstream distance is equal to upstream distance, then

(a) Average speed during whole journey $= \frac{(x + y)(x - y)}{x}$

(b) Time taken to cover the whole journey $= \frac{x \times d}{(x - y)(x + y)}$

where, d is the total distance.

(c) The distance between the two places $= \frac{t(x + y)(x - y)}{2x}$

where, t = time taken to cover the whole journey

(iv) If the boat/swimmer cover a distance in t_1 time and returns the same distance in t_2 time, then

$$x = \frac{y(t_1 + t_2)}{(t_2 - t_1)} \text{ and } y = \frac{x(t_2 - t_1)}{(t_1 + t_2)},$$

where, x = Speed of boat/river in still water

and y = Speed of flowing water.

Pipes and Cisterns

Cistern A vessel, which is used to store water, is called cistern, it is connected by two pipes.

Inlet A pipe connected to cistern, which is used to fill the cistern is called inlet.

Outlet A pipe connected to cistern, which is used to empty the cistern, is called outlet.

Leak A hole in the cistern, through which water flows out of the cistern.

Formulae Related to Pipes and Cisterns

(i) Suppose three pipes A, B and C takes a, b and c time respectively to fill/empty the cistern, then

(a) The part of the cistern filled/emptied by pipe A in 1 h $= \frac{1}{a}$, similar for pipe B and C.

(b) Part of the cistern, filled/emptied by pipe A in n hour $= \frac{n}{a}$, similar for pipe B and C.

(c) If pipe A and B both are working as inlet pipe, then part of the cistern, filled by A and B, both in 1 h $= \frac{1}{a} + \frac{1}{b} = \frac{a+b}{ab}$

(d) If pipes A, B and C are all working as inlet, then part of the cistern, filled by A, B and C in 1 h $= \frac{1}{a} + \frac{1}{b} + \frac{1}{c} = \frac{ab+bc+ca}{abc}$

or the time taken to fill the cistern completely $= \frac{abc}{ab+bc+ca}$

(e) If the cistern is full and pipe A and B working as an outlet, the part of the cistern emptied in 1 h $= \frac{1}{a} + \frac{1}{b} = \frac{a+b}{ab}$

or the time taken to empty the cistern $= \frac{ab}{a+b}$

(f) If the cistern is full and pipes A, B and C working together as an outlet, then the part of the cistern emptied in 1 h

$$= \frac{1}{a} + \frac{1}{b} + \frac{1}{c} = \frac{ab+bc+ca}{abc}$$

or the time taken to empty the cistern $= \frac{abc}{ab+bc+ca}$

(g) If pipe A is working as inlet and B as outlet, then the part of the cistern filled (if $b > a$) when both are opened $= \frac{1}{a} - \frac{1}{b} = \frac{b-a}{ab}$ or the time taken to fill the tank $= \frac{ab}{b-a}$

(h) If the cistern is empty and pipes A and B are working as inlet and C as outlet, then part of the cistern filled in 1 h

$$=\frac{1}{a}+\frac{1}{b}-\frac{1}{c}=\frac{bc+ca-ab}{abc}$$

or time taken to fill the tank $=\dfrac{abc}{bc+ca-ab}$

(ii) If only pipe A is working as inlet, which fills it in time a and because of a leak in the cistern, takes x units of time more to fill the cistern. Now, if the cistern is full, then the time taken to empty the cistern due to leak is given by $a\left(1+\dfrac{a}{x}\right)$.

(iii) If A and B are working together to fill the tank, takes x units of time. When A works alone takes y units of time more than x and when B works alone takes z units of time more than x , then $x^2 = yz$.

Clock

Clocks consists of two arms, longer arm which shows minute is called **minute hand** and shorter arm which shows hour is called **hour hand**.

Dial

Dial of a clock is a circle, whose circumference is divided into 12 equal parts called 'hour space'. Each hour space is further divided into 5 parts, called 'minute space'.

Value Points

(i) The minute hand is 12 times faster than hour hand.

(ii) In an hour, the minute hand covers 60 min spaces, while hour hand covers 5 min spaces. So, in an hour, the minute hand gains 55 min space.

(iii) Minutes space gained by minute hand in 1 min $=\dfrac{55}{60}$.

(iv) In 1 h, minute hand covers 360°, so in one minute it covers 6°.

(v) In 1 h, hour hand covers $\dfrac{360°}{12}=30°$, so in one minute, hour hand covers (1/2)°. So, in 1 min, the minute hand gains $\left(5\dfrac{1}{2}\right)^{\circ}$.

(vi) In 1 h, both the hands coincide once, but in 12 h, they coincide 11 times.

(vii) Two hands are at right angle, when they are 15 min space apart, this happens two times in an hour, but 22 times in 12 h.

(viii) Two hands are in opposite direction when they are 30 min space apart, this happens one time in an hour and 11 times in 12 h.

(ix) If both hands start together from the same position, both will coincide after $65\frac{5}{11}$ min.

(x) **Slow Clock** A clock in which both hands coincide at an interval more than $65\frac{5}{11}$ min, is called slow clock.

(xi) **Fast Clock** A clock in which both hands coincide at an interval less than $65\frac{5}{11}$ min, is called fast clock.

(xii) Angle between the hour hand and minute hand at time $xx : yy$, is given by

(a) If hour hand is behind minute hand, then angle

$$= \left(yy \times \frac{11}{2} - xx \times 30 \right)^\circ$$

(b) If minute hand is behind hour hand, then angle

$$= \left(xx \times 30 - yy \times \frac{11}{2} \right)^\circ$$

(xiii) If hour hand and minute hand coincide at $xx : yy$, then

$$yy = \frac{60}{11} \times xx$$

(xiv) Between x and $(x+1)$ O'clock, the two hands will coincide at

$$5 \times x \times \left(\frac{60}{55}\right) \text{ min past } x.$$

(xv) For a slow clock, total time lost in n hours $= n \times 60 \left(\dfrac{x - 65\frac{5}{11}}{x} \right)$ min

where, x is the time in which the hands of slow clock coincide.

(xvi) For a fast clock, total time gained in n hours

$= n \times 60 \left(\dfrac{65\frac{5}{11} - x}{x} \right)$ min, where x is the time in which the hands of the fast clock coincide.

Calendar

Calendar is a measure of time having day as the smallest unit.

Ordinary Year A year having 365 days, is called ordinary year.

Leap Year A year having 366 days, is called leap year.

Odd Days Number of days more than the complete numbers of weeks in a given period is called odd days.

Important Points

(i) Every year, except a centurial year is leap year, if it is divisible by 4.

(ii) Every 4th century is a leap year. A centurial year is a leap year, if it is divisible by 400.

(iii) An ordinary year have only one odd day.

(iv) A leap year have only two odd days.

(v) 100 yr = 76 ordinary years + 24 leap years

(vi) 100 yr i.e. 1 century contains

$$76 + 24 \times 2 = 76 + 48 \text{ odd days}$$
$$= 124 \text{ odd days}$$
$$= 17 \text{ weeks} + 5 \text{ odd days}$$

So, 100 yr have 5 odd days.

(vii) 200 yr contain 5×2 odd days = 1 week + 3 odd days

So, 200 yr contain 3 odd days.

Similarly, 300 yr contain 1 odd day and

400 yr contain $5 \times 4 + 1$ odd day = 21 odd days = 3 week

i.e. 400 yr contain no odd days.

(viii) Last day of a century can not be either Tuesday, Thursday or Saturday.

(ix) The first day of a century must be either Monday, Tuesday, Thursday or Saturday.

Percentage

The word 'per cent', means 'per hundred' or 'out of hundred', symbol % is used to express percentage.

1. To convert a fraction into percentage, multiply the fraction by 100.

   If fraction $= \frac{x}{y}$, then its percentage $= \left(\frac{x}{y} \times 100\right)\%$.

2. Percentage can be converted into fraction, by dividing the percentage by 100.

   If percentage is $a\%$, then its fraction will be $a/100$.
3. To convert decimal into percentage, multiply it by 100.
4. To convert percentage into decimal, divide it by 100.
5. $x\%$ of $y = y\%$ of x

Formulae Related to Percentage of a Quantity

- To express x as a percentage of y percentage $= \left(\frac{x}{y} \times 100\right)\%$
- If $x\%$ of a number is y, then the number is $\frac{y}{x} \times 100$.
- If a quantity is increased, then

  Percentage increases $= (x\%) = \left(\frac{\text{increase in quantity}}{\text{original quantity}} \times 100\right)\%$

  and new quantity $= \left(\frac{100 + x}{100}\right) \times$ original quantity.
- If a quantity is decreased, then

  Percentage decrease $= (x\%) = \left(\frac{\text{decrease in quantity}}{\text{original quantity}} \times 100\right)\%$

  and new quantity $= \left(\frac{100 - x}{100}\right) \times$ original quantity.
- If a quantity x is $r\%$ more than another quantity y, then y is less than x by $\left(\frac{r}{100 + r} \times 100\right)\%$.

- If a quantity x is $r\%$ less than another quantity y, then y is more than x by $\left(\frac{r}{100-r}\times 100\right)\%$.
- If two quantities are $x\%$ and $y\%$ more than a third quantity, then the first is $\left(\frac{100+x}{100+y}\times 100\right)\%$ of the second.
- If a quantity x is $x\%$ of z and y is $y\%$ of z, then x is $\frac{x}{y}\times 100\%$ of y.
- If a quantity is first increased by $x\%$ and then decreased by $y\%$, then there percentage change in the quantity $=\left(x-y-\frac{xy}{100}\right)\%$ (increase, if percentage is +ve and decrease, if percentage is –ve).
- If a quantity is first increased by $x\%$, and then increased by $y\%$, then final increase percentage is $\left(x+y+\frac{xy}{100}\right)\%$.
- If $x\%$ of a quantity is taken by the first person, $y\%$ is taken by second and $z\%$ of the remaining is taken by the third person and quantity p is left, then total quantity in the beginning was

$$\frac{p\times 100\times 100\times 100}{(100-x)(100-y)(100-z)}$$

- If we have initial quantity A and $x\%$ of the quantity is added to it, then $y\%$ is added, then $z\%$ is added and final quantity becomes B, then

$$A=\frac{B\times 100\times 100\times 100}{(100+x)(100+y)(100+z)}$$

Formulae Related to Population

(i) If the population of a town is A. Suppose, in first year, it increases by $x\%$, in second year by $y\%$ and in third year by $z\%$, then population after 3 yr

$$=\frac{A\times(100+x)(100+y)(100+z)}{100\times 100\times 100}$$

(ii) In the above case, if the population 'A' 'decreases' in third year, then population after 3 yr

$$=\frac{A\times(100+x)(100+y)(100-z)}{100\times 100\times 100}$$

1. Formulae Related to Commodity

(i) If the price of a commodity increases by $x\%$, then to keep the expenses same, decrease in the consumption will be $\left(\frac{x}{100+x}\times 100\right)\%$.

(ii) If the price of a commodity decreases by $x\%$, then to keep the expenses same, increases in the consumption will be $\left(\frac{x}{100-x}\times 100\right)\%$.

(iii) If the price of the commodity is increased by $x\%$, such that the customer buy n units less for ₹ y, then increased price of the commodity is ₹ $\left(\frac{xy}{100n}\right)$ and original price was ₹ $\left(\frac{xy}{(100+x)n}\right)$ per unit.

(iv) If the price of the commodity is decreased by $x\%$, such that the customer buy n units more for ₹ y, then decreased price is ₹ $\left(\frac{xy}{100n}\right)$ per unit and original price was ₹ $\left(\frac{xy}{(100-x)n}\right)$ per unit.

2. Formulae Related to Marks

(i) If in an examination, pass percentage is $x\%$ and a candidate scoring y marks fails by z marks, then maximum marks in the examination is $\frac{100(y+z)}{x}$.

(ii) In an examination, if a candidate scoring $x\%$ fails by a marks and another candidate scoring $y\%$ gets b marks more than the minimum marks required to pass. Then, maximum marks in the examination will be $\frac{100(a+b)}{y-x}$.

Profit, Loss and Discount

Some Basic Terms

(i) **Cost Price** (CP) The price paid by a customer or shopkeeper to purchase an article.

(ii) **Selling Price** (SP) The price at which a shopkeeper sells an article.

(iii) **Overhead Charges** Money spent on the article for transporting, handling, installation after purchasing it.
(iv) **Marked Price** (MP) The printed or original price of an article.
(v) **Discount** Amount deducted from the marked price.
(vi) **Net Price** Amount paid by the customers to purchase an article after deducing the discount.
(vii) **Gross Profit** The total profit without deducing tax.
(viii) **Net Profit** Profit after deducing tax.

Important Points

- The gain (profit) or loss per cent is calculated on cost price.
- Overhead charges should be included in the cost price.
- Discount is always calculated on Marked Price (MP).
- Discount series $x\%$, $y\%$ and $z\%$,..., $x\%$, $z\%$, $y\%$, ... or $z\%$, $x\%$, $y\%$, ... any combination will give the same Selling Price (SP).

Formulae Related to Profit and Loss

1. Gain (Profit) = SP – CP
2. Loss = CP – SP
3. $\text{Profit / Loss\%} = \left(\dfrac{\text{Amount of profit / loss}}{\text{CP}} \times 100\right)\%$
4. If profit is $x\%$, then
$$SP = \frac{100 + x}{100} \times CP \text{ and } CP = \frac{100}{100 + x} \times SP$$
5. If loss is $y\%$, then
$$SP = \frac{100 - y}{100} \times CP \text{ and } CP = \frac{100}{100 - y} \times SP$$
6. (i) When there are two successive profits of $x_1\%$ and $x_2\%$, then resultant profit will be $\left(x_1 + x_2 + \dfrac{x_1 x_2}{100}\right)\%$.

(ii) If there is a profit of $x\%$ and loss of $y\%$ in a transaction, then profit or loss will be $\left(x - y - \dfrac{xy}{100}\right)\%$.

If it is +ve, then there is profit and if it is –ve, then there will be loss.

(iii) If there are two successive loss of $x\%$ and $y\%$, then resultant loss will be $\left(x + y - \dfrac{xy}{100}\right)\%$.

(iv) If the same article is sold at successive profits $x_1\%, x_2\%, x_3\%, \ldots$ and successive losses $y_1\%, y_2\%, \ldots$, then CP will be

$$SP \times \left(\frac{100}{100+x_1} \times \frac{100}{100+x_2} \times \ldots \times \frac{100}{100-y_1} \times \frac{100}{100-y_2} \times \ldots\right)$$

Dishonest Dealer

(i) If a shopkeeper sells an article at its cost price but cheats the customer by using false weight, then percentage gain

$$= \frac{\text{True weight} - \text{False weight}}{\text{False weight}} \times 100\%$$

or $\quad \text{percentage gain} = \dfrac{\text{Error}}{\text{True weight} - \text{Error}} \times 100\%$

(ii) If a shopkeeper uses A g in place of 1 kg (1000 g) to sell his goods and bears a loss of $y\%$, then his actual gain/loss is

$$(100-y)\left(\frac{100}{A}\right) - 100.$$

(iii) If a shopkeeper uses A g in place of 1 kg (1000 g) and gains a profit of $x\%$, then his actual profit/loss is $(100+x)\left(\dfrac{100}{A}\right) - 100.$

(iv) If a shopkeeper sells an objects with a profit $x\%$ and uses a weight to measure it which is $l\%$ less than its original weight, then total profit $= \dfrac{x+l}{100-l} \times 100\%.$

False Weight

If a shopkeeper sells a substance at its cost price but uses an incorrect weight (by mistake weighing more than that marked on it), then percentage loss will be

$$\text{Pecentage loss} = \frac{\text{Error}}{\text{True value} + \text{Error}} \times 100\%$$

(i) If $d_1\%, d_2\%, d_3\%, \ldots$ are the successive discounts given on an article, then

$$SP = MP \times \left(\frac{100-d_1}{100}\right) \times \left(\frac{100-d_2}{100}\right) \times \left(\frac{100-d_3}{100}\right) \times \ldots$$

(ii) If two items are sold at same SP, one at a loss of $x\%$ and other at a gain of $x\%$, then there is a loss of $\dfrac{x^2}{100}\%$ or $\left(\dfrac{x}{10}\right)^2\%$.

(iii) If CP of two items is same, if one is sold with a loss of x% and other is sold with a gain of x%, then there is no loss or no gain.

(iv) If a man purchases x items for ₹ y and sell y items for ₹ x, then profit or loss (depending upon +ve or –ve sign) is $\frac{x^2 - y^2}{y^2} \times 100\%$.

(v) If cost price of x articles is equal to the selling price of y articles, then profit/loss is $\frac{x - y}{y} \times 100\%$.

(vi) If a shopkeeper gains a profit of x_1% on an article, if he sells it ₹ R more, then he makes a profit of x_2%, then

$$CP = ₹\left(\frac{R \times 100}{x_2 - x_1}\right).$$

(vii) If a shopkeeper sells an article at a loss of y%, if he sells it ₹ 'R' more, he would make profit x%, then

$$SP = \frac{R(100 + x)}{x + y}$$

(viii) If a shopkeeper sells an article at ₹ R, at a loss of x%, then to gain x%, the

$$SP = \left(\frac{100 + x}{100 - x}\right) \times R.$$

(ix) If CP and SP of an article is reduced by same amount (say R) and profit is increased from x_1% to x_2%, then

$$\text{Actual CP} = \frac{x_2 \times R}{x_2 - x_1}.$$

Transaction in Part

(i) If m part of a consignment is sold at x_1% profit, n part is sold at x_2% profit and l part at x_3% profit and overall profit is ₹ R, then value of total consignment $= \frac{R \times 100}{mx_1 + nx_2 + lx_3}$.

(ii) If a man purchases a certain number of articles at R_1 and the same number at R_2 and after mixing them together, he sells them at R_3, then gain or loss

$$\text{(according +ve or –ve sign)} = \left[\frac{2R_1R_2}{R_3(R_1 + R_2)} - 1\right] \times 100\%.$$

(iii) If a shopkeeper marks an article at $x\%$ above its cost price and gives purchasers as discount of $d\%$, then the profit/loss (depending upon +ve or –ve sign) is $\left(x-d-\frac{dx}{100}\right)\%$.

(iv) If a person buys two articles at total cost of ₹ R and sells one at a loss of $y\%$ and other at a profit of $x\%$, then

$$\text{Cost of one article} = \frac{\text{CP of both} \times y}{x+y}.$$

$$\text{Cost of second article} = \frac{\text{CP of both} \times x}{x+y}.$$

(v) When each of the two articles is sold at same price and a profit of $x\%$ is on first and a loss of $y\%$ is on second, then gain or loss (depending upon +ve or –ve sign) is

$$\frac{100(x-y)-2xy}{(100+x)+(100-y)}.$$

(vi) If a discount is $d_1\%$, then shopkeeper makes a profit of $x_1\%$ and if the discount is $d_2\%$, then profit

$$x_2\% = (100+x_1)\left(\frac{100-d_2}{100-d_1}\right) - 100\%.$$

Simple Interest

Some Basic Terms

(i) **Interest** (I) Interest is the amount of money which is paid by the borrower to the lender for the use of the money lent.

(ii) **Principal** (P) The money borrowed by the borrower from the lender.

(iii) **Rate of Interest** (R) The money paid by the borrower to the lender for 1 yr use of money lent is called rate of interest per annum.

(iv) **Time** (T) The duration for which the money is borrowed by the borrower.

(v) **Amount** (A) Principal together with the amount of interest is called amount.

(vi) **Simple Interest** (SI) If the interest is calculated on the original sum (principal) for any period of time, is called simple interest.

Some Important Formulae

1. $SI = \dfrac{P \times R \times T}{100}$ 2. $R = \dfrac{SI \times 100}{P \times T}$

3. $T = \dfrac{SI \times 100}{P \times R}$ 4. $A = P + SI$

5. $A = P\left(1 + \dfrac{T \times R}{100}\right)$ 6. $P = \dfrac{A \times 100}{100 + TR}$

Formulae Related to Simple Interest

(i) If rate of interest is R_1% for T_1 years, R_2% for next T_2 years, R_3% for next T_3 years and so on and the total interest is SI, then principal amount is

$$P = \frac{SI \times 100}{R_1T_1 + R_2T_2 + R_3T_3 + \ldots}.$$

(ii) When the sum of money (principal) become n times in T years, then rate of interest is given by

$$R = \frac{100(n-1)}{T} \text{ \% per annum.}$$

(iii) The annual payment that will discharge a debt of ₹ A in T years at the rate of interest R% per annum is

$$\frac{100A}{100T + \dfrac{RT(T-1)}{2}}.$$

(iv) If a sum of amounts to ₹ A_1 in T_1 years and ₹ A_2 in T_2 years at simple interest, then rate of interest is given by

$$R = \frac{100(A_2 - A_1)}{A_1T_2 - A_2T_1}$$

(v) If a sum of amounts to ₹ A_1 at rate R_1% per annum and ₹ A_2 at rate R_2% per annum for the same duration, then time is

$$T = \frac{100(A_2 - A_1)}{A_1R_2 - A_2R_1}$$

(vi) If a sum is put at simple interest at the rate R_1%, for T years to obtain simple interest SI_1, if it had been put at rate R_2% for same years, then simple interest is SI_2, then the sum was

$$P = \frac{(SI_2 - SI_1) \times 100}{T \times (R_2 - R_1)}.$$

(vii) If a sum of ₹ P is lent on simple interest in n parts such that the interest on first part at R_1% for T_1 years, interest on second part at R_2% for T_2 years, interest on third part at R_3% for T_3 years and so on, then the ratio in which the sum was divided in n parts, is given by $\frac{1}{R_1T_1} : \frac{1}{R_2T_2} : \frac{1}{R_3T_3} : \dots : \frac{1}{R_nT_n}$

(viii) If a sum of ₹ P is lent on simple interest in n parts such that the amount of first part lent at R_1% for T_1 years, the amount of second part lent at R_2% for T_2 years, the amount of third part lent at R_3% for T_3 years and so on. Then, the ratio in which the sum was divided in n parts, is given by

$$\frac{1}{100 + R_1T_1} : \frac{1}{100 + R_2T_2} : \frac{1}{100 + R_3T_3} : \dots : \frac{1}{100 + R_nT_n}$$

Compound Interest

Money is said to be lent at **Compound Interest** (CI), if the interest at the end of year or a fixed period of time is not paid by the borrower to the lender, it is added to the principal and thus the amount obtained becomes the new principal for the next period and so on.

Value Points

(i) For 1 yr, compound interest is equal to the simple interest.

(ii) Compound interest for more than one year is always greater than the simple interest.

(iii) The amount of the previous year becomes the principal for the successive year.

(iv) The difference between two consecutive amounts is the interest on the preceeding amount.

Formulae Related to Compound Interest

If R is the rate of interest per annum, T is the duration in years, A is the amount and P is the principal.

1. (i) If interest is compounded annually, then

(a) $A = P\left(1 + \frac{R}{100}\right)^T$ (b) $P = \frac{A}{\left(1 + \frac{R}{100}\right)^T}$

(ii) If the interest is compounded half-yearly, then

$$A = P\left(1 + \frac{R/2}{100}\right)^{2T}$$

(iii) If the interest is compounded quaterly, then

$$A = P\left(1 + \frac{R/4}{100}\right)^{4T}.$$

(iv) If the rate of interest is $R_1\%$, $R_2\%$, $R_3\%$, respectively for I, II and III years, then

$$A = P\left[1 + \frac{R_1}{100}\right]\left[1 + \frac{R_2}{100}\right]\left[1 + \frac{R_3}{100}\right].$$

2. Compound Interest, $\text{CI} = A - P$
3. If interest is compounded annually and time is in fraction of years, say $n\frac{p}{q}$ years, then $A = P\left(1 + \frac{R}{100}\right)^n \left[1 + \frac{\frac{p}{q}R}{100}\right]$.
4. If a sum becomes x times in y years at compound interest, then after ny years it will be $(x)^n$ times.
5. If a certain sum becomes n times in T years, then rate of interest is $R = 100[(n)^{1/T} - 1]$.
6. Relation between SI and CI,

$$\text{SI} = \frac{R \times T}{100\left[\left(1 + \frac{R}{100}\right)^T - 1\right]} \times \text{CI}$$

7. Difference between CI and SI,

$$\text{CI} - \text{SI} = P\left[\left(\frac{100 + R}{100}\right)^T - \frac{RT}{100} - 1\right]$$

8. Annual instalment, compounded annually is given by

$$\text{instalment} = \frac{P}{\left(1 + \frac{R}{100}\right)^T} = P\left(\frac{100}{100 + R}\right)^T.$$

9. If the difference between CI and SI for 2 yr at rate $R\%$ is ₹ x, on a certain sum of money, then sum is given by $P = x\left(\frac{100}{R}\right)^2$.

10. If the difference between CI and SI on a certain sum (principal) for 3 yr at rate of interest $R\%$, is ₹ x, then the sum is given by

$$P = \frac{x(100)^3}{R^2(300 + R)}.$$

11. If a certain sum becomes ₹ A_1 in n years and ₹ A_2 in $(n + 1)$ years at compound interest, then

(i) rate of interest, $R = \dfrac{(A_2 - A_1) \times 100}{A_1}\%$.

(ii) sum $= A_1\left(\dfrac{A_1}{A_2}\right)^n$

12. If a certain sum becomes ₹ A_1 in T_1 years at compound interest, then after T_2 years, the amount will be $A_2 =$ ₹ $\dfrac{(A_1)^{T_2/T_1}}{(P)^{T_2/T_1 - 1}}$, where P is the principal.

13. If the compound rate of interest is $R_1\%$ for first T_1 years, $R_2\%$ for next T_2 years, $R_3\%$ for next T_3 years and so on, then

$$A = P\left[1 + \frac{R_1}{100}\right]^{T_1}\left[1 + \frac{R_2}{100}\right]^{T_2}\left[1 + \frac{R_3}{100}\right]^{T_3} \dots$$

14. If certain sum at compound interest becomes x times in n_1 year and y times in n_2 year, then $x^{1/n_1} = y^{1/n_2}$.

Growth and Depreciation

Some Basic Terms

(i) **Growth** Increase in price of an article or quantity with respect to time, is called growth or appreciation.

(ii) **Depreciation** Decrease in price of an article or quantity with respect to time, is called depreciation.

(iii) **Rate of Growth/Depreciation** (R) The rate at which the price of an article or quantity increases/decreases is called the rate of growth/depreciation.

(iv) **Original Value** (P) The price of an article/quantity at beginning of the period is called original value.

(v) **Final Value** (A) Price of an article/quantity at the end of the period is called final value.

Important Points

(i) Appreciated value is always greater than the original value.

(ii) Depreciated value is always less than the original value.

(iii) The same item may growth in one year and depreciate in another year.

Formulae Related to Growth and Depreciation

1. If original value is P and final value is A, rate of growth/depreciation is R% per annum and time period is T years.

(i) **For growth**

(a) $A = P\left(1 + \frac{R}{100}\right)^T$ (b) increase $= A - P$

(ii) **For depreciation**

(a) $A = P\left(1 - \frac{R}{100}\right)^T$ (b) decrease $= P - A$

2. If time is in fraction of year, say $n\frac{p}{q}$, then

(i) **For growth** $A = P\left(1 + \frac{R}{100}\right)^n\left(1 + \frac{\frac{p}{q} \times R}{100}\right)$

(ii) **For depreciation** $A = P\left(1 - \frac{R}{100}\right)^n\left(1 - \frac{\frac{p}{q} \times R}{100}\right)$

3. If there is increase of R_1% in T_1 years, decrease of R_2% in next T_2 years and an increase of R_3% in next T_3 years, then

$$A = P\left(1 + \frac{R_1}{100}\right)^{T_1}\left(1 - \frac{R_2}{100}\right)^{T_2}\left(1 + \frac{R_3}{100}\right)^{T_3}$$

Applications

1. **Population** If there is an increase/decrease of R% per annum in the population, then

(i) population after n years will be

$$A = P\left(1 + \frac{R}{100}\right)^n, P = \text{Present population.}$$

(ii) population n years ago will be

$$A=\frac{P}{\left(1+\frac{R}{100}\right)^n}$$

2. **Old Wooden Objects** If Old wooden objects decays at a constant rate of $R\%$ per annum, then after n years, its value will be

$$A=P\left(1-\frac{R}{100}\right)^n, P = \text{Present value}$$

Partnership

Partnership is an association of two or more persons who put their money together to carry out on a certain business. These persons are called partners.

(i) **Active or Working Partners** Partners who actively participate in managing the process of the business.

(ii) **Sleeping Partners** Partners who only invest their money in the business and do not actively participate in it.

Types of Partnership

1. **Simple Partnership** If partners of the business invest their money/capital in the business for same duration of time, the partnership is called simple partnership.

In this case, the profit/loss is divided in the ratio of their investment.

(i) If two partners P and Q invest their money in a business, then Investment of P : Investment of Q = Profit/loss of P : Profit/loss of Q.

(ii) If there are three partners P, Q and R to invest, then Investment of P : Investment of Q : Investment of R = Profit/loss of P : Profit/loss of Q : Profit/loss of R.

2. **Compound Partnership** If the partners of the business invest their money for different duration of time, then it is called compound partnership.

In this case, the profit/loss is divided in the ratio of their equivalent investment for a unit of time.

Equivalent investment = Investment × Number of Units of time

(i) If two partners P and Q invest amount of ₹ x_1 and ₹ x_2, respectively for time t_1 and t_2 (units), then their profit/loss will be in the ratio. Profit/Loss of P : Profit/Loss of $Q = x_1t_1 : x_2t_2$.

(ii) If three partners P, Q and R invest their money of ₹ x_1, ₹ x_2 and ₹ x_3 for time t_1, t_2 and t_3 (units) respectively, then their profit/loss will be in the ratio.

Profit/Loss of P : Profit/Loss of Q : Profit/Loss of $R = x_1t_1 : x_2t_2 : x_3t_3$

Similarly, for more partners, profit/loss can be calculated.

Share and Debenture

Some Basic Terms

(i) **Capital** Total amount of money required to start or expand a company.

(ii) **Share** Capital is divided into smaller units, which are called share.

(iii) **Face Value/Nominal Value** (FV) The original value issued by a company for a share. It is the printed value of the share.

(iv) **Market Value** (MV) The value at which a share is available in the share market, depending on market value. Three types of shares are available.

(a) Share at Par If MV = FV, the share is said to be at par.

(b) Share at Premium If FV < MV, then the share is said to be 'above par' or 'at premium'.

(c) Share at Discount If FV > MV, then the share is said to be 'below par' or 'at discount'.

(v) **Stock** Total face value of the shares held by a shareholder.

$$\text{Stock} = \text{FV} \times \text{Number of shares}$$

(vi) **Investment** Total amount of money paid by a shareholder to the shares.

$$\text{Investment} = \text{MV} \times \text{Number of shares}$$

(vii) **Proceeds** If a shareholder sells his shares, then total amount of money, obtained after selling the shares, is called proceeds.

$$\text{Proceeds} = \text{MV} \times \text{Number of shares}$$

(viii) **Dividend** Shareholder are entitled to the profit of the company subject to certain legal compliance, this profit is called dividend.

$$\text{Dividend} = \text{Stock} \times \frac{\text{Rate of Dividend}}{100}$$

(ix) **Return Per cent** This is the actual earning per cent of the investor.

$$\text{Return\%} = \frac{\text{Dividend}}{\text{Investment}} \times 100\%$$

(x) **Debenture** Company can obtain loans from public at fixed percentage of interest; the small unit of the loan granted by the public is called debenture.

(xi) **Broker** Shares, stocks and debentures are sold or purchased through a person, called broker.

(xii) **Brokerage** Amount paid to the broker for selling or purchasing of shares is called brokerage.

Value Points

(i) Dividend on share is calculated on its face value.

(ii) Interest on debenture is calculated on face value of debenture.

(iii) Same rules and formulae used for shares can be applied to debenture.

(iv) Brokerage is calculated on market value of share or debentures.

Formulae Related to Shares and Investment

1. When the stock is at premium sale, then
$$MV = 100 + \text{Premium}$$
2. When the stock is at discount sale, then
$$MV = 100 - \text{Discount}$$
3. $\text{Number of shares} = \dfrac{\text{Stock}}{FV} = \dfrac{\text{Investment}}{MV} = \dfrac{\text{Total dividend}}{\text{Dividend per share}}$
4. Income per share = Rate of dividend × FV
5. Total income = Income per share × Number of share
6. $\text{Brokerage on 1 share} = MV \times \dfrac{\text{Rate of brokerage}}{100}$
7. $\text{Total brokerage paid} = \text{Investment} \times \dfrac{\text{Rate of brokerage}}{100}$
8. $\text{Purchase value for one share} = MV\left(1 + \dfrac{\text{Rate of brokerage}}{100}\right)$
9. $\text{Sale value for 1 share} = MV\left(1 - \dfrac{\text{Rate of brokerage}}{100}\right)$
10. $\text{Rate of interest on the investment} = \dfrac{\text{Total income} \times 100}{\text{Total investment}}$

11. Rate of interest on the investment $= \dfrac{\text{Dividend \%} \times \text{FV}}{\text{MV}\left(\dfrac{1+\text{Rate of brokerage}}{100}\right)}$

12. Amount of stock $= \dfrac{\text{Investment} \times 100}{\text{MV}} = \dfrac{\text{Investment} \times 100}{\text{Rate per cent}}$

13. Annual income $= \dfrac{\text{Amount of stock} \times \text{Rate per cent}}{100}$

$= \dfrac{\text{Investment} \times \text{Rate per cent}}{\text{MV}}$

Alligation or Mixture

1. When two or more types of quantities of things are mixed, a **mixture** is produced.
2. **Alligation** is a rule that enables us to find.
   (a) The proportion in which two or more ingrediants of the given prices must be mixed to produce a mixture at a given price.
   (b) The mean price of the mixture when the prices of the ingrediants and the proportions in which they are mixed is known.
3. **Rule of alligation**

$$\frac{\text{Quantity of cheaper ingrediant}}{\text{Quantity of dearer ingrediant}} = \frac{\text{CP of dearer} - \text{Mean price}}{\text{Mean price} - \text{CP of cheaper}}$$

4. **Mean price** $= \dfrac{\left(\begin{array}{c}\text{Quantity of cheaper} \times \text{CP of cheaper} \\ + \text{Quantity of dearer} \times \text{CP of dearer}\end{array}\right)}{\text{Quantity of cheaper} + \text{Quantity of dearer}}$

5. Two vessels of equal size are full with mixtures of liquids A and B in the ratios $a_1 : b_1$ and $a_2 : b_2$ respectively. The contents of both vessels are emptied into a single large vessel. Then,

$$\frac{\text{Quantity of liquid } A}{\text{Quantity of liquid } B} = \frac{\left(\dfrac{a_1}{a_1+b_1} + \dfrac{a_2}{a_2+b_2}\right)}{\left(\dfrac{b_1}{a_1+b_1} + \dfrac{b_2}{a_2+b_2}\right)}$$

6. Three vessels of size equal are full with mixtures of liquids A, B and C in the ratios $a_1 : b_1, a_2 : b_2$ and $a_3 : b_3$, respectively. The contents of all three vessels are emptied into a single large vessel. Then,

$$\frac{\text{Quantity of liquid } A}{\text{Quantity of liquid } B} = \frac{\left(\frac{a_1}{a_1+b_1} + \frac{a_2}{a_2+b_2} + \frac{a_3}{a_3+b_3}\right)}{\left(\frac{b_1}{a_1+b_1} + \frac{b_2}{a_2+b_2} + \frac{b_3}{a_3+b_3}\right)}$$

7. Two vessels of capacities c_1 and c_2 have mixtures of liquids A and B in the ratio $a_1 : b_1$ and $a_2 : b_2$, respectively. The contents of both vessels are emptied into a single large vessel. Then,

$$\frac{\text{Quantity of liquid } A}{\text{Quantity of liquid } B} = \frac{\left(\frac{a_1c_1}{a_1+b_1} + \frac{a_2c_2}{a_2+b_2}\right)}{\left(\frac{b_1c_1}{a_1+b_1} + \frac{b_2c_2}{a_2+b_2}\right)}$$

8. Three vessels of capacities c_1, c_2 and c_3 are full with mixtures of liquids A and B in the ratio $a_1 : b_1, a_2 : b_2$ and $a_3 : b_3$, respectively. The contents of all three vessels are emptied into a single large vessel. Then,

$$\frac{\text{Quantity of liquid } A}{\text{Quantity of liquid } B} = \frac{\left(\frac{a_1c_1}{a_1+b_1} + \frac{a_2c_2}{a_2+b_2} + \frac{a_3c_3}{a_3+b_3}\right)}{\left(\frac{b_1c_1}{a_1+b_1} + \frac{b_2c_2}{a_2+b_2} + \frac{b_3c_3}{a_3+b_3}\right)}$$

9. A vessel contains x litre of liquid A. From this vessel, y litre $(y < x)$ are withdrawn and replaced by y litre another liquid B. Next y litre of this mixture is withdrawn and replaced by y litre of liquid B. This operation is repeated n times.

Then,

$$\frac{\text{Quantity of liquid } A \text{ left after } n\text{th operation}}{\text{Quantity of liquid } A \text{ initially present}} = \left(\frac{x-y}{x}\right)^n \text{ or } \left(1-\frac{y}{x}\right)^n$$

Elementary Algebra

Polynomial

An expression of the form $a_0x^n + a_1x^{n-1} + a_2x^{n-2} + \ldots + a_{n-1}x + a_n$, where $a_0, a_1, \ldots, a_n$ are real numbers and n is a non-negative integer, is called a polynomial in the variable x. Polynomial in the variable x are usually denoted by $f(x)$, $g(x)$ and $h(x)$ etc.

Thus, $f(x) = a_0x^n + a_1x^{n-1} + a_2x^{n-2} + \ldots + a_{n-1}x + a_n$.

Important Points

(i) If $a_0 \neq 0$, then n is called the **degree** of the polynomial $f(x)$; it is written as $\deg f(x) = n$.

(ii) $a_0x^n, a_1x^{n-1}, a_2x^{n-2}, \ldots, a_{n-1}x$, a_n are called the **terms** of the polynomial $f(x)$; a_n is called the **constant term**.

(iii) $a_0, a_1, a_2, \ldots, a_{n-1}, a_n$ are called the **coefficients** of the polynomial $f(x)$.

(iv) If $a_0 \neq 0$, then a_0x^n is called the **leading term** and a_0 is called the **leading coefficient** of the polynomial.

(v) If all the coefficients $a_0, a_1, a_2, \ldots, a_{n-1}, a_n$ are zero, then $f(x)$ is called a **zero polynomial**. It is denoted by the symbol 0. The degree of the zero polynomial is never defined.

Degree of a Polynomial

(i) **In One Variable** The highest power of the variable is called the degree of the polynomial.

(ii) **In Two Variables** The sum of the powers of the variables in each term is obtained and the highest sum, so obtained is the degree of that polynomial.

Types of Polynomials

(i) **Constant Polynomial** A polynomial having degree zero.

(ii) **Linear Polynomial** A polynomial having degree one.

(iii) **Quadratic Polynomial** A polynomial having degree two.

(iv) **Cubic Polynomial** A polynomial having degree three.

(v) **Biquadratic Polynomial** A polynomial having degree four.

Fundamental Operations on Polynomial

(i) **Addition of Polynomials** To calculate the addition of two or more polynomials, we collect different groups of like powers together and add the coefficients of like terms.

(ii) **Subtraction of Polynomials** To find the subtraction of two or more polynomials, we collect different groups of like powers together and subtract the coefficient of like terms.

(iii) **Multiplication of Polynomials** Two polynomials can be multiplied by applying distributive law and simplifying the like terms.

(iv) **Division of Polynomials** When a polynomial $p(x)$ is divided by a polynomial $q(x) \neq 0$, we get two polynomials $g(x)$ and $r(x)$ such that

$$p(x) = q(x)g(x) + r(x)$$

Synthetic Division Method (Horner's Method)

This method is to find the quotient and the remainder when a polynomial is divided by a binomial.

Rule for Synthetic Division

1. First complete the given polynomial $f(x)$ by adding the missing term with zero coefficients.
2. Write the successive coefficients $a_0, a_1, a_2, \ldots, a_n$ of the polynomial $f(x)$.
3. If we want to divide the polynomial by $x - h$, then write h in the left corner.
4. In third row write b_0 below a_0, where $b_0 = a_0$ and then multiply b_0 by h to get the product hb_0.
5. Adding hb_0 to a_1, we get b_1. Similarly by adding hb_1 to a_2, we get b_2 and so on

h	a_0	a_1	a_2	....	a_n
		$+hb_0$	$+hb_1$	....	
	b_0	b_1	b_2	....	

6. Repeat this till you get last term which is remainder R.

   If $R = 0$, then h is the root of the polynomial $f(x) = 0$ and the equation can be reduced by one dimension.

Factorisation of Polynomials

(i) $(x - a)^2 = x^2 - 2xa + a^2$ (ii) $(x + a)^2 = x^2 + 2xa + a^2$

(iii) $(x + a)^3 = x^3 + 3x^2a + 3a^2x + a^3$

(iv) $(x - a)^3 = x^3 - 3x^2a + 3a^2x - a^3$

(v) $(x + y + z)^2 = x^2 + y^2 + z^2 + 2xy + 2yz + 2zx$

(vi) $(w + x + y + z)^2 = w^2 + x^2 + y^2 + z^2 + 2w(x + y + z) + 2x(y + z) + 2yz$

(vii) $a^3+b^3+c^3-3abc=(a+b+c)\cdot(a^2+b^2+c^2-ab-bc-ca)$

(viii) If $a+b+c=0 \Rightarrow a^3+b^3+c^3=3abc$

Some Special Products

(i) $(x-a)(x+a)=x^2-a^2$

(ii) $(x-a)(x^2+xa+a^2)=x^3-a^3$

(iii) $(x+a)(x^2-xa+a^2)=x^3+a^3$

(iv) $(x-a)(x+a)(x^2+a^2)=x^4-a^4$

(v) $(x^2+xa+a^2)(x^2-xa+a^2)=x^4+x^2a^2+a^4$

(vi) If n is a natural number, then

$$(x-a)(x^{n-1}+x^{n-2}a+x^{n-3}a^2+\ldots+a^{n-1})=x^n-a^n$$

(vii) If n is an even natural number, then

$$(x+a)(x^{n-1}-x^{n-2}a+x^{n-3}a^2-\ldots-a^{n-1})=x^n-a^n$$

(viii) If n is an odd natural number, then

$$(x+a)(x^{n-1}-x^{n-2}a+x^{n-3}a^2-\ldots+a^{n-1})=x^n+a^n$$

Identities of Polynomial

1. $x^2+a^2=(x+a)^2-2xa=(x-a)^2+2xa$
2. $x^3+a^3=(x+a)^3-3xa(x+a)$
3. $x^3-a^3=(x-a)^3+3xa(x-a)$
4. $(x+a)^2=(x-a)^2+4xa$
5. $(x-a)^2=(x+a)^2-4xa$
6. $(x+a)^2+(x-a)^2=2(x^2+a^2)$
7. $(x+a)^2-(x-a)^2=4xa$
8. $(x+a)^3+(x-a)^3=2x(x^2+3a^2)$
9. $(x+a)^3-(x-a)^3=2a(3x^2+a^2)$
10. $x^2+\frac{1}{x^2}=\left(x+\frac{1}{x}\right)^2-2$
11. $x^2+\frac{1}{x^2}=\left(x-\frac{1}{x}\right)^2+2$
12. $\left(x-\frac{1}{x}\right)^2=\left(x+\frac{1}{x}\right)^2-4$
13. $\left(x+\frac{1}{x}\right)^2=\left(x-\frac{1}{x}\right)^2+4$
14. $x+\frac{1}{x}=\sqrt{\left(x^2+\frac{1}{x^2}\right)+2}$
15. $x-\frac{1}{x}=\sqrt{\left(x^2+\frac{1}{x^2}\right)-2}$
16. $\left(x+\frac{1}{x}\right)^2+\left(x-\frac{1}{x}\right)^2=2\left(x^2+\frac{1}{x^2}\right)$
17. $\left(x+\frac{1}{x}\right)^2-\left(x-\frac{1}{x}\right)^2=4$
18. $x^3+\frac{1}{x^3}=\left(x+\frac{1}{x}\right)^3-3\left(x+\frac{1}{x}\right)$
19. $x^3-\frac{1}{x^3}=\left(x-\frac{1}{x}\right)^3+3\left(x-\frac{1}{x}\right)$

Value of a Polynomial $f(x)$ at $x=\alpha$

Let $f(x) = a_0x^n + a_1x^{n-1} + a_2x^{n-2}+...+a_n$ be a polynomial in x and α be a real number, then the real number

$a_0\alpha^n + a_1\alpha^{n-1} + a_2\alpha^{n-2} +...+ a_n$ is called the value of $f(x)$ at $x = \alpha$.

Thus, if $f(x)$ is a polynomial in x and α is a real number, then the value obtained by replacing x by α in $f(x)$ is called the value of $f(x)$ at $x = \alpha$. It is denoted by $f(\alpha)$.

Remainder Theorem

If $p(x)$ is a polynomial in x of degree ≥ 1 and a be any real number such that, if $p(x)$ is divided by a polynomial of the form $(x - a)$, then the remainder is $p(a)$.

Factor Theorem

If $p(x)$ is a polynomial in x of degree ≥ 1 and a be any real number such that $p(a) = 0$, then $(x - a)$ is a factor of $p(x)$.

Zeroes/Roots of a Polynomial

A real number α is a zero of the polynomial $p(x)$, if and only if $f(\alpha) = 0$.

If $p(x)$ is a polynomial of order n, such that

$p(x) = a_0x + a_1x^{n-1} + a_2x^{n-2} + ... + a_{n-1}x + a_n = 0$,

where $a_0, a_1, a_2, ..., a_n \in R$ and $p(x)$ have roots $\alpha_1, \alpha_2, \alpha_3, ..., \alpha_n$, then

(i) Sum of roots $\alpha_1 + \alpha_2 + ... + \alpha_n = (-1)^1 \dfrac{a_1}{a_0}$

(ii) Sum of product of two roots at a time,

$$\alpha_1\alpha_2 + \alpha_1\alpha_3 + ... = (-1)^2 \frac{a_2}{a_0}$$

(iii) Sum of product of three roots at a time,

$$\alpha_1\alpha_2\alpha_3 + \alpha_2\alpha_3\alpha_4 + ... = (-1)^3 \frac{a_3}{a_0}$$

(iv) Product of all roots

$$\alpha_1\alpha_2\alpha_3... \alpha_n = (-1)^n \frac{a_n}{a_0}$$

Number of Zeroes of a Polynomial

(i) A quadratic polynomial can have atmost 2 zeroes.

(ii) A cubic polynomial can have atmost 3 zeroes.

(iii) A polynomial of degree $(n > 1)$ can have atmost n zeroes.

Value Points

(i) If a polynomial $p(x)$ is divided by $(ax - b)$, then remainder is $p(b/a)$.

(ii) If a polynomial $p(x)$ is divided by $(ax + b)$, then remainder is $p(-b/a)$.

(iii) If a polynomial $p(x)$ is divided by $(b - ax)$, then remainder is $p(b/a)$.

(iv) The set of polynomials has closure, commutative and associative properties under addition as well as multiplication.

Subtraction is not commutative in the set of polynomials.

(v) 0 is the identity element under addition.

(vi) 1 is the identity element under multiplication.

(vii) Every polynomial has an additive and multiplicative inverse.

HCF of Monomials

To find the HCF of two or more monomials, we multiply the HCF of the numerical coefficients of the monomials by the highest power of each of the letters common to both the polynomials.

LCM of Monomials

To find the LCM of two monomials, we multiply the LCM of the numerical coefficient of the monomials by all the factors raised to the highest power which it has in either of the given polynomials.

Formulae on LCM and HCF

(i) $\text{LCM of two polynomials} = \dfrac{\text{Product of polynomials}}{\text{HCF of polynomials}}$

(ii) $\text{HCF of two polynomials} = \dfrac{\text{Product of polynomials}}{\text{LCM of polynomials}}$

(iii) For any two polynomials $p(x)$ and $q(x)$;
$p(x) \times q(x) = [\text{HCF of } p(x) \text{ and } q(x)] \times [\text{LCM of } p(x) \text{ and } q(x)]$

Linear Equations

(i) **Equation** A statement of equality of two algebraic expressions involving two or more unknown variable, is called equation.

(ii) **Linear Equation** An equation involving the variables in maximum of order 1 is called a linear equation. Graph of linear equation is a straight line.
Linear equation in one variable is of the form $ax + b = 0$.
Linear equation in two variables is of the form $ax + by + c = 0$.

(iii) **Solution of an Equation** A particular set of values of the variables, which when substituted for the variables in the equation makes the two sides of the equation equal, is called the solution of an equation.

(iv) **Simultaneous Linear Equation** A set of linear equation in two variables is said to form a system of simultaneous linear equation, if both equations have same solution.

(v) **Consistency of Simultaneous Linear Equation** If a system of simultaneous linear equation has atleast one solution, then the system of linear equation is called consistent.

(vi) **Inconsistency of Simultaneous Linear Equation** If a system of simultaneous linear equation has no solution, then the system of linear equation is called inconsistent.

Solving Linear Equation of One Variable

1. Rules for Solving a Linear Equation

(a) Same quantity can be added/subtracted both sides of an equation without changing the equality.

(b) Both the sides of an equation, can be multiplied/divided by the same non-zero number, without changing the quantity.

2. Steps for Solving Linear Equation

***Step* I** Obtain the linear equation and do cross-multiplication, if necessary.

***Step* II** Transpose the terms involving the variables on the left hand side and those not involving the variables to the right hand side.

***Step* III** Simplify the two sides to obtain the equation of the form $ax = b$.

***Step* IV** Find the value of x as $x = \frac{b}{a}$.

Solving Linear Equation of Two Variables

1. Elimination by Substitution

***Step* I** Find the value of one variable (say y) in terms of another variable (say x).

***Step* II** Substitute this value in another equation to obtain the value of another variable (say x).

***Step* III** Substituting this obtained value of variable (x) in the first equation, the value of first variable to be obtained.

2. Elimination by Equating the Coefficient

***Step* I** Multiply the equations by suitable non-zero constants so to make the coefficients of one of the variable same.

Step II Add or subtract the equations obtained, to eliminate one of the variable.

Step III Solve the linear equation in one variable obtained in step II and get the value of one variable.

Step IV Substitute the value of the variable obtained in above step in any of the given equations and find the second value.

3. Cross-multiplication Method

Step I Consider the system of simultaneous linear equations, in two variables x and y.

i.e. $a_1x + b_1y + c_1 = 0$

and $a_2x + b_2y + c_2 = 0$

Step II Now, cross-multiply the terms, according to the arrow, given below.

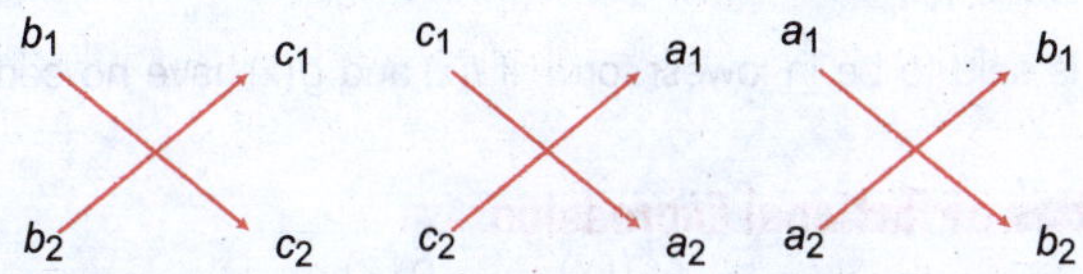

Step III Now, find the value of x and y according to the following relation

$$\frac{x}{b_1c_2 - b_2c_1} = \frac{y}{c_1a_2 - c_2a_1} = \frac{1}{a_1b_2 - a_2b_1}$$

which gives

$$x = \frac{b_1c_2 - b_2c_1}{a_1b_2 - a_2b_1} \text{ and } y = \frac{c_1a_2 - c_2a_1}{a_1b_2 - a_2b_1}$$

4. Graphical Method

When we draw the graph of each of the two equations, we have the following possibilities.

(a) If two lines intersect at one point, then it has a unique solution and point of intersection gives the solution.

(b) If two lines are parallel, then it has no solution.

(c) If two lines are coincide, then it has infinite solutions.

Solution for Linear Equation in Two Variables

When two linear equations $a_1x + b_1y = c_1$ and $a_2x + b_2y = c_2$ are given

Case I If $\frac{a_1}{a_2} \neq \frac{b_1}{b_2}$ then the system is consistent with unique solution.

***Case* II** If $\frac{a_1}{a_2} = \frac{b_1}{b_2} \neq \frac{c_1}{c_2}$, then the system is inconsistent with no solution.

***Case* III** If $\frac{a_1}{a_2} = \frac{b_1}{b_2} = \frac{c_1}{c_2}$, then the system is consistent (dependent), with infinitely many solutions.

Rational Expression

If $f(x)$ and $g(x)$ are two polynomials and $g(x) \neq 0$, then quotient $\frac{f(x)}{g(x)}$ is called a rational expression.

Remember that

- Every polynomial is a rational expression but every rational expression is not a polynomial.
- $\frac{f(x)}{g(x)}$ is said to be in lowest form, if $f(x)$ and $g(x)$ have no common factor.

Properties of Rational Expression

(i) **Addition** Addition of $\frac{f(x)}{g(x)}$ and $\frac{p(x)}{r(x)}$ is defined as

$$\frac{f(x)}{g(x)} + \frac{p(x)}{r(x)} = \frac{f(x) \cdot r(x) + p(x) \cdot g(x)}{g(x) \cdot r(x)}$$

(ii) **Subtraction** When we subtract $\frac{f(x)}{g(x)}$ from $\frac{p(x)}{r(x)}$, then

$$\frac{p(x)}{r(x)} - \frac{f(x)}{g(x)} = \frac{p(x) \cdot g(x) - f(x) \cdot r(x)}{r(x) \cdot g(x)}$$

(iii) **Multiplication** When $\frac{f(x)}{g(x)}$ and $\frac{p(x)}{r(x)}$ are multiplied, then as $\frac{f(x)}{g(x)} \times \frac{p(x)}{r(x)} = \frac{f(x) \cdot p(x)}{g(x) \cdot r(x)}$

(iv) **Division** When $\frac{f(x)}{g(x)}$ is divided by $\frac{p(x)}{r(x)}$, we get it as

$$\frac{f(x)}{g(x)} \div \frac{p(x)}{r(x)} = \frac{f(x)}{g(x)} \cdot \frac{r(x)}{p(x)}$$

Logarithms

If a is a positive real number other than 1 and $a^x = m$, then x is called the logarithm of m to the base a, written as $\log_a m$. In $\log_a m$, m should be always positive.

Value Points

(i) If $m < 0$, then $\log_a m$ will be imaginary and if $m = 0$, then $\log_a m$ will be meaningless.

(ii) $\log_a m$ exists only, if $m, a > 0$ and $a \neq 1$.

(iii) The another way of $\log_e x$ can be represented as ln.

(iv) In a logarithmic expression when the base is not mentioned, it is taken as 10.

Types of Logarithms

1. **Natural** (or Napier) **Logarithms** The logarithm with base e ($e = 2.718$) is called natural logarithms.

   e.g. $\log_e x, \log_e 25$ etc.

2. **Common** (or Brigg's) **Logarithms** The logarithm with base 10 is called common logarithm.

   e.g. $\log_{10} x, \log_{10} 75$ etc.

- The another way of $\log_e x$ can be represented as ln.
- In a logarithmic expression when the base is not mentioned, it is taken as 10.

Characteristic and Mantissa of a Logarithm

The logarithm of positive real number n consists of two parts.

(i) The integral part is known as the **characteristic**. It is always an integer positive, negative or zero.

(ii) The decimal part is called as the **mantissa**. The mantissa is never negative and is always less than one.

Method to Find the Characteristic

***Case* I When number is greater than 1.**

The characteristic is one less than the number of digits in the left of decimal point in the given number.

Number (x)	:	6.125	61.321	725.132
Number of digits in the integral part of x	:	1	2	3
Characteristic of $\log x$	:	$1-1=0$	$2-1=1$	$3-1=2$

***Case* II When number is less than 1**.

The characteristic of the logarithm of a positive number less than 1 is negative and is numerically greater by 1 than the number of zeroes between the decimal sign and the first significant figure of the number.

e.g.

Number (x)	:	0.7684	0.06712	0.00031
Number of zeroes after the decimal point	:	0	1	3
Characteristic of log x	:	$-(0+1)$ $=-1=\overline{1}$	$-(1+1)$ $=-2=\overline{2}$	$-(3+1)$ $=-4=\overline{4}$

In place of -1 or -2 etc., we use $\overline{1}$ (one bar) and $\overline{2}$ (two bar) etc.

Properties of Logarithms

(i) A negative number can never be expressed as the power of 10, mantissa should always be kept positive. Hence, whenever characteristic is negative, minus sign is placed above the characteristic and not to its left to show that the mantissa is always positive.

(ii) Mantissa of the logarithm of all the numbers having same digits in the same order will be the same, irrespective of the position of the decimal point.

Anti logarithm

The positive number a is called the anti logarithm of a number b, if a is anti logarithm of b, then we write $a=$ antilog b.

So, $a=\text{antilog } b \Leftrightarrow \log a=b$.

Important Points

(i) $a^{\log_a x}=x; a\neq 0, \neq \pm 1, x>0$

(ii) $a^{\log_b x}=x^{\log_b a}; a>0, b>0, \neq 1, x>0$

(iii) $\log_a a=1, \log_a 1=0; a>0, \neq 1$

(iv) $\log_a x=\dfrac{1}{\log_x a}; x, a>0, \neq 1$

(v) $\log_a x=\log_a b\times\log_b x=\dfrac{\log_b x}{\log_b a}; a, b>0, \neq 1, x>0$

(vi) For $m, n > 0$, $a > 0$ and $a \neq 1$

(a) $\log_a (mn) = \log_a m + \log_a n$ (b) $\log_a \left(\frac{m}{n}\right) = \log_a m - \log_a n$

(c) $\log_a (m)^n = n \log_a m$

(vii) For $x > 0, a > 0, \neq 1$

(a) $\log_{a^n} (x) = \frac{1}{n} \log_a x$

(b) $\log_{a^n} x^m = \frac{m}{n} \log_a x$

(viii) For $x > y > 0$

(a) $\log_a x > \log_a y$, if $a > 1$

(b) $\log_a x < \log_a y$, if $0 < a < 1$

(ix) If $a > 1$, then

(a) $\log_a x > p \Rightarrow x > a^p$

(b) $0 < \log_a x < p \Rightarrow 0 < x < a^p$

(x) If $0 < a < 1$, then

(a) $\log_a x > p \Rightarrow 0 < x < a^p$

(b) $0 < \log_a x < p \Rightarrow a^p < x < 1$

(xi) (a) $\log_a x > 0 \Leftrightarrow x > 1, a > 1$ or $0 < x < 1, 0 < a < 1$

(b) $\log_a x < 0 \Leftrightarrow x > 1, 0 < a < 1$ or $0 < x < 1, a > 1$

(xii) (a) $\log_b a \to -\infty$, if $b > 1$ and $a \to 0^+$

(b) $\log_b a \to \infty$, if $b > 1$ and $a \to \infty$

(c) $\log_b a \to \infty$, if $0 < b < 1$ and $a \to 0^+$

(d) $\log_b a \to -\infty$, if $0 < b < 1$ and $a \to \infty$

Graph of $y = \log_b a$ is as follows

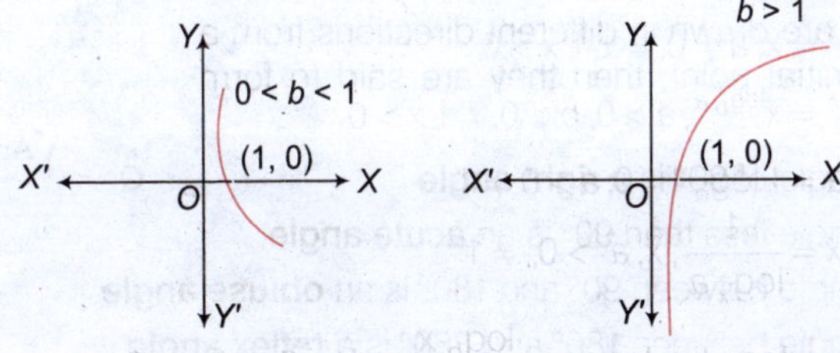

Geometry

Point

A fine dot on paper or a location on plane is called point. Point has no length, breadth or thickness.

Line

A line is defined as set of points that extend infinitely in both directions.

Line Segment

A line segment is a part of straight line that is bounded by two distinct end points and contains every point on the line that is between its end points.

Ray

If a line segment is extended to unlimited length on one of the end points, then it is called a ray.

Value Points

(i) A line contains infinite points.

(ii) Infinite lines can pass through a point.

(iii) Two distinct lines in a plane cannot have more than one point common.

Angle

If two rays are drawn in different directions from a common initial point, then they are said to form an angle.

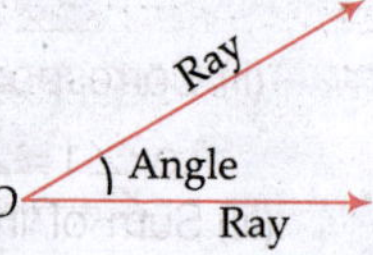

(i) An angle of 90° is a **right angle**

(ii) An angle less than 90° is an **acute angle**.

(iii) An angle between 90° and 180° is an **obtuse angle**.

(iv) An angle between 180° and 360° is a **reflex angle**.

(v) The sum of all angles on one side of a straight line is 180°.

(vi) When any number of straight lines joined at a point, then the sum of all the angles around that point is 360° which is called as **complete angle**.

Competition Insight

Two angles whose sum is 90° are said to be **complementary** to each other and two angles whose sum is 180° are said to be **supplementary** to each other.

Intersecting Lines

When two straight lines intersect each other, then vertically opposite angles are equal.

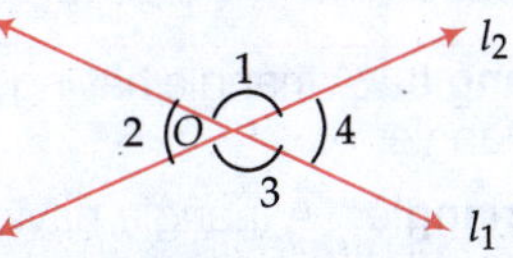

i.e. $\angle 1 = \angle 3$ and $\angle 2 = \angle 4$

Parallel Lines

When a straight line *XY* cuts two parallel lines l_1 and l_2 as shown in the figure, the line *XY* is called the transversal line.

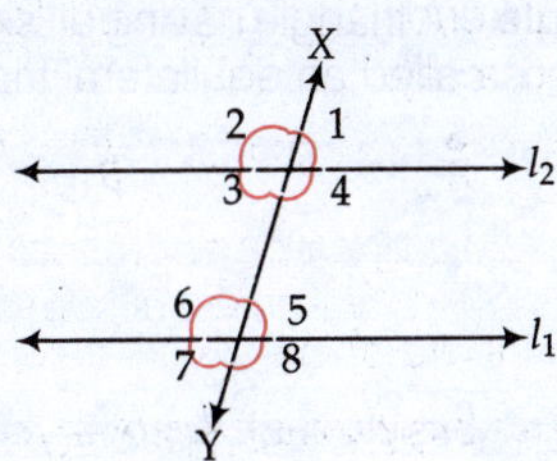

The following are the relationships between various angles that are formed.

(i) Alternate angles are equal.
i.e. $\angle 1 = \angle 7$ and $\angle 2 = \angle 8$ [alternate exterior angles]
$\angle 3 = \angle 5$ and $\angle 4 = \angle 6$ [alternate interior angles]

(ii) Corresponding angles are equal.
i.e. $\angle 1 = \angle 5$, $\angle 2 = \angle 6$, $\angle 3 = \angle 7$ and $\angle 4 = \angle 8$.

(iii) Sum of interior angles on the same side of the transversal line is equal to 180°.
i.e. $\angle 3 + \angle 6 = 180°$ and $\angle 4 + \angle 5 = 180°$
These angles are also known as cointerior angles.

(iv) Sum of exterior angles on the same side of the transversal is equal to 180°.
i.e. $\angle 1 + \angle 8 = 180°$ and $\angle 2 + \angle 7 = 180°$.
These angles are also known as coexterior angles.

Triangles

A figure bounded by three line segments in a plane is called a triangle. It has three vertices, three sides and three angles.

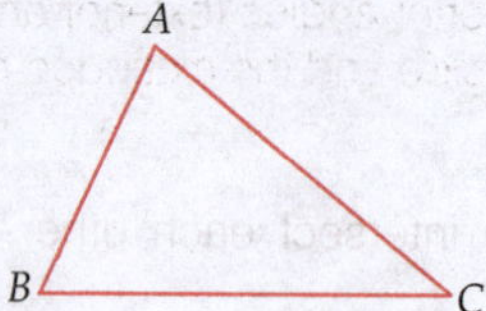

(i) **Acute Angled Triangle** A triangle having all angles acute, is called an acute angled triangle.

(ii) **Obtuse Angled Triangle** A triangle having one obtuse angle and two acute angles is called an obtuse angled triangle.

(iii) **Scalene Triangle** A triangle having three sides of different lengths, is called a scalene triangle i.e. $AB \neq BC \neq AC$.

(iv) **Isosceles Triangle** A triangle having two sides or two angles are equal, is called an isosceles triangle.

(v) **Equilateral Triangle** A triangle having all sides equal or each angle of measure is 60°, is called an equilateral triangle.

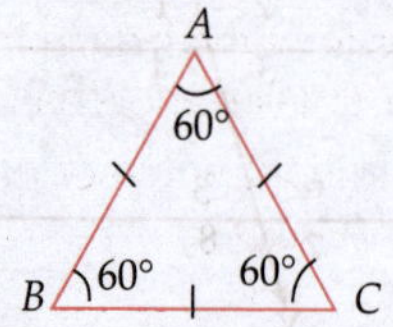

i.e. $AB = BC = AC$

or $\angle A = \angle B = \angle C = 60°$

(vi) **Right Angled Triangle** A triangle having one angle of measure 90° is called a right angled triangle. The side opposite to the right angle is called its **hypotenuse** and the remaining two sides are called **perpendicular** and **base**.

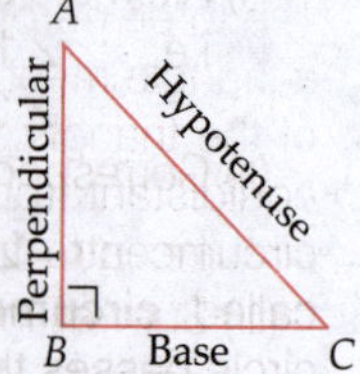

Here, $AC^2 = AB^2 + BC^2$

which is known as Pythagoras theorem i.e. In a right triangle, the square of the hypotenuse is equal to the sum of the square of the other two sides.

Important Properties of Triangles

(i) Sum of the three angles of a triangle is 180°.

(ii) Sides opposite to equal angles are equal and *vice-versa*.

(iii) In an isosceles right angled triangle, one angle is 90° and other two angles are 45° each.

(iv) The exterior angle of a triangle (at each vertex) is equal to the sum of its two opposite interior angles (exterior angle is the angle formed at any vertex, by one side and the extended portion of the second side at that vertex)

i.e. $\angle Z = \angle X + \angle Y$.

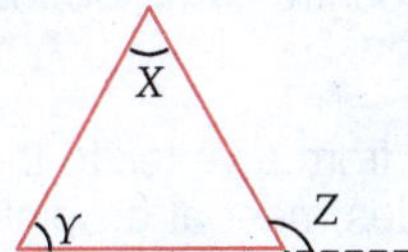

(v) Side opposite to the greatest angle is the longest side and vice-versa.

Also, side opposite to the smallest angle is the smallest side and vice-versa.

(vi) If the sides are arranged in the ascending order of their measurement, then the angles opposite to the side (in the same order) will also be in ascending order (i.e. greater angles has greater side opposite to it). If the sides are arranged in descending order of their measurement, then the angles opposite to the side in the same order will also be in descending order. (i.e. smaller angle has smaller side opposite to it).

(vii) There can be only one right angle or only one obtuse angle in any triangle.

Different Centre of a Triangle

1. Circumcentre

The three perpendicular bisectors of the sides of a triangle meet at a point is called **circumcentre** of the triangle. The circumcentre of a triangle is equidistant from its vertices and the distance of circumcentre from each of the three vertices is called **circumradius** (R) of the triangle. The circle passes through all the three vertices of the triangle is called **circumcircle**.

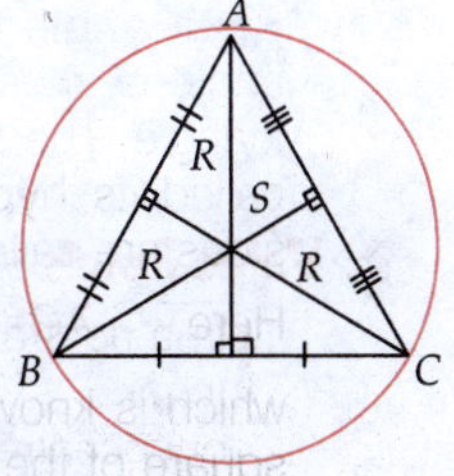

2. Incentre and Excentre

If I is the centre, then $\angle BIC = 90° + \frac{\angle A}{2}$.

The internal bisectors of the three angles of a triangle meet at a point is called **incentre** (I) of the triangle. Incentre is equidistant from the three sides of the triangle, i.e. the perpendiculars drawn from the incentre to the three sides are equal in length and this length is called the **inradius** (r) of the triangle.

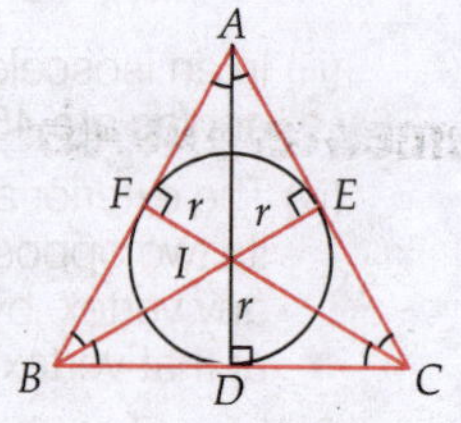

The circle drawn with incentre as centre and touches all three sides on the inside is called **incircle**. The point of intersection of two external angle bisectors and one internal angle bisector is called an **excentre**.

Any triangle has three excentres, one opposite to each vertex.

3. Orthocentre

The perpendicular drawn from a vertex to the opposite side is called an **altitude**. The three altitudes meet at a point is called orthocentre.

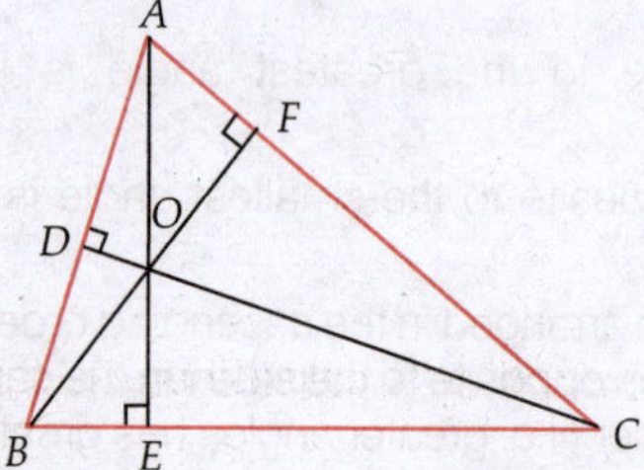

4. Centroid

Median is the line joining the mid-point of a side to the opposite vertex. The three medians of a triangle meet at a point is called the centroid G. Centroid divides the median in the ratio 2 : 1.

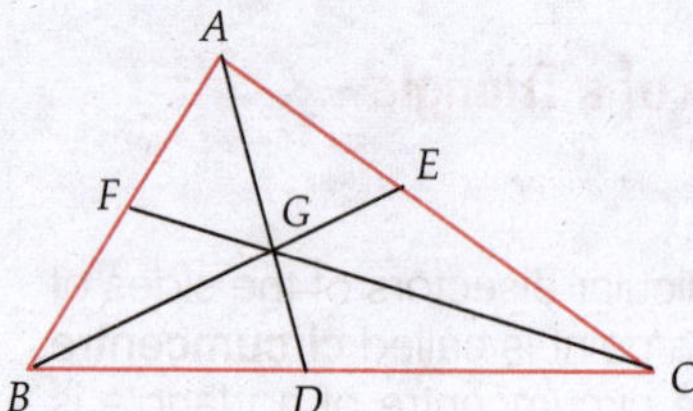

Value Points

(i) In a right angled triangle, the vertex where the right angle is formed (i.e. the vertex opposite to the hypotenuse) is the orthocentre.

(ii) In an obtuse angled triangle, the orthocentre lies outside the triangle.

(iii) Centroid divides each of the medians in the ratio 2 : 1, the part of the median towards the vertex being twice in length to the part towards the side.

(iv) In a right angled triangle, the length of the median drawn to the hypotenuse is equal to half of the hypotenuse. This median is also the circumradius and mid-point of the hypotenuse is the circumcentre.

(v) In an isosceles triangle, centroid, orthocentre, circumcentre and incentre all lie on the median to the base.

(vi) In an equilateral triangle, centroid, orthocentre, circumcentre and incentre all coincide.

(vii) The ratio of circumradius and inradius of an equilateral triangle is 2 : 1.

Congruency of Triangles

Two triangles are identical in all respects are said to be congruent and it is denoted by the symbol $\cong$. In two congruent triangles,

(i) the corresponding sides are equal.

(ii) the corresponding angles are equal.

Two triangles will be congruent, if atleast one of the following conditions is satisfied.

(i) Three sides of one triangle are respectively equal to the three sides of the second triangle. (SSS)

(ii) Two sides and the included angle of one triangle are respectively equal to two sides and the included angle of the second triangle. (SAS)

(iii) Two angles and the included side of a triangle are respectively equal to two angles and the corresponding side of the second triangle. (ASA) or (AAS)

(iv) Two right angled triangles are congruent, if the hypotenuse and one side of one triangle are respectively equal to the hypotenuse and one side of the second right angled triangle. (RHS)

Similarity of Triangles

Two triangles are said to be similar, if they are alike in shape only and it is denoted by the symbol ($\sim$). The corresponding angles of two similar triangles are equal but the corresponding sides are proportional but not equal. Two triangles are similar, if

(i) the three angles of one triangle are respectively equal to the three angles of the second triangle. (AAA) or (AA)

(ii) two sides of one triangle are proportional to two sides of the other and the included angles are equal. (SAS)

(iii) the corresponding sides of two triangles are in the same ratio, then triangles are similar. (SSS)

Some Important Theorems

1. **Pythagoras Theorem** In ΔABC, if $\angle B = 90^\circ$, then $AC^2 = AB^2 + BC^2$.

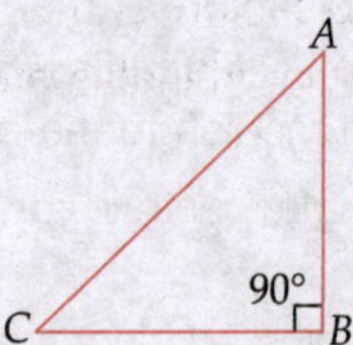

2. In ΔABC, if AD is the angle bisector intersecting BC at D, then $\frac{AB}{AC} = \frac{BD}{DC}$.

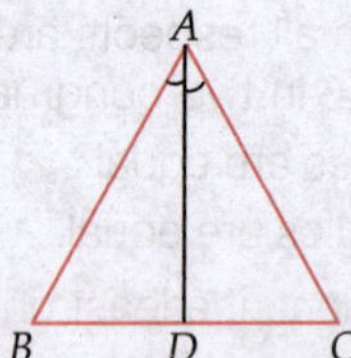

3. If D and E divide AB and AC in the ratio $m:n$ respectively, then $DE = \frac{m}{m+n} BC$.

4. **Mid-point Theorem** The line segment joining mid-points of two sides of a triangle is parallel to the third side and equal to half of it.

   i.e. $BC \parallel DE$ and $DE = \frac{1}{2} BC$

5. In ΔABC, if D and E are the points on AB and AC, respectively such that DE is parallel to BC, then $\frac{AD}{AB} = \frac{AE}{AC}$.

6. In ΔABC, if AD is the median from A to side BC meeting BC at its mid-point D, then $2(AD^2 + BD^2) = AB^2 + AC^2$. This is called the **Apollonius theorem**.

7. The ratio of areas of two similar triangles is equal to the ratio of the squares of any two corresponding sides.

8. The areas of two similar triangles are in the ratio of the squares of corresponding altitudes.

9. The areas of two similar triangles are in the ratio of the squares of the corresponding medians.
10. The areas of two similar triangles are in the ratio of the squares of the corresponding angle bisector segments.
11. If the areas of two similar triangles are equal, then the triangle are congruent and *vice-versa.*

Quadrilaterals

A plane closed figured bounded by four segments is called quadrilateral.

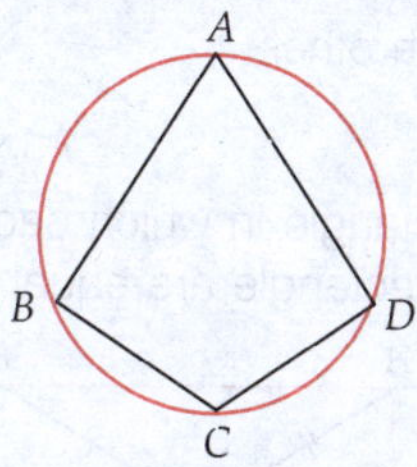

1. The sum of four angles of a quadrilateral is equal to 360°.
2. If the four vertices of a quadrilateral lie on the circumference of a circle i.e. if the quadrilateral can be inscribed in a circle, it is called a cyclic quadrilateral.

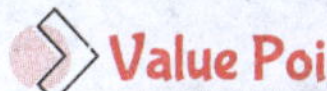

Value Points

In a cyclic quadrilateral, the sum of opposite angles is 180°
i.e. $A + C = 180°$ and $B + D = 180°$.

Parallelogram

A quadrilateral having opposite sides parallel is called a parallelogram. In a parallelogram,

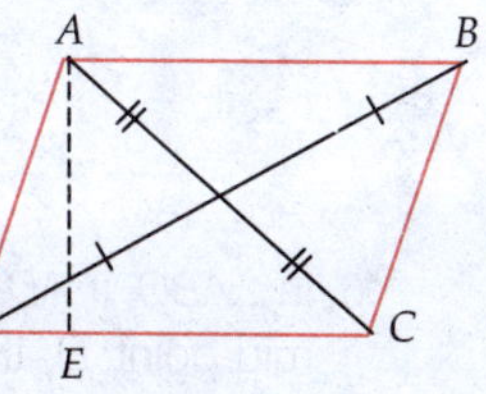

(i) opposite sides are equal.
(ii) opposite angles are equal.
(iii) each diagonal divides the parallelogram into two congruent triangles.
(iv) sum of any two adjacent angles is 180°.
(v) the diagonals bisect each other.

Rhombus

A parallelogram is a rhombus in which every pair of adjacent sides are equal (all four sides of a rhombus are equal).

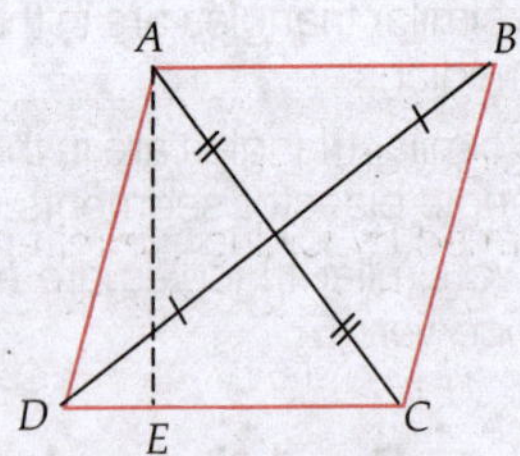

Since, a parallelogram is a rhombus, all the properties of a parallelogram apply to a rhombus. Further, in a rhombus, the diagonals are perpendicular to each other.

Rectangle

A parallelogram is a rectangle in which each of the angles is equal to 90°. The diagonals of a rectangle are equal.

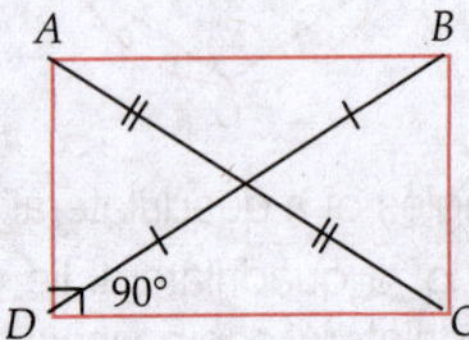

A rectangle is also a special type of parallelogram and hence all properties of a parallelogram apply to rectangles also.

Square

A rectangle is a square in which all four sides are equal (a rhombus in which all four angles are equal, all are right angles).

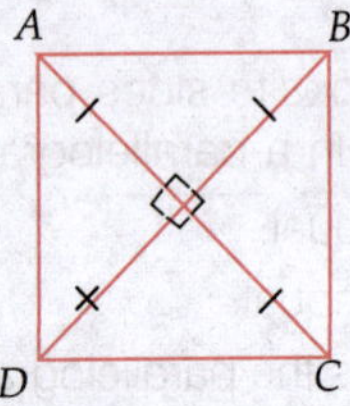

Hence, the diagonals are equal and they bisect at right angles.

Trapezium

If one pair of opposite sides of a quadrilateral are parallel, then it is called a trapezium.

In the figure, side *AD* is parallel to *BC*. Any trapezium is said to be an isosceles trapezium, if $CD = AB$.

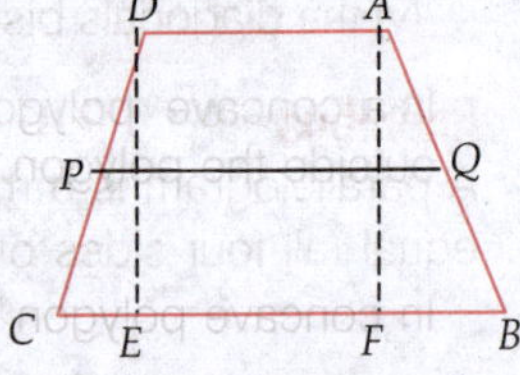

Value Points

(i) The quadrilateral formed by joining the mid-points of the consecutive sides of a rectangle is a rhombus and *vice-versa.*

(ii) The figure formed by joining the mid-points of the pairs of consecutive sides of a quadrilateral is a parallelogram.

(iii) The quadrilateral formed by joining the mid-points of the sides of a square, is a square.

(iv) Two parallelograms on the same base and between the same parallel lines have equal areas.

(v) One parallelogram and one rectangle on the same base and between same parallel lines have equal areas.

(vi) Two triangles on the same base and between the same parallel lines have equal areas.

Polygon

Any figure bounded by three or more line segments is called a polygon. A regular polygon is one in which all sides are equal and all angles are equal. A regular polygon can be inscribed in a circle.

The name of polygons with three, four, five, six, seven, eight, nine and ten sides are respectively triangle, quadrilateral, pentagon, hexagon, heptagon, octagon, nonagon and decagon.

Convex Polygon

In a convex polygon, a line segment joining any two points inside it, never goes outside the polygon.

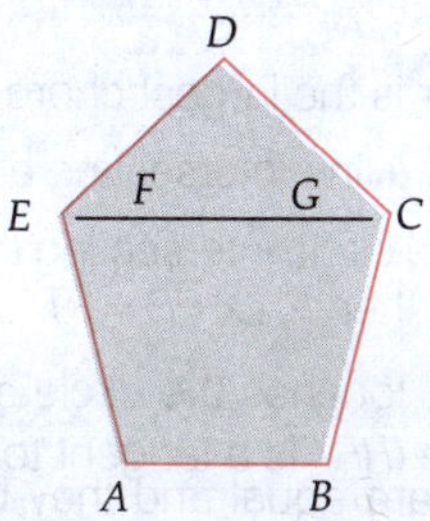

Concave Polygon

In a concave polygon, a line segment joining two points inside it, goes outside the polygon.

Or

In concave polygon atleast one of the interior angle is more than 180°.

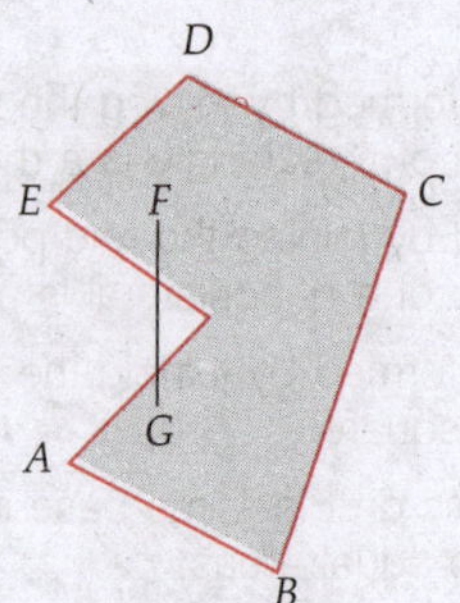

Value Points

(i) The sum of all the angles in a convex polygon is $(2n-4)90°$.

(ii) Exterior angle of a regular polygon is $\frac{360°}{n}$.

(iii) Interior angle of a regular polygon is $\left(180° - \frac{360°}{n}\right)$

(iv) Number of diagonals of a convex polygon with n sides is $\frac{n(n-3)}{2}$.

Circles

A circle is a set of points which are at a constant distance from a fixed point (i.e. centre) in the plane.

1. **Radius** Radius is the shortest distance between the centre of the circle and a point on the circumference of the circle.
2. **Chord** A chord is a line joining two points on the circumference of a circle.
3. **Diameter** Diameter is the largest chord of a circle.
4. **Secant** A secant is a line intersecting a circle in two distinct points.
5. If PAB is a secant to a circle intersecting the circle at A and B and PT is a tangent segment, then $PA \times PB = PT^2$.
6. **Tangent** A line that touches the circle at only one point is called a tangent to the circle (RR' is a tangent touching the circle at R).

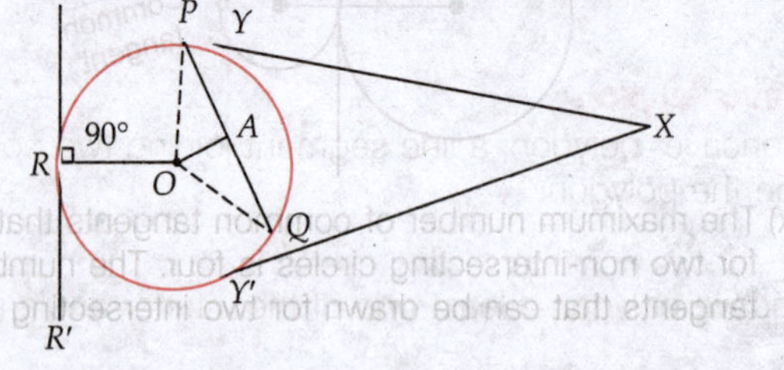

Properties of Circle

(i) If two chords APB and CPD intersect at P, then

$$PA \cdot PB = PC \cdot PD.$$

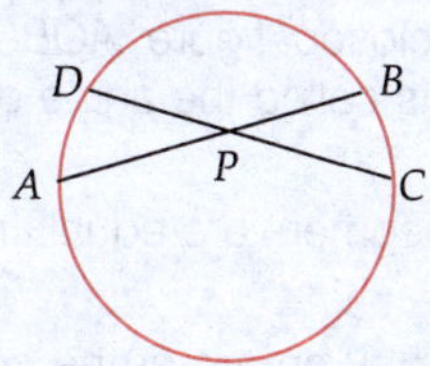

(ii) A tangent is perpendicular to the radius drawn at the point of tangency ($RR' \perp OR$) i.e. at R.

(iii) Two tangents can be drawn to the circle from any point outside the circle and these two tangents are equal in length (in figure X is the external point and the two tangents XY and XY' are equal.)

(iv) One and only one circle passes through any three given non-collinear points.

(v) Two circles are said to touch each other, if a common tangent can be drawn touching both the circles at the same point. This is called the **point of contact** of the two circles. When two circles touch each other, then the point of contact and the centres of the two circles are collinear.

(vi) If two circles touch internally, then the distance between two centres is equal to the difference of their radii.

(vii) If two circles touch externally, then the distance between two centres is equal to the sum of their radii.

(viii) A common tangent drawn to two circles is called a direct common tangent, if the tangent cuts the line passing through the centres between the two circles but not on one side of the circles.

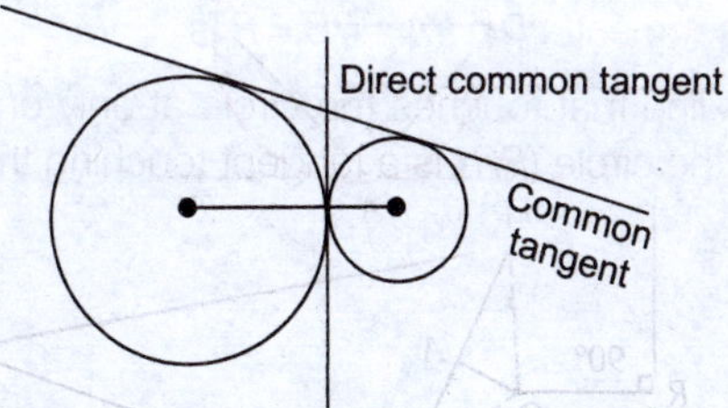

(ix) The maximum number of common tangents that can be drawn for two non-intersecting circles is four. The number of common tangents that can be drawn for two intersecting circle is 2.

Arc and Sector

An arc is a segment of a circle. In the figure, ACB is called minor arc and ADB is called **major arc**. In general, when we say it is an arc AB, we refer to the **minor arc**. The closed figure $AOBCA$ is called the **sector**. $\angle AOB$ is called the angle of the **sector**.

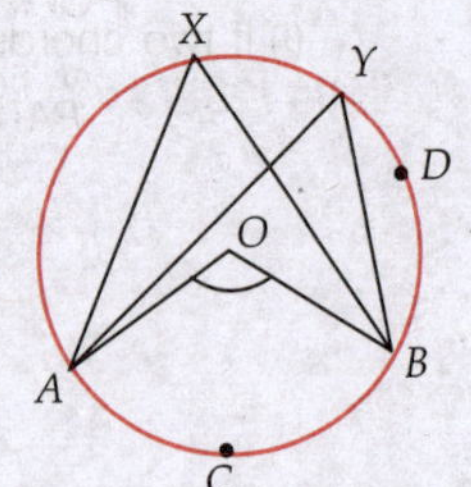

(i) Angles in the same segment are equal. In the figure, $\angle AXB = \angle AYB$.

(ii) The angle subtended by an arc at the centre is double the angle subtended by the arc in the remaining part of the circle. In the figure, $\angle AOB = 2 \times \angle AXB = 2 \times \angle AYB$.

Some Important Theorems

1. If two arcs of a circle are congruent, then the corresponding chords are equal.
2. The perpendicular from the centre of a circle to a chord bisects the chord.
3. The line joining the centre to the mid-point of a chord is perpendicular to the chord.
4. Chords which are equidistant from the corresponding centres are equal.
5. Equal chords of a circle are equidistant from the centre.
6. The angle at the circumference in a semi-circle is a right angle.
7. **Alternate Segment Theorem** The angle formed between the tangent and the chord through the point of contact of the tangent is equal to the angle formed by the chord in the alternate segment i.e. $\angle BAT = \angle ADB$.

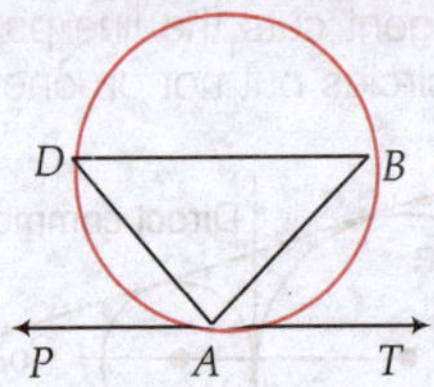

Perimeter and Area of Plane Figure

Plane Figure A figure enclosed by three or more sides or by a circular boundary.

Perimeter Total length of the sides of a plane figure.

Area Space covered by a plane figure.

Triangle

For any triangle having sides a, b and c, then

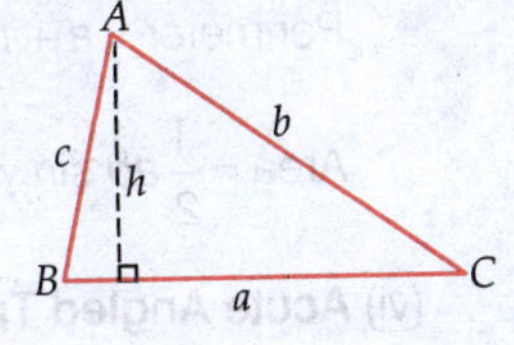

Perimeter $= a + b + c = 2s$

Area = Base × Height $= \frac{1}{2}(a \times h)$

or Area $= \sqrt{s(s-a)(s-b)(s-c)}$, it is called **Heron's formula**

where, $s = \frac{a+b+c}{2}$ = semi-perimeter of the triangle.

Different Types of Triangles

(i) **Right Angled Triangle**

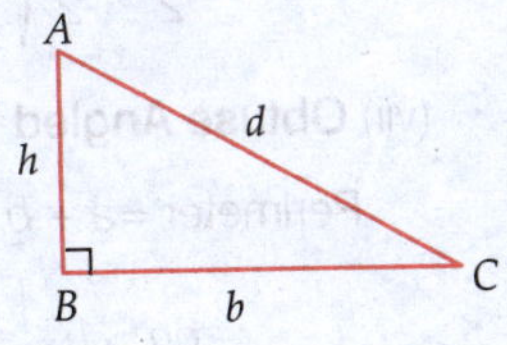

Perimeter $= b + d + h$

Area $= \frac{1}{2}(b \times h)$

Hypotenuse $= d = \sqrt{h^2 + b^2}$

(ii) **Equilateral Triangle**

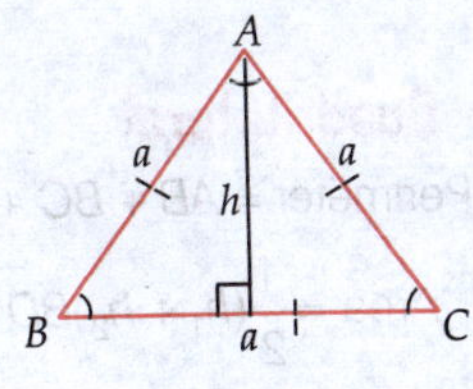

Perimeter $= 3a$

Altitude = Height $(h) = \frac{\sqrt{3}}{2}a$

Area $= \frac{\sqrt{3}}{4}a^2$

(iii) **Isosceles Triangle**

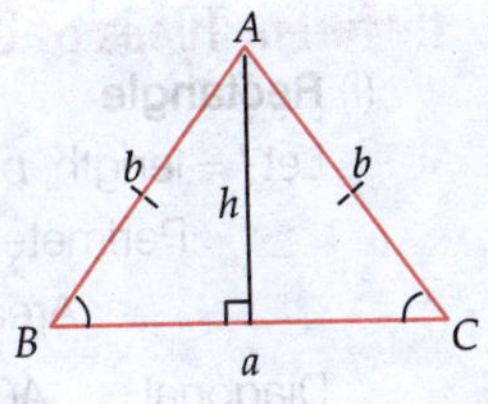

Perimeter $= a + 2b$

Altitude = Height $(h) = \frac{\sqrt{4b^2 - a^2}}{2}$

Area $= \frac{a}{4}\sqrt{4b^2 - a^2}$

(iv) **Isosceles Right Triangle**

$$\text{Perimeter} = 2a + \sqrt{2}a$$

$$\text{Hypotenuse } (b) = \sqrt{2}a$$

$$\text{Area} = \frac{1}{2}a^2$$

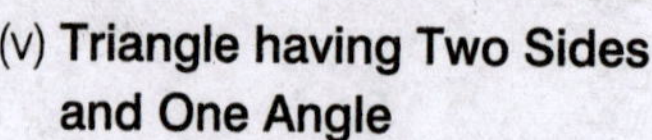

(v) **Triangle having Two Sides and One Angle**

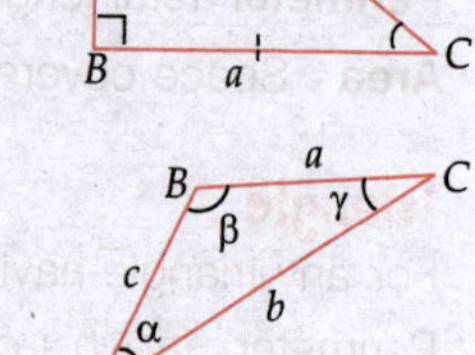

$$\text{Perimeter} = a + b + c$$

$$\text{Area} = \frac{1}{2}ab\sin\gamma = \frac{1}{2}bc\sin\alpha = \frac{1}{2}ac\sin\beta$$

(vi) **Acute Angled Triangle**

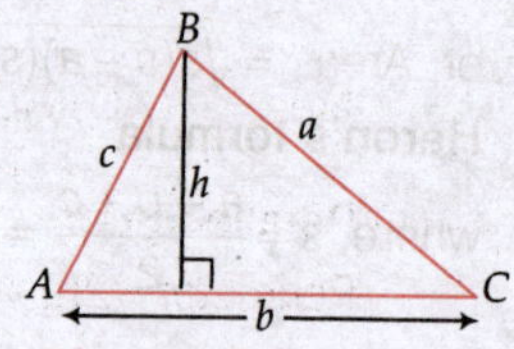

$$\text{Perimeter} = a + b + c$$

$$\text{Area} = \frac{bh}{2} = \frac{b}{2}\sqrt{a^2 - \left(\frac{a^2 + b^2 - c^2}{2b}\right)^2}$$

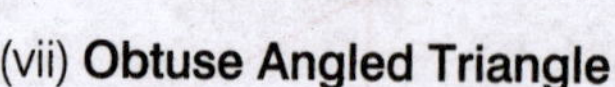

(vii) **Obtuse Angled Triangle**

$$\text{Perimeter} = a + b + c$$

$$\text{Area} = \frac{bh}{2} = \frac{h}{2}\sqrt{a^2 - \left(\frac{c^2 - a^2 - b^2}{2b}\right)^2}$$

Quadrilateral

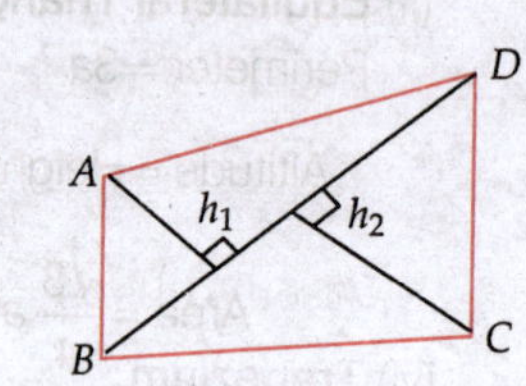

$$\text{Perimeter} = AB + BC + CD + DA$$

$$\text{Area} = \frac{1}{2}(h_1 + h_2)BD$$

Different Types of Quadrilaterals

(i) **Rectangle**

Let l = length, b = breadth

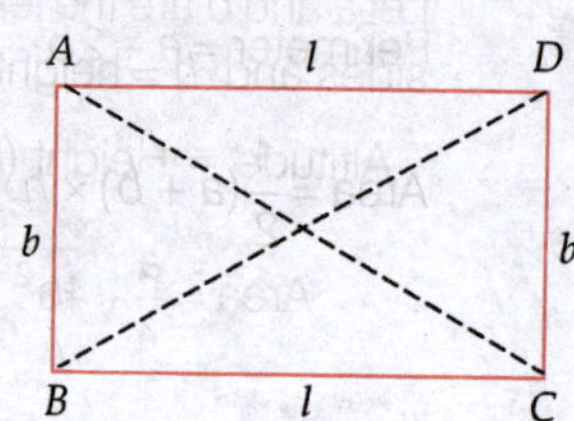

$$\text{Perimeter} = 2(l + b)$$

$$\text{Area} = l \times b$$

$$\text{Diagonal, } AC = BD = \sqrt{l^2 + b^2}$$

(ii) Rectangular Path

Let w be the width of the path.

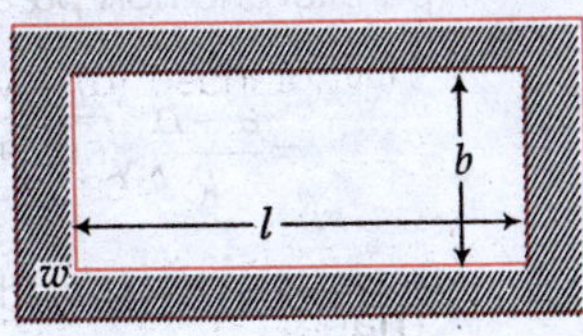

Perimeter of outer path

$$= 2[(l + 2w) + (b + 2w)]$$

Area of outer rectangle

$$= (l + 2w)(b + 2w)$$

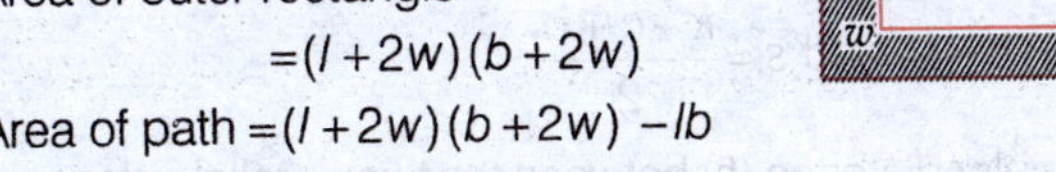

Area of path $= (l + 2w)(b + 2w) - lb$

(iii) Square

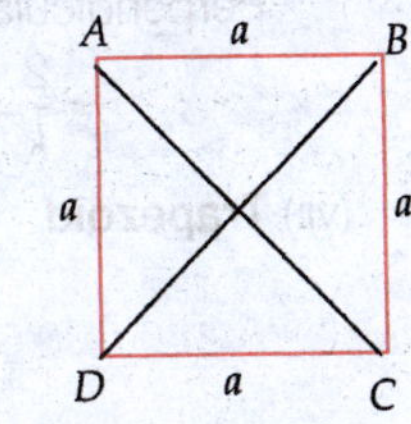

Perimeter $= 4a$

Diagonal, $AC = BD = \sqrt{2}a = \sqrt{2 \times \text{Area}}$,

where Area $= a^2$

$$\text{Area} = \frac{1}{2}(AC)(BD) = \frac{1}{2}(AC)^2 = \frac{1}{2}(BD)^2$$

(iv) Parallelogram

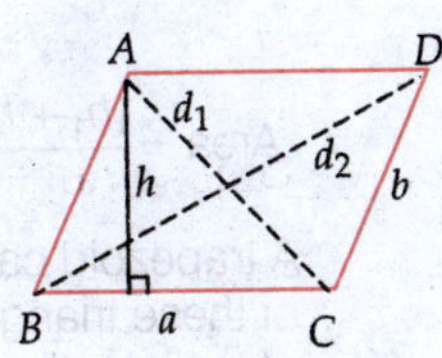

Perimeter $= 2(a + b)$

Area $= a \times h$

Also, $d_1^2 + d_2^2 = 2(a^2 + b^2)$ or

$$\text{Area} = 2\sqrt{s(s - a)(s - b)(s - d)},$$

where $s = \dfrac{a + b + d}{2}$

(v) Rhombus

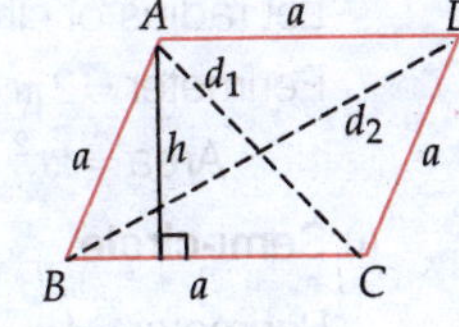

Perimeter of rhombus $= 4a$

Area of rhombus $= a \times h$

Area of rhombus $= \dfrac{1}{2}d_1 d_2$

Also, $d_1^2 + d_2^2 = 4a^2$

(vi) Trapezium

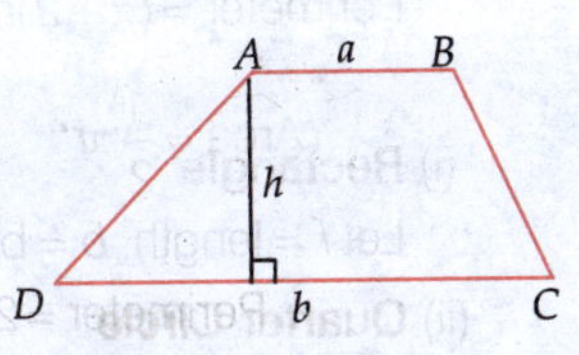

Let a and b are the length of the parallel sides and h = height

$$\text{Area} = \frac{1}{2}(a + b) \times h$$

Area of trapezium, when the lengths of parallel and non-parallel sides are given

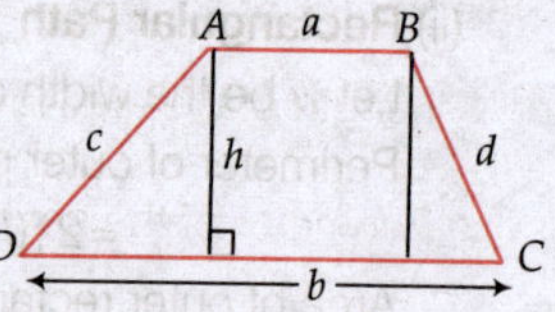

$$=\frac{a+b}{k}\sqrt{s(s-k)(s-c)(s-d)},$$

where $k=(b-a)$ and $s=\dfrac{k+c+d}{2}$

Perpendicular distance (h) between the two parallel sides

$$=\frac{2}{k}\sqrt{s(s-k)(s-c)(s-d)}$$

(vii) **Trapezoid**

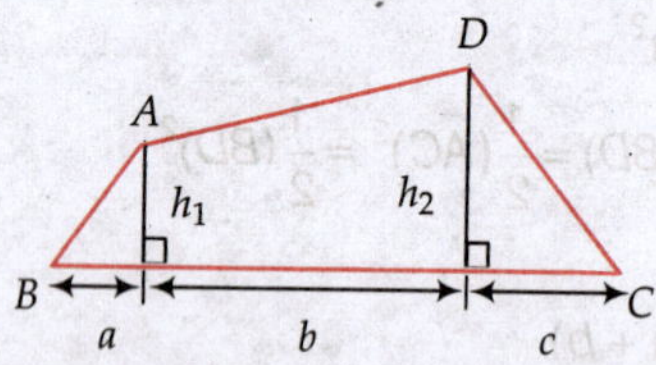

$$\text{Area}=\frac{(h_1+h_2)b+ah_1+ch_2}{2}$$

A trapezoid can also be divided into two triangles. The area of each of these triangles is calculated and the result added to find the area of trapezoid.

Circle

Let radius of circle $= r$, diameter $= d$

Perimeter $= 2\pi r = \pi d \qquad (\because d = 2r)$

Area $= \pi r^2$

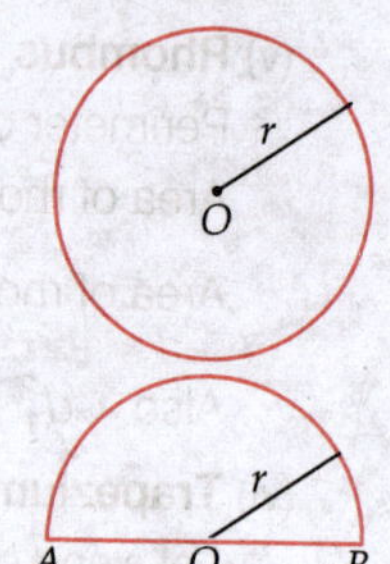

(i) **Semi-circle**

Perimeter $= (\pi+2)r = \pi r + d = \dfrac{36}{7}r$

Area $= \dfrac{1}{2}\pi r^2$

(ii) **Quarter Circle**

Perimeter $= \left(\dfrac{\pi}{2}+2\right)r$

Area $= \dfrac{1}{4}\pi r^2$

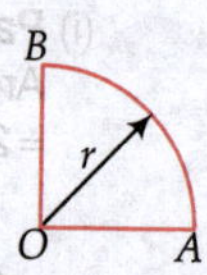

(iii) **Sector of a Circle**

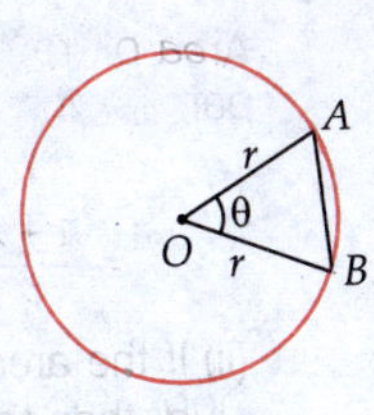

Length of the arc $AB = \frac{2\pi r}{360°}\theta$

Perimeter of the sector $AOB = 2r + \frac{2\pi r\theta}{360°}$

Area of the sector $AOB = \frac{\pi r^2}{360°}\theta$

Area of the sector $AOB = \frac{1}{2} \times \text{arc } AB \times r$

(iv) **Segment of a Circle**

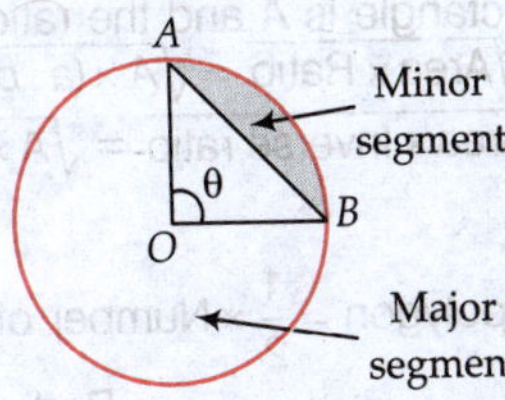

Area of minor segment $= \frac{r^2}{2}\left[\frac{\theta\pi}{180°} - \sin\theta\right]$

Area of major segment $= \frac{r^2}{2}\left[\frac{(360° - \theta)\pi}{180°} + \sin\theta\right]$

Area of minor segment = Area of sector – Area of triangle, where Area of triangle $= \frac{1}{2}r^2 \sin\theta$ and Area of major segment = Area of circle – Area of minor segment

Concentric Circles

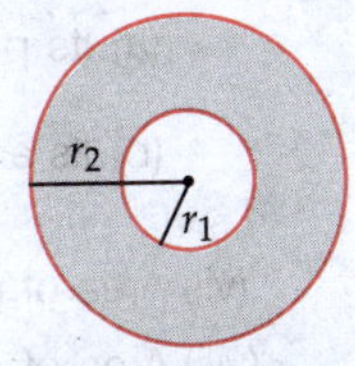

Perimeter $= 2\pi(r_1 + r_2)$

Area of the shaded region

$$= \pi(r_2^2 - r_1^2)$$

$$= \pi(r_2 + r_1)(r_2 - r_1)$$

If two circles are concentric, then they have the same centre but always have different radii.

Formulae on Area of Different Objects

(i) **Path Around a Garden/Verandah Around a Room**

Area of the verandah

= 2 (Width of verandah) × [Length + Breadth of room + 2 (Width of verandah)]

$= 2 \times d \times [l + b + 2d]$

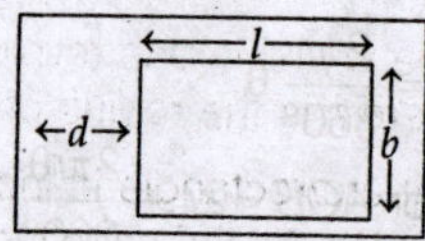

(ii) If the area of the verandah is A and the width of the verandah is d, then the area of the 'square shaped' garden/room is given by

$$\text{Area of garden/room} = \left[\frac{A - 4d^2}{4d}\right]^2$$

(iii) If the area of a rectangle is A and the ratio of its sides is $a : b$, then First side $= \sqrt{\text{Area} \times \text{Ratio}} = \sqrt{A \times (a : b)}$

Second side $= \sqrt{\text{Area} \times \text{Inverse ratio}} = \sqrt{A \times (b : a)}$

(iv) **Regular Polygon**

Area of a regular polygon $= \frac{1}{2} \times$ Number of sides $\times$ Radius of the inscribed circle

(a) Area of regular hexagon $= \frac{3\sqrt{3}}{2} \times (\text{Side})^2$

(b) Area of regular octagon $= 2(\sqrt{2} + 1)(\text{Side})^2$

(v) If the area of the square is A, then area of the circle formed by the same perimeter $= \frac{4A}{\pi}$.

(vi) If all the measuring sides of a plane figure, is increased/decreased by $x\%$, then

(a) Its perimeter increases/decreases by $x\%$.

(b) Its area increases or decreases by $\left(2x + \frac{x^2}{100}\right)\%$ or $\left(2x - \frac{x^2}{100}\right)\%$.

(vii) Area of room = Length × Breadth

(viii) Area of 4 walls of a room = 2(Length + Breadth) × Height

(ix) Radius of incircle of an equilateral triangle of side 'a' $= \frac{a}{2\sqrt{3}}$

(x) Radius of circumcircle of an equilateral triangle of side 'a' $= \frac{a}{\sqrt{3}}$

(xi) Angle inscribed by minute hand in 60 min = 360°

(xii) Angle inscribed by hour hand in 12 h = 360°

(xiii) Angle inscribed by minute hand in 1 min = 6°

(xiv) Distance moved by a wheel in one revolution = Circumference of the wheel $=2\pi r$, where r is the radius of a circle

(xv) If the length of a square/rectangle is increased by x% and the breadth is decreased by y%, the net effect on the area is given by

Net effect $=\left[x-y-\frac{xy}{100}\right]\%$

(xvi) If the side of a square/rectangle/triangle is doubled, then area is increased by 300%, i.e. the area becomes four times of itself.

(xvii) If the radius of a circle is decreased by x %, the net effect on the area is $\left(-\frac{x^2}{100}\right)\%$ i.e. the area is decreased by $\left(\frac{x^2}{100}\right)\%$.

(xviii) If a floor of dimensions $(l \times b)$ is to be covered by a carpet of width w metre, then the length of the carpet is $\left(\frac{lb}{w}\right)$ m.

(xix) If a floor of dimensions $(l \times b)$ m is to be covered by a carpet of width w metre at the rate ₹ X per metre, then the total amount required is ₹$\left(\frac{Xlb}{w}\right)$.

(xx) If a room of dimensions $(l \times b)$ m is to be paved with square tiles, then
(a) the side of the square tile = HCF of l and b
(b) the number of tiles required $=\frac{l \times b}{(\text{HCF of } l \text{ and } b)^2}$

(xxi) If the sides of a rectangular field of area x sq m are in the ratio $m:n$, then the sides are given by $\sqrt{x \cdot \frac{m}{n}}$ and $\sqrt{x \cdot \frac{n}{m}}$.

(xxii) If the side of a regular polygon is a and the polygon has n sides, then the area of the polygon is $\left[\frac{n}{4}\cot\left(\frac{\pi}{n}\right)\right]a^2$ sq units.

(xxiii) The area of a square inscribed in a circle of radius r is $2r^2$ and the side of a square inscribed in a circle of radius r is $\sqrt{2}r$.

(xxiv) The area of the largest triangle inscribed in a semi-circle of radius r is r^2.

(xxv) The number of diagonals of a regular polygon of n sides is given by $\frac{n(n-3)}{2}$.

(xxvi) (a) If a square hall x metre long is surrounded by a verandah (on the outside of the hall) d metre wide, then the area of the verandah is given by $4d\,(x + d)$ sq m.

(b) If the verandah is made inside the hall, then the area of verandah is given by $4d\,(x - d)$ sq m.

Surface Area and Volume of Solid Figure

Surface Area Area covered by the outer surface of a solid.

Volume Amount of space occupied by a solid.

Value Points

(i) The capacity of a container is equal to its volume.

(ii) The volume of the material in a hollow body is equal to the difference between the external volume and internal volume.

(iii) To find the cost of polishing/covering/painting of a solid, firstly we will have to find its exposed surface area and then multiply it by unit cost.

(iv) To find the quantity of a substance continued in a solid, we find its volume.

(v) Volume of water accumulated on a roof after rain

= Surface area of roof × Rain falls

Solid Figure

The objects which occupy space (i.e. they have three dimensions) are called solids.

1. Cuboid (Parallelopiped)

A figure which is surrounded by six rectangular surfaces is called cuboid.

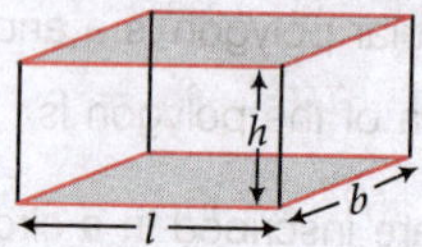

Lateral surface area $= 2\,(l + b)h$

Total surface area $= 2(lb + bh + lh)$

Volume $= lbh$

Length of the diagonal $= \sqrt{l^2 + b^2 + h^2}$

$$\text{Volume} = \sqrt{\text{Area of base / top} \times \text{Area of side face} \times \text{Area of other side face}}$$

2. Cube

A cuboid whose length, breadth and height are same is called a cube.

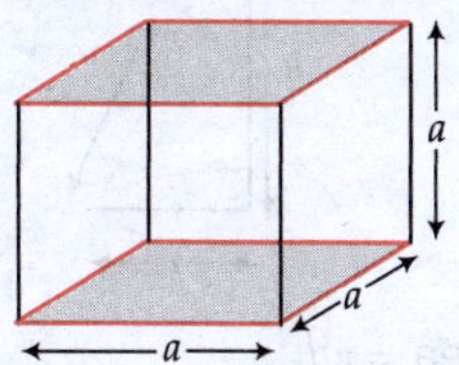

Let side of a cube be a.

$$\text{Lateral surface area} = 4a^2$$

$$\text{Total surface area} = 6a^2$$

$$\text{Volume} = a^3$$

$$\text{Length of the diagonal} = \sqrt{3}a$$

$$\text{Edge of a cube} = \sqrt[3]{\text{Volume}}$$

3. Right Circular Cylinder

A right circular cylinder is considered as a solid generated by the revolution of a rectangle about one of its sides.

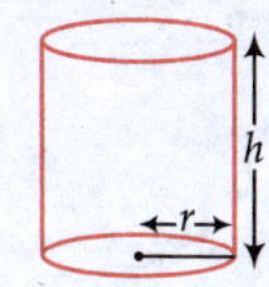

$$\text{Curved surface area} = 2\pi rh = \pi dh$$

$$\text{Total surface area} = 2\pi rh + 2\pi r^2$$

$$= 2\pi r(r + h) = \pi d\left(\frac{d}{2} + h\right)$$

$$\text{Volume} = \pi r^2 h = 0.7857\, d^2 h$$

4. Hollow Cylinder

$$\text{Curved surface area} = 2\pi (R + r)h$$

$$\text{Total surface area} = 2\pi (R + r)(h + R - r)$$

$$\text{Volume} = \pi h (R^2 - r^2)$$

$$\text{or Volume of material} = \pi(R^2 - r^2)h$$

5. Right Circular Cone

A right circular cone is a solid generated by revolving of a right angled triangle through one of its sides (other than hypotenuse) containing the right angle as axis.

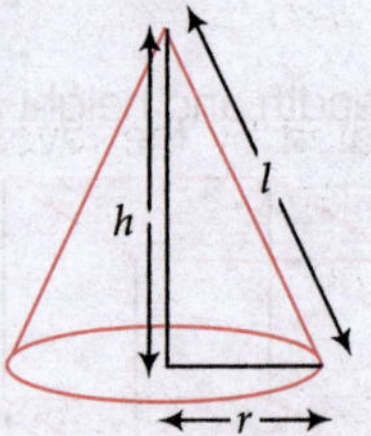

Curved surface area $= \pi rl$

Total surface area $= \pi rl + \pi r^2 = \pi r(l + r)$

$$\text{Volume} = \frac{1}{3}\pi r^2 h$$

Slant height, $l = \sqrt{h^2 + r^2}$

A cone has only one round surface at the bottom and a curved lateral surface on the sides.

6. Frustum of Right Circular Cone

If a right circular cone is cut off by a plane parallel to its base, then the portion of the cone between the cutting plane and the base of the cone is called a frustum of the cone.

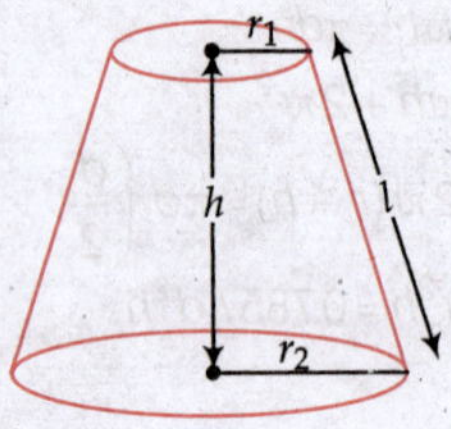

Slant height $= l = \sqrt{h^2 + (r_2 - r_1)^2}$

Curved surface area $= \pi(r_1 + r_2)l$

Total surface area $= \pi[(r_1 + r_2)l + r_1^2 + r_2^2]$

$$\text{Volume} = \frac{\pi h}{3}(r_1^2 + r_2^2 + r_1 r_2)$$

7. Sphere

A sphere is a solid generated by the revolution of a semi-circle about its diameter.

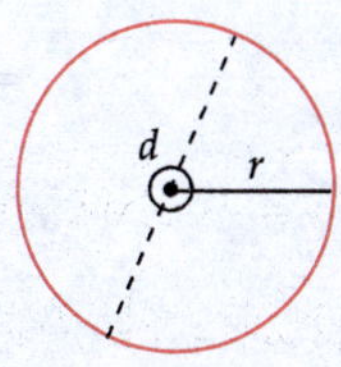

$$\text{Surface area} = 4\pi r^2 = \pi d^2$$

$$\text{Volume} = \frac{4}{3}\pi r^3 = \frac{\pi}{6}d^3$$

8. Hemisphere

A plane passing through the centre of a sphere, divides the sphere into two equal parts. Each part is called a hemisphere.

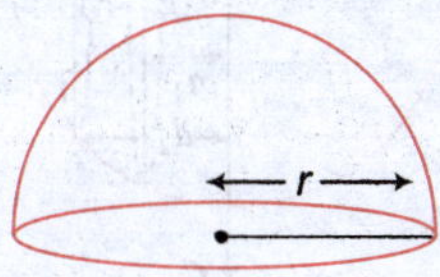

$$\text{Curved surface area} = 2\pi r^2$$

$$\text{Total surface area} = 2\pi r^2 + \pi r^2 = 3\pi r^2$$

$$\text{Volume} = \frac{2}{3}\pi r^3$$

9. Hollow Sphere (Shell)

The solid enclosed between two concentric spheres is called a hollow sphere.

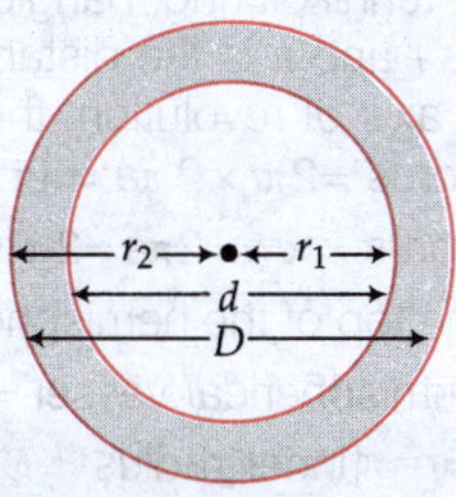

$$\text{Volume of the material} = \frac{4}{3}\pi(r_2^3 - r_1^3)$$

$$= \frac{\pi}{6}(D^3 - d^3)$$

10. Frustum of a Sphere

$$\text{Volume} = \frac{\pi d}{6}\{3(a^2 - d_1^2) + 3(a^2 - d_2^2) + d_2^2 - 2d_1 d_2 + d_1^2\}$$

$$= \frac{\pi d}{6}(3r_1^2 + 3r_2^2 + d^2), \text{ where } d = d_2 - d_1$$

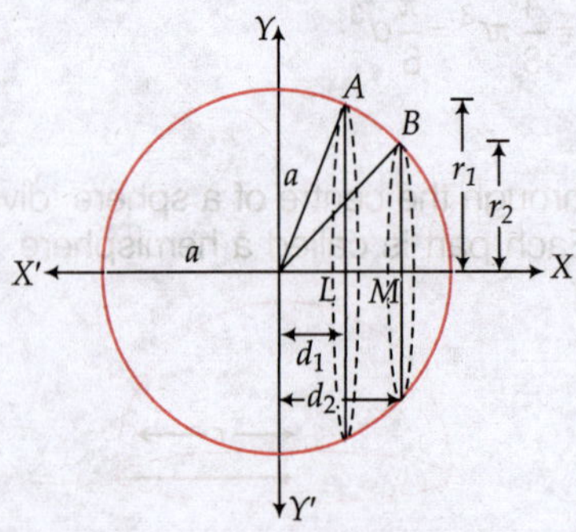

$$\text{Curved surface area} = 2\pi a(d_2 - d_1) = 2\pi ad$$

$$\text{Total surface area} = 2\pi ad + (\pi r_1^2 + \pi r_2^2)$$

$$= \pi(2ad + r_1^2 + r_2^2)$$

11. Torus (Solid Ring)

Torus is a solid revolution of three dimensions obtained when a circle is rotated about an axis lying in its plane but not intersecting the circle. e.g. A cycle tubes, rings, tennikoit ring, bangles and life belt. If radius of the circle which rotates is r and a is the distance between centre of the surface of circle and the axis of revolution, then

Curved surface area of torus $= 2\pi r \times 2\pi a = 4\pi^2 ra$

$$\text{Volume of the torus} = \pi r^2 \times 2\pi a = 2\pi^2 r^2 a$$

Area of the ring around the top of the hemispherical vessel $= \pi(R^2 - r^2)$

Total surface area of a hemispherical vessel $= 3\pi(R^2 + r^2)$,

where R = Outer radius, r = Inner radius

12. Right Prism

A right prism is a prism in which the joining edges and faces are perpendicular to the base faces.

Lateral surface area = Perimeter of base × Height

Whole surface area = Lateral surface area + 2 × Area of base

Volume = Area of base × Height

(i) **Triangular Prism**

A three sided prism having parallel bases and in equilateral triangle. Lateral surface area = $3ah$

$$\text{Total surface area} = 3ah + \frac{\sqrt{3}}{4}a^2$$

$$\text{Volume} = \frac{\sqrt{3}}{4}a^2 \times h$$

(ii) **Pentagonal Prism**

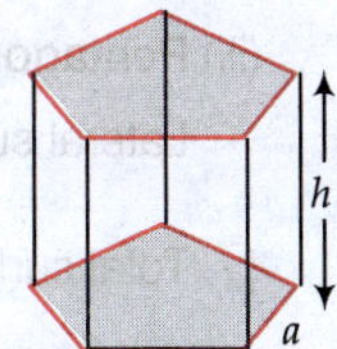

Surface area of pentagonal $= \sqrt{3}a^2$

Lateral surface area $= 5a \times h = 5ah$

Total surface area $= 5ah + 2\sqrt{3}a^2$

Volume $= \sqrt{3}a^2 \times h = \sqrt{3}a^2h$

(iii) **Hexagonal Prism**

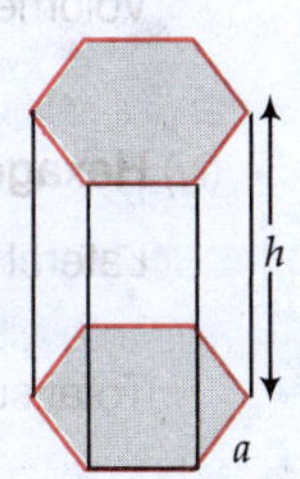

$$\text{Surface area of hexagonal} = \frac{3\sqrt{3}}{2}a^2 = 2.5981a^2$$

Lateral surface area $= 6a \times h = 6ah$

$$\text{Total surface area} = 6ah + \frac{3\sqrt{3}}{2}a^2$$

$$\text{Volume} = \frac{3\sqrt{3}}{2}a^2h = 2.5981a^2h$$

13. Pyramid

It is a structure whose outer surfaces are triangular and converge to a single point at the top.

$$\text{Lateral surface area} = \frac{1}{2} \times \text{Perimeter of base} \times \text{Slant height}$$

Total surface area = Lateral surface area + Area of base

$$\text{Volume} = \frac{1}{3} \times \text{Area of base} \times \text{Height}$$

(i) **Triangular Pyramid**

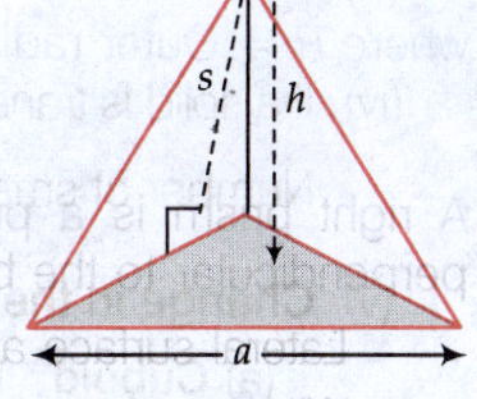

$$\text{Lateral surface area} = \frac{1}{2}(3a) \times s = \frac{3}{2}as$$

$$\text{Total surface area} = \frac{3}{2}as + \frac{\sqrt{3}}{4}a^2$$

$$\text{Volume} = \frac{1}{3} \times \frac{\sqrt{3}}{4}a^2 \times h = \frac{\sqrt{3}}{12}a^2h$$

(ii) **Square Pyramid**

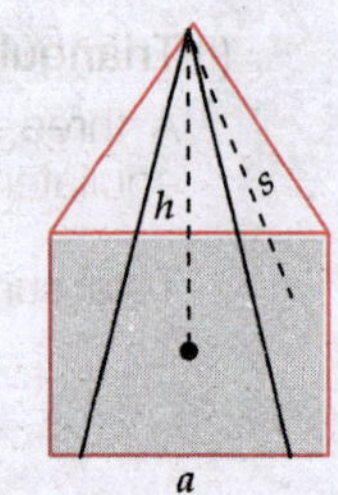

Lateral surface area $= \frac{1}{2} \times 4a \times s = 2as$

Total surface area $= 2as + a^2$

Volume $= \frac{1}{3} \times h \times a^2 = \frac{a^2h}{3}$

(iii) **Pentagonal Pyramid**

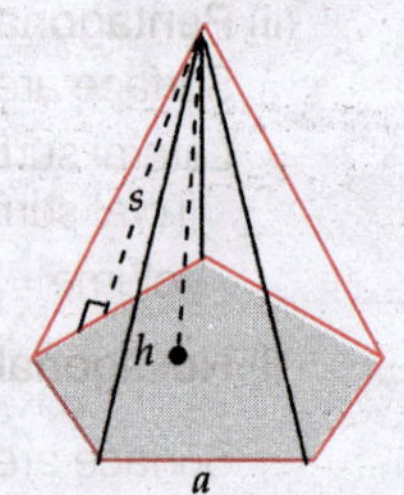

Lateral surface area $= \frac{1}{2} \times 5a \times s = \frac{5}{2}as$

Total surface area $= \frac{5}{2}as + \sqrt{3}a^2$

Volume $= \frac{1}{3} \times \sqrt{3}a^2 = \frac{1}{\sqrt{3}}a^2$

(iv) **Hexagonal Pyramid**

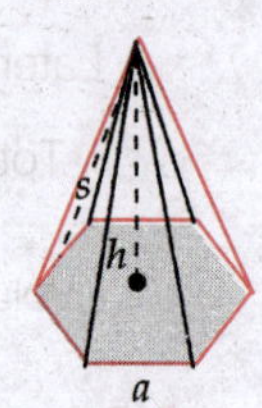

Lateral surface area $= \frac{1}{2} \times 6a \times s = 3as$

Total surface area $= 3as + \frac{3\sqrt{3}}{2}a^2$

Volume $= \frac{\sqrt{3}}{2}a^2h$

Formulae on Volume of Different Objects

(i) If a cuboid has length, breadth and height be a, b and c, each of thickness d, then capacity $= (a - 2d)(b - 2d)(c - 2d)$
Volume of material $= abc - [(a - 2d)(b - 2d)(c - 2d)]$

(ii) If three cubes of sides a, b and c are melted and a new cube is formed of side x, then $x = \sqrt[3]{a^3 + b^3 + c^3}$.

(iii) Volume of water released by a pipe
$=$ Rate of flow $\times$ Area of cross section $\times$ Time

(iv) If a solid is transformed into a number of small identical solids, then

$$\text{Number of small solids} = \frac{\text{Volume of large solid}}{\text{Volume of small solid}}$$

(v) **Change in the Dimensions**

(a) **Cuboid** If length, breadth and height of a cuboid is increased by $x\%$, $y\%$ and $z\%$ respectively, then increase in its volume is given by $\left[x + y + z + \frac{xy + yz + zx}{100} + \frac{xyz}{(100)^2}\right]\%$.

(b) **Cube** If the sides of the cube are changed by x%, then change in the volume is given by $\left[3x+\frac{3x^2}{100}+\frac{x^3}{(100)^2}\right]\%$

or $\left[\left(1+\frac{x}{100}\right)^3-1\right]\times 100\%$.

(c) **Sphere** If the radius of a sphere is changed by x%, then the change in its volume is given by

$$\left[3x+\frac{3x^2}{100}+\frac{x^3}{100^2}\right]\% \text{ or } \left[\left(1+\frac{x}{100}\right)^3-1\right]\times 100\%.$$

(d) **Cylinder** If height of a cylinder is changed by x%, then the change in its volume = x%.

(i) If height and radius are changed by x% and y% respectively, then the change in its volume is given by

$$\left[2x+y+\frac{x^2+2xy}{100}+\frac{x^2y}{(100)^2}\right]\%.$$

(ii) If height and radius are changed by x%, then change in the volume is given by

$$\left[3x+\frac{3x^2}{100}+\frac{x^3}{(100)^2}\right]\%.$$

(e) If the length, breadth and height of cuboid are made x, y and z times respectively, its volume is increased by $(xyz-1)\times 100\%$.

(f) If the sides and diagonal of a cuboid are given, then the total surface area in terms of diagonal and sides is given by

Total surface area = (Sum of the sides)^2 – (Diagonal)^2.

(g) If the side of a cube is increased by x%, then surface area is increased by $\left[2x+\frac{x^2}{100}\right]\%$.

(h) If each side of a cube is doubled, its volume becomes 8 times i.e. Volume is increased by 700%.

Appendices

Some Great Mathematicians & Their Contributions

Archimedes

The greatest mathematicians of ancient era, Archimedes made phenomenal contribution in the field of Mathematics. His works include integral calculus studies and finding various computation techniques to determine volume and area of several shapes including the conic section.

Euclid

Euclid, the 'father of Geometry', wrote the book ,"Euclid's Elements", that is considered to be the greatest piece of historical works in Mathematics. The book is divided into 13 parts and in it, Euclid has discussed in details about geometry (what is now called Euclidean geometry). His contributions are also famous in the fields of spherical geometry, conic sections and number theory.

Aryabhatta

Aryabhatta, the greatest Indian mathematician of ancient era, has been famous for his mathematical works and theorems on astronomical bodies that have been found to be very accurate in terms of modern calculations. "Aryabhatiya", his only work to have survived has given the world innumerable theorems and research subjects. His two other major contributions are the introduction of zero to the world and calculating the approximate value of pie. His works are also spread in fields like include algebra, arithmetic, trigonometry, quadratic equations and the sine table.

Ramanujan

Srinivasa Ramanujan Iyengar, the greatest Indian mathematician of 20 th century, contributed immensely in fields like number theory, mathematical analysis, string theory and crystallography.

His genius has been admired by some greatest contemporary mathematicians of his time. He is hailed to be one of the most famous mathematicians in the field of number theory. Although he lived for a short span of 32 yr, he compiled nearly 3900 phenomenal results that leave even the best mathematical brains of today in sheer awe and wonder!

Brahmagupta

He gave four methods of multiplication. He gave the following formula, used in GP series $a+ar+ar^2+ar^3+\ldots+ar^{n-1}=(ar^{n-1})\div(r)$. He gave the following formulae: Area of a cyclic quadrilateral with side a, b, c and d is $\sqrt{(s-a)(s-b)(s-c)(s-d)}$, where $2s=a+b+c+d$.

Rene Descartes

The French philosopher and mathematician, Rene Descartes was famous for his method of expressing geometric shapes in the form of algebraic equation. It was because of Rene Descartes that we got introduced to the beautiful branch of coordinate geometry. The Cartesian coordinates, in fact, refer to his name. Besides this Rene made valuable contributions in the field of optics and energy conservation.

Leonhard Euler

Euler, a Swiss mathematician and physicists is widely acclaimed for his contributions in the field of function notation. His mathematical genius has been proved by his contribution in the fields of infinitesimal calculus and graph theory. His mathematical works and research in optics, mechanics, fluid dynamics have been hailed to be very influential.

Fibonacci

Leonardo of Pisa, the greatest European Italian mathematician, popularly known as Fibonacci, was the first mathematician to introduce Hindu - Arabic system in Europe, that is the positional system of using ten digits with a decimal point and zero. He is popular for using Fibonacci number sequence, that is, 0, 1, 1, 2, 3, 5, 8, 13, ... in the book authored by him, known as Book of Calculation, the Liber Abaci.

Carl F. Gauss M

Carl F. Gauss, a German mathematician, known as Princeps mathematicorum meaning, 'the Prince of Mathematicians' or 'the foremost of mathematicians' was a child prodigy and a genius. Even as a teenager, he is believed to have made remarkable mathematical contributions. Carl F. Gauss made path breaking contributions in fields like set theory, statistics, differential analysis, geophysics, electrostatics, number theory and astronomy. He proved the fundamental theorem of Algebra and made various contribution in number theory.

Sir Isaac Newton

Sir Isaac Newton was one of the greatest mathematician and physicist, the world has ever produced. His contributions in mathematics are spread in almost every field.

However, he developed Calculus, both differential and integral, that are still the most important aspects of higher Mathematics. Using Calculus, he made it easier to find the area bounded by closed curves. In Physics, his most famous and world changing contribution was the discovery of existence of gravitation force in our surrounding.

Blaise Pascal

Blaise Pascal, French philosopher, mathematician and physicist, contributed in several areas of Mathematics, but he is widely known for Pascal's triangle. He invented the first mechanical adding machine in the year 1642.

The unit of atmospheric pressure, Pascal (Pa) has been named in his honor. He also made contributions in the field of computer and the programming language pascal was named after him, in 1972.

Pythagoras

The Greek mathematician and philosopher, known as the 'father of numbers', is famous for the discovery of Pythagorean theorem formula, which states that in a right angled triangle, the square of the hypotenuse (z), is equal to the sum of the squares of the other two sides, x and y that is $x^2 + y^2 = z^2$.

Benjamin Banneker

A child prodigy, a watch designer and a mathematician, Bannerker discovered many puzzles in fields of trigonometry. He was a genius in logarithms and used them extensively in trigonometry. He is still regarded as the most popular black mathematician.

John Von Neumann

The Hungarian-American mathematician, physicist, John made valuable contribution in several fields like set theory, functional analysis, quantum mechanics, ergodic theory, continuous geometry and statistics.

His operator theory in mechanics is still regarded as one of his most pioneering works. He was also a key figure in the development of game theory.

Joseph Fourier

The Fourier's law and Fourier transform are named after him. He is also accredited with the discovery of the green house effect. He is popular for discovering Fourier series and its uses in determining the application of real life examples in heat transfer and vibrations.

Sophie Germain

Especially known for her work on 'Fermat's Last Theorem', Sophie was one of the initiators of the elasticity theory and also contributed to number theory and philosophy. She was regarded as 'the revolutionary mathematician' of her times.

Amalie Emmy Noether

She gave path breaking theorems in algebra field. The most popular, 'Noether's Theorem' connects symmetry and conservation laws in Physics. She also made valuable contributions to the theories of algebraic invariants and number fields.

Albert Einstein

The scientific world was amused by the Einstein's theory of relativity. Although Albert Einstein was physicist, his applied mathematical theorems to reach to apt conclusions. Known as 'Father of Physics', he can be best described as a mathematical physicist. He also won the Nobel Prize in 1921 for his contributions to Physics and the discovery of law of photoelectric effect.

Table of Symbols

Symbol	Reference
$\equiv$	identity
$\simeq$	approximately equal to
$\rightarrow$	approaches, ray
$<<$	much less than
$>>$	much greater than
$a \times b$, $a \cdot b$	multiplication
$a \div b$, a/b	division
$\therefore$	therefore
$\because$	since
$\wedge$	conjunction (and)
$\vee$	disjunction (or)
$\Rightarrow, \Leftrightarrow$	implication
$\sim$	negation, equivalence relation
$\exists, \forall$	quantifier
$\subseteq, \supseteq$	subset
$\subset, \supset$	proper subset
$\cup, \bigcup$	union
$\cap, \bigcap$	intersection
$A', \overline{A}$	complement
$A \times B$	cartesian product
$A - B$	difference set
$A \Delta B$	symmetric difference
$n(A), \#(A)$	cardinality
$[a,b]$	closed interval, least common multiple
(a,b)	open interval, greatest common divisor
$[a,b), (a,b]$	interval open at one end

Symbol	Reference
$[x]$	integer part
$\{x\}$	fractional part
(x)	least integer
$\Sigma, \sum$	summation
$\Pi, \prod$	product
π	pi
$f: x \to y$	function, mapping
$f: S \to T$	function, mapping
$x \to h$	limit
fog	composition
f^{-1}	inverse function, inverse mapping
$f', \frac{df}{dx}, y', \frac{dy}{dx}$	derivative, derived function
$f'', f''', \ldots, f^{(n)}, \frac{d^2 f}{dx^2}, \ldots, \frac{d^n f}{dx^n}$	higher derivative
$y'', y''', \ldots, y^{(n)}, \frac{d^2 y}{dx^2}, \ldots, \frac{d^n y}{dx^n}$	higher derivative
$f_x, f_y, f_1, f_2, \frac{\partial f}{\partial x}, \frac{\partial f}{\partial y}$	partial derivative
$f_{xx}, f_{xy}, \ldots, f_{11}, f_{12}, \ldots, \frac{\partial^2 f}{\partial x^2}, \frac{\partial^2 f}{\partial x \partial y}, \ldots$	higher order partial derivative
$\dot{x}, \ddot{x}$	rate of change
$\mathbf{a} \cdot (\mathbf{b} \times \mathbf{c}), [\mathbf{a}\,\mathbf{b}\,\mathbf{c}]$	scalar triple product
$\mathbf{a} \times (\mathbf{b} \times \mathbf{c})$	vector triple product
$\langle G, O \rangle$ or (G, O)	group
$\langle R, +, \times \rangle$ or $(R, +\times,)$	ring
$E(X)$	expected value

Conversion of Time

60 seconds	=	1 minute
60 minutes	=	1 hour
24 hours	=	1 day
7 days	=	1 week
15 days	=	1 fortnight
28, 29, 30 or 31 days	=	1 month

12 months	=	1 year
365 days	=	1 year
366 days	=	1 leap year
10 years	=	decade
25 years	=	silver jubilee
50 years	=	golden jubilee
60 years	=	diamond jubilee
75 years	=	radium jubilee or platinum jubilee
100 years	=	century
1000 years	=	10 centuries or 1 millenium

Equivalents of Units

Units of Lengths

12 inches	=	1 feet (ft) = 0.348 metres
3 feet	=	1 yard (d)
1 yard	=	0.9144 metres
22 yards	=	1 chain
1 kilometre	=	0.621 mile or 10^3 metres
1 mile	=	1.6093 kilometres or 1760 yards
1 inche	=	2.54 centimetres
1 hectare	=	2.471 acres

Units of Area

1 square feet	=	144 square inches
	=	0.0929 square metres
1 square metre	=	1.196 square yards
1 square yard	=	0.836 square metres
1 square kilometre	=	0.3861 square miles
	=	1000 hectares
1 square mile	=	2.59 square kilometres
	=	640 acres
1 acre	=	4840 square yards
	=	4046.86 square metres
100 square metres	=	1 acre
100 acres	=	1 hectare
	=	1000 square metres

Derivatives of Different Functions

y	$\frac{dy}{dx}$	y	$\frac{dy}{dx}$
x^n	nx^{n-1}	$\cosh x$	$\sinh x$
$u + v$	$\frac{du}{dx} + \frac{dv}{dx}$	$\tanh x$	$\text{sech}^2 x$
uv	$u\frac{dv}{dx} + v\frac{du}{dx}$	$\text{cosech}\, x$ $\text{sech}\, x$	$-\text{cosech}\, x \coth x$ $-\text{sech}\, x \tanh x$
$\frac{u}{v}$	$\frac{1}{v^2}\left(v\frac{du}{dx} - u\frac{dv}{dx}\right)$	$\coth^{-1} x$	$\frac{1}{1-x^2}$
ax	a	$\sinh^{-1} x$	$\frac{1}{\sqrt{(x^2+1)}}$
$\sin x$	$\cos x$	$\cosh^{-1} x$	$\frac{1}{\sqrt{(x^2-1)}}$
$\cos x$	$-\sin x$	$\tanh^{-1} x$	$\frac{1}{x^2-1}$
$\tan x$	$\sec^2 x$	$\text{cosech}^{-1} x$	$-\frac{1}{x\sqrt{(1+x^2)}}$
$\text{cosec}\, x$	$-\text{cosec}\, x \cot x$	$\text{sech}^{-1} x$	$-\frac{1}{x\sqrt{(1-x^2)}}$
$\sec x$	$\sec x \tan x$	$\coth^{-1} x$	$-\frac{1}{x^2-1}$
$\cot x$	$-\text{cosec}^2 x$	$\cot^{-1} x$	$-\frac{1}{1+x^2}$
$\sin^{-1} x$	$\frac{1}{\sqrt{(1-x^2)}}$	$\sec^{-1} x$	$\frac{1}{x\sqrt{(x^2-1)}}$
$\cos^{-1} x$	$-\frac{1}{\sqrt{(1-x^2)}}$	$\text{cosec}^{-1} x$	$-\frac{1}{x\sqrt{(x^2-1)}}$
$\tan^{-1} x$	$\frac{1}{1+x^2}$	$\log x$	$\frac{1}{x}$
e^x	e^x	a^x	$a^x \log a$
e^{-x}	$-e^{-x}$	$\sinh x$	$\cosh x$

Reduction Formulae

For a positive integer

(i) $\int \sin^n ax\, dx = -\frac{\sin^{n-1} ax \cos ax}{na} + \frac{n-1}{n}\int \sin^{n-2} ax\, dx$

(ii) $\int \cos^n ax\, dx = \frac{\cos^{n-1} ax \sin ax}{na} + \frac{n-1}{n}\int \cos^{n-2} ax\, dx$

(iii) When $n > 1$, $\int \tan^n ax\, dx = \frac{1}{a(n-1)}\tan^{n-1} ax - \int \tan^{n-2} ax\, dx$

(iv) $\int x^n e^{ax} dx = \frac{1}{a} x^n e^{ax} - \frac{n}{a}\int x^{n-1} e^{ax} dx$

(v) $\int (\ln x)^n dx = x(\ln x)^n - n\int (\ln x)^{n-1} dx$